THE IRWIN GUIDE
TO USING
THE WALL STREET JOURNAL

THE IRWIN GUIDE
TO USING
THE WALL STREET JOURNAL

SEVENTH EDITION

MICHAEL B. LEHMANN

McGraw-Hill

New York   Chicago   San Francisco   Lisbon   London
Madrid   Mexico City   Milan   New Delhi
San Juan   Seoul   Singapore   Sydney   Toronto

The *McGraw-Hill* Companies

4 5 6 7 8 9 0 DOC/DOC 0 9 8 7 6

ISBN 0-07-141664-1

McGraw-Hill books are available at special discounts to use as premiums and sales promotions, or for use in corporate training programs. For more information, please write to the Director of Special Sales, Professional Publishing, McGraw-Hill, Two Penn Plaza, New York, NY 10121-2298. Or contact your local bookstore.

 This book is printed on recycled, acid-free paper containing a minimum of 50% recycled de-inked paper.

Library of Congress Cataloging-in-Publication Data

Lehmann, Michael B.
    The Irwin guide to using the Wall Street journal / Michael B. Lehmann.— 7th ed.
      p. cm.
    Includes bibliographical references and index.
    ISBN 0-07-141664-1 (hardcover : alk. paper)
    1. Business cycles—United States.   2. Economic indicators—United States.
   3. Investments—United States.   4. Wall Street journal. I. Title.
   HB3743.L44 2005
   332.6—dc21

                                        2004023293

PREFACE

When I first proposed this book, the publisher asked me if its purpose was to show the reader "how to be your own economist." Not exactly, I said. The objective was to show the reader "how to use *The Wall Street Journal* to be your own economist." After all, the *Journal* is the authoritative source for business news in America; it is published coast to coast; and it has one of the largest daily circulations of any newspaper in the country. By focusing on a handful of key statistical reports in the *Journal*, you can acquire a surprisingly quick and firm comprehension of the ups and downs of the American business economy. This book will facilitate that comprehension, clearly and accurately—but, I hope, in a pleasing and nontechnical manner.

The Irwin Guide to Using The Wall Street Journal is designed to help you develop a sound overview of our economy, thus making your grasp of economic events as well as your business and investment decisions more informed and more confident. But it is not a get-rich-quick manual. You should always seek competent professional counsel before placing business or personal capital at risk.

Michael B. Lehmann

ACKNOWLEDGMENTS

I wish to express my gratitude to Eric Hsu and Sarah Hilliker for their assistance in preparing the text and organizing *The Wall Street Journal* sources.

Once again, I wouldn't have much to work with had it not been for the editorial assistance on earlier editions of my wife, Millianne Lehmann, and my colleague, Alan Heineman. My indebtedness to them continues through this edition.

Robert H. Meier of Chicago, Illinois, revised the list of suggested further reading in Appendix D, which he had kindly contributed to the sixth edition. This is an education in itself. Don't miss it.

My thanks also to Bruce Wydick, Chairman of the University of San Francisco's Department of Economics, and Jennifer Turpin, Dean of its College of Arts & Sciences, for their past and continuing support of my writing and research efforts.

Finally, my thanks to Kelli Christiansen, my editor at McGraw-Hill, who is a pleasure to work with and for.

M.B.L.

CONTENTS

PART I

THE BIG PICTURE: THE ECONOMIC CLIMATE AND THE INVESTMENT OUTLOOK   1

PART II

YOUR CHOICE OF INVESTMENTS   209

THE IRWIN GUIDE
TO USING
THE WALL STREET JOURNAL

THE BIG PICTURE: THE ECONOMIC CLIMATE AND THE INVESTMENT OUTLOOK

1

INTRODUCTION

THE MILLENNIUM BUBBLE

CHART 1–1 ON PAGE 3 PROVIDES a clear picture of the stock market's surge in the 1980s and 1990s, the millennium bubble of the late 1990s, and the bubble's subsequent collapse.

The S&P 500, which represents a broad cross section of the American economy, made extraordinary gains in the 1990s and hit 1,500 in 2000. By 2003 it had lost 40 percent of its value and fallen below 900. Even the blue-chip Dow Jones Industrial Average tripled in the 1980s and tripled again in the 1990s, rising to a peak of almost 12,000 in the year 2000, and then fell back below 7,500 in 2003. The technology-heavy NASDAQ climbed tenfold in the 1990s, cresting over 5,000 in the spring of 2000, and then surrendered three-fourths of that height—down to 1,300—by 2003.

However, the stock market was merely a reflection of the underlying economy's powerful surge, of industry's extraordinary performance and its subsequent decline. The technology boom propelled profits and employment swiftly forward. The world was abuzz with tales of a New Economy that promised blue skies forever. Then the bubble burst, confronting us with business failures and unemployment.

What forces propelled the economy and stock market to new heights in the 1980s and 1990s? What caused the subsequent debacle? Could the savvy observer and investor (could you?) have grasped the root causes of the boom, bubble, and bust? Could you have discerned omens of the coming crash? Do these past events provide clues to the future?

CHART 1–1 Standard & Poor's 500: Stock Market Average

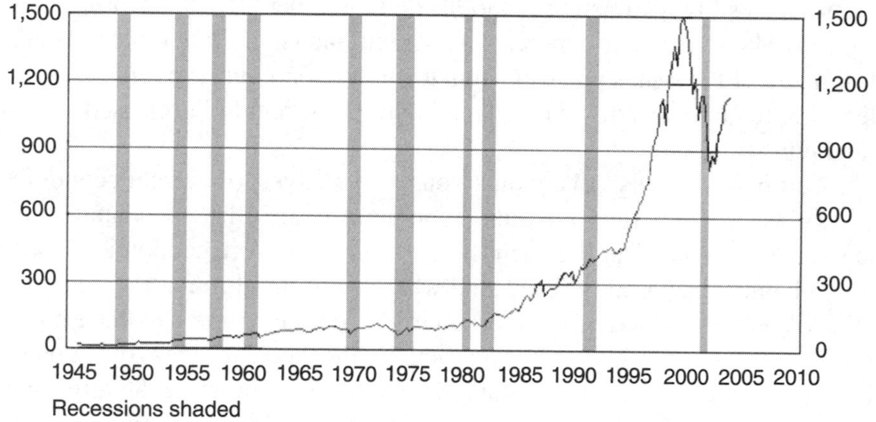

Recessions shaded

Source: Standard & Poor's Statistical Services.

ON YOUR OWN

The answer is yes. You can be that savvy observer and investor. You *can* do it on your own, without an interpreter. With a little assistance *you* will be able to decipher the stock market, GDP, capacity utilization, price/earnings ratios, and other statistical series and reports. You will gain an understanding of developing economic, business, and investment trends so that you can make your own analysis and your judgments and opinions are not based merely on (and therefore biased by) popular analyses and secondary sources.

It's worth some time and effort to learn how to deal with the data on your own, because until you come to grips with the data you can't honestly say that you have formed your own opinion about current economic and business events, let alone about what the future holds. The experts in the news media now serve as intermediaries between you and the data. However, no matter how many experts are quoted, you still aren't dealing with the facts, only with someone else's interpretation of them. Furthermore, these interpretations are often contradictory—and therefore confusing. At some point you have to wonder: Do the "experts" know what they're talking about? And while you are waiting for them to sort things out, your investment opportunities may have passed.

On the other hand, your desire to master the data may also stem from your own business needs. Will demand for your product be weak or strong two quarters from now or two years from now? Is this the time to lay in additional inventory, hire key personnel, and build more plant? Or, despite the current level of orders, would it be more prudent to put those plans on hold? Can you beat the competition to the punch, one way or another? Are interest rates likely to rise or to fall? Is deflation merely a buzzword, or are we truly about to embark upon an era of continuously falling prices? That's just a hint of the issues you can begin to analyze on your own; all it takes is learning to come to grips with a small number of regularly released statistical reports.

You may also wish to conduct your own analysis of current economic events because they form the foundation for so many other social and political developments. Can President Bush's tax cuts restore economic growth *and* a balanced federal budget? And what about our chronic trade deficit? What does it mean and how important is it? Do your answers to these questions reflect your analysis of the data, your political point of view, or the opinions of your favorite commentator? Maybe they should reflect all three, but they can reflect only the last two until you learn to deal with the numbers on your own. Once you do that, your own judgment will be of greater importance to you and others.

Don't misunderstand: Dispensing with expert advice is not your objective. Even the world's leading authorities on a subject must consult other experts as a continual check on their understanding. Challenges of authority help prevent sloppy thinking. The point is: If you become the expert by handling the data on your own, you will know whether the advice offered by other experts makes sense. Without the requisite knowledge, you'll never be certain whether you're receiving sound or flimsy advice.

If you want to be your own economist and investment adviser, if you wish to master the daily data, you need two things: (1) a readily available, reliable, and comprehensive statistical source and (2) a guide to organizing and interpreting the information you receive.

As to the first requirement, *The Wall Street Journal* (in print or online) is your best daily source of investment, business, and economic information; you really don't need anything else. It contains all the reports necessary to conduct your own analysis.

With respect to the second requirement, this book can be your guide. *The Irwin Guide to Using the Wall Street Journal* explains the statistics you need so that what they measure and how they are computed will be clear. GDP, capacity utilization, the price/earnings ratio, and the Dow Jones Industrial Average cannot remain vague and indefinite terms if you are going to be in control of the information.

For example, if the *Journal* reports that the money supply has increased, it is important to know that this fact has virtually nothing to do with the availability of currency. The money supply is composed largely of checking accounts; currency is the petty cash of the economy.

Understanding the nature of the various statistical series is, of course, not enough. You must be able to place them in both historical and contemporary context. For instance, the price/earnings (P/E) ratio for the Dow stocks hit a high of 22 in August 1987, just as the Dow peaked immediately prior to the October 1987 crash. In 1998, the P/E for the Dow climbed past 22 as the millennium bubble grew. The wise investor understood this sign of stock-market speculation and was prepared to act on it.

You will develop these essential skills and gain strength in their use with each chapter. Your historical perspective will deepen, providing the background or benchmark for evaluating contemporary events. When a *Journal* article states that the trade deficit is the largest ever, or that the Dow Jones Industrial Average has hit a new high, the comparison can provide perspective only if you grasp the frame of reference. Knowledge of the past aids evaluation of the present by providing a standard against which recent developments are measured. For instance, motor-vehicle sales and housing starts may be slightly higher or lower than they were a year ago, but your knowledge of their relationship to the historic peaks will provide needed insight.

As you read on, you will become aware that none of the statistical reports stands alone. Understanding the relationships among them provides insight into the economy's operation and the investment scene; each is a piece of the puzzle, and together they compose the picture. For instance, mortgage interest rates and home construction were featured in the *Journal* throughout 2002. As mortgage interest rates fell, home construction grew and sustained a drooping economy. When interest rates bottomed and rebounded in 2003, however, wise observers wondered whether residential construction would continue to bolster the economy.

Consider another example. In 2003 the United States asked China to stop linking its currency's value to ours and let the yuan float upward, i.e., permit the dollar to fall in value against the yuan. The hope was that more expensive yuan (cheaper dollars)—and hence higher prices for Chinese goods in U.S. markets—would reduce our imports and thereby assist U.S. manufacturers. Thus, the statistical reports on the value of the dollar and other currencies and on our ability to compete internationally are inextricably linked, as you will see in more detail in Chapter 10.

All of the statistics analyzed in this book can be interrelated in this fashion, so they need not be a series of isolated events, released piecemeal on a day-to-day basis. Instead, they will form an unfolding pattern that clearly reveals the direction of economic and business activity.

Finally, you need a framework, a device to give a coherent shape to these historical insights and contemporary interrelationships. The business cycle, the wave-like rise and fall of economic activity, provides that necessary framework. You are already familiar with the cycle in your own investing, business, or personal situation, and the news media have provided increased coverage of the ups and downs of the economy in recent years. Economic expansion and contraction, easy or tight credit conditions, inflation and unemployment are recurring facts of life. No one escapes them.

The business cycle is the best vehicle for illuminating the *Journal*'s regularly appearing statistical series. Its phases bring life and meaning to the statistical reports and establish the perspective through which the illustrations and examples in the book are interwoven into a unified exposition.

Each chapter will introduce one or more statistical series and will be devoted to a theme (such as the money and credit markets) that is used to describe and explain the statistical series introduced in the chapter. The explanation will begin with the simplest and most basic elements of the business cycle and proceed to additional topics that will complete your understanding. This step-by-step progression of topics will not, however, prevent you from breaking into any chapter, out of order, if you wish to examine a particular statistical series or group of series. Indeed, you may already have a firm grasp of some of these topics and need only to fill in the missing elements to round out your comprehension of the essential workings of American business. A complete listing of all the statistical series discussed in this guide can be found in the appendices following Chapter 16.

Each chapter will describe its statistical series in the context of the business cycle and explain the relationship of the new series to the overall picture. Analysis will be based on charts drawn from official sources so that you can visualize the data and put the current information in perspective. Recent articles in *The Wall Street Journal* containing the statistical series will be reproduced and discussed to help you interpret the data presented in the charts. Finally, you will be alerted to what future developments can be expected.

You will enjoy putting the puzzle together yourself. Anyone can do it, with a little help. The ebb and flow of the business cycle will channel the stream of data that now floods you in seemingly random fashion, and you will experience a genuine sense of accomplishment in creating order out of something that may previously have appeared chaotic.

A word of caution before you begin. This will not be an economics or business-cycle course or text, nor will it be a precise forecasting device. There will be no formula or model. The business cycle is used strictly as a vehicle to make the statistical information usable in as easy a manner as possible. The objective is not to make a professional economist out of you, but to enable you to conduct your own analysis of the data as soon as possible. You will dive into the data and "get your hands dirty" by taking apart the cycle, analyzing it, and reassembling it. When you have finished this book, you will feel confident that you can deal with the data on your own.

In order to expedite your reference to these data, turn to Appendixes A, B, and C on pages 359, 364, and 369. These appendices list the statistical series discussed in this book, and provide them in alphabetical, chapter and page, and chronological order. They will furnish you with a quick guide to the key data published in the *Journal*'s print edition.

The next section introduces you to the *Journal*'s online edition.

THE ONLINE EDITION

Gaining access to the *Journal*'s print edition is easy. You need only turn the pages. The online edition may be more intimidating for some, but it need not be.

Just go to the Web site of the *Journal* by typing in the following address: http://online.wsj.com. That will bring up the home page of *The Wall Street Journal Online* (see the example on page 8). You can subscribe by clicking on the appropriate link at the top of the page. If you choose the option of storing your password, you can avoid providing your password each time you log on.

Once you have subscribed to the online edition, you can, of course, explore the home page and its links at your leisure. However, this book will make use of four sets of data-gathering procedures with which you may wish to familiarize yourself now: (1) news articles, (2) company-specific information, (3) data on and analysis of the economy, and (4) market information. Just follow the instructions below after you have subscribed:

News Article Retrieval.   The home page has links to both current and old news stories. To retrieve news stories in the *Journal*'s archive, click on Article Archives (under Research) and follow the instructions provided on the linked page.

Company Information (stock quotes, financial data, etc.).   On the home page under Research, type in the company name or stock symbol and click on the arrow.

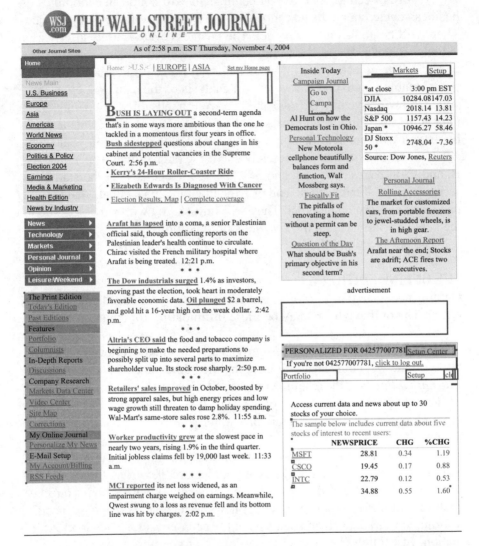

Data on and Analysis of the Economy. Click on Economy in the home page's left-hand menu-bar and then select one of the following options under Data and Resources at the top right of the linked page (see page 9 for an example).

   Economic Indicators for the latest government report

   Chartbook for an up-to-date chart

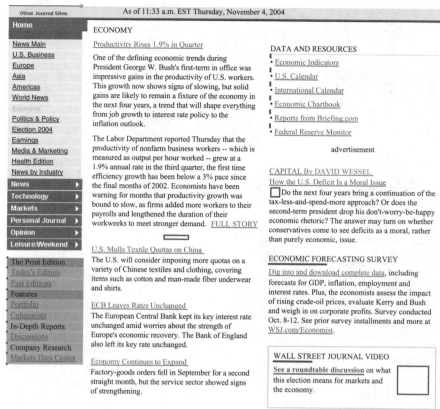

Reports from Briefing.com for this firm's analyses

Federal Reserve Monitor to track Federal Reserve policy and
     actions

Market Information (stocks, bonds, commodities, currency, etc.). Click
on Markets and Markets Data Center in the home page's left-hand menu-bar
and then go to the links provided (see page 10).

Appendix D on page 374 furnishes you with a quick guide to the
Journal's online edition. It not only lists the data available and how to
retrieve it, this appendix also presents the chapter and page which discuss
the data.

MARKETS DATA
SECTION INDEX ▶

Markets Data Center

Data Bank
- Data Bank
- Closing Stock Diary
- Closing Stock Data Bank

U.S. Stocks
Market Wrap
- Quotes Search
- Most Actives - Summary
- Leaders - Summary
- Losers - Summary
- Volume Pctg Leaders - Summary
- Most Actives - Top 100
- Leaders - Top 100
- Losers - Top 100
- Volume Pctg Leaders - Top 100
- NYSE Highs/Lows
- NMS Highs/Lows
- AMEX Highs/Lows
- OTC Bulletin Board Most Actives
- DJIA Hour by Hour
- Index Charts
- Closing Stock Tables
After Hours
- Most Actives: 4-6:35 p.m.
- Leaders/Losers: 4-6:35 p.m.
Statistics
- Dividends
- Index Components
- Money Flow - Summary
- Money Flow - Top Gainers
- Money Flow - Top Decliners
- New Securities Issues
- New Stock Listings
- Odd Lot Trading
- Short Interest
- Stock Splits
- Yields On Dow Stocks
Historical Index Data
Dow Jones Industrial Average
- One-Day Gains/Losses, All Time
- One-Day Gains/Losses, 2004
- One-Day Gains/Losses, 2003
- One-Day Gains/Losses, 2002
- Intraday Point swings
S&P 500 Index
- One-Day Gains/Losses, All Time
- One-Day Gains/Losses, 2004
- One-Day Gains/Losses, 2003
- One-Day Gains/Losses, 2002
Nasdaq Composite
- One-Day Gains/Losses, All Time
- One-Day Gains/Losses, 2004
- One-Day Gains/Losses, 2003
- One-Day Gains/Losses, 2002
- Volume Records
NYSE
- Volume Records
Major Indexes
- Highs/Lows, All Time
Options/Futures
- Index Options
- LEAPS
- Listed Options
- Most Active Options
- Options Summaries
- Unusual Intraday Option Activity
- Unusual Daily Option Activity
- Index Futures, U.S.
- Index Futures, Non-U.S.

Industry Groups/Sectors
- DJ Industry Group Center

Global Indexes
- DJ Global Indexes
- World Leading Groups
- World Lagging Groups
- Americas Groups
- Asian Groups
- European Groups
- U.S. Leading & Lagging Groups
- DJ Global Portfolio Indexes
- DJ Industry Group Center

Bond Markets
- Bond Indexes
- Bond Yields
- Bond Diaries
- Federal Reserve Data
- Federal Reserve Monitor
- Guaranteed Investment Contracts
- International Government Bonds
- Returns on International Gov't Bonds
- Key Rates
- Money Rates
- Mortgage- Backed Securities & CMOs
- Treasury Quotes
- Tax-Exempt Bonds
- Mortgage & Banking Rate Center

Commodities
Agriculture
- Food, Fiber
- Livestock, Meat
- Oats, Corn, Rice
- Oilseeds
- Wheat
Energy
- Electricity
- Petroleum
Index
- U.S.
- Non-U.S.
Interest Rate
- Americas
- Europe
- Euro
- EuroDollar, Yen
- Asian, Pacific
Other
- Currency
- Metals
- Lumber
- Weather
- Commodities Weekly Settlement
Futures Options
- Agricultural
- Currency
- Index
- Interest Rate
- Livestock
- Metals
- Oil
- Other
- Futures Options Weekly Settlement
Spot Prices
- Cash Prices
- Electricity Prices
- Oil Statistics
- London Metal Exchange Prices

Currencies
- Exchange Rates
- Hourly Exchange Rates
- Key Cross Rates
- Currency Futures

The chapters that follow provide many illustrations from the *Journal's* print and online editions. On occasion, however, in order to conserve space on these pages, instructions will show you how to retrieve this information even though the chapter provides no illustration.

Now, before exploring the data in detail, let's take time for a leisurely overview of the business cycle in Chapter 2.

2

THE BUSINESS CYCLE

A BIT OF HISTORY

THE BUSINESS CYCLE IS NOTHING NEW. It's been a characteristic of every capitalist economy in the modern era. Nations have endured boom followed by bust, prosperity and then depression—periods of growth and confidence trailing off into a decade of despair.

It is all so familiar to us that images of its human effects are scattered among our popular stereotypes. Men in top hats peer at ticker tape emerging from a little glass dome. They wheel and deal, corner wheat markets, play with railroads, and organize steel companies. Fortunes are quickly won and just as quickly lost. Former tycoons are seen selling apples on street corners. Factory gates shut and signs go up saying, "No help wanted." Soup kitchens appear, and desperate families flee the dust bowl in Model A pickup trucks.

These caricatures—based on real history, actual power, blows of ill fortune, human suffering—persist in our collective consciousness, permanently etched by the Great Depression. Although the stock market collapse of 1929 is the most notorious such event in our history, it is by no means unique. Cycles in the American economy can be traced and analyzed going back to the beginning of the 19th century. And, as you are very well aware, despite all the talk of a "new economy" at the end of the 1990s—an economy that would grow smoothly forever, driven by high tech and undeterred by the vicissitudes of the cycle—we were hit by the cycle's nasty downdraft when the millennium bubble burst in the year 2000. The business cycle has been part and parcel of American economic history from the beginning.

The settlement of the West is an example. The frontier assumes such importance in our history and folklore that we tend to think of the westward migration as a smooth, if hazardous, inevitable flow, driven by the doctrine of manifest destiny. It didn't happen that way. The settlement of the West proceeded in a cyclical pattern.

Farmers and ranchers were (and are) businesspeople. The sod house and subsistence farming of the 1800s were temporary inconveniences, converted as quickly as possible to growing cash crops and raising livestock for the market. The settlers wanted to know the bottom line, the difference between revenue and expense. They wanted the best price for their cotton, corn, cattle, wheat, and hogs. They wanted to maximize production and minimize cost by using modern cultivation techniques and the latest equipment. Railroads and banks concerned them, because transportation and interest rates affected the cost of doing business and thus their profit margin. Finally, and most important, farmers wanted their capital to grow. They expected their net worth to increase as their farms appreciated in value and their mortgages were paid.

This experience was not confined to the United States; European settlers in Canada, Australia, and Argentina produced the same commodities under similar conditions. All were part of the growing world economy. Farmers and ranchers counted on industrialization and urbanization at home and in Europe to build demand for their commodities.

As worldwide demand for food and fiber increased rapidly, farmers and ranchers responded by boosting production as best they could on existing holdings. Eventually, however, their output reached its limit, even though demand continued to grow. As a result, prices began to creep, and then race, upward. The venturesome dreamed of moving west and doubling or tripling their acreage. Record crop and livestock prices made the costs of moving and financing a new spread seem manageable, and existing farms could always be sold to the less intrepid. Thousands upon thousands of families streamed across the frontier, claiming millions of acres offered by generous government policies or buying from speculators who held raw land.

Nobody planned the westward migration; nobody coordinated it; nobody governed it. Individuals made their own calculation of the market. Farmers and ranchers borrowed money to purchase land and building materials and to buy livestock, seed, and equipment. Newly opened banks faced an insatiable demand for credit. Towns sprang up at railroad sidings where grain elevators and livestock yards were constructed. Merchants and Main Street followed. High prices brought a land boom, and the land boom brought settlement and opened the West.

It took a while for the newly converted prairie to produce a cash crop. But when it did, thousands of new farms began dumping their output on the market. The supply of agricultural commodities increased dramatically. Shortage changed to surplus, and prices dropped. Time after time during the 19th century, commodity prices fell to record lows after a period of inflation and the subsequent land rush.

Many farmers and ranchers were wiped out. They could not pay their debts while commodity prices scraped bottom, and banks foreclosed on their property. If a bank made too many loans that went bad, then it was dragged down too. Merchants saw their customers disappear and had to close up shop. Settlers abandoned their land, and boomtowns became ghost towns.

Prices inevitably remained low for years, and most farmers, living on returns far below expectations, barely made it. In every instance, it took a while before the steady growth in world demand absorbed the excess agricultural commodities.

As time passed, the cycle would repeat itself. After the inflation that accompanied the Civil War, western settlement continued to occur in waves until the end of the century, despite 30 years of deflation. The process happened at least half a dozen times until the frontier closed in the last years of the 19th century.

By the turn of this century, progress had been spectacular. Many thousands of acres of prairie had been transformed into productive field and pasture. Commodities worth billions of dollars were produced annually for the domestic and world markets. Billions of dollars of wealth had been created in the form of improved farmland. But the discipline of the business cycle governed the advance. For every two steps forward, there had been one step backward, as those who borrowed or lent the least wisely, settled the poorest land, or had the worst luck went broke.

Things haven't changed. Agriculture's fortunes are still guided by the cycle. Remember the boom of the early 1970s? Consumption of beef was up; President Nixon negotiated the wheat deal with Russia; the Peruvian anchovy harvest had failed, and soy beans were used to fill the gap (as a protein extender). Agricultural commodity prices doubled, even tripled, causing farm income to shoot up. As a result, farmers spent the rest of the decade investing heavily in land and equipment. Ultimately, supply outstripped demand, and farm prices deteriorated throughout the early 1980s.

We've seen the result. It's nothing that hasn't happened before: foreclosures, bankruptcies, falling land values, broken families, and ruined lives. Eventually, of course, prices stabilize—until the next cycle comes along to start the process all over again.

Oil presents a similar picture. Billions were spent in the 1970s on exploration, recovery, and production projects in Texas, Louisiana, Oklahoma, Wyoming, Colorado, and Alaska when prices were high. Houston, Dallas, Denver, and Anchorage were boomtowns in the early 1980s. Then, when prices fell (and they always do), the money dried up. Soon you could get a condominium in Anchorage or Denver for $15,000 because whole city blocks of new housing developments were abandoned—left by their owners for bank foreclosure.

What was true for farming and oil was equally true for the nation's railroads: They developed in the same cyclical pattern. On the eve of World War I, America's railway system was complete, representing a total capital investment second only to that of agriculture. It was a remarkable feat of creative engineering and equally creative financing.

We marvel at the colorful exploits of the Goulds, Fisks, Drews, Vanderbilts, Stanfords, Hills, and others. History refers to some of them as "robber barons"; they seemed to skim off one dollar for every two invested, and it's a wonder that the railway system was ever completed or operated safely. Yet there it was, the largest in the world, a quarter of a million miles of track moving the nation's freight and passenger traffic with unparalleled efficiency.

Promoters speculatively pushed the railroads westward in anticipation of the freight and passenger traffic that settlement would bring. Federal, state, and local governments, vying for the routes that would generate progress and development, gave the railroad companies 10 percent of the nation's land. Improving rights-of-way; laying track; building trestles, stations, and marshaling yards; and purchasing locomotives and rolling stock required the railway companies to raise more capital than had ever been mobilized for any other single business venture. The companies floated billions of dollars in stocks and bonds, and investors eagerly ventured their capital to take advantage of prospective success.

Flush with funds, the railroads raced toward the Pacific Coast, hoping that revenue would grow quickly enough to justify their huge investment. Periodically, however, the generous rate of expansion exceeded the growth in traffic. Prospects for profits, which had seemed so bright, grew dim. Investors stopped providing funds, and railroad track construction came to a halt. Since operating revenues could not recover costs, many railroads were forced into receivership and were reorganized. Stock and bond prices plunged, wiping out investors long after the promoters had made off with their killings.

Eventually, traffic grew sufficiently to justify existing lines and raise hopes that construction could profitably resume. Investors were once again lured into advancing their funds, and a new cycle of railway expansion began. It, too, was followed by a bust, and then by another wave of construction, until the nation's railway system was complete.

The tracks spanned a continent, from New York, Philadelphia, and Baltimore to Chicago, and from there to New Orleans, Los Angeles, San Francisco, Portland, and Seattle. Profit had motivated the enterprise, and enormous tangible wealth had been created. Losses had periodically and temporarily halted the undertaking and impoverished those who had speculated unwisely or who had been duped. Construction had proceeded in waves. It was an unplanned and often disorganized adventure, but, given the institutions of the time, no other method could have built the system as rapidly.

In this and the preceding century, we have seen the business cycle not only in the heroic proportions of the Roaring Twenties and the Great Depression, but also during every succeeding business expansion or recession. The 1990s boom and subsequent bust were merely its latest incarnation, reminding us of the 19th-century railway booms and busts. Everybody had to have a personal computer on his or her desk, plus the software to run the requisite word processing programs and spreadsheets. Then came the Internet and the telecommunications boom that promised to meld television and the World Wide Web, bringing interconnectivity into every office and home. Quickly the boom got ahead of itself and tripped on its own feet. It became clear that promoters had (once again) built too far ahead of demand. Soon there were accusations of skullduggery and a new set of robber barons emerged. As the economy recoiled in recession, the 21st century began with a reminder of the past.

We're in the cycle now, and we will be tomorrow and next year. Business activity always expands and then contracts. There are periods when production, employment, and profits surge ahead, each followed by a period when profits and output fall and unemployment increases. Then the entire cycle repeats itself once again. During the expansion, demand, production, income, and wealth grow. Homes and factories are constructed, and machinery and equipment are put in place. The value of these assets also grows as home prices and common stock prices increase. But then comes the inevitable contraction, and all the forces that mark the expansion shift into reverse. Demand, production, and income fall. The level of construction and the production of machinery and equipment are drastically curtailed. Assets lose their value as home prices and common stock prices fall.

No doubt you already realize that business cycles occur and repeat themselves in this way. But why? No completely satisfactory theory has yet been created. No one can accurately predict the length and course of each cycle. Economics, unlike physics, cannot be reduced to experiments and repeated over and over again under ideal conditions. There is no economic equivalent to Galileo on the Tower of Pisa, proving that objects of unequal weight fall with equal speed, because the economic "tower" is never quite the same height; the "objects" keep changing in number, size, and even nature; and the "laws of gravity" apply unequally to each object.

Yet one thing is certain: The business cycle is generated by forces within the economic system, not by outside forces. These internal forces create the alternating periods of economic expansion and contraction. And you should recognize that certain crucial features of the cycle will endure.

A THUMBNAIL SKETCH

Each business cycle is driven by five basic principles, as follows:

1. *First, the forces of supply and demand condition every cycle.* Our ability to enjoy increasing income depends on our ability to supply or create increased production or output; we must produce more to earn more. But the level of demand—the expenditures made in purchasing this output—must justify the level of production. That is, we must sell what we produce in order to earn. With sufficient demand, the level of production will be sustained and will grow, and income will increase; if demand is insufficient, the reverse will occur. During the expansionary phase of the cycle, demand and supply forces are in a relationship that permits the growth of production and income; during the contractionary phase, their relationship compels a decrease in production and income.

2. *Second, neither consumers nor businesses are constrained to rely solely on the income they have generated in the process of production.* They have recourse to the credit market; they can borrow money and spend more than they earn. Spending borrowed funds permits demand to take on a life of its own and bid up a constantly and rapidly growing level of production. This gives rise to the expansionary phase of the cycle. Eventually, the growth in production becomes dependent on the continued availability of credit, which sustains the growth in demand. But once buyers can no longer rely on borrowed funds (because of market saturation, the exhaustion of profitable investment opportunities, or tight credit), demand falls and, with it, the bloated level of production and income. The contractionary phase has begun.

3. *Third, every expansion carries with it the inevitability of "over-expansion," the creation of excess productive capacity and subsequent contraction.* Overexpansion may be propelled by businesses that invest too heavily in new plant and equipment in order to take advantage of a seemingly profitable opportunity, thereby creating excess productive capacity. Consumers who borrow too heavily in order to buy homes, autos, or other goods can also spur on overexpansion. But when businesses realize the expected level of sales will not support the newly created excess, let alone investments in and purchases of additional plant and equipment, and when consumers realize they will have difficulty paying for that new home or car, then both businesses and consumers curtail their borrowing and expenditures. Since production and income have spurted ahead to meet the growth in demand, they fall when the inevitable contraction in demand takes place.

4. *Fourth, during contractions, production and income recede to a sustainable level; that is, they fall to a level not reliant on a continuous growth in credit.* The contraction returns the economy to a more efficient level of operation.

5. *Fifth, every contraction sows the seeds of the subsequent recovery.* Income earned in the productive process, rather than bloated levels of borrowing, maintains the level of demand. Consumers and businesses repay their debts. Eventually, lower debt burdens and interest rates encourage consumer and business borrowing and demand. The economy begins expanding once more.

There is progress nevertheless over the course of the cycle. Overall growth takes place because some, or even most, of the increase in output remains intact. Nor is all the created wealth subsequently destroyed. The abandoned steel mills of the "rust belt" will be scrapped, but the plant and equipment used to make personal computers will remain on-stream. Residential construction completed in 1986 turned a profit for its developers, while homes completed in 1990, at the peak of that cycle, were liquidated at a loss after standing empty for a year. The Internet is here to stay, but much of the telecommunication industry's productive capacity—installed in the late 1990s—will remain idle until demand grows sufficiently to justify its existence. These are but a few examples of how the economy expands. The tree grows, but the rings in its trunk mark the cycles of seasons that were often lush but on occasion were beset by drought.

In the 1990s some thought that the business cycle had been repealed. They were cruelly disappointed. The chapters that follow will discuss not only the cycle's dynamic but also the forces that "stretched out" the cycle in the 1990s and postponed recession's onset. You will also learn how that cycle was unique in our post–World War II history. Consumer expenditures drove earlier cycles, while expenditures on plant and equipment drove the 1990s boom. In earlier cycles business waited for consumers to spend before venturing its capital. This time business led and consumers followed.

As you may already suspect, the business cycle does not operate in a vacuum. It is conditioned, shortened, and stretched, as well as initiated and forestalled, by the institutions of our economy. The Federal Reserve and the federal government have enormous influence on economic activity. You'll learn how they act to influence the cycle, and you'll learn when and why their actions have succeeded and when and why their actions have failed. That discussion must wait, however, until you have completed a fundamental analysis of the most recent cycle's origin and demise.

The analysis begins in Chapter 3 with an examination of the stock market, one of the economy's most sensitive indicators of underlying strength or weakness.

3

STOCKS

EARLY WARNING

HART 3–1 ON PAGE 21 (WHICH IS A REPEAT OF CHART 1–1) SHOWS the 1990s stock-market bubble and its collapse at the start of the new millennium.

Could the savvy investor have forecast the impending reversal and bailed out in time? Were there any omens or early warnings?

Analysts have developed an indicator—known as the price/earnings (P/E) ratio—that measures the relationship between share prices and earnings and thereby indicates the degree of speculative fever. Chart 3–2 on page 21 shows the S&P, the earnings per share (EPS) for the S&P, and the S&P's P/E ratio—the S&P divided by earnings per share. You'll have an opportunity to examine these measures in more detail below, but for the time being think of the P/E ratio as an indicator of the relative strength of the S&P compared with the earnings of the companies in the S&P. If the S&P rises more rapidly than the earnings of the companies in the S&P and the P/E ratio therefore rises as well, that can be a sign of speculation. Overly enthusiastic investors are bidding up stock prices beyond any reasonable expectation of earnings growth. That's a warning for prudent investors to leave the market.

That is precisely what happened in the late 1990s. Chart 3–2 clearly shows that the S&P's P/E ratio rose to levels higher than had prevailed at any time since World War II. (You can probably observe an average P/E of about 15 for these postwar years.) While it is true that the stock market will advance

CHART 3–1 Standard & Poor's 500: Stock Market Average

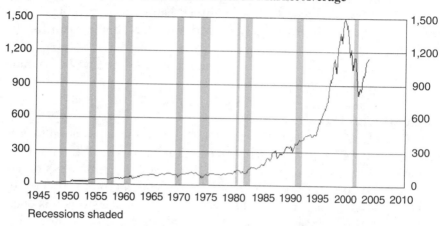

Recessions shaded

Source: Standard & Poor's Statistical Services.

whenever investors anticipate rising earnings, if stock-market values significantly and persistently rise more rapidly than earnings, that is a sign of speculation. Investors considered a P/E ratio of 15 a good rule of thumb in the decades following World War II. As the S&P's P/E climbed to 30 and beyond in the late 1990s, savvy investors got out.

To ask the obvious, Why did investors drive up the stock market so

CHART 3–2 S&P 500: Price, Earnings per Share, and Price/Earnings Ratio

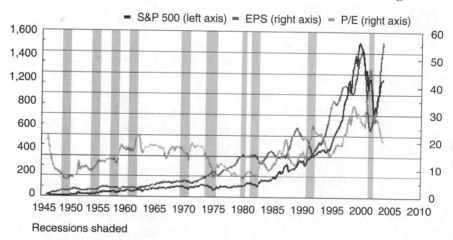

Recessions shaded

Source: Standard & Poor's Statistical Services.

much more rapidly than the earnings of the companies represented by the market? Or, reversing the inquiry, What happened to earnings? Why couldn't corporate profits keep pace with investors' enthusiasm for the stock market?

Before you deal with that issue, be sure you fully understand the P/E ratio and the concept that underlies it.

THE PRICE/EARNINGS RATIO

The price of a share of stock reflects the ability of the corporation to earn profits. As stated above, this relationship is expressed as the P/E ratio (price divided by per share earnings), or the ratio between the price of the stock and the profits per share of stock earned by the corporation (profits divided by number of shares outstanding). The price/earnings ratio answers this question: What price must an investor pay to capture a dollar of earnings? For instance, a P/E ratio of 10 might mean that a share sold for $100 and that a company earned $10 per share per annum. In that case you must pay $100 to capture $10 in earnings (the equivalent of $10 to capture $1 in earnings). Or it might mean that a share sold for $70 and that a company earned $7 per share per annum. Once again the investor pays $10 to capture a dollar of earnings.

The investor, of course, seeks the highest yield consistent with safety. The earnings yield is annual profit expressed as a percentage of the market price of the investment. If you earn $100 a year on an investment of $1,000, the yield is 10 percent. A P/E ratio of 10 (10/1) represents a 10 percent yield, because earnings are 1/10 (10 percent) of the price per share (as, for instance, when earnings per share were $10 and a share sold for $100). Similarly, a P/E ratio of 5 (5/1) is the equivalent of a 20 percent yield, because earnings per share are a fifth (20 percent) of invested capital. A P/E ratio of 20 (20/1) represents a 5 percent earnings yield.

You can follow the S&P's P/E daily in the *Journal*'s print edition on the second page (C2) of the third section, called *Money and Investing*. An example from the Tuesday, December 23, 2003, *Journal* appears on page 23. Notice the *reported* P/E ratio of 27 and the *estimated* P/E ratio of 19. The reported (higher) figure employs the latest reported earnings data, i.e., historical facts. The estimated (lower) figure employs the latest estimate of corporate earnings, i.e., a projection. In this case, a higher (rosy) earnings estimate produced a lower P/E.

P/E data is also available in the *Journal*'s online edition (http://online. wsj.com). Follow these steps (you may wish to review the general directions beginning on page 7 of Chapter 1 as well as Appendix D on page 374):

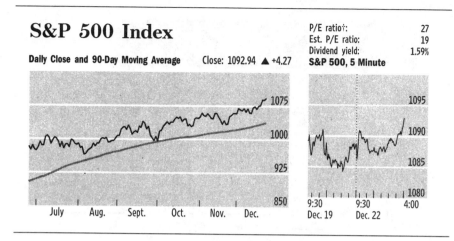

S&P 500 Index

Daily Close and 90-Day Moving Average   Close: 1092.94 ▲ +4.27

P/E ratio†:	27
Est. P/E ratio:	19
Dividend yield:	1.59%

S&P 500, 5 Minute

1. Scroll down the home page's left-hand menu-bar and click on Barron's Online.
2. Click on Market Lab under Home in the left-hand menu-bar.
3. Click on Index P/Es & Yields under Stocks.
4. Scroll down for the S&P 500 reported-earnings P/E ratio. (You can observe the Dow's P/E on the way.)

The Tuesday, January 27, 2004, edition of Barron's Online (see page 24) reported a P/E ratio of 29.59 (as of Monday, January 26, 2004) for the S&P 500 in the latest week. Note that the ratio was only slightly higher than a year earlier despite a rise in the S&P that exceeded 20 percent. That's testimony to the strong growth of earnings in the intervening year. Earnings grew so rapidly that the stock market could appreciate dramatically without significantly pushing up the ratio of share prices to profits.

As mentioned previously, by the late 1990s a binge of speculation had boosted the P/E upward far more rapidly than earnings. As the ratio hit an all-time high, warning investors that the stock market had reached an unsustainable level, the message was clear: Get out now!

What went wrong? Why didn't earnings keep up?

PROFITS AND PROFIT MARGINS

Let's examine the corporate earnings' record before probing the underlying causes behind earnings' failure to grow. Chart 3–3 on page 25 mea-

BARRON'S Online

Home
This Week's
Magazine
Companies
Markets
Technology
Funds/Q&A
Market Lab
Portfolio
Online Exclusives
Past Editions
MarketGauge
See what stocks and
sectors are moving
today's markets.
FREE Markets
Tools
•Stock & Fund
Listings
•Futures
•Options
•Annuities
•Economic Calendar
•Markets Calendar
Help
Contact Us

MONDAY, JANUARY 26, 2004

Indexes' P/Es & Yields

DJ latest 52-week earnings and dividends adjusted by Dow Divisors at Friday's close. S&P Dec. 4-quarter's earnings as reported and indicated dividends based on Friday close. S&P 500 P/E ratios based on earnings as reported. For additional earnings series, please refer to www.spglobal.com/earnings.html. DJ latest available book values for FY 2002 and 2001, and S&P latest for 2002 and 2001.

	Last Week	Prev. Week	Year Ago Week
DJ Industrial Average	10568.29	10600.51	8131.01
P/E Ratio	21.65	22.25	20.52
Earnings Yield (%)	4.62	4.49	4.87
Earns $	488.14	476.40	396.22
Dividend Yield (%)	2.00	1.99	2.32
Dividends ($)	211.14	210.81	188.61
Market to Book	4.62	4.64	3.30
Book Value ($)	2286.69	2286.69	2463.72
DJ Transporation Average	3072.94	3036.28	2163.33
P/E Ratio	42.40	Nil	Nil
Earnings Yield (%)	2.36	Nil	Nil
Earns $	72.47	-.07	-115.23
Dividend Yield (%)	1.09	1.10	1.37
Dividends ($)	33.37	33.37	29.68
Market to Book	2.47	2.41	1.20
Book Value ($)	1241.65	1241.65	1809.28
DJ Utility Average	271.29	266.81	210.66
P/E Ratio	Nil	Nil	14.20
Earnings Yield (%)	Nil	Nil	7.04
Earns $	-3.58	-3.36	14.84
Dividend Yield (%)	3.61	3.67	5.44
Dividends ($)	9.78	9.78	11.46
Market to Book	1.91	1.88	1.26
Book Value ($)	141.77	141.77	167.48
S&P 500 Index	1141.55	1139.83	861.40
P/E Ratio	29.59	29.51	28.68
Earnings Yield (%)	3.38	3.39	3.49
Earns $	38.58	38.62	30.04
Dividend Yield (%)	1.61	1.59	1.87
Dividends ($)	18.38	18.12	16.11
Market to Book	3.52	3.52	3.96
Book Value ($)	324.14	324.14	217.32

P/E Ratio ⟶ (P/E Ratio)

THE WALL STREET JOURNAL ONLINE
WSJ.com

BARRON'S
Get Free
Weeks of Barron's

CHART 3–3 After-Tax Corporate Profits

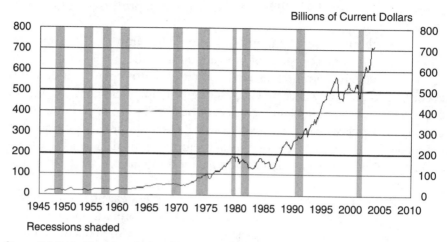

Billions of Current Dollars

Recessions shaded

Source: U.S. Dept. of Commerce, Bureau of Economic Analysis, *National Income & Product Accounts,*
Table 1.12, line 46.

sures corporate profits as compiled by the Bureau of Economic Analysis
of the Department of Commerce. It illustrates corporate earnings' rapid rise
in the 1990s, their peak in the summer of 1997, and their failure to regain
that peak despite a brief surge associated with the Y2K boom in 2000.
Manufacturers' profits (see Chart 3–4), as compiled by the Census Bureau,

CHART 3–4 Manufacturers' After-Tax Profits

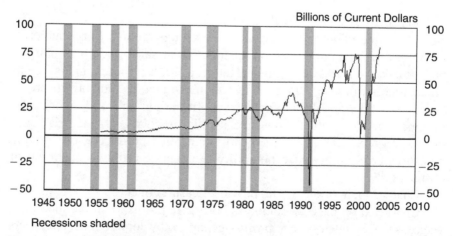

Billions of Current Dollars

Recessions shaded

Source: U.S. Census Bureau, *Quarterly Financial Report for Manufacturing Corporations,* Table 2, Part B.

exhibit a similar pattern. They peak in early 1998, then dip before a last hurrah in 2000. By 1997–1998 the sharp run-up in profits was drawing to a close.

These charts raise an important issue: Why didn't EPS reflect the 1997–1998 profit peak instead of growing until 2000?

Unfortunately, corporations were not required to report their earnings according to generally accepted accounting principles. Some firms did not even report their earnings on a consistent basis. The worst of these short-comings have now been corrected following the widespread disclosures of corporate skullduggery. The government agencies whose data underlie Charts 3–3 and 3–4 do, of course, report corporate profits on a consistent and mean-ingful basis.

The Wall Street Journal can also help you assess earnings on a timely basis. Its survey of corporate profits for over 1,500 corporations, including industry-wide statistics on earnings and net income, appears about two months after the close of the quarter. The second paragraph of the Tuesday, August 5, 2003, online edition article on page 27 reports a 63 percent earnings increase over the year-earlier (second) quarter. The *Journal* also summarizes the Com-merce Department's Bureau of Economic Analysis accounting for corporate profits. The second paragraph of its Wednesday, November 26, 2003, online article (see page 28) informs you of a 30 percent increase in corporate prof-its from the same (third) quarter a year ago.

You can gain access to any *Journal* online article by clicking on Article Archives under Research on the home page and following the instructions provided.

PROFIT MARGINS AND PROFITABILITY

Now it is time to probe further into the earnings reports. Corporate prof-its reflect the amount earned on each dollar of sales (the profit margin) multiplied by dollar-sales volume. Thus, if a firm's profit margin is 5 cents on each dollar of sales and it sells $100 of product, its total profits are $5 ($0.05 × $100 = $5). If you focus on profit margin only and ignore sales volume, you can evaluate how successfully the firm is able to price each unit of product above its cost of producing that product. Profit margin measures profitability, i.e., the ability to generate profit on each unit of output sold.

Charts 3–5, 3–6, and 3–7 all provide measures of corporate profitability.

Chart 3–5 on page 29 compares corporate profits to all the income—wages, salaries, interest, rent, profit—generated by corporations. It answers this question: What percent is corporate profits of the total income generated

THE WALL STREET JOURNAL.
O N L I N E

Other Journal Sites

As of 7:14 p.m. EDT Tuesday, August 5, 2003

Home
News ▶
Technology ▶
Markets ▶
Personal Journal ▶
Opinion ▶
Leisure/Weekend ▶

In Today's Paper
Columnists
Portfolio
Setup Center
Site Map
Discussions
Help
Contact Us
Log In

THE WALL STREET JOURNAL
Print Editions
Customer Service

Today In:

BARRON'S Online

PAGE ONE

Profits at Big Companies Show Solid Gains in Second Period

Some Executives Are Remaining Cautious
Despite Signs Recovery Is Gaining Steam

By JON E. HILSENRATH
Staff Reporter of THE WALL STREET JOURNAL

It's been a long time coming, but the growth in corporate profits appears to be picking up momentum.

Net income rose 63% in the second quarter among companies tracked by Dow Jones & Co. that had reported earnings as of Friday. At present levels, net income is approaching historic highs and falls just short of the $122.9 billion recorded when the economy was still booming during the second quarter of 2000. The profit improvement, if sustained in the coming months, could contribute to the stronger economic recovery that so many economists are now predicting.

Corporate Earnings

HIT OR MISS?

 See an interactive graphic of select companies that hit the bull's eye and that missed the mark.

Still, some executives, in talking about their earnings progress, remained cautious in conference calls with investors in recent weeks. "I don't need to remind investors that second-half economic recoveries were expected back in 2001 and again in 2002," John Joyce, International Business Machines Corp.'s chief financial officer, said in mid-July after the company beat analyst expectations with its earnings report. "While some may argue that it's more likely this year, we're going to take a very pragmatic view."

Dow Jones, which publishes The Wall Street Journal, tracks more than 1,500 companies in its US Total Market Index. Of these, 1,251 companies had reported earnings for the second quarter as of Friday. Combined net income for those companies was $112.5 billion, up from $69.2 billion a year earlier. The figures are those actually reported by listed companies under generally accepted accounting principles, without the many special adjustments that Wall Street analysts often make to the numbers. Helping to make comparisons to a year ago more favorable, the latest results included fewer charges and asset write-offs than last year, when many companies were cleaning their books due in part to new accounting rules and a wave of bookkeeping scandals. Nevertheless, analysts said the second-quarter increase in profits was real.

Corporate Earnings–Second Paragraph

Net income rose 63% in the second quarter among companies tracked by Dow Jones & Co. that had reported earnings as of Friday. At present levels, net income is approaching historic highs and falls just short of the $122.9 billion recorded when the economy was still booming during the second quarter of 2000. The profit improvement, if sustained in the coming months, could contribute to the stronger economic recovery that so many economists are now predicting.

As of Wednesday, November 26, 2003

Other Journal Sites

- Home
- News
- Technology
- Markets
- Personal Journal
- Opinion
- Leisure/Weekend

In Today's Paper
Columnists
Portfolio
Setup Center
Site Map
Discussions
Help
Contact Us

THE WALL STREET JOURNAL
Print Editions
Customer Service

Today In:

BARRON'SOnline

@ Your Service
Lind-Waldock
FREE report! Get your
Stock Market Outlook
CLICK HERE
More Insights. Better
Decisions. Visit The
Business Insight Center.
Avoid the lines.
continental.com check-in.
Give the perfect gift:
The Online Journal

PAGE ONE

Company Profits Soared By 30% in 3rd Quarter

Biggest Gain in Two Decades Came as GDP Is Revised Up; Red-Hot Pace Seen Cooling

By JON E. HILSENRATH
Staff Reporter of THE WALL STREET JOURNAL

The economic recovery has picked up momentum, boosting the bottom lines of a wide range of U.S. corporations.

The Commerce Department reported that profits at American companies rose 30% in the third quarter, compared with a year earlier. That was the largest year-over-year growth in profits in 19 years and was enough to lift the annual pace of profits above $1 trillion for the first time in history.

Corporate Earnings

The corporate profit figures were part of a broader report on economic output, or gross domestic product. The government revised up its estimate of the annual rate of third-quarter GDP to 8.2% from the previously reported annual pace of 7.2%. The revision in GDP -- the total value of the nation's goods and services -- occurred largely because companies didn't reduce inventories as aggressively as previously thought in the face of booming consumer demand. Less inventory reduction meant companies had to produce more goods to keep up with demand.

For many companies, the combination of faster economic growth (which spurs revenue gains) and rapid productivity improvement (which helps contain costs) translates to stronger profits. Better profits, in turn, are expected to give business executives added confidence to hire more workers and invest more aggressively in new projects.

"This is making us more confident that this [recovery] is sustainable," said James Glassman, an economist with J.P. Morgan Chase & Co. "Hiring is already under way and my guess is it is going to accelerate."

Underscoring that point, the Conference Board said its index of consumer confidence rose to 91.7 in November from 81.7 in October, as fewer of the 5,000 people contacted in the group's monthly mail survey said jobs were hard to get.

Corporate Earnings–Second Paragraph

The Commerce Department reported that profits at American companies rose 30% in the third quarter, compared with a year earlier. That was the largest year-over-year growth in profits in 19 years and was enough to lift annual pace of profits above $1 trillion for the first time in history.

CHART 3–5 Ratio: Corporate Profits to Corporate Income

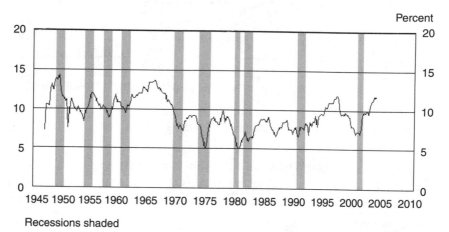

Recessions shaded

Source: The Conference Board, *Business Cycle Indicators,* Series A0Q081.

CHART 3–6 Ratio: Implicit Price Deflator to Unit Labor Costs, Nonfarm Business

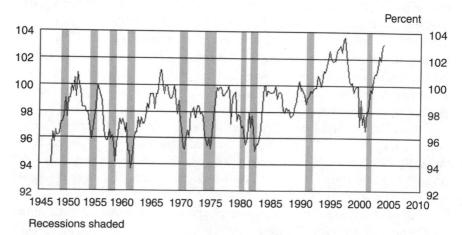

Recessions shaded

Source: U.S. Bureau of Labor Statistics.

CHART 3–7 After-Tax Profits in Cents per Dollar of Sales: Manufacturing

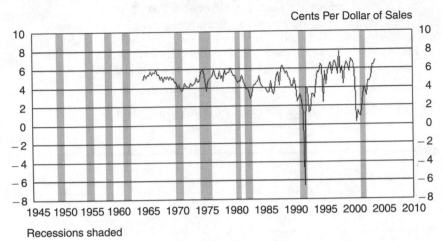

Cents Per Dollar of Sales

Recessions shaded

Source: U.S. Census Bureau, *Quarterly Financial Report for Manufacturing Corporations,* Table 1, Part A.

by American corporations? The answer is an approximate expression of corporate profits as a share of sales revenue. You can see that the ratio grew from less than 8 percent in 1990 to more than 12 percent in 1997, and then began to fall.

Chart 3–6 on page 29 portrays the ratio of price to unit labor cost. This is a fraction in which price is the numerator (top half) and cost is the denominator (bottom half). This ratio informs you of the extent of labor cost's encroachment on prices, business's ability to hold down labor costs in relation to the price received, and it is therefore a proxy for profit margins. Chart 3–6 shows that the ratio fluctuated in a range between 96 and 102 prior to the 1990s and how, in a steep and dramatic climb, it rose to 105 in 1997–1998. In little more than a decade, price—the revenue generated on each unit of output—had grown 5 percent more than the costs associated with each unit of output. American business had posted an unprecedented improvement in profitability. Then the decline began.

Manufacturers profits in cents per dollar of sales (see Chart 3–7) tell a similar story. They had occasionally reached a high of 6 cents per dollar of sales. By 1995 and 1996 they were over 6 cents and peaked at 8 cents in 1997 and 1998. For a couple of years afterward, they fluctuated around 6 cents before slipping away.

These charts present a phenomenal and unprecedented growth in the profitability of American business from 1990 to 1997–1998. But, as a glance reveals, the earnings boom ended as quickly as it began.

What happened? Why did profits and profitability hit a wall two or three years before the boom ended and before the stock market peaked? You can see the early-warning signs, but what causes lay at their root?

Wait a minute, you may say. It's all well and good to explore the roots of the bubble economy's demise, yet the investigation would be incomplete if it did not delve into the economy's rebound from the bubble's collapse.

Chapter 4 delves into the causes of the New Economy's demise and also explores the sharp recovery following the 2001 recession.

C H A P T E R

4

OUTPUT, EFFICIENCY, AND COSTS

NEW ECONOMY VS. OLD ECONOMY

ROFITS FELL AND PROFIT MARGINS SHRANK IN THE LATE 1990s, warning investors that the stock-market bubble was about to burst. This chapter will show that rising wages, the obvious product of full employment, lay at the root of this profit squeeze. Since these developments and facts were not hidden from investors' view, why didn't investors make a connection between full employment, rising wages, and the profit squeeze that would ultimately sink the stock market?

Unfortunately, widespread belief that a "New Economy" was at hand convinced many investors that rising productivity (efficiency, or output per worker) would solve all problems. The New Economy advocates argued that the personal-computer revolution, along with the Internet and all the other accoutrements of the interconnected age, would raise output per worker (productivity) so rapidly that businesses' costs had to continually fall and profitability regularly rise regardless of the increase in wages.

For instance, citing a crude example, even if a business must pay its employees twice as much per hour, that business's cost per unit of output will fall by half if each employee produces four time as much per hour. Why will those employees' productivity quadruple? Because they are using their computers and the Web to work faster, smarter, and more efficiently. As per-unit costs slid relentlessly downward with the computer age's advance, profit margins and profits would rise equally relentlessly with the growing gap between prices and costs. Earnings' upward spiral would lift the stock market with it, said the New Economy advocates. The good times would never end.

The New Economy advocates said, "This time it's different." There would be no surging costs and no shrinking profit margins to disable the boom because they believed that the Old Economy's rules no longer applied. In the Old Economy, their analysis went, rapidly rising output strained facilities, reduced efficiency and raised costs, thereby depressing profit margins and profits. In other words, every boom contained the seeds of its own demise.

The reasons were straightforward. At the peak of the cycle, when output is at its maximum, production facilities are strained to the point where production costs rise sharply. Overburdened equipment fails, accelerating the expense of maintenance and repair. The quantities of labor added to the production process are relatively greater than the increase in output. Inevitable inefficiencies force up costs. If, because of competitive pressures, management cannot raise prices in lock-step with increasing costs, and costs rise more rapidly than prices, profit margins are squeezed and profits fall. Eventually, inflation increases if shrinking profit margins do not bear the entire burden of rising costs and management is able to raise prices. The worst of all worlds transpires: shrinking profits, rising prices, and a falling stock market.

So much for the Old Economy's rules. This time, in the 1990s, the New Economy advocates said it was different. Under the New Economy's rules, businesses' continual addition of new plant and equipment, especially new computer hardware and software, would boost productivity (efficiency, or output per worker) to such an extent that output could increase limitlessly without compromising efficiency, raising costs, squeezing profit margins, and generating inflation.

In a way, the economy would never reach the top of the cycle. Rather, the economy would grow and grow without straining facilities and raising costs. Put differently, productivity would increase continually and effortlessly. Under these circumstances, profit margins would not shrink and inflation would not occur. The stock market could continue on its upward trajectory, uninterrupted by the Old Economy business cycle and its inevitable crimp on profit growth.

Unfortunately, the New Economy advocates did not anticipate that full employment would undo their forecast. Rising output required more workers, and before long employers were raiding one another's work forces in order to recruit new employees. As employers bid wages upward, output per worker could not keep pace with rapidly escalating wages.

✕ This point requires emphasis. Productivity—efficiency or output per worker—continued to climb. It's just that wages rose more rapidly than the gain in productivity. Therefore, employment costs rose despite productivity's continued ascent. As employment costs rose, profit margins fell and the stock market and the economy inevitably slumped as businesses cut back their expansion in a climate of reduced profitability. The New Economy had met its match.

The connections between output, efficiency, costs, and profits form this chapter's central theme. Let's turn now to an examination of the statistical releases that will be of particular importance in charting the course of production and the interaction of efficiency, inflation, and profit margins as the economy moves through the business cycle.

Take the time and have the patience to acquaint yourself with these indicators, because they will unlock your understanding of corporate profits. Gross domestic product, industrial production, and capacity utilization measure the economy's output; productivity measures its efficiency. Let's start with gross domestic product, industrial production, and capacity utilization before moving to productivity.

GROSS DOMESTIC PRODUCT

Gross domestic product (GDP) is a good place to start. As the broadest available measure of economic activity, it provides the official scale with which fluctuations in the economy are measured.

The Wall Street Journal publishes data from the U.S. Department of Commerce's quarterly release on the GDP about one month after the close of the quarter. Then, near the end of the two subsequent months, it reports revisions of the data. The third quarter 2003 figures appeared in the Friday, October 31, 2003, print edition (see page 35).

A front-page chart accompanies some GDP articles in the print edition. See, for instance, the excerpt from the October 31, 2003, *Journal* on page 35.

The second paragraph of the October 31, 2003, story tells you the economy grew at a 7.2 percent annual rate in the third quarter of 2003. What does this figure mean?

Constant-dollar (real) GDP measures the final output of goods and services produced in the U.S. in a year, without including the impact of changed prices on the value of those goods. Thus, this year's output (as well as last year's output, next year's, or any year we wish to measure) is calculated in the prices of the base year (2000).

This kind of aggregate measure was once referred to as the gross national product (GNP), and there is a slight difference between the two. Put simply, GNP measures the output and earnings of Americans, no matter where they

Higher Gear

Economy Turned In Its Best Quarter In Nearly 2 Decades

GDP Surged 7.2% in Quarter On Broad-Based Gains; Bush Team Trumpets Data

Employment Continues to Lag

By Jacob M. Schlesinger
And Jon E. Hilsenrath

The U.S. economy shot out of the doldrums to its best quarterly growth rate in nearly two decades, giving a potentially powerful political lift to President Bush despite chronic weakness in the job market.

The 7.2% annualized rise in gross domestic product in the third quarter was the strongest pace of growth since the first quarter of 1984 and the broadest-based gain in the economy in the three years since the stock-market-fueled boom years of the 1990s.

Spending by consumers, exports and residential construction all registered sharp gains. But the news economists found most significant was that investment by businesses grew at an 11% annual clip, the fastest rate since early 2000.

The burst of growth was in different measures both an economic and a political achieve-

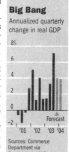

Big Bang

Annualized quarterly change in real GDP

Forecast

'01 '02 '03 '04

Sources: Commerce
Department via
-Economy.com; WSJ.com

GDP

ment for President Bush. As the economy sputtered after the stock market tanked in 2000 and the terrorist attacks of 2001, he pushed through the biggest tax cuts in history, adding fiscal fuel to the monetary stimulus of lower interest rates set by the Federal Reserve.

While the economy certainly won't keep up the third quarter's blistering pace in the months ahead, most economists believe the quarter marks a distinctive shift into a more-robust expansion that could stretch to next year's presidential election. "We're not going to see 7% growth again, but we could well see over 4% over the course of the next year," said Richard Berner, an economist with Morgan Stanley in New York.

The darkest shadow over the economy now is unemployment, which remains above 6% of the labor force. Yesterday's GDP number was also just a preliminary estimate by the Commerce Department and could be revised in a few months. Some economists questioned whether steady growth could continue once the short-term effects of pump-priming from tax cuts and low interest rates wear off. Moreover, critics of the tax cuts argue that their contribution to the latest burst of growth comes at a steep cost: mounting federal budget deficits.

But yesterday's report will take some sting out of the most potent attack Democrats have been honing for the 2004 campaign: that Mr. Bush, like his father, is presiding over a weak economy and doesn't deserve another term. By early afternoon, Mr. Bush's campaign aimed to take advantage, e-mailing a giddy report with the subject line, "Breaking News: Largest economic growth in 19 years."

"There is no precedent in the last generation and a half of an American president losing an election when the economy is booming," says Republican pollster William McInturff. The last president to enjoy such a strong quarter was Ronald Reagan, who successfully managed the shift from economic gloom to optimism to win a second term after a deep recession.

Strong growth, if sustained, helps Mr. Bush in his running argument with Democrats about the wisdom of his aggressive tax-cutting, the centerpiece of his economic policy. As retired Gen. Wesley Clark, one of the nine Democrats competing to challenge Mr. Bush, said in a debate in Detroit earlier this week: "They said tax cuts would help us.... They didn't." Mr. Bush was quick to offer a rebuttal in a
Please Turn to Page A6, Column 4

---

live and work, whereas GDP measures output and earnings in the U.S. regardless of the earner's nationality. For instance, GNP includes the profits of American corporations overseas and excludes the profits of foreign corporations in America, while GDP excludes the former and includes the latter.

GDP includes only final goods and services. This eliminates measuring the same thing more than once at various stages of its production. For instance, bread purchased by the consumer appears in GDP, but both the flour from which the bread is baked and the wheat from which the flour is milled are omitted, because the value of the bread comprises the value of all its ingredients. Thus, the economy's output of *all* goods and services is far

GDP–Second Paragraph

The 7.2% annualized rise in gross domestic product in the third quarter was the strongest pace of growth since the first quarter of 1984 and the broadest-based gain in the economy in the three years since the market boom years of the 1990s.

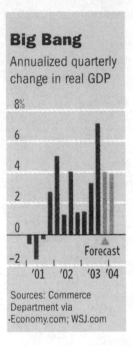

Big Bang

Annualized quarterly change in real GDP

greater than its output of *final* (GDP) goods and services. We use very little steel, chemicals, or advertising agency services directly. Their value is subsumed in our purchases of well-promoted Chevrolets and Saran Wrap.

The second paragraph of the October 31, 2003, article (see above) refers to a 7.2 percent increase of final output in 2003's third quarter. This measurement was made at a *seasonally adjusted annual rate*. Adjusting for seasonal factors merely means correcting the distortion in the data arising from the measurement being taken during this rather than any other quarter. Obviously, no seasonal adjustment is required when a whole year's data is measured, but when the year is divided up and data extracted for a run of months, the risk of distortion attributable to the season is great. For instance, retail trade is particularly heavy around Christmas and particularly light immediately after the first of the year; you could not make a useful comparison of the first quarter's retail sales with the last quarter's without first making a seasonal adjustment.

The reference to "annual rate" shows that the data for the third quarter, which of course covers only three months' activity, has been multiplied by 4 to increase it to a level comparable to annual data.

The constant-dollar or real GDP calculation is made in order to compare the level of output in one time period with that in another without inflation's distorting impact. If the inflation factor were not removed, you would not

CHART 4–1 GDP in 2000 Dollars; Change in Constant (2000) Dollar GDP

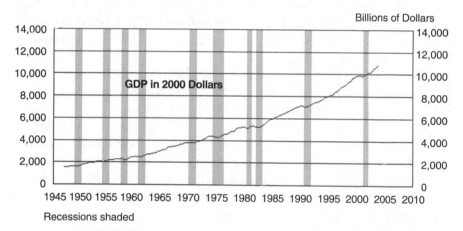

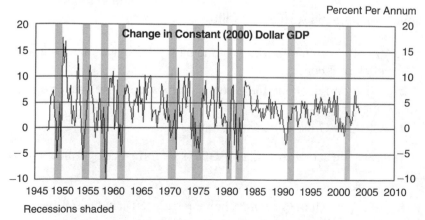

Source: U.S. Dept. of Commerce, Bureau of Economic Analysis, *National Income & Product Accounts*, Table 1.1.6, line 1, and Table 1.1.1, line 1.

GDP per capita!
↳ Population
Growth Rate?

Kids eventy producers?

know whether differences in dollar value were due to output changes or price changes. Real GDP gives you a dollar value that measures output changes only.

One last point should be made before moving on. A glance at Chart 4–1 shows a steady and robust rise in GDP throughout the 1990s. A 3 percent annual increase in GDP is well above the rate of population growth, providing a substantial per capita gain, without getting to an unsustainable rate of more than 5 percent, which, for any length of time, strains our productive capacity. The 7.2 percent gain reported for the third quarter could not long continue.

Now you are ready to put GDP's current performance in historical perspective. Compare it with Chart 4–1 on page 37.

The top graph portrays the actual level of GDP, while the bottom graph depicts quarterly percentage changes at annual rates. When the bottom series is above the zero line, GDP has increased; a drop in GDP is indicated by points below the zero line.

As you look at these graphs, pay special attention to GDP's setback during the recessions of 1990–1991 and 2001. "Two consecutive quarters of declining GDP" is the traditional definition of recession.

The *Journal*'s online edition (http://online.wsj.com) can also help you grasp GDP's trend by providing you with the government's GDP report, an up-to-date chart, and a private research firm's (Briefing.com) analysis. You may wish to review the general directions for retrieving online information on page 7 of Chapter 1. Appendix D on page 374 also furnishes you with a quick guide to the *Journal*'s online edition.

You can find the latest GDP report by the Commerce Department's Bureau of Economic Analysis as follows:

1. Scroll down the *Journal*'s home page's left-hand menu-bar and click on Economy.
2. Click on Economic Indicators under Data and Resources on the upper right.
3. Click on Gross Domestic Product.

You can gain access to a chart of GDP's performance by following these steps:

1. Scroll down the *Journal*'s home page's left-hand menu-bar and click on Economy.
2. Click on Economic Chartbook under Data and Resources.

Home

News   Technology   Markets   Your Money

MARKETS DATA
SECTION INDEX ⊕

Economic Chartbook

U.S. Economic Calendar   Economic Indicator Archive   Reports From Briefing.com

Charts: Industrial Production I Purchasing Managers I Retail Sales I Consumer Spending
Consumer Confidence I Consumer Prices I Producer Prices I Housing Starts I Existing-Home Sa
International Trade

Economic Growth and Employment

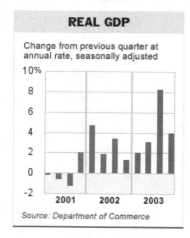

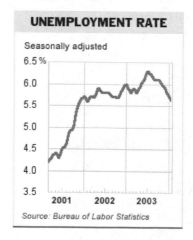

Q4: +4% Full report BEA Revisions (1929-2003)	**January: 5.6%** Full report

The chart from the Thursday, January 8, 2004, edition of the online *Journal* appears above.

Here's how to find Briefing.com's latest GDP analysis:

1. Scroll down the *Journal*'s home page's left-hand menu-bar and click on Economy.

2. Click on Reports from Briefing.com under Data and Resources.
3. Click on GDP—Prel.

Consider the example below taken from the Thursday, February 19, 2004, edition of the online *Journal*. (The chain deflator—the less-volatile line—measures inflation.)

These reports bear witness to GDP's formidable surge in 2003's third quarter and show that consumption expenditures, residential construction, and technology investments played key roles in the advance.

WSJ.com THE WALL STREET JOURNAL.
O N L I N E

Home

News   Technology   Markets   Personal Journal

MARKETS DATA
SECTION INDEX ▶

Briefing.com

Thursday, February 19, 2004

Q4 GDP-ADV.

Commentary and background from Briefing.com. See an index of reports.

BRIEFING.COM°
Live Market Analysis

Updated: 30-Jan-04 | Archive | Glossary

Return to Economic Calendar

GDP & Chain Deflator
year-on-year % change

```
6.0%

4.0%

2.0%

0.0%

-2.0%
      Q1 90   Q1 92   Q1 94   Q1 96   Q1 98   Q1 00   Q1 02
```

Updated: 30-Jan-04   ——— GDP ——— Chain Deflator

So far so good. GDP's growth and fluctuation provide a clear measure of the economy's performance. Rapid growth and recession are easy to observe. But the clash of the Old Economy and New Economy has not been resolved. In order to deal with this issue, you will need a more volatile and sensitive measure of the economy's performance.

Industrial production and capacity utilization will mirror GDP's record and also provide important additional detail, so you should now become acquainted with these series.

INDUSTRIAL PRODUCTION

The Wall Street Journal reports data from the Federal Reserve's report on *industrial production* in an article that usually appears mid-month. The Tuesday, September 16, 2003, print edition's release (see page 42) is a typical example. The second paragraph, statistical table, and chart summarize matters, while the article provides detail and commentary.

The index of industrial production measures changes in the output of the mining, manufacturing, and gas and electric utilities sectors of our economy. Industrial production is a narrower concept than GDP, because it omits agriculture, construction, wholesale and retail trade, transportation, communications, services, finance, and government. Industrial production is also more volatile than GDP, because GDP, unlike industrial production, includes activities that are largely spared cyclical fluctuation, such as services, finance, and government. The brunt of cyclical fluctuations falls on the mining, manufacturing, and public utilities sectors. Nonetheless, GDP and industrial production move in parallel fashion.

Industrial production is measured by an *index*, a technique that focuses on the relative size and fluctuation of physical output without concern for its dollar value. See Chart 4–2 on page 44. To construct the index, a base year (1997) was selected to serve as a benchmark and assigned a value of 100.0. (Think of it as 100 percent.) Data for all other months and years is then expressed in relative proportion (numerical ratio) to the data for the base year. For example, according to the statistical summary included with the article, industrial production had an index value of 110.2 in August 2003. This placed August 2003's industrial production 10.2 percent higher than the average rate of production in 1997. These developments are reflected in the rate of capacity utilization and in the efficiency with which the economy operates.

CAPACITY UTILIZATION

The Wall Street Journal publishes information from the Federal Reserve's monthly statistical release on *capacity utilization*, or, as it is often called, the

Industrial Output in U.S. Edges Up

*High-Tech Shows Strength,
But Economists Question
The Durability of Rebound*

BY PATRICK BARTA

Industrial production edged up in August, but at a less vigorous pace than in July, leading some economists to question the durability of the recent manufacturing rebound.

On a day filled with conflicting economic reports, the Federal Reserve said industrial production rose 0.1%, following a revised 0.7% rise in July. That month was previously estimated as a 0.5% gain. Production of high-tech goods such as semiconductors was very strong, but other industries, including primary metals and motor vehicles, showed declines, and overall manufacturing output fell 0.1%.

The data almost certainly wasn't weak enough to cause Federal Reserve officials to change interest rates when they meet today. Over the past several weeks, numerous other reports have pointed to a re-

[Industrial Production]

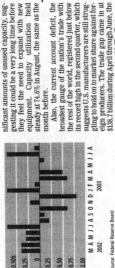

Less Productive

Month-to-month percentage change in industrial production.

M A M J J A S O N D J F M A M J J A
2002   2003

Source: Federal Reserve Board

INDUSTRIAL PRODUCTION

Here is a summary of the Federal Reserve Board's report on industrial production in August 2003. Figures are seasonally adjusted.

	% Chg. From	
	July 2003	August 2002
Total	0.1	–1.0
Consumer goods	–0.2	–0.6
Business equipment	0.5	–1.7
Defense and space	1.2	6.5
Manufacturing only	–0.1	–1.4
Durable goods	–0.2	–0.9
Nondurable goods	–0.1	–2.4
Mining	0.2	–0.4
Utilities	1.9	2.9

The industrial production index for August stood at 110.2% of the 1997 average.

[Statistical Summary]

bounding economy, and some analysts took a glass-half-full approach to the industrial-production data, viewing it as evidence that many parts of the factory sector, while not exactly booming, are at least starting to stabilize.

Highlighting that optimism, the National Association for Business Economics said its forecasters now expect the economy to show an annual growth rate of 2.6% for 2003, up from an estimate of 2.3% four months ago. The forecasters raised their 2004 estimate to 4% from 3.6%.

Even so, the industrial production report wasn't as strong as some economists had hoped, and it contained a few disquieting elements. For example, it included a 3.1% decline in primary metals production and a 2.6% drop in motor-vehicle production, though the latter was likely influenced by last month's power outage. Other categories that showed weakness included textile and apparel production. Technology production increased 2.3%, while semiconductor production climbed 2.6%.

The latest report "is more evidence

that manufacturing activity is improving, but also indicates that the gains are neither uniform over time nor by industry," said Steve Wood, chief economist at Insight Economics in Danville, Calif.

Factories continue to operate with significant amounts of unused capacity, suggesting it could be a very long time before they feel the need to expand with new equipment. Capacity utilization held steady at 74.6% in August, the same as the month before.

[Capacity Utilization]

Also, the current account deficit, the broadest gauge of the nation's trade with the rest of the world, registered just below its record high in the second quarter, which suggests U.S. manufacturers are still struggling to hold on to market share against foreign producers. The trade gap came in at $138.7 billion during April through June, the Commerce Department said. The first quarter's current account deficit was revised to $138.7 billion from a previously-reported $136.1 billion.

Yesterday, Commerce Secretary Don Evans said he plans to travel to China in a few weeks and intends to have a Commerce Department official in China "once a month" to raise issues of concern to American manufacturers. Among those issues are currency manipulation, trade barriers, piracy of intellectual property and insulated capital markets.

*— Rebecca Christie of Dow Jones
Newswires contributed to this article.*

Industrial Production–Second Paragraph

On a day filled with conflicting economic reports, the Federal Reserve said industrial production rose 0.1%, following a revised 0.7% rise in July. That month was previously estimated as a 0.5% gain. Production of high-tech goods such as semiconductors was very strong, but other industries, including primary metals and motor vehicles, showed declines, and overall manufacturing output fell 0.1%.

INDUSTRIAL PRODUCTION

Here is a summary of the Federal Reserve Board's report on industrial production in August 2003. Figures are seasonally adjusted.

	% Chg. From July 2003	August 2002
Total	0.1	−1.0
Consumer goods	−0.2	−0.6
Business equipment	0.5	−1.7
Defense and space	1.2	6.5
Manufacturing only	−0.1	−1.4
Durable goods	−0.2	−0.9
Nondurable goods	−0.1	−2.4
Mining	0.2	−0.4
Utilities	1.9	2.9

The industrial production index for August stood at 110.2% of the 1997 average.

Less Productive

Month-to-month percentage change in industrial production.

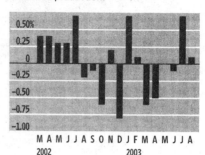

M A M J J A S O N D J F M A M J J A
2002   2003

Source: Federal Reserve Board

factory operating rate, along with the industrial production figures. The third paragraph from the end of the September 16, 2003, print article, below, reports capacity utilization's 74.6 percent rate in August 2003.

Capacity utilization is the rate at which mining, manufacturing, and public utilities industries operate, expressed as a percentage of the maxi-

---

Capacity Utilization–Third from Last Paragraph

Factories continue to operate with significant amounts of unused capacity, suggesting it could be a very long time before they feel the need to expand with new equipment. Capacity utilization held steady at 74.6% in August, the same as the month before.

CHART 4–2 Industrial Production Index

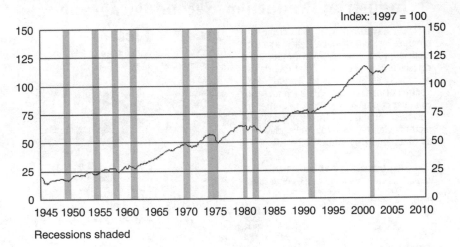

Recessions shaded

Source: Federal Reserve.

mum rate at which they could operate under existing conditions. Putting the matter differently, think of capacity utilization as measuring what these industries are currently producing compared (in percentage terms) to the most they could produce using all of their present resources. Thus, if an industry produces 80 tons of product in a year, while having plant and equipment at its disposal capable of producing 100 tons a year, that industry is operating at 80 percent of capacity; its capacity utilization is 80 percent.

Capacity utilization is a short-run concept determined by a company's current physical limits; at any moment in which capacity utilization is reported, it is assumed that the company's plant and equipment cannot be increased, although labor and other inputs can. This defines the short run.

Although manufacturing industry continually adds new plant and equipment, it is useful to snap a photograph at a particular moment to enable measurement and comparison.

What bearing does capacity utilization have on the efficiency or productivity of industry? The following analogy is crucial to your understanding of the New Economy advocates' analysis of the Old Economy's operation. The New Economy advocates argued that the personal computer and the Internet would free the economy from the Old Economy constraints, as illustrated by the following hypothetical analogy.

Your car operates more efficiently at 50 miles per hour than at 70 miles per hour if its maximum speed is 80, for you will obtain better gas mileage at the lower speed.

Efficiency is expressed as a relationship between inputs (gas gallons) and outputs (miles driven). Your car's engine operates more efficiently at lower speeds, or at lower levels of capacity utilization.

You are therefore confronted with the problem of diminishing returns: As your speed increases, you obtain fewer miles for each additional gallon of gas. At 50 miles per hour, you can go 30 miles on an additional gallon of gas; at 52 miles per hour, 29 miles on an additional gallon; at 54 miles per hour, 28 miles; and so on. Your output (miles) per unit of input (gallon) falls as you push toward full capacity utilization (maximum speed).

Likewise, as capacity utilization increases, an industry also passes the point of diminishing returns. This may be at 70 percent, 80 percent, or 90 percent of capacity utilization, depending on the industry, but the point will ultimately be reached where the percentage increases in output will become smaller than the percentage increases in input. For instance, a 15 percent increase in labor input, once we have passed the point of diminishing returns, may provide only a 10 percent increase in output. This phenomenon does not occur because of some mystical mathematical relationship, nor because people are just like automobile engines. There are common-sense reasons for it, and you probably know many of them already.

First, at low levels of capacity utilization, there is ample time to inspect, maintain, and repair equipment; accidental damage can be held to a minimum; and production increases can be achieved easily in a smoothly efficient plant. Above a certain level of capacity utilization, however, management finds it more difficult to inspect, maintain, and repair equipment because of the plant's heavier operating schedule. Perhaps a second shift of workers has been added or additional overtime scheduled. There is less time for equipment maintenance, and accidental damage becomes inevitable. The labor force is in place and on the payroll, and production does increase, but not as rapidly as does labor input, because equipment frequently breaks down.

Second, as production increases and more labor is hired, the last people hired are less experienced and usually less efficient than the older workers; furthermore, crowding and fatigue can become a problem if more overtime is scheduled. Poor work quality and accidental damage result. All of this ensures that output will not increase as rapidly as labor input.

Third, low levels of capacity utilization occur at the trough of a recession. Business firms typically suffer a sharp drop in profit, if not actual losses, and, under these circumstances, the employer reduces the work force as much as possible. In fact, the firm usually reduces the work force more than the drop in output, once the decision to cut back has been made. Why more than the drop in output? Because by the trough of recession, the seriousness of the situation is recognized, and industry has embarked on a thorough restructuring. The alarm has sounded and costs (work force) are slashed. That's why recession often generates the sharpest increases in efficiency.

Even after output has begun to recover, an extended period of labor reduction may continue as part of a general cost-cutting program. As recovery boosts capacity utilization, however, hiring additional workers becomes inevitable. When a factory reaches full capacity utilization near the peak of a boom, the cost-cutting program will be long forgotten as management scrambles for additional labor in order to meet the barrage of orders. At this point, additions to labor are greater than increments in output, even though (to repeat) output will be rising somewhat.

You can summarize business's decisions regarding labor as follows. During rapid expansion and into economic boom, when orders are heavy and capacity utilization is strained, business will sacrifice efficiency and short-run profits to maintain customer loyalty. Management adds labor more rapidly than output increases in order to get the job done. But, when the recession hits in earnest, and it becomes apparent that orders will not recover for some time, management cuts labor costs to the bone with layoffs and a freeze on hiring. This is especially true during a prolonged recession, such as that of 1981–1982, which followed on the heels of an earlier recession (in 1980) and an incomplete recovery. Even after recovery and expansion begin, however, business will still attempt to operate with a reduced labor force in order to reap the benefits of cost cutting in the form of higher profits. Operating efficiency (productivity) improves rapidly, and it will not be threatened until the expansion heats up and boom conditions develop.

Remember the motor in your car? Efficiency is expressed as the relationship between inputs (fuel) and outputs (distance traveled). It is useful to think of the economy as if it were a machine, like the engine in your car.

Since your engine is fixed in size (at any moment in time), you can only push a finite amount of fuel through it. Depressing the accelerator rapidly increases your speed and the distance traveled, but the increment in fuel used is greater than the increment in speed and distance. Hence, the efficiency of your engine falls, despite your greater speed and distance. You are getting fewer miles per gallon, and it's taking more fuel to go a mile, because you are driving faster.

Just as a bigger engine would help you accelerate more quickly, more industrial capacity would permit the economy to operate more efficiently. But, for the moment, the economy is limited to the amount of capacity on hand, making it useful to speak about the rate of capacity utilization at any moment in time. And it is important to realize that, like your car engine, the economy becomes less efficient if it is pushed too hard.

Now compare capacity utilization's historical record with that of GDP. See Chart 4–3 below. Note that the figure did not rise above the 85 percent

CHART 4–3 GDP and Capacity Utilization

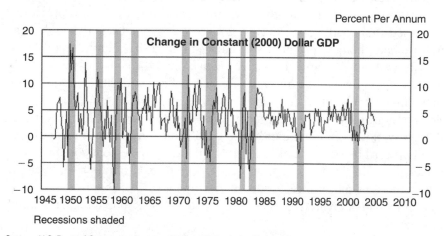

Recessions shaded

Source: U.S. Dept. of Commerce, Bureau of Economic Analysis, *National Income & Product Accounts,*
Table 1.1.1, line 1.

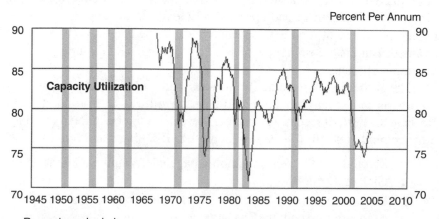

Recessions shaded

Source: Federal Reserve.

range throughout the 1990s. This evidence of relaxed growth in GDP kept our economic machinery cool and prevented overheating.

These observations return you to the Old Economy vs. New Economy controversy. The New Economy advocates made two points. First, they said that personal computer and Internet capabilities had dramatically upgraded industrial capacity's quality. The equipment of the 1990s was better than that of earlier periods. Second, they said that business continued to add capacity so rapidly throughout the 1990s that utilization rates could not climb to dangerous levels. Returning to the automobile-engine analogy, it was as if the New Economy advocates were insisting that the economy's engine grew bigger and better as the economy accelerated, thereby avoiding increased strain and costs. The New Economy argument said that high technology had changed production relationships so that output could grow rapidly without straining productive capacity and the economy.

The New Economy advocates seemed to have it right for a while, but they did not anticipate rising wages' squeeze on profit margins. Rapid additions of high-technology equipment boosted output and productivity, holding prices down. But that didn't stop costs from surging when wages spiraled upward in a climate of full employment. Management couldn't raise prices as swiftly as it wished, but it did have to pay rapidly rising wages. Profit margins and profits eroded in a climate of low inflation. The Old Economy had not reared its ugly head, but the New Economy had not fared any better.

Returning to the analogy of the automobile engine, fuel efficiency could not reduce fuel costs because fuel prices had risen more rapidly than engine efficiency. Management had operated efficiently in the engineering sense by adding plenty of high-tech productive capacity. Facilities had not been strained. But costs rose nonetheless as rising wages undid any gain from operating efficiency.

The *Journal*'s online edition provides you with up-to-date charts and reports on industrial production and capacity utilization from the Federal Reserve and Briefing.com. Just follow these steps to obtain them (see page 38 to remind yourself of how you found the GDP charts and reports).

1. Scroll down the *Journal*'s home page's left-hand menu-bar and click on Economy.
2. Click on Economic Indicators, Economic Chartbook and Reports from Briefing.com under Data and Resources.

The next series in this chapter, labor productivity and unit labor costs, will provide the statistical measurements needed to calibrate these fluctuations in efficiency and wage cost. But first, a brief note on the Purchasing Managers' Index.

PURCHASING MANAGERS' INDEX

You can buttress your analysis of manufacturing activity by tracking the Purchasing Managers' Index (PMI) as reported by the Institute of Supply Management. Purchasing managers at industrial corporations report whether key material inputs required in manufacturing operations (such as steel, lumber, cement, chemicals, etc.) are easier or more difficult to obtain. Their observations provide a measure of whether manufacturing operations are expanding or contracting. A reading over 50 indicates expanding activity; a reading under 50 indicates the opposite.

See the example below from the Tuesday, December 3, 2003, print edition of the *Journal*, especially the graph and the second paragraph. Also see

U.S. Manufacturing Activity Surges

Sector's Jobs Rise Sharply; Even Optimistic Forecasts Are Topped by the Results

By MICHAEL SCHROEDER

WASHINGTON—U.S. manufacturing last month showed the most robust activity in two decades, lifting employment in the sector to the highest level in more than three years.

The private Institute for Supply Management said its November index of manufacturing activity came in at 62.8, up from 57 for October. Providing solid evidence of an improving manufacturing jobs picture, the ISM's employment index climbed to 51 from 47.7. It marks the first time since September 2000 the gauge exceeded 50.

Readings of at least 50 indicate growth in the U.S. industrial sector, which has lagged behind other areas of the American economic recovery.

The economic data were stronger than even optimistic forecasts. Economists surveyed by Dow Jones Newswires and CNBC had expected the overall industrial index to rise to 59 for November.

In addition, order backlogs increased and supplier deliveries slowed, indicating that demand is outstripping production.

"More and more sectors of manufacturing are beginning to be influenced by the recovery," including steel, said Jerry Jasinowski, president of the National As-

Expanding

The ISM Manufacturing Index; values above 50 indicate an expanding factory sector

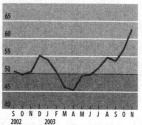

Source: Institute for Supply Management via Economy.com

sociation of Manufacturers.

Wall Street cheered the improvement, with major stock indexes extending earlier gains on the news and bond prices, which are sensitive to interest rates, falling. The Dow Jones Industrial Average gained 116.59, or 1.2%, to 9899.05, and the Nasdaq Composite Index gained 29.56, or 1.5%, to 1989.82. The dollar rallied. The euro, which had risen to a high of $1.2040 in London trading, weakened to $1.1975, down from $1.1991 late Friday in New York. The dollar advanced mainly against major European currencies, while heavy selling of euros against the yen limited the dollar's

Purchasing Managers' Index

strength against the Japanese currency.

Calling the survey results "astonishing," Ian Shepherdson, chief U.S. economist at High Frequency Economics Ltd. in Valhalla, N.Y., said the November reading is consistent with an economic growth rate of about 7%. He said the employment survey suggests "the three-year run of industrial-job losses will soon end."

Meanwhile, the U.S. Commerce Department said construction spending for October increased a higher-than-expected 0.9%, as residential home building reached unprecedented levels. Big gains also were registered in public projects as federal and state governments have ramped up spending.

Overall construction spending rose to a seasonally adjusted annual rate of $922 billion from an upwardly revised $913.5 billion for September.

While private residential-construction spending rose 2.2% to a record $484.1 billion from $473.6 billion, private nonresidential construction slipped 2.1%. The decline, the steepest since a 2.3% drop in December 2002, was driven by weakness in construction of commercial facilities, power plants and factories.

The economic reports indicate that U.S. growth is likely to continue. "Based on this data, it appears that the recovery is gaining momentum," said Norbert Ore, who directs the survey for the ISM. "Indications are that the manufacturing sector is ending 2003 on a very positive note, and all of the indexes support continued strength into 2004," he said.

Second Paragraph–Purchasing Managers' Index

The private Institute for Supply Management said its November index of manufacturing activity came in at 62.8, up from 57 for October. Providing solid evidence of an improving manufacturing jobs picture, the ISM's employment index climbed to 51 from 47.7. It marks the first time since September 2000 the gauge exceeded 50.

Expanding

The ISM Manufacturing Index; values above 50 indicate an expanding factory sector

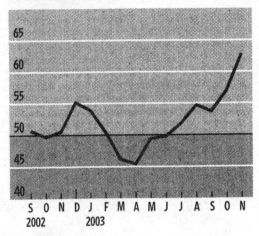

Source: Institute for Supply Management via Economy.com

Chart 4–4 on page 51. The *Journal* article with its graph and Chart 4–4 tell you that manufacturing activity surged in late 2003.

You can also check the PMI online:

1. Scroll down the *Journal*'s home page's left-hand menu-bar and click on Economy.
2. Click on Economic Indicators under Data and Resources and then click on Purchasing Index.
3. Click on Economic Chartbook under Data and Resources.

CHART 4–4 Purchasing Managers' Index

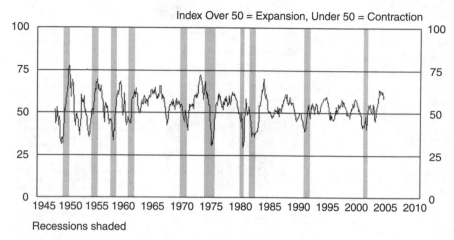

Recessions shaded

Source: Institute for Supply Management.

4.   Click on Reports from Briefing.com under Data and Resources and then click on ISM Index.

LABOR PRODUCTIVITY AND UNIT LABOR COSTS

The Wall Street Journal reports figures from the U.S. Department of Labor's preliminary release on *nonfarm labor productivity* about a month after the end of the quarter and publishes a revision about a month later. The Thursday, December 4, 2003, print article presents revised data for the third quarter of 2003 (see page 52). Also note the article's second paragraph and the graph that frequently accompanies the report.

Chart 4–5 on page 53 presents the record for all business (including farms). The difference between a chart with farm data and one without is so small as to be meaningless.

The December 4, 2003, article reported an upwardly revised 9.4 percent productivity gain, which was an improvement over the initial report of 8.1 percent published a month earlier.

Labor productivity measures output or production per unit of labor input (e.g., output per hour) and is *the most important gauge* of our nation's efficiency. Its significance cannot be overemphasized, for *per capita real income cannot improve*—and thus the country's standard of living cannot rise—*without an increase in per capita production.*

Unit labor cost measures the cost of labor per unit of output. Thus, unit labor cost is the *inverse* of labor productivity, since unit labor costs

Productivity Rises at 9.4% Rate

Best Performance in 20 Years Bolsters Corporate Profits, But May Not Be Sustained

By GREG IP
And JOSEPH REBELLO

WASHINGTON—In a performance with bullish implications for Americans' standard of living, the productivity of U.S. workers rose at the fastest rate in 20 years in the third quarter, revised data show.

Output per worker at nonagricultural businesses in the third quarter rose at an annual rate of 9.4%, the Labor Department said, even better than its earlier estimate of 8.1%. That is the best quarterly performance since 1983, and brought the 12-month rate of increase to 5%. For the two years ended Sept. 30, productivity growth averaged 5.5%, the best two-year performance since 1953, according to Banc of America Securities.

Increased productivity means companies can produce more per worker, earn more profits and pay higher wages without raising prices. It is the key to rising standards of living over the long run.

If sustained, the third-quarter performance would lead to a doubling in the U.S. standard of living in just eight years. However, productivity likely has been temporarily elevated by companies' ability to boost output without adding to capacity and by their reluctance to hire amid uncertainty about the sales outlook.

As that outlook has brightened, hiring has picked up in the past three months. Combined with a slowing in growth from the third quarter's 8.2% pace, that means

More Efficient

Seasonally adjusted annual rates of productivity growth in the nonfarm business sector

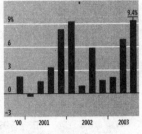

Source: Labor Department via Economy.com

productivity will probably rise less than 2% in the current quarter, said Jade Zelnik, economist at RBS Greenwich Capital.

In the short run, the strong productivity performance bolsters corporate profits and encourages the Federal Reserve to take its time about raising interest rates. "This is going to be extremely important for the sustainability of the recovery," said Scott Anderson, a senior economist with Wells Fargo & Co. in Minneapolis. "It means corporate profitability will remain strong, and that will allow businesses to ramp up hiring and investment spending while keeping costs contained."

In the long run, the recent performance likely means the economy's long-term growth rate could have risen to as much as 4%, from about 2.5% between the early 1970s and mid-1990s.

— **Productivity**

Meanwhile, another report showed U.S. business activity continued to expand in November, although at a slower pace than in October. The Institute for Supply Management said its index of nonmanufacturing business activity fell to 60.1 from 64.7. Any number above 50 indicates an expansion. The index has been above that threshold since March.

The subindex for employment rose to 54.9 from 52.9 in October, suggesting hiring has accelerated. The combination of slowing output growth with quickening hiring suggests a slowdown in productivity gains.

Yesterday's revision in third-quarter productivity growth mainly reflected a previously reported upward revision of growth in gross domestic product in the third quarter to 8.2%. Workers' hours, meanwhile, grew 0.8%, the fastest gain in 3½ years. Because output per hour rose so much faster than labor compensation per hour, the cost in salaries and benefits of producing a unit of output dropped 5.8%, the biggest annual decline in 20 years.

Productivity in the durable-goods manufacturing sector rose 14.8%, the biggest gain in 32 years, the Labor Department said.

Productivity in the nonfinancial corporate sector rose an impressive 9.2%, a two-year high. The sector excludes hard-to-measure unincorporated businesses and financial firms, and, as a result, is considered by Fed Chairman Alan Greenspan a "more accurate" gauge of general productivity trends.

Productivity–Second Paragraph

Output per worker at nonagricultural businesses in the third quarter rose at an annual rate of 9.4%, the Labor Department said, even better than its earlier estimate of 8.1%. That is the best quarterly performance since 1983, and brought the 12-month rate of increase to 5%. For the two years ended Sept. 30, productivity growth averaged 5.5%, the best two-year performance since 1953, according to Banc of America Securities.

CHART 4–5 Productivity: Output per Hour, Business Sector (1992 = 100); Change in Output per Hour

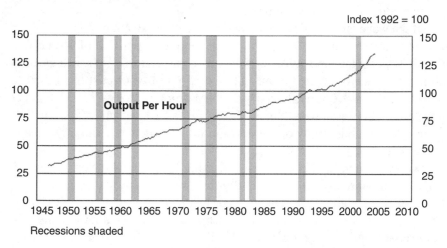

Recessions shaded

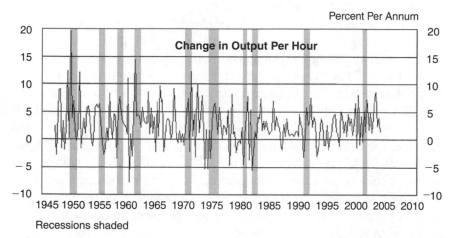

Recessions shaded

Source: U.S. Bureau of Labor Statistics.

fall as labor productivity rises, and vice versa. Unit labor cost tells you how much added labor is required to produce an additional unit of output. Because labor is hired for a wage, requiring more labor time to produce each unit of output will raise labor costs per unit of output, and vice versa.

Consider, for instance, a factory that assembles handheld calculators. If the production of a calculator has required an hour of labor and a technological innovation permits the production of two calculators per hour, labor productivity has doubled from one to two calculators per hour. The output per hour of work is twice what it was.

If the wage rate is $20 per hour, and before the innovation an hour of work was required to produce a calculator, the labor cost per unit of output was then $20. After the innovation, however, two calculators can be produced in an hour, or one calculator in half an hour, so unit labor cost has fallen to $10. Note that as labor productivity doubled, from one to two calculators per hour, unit labor costs were halved, from $20 to $10 per unit of output. The gain in labor productivity drove down unit labor costs without any change in the wage rate.

Keep in mind, however, when reflecting upon Old vs. New Economy issues, if wage rates rise more rapidly than productivity, as they did in the late 1990s, unit labor cost will rise. For instance, returning to the example above, if wages rise to $60 per hour while productivity doubles, the unit labor cost of producing a calculator will rise to $30 ($60 per hour wage divided by two calculators) despite the gain in productivity.

Now compare the record of labor productivity and unit labor costs with the other indicators examined so far (see Chart 4–6 on page 55).

The discussion begins with an Old Economy example drawn from the 1970s. This will lead to the New Economy analysis and its failure to anticipate rising costs and the squeeze on profits in the late 1990s.

GDP, industrial production, and capacity utilization together defined the business cycle in the 1970s. Their fluctuations indicate prosperity and recession. You can also see that labor productivity plunged and unit labor costs soared with the peak of each cycle in the 1970s. Labor productivity improved and unit labor costs declined with each recession and into the next recovery. But as soon as expansion got under way, labor productivity's growth began to weaken and unit labor costs began to rise, until productivity slumped and costs peaked at the end of the boom.

And this brings you full circle to the discussion of efficiency included in the earlier investigation of capacity utilization: The economy's efficiency deteriorated in the 1970s with each boom and improved in each recession and into recovery. All that this section has done is to provide the labels and devices (labor productivity and unit labor costs) necessary to measure that efficiency. During boom conditions, efficiency (labor productivity) declines and expenses (unit labor costs) mount. During recession the opposite is true.

At first you might ask yourself: Why would management ever place itself in the position of risking a drop in the efficiency of its operations

CHART 4–6 Unit Labor Cost, Labor Productivity, Capacity Utilization, and GDP

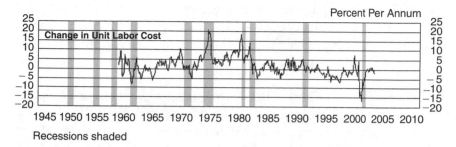

Recessions shaded

Source: U.S. Bureau of Labor Statistics.

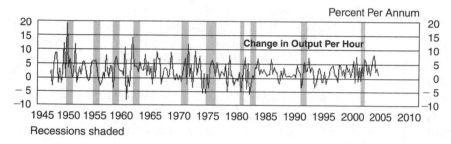

Recessions shaded

Source: U.S. Bureau of Labor Statistics.

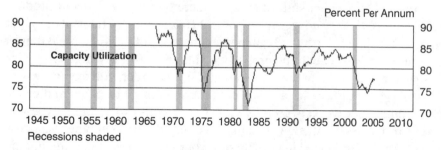

Recessions shaded

Source: Federal Reserve.

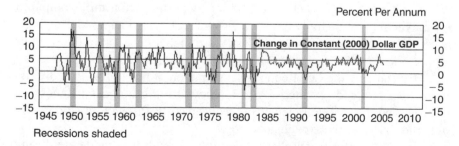

Recessions shaded

Source: U.S. Dept. of Commerce, Bureau of Economic Analysis, *National Income & Product Accounts,*
Table 1.1.1, line 1.

in order to push output and capacity utilization too far? Why not limit production to an efficient level of operations, at, say, 80 percent capacity utilization, rather than risk declining productivity at 90 percent of capacity utilization? The answer is easy, if you put yourself in management's shoes.

Suppose you're the boss at Bethlehem Steel, and Ford Motor Co. is your best customer. Suppose also that you're running two production shifts at your mill, 16 hours a day, and a small maintenance crew is employed during the remaining 8-hour shift. The maintenance crew inspects, maintains, and repairs the equipment so that everything is up and running during the daily 16 hours of production.

Now Ford calls and says that their sport-utility vehicles have been a big success and they need more steel in a hurry. Do you tell Ford that you're sorry, that you're running flat out, that you have no idle capacity, and that they should come back during the next recession when you will have plenty of idle capacity and would be happy to take their order? Only if you want to lose your best customer. No, you tell them you will move heaven and earth to fill their order, and you cancel the maintenance shift and put on another production shift.

Putting on another shift of workers increases the size of your production crew (and labor costs) by 50 percent (from 16 to 24 hours a day), yet your output increases by only 30 percent because of periodic breakdowns in equipment that cannot be properly maintained. But if you only require a 30 percent increase in output in order to fill the order, you may very well be willing to put up with a 50 percent increase in labor hours and costs. Sure, output per worker (productivity) falls on this order, and maybe you won't turn a profit either. That's okay as long as you keep your best customer. You're interested in maximizing your profit in the long run, not the short run.

As a result, you've met your deadline by pushing your mill's output to the maximum. Productivity has declined and costs have increased. But that's acceptable, especially if you can pass those higher costs on in the form of higher prices (the subject of the next section of this chapter).

That sums up the Old Economy explanation of the 1970s. Rapidly rising output reduced productivity/efficiency, driving up costs. Recession improved productivity/efficiency and reduced costs. Productivity did poorly over the course of these cyclical swings.

The charts inform you that productivity growth was moderate during the 1980s, as output grew more rapidly than labor input. The economy was far better off than in the 1970s, when periodic declines in productivity were associated with excessive rates of capacity utilization.

Notice as well that productivity improved nicely coming out of the 1990–1991 recession and then grew continually throughout the 1990s, although not at the strong, sustained rate it enjoyed in some previous periods such as the early 1960s.

Here is where the New Economy argument enters. The New Economy advocates said that the economy could grow rapidly while productivity and efficiency improved just as quickly. They said that business added new capacity of an improved quality so rapidly in the 1990s that higher rates of capacity utilization never threatened improvement of productivity and efficiency. Capacity utilization did not rise, despite rapidly rising output, because of capacity's new, hi-tech caliber and its swift increase. This, the argument continued, translated into swiftly rising productivity and efficiency, holding unit labor costs in check.

All this proved true, as far as it went. Problems arose when rapidly growing output demanded a rapidly rising workforce. Soon employers began hiring employees away from other employers because the available labor pool had dried up. Unit labor costs rose despite productivity's continued improvement, squeezing profit margins because businesses could not raise prices rapidly enough. Supply grew so swiftly that businesses had no pricing strength. Profit margins, and then profits, began to decline.

Rising productivity in the 1990s should have translated into rising profit margins and profits, and it did up to a point. But surging output eventually derailed the New Economy in a new (rising wages) business cycle, just as it had once derailed the Old Economy in an old (falling productivity) business cycle. In both cases, rising costs squeezed profit margins and profits. Unlike the Old Economy, however, rising costs did not propel the New Economy into inflation. In the Old Economy 1970s, escalating demand—fueled by consumer borrowing—dragged supply along and bid prices rapidly upward. In the New Economy 1990s, surging supply set the pace and kept inflation at bay.

The *Journal*'s online edition will allow you to research the latest data on productivity and labor costs:

1. Scroll down the *Journal*'s home page's left-hand menu-bar and click on Economy.
2. Click on Economic Indicators under Data and Resources and then click on Business Productivity.

3. Click on Reports from Briefing.com under Data and Resources
    and then click on Productivity-Prel.

Strong output growth in 2003's third quarter, when combined with slow
hiring, generated a burst of improved productivity and reduced labor costs.
As productivity surged in 2003, unit labor costs plunged. You should remain
aware, however, that slowly rising wages—due to the 2001 recession—were
the chief restraints on labor costs in the new millennium.

Productivity and the Cycle

- The economy is like your car's engine—far more efficient at a steady,
  moderate pace than in stop-and-go traffic.
- If you push the accelerator to the floor and rev the engine (high capacity utilization), efficiency (productivity) drops.

Let's turn now to producer prices, which provide us with a direct measure of inflation.

PRODUCER PRICES

The *producer price index*, once referred to as the wholesale price index, is
compiled by the U.S. Department of Labor and shows the changes in prices
charged by producers of finished goods—changes that are, of course, reflected
in the prices consumers must pay. Data from the Labor Department's news
release on producer prices is usually published by *The Wall Street Journal*
in mid-month.

The Monday, November 17, 2003, print-edition article on page 59 is an
example, and the second paragraph tells you the producer price index rose
0.8 percent in October of 2003.

You can use the *Journal*'s online edition to delve deeper, if you wish.
Here's how.

1. Scroll down the home page's left-hand menu-bar and click on
    Economy.
2. Click on Economic Indicators under Data and Resources and then
    click on Producer Price Index.
3. Click on Economic Chartbook under Data and Resources and
    scroll down to producer prices.
4. Click on Reports from Briefing.com under Data and Resources
    and then click on PPI.

Producer Prices Rose in October, Driven Higher by Auto Stickers

By JON E. HILSENRATH

Automobile makers raised prices and reduced dealer incentives on 2004 car models in October while California, the nation's biggest auto market, increased car taxes—moves that prompted consumers to cut back on purchases.

Producer Prices

That was the upshot of a slew of government data released Friday. The Bureau of Labor Statistics reported that producer prices rose a larger-than-expected 0.8% on a seasonally adjusted basis in October from the month before, largely because of higher auto prices. Meanwhile, the U.S. Census Bureau reported retail sales slipped 0.3% in October, largely due to declining auto sales.

"Manufacturers are adjusting incentives in part to see how well their products can do without incentives as the economy strengthens," said Robert Schnorbus, chief economist at J.D. Power & Associates, a market research company. "Consumers, being finicky as they are, just don't like to see incentives go down, and they're pulling back."

The Federal Reserve also reported that industrial production rose for the fourth straight month in October, but the pace of increases was curtailed by a slowdown in motor vehicle assemblies.

Some auto makers responded by fattening incentives in November. This is leading some economists to predict the October sales slowdown and the spike in prices will be temporary. "It is the pregnant pause of a wiser consumer," said David Littman, chief economist of Comerica Bank in Detroit. Underscoring expectations of a pickup in consumer spending later in the year, the University of Michigan's index of consumer sentiment rose to 93.5 in early November, stronger than the late October reading of 89.6.

Paul Taylor, chief economist at the National Automobile Dealers Association, said California played a role in the consumer spending slowdown in October. Wildfires raged in parts of the state, and California consumers were hit with a sudden increase in vehicle-registration fees, which Gov.-elect Arnold Schwarzenegger has promised to reverse. That left some potential car buyers sitting on the fence until the outlook for the fees became more clear. (See related article, A8).

Mr. Taylor estimates October car sales in California were down more than 10% from a year earlier because of these factors. Since Californians buy one out of every eight cars sold nationwide, it had a large impact on the latest data. Nationwide, retail sales at auto dealers were down 1.9% on a seasonally adjusted basis in October.

Two broader economic themes were underlined by the reports released Friday. The first was that consumer spending appears to be slowing after a sizzling summer. However, the slowdown doesn't yet

Please Turn to Page A12, Column 6

Chart 4–7 (see page 60) confirms that in the 1990s, inflation, as measured by the producer price index, continued to fall and remained well below the double-digit levels of the 1970s. The drop since the 1979–1980 peak has been dramatic, and some forecasters continue to fear deflation (declining prices) in the first decade of the 21st century.

You can also see from Chart 4–8 on page 61 that in the 1970s Old Economy the cyclical trends in producer prices mirrored those of unit labor costs. With each boom in output and capacity utilization, productivity dropped and unit labor costs rose, driving producer prices up. Then, when recession hit and output and capacity utilization fell, improved labor productivity and lower unit labor costs were reflected in reduced inflation. The 1981–1982

CHART 4–7 Producer Price Index (1982 = 100); Change in Index at Monthly Rate

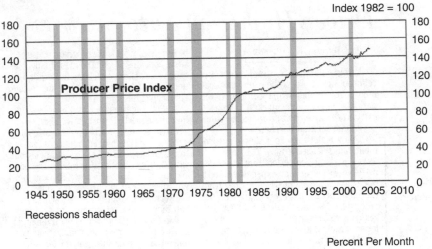

Index 1982 = 100

Producer Price Index

1945 1950 1955 1960 1965 1970 1975 1980 1985 1990 1995 2000 2005 2010

Recessions shaded

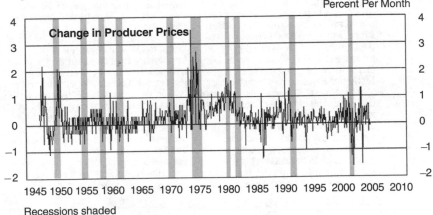

Percent Per Month

Change in Producer Prices

1945 1950 1955 1960 1965 1970 1975 1980 1985 1990 1995 2000 2005 2010

Recessions shaded

Source: U.S. Bureau of Labor Statistics.

recession illustrates the principle: Inflation's trend followed unit labor costs downward. As the economy's efficiency improved, stable prices followed on the heels of stable costs. Inflation remained low throughout the 1980s and early 1990s because unit labor costs increased at a moderate pace.

The full employment of the late 1990s New Economy didn't generate "wage inflation" precisely because the competitive conditions generated by rapidly rising output prevented employers from raising prices despite rising wages. Business added new capacity (additional plant and equipment) at

CHART 4–8 Changes in Unit Labor Cost and Producer Pri

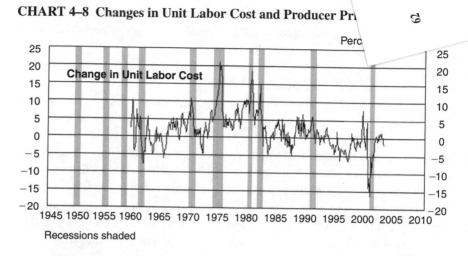

Perc

Change in Unit Labor Cost

Recessions shaded

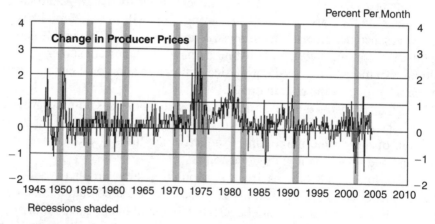

Percent Per Month

Change in Producer Prices

Recessions shaded

Source: U.S. Bureau of Labor Statistics.

such a torrid pace that capacity utilization rates remained moderate and supply (output) grew sufficiently rapidly to hold prices in check. As the decade neared its end, employers found themselves squeezed between the need to offer their workers higher wages and the competitive realities of the marketplaces in which they sold their goods. Rising costs, coupled with the inability to boost prices because of the rapid growth in the quantity of output, squeezed profit margins and constrained and eventually reduced corporate earnings.

The 2001 recession reduced unit labor costs and producer prices (see Chart 4–8). Even during recovery from recession, moderate wage gains restrained unit labor costs and inflation.

THE COST/PRICE DYNAMIC: A SUMMARY

You can begin to summarize the issues by considering the Old Economy (1965–1995) analysis of inflation's dynamic in the following context.

If you ask a businessperson why prices rise, he or she will answer, "Rising costs," probably referring to personal experience. When you ask an economist the same question, the response will be, "Demand exceeds supply at current prices, and therefore prices rise," probably referring to the textbook case. These points of view seem to have nothing in common, yet an Old Economy analysis of economic expansion shows that they meld into a single explanation. Consider an idealized (and hypothetical) situation.

Suppose all the indicators of economic expansion (demand)—auto sales, consumer credit, housing starts—are strong. This will initiate broad-based growth as incomes increase in the construction, auto, and other durable goods industries, spilling over and boosting demand for other consumer goods. Boom conditions will intensify as business invests in additional factories and machinery to meet the rush in orders.

As the expansion unfolds, capacity utilization increases with the growth in demand and production. Soon factories move from, say, 70 percent to 90 percent of their rated maximum. Productive facilities strain to meet the demand and retain the loyalty of customers.

Next, high levels of capacity utilization drive labor productivity down and unit labor costs up; efficiency is sacrificed for increased output. Machinery that is always in use cannot be adequately maintained, and so it breaks down. Inexperienced workers often do not make the same contribution as old hands. The amount of labor employed increases more rapidly than output, and, as output per worker falls, the labor cost per unit of output rises. This generates a surge in production costs.

Finally, rapidly increasing costs are translated into rapidly increasing prices, and a renewed round of inflation begins. (Read ↑ as "up," ↓ as "down," and → as "leads to.")

GDP ↑→ Industrial production ↑+
Purchasing managers' index ↑→ Capacity utilization ↑→
Labor productivity ↓→ Unit labor costs ↑→ Producer prices ↑

So the practical (businessperson's) and the theoretical (economist's) explanations of Old Economy inflation are not at odds. During expansion, demand bids production to a level that is inefficient and costly. The businessperson experiences the increased cost and attributes inflation directly to that experience. The economist sees increased demand as the ultimate cause of the production gain that drives costs up. Each explanation covers different aspects of the single phenomenon, economic expansion.

Now consider the Old Economy's logical progression of events after the business cycle peaks and the economy tumbles into recession. When GDP and industrial production fall, capacity utilization declines. This leads to an increase in labor productivity and a drop in unit labor costs, driving down the rate of inflation as measured by producer prices.

GDP $\downarrow\rightarrow$ **Industrial production** $\downarrow+$
Purchasing managers' index $\downarrow\rightarrow$**Capacity utilization** $\downarrow\rightarrow$
Labor productivity $\uparrow\rightarrow$ **Unit labor costs** $\downarrow\rightarrow$ **Producer prices** $\downarrow$

Like the reveler's hangover, recession grips the Old Economy following the bender of boom and inflation. Rest is the only cure, and recovery is marked not by a renewed round of expansion and growth, but by a slack period in which steadiness is restored.

The New Economy analysis leaves much, but not all, of this tale behind. In the New Economy, as envisioned by its 1990s proponents, production could grow continually, without cyclical limit, without squeezing profit margins, and without generating inflation because the continual high-tech expansion of productive capacity continually boosted production *and* productivity. As businesses rapidly added hi-tech capacity, boom conditions would not generate their own demise because productivity growth would not falter and costs would not rise. Even if prices remained flat, or even fell because of output's rapid increase, profit margins would stay strong as surging productivity pushed unit labor costs ever downward. Production, productivity, and profits would spiral relentlessly upward.

The New Economy advocates never envisioned that full employment could force wages so rapidly upward that unit labor costs would rise despite strong productivity growth. Profit margins and profits melted away in the late 1990s as their rosy scenario unraveled.

The new millenium began with recession. That restrained wage gains and labor costs, boosting profit margins while suppressing inflation.

SUMMARY AND CONCLUSION

If all of this makes sense, fine. If it bears repeating, consider the following.

Profits measure efficiency by comparing revenues to costs. In the Old Economy, efficiency typically improved during the early phases of the business cycle and deteriorated during the latter phases. Thus, profits usually grew during recovery and expansion and deteriorated during peak and contraction.

Keep in mind the two elements that determine corporate profits. The first is the profit realized on each unit of sales, or profit margins, multiplied by the second, which is the volume of output. Profit margins, or profit per unit of output, are crucial for any analysis of corporate earnings.

A bit of logic reveals the relationship between general changes in economic efficiency over the cycle and the specific measurement of profit. Efficiency rose early in the Old Economy cycle because factories operated with excess capacity and produced less than maximum output. The general reduction in costs due to enhanced productivity increased the spread between prices and costs, known as the profit margin or profit per unit of output. As sales increased, total profit grew because of both higher output and higher profits per unit of output.

Efficiency deteriorated late in the cycle as factories strained to produce maximum output. Costs rose as productivity fell, and industry was forced into a "profit squeeze," meaning that costs pushed up against prices. Total profits fell as sales volume stopped growing, or actually contracted with the onset of recession, and profit per unit of output (the profit margin) fell.

It may help to think of what happened in these terms: Costs rose as output increased and industry reached full capacity utilization. As costs came up from below, they bumped prices upward. But competition prevented management from raising prices as rapidly as it liked. If costs rose more rapidly than prices, that squeezed the margin between price and cost. Profit margins declined even as prices rose ever-more rapidly.

On the other hand, management had the opportunity to rebuild its profit margins in the slack period following recession. Costs were no longer rising as rapidly, because capacity utilization was low. This provided management with the opportunity to recover profit margins by raising prices more rapidly than costs.

Thus, paradoxically, profit margins shrunk when prices rose most rapidly, typically before the peak of the cycle, and grew when inflation abated in the slack period immediately after recession and when recovery began.

That's why both productivity and profitability recovered nicely as the economy emerged from most recessions after World War II. There was a strong correlation between productivity and profit margins. As the economy's efficiency improved, so did the spread between price and cost. Business earned more per unit of output. But in the superheated economy at the business cycle's peak, such as during the highly volatile Old Economy 1970s, efficiency and profitability deteriorated. Profit margins shrank.

Events unfolded somewhat differently in the late 1990s. Businesses had added so much new and improved plant and equipment throughout the 1990s that firms churned out a larger and larger supply of goods and services and prices remained in check. Labor markets, however, became tighter and tighter as businesses hired more and more help in order to meet orders. By 1997 and 1998 we had reached full employment. Businesses had to compete with one another for employees, hiring workers away from other businesses because the pool of unemployed had dried up. Wages now rose more rapidly than prices, squeezing profit margins in a climate of low inflation.

Rising wages defeated the New Economy in the late 1990s, because businesses had rapidly added productive capacity, enabling strong growth in supply that held prices in check just as labor costs climbed. With the onset of the 2001 recession (contracting demand) in the new decade, some economists have forecasted a sustained downward price trend. They have said that deflation seems just around the corner. We'll see if their forecast bears fruit.

Meanwhile, you should turn your attention to business investment in plant, equipment, and inventory, the subject of the next two chapters, because this investment was the key ingredient in the New Economy's bubble and its subsequent pop.

5

BUSINESS CAPITAL EXPENDITURES

BUSINESS LEADS THE BOOM

BUSINESS CAPITAL EXPENDITURES LED THE 1990s NEW ECONOMY BOOM. Some called it the *personal computer revolution*. Everyone had to have a computer on his or her desk or lap, and that decision called forth all the peripherals. Rounding out the system required the Internet, multimedia, word processing, spreadsheets, networks, servers, databases, and the telecommunications revolution. By 1994 a tidal wave of technology expenditures began to build, rose throughout the decade, and then came crashing down in the 2001 recession. The phenomenon reminded many of the 19th-century railroad booms.

This leading role was an unaccustomed one for business capital expenditures. Consumer outlays had driven earlier post–World War II Old Economy business cycles. Households purchased new homes, new automobiles, and other durable goods, and then business took its cue from the consumer by adding plant and equipment. When residential construction soared, forest product companies built new lumber mills, and when auto sales climbed, automobile manufacturers built new auto plants. The consumer set the trend, and business followed.

Then, in the New Economy 1990s, the roles reversed. Now business set the trend and the consumer followed. As business investment in new plant and equipment reached unprecedented levels, igniting a general boom that spurred employment and instigated rising wages and salaries, households splurged on new homes and cars. To repeat, business led the 1990s boom and consumers followed.

This chapter will acquaint you with a readily available statistical series that portrays business capital expenditures. Before turning to the data, however, let's consider in more detail the reasons why business invests.

WHY BUSINESS INVESTS

There are six principal factors influencing business decisions to spend on new plant and equipment.

First, old facilities may wear out and need to be replaced.

Second, the rate of capacity utilization may be high. Recall the Old Economy 1970s business cycle. Putting it simply, if sales are strong, business will invest in new machinery and equipment in order to have the capacity necessary to fill the orders. During a recession, however, the rate of capacity utilization is low and business has more than enough plant and equipment on hand to satisfy the low volume of orders. Why add to plant and equipment when the existing level is already more than adequate?

Third, old facilities, whether fully utilized or not, will be scrapped and replaced by new facilities if operating costs can be sufficiently reduced through innovation in the process of production. Think of the 1990s New Economy investment binge, fueled by the hope of rising productivity. Competition leaves business no choice: If equipment is no longer cost-effective, it must be replaced, even though it could still be used.

Fourth, new plant and equipment may be required to produce a new or redesigned product, even if existing facilities have a continued useful life. Model and style changes have forced the automobile industry to spend billions replacing still-functional equipment, for instance. The New Economy required PCs, PC components, and PC peripherals that didn't exist in the Old Economy.

Fifth, spending on plant and equipment is sensitive to current and anticipated profits. Business will invest in additional facilities if it expects long-range profit growth beyond any short-run cyclical fluctuation. The telecommunications industry invested billions in Internet transmission facilities in the late 1990s. In addition, profits plowed back into the business provide the cash flow necessary to finance capital expenditures. A recession will limit business's ability to finance capital expenditures, and expansion will generate the necessary cash flow.

The sixth factor factor is interest rates. Business must borrow to finance plant and equipment expenditures if internally generated funds are not adequate. When interest rates are very high, the cost of borrowing may be prohibitive, and so business firms postpone or cancel their capital expenditure plans. Or they may feel that, for the time being, they can get a better return by investing their own funds at high rates of interest than by making expenditures on new productive facilities.

It seems that reasons three, four, and five best fit 1990s New Economy developments, while reason two explains earlier Old Economy cycles. Whether or not the desktop or the laptop actually reduced all businesses' operating costs, every business came to believe that the personal computer and its peripherals were office essentials. Not to have these pieces of equipment meant a firm was old-fashioned or eccentric.

Once managements across the country had made the decision to join the PC revolution, the existing and start-up firms that wished to enable that revolution made huge expenditures on new capacity. Hardware and software purveyors of the Internet, multimedia, word processing, spreadsheets, networks, servers, databases, and telecommunications ramped up by spending billions on new plant and equipment. Users and suppliers set the trend.

You can keep abreast of capital expenditures by following a series published monthly in *The Wall Street Journal*: the Commerce Department report on new orders for nondefense capital goods.

NONDEFENSE CAPITAL GOODS

The Wall Street Journal publishes the previous month's preliminary data for nondefense capital goods in the last week of the month as part of an overall report on durable goods, and then publishes the revised data about a week later in a release on manufacturers' new orders. See the Wednesday, August 27, 2003, print-edition article on page 69. The statistical summary accompanying the article states that orders for nondefense capital goods were $58.16 billion in July of 2003 and had grown by 1.2 percent since the previous month.

The *Journal*'s online edition (http://online.wsj.com) can also help you.

You may wish to review the general directions for retrieving on-line information on pages 7 through 11 of Chapter 1. Appendix D on page 374 also furnishes you with a quick guide to the *Journal*'s online edition.

Durable-Goods Orders Climb Again

July Gain of 1% Lifts Hopes Of Manufacturing Growth; Consumer Optimism Rises

By MICHAEL SCHROEDER

WASHINGTON—Demand for big-ticket products increased solidly for the second straight month in July, bolstering hopes the U.S. manufacturing sector may be rebounding.

The Commerce Department reported that new orders for durable goods—expensive items such as kitchen appliances that are built to last three years or more—climbed 1% in July after a rise of 2.6% a month earlier. New orders had fallen 1.4% in April and were flat in May.

The report also showed that business spending is picking up. In particular, shipments of nondefense capital goods, excluding aircraft, jumped 2.9% in July. Were that pace to continue for the full third quarter, it would represent a double-digit increase over second-quarter shipments on an annualized basis, economists said.

In addition, orders for nondefense capital goods, which are items meant to last 10 years or more, rose 0.4% in July, a third consecutive monthly gain.

"This represents the most meaningful evidence of a pickup in business capital spending seen in the expansion to date," said Peter Kretzmer, an economist at Bank of America Corp.

Meanwhile, the Conference Board, a private research group, said that its index of consumer confidence rose to 81.3 in August from a revised figure of 77 in July. Economists had generally predicted the index would rise only to 80 in August. The index was 100 in 1985.

Based on a survey of 5,000 U.S households, the index measures the general optimism of U.S. consumers. But the survey also noted one downbeat note within the generally positive August results, in the form of lingering doubts about employment prospects in the current economy.

In particular, many consumers are worried their jobs will be outsourced to foreign countries, said Delos Smith, a Conference Board senior business analyst.

A few other economic indicators have also hinted at weakness. The U.S. housing market showed its first signs of cooling after months of hot sales that have helped stabilize the economy. Although record-low mortgage-interest rates and rising home values have kept the market strong, a recent increase in interest rates is expected to put the brakes on new sales and crimp consumers' ability to spend cash taken out from refinanced mortgages.

New-home sales dropped 2.9% in July to a seasonally adjusted annual rate of 1.165 million, the Commerce Department said. In June, new-home sales rose to a record annual rate of 1.2 million, an 8.3% gain from the previous month. An earlier preliminary estimate showed a 4.7% increase to a 1.16 million annual rate.

The median price of a new home rose 3.7% to $191,500 in July, compared with an increase of 9.1% in the year-earlier month.

On Monday, the National Association of Realtors reported that sales of existing homes peaked in July at a record 6.12 million annual rate, another indicator of the overall strength of the housing market. But Realtors also said that rising interest rates are beginning to slow mortgage applications.

In manufacturing, the gains in big-ticket products were broad based. Sales of motor vehicles and parts surged 5.5%, boosted by aggressive incentives and low interest rates. Machinery orders also had a strong showing, climbing 1.8%, while orders of computers and electronic products rose 1.9%. Defense capital goods orders dropped by 12.2% in July.

—Jennifer Corbett Dooren contributed to this article.

Statistical Summary

DURABLE GOODS
Here are the Commerce Department's latest figures on new orders for durable goods, seasonally adjusted, in billions:

	July '03	June '03	% Chg.
Total	$173.98	$172.32	1.0
Primary metals	10.79	10.60	1.8
Nonelect. machinery	20.92	20.55	1.8
Electrical machinery	8.37	8.36	0.1
Transportation equip.	51.88	52.30	−0.8
Capital goods	65.53	65.84	−0.5
Nondefense	58.16	57.45	1.2
Defense	7.37	8.39	−12.2

Statistical Summary

DURABLE GOODS

Here are the Commerce Department's latest figures on new orders for durable goods, seasonally adjusted, in billions:

	July '03	June '03	% Chg.
Total	**$173.98**	**$172.32**	**1.0**
Primary metals	10.79	10.60	1.8
Nonelect. machinery	20.92	20.55	1.8
Electrical machinery	8.37	8.36	0.1
Transportation equip.	51.88	52.30	−0.8
Capital goods	65.53	65.84	−0.5
Nondefense	58.16	57.45	1.2
Defense	7.37	8.39	−12.2

The Tuesday, January 6, 2004, article in the online edition provides an example of the full report on manufacturers' new orders. The third from the last paragraph reported a 5.7 percent drop in November 2003 orders for nondefense capital goods, but did not provide the dollar amount.

You can delve deeper into the subject online as follows:

1. Scroll down the online edition's home page's left-hand menu-bar and click on Economy.
2. Click on Economic Indicators under Data and Resources; click on Durable-Goods Orders (PDF); and then scroll down to CAPITAL GOODS INDUSTRIES, NONDEFENSE.
3. Click on Reports from Briefing.com under Data and Resources and then click on Durable Orders.

This series presents new orders received by manufacturers of durable goods other than military equipment. (Durable goods are defined as those having a useful life of more than three years.) Nondefense capital goods represent approximately one-fifth to one-third of all durable goods production. The series includes engines; construction, mining, and materials handling equipment; office and store machinery; electrical transmission and distribution equipment and other electrical machinery (excluding household appliances and electronic equipment); and railroad, ship, and aircraft transportation equipment. Military equipment is excluded because new orders for such items do not respond directly to the business cycle.

Chart 5–1 (page 72) provides a good illustration of the relationship between nondefense capital goods orders and the business cycle. The series tracks orders rather than shipments in order to obtain maximum advance notice of business cycle developments and turning points.

Orders for nondefense capital goods surged in the 1990s, rising to $80 billion before dropping back to less than $60 billion when recession hit. Notice how rapidly the chart climbs toward the end of the decade. The boom reached frenzied proportions with the Y2K panic and the excesses of the telecommunications bubble.

Then the bubble burst in 2001. The boom was over. Just as the railroad tycoons built their networks ahead of demand, sometimes running out of cash in North Dakota on their way from Chicago to Seattle, so the telecommunications industry had built its networks ahead of demand before the millennium bubble burst. In each case, business's dreams and its investment in those dreams pulled the economy forward, only to relapse into hard times

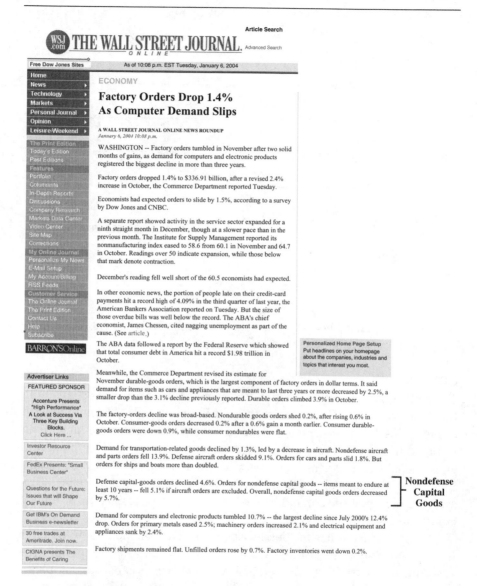

Article Search
Advanced Search

THE WALL STREET JOURNAL ONLINE

Free Dow Jones Sites   As of 10:08 p.m. EST Tuesday, January 6, 2004

Home
News
Technology
Markets
Personal Journal
Opinion
Leisure/Weekend

The Print Edition
Today's Edition
Past Editions
Features
Portfolio
Columnists
In-Depth Reports
Discussions
Company Research
Markets Data Center
Video Center
Site Map
Corrections
My Online Journal
Personalize My News
E-Mail Setup
My Account/Billing
RSS Feeds
Customer Service
The Online Journal
The Print Edition
Contact Us
Help
Subscribe

BARRON'S Online

Advertiser Links
FEATURED SPONSOR

Accenture Presents
"High Performance"
A Look at Success Via
Three Key Building
Blocks.
Click Here ...

Investor Resource
Center

FedEx Presents: "Small
Business Center"

Questions for the Future:
Issues that will Shape
Our Future

Get IBM's On Demand
Business e-newsletter

30 free trades at
Ameritrade. Join now.

CIGNA presents The
Benefits of Caring

ECONOMY

Factory Orders Drop 1.4%
As Computer Demand Slips

A WALL STREET JOURNAL ONLINE NEWS ROUNDUP
January 6, 2004 10:08 p.m.

WASHINGTON -- Factory orders tumbled in November after two solid months of gains, as demand for computers and electronic products registered the biggest decline in more than three years.

Factory orders dropped 1.4% to $336.91 billion, after a revised 2.4% increase in October, the Commerce Department reported Tuesday.

Economists had expected orders to slide by 1.5%, according to a survey by Dow Jones and CNBC.

A separate report showed activity in the service sector expanded for a ninth straight month in December, though at a slower pace than in the previous month. The Institute for Supply Management reported its nonmanufacturing index eased to 58.6 from 60.1 in November and 64.7 in October. Readings over 50 indicate expansion, while those below that mark denote contraction.

December's reading fell well short of the 60.5 economists had expected.

In other economic news, the portion of people late on their credit-card payments hit a record high of 4.09% in the third quarter of last year, the American Bankers Association reported on Tuesday. But the size of those overdue bills was well below the record. The ABA's chief economist, James Chessen, cited nagging unemployment as part of the cause. (See article.)

The ABA data followed a report by the Federal Reserve which showed that total consumer debt in America hit a record $1.98 trillion in October.

Meanwhile, the Commerce Department revised its estimate for November durable-goods orders, which is the largest component of factory orders in dollar terms. It said demand for items such as cars and appliances that are meant to last three years or more decreased by 2.5%, a smaller drop than the 3.1% decline previously reported. Durable orders climbed 3.9% in October.

The factory-orders decline was broad-based. Nondurable goods orders shed 0.2%, after rising 0.6% in October. Consumer-goods orders decreased 0.2% after a 0.6% gain a month earlier. Consumer durable-goods orders were down 0.9%, while consumer nondurables were flat.

Demand for transportation-related goods declined by 1.3%, led by a decrease in aircraft. Nondefense aircraft and parts orders fell 13.9%. Defense aircraft orders skidded 9.1%. Orders for cars and parts slid 1.8%. But orders for ships and boats more than doubled.

Defense capital-goods orders declined 4.6%. Orders for nondefense capital goods -- items meant to endure at least 10 years -- fell 5.1% if aircraft orders are excluded. Overall, nondefense capital goods orders decreased by 5.7%. ⎤ **Nondefense**
⎬ **Capital**
⎦ **Goods**

Demand for computers and electronic products tumbled 10.7% -- the largest decline since July 2000's 12.4% drop. Orders for primary metals eased 2.5%; machinery orders increased 2.1% and electrical equipment and appliances sank by 2.4%.

Factory shipments remained flat. Unfilled orders rose by 0.7%. Factory inventories went down 0.2%.

Nondefense Capital Goods—Third Paragraph from End

Defense capital-goods orders declined 4.6%. Orders for nondefense capital goods -- items meant to endure at least 10 years -- fell 5.1% if aircraft orders are excluded. Overall, nondefense capital goods orders decreased by 5.7%.

CHART 5–1 Orders for Nondefense Capital Goods

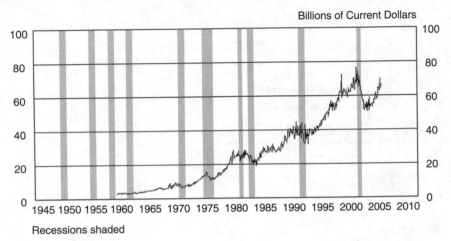

Billions of Current Dollars

Recessions shaded

Source: U.S. Census Bureau.

and disappointment. Orders for nondefense capital goods had not fully recovered several years after the recession's end.

CONCLUSION

The role of business capital expenditures in the business cycle changed in the post–World War II era. Under the Old Economy rules, through the end of the 1970s, business capital expenditures reinforced the cycle rather than initiated it. Business responded to consumer orders by adding plant and equipment. As the expansion developed into the peak of the cycle, straining productive capacity, business added facilities and equipment. This swelled the level of demand and contributed to generally inflationary conditions.

After recession began, businesses typically canceled some of their investment projects. Yet most were completed, and these expenditures eased the downturn. Time elapsed before a new cycle's expansionary phase encouraged another round of capital expenditures. Until that occurred, however, depressed levels of plant and equipment expenditures restrained demand and prevented the economy from heating up too quickly. When capital expenditures did recover, the economy once again approached the cycle's peak.

But the New Economy cycle of the 1990s developed differently. Business capital expenditures now played a more independent and important role. Capital expenditures did not merely respond to consumer demand, they now drove the cycle forward. This time business led and households followed.

Now let's consider the place of inventories in the cycle's dynamic. The role played by inventories also changed in the New Economy, and they are the subject of Chapter 6.

6

INVENTORIES

A DESTABILIZING FORCE

I NVENTORIES ARE STOCKS OF GOODS ON HAND: raw materials, goods in process, or finished products. Individual businesses use them to bring stability to their operations, and yet you'll see that they actually have a destabilizing effect on the business cycle.

Businesses view inventories as a necessary evil. A manufacturer, wholesaler, or retailer can't live from hand to mouth, continually filling sales orders from current production. Stocks of goods "on the shelf" are a cushion against unexpected orders and slowdowns in production. On the other hand, inventories are an investment in working capital and incur an interest cost. If the firm borrows capital to maintain inventories, the direct interest cost is obvious. Even if the firm has not borrowed, however, working capital tied up in inventories represents an interest cost. Any funds invested in inventories could have earned the going interest rate in the money market, and this loss can substantially crimp profits.

Therefore, business attempts to keep inventories at an absolute minimum consistent with smooth operations. For a very large business, literally millions of dollars are at stake. This is why you see modern automated cash registers (i.e., the ones that automatically "read" the black and white bar code on packages) in large chain supermarkets and retail establishments.

These cash registers came into use not chiefly because they record your purchases more quickly and accurately (which of course they do), but because they also tie into a computer network that keeps track of inventories of thousands of items on a daily basis.

But why do inventories, so necessary to the smooth functioning of an individual business, exacerbate the business cycle?

The late-1990s New Economy boom and 2001 recession provide a good example. As demand rose, businesses boosted production to meet the growing volume of orders. If business had not been quick enough, an unplanned draw-down of inventories would have occurred. This is known as involuntary inventory depletion. If inventories are severely depleted, shortages can result and sales may be jeopardized because goods are not available. To protect itself against such a development once it became confident of the unfolding 1990s expansion, business boosted output and defensively accumulated inventories. For the entire economy, production gained more rapidly than sales as firms stockpiled, rather than sold, output as inventories to prevent shortages, accentuating the cyclical expansion. In summary, inventory accumulation exacerbated the boom.

Now consider the 2001 downswing of the cycle. No firm willingly maintains production in a sales slump because unsold goods would pile up on the shelf. As sales weaken and fall, business curtails production in order to prevent involuntary inventory accumulation. Indeed, once business recognizes the severity of the slump, it will begin to liquidate the large volume of (now unnecessary) inventories built up during the previous expansion. These stockpiles of goods are no longer needed and can be disposed of. But as goods are sold from inventories, output and employment are reduced more than sales because orders can be filled from inventories rather than from current production. Firms can cut production sharply as they sell goods out of inventory. This aggravates the cycle's downturn.

It also helps explain the shock brought on by the 2001 recession. Inventory accumulation sharpened the late-1990s New Economy boom, driving production forward more rapidly than sales. Then, when the first hint of weakness struck, businesses switched from accumulating their inventories to disposing of them. Production, which had been in overdrive, shifted into reverse. The recession was on.

Thus, inventories play an important destabilizing role in the cycle through their influence on industrial production, boosting output during expansion and depressing it during a slump. Inventory's impact on inflation in the Old Economy 1970s compounded this destabilizing influence. Inventory accumulation heightened rapid expansion, contributing to inflationary pressures. Business firms increased their inventory buildup, intending to stockpile goods at current prices and sell them later at inflated prices. And when inventory liquidation in a recession contributed to deflationary pressures, as occurred in 1981–1982, falling prices triggered a panic sell-off that drove prices down even more steeply.

Here's how it worked during the inflationary Old Economy 1970s. Business stockpiled goods during the expansionary phase of the cycle to prevent involuntary inventory depletion and shortages, and prices started to rise. Firms quickly discovered that goods held in inventory increased in value along with the general rise in prices. They had an incentive to buy now while prices were low, hold the goods in inventory, and sell them later at higher prices and profits. As soon as prices rose rapidly enough, widespread speculation set in, adding to the general increase in production and reinforcing the inflation.

Recall, for example, the rapid increase in sugar prices in 1973–1974. Sugar manufacturers and industrial users of sugar (canners, soft drink bottlers, confectioners, and bakers) produced sugar and sweetened products and held them in inventory while their prices were low, hoping to make large profits from sales when their prices rose. This speculative stockpiling contributed to the price increase by bidding up production (and costs) out of proportion to sales. Of course, when the inevitable contraction came, liquidation of the inventory overhang helped halt the inflationary spiral. Businesses panicked in 1975 when faced with the prospect of selling at a price that did not recoup interest costs. The sell-off reduced sugar prices. More important, industry output plummeted and layoffs mounted as orders were filled from the shelf.

Liquidation continued until inventories fell to a proper relation to sales. Thus, speculative inventory accumulation and liquidation became a self-fulfilling prophecy. Firms piled up inventories in anticipation of a price increase, and the large volume of orders sent prices upward. When the bubble burst, firms liquidated inventories in haste, afraid of a drop in prices, and the sell-off forced prices downward.

Now you understand why inventories and their relationship to sales are such important economic indicators. They not only confirm the stage of the cycle, they also provide advance warning of turning points and of the strength or severity of impending boom and bust.

And you also understand the irony that inventories exacerbate the business cycle, even though individual businesses use inventories to smooth operations. Production will rise more rapidly than sales during cyclical expansion, the difference accumulating as inventories, intensifying the expansion and hastening recession. After recession begins, firms will reduce output more rapidly than the drop in sales, drawing upon inventories to make up the difference. Therefore, the cycle's downswing will be more severe.

RECENT EXPERIENCE

The Wall Street Journal publishes the Commerce Department's inventory data (see below) for manufacturing and wholesale and retail trade around the middle of each month. (No inventory data are published for other sectors of the economy.) The excerpt below from the *Journal*'s Tuesday, November 18, 2003, print edition informs you in the first paragraph that inventories grew by $3.6 billion, while the third paragraph from the end of the article reports that inventories were 1.36 times sales.

The same day's online edition also carried the report (http://online. wsj.com). You may wish to review the general directions for retrieving online

---

September Rise In Inventories Is Good for GDP

By JON E. HILSENRATH

Inventory Accumulation — Businesses increased inventories by a seasonally adjusted $3.6 billion in September from August, the Commerce Department said in a report that suggested economic growth during the summer was even stronger than the supercharged pace initially estimated.

The government announced last month that the nation's gross domestic product grew at a 7.2% annual rate during the third quarter. When it made that preliminary GDP estimate, it assumed businesses pared inventories by $35.8 billion, at an annual rate, in the process as consumer spending was rising. Yesterday's reported increase in

Several forecasting firms revised upward their third-quarter growth estimates.

September inventories suggests businesses were less aggressive about clearing off shelves during the third quarter than estimated and that they instead produced more cars, building materials and other products to meet rising consumer demand.

As a result, several economic forecasting firms revised upward their estimates for third-quarter growth. For ex-
ample, Macroeconomic Advisers LLP estimates the stronger-than-expected inventory figures, in addition to recent strong construction data, mean GDP grew by more than 8% during the third quarter. The Commerce Department's Bureau of Economic Analysis will make its regularly scheduled revision of GDP data a week from today.

Inventory/Sales Ratio — The September increase in inventories amounted to a 0.3% gain on a seasonally adjusted basis from August, the first monthly increase since March. The increase exceeded the 0.1% drop expected by analysts. Inventories rose at auto dealers, furniture stores, building suppliers and general-merchandise stores. But the ratio of inventories to sales—a closely followed measure of how lean inventories remain—was unchanged at 1.36, a record low.

Many economists are expecting inventory building to continue in the fourth quarter, providing a boost to economic output. Some economists counter, however, that businesses are unlikely to build inventories much in the months ahead because executives are focused on operating more efficiently, with as little inventory as possible.

Separately, the Federal Reserve Bank of New York reported its monthly index of manufacturing activity improved to a record 41 in November from an upwardly revised 34 in October. Indexes for new orders and shipments topped the previous record set in October, and the inventories index was slightly positive. Indexes on employment and the length of the workweek also were positive and near last month's level.

information on pages 7 through 11 of Chapter 1. Appendix D on page 374 also furnishes you with a quick guide to the *Journal*'s online edition.

Economic Indicators and Briefing.com present these data in easy-to-use text, table, and chart form:

1. Scroll down the online edition's home page's left-hand menu-bar and click on Economy.

2. Click on Economic Indicators under Data and Resources and then click on Business Inventories (PDF).

3. Click on Reports from Briefing.com under Data and Resources and then click on Business Inventories.

Inventories and sales are straightforward concepts. The inventory/sales ratio tells you how many months it would take to sell off inventories at the prevailing sales pace. You can calculate the ratio by dividing monthly inventory by monthly sales. Historically, inventories had been roughly 1.5 times sales over the cycle, although the ratio fell during the New Economy 1990s. A rise in the ratio indicates that inventories are growing out of proportion to sales and that inventory liquidation and recession are imminent. A fall in the ratio informs you that sales are outpacing inventory growth and that economic expansion is under way. This is a key indicator; you should follow it closely.

Charts 6–1 (below) and 6–2 (on page 79) illustrate inventories' role in the New Economy late-1990s boom and the 2001 recession. This cycle con-

CHART 6–1 Change in Book Value of Manufacturing and Trade Inventories

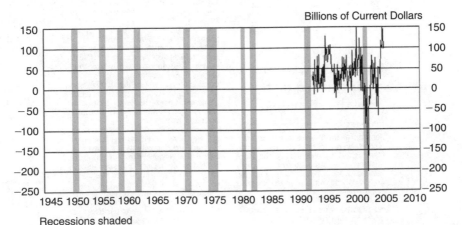

Recessions shaded

Source: U.S. of the Census Bureau.

CHART 6–2 Manufacturing and Trade Inventory/Sales Ratio

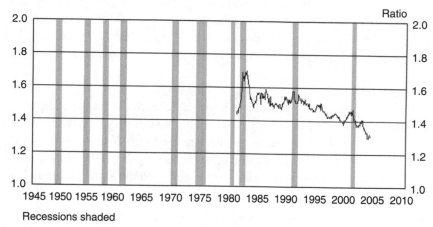

Recessions shaded

Source: U.S. Census Bureau.

cluded with a good example of inventory accumulation and speculation followed by inventory liquidation.

Begin with Chart 6–1 and follow the steep rise in inventories from 1995 through 2000 and the 2001 liquidation. Then turn to Chart 6–2 and notice that the inventory/sales ratio had fallen to an unusually low level by the end of the 1990s as sales gains outstripped inventory growth. As the cycle's peak approached, however, sales stopped growing and unplanned inventory accumulation became a problem. Business firms had to deal with ever-larger stockpiles of goods, and the inventory/sales ratio rose. Sensing that a sell-off was around the corner, businesses tried to bring inventories under control. Unfortunately, this was more easily said than done. Orders had to be canceled and production curtailed more than once because business underestimated the shortfall in orders.

But beginning in late 2000 and continuing into 2001, inventory liquidation finally began (see Chart 6–1). Under panic conditions, business desperately dumped goods on the market. Industrial production dropped as business firms cut output sharply and filled their meager volume of orders from overstocked inventories. In less than two years conditions deteriorated from $150 billion of inventory buildup to over $150 billion of inventory sell-off. There is no doubt that inventory accumulation and liquidation played a key role in the New Economy boom and recession.

Then, by late 2002, businesses realized they had overshot the mark and excessively depleted inventories. Their renewed inventory accumulation began to spark recovery (see Chart 6–1) as inventory accumulation swung back to prerecession levels. As soon as businesses began restoring their inventories to a more normal level, production stopped falling and the recession was over. Finally, the inventory/sales ratio (see Chart 6–2) started to fall once again as sales eventually grew more rapidly than inventories.

CONCLUSION

Expenditures on new equipment and inventory accumulation were important ingredients in the New Economy's boom and bust. It may be a while before we return to the heroic numbers of the late 1990s. If boom conditions do return, however, observe these indicators for new signs that business investment in equipment and inventories has exacerbated the cycle and may hasten the onset of the next recession.

Investor's Tip

- Watch inventory figures carefully. If boom conditions drive inventories out of moderate proportion to sales and the inventory/sales ratio rises rapidly, you know recession can't be far behind.

Turn now to Chapter 7 for an analysis of the consumer's role in recent economic developments.

C H A P T E R 7

THE POSTWAR
BUSINESS CYCLE:
THE ROLE OF
CONSUMER DEMAND

THE CONSUMER TO THE RESCUE

S TRONG CONSUMER DEMAND as a result of falling interest rates sustained the economy in 2001, 2002, 2003, and 2004. As rates fell, residential construction and auto sales remained strong because household spending, which relies heavily on borrowing to finance these expenditures, helped offset the slump in business capital investment. The economy limped along, but it would have collapsed entirely without strong consumer demand.

Low interest rates restored consumer expenditures to the key role they had played before the 1990s. You have seen that business investment rather than consumer demand led the New Economy's advance in the 1990s. In that decade, consumers reinforced the business cycle; they did not lead the cycle. In earlier decades, however, and especially in the Old Economy 1960s and 1970s, consumers led the business cycle and provided its key dynamic. Consumer borrowing and therefore interest rates played a crucial role in the Old Economy. However, the consumer's role changed dramatically with the passage from Old Economy to New Economy. Here's how.

CONSUMER DEMAND AND THE OLD ECONOMY

In the Old Economy consumers borrowed continually and prodigiously to finance purchases of residential construction, automobiles, and other durable goods. The level of activity grew decade after decade and with each cycle, so that in the 1970s tidal waves of credit roared through the system, rapidly swelling demand to record levels.

It started in the 1920s, a kind of brief test run for the full-scale activity that followed World War II. Credit-backed demand included kitchen and laundry appliances; furniture and furnishings; electronic equipment such as television sets, VCRs, stereos, and personal computers; residential construction; and automobiles. All were financed by credit, and the terms became more liberal over time, even as interest rates rose. The American consumer was encouraged—indeed, came to feel obligated—to mortgage the future so that present expenditures could exceed present income, with borrowing covering the difference.

The economy's health thus developed a dependence on the chronic fix of greater consumer expenditures, financed by borrowing. Full production and employment became the hostages of ever-larger waves of consumer expenditure on discretionary purchases financed by borrowing.

Unfortunately, these surges in consumer demand always led to their own demise, because expansion brought inflation, which depleted real incomes and generated the downturn of the cycle. Only then did inflation abate, real income recover, and expansion begin anew. Thus, every boom inevitably went bust, and each recession was also self-correcting and carried with it the seeds of economic recovery.

But why did the business cycle always rebound from recession, never falling into permanent depression, and why wasn't expansion continuous? Well, to begin with, every expansion ended inevitably in recession, because every expansion was fueled by credit. Consumers and businesses borrowed to buy new homes, cars, factories, and machinery. The more they borrowed and spent, the faster demand grew, pushing production into high gear in order to keep pace with demand. But, sooner or later, the upward spiral of borrowing and spending came to an end. The strain on productive facilities forced costs higher, pushing prices up, too. Inflation depressed consumer sentiment, and consumers responded by curtailing their expenditures.

Consumers also found that their incomes could not support the burden of additional debt repayment. Businesses, having accomplished their targeted growth in plant and equipment, cut back or ceased their expenditures in this area. Once business and consumer borrowing and spending started to decline, the slump began, and production and income fell. Inflation subsided with the drop in demand.

The recessions hit bottom just before consumers recovered their confidence, due to inflation's decline, and began spending again. Components of demand that were financed by credit stopped shrinking. Remember that these components were a limited, though highly volatile, share of total demand. (The demand for many items that were not financed by credit, such as food and medical care, hardly declined at all during recession.) As consumers and businesses ceased borrowing and turned their attention to liquidating their expansion-generated debts, the price of credit, namely interest rates, fell until, finally, the debt burden and interest rates were low enough that consumers and businesses could borrow and spend again. At this juncture, auto production, home construction, and business investment in new plant and equipment stopped falling, the slide ended, and economic recovery was in sight.

Generally speaking, expansion ceased when consumers were no longer willing to borrow and spend; contraction ended when their confidence returned. In the 1970s, these cyclical changes in consumer confidence were closely tied to the rate of inflation. Rapid economic expansion brought swiftly rising prices with an attendant and sobering drop in real income and consumer confidence. Recession cooled the pace of inflation, encouraging a resurgence of confidence.

So far, the business cycle has been painted with fairly broad strokes. The time has come to take up a finer brush, so that essential details and connections can be clearly drawn. This chapter shows you how to use *The Wall Street Journal* to understand each step in the growth of consumer demand.

The first statistical series to be examined in this chapter is the *consumer price index* (CPI), whose fluctuations chart the course of inflation. In the Old Economy, lower inflation led to improved consumer sentiment and demand, which drove economic expansion forward. You can gauge the latter through data on auto sales, consumer credit, housing starts, and home sales, which will serve as the leading indicators of consumer demand.

CONSUMER PRICE INDEX

The Bureau of Labor Statistics' CPI release usually appears mid-month in *The Wall Street Journal*. In the Wednesday, November 10, 2003, print-edition article, the second paragraph informs you that the CPI remained unchanged in October 2003. Although multiplying the monthly data by 12 will provide a rough approximation of inflation's annual rate for that month, you can see from the second paragraph that the CPI had increased 2 percent in the year ending October 2003. (See page 84.)

Consumer Prices Hold Steady In Face of Accelerating Growth

By Jon E. Hilsenrath
And Joseph Rebello

Consumer prices held steady in October, indicating the recent burst of economic growth isn't fanning inflation for households.

CPI — The consumer-price index was unchanged after rising in four straight months. A decline in energy and automobile prices offset increases in prices for meat and lodging, the Labor Department said. During the past 12 months, consumer prices were up 2%. The core consumer-price index, a more stable inflation indicator that excludes volatile food and energy prices, rose 0.2%. That was slightly more than expected but still up just 1.3% from a year earlier.

A separate report last week showed wholesale prices—the prices charged by manufacturers—rose for the fifth straight month in October.

Taken together, the data appeared unlikely to move Federal Reserve officials from their view that they can keep short-term interest rates low, even though economic growth has accelerated in recent months. In the past, faster economic growth has fanned fears of inflation and rising interest rates. But Fed policy makers say the labor market remains weak and manufacturers still have ample unused production capacity, factors that will prevent companies from raising prices very aggressively.

"There's still room for some pretty strong growth before the risk of inflationary pressures becomes a primary concern," said Robert Parry, president of the Federal Reserve Bank of San Francisco.

Private economists tended to agree with that assessment, though some said the latest inflation data included faint hints that inflation might not fall much further. James O'Sullivan, an economist with UBS Ltd. in New York, noted that core consumer prices rose at a 1.5% annual rate during the past three months, faster than the 1% annual growth registered in the three months ended in June and the 0.4% growth rate in the three months ended in April.

"Our own leading indicator of inflation

Please Turn to Page A12, Column 1

Stabilizing

Consumer prices, excluding food and energy; three-month change at a seasonally adjusted annual rate

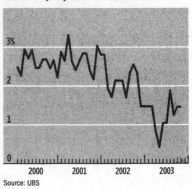

Source: UBS

You can also go to the online edition for this report (http://online.wsj.com). General directions for retrieving online information appear in Chapter 1 on pages 7 through 11. Appendix D on page 374 also furnishes you with a quick guide to the *Journal*'s online edition.

The online edition lets you examine the Bureau of Labor Statistics' report and also presents CPI data in chart form:

1. Scroll down the online edition's home page's left-hand menu-bar and click on Economy.
2. Click on Economic Indicators under Data and Resources and then click on Consumer Price Index.
3. Click on Economic Chartbook under Data and Resources and then scroll down to Consumer Prices.
4. Click on Reports from Briefing.com under Data and Resources and then click on CPI.

The CPI compares relative price changes over time. An index must be constructed because consumers purchase such a wide variety of goods and services that no single item could accurately reflect the situation. (See Chart 7–1 on page 86.)

After a base period (1982–1984) is selected and assigned an index number of 100.0, prices for other periods are then reported as percentage changes from this base. For instance, if prices rose 5 percent, the index would be 105.0. If prices fell by 10 percent, the index would be 90.0.

The Bureau of Labor Statistics (BLS) calculates the CPI by compiling a list of the goods and services purchased by the typical consumer, including such items as food, clothing, shelter, public utilities, and medical care. These make up the "market basket." The base-period price of each item is recorded and assigned a weight according to its relative importance in the basket. Changes in the price of each item are noted, and the percentage change in the total price is reflected in the change of the index number.

The ways consumers spend are continuously shifting, because tastes change, as do incomes and the relative prices of goods. New goods and services are frequently introduced. It would be impossible, however, to generate a consistent index of consumer prices if the components of the market basket were constantly changed; a balance must be struck between the need for consistency and the need for an accurate reflection of consumer buying patterns. Therefore, the BLS revises the contents of the market basket only occasionally, after conducting a survey of consumer expenditure patterns. Contrary to the popular image, the CPI is not really a "cost-of-living" index. The BLS's market basket is fixed; the individual consumer's is not. Substitutions are made with changes in prices and with changes in income. Your cost of living can vary (or can be made to vary) independently of any change in the CPI.

Make a mental note that the *Journal*'s November 10, 2003, report, as well as Chart 7–1, confirms inflation's continued abatement since the peak in the

CHART 7–1 Consumer Price Index, 1982–1984 = 100; Change in Index at Monthly Rate

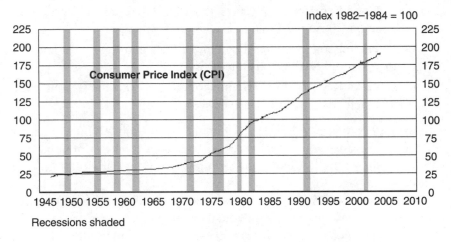

Recessions shaded

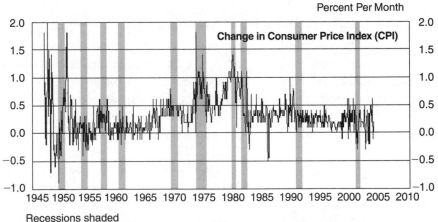

Recessions shaded

Source: U.S. Bureau of Labor Statistics.

late 1970s; the CPI increased by about 5 percent annually in the middle and late 1980s, fell to half that level with the 1990–1991 recession, and remained at 1 or 2 percent annually at the end of the 1990s and into the new millennium.

When the economy emerged from the 2001 recession, some feared that deflation would also emerge with continued constrained demand and rapidly rising output. More on that concern later in the chapter.

EMPLOYMENT DATA

The Wall Street Journal usually publishes the Labor Department's *monthly employment report* on Monday of the second week. February 2004 data appeared in the Monday, March 8, 2004, online edition (see page 88). The second paragraph reported that unemployment remained at 5.6 percent and that nonfarm employment grew by 21,000 in February 2004. Chart 7–2 on page 89 puts this figure in historical perspective.

Charts 7–2 and 7–3 (on page 90) show the protracted 1990s decline in the unemployment rate and its jump in the 2001 recession as well as nonfarm employment's strength in the 1990s and its collapse in the 2001 recession and its subsequent recovery.

You should also track the *average workweek* and *factory overtime* because they, too, portray the economy's strength and are important determinants of consumer sentiment. These data appear in the statistical summary that frequently accompanies the print-edition story. Charts 7–4 and 7–5 on pages 90 and 91 clearly show that both the workweek and overtime generally improve during expansion, flatten with boom conditions, and plummet in recession. A strong economy provides big paychecks.

These charts provide ample evidence of the New Economy's positive impact on labor markets in the late 1990s. During these years of full employment (see Chart 7–3), nonfarm employment grew dramatically (see Chart 7–2), as did the workweek (see Chart 7–4) and overtime (see Chart 7–5). Together with the low rate of inflation, these data will help explain the record robust levels of consumer sentiment during the advent of the New Economy in the 1990s.

The *Journal*'s online edition lets you examine the Bureau of Labor Statistics' employment report and charts that illustrate the unemployment rate as well as nonfarm payroll changes and the workweek:

1. Scroll down the online edition's home page's left-hand menu-bar and click on Economy.
2. Click on Economic Indicators under Data and Resources and then click on Consumer Price Index.
3. Click on Economic Chartbook under Data and Resources and see the chart that depicts the unemployment rate.
4. Click on Reports from Briefing.com under Data and Resources and then click on Nonfarm Payrolls to view the chart portraying payroll changes.

A weekly statistic can also help keep you informed of labor-market developments. On Fridays the *Journal* publishes a report summarizing the

As of Monday, March 8, 2004

ECONOMY
Job Growth Falls Short of Estimates

**February Data on Payrolls
Fuel Worries Consumers
May Slow Their Spending**

By JAMES R. HAGERTY and JON E. HILSENRATH
Staff Reporters of THE WALL STREET JOURNAL
March 8, 2004

Until recently, economists were merely puzzled that the expanding U.S. economy was failing to produce many new jobs. Now they are starting to get worried about it.

In a report described by one government economist as a "limp handshake," the Labor Department said Friday that just 21,000 payroll jobs were created in February; economists had expected about 125,000. The unemployment rate remained at 5.6%, but that was because more Americans dropped out of the labor market, many deciding that job hunting was a waste of time.

Job Growth

REACTIONS

Economists: The 21,000 jobs added to payrolls fell well short of the 125,000 economists had expected. Read a roundup of economists' reactions to the report.

Financial Markets: Stocks skidded and bond prices soared following the report's release. See continuously updated market coverage at wsj.com/ markets.

Unless job creation picks up within the next few months, consumers may grow more jittery, as they watch friends and neighbors struggle to find work. That, in turn, could prompt Americans to slow spending, warned Sung Won Sohn, chief economist at Wells Fargo & Co. "The risk of economic slowdown has clearly increased," he said.

The positive news in Friday's report was that it underlined continued improvements in productivity as companies find ways to raise output without expanding their work forces. While painful for many workers, these productivity gains have helped boost corporate profits and held down interest rates. In another positive development, job losses in manufacturing are slowing. Factories shed 3,000 jobs in February, down from 13,000 in January and a range of 40,000 to 60,000 a month last summer.

Still, the job-market stagnation portrayed in Friday's report was more bad news for President Bush. Even if the labor market does get better soon, as many economists expect, that could come too late for the president to get credit before the November election.

Mr. Bush's predicament is all the more difficult because there is little more that Washington can do to pump up growth during coming months. The Bush administration's mammoth tax cuts have given the economy some juice during the past two years, but the resulting record budget deficits make it impossible to push through new reductions soon.

Job Growth–Second Paragraph

In a report described by one government economist as a "limp handshake," the Labor Department said Friday that just 21,000 payroll jobs were created in February; economists had expected about 125,000. The unemployment rate remained at 5.6%, but that was because more Americans dropped out of the labor market, many deciding that job hunting was a waste of time.

Labor Department's release on initial claims for unemployment insurance, which provides a running tabulation of weekly job losses. (Unlike the monthly nonfarm employment data—see Chart 7–2 below—that appears with the unemployment rate, this statistic reports gross job losses only and is not a *net* job growth—or loss—statistic.)

The second paragraph of the Friday, November 2, 2003, story on page 92 informs you of 355,000 jobless claims in the latest week and of the 367,000 four-week average. The article goes on to express optimism in a number lower than 400,000, and the chart clearly illustrates the drop in claims and the improved employment picture in late 2003. You can examine the historical record in Chart 7–6 (on page 93).

PERSONAL INCOME
The Commerce Department's monthly personal income report appears in *The Wall Street Journal* during the fourth week or the following week. The

CHART 7–2 Job Growth

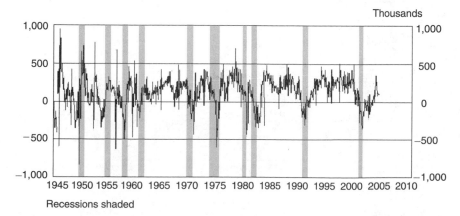

Recessions shaded

Source: U.S. Bureau of Labor Statistics.

CHART 7–3 Unemployment Rate

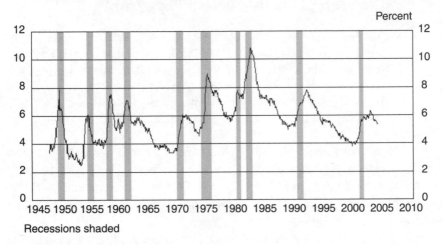

Recessions shaded

Source: U.S. Bureau of Labor Statistics.

statistical summary at the end of the Monday, June 30, 2003, *Journal* print-edition article on page 93 informs you that personal income rose to a seasonally adjusted rate of $9.164 trillion in May of 2003. The second paragraph and statistical summary also inform you that consumption expenditures grew to $7.575 trillion, a gain of 0.1 percent. These are current, not constant dollars; there is no adjustment for inflation.

CHART 7–4 Average Workweek of Manufacturing Production Workers

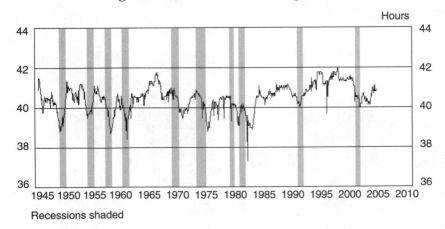

Recessions shaded

Source: U.S. Bureau of Labor Statistics.

CHART 7–5 Average Weekly Overtime of Manufacturing Production Workers

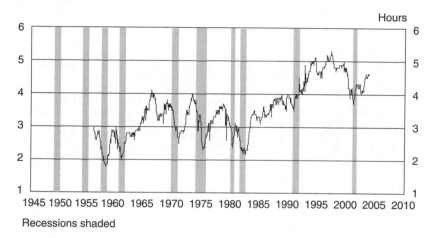

Recessions shaded

Source: U.S. Bureau of Labor Statistics.

Personal income and spending data, in table and chart form, are available in the *Journal*'s online edition:

1. Scroll down the online edition's home page's left-hand menu-bar and click on Economy.
2. Click on Economic Indicators under Data and Resources and then click on Personal Income.
3. Click on Economic Chartbook under Data and Resources and scroll down to Consumer Spending.
4. Click on Reports from Briefing.com under Data and Resources and then click on Personal Income to view the charts portraying personal income and personal consumption expenditures.

Personal income is all the income we earn (wages, salaries, fringe benefits, profit, rent, interest, and so on) plus the transfer payments we receive (such as veterans' benefits, social security, unemployment compensation, and welfare) minus the social security taxes we pay to the government.

Therefore, the federal government's ability to borrow from banks and use these borrowed funds to pay out to us in transfer payments more than it receives from us in taxes provides a cushion that keeps personal income

Jobs Claims Fall Again; Indicators Up

By Jon E. Hilsenrath

In another sign the job market is healing, the Labor Department said fewer people are filing new claims for unemployment benefits. The improving labor market, in turn, pushed up a closely watched index used to forecast future economic activity.

Initial jobless claims decreased by 15,000 to 355,000 in the week ending Nov. 15, the Labor Department said. The four-week average of claims dropped 9,000 to 367,250, its lowest level since February 2001. Claims are down by nearly 100,000 from a 2003 peak of 459,000 set in April.

Initial unemployment claims offer a hint about the latest trend in unemployment. The job market is generally considered to be improving as fewer people file claims. A sustained drop below 400,000 is generally considered to be a benchmark for rising national employment.

Meanwhile, the Conference Board, a private research group, said its index of leading economic indicators rose 0.4% in October to 113.6. The index tracks indicators that tend to be at the leading edge of coming trends in the economy, such as jobless claims, stock prices, permits for new building activity or new orders for durable goods. During the six months ended Oct. 31, the leading index rose at a 5.7% annual rate, with all 10 components showing improvement.

"This improvement that we've been looking at in the economy during last couple of months is probably going to continue into 2004," said Ken Goldstein, economist at the Conference Board.

Six of the 10 indicators used to compile the leading index increased in October. One of the biggest contributors to the improvement was the decline in jobless claims.

The job-market improvement occurs as debate heats up in Washington about whether Congress should continue funding emergency unemployment benefits, which provides coverage for an additional 13 weeks to people who haven't found a job after regular benefits have expired. Unless the program is extended

Please Turn to Page A7, Column 5

Jobless Claims [bracket annotation beside second paragraph]

Claims Drop

Four-week moving average of initial unemployment insurance claims

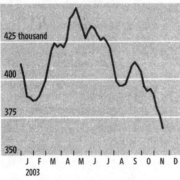

Source: Labor Department via Economy.com

---

growing even in recession, when earned income is down. The federal deficits generated during recession help maintain personal income despite rising unemployment, and thereby maintain a floor under personal consumption expenditures. As you can see from the historical data (see Chart 7–7 on page 94), personal income has grown so steadily that it is difficult to use as a cyclical indicator.

CHART 7–6 Initial Claims for Unemployment Insurance

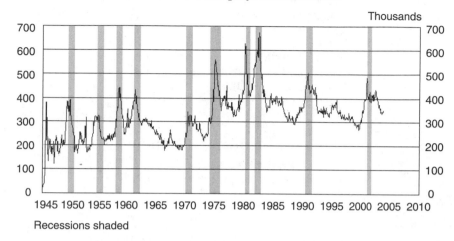

Thousands

Recessions shaded

Source: The Conference Board, Business Cycle Indicators, Series A0M005.

Consumers' Spending, Income Rise

By MICHAEL SCHROEDER

WASHINGTON—Consumer spending and income rose modestly in May, evidence of cautious advancements in the lackluster economy.

Consumer Spending
The Commerce Department reported that consumer spending rose 0.1% in May from April, a bit below expectations. Adjusted for inflation in May, consumer outlays increased 0.3%, up from a 0.1% increase in April. The April figure was revised from the department's initial estimate of a 0.1% decline.

Continued low prices may have acted as a spending stimulus. The core inflation rate, as measured by the 12-month change in the personal consumption expenditure price index, moved lower, to 1.2% in May from 1.3% a month earlier.

The reports "showed distinct improvement," said Peter Kretzmer, a senior economist at Bank of America Corp.

Consumer spending has begun to rebound since a dismal period earlier in the year. Driven by low interest rates, consumers are still refinancing mortgages at high levels and using the savings—albeit cautiously—on new purchases.

Inflation-adjusted spending for durable goods, including such big-ticket items as cars, fell 0.1% in May. But retail sales helped increase spending on nondurable goods by 0.5%.

Pressure on Prices
Year-over-year change in the chained-price index of consumer expenditure, excluding food and energy

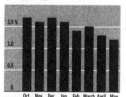

Oct. Nov. Dec. Jan. Feb. March April May
2002   2003
Source: Bureau of Economic Analysis

Inflation-adjusted income, including wages, interest and government benefits, rose 0.4% last month, the largest increase since June 2002—offsetting April's decline. If the trend continues, spending will build in the future. Consumer spending accounts for two-thirds of all economic activity in the U.S.

Despite the recent monthly increases, personal income has been hurt by limited growth in new jobs. Personal income grew at a 2.9% annual pace in May, down from 3.1% in April, and well below the 3.5% pace at the beginning of the year.

Consumer-confidence numbers are sending mixed signals. The University of Michigan said its index of consumer sentiment edged down to 89.7 in June from 92.1 in May. But the reading at the end of the month was a significant improvement over the initial mid-June reading of 87.2. That might reflect improvements in the stock and bond markets and the expectation that the Federal Reserve would lower short-term interest rates. Last Wednesday, the Fed lowered its federal-funds rate by a quarter of a percentage point to 1%, the lowest level in more than four decades.

PERSONAL INCOME
Here is the Commerce Department's latest report on personal income. The figures are at seasonally adjusted annual rates in trillions of dollars.

	May 2003	April 2003
Personal income	$9.164	$9.137
Wages and salaries	5.091	5.083
Factory payrolls	.749	.749
Transfer payments	1.365	1.355
Disposable personal income	8.074	8.051
Personal outlays	7.790	7.780
Consumption expenditures	7.575	7.564
Other outlays	.215	.215
Personal savings	.283	.272

Summary

Consumer Spending–Second Paragraph

The Commerce Department reported that consumer spending rose 0.1% in May from April, a bit below expectations. Adjusted for inflation in May, consumer outlays increased 0.3%, up from a 0.1% increase in April. The April figure was revised from the department's initial estimate of a 0.1% decline.

Personal Income–Summary

PERSONAL INCOME

Here is the Commerce Department's latest report on personal income. The figures are at seasonally adjusted annual rates in trillions of dollars.

	May 2003	April 2003
Personal Income	$9.164	$9.137
Wages and salaries	5.091	5.083
Factory payrolls	.749	.749
Transfer payments	1.365	1.355
Disposable personal Income	8.074	8.051
Personal outlays	7.790	7.780
Consumption expenditures	7.575	7.564
Other outlays	.215	.215
Personal savings	.283	.272

CHART 7–7 Personal Income

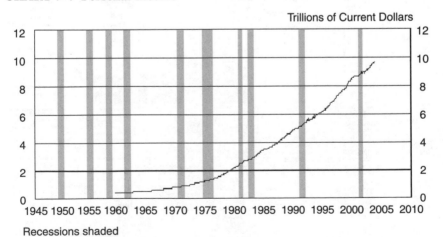

Trillions of Current Dollars

Recessions shaded

Source: U.S. Dept. of Commerce, Bureau of Economic Analysis, *National Income & Product Accounts,* Table 2.6, line 1.

94

CONSUMER SENTIMENT

Now consider the impact of inflation and employment data on the consumer. Chart 7–8 provides ample evidence of consumer sentiment's record surge in the New Economy 1990s and subsequent collapse in the 2001 recession.

The Survey Research Center at the University of Michigan compiles the *Index of Consumer Sentiment*. Consumers are asked a variety of questions regarding their personal financial circumstances and their outlook for the future. Responses are tabulated according to whether conditions are perceived as better or worse than a year earlier, and an index is constructed comparing the outcome to that for a base year (1966).

The Wall Street Journal occasionally publishes this index, as it did in the print edition of Monday, June 16, 2003 (see page 96), when the Survey Research Center reported consumer sentiment of 87.2 in early June of 2003 (the final report appears the following month). More often the *Journal* publishes the Conference Board's *Index of Consumer Confidence*.

A glance at Chart 7–8 below shows you that the Michigan and Conference Board indexes have similar records, although the Conference Board index is more volatile.

The second paragraph of the *Journal*'s online article (see page 97) for Tuesday, February 24, 2004, reported a sharp drop in consumer confidence, although the remainder of the article revealed a variety of views on the decline's significance.

CHART 7–8 Consumer Sentiment: Michigan and Conference Board Surveys

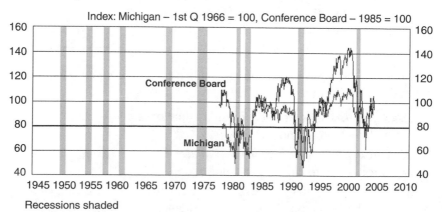

Recessions shaded

Source: The Conference Board, *Business Cycle Indicators,* Series U0M058 and U0M122.

Consumer Confidence Slips in Aftermath of War

By Greg Ip

WASHINGTON—Consumers' spirits have begun slipping again after a sharp postwar bounce, further clouding the economic outlook.

Expectations of inflation also have begun dropping, according to the University of Michigan, something that might foreshadow an increased risk of deflation, or generally falling prices.

Other reports show that wholesale prices declined in May from April and the U.S. international trade deficit narrowed slightly in April from March. Both developments were due heavily to the declining cost of oil.

In a report released Friday, the University of Michigan's index of consumer sentiment fell to 87.2 in early June from 92.1 in May, though it remains well above its recent low of 77.6 in March as worries over war with Iraq peaked. Much like in the aftermath of the 1991 Gulf War, "a still-weak labor market appears set to erode confidence over the next few months," said Lehman Brothers economist Drew Matus.

The deterioration in sentiment was hardly catastrophic. It was mostly because of consumers' declining confidence in the future. The index of expectations fell to 84.2, from 91.4 in May, but that is

after expectations had shot up sharply after war jitters began to ease in March. The index of consumers' views on current conditions edged down to 92 from 93.2, changing little since March.

In the wake of the consumer confidence data Friday, the Dow Jones Industrial average fell 79.43, or 0.86%, to 9117.12.

This corresponds to what is going on in the overall economy and the markets. While forward-looking investors have bid up stocks and corporate bonds in anticipation of a strong postwar recovery, hard data show only a stabilization, not an acceleration, in economic activity.

The strengths of consumer confidence and financial markets have been among the few signs supporting widely held expectations of a strong second-half recovery. If confidence is slipping, markets may soon, as well, and that is likely to worry Federal Reserve officials. On Friday, futures markets indicated an increased expectation that the Fed will cut its short-term interest-rate target, now at 1.25%, by as much as half a percentage point on June 25.

Another potentially troubling sign for those worried about deflation is that consumers' median expectation of inflation over the next five to 10 years slipped to 2.6% from 2.8%, out of the 2.7%-3.1% range that had prevailed since 1997, other than a dip to 2.5% in September

2002. "This is an indication consumers are in the process of changing their long-term inflation expectations" in response to the weaker prices they see throughout the economy, said Richard Curtin, director of the university's surveys of consumers. But he said only 4% of the 300 respondents to the early June survey expect deflation over the next five to 10 years, within the 2%-7% range of recent years.

"Fed officials will undoubtedly keep an eye on this measure to see whether June's reading turns out to be a blip or the beginning of a persistent shift in price perceptions," said RBS Greenwich Capital economist Steve Stanley.

The Fed has regarded the risk of deflation as low in part because consumers have expected steady inflation. As long as people expect prices to rise, they will set their spending and salary demands accordingly. Expectations of deflation can help make it reality.

Separately, the Labor Department on Friday said producer prices fell 0.3% in May from April, the second consecutive monthly drop, but that mostly reflected the decline in petroleum-related prices from their Iraq-war heights. Excluding food and energy, "core" producer prices rose 0.1%. Core prices are still down 0.1% from a year ago. On balance, the report suggested that deflationary forces aren't

Please Turn to Page A4, Column 5

Consumer Sentiment

Consumer Sentiment–Fourth Paragraph

In a report released Friday, the University of Michigan's index of consumer sentiment fell to 87.2 in early June from 92.1 in May, though it remains well above its recent low of 77.6 in March as worries over war with Iraq peaked. Much like in the aftermath of the 1991 Gulf War, "a still-weak labor market appears set to erode confidence over the next few months," said Lehman Brothers economist Drew Matus.

Charts depicting both consumer confidence and consumer sentiment are available in the *Journal's* online edition:

1. Scroll down the online edition's home page's left-hand menu-bar and click on Economy.

2. Click on Economic Chartbook under Data and Resources and scroll down to Consumer Confidence.

3. Click on Reports from Briefing.com under Data and Resources and then click on Consumer Confidence to view the charts portraying both consumer confidence and consumer sentiment.

Other Journal Sites

As of 12:30 p.m. EST Tuesday, February 24, 2004

Home
News
Technology
Markets
Personal Journal
Opinion
Leisure/Weekend

The Print Edition
Today's Edition
Past Editions
Features
Columnists
In-Depth Reports
Discussions
Company Research
Markets Data Center
Site Map
My Online Journal
Portfolio
Personalize My News
E-Mail Setup
My Account/Billing
Customer Service
The Online Journal
The Print Edition
Contact Us
Help

Subscribe

BARRON'S Online

ECONOMY

Consumer Confidence Drops Amid Job-Market Concerns

A WALL STREET JOURNAL ONLINE NEWS ROUNDUP
February 24, 2004 12:30 p.m.

NEW YORK -- Consumer confidence in February fell at its fastest pace in a year amid rising concerns about the slow pace of job creation, according to a private research group.

The Conference Board reported early Tuesday that its consumer-confidence index tumbled to 87.3 from 96.4 last month. That was the steepest one-month decline since February 2003, when the index dropped 14 points. The index stood at 100 in 1985, its base year.

Consumer Confidence

"Consumers began the year on a high note, but their optimism has quickly given way to caution," said Lynn Franco, director of the group's Consumer Research Center. "At the core of their disenchantment is the labor market. While the current expansion has generated jobs over the past several months, the pace of creation remains too tepid to generate a sustainable turnaround in consumers' confidence."

Economists had expected a reading of 92, according to a survey by Dow Jones Newswires and CNBC.

But some economists said that bad winter weather was largely to blame. "We think it likely that much, if not all this decline is due to the severe weather," wrote Ian Shepherdson, chief U.S. economist at High Frequency Economics, in a note to clients. "Widespread storms temporarily boosted layoffs in the early part of the month." However, he noted that big snowstorms in January 1996 sent the headline number down 10.8 points, which then rebounded 9.6 points in the following month, adding that "We expect a repeat now."

CONSUMER CONFIDENCE

Index stood at 100 in 1985, its base year

Source: Conference Board

Other economists noted that, while the drop was steep, the index remains at a high level, given where it has been in the last year, which bodes well for consumer spending. The index reached as low as 61.4 in March before rebounding in April.

Bear Stearns Chief Market Economist John Ryding said: "We think that the decline in confidence more likely reflects the trash-talking on the economy arising from the presidential primary season rather than reflecting a deterioration in economic conditions,"adding that jobless claims dropped last week and that same-store sales are on the rise. "We look for confidence to rebound, especially as tax refunds begin to flow in over the next two months."

Consumer Confidence–Second Paragraph

The Conference Board reported early Tuesday that its consumer-confidence index tumbled to 87.3 from 96.4 last month. That was the steepest one-month decline since February 2003, when the index dropped 14 points. The index stood at 100 in 1985, its base year.

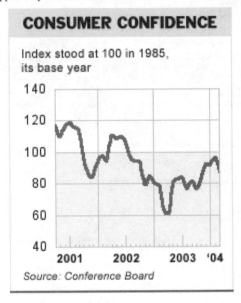

CONSUMER CONFIDENCE

Index stood at 100 in 1985, its base year

Source: Conference Board

Now that you are acquainted with consumer sentiment and consumer confidence and their key determinants, take time to consider consumer sentiment's central role in the Old Economy's dynamic. As you recall, consumer demand drove the Old Economy, and consumer sentiment and consumer confidence drove consumer demand. Compare the CPI with the Michigan index (see Chart 7–9 on page 99), and you will find that inflation and consumer sentiment moved in opposite directions during the Old Economy 1970s, as consumers responded to the rate of inflation.

Begin by contrasting the years 1955 through 1965 with 1965 through 1980. The principal difference between these periods is the moderate rate of inflation in the first decade and the cyclical increase of inflation after that. With each boom (1969, 1974, 1979), the rate of inflation hit a new high and consumer sentiment reached a new low. Although the recession in the mid-

CHART 7–9   Index of Consumer Sentiment

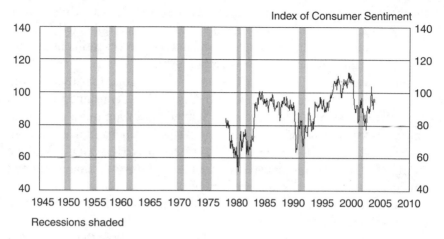

Recessions shaded

Source: The Conference Board, *Business Cycle Indicators,* Series U0M058.

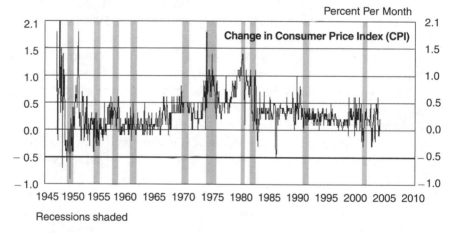

Recessions shaded

Source: U.S. Bureau of Labor Statistics.

1970s was worse than the 1970 recession, the rate of inflation did not drop to as low a number. No wonder consumer sentiment deteriorated for 15 years: Inflation and the attendant swings of the business cycle were becoming more severe. Once inflation's grip was broken in the early 1980s, however, consumers began feeling positively upbeat again for the first time in 20 years. The key had been the interruption of the inflationary boom–bust cycle.

Consumers are influenced by more than inflation. Employment opportunities, interest rates, and current events (like the Persian Gulf War of 1990–1991) all play a role. Consumer psychology is complicated. Yet you can see inflation's singular impact; inflation and consumer sentiment demonstrated a clear and predictable inverse relationship.

Iraq's invasion of Kuwait on August 2, 1990, broke that relationship and depressed consumer sentiment for two reasons. First, consumers expected that gasoline prices would rise quickly. Second, and even more important, no one knew whether we would be drawn into the conflict and what the consequences would be. How many lives would be lost? How long would the fighting last? As a result, consumer sentiment plunged dramatically and drastically without a severe and protracted surge of inflation.

Consumer sentiment remained in the doldrums until the fighting stopped, and then snapped back, only to fade as the recession lingered. For the first time in two decades, consumer sentiment seemed to follow the cycle rather than lead it. But by late 1994, consumer confidence had climbed out of the doldrums and was back in its 1980s range. By the mid-1990s, both consumer sentiment and consumer demand were robust again.

However, that was nothing compared to the New Economy surge in consumer confidence in the late 1990s. Inflation remained low, as you can see from Chart 7–9 on page 99, and then employment opportunities bloomed as Charts 7–2 through 7–6 on pages 89–93 illustrate. Business investment in technology (hardware and software) pushed the economy to its limits, providing jobs for everyone. Consumer confidence soared to an all-time record (see Charts 7–8 and 7–9 on pages 95 and 99) with the New Economy.

Which brings us to the nub of this discussion: *New Economy or Old Consumer sentiment drove consumer borrowing and spending.* You'll see below that strong consumer sentiment propelled consumer demand forward, while low consumer sentiment depressed consumer demand.

Feelings Are Facts

- When consumer sentiment falters, watch out for recession.

CONSUMER DEMAND

The Wall Street Journal regularly publishes articles on four indicators of consumer demand that merit your close attention: new-vehicle sales, consumer credit, housing activity, and retail sales. Let's examine each in turn.

New-Vehicle Sales

Around the 5th of the month, *The Journal* reports new-vehicle sales data compiled by the manufacturers. According to the second paragraph of an article in the Wednesday, March 3, 2004, online edition (see below), February 2004 new-vehicle sales (sedans, pickups, vans, and sport-utility vehicles) were

Other Journal Sites   As of 12:14 a.m. EST Wednesday, March 3, 2004

Home
News
Technology
Markets
Personal Journal
Opinion
Leisure/Weekend

The Print Edition
Today's Edition
Past Editions
Features
Columnists
In-Depth Reports
Discussions
Company Research
Markets Data Center
Site Map
My Online Journal
Portfolio
Personalize My News
E-Mail Setup
My Account/Billing
Customer Service
The Online Journal
The Print Edition
Contact Us
Help

BARRON'S Online

Lind-Waldock

Korea & NE Asia
Business Conf.

FREE report! Get
your Stock Market
Outlook. CLICK
HERE

U.S. BUSINESS NEWS

Car, Light-Truck Sales Increase 4.8% in U.S.

By SHOLNN FREEMAN and KAREN LUNDEGAARD
Staff Reporters of THE WALL STREET JOURNAL
March 3, 2004 12:14 am.

DETROIT -- U.S. car and light-truck sales rose 4.8% last month against a weak year-earlier comparison as a stronger economy drew more buyers to car lots. Major Japanese auto makers outperformed the overall market and Detroit's Big Three.

Industry sales executives said the market beat expectations. Lifted by strong truck and luxury vehicle sales, U.S. car and light-truck sales totaled 1,277,705 vehicles, according to research firm Autodata. The February figure translates to a seasonally adjusted annual selling rate of 16.4 million vehicles, above the sluggish 15.6 million in the month a year ago. Last year's results reflected consumer nervousness about a looming war with Iraq, which depressed sales and led General Motors Corp. and Ford Motor Co. to slash production.

New-Vehicle Sales

The rise in sales comes as many auto makers look forward to a strengthening economy yet still struggle to sell cars without costly incentives, like low-cost financing and rebates. So far, auto makers, who had been looking to ease off incentives, have had trouble doing so. Plus, both GM and Ford finished the month with high inventories, which could make it difficult to cut incentives soon.

Among U.S. auto makers, GM and DaimlerChrysler AG's Chrysler division reported higher sales, while Ford's sales fell. GM, the world's biggest car maker in terms of cars sold, reported February sales rose 5.6% to 353,117 units.

DaimlerChrysler reported Chrysler division sales grew 1.2% to 172,647 in the month over February 2003. Mercedes-Benz, also owned by DaimlerChrysler, said sales edged up 0.5% to 16,174.

New Vehicle Sales–Second Paragraph

Industry sales executives said the market beat expectations. Lifted by
strong truck and luxury vehicle sales, U.S. car and light-truck sales
totaled 1,277,705 vehicles, according to research firm Autodata. The
February figure translates to a seasonally adjusted annual selling rate of
16.4 million vehicles, above the sluggish 15.6 million in the month a
year ago. Last year's results reflected consumer nervousness about a
looming war with Iraq, which depressed sales and led General Motors
Corp. and Ford Motor Co. to slash production.

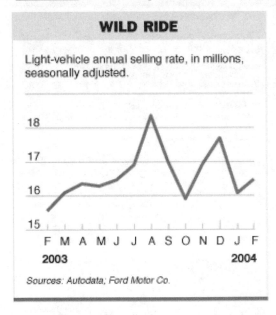

WILD RIDE

Light-vehicle annual selling rate, in millions,
seasonally adjusted.

Sources: Autodata; Ford Motor Co.

16.4 million (at a *seasonally adjusted annual rate*) and stronger than the
same month a year earlier (see Chart 7–10 on page 103 for a historical comparison).

The seasonally adjusted annual rate is an important statistic. Use it whenever you compare a variety of months in a variety of years.

Briefing.com (in the *Journal*'s online edition) provides good, up-to-date
charts on new-vehicle sales, but you should be aware that Briefing.com presents the data on a different basis than the *Journal* report. The *Journal* article excludes heavy-truck sales, while Briefing.com includes them. To find
the Briefing.com charts:

1. Scroll down the online edition's home page's left-hand menu-bar and click on Economy.
2. Click on Reports from Briefing.com under Data and Resources and then click on Auto Sales.

The well-equipped auto has symbolized the American consumer economy since the 1920s. The automobile industry pioneered such now familiar techniques as planned obsolescence, mass production, and mass marketing and advertising campaigns in the 1920s and 1930s. Henry Ford's Model T was the first mass-produced automobile. His assembly-line production methods were state of the art; his marketing concept, however, was vintage 19th century. He emphasized the cheapest possible serviceable car at the lowest price. Henry Ford reduced the price of a Model T to $300 in the early 1920s and provided customers with any color they wanted, as long as it was black. Ford dominated the market until the late 1920s, when General Motors saw the profit potential in continually inflating the product by offering colors, options, model changes, and increased size, weight, and speed. This strategy enabled GM to take the sales lead from Ford; from then on, competition in autos meant more (and different) car for more money, not the same car for a lower price. The option of less cars for less money was eliminated until the German and Japanese imports arrived.

Ford had grafted 20th-century technology onto 19th-century marketing techniques, driven the price down as far as it could go, and seen sales go flat

CHART 7–10 New-Vehicle Sales

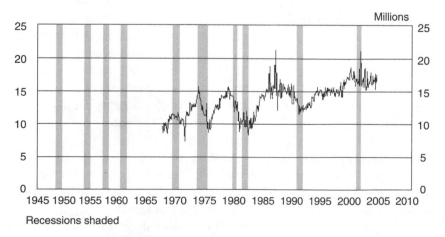

Recessions shaded

Source: U.S. Dept. of Commerce, Bureau of Economic Analysis.

in the mid-1920s, as the market became saturated. GM pioneered the 20th-century marketing technique of product inflation on a mass scale and gambled that the consumer would borrow ever more in order to buy next year's model.

Product inflation boosts sales by cajoling the consumer into buying something new at a higher price. The customer isn't swindled, just convinced by marketing and advertising techniques that he or she needs an improved product for more money. Planned obsolescence is a corollary, because style and model changes, as well as product improvement, aid in persuading the consumer that the present (and still serviceable) model should be replaced with a better, more expensive model, not a lower-cost repeat of the old model.

That set the pattern for American marketing of consumer goods. You can see it in your kitchen, laundry room, and living room, not just your driveway. TV replaced radio, color TV replaced black-and-white TV, and DVDs (not yesteryears' VCRs) are now perceived as near-compulsory accessories. With each innovation, the price goes up and so does debt.

The 1970s and 1980s, however, brought a rude shock to the domestic automobile manufacturers. The American public was no longer willing to buy whatever the manufacturers wished to sell. Consumers balked at continued product inflation, especially if it meant buying features, such as increased size and weight, that were no longer attractive. In addition, consumers were willing to accept less car for less money, especially if it meant a better-made and more fuel-efficient vehicle. As a result, the domestic manufacturers lost market share to the imports, and they have only recently stemmed the tide.

New-vehicle sales led the cycle into both expansion and contraction throughout the years of the Old Economy. You can see that sales turned down as soon as escalating inflation eroded consumer sentiment (see Chart 7–9 on page 99 and Chart 7–10 on page 103) and recovered quickly when inflation subsided and consumer sentiment improved. New-vehicle sales responded favorably to the New Economy's full employment of the late1990s, when consumer confidence reached record highs. Sharply falling interest rates accompanying the 2001 recession maintained auto sales at a record pace despite low consumer sentiment.

The fortunes of the auto industry may no longer lead the New Economy business cycle, foretelling recession and prosperity the way it did in the days of the Old Economy. Whereas what's good for GM may not necessarily be good for America, you should nonetheless regularly track new-vehicle sales. Not only does the auto industry, along with the cluster of industries that depends upon it (e.g., rubber tires, steel, glass, upholstery, fuzzy dice), represent a significant share of total economic activity, but it remains a crucial factor in the economy's success even in the days of the New Economy (or its aftermath).

Consumer Credit

The Wall Street Journal publishes the Commerce Department's release on consumer installment debt in the second week of the month. Changes in consumer credit have been an important barometer of consumer activity, because consumers have borrowed heavily to finance purchases of autos and other expensive and postponable items. The Monday, November 10, 2003, print-edition article reproduced on page 106 informs you that consumers borrowed $15.1 billion at a *seasonally adjusted monthly rate* in September 2003, for an approximate increase of $181.2 billion (times 12) at an annual rate.

The *Journal*'s online edition provides access to the Federal Reserve's latest bulletin on consumer credit as well as chart displays of consumer credit's growth.

1. Scroll down the online edition's home page's left-hand menu-bar and click on Economy.

2. Click on Economic Indicators under Data and Resources and then click on Consumer Credit. You will have to subtract the previous month's total from the most recent month's figure for total consumer credit outstanding in order to obtain the monthly increase. Then multiply by 12 to approximate the annual rate.

3. Click on Reports from Briefing.com under Data and Resources and then click on Consumer Credit.

Chart 7–11 on page 107 illustrates consumer credit's Old Economy role and its traditional dependence on consumer confidence (see Chart 7–8 on page 95). Households' reliance on consumer credit rose gradually and cyclically before its explosive growth in the 1970s. You can see the cyclical maximums of $10 billion in the late 1960s, $20 billion in the early 1970s, $50 billion in the late 1970s, $80 billion by the mid-1980s, and $150 billion in the 1990s.

But business capital expenditures, not consumer credit, led the New Economy of the late 1990s. By the end of the decade consumer installment borrowing fluctuated no higher than the levels reached in the early 1990s. Then consumer credit trailed consumer sentiment south during the 2001

Consumer Debt Rose
At a Greater Rate
Than Was Expected

Dow Jones Newswires

Consumers increased their debt loads in September at the fastest pace since January, the Federal Reserve said Friday.

Consumer Credit

Consumer-credit balances on auto loans, credit-card loans and other debt rose $15.1 billion in September to $1.972 trillion. That follows a revised $8.8 billion rise in August to $1.957 trillion, originally reported up $8.2 billion. The September consumer-credit increase was more than twice as large as Wall Street analysts expected.

The September consumer-credit increase was led by nonrevolving credit, which is mostly auto loans. Nonrevolving credit climbed by $12.1 billion in September, after rising by a revised $7.1 billion in August.

In addition to auto loans, nonrevolving credit includes education loans and loans on motor homes, boats, trailers or vacations.

Revolving credit, mostly credit cards, jumped $3.0 billion in September after rising by a revised $1.7 billion in August, first reported up $1.2 billion.

In annual terms, consumer credit rose at a 9.7% rate in September after growing at a revised 5.5% annual growth rate in August, the Fed said.

Revolving credit grew at a 5.0% annual rate in September after rising at a revised 2.9% annual rate in August. Nonrevolving credit climbed at a 13% annual rate in September, up sharply from a 1.7% rate in August.

CHART 7–11 Change in Consumer Installment Credit

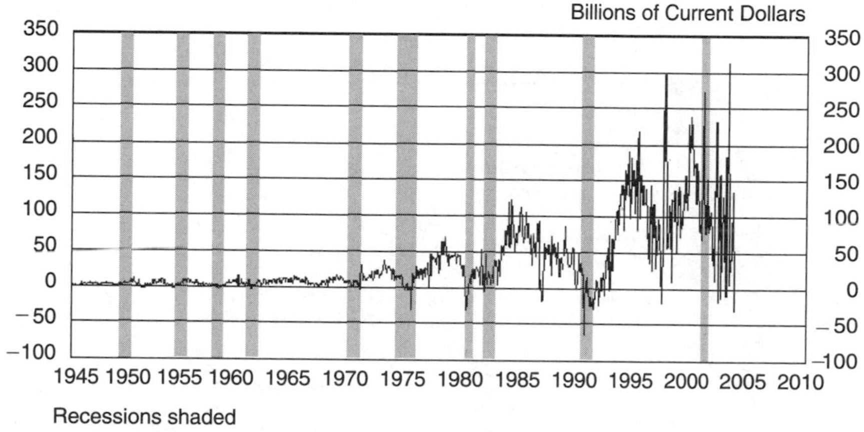

Billions of Current Dollars

Recessions shaded

Source: Federal Reserve.

recession, and both remained weak for a couple of years thereafter. Although zero-percent financing boosted automobile sales and automobile-related borrowing, anemic consumer sentiment prevented a general rebound in consumer credit.

Housing Activity

Housing starts and sales of existing and new homes are significant indicators of consumer demand. You should follow all three.

Housing Starts. The Commerce Department's monthly release on *housing starts* is usually published in *The Wall Street Journal* from the 17th through the 20th of the month. Always direct your attention to the seasonally adjusted monthly figure, presented at an annual rate. The second paragraph of the online edition's Wednesday, March 17, 2004, article on page 108 indicated that housing starts remained strong, at 1.86 million, through the early months of 2004.

The *Journal*'s online edition lets you browse the Census Bureau's official report and peruse a number of charts depicting residential construction activity.

1.   Scroll down the online edition's home page's left-hand menu-bar and click on Economy.
2.   Click on Economic Indicators under Data and Resources and then click on Housing Starts to obtain the Census Bureau's report.

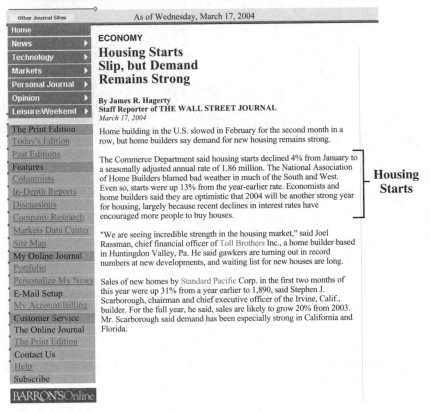

ECONOMY

Housing Starts Slip, but Demand Remains Strong

By James R. Hagerty
Staff Reporter of THE WALL STREET JOURNAL
March 17, 2004

Home building in the U.S. slowed in February for the second month in a row, but home builders say demand for new housing remains strong.

The Commerce Department said housing starts declined 4% from January to a seasonally adjusted annual rate of 1.86 million. The National Association of Home Builders blamed bad weather in much of the South and West. Even so, starts were up 13% from the year-earlier rate. Economists and home builders said they are optimistic that 2004 will be another strong year for housing, largely because recent declines in interest rates have encouraged more people to buy houses.

"We are seeing incredible strength in the housing market," said Joel Rassman, chief financial officer of Toll Brothers Inc., a home builder based in Huntingdon Valley, Pa. He said gawkers are turning out in record numbers at new developments, and waiting list for new houses are long.

Sales of new homes by Standard Pacific Corp. in the first two months of this year were up 31% from a year earlier to 1,890, said Stephen J. Scarborough, chairman and chief executive officer of the Irvine, Calif., builder. For the full year, he said, sales are likely to grow 20% from 2003. Mr. Scarborough said demand has been especially strong in California and Florida.

Housing Starts

Housing Starts–Second Paragraph

The Commerce Department said housing starts declined 4% from January to a seasonally adjusted annual rate of 1.86 million. The National Association of Home Builders blamed bad weather in much of the South and West. Even so, starts were up 13% from the year-earlier rate. Economists and home builders said they are optimistic that 2004 will be another strong year for housing, largely because recent declines in interest rates have encouraged more people to buy houses.

3. Click on Economic Chartbook under Data and Resources and then scroll down to Housing Starts.

4. Click on Reports from Briefing.com under Data and Resources and then click on Housing Starts for additional chart displays.

The cyclical sensitivity of residential construction to consumer sentiment and the availability of mortgage credit were hallmarks of the Old Economy. Housing starts were an important leading indicator of overall economic activity. (See Chart 7–8 on page 95 and Chart 7–12 below.) Housing starts turned down well before the onset of recession, as soon as rising inflation reduced consumer confidence and drove interest rates north, drying up mortgage credit. But you can see that they often turned back up even before the recession ended, as consumer confidence returned with the decline of inflation and the easing of interest rates.

With the advent of the New Economy in the late 1990s (see Chart 7–12), housing starts once again flirted with levels reminiscent of the late 1980s. But the remarkable story for housing starts is their continued strength through the 2001 recession and immediately afterward. Plunging interest rates held them, as well as auto sales, buoyantly aloft.

What was said earlier about industries related to auto sales can be repeated for residential construction. Lumber, cement, glass, roofing materials, heating, plumbing and electrical supplies, kitchen and laundry appli-

CHART 7–12 Housing Starts

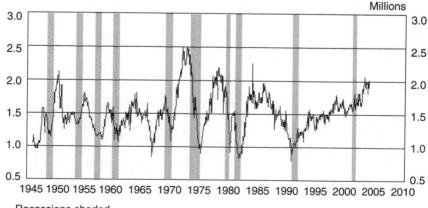

Recessions shaded

Source: U.S. Census Bureau.

WSJ.com THE WALL STREET JOURNAL. ONLINE

As of 12:36 p.m. EST Monday, March 1, 2004

ECONOMY

Existing-Home Sales Drop But Market Remains Strong

A WALL STREET JOURNAL ONLINE NEWS ROUNDUP
March 1, 2004 12:36 p.m.

WASHINGTON – Sales of existing single-family homes declined last month, a trade group reported. Economists attributed much of the drop to bad winter weather and noted that sales overall remained at a historically high level.

The National Association of Realtors said Wednesday that existing-home sales declined 5.2% in January to a seasonally adjusted annual rate of 6.04 million units, from a downwardly revised pace of 6.37 million a month earlier. December sales had originally been recorded at 6.47 million.

Existing-Home Sales

Economists had been expecting January sales of 6.26 million homes.

After peaking at a record 6.68 million homes in September, sales dropped steadily for two months before a slight uptick in December.

"Some of the recent weakness has been due to severe winter weather," wrote Steven Wood, chief economist at Insight Economics, in a note to clients. "However, low mortgage rates are still stimulating demand and keeping home sales at very high levels."

"We have to keep in mind that the level of home-sales activity over the last six months has been the strongest on record," said David Lereah, NAR's chief economist, adding that the trend is for home sales to stay close to record levels this year.

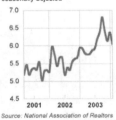

EXISTING-HOME SALES

Annual rate, in millions of units, seasonally adjusted

7.0
6.5
6.0
5.5
5.0
4.5

2001   2002   2003

Source: National Association of Realtors

In annual terms, sales were 2% above the 5.92 million-unit pace in January 2003.

The housing market has been strong the past several years, weathering the recession and sizzling as mortgage rates last year tumbled to record lows. According to Freddie Mac, the national average commitment rate for a 30-year, conventional, fixed-rate mortgage was 5.71% in January, down from 5.88% in December; it was 5.92% in January 2003.

Existing Home Sales–Second Paragraph

The National Association of Realtors said Wednesday that existing-home sales declined 5.2% in January to a seasonally adjusted annual rate of 6.04 million units, from a downwardly revised pace of 6.37 million a month earlier. December sales had originally been recorded at 6.47 million.

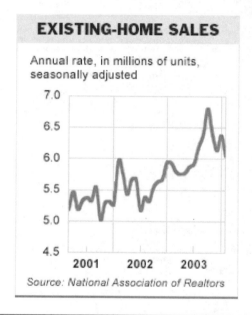

EXISTING-HOME SALES

Annual rate, in millions of units, seasonally adjusted

Source: National Association of Realtors

ances, and furniture and furnishings are all part of the cluster of industries that fluctuate with housing starts. Residential construction is an engine that pulls a long train.

Home Sales. Two additional reports that exclude apartment-house activity will help you follow the market for single-family homes, and thereby provide an insight into new construction activity.

In the last week of each month, *The Wall Street Journal* publishes the National Association of Realtors' report on *existing-home sales* for the prior month. The report and accompanying chart in the Monday, March 1, 2004, online edition (see page 110) reported a 2003 surge in existing-home sales and stated that sales remained above six million into the new year.

Free Dow Jones Sites

As of Friday, June 25, 2004

Home
News
Technology
Markets
Personal Journal
Opinion
Leisure/Weekend

The Print Edition
Today's Edition
Past Editions
Features
Portfolio
Columnists
In-Depth Reports
Discussions
Company Research
Markets Data Center
Video Center
Site Map
Corrections
My Online Journal
Personalize My News
E-Mail Setup
My Account/Billing
RSS Feeds
Customer Service
The Online Journal
The Print Edition
Contact Us
Help
Subscribe

BARRON'S Online

Advertiser Links

FEATURED SPONSOR

Accenture Presents
"High Performance"
A Look at Success Via
Three Key Building
Blocks.
Click Here ...

Investor Resource
Center

FedEx Presents: "Small
Business Center"

ECONOMY

New-Home Sales Leapt Last Month

**Increasing Mortgage Rates
May Have Stoked Buying;
Durable-Goods Orders Fell**

By MARY KISSEL
Staff Reporter of THE WALL STREET JOURNAL
June 25, 2004; Page A2

Sales of new, single-family homes soared in May, despite higher mortgage rates that are expected to slow the housing market eventually. Separately, the manufacturing sector hit a speed bump as durable-goods orders slipped, and jobless claims ticked up slightly.

Economists pointed to rising employment, increasing personal income and continued low interest rates as strong contributing factors to the new-home sales data, as well as a rush by fence-sitters to buy before mortgage rates rose more. Analysts were divided, however, on why average new-home sale prices showed an unusual decline, especially in light of recent widespread fears of escalating sticker prices.

THE JOURNAL REPORT

 The party can't last forever. Over the next five or 10 years, analysts say, home prices are likely to yield a less-impressive return, while the market slows to catch its breath. What's a home investor to do?

Builders may be cutting prices to remain competitive in the face of higher interest rates, said Drew Matus, an economist at Lehman Brothers. "A one percentage point increase in mortgage rates leads to about a 10% drop in home affordability," Mr. Matus said. "That 10% has got to come from somewhere."

David Seiders, chief economist at the National Association of Home Builders, pointed to strong sales in the South, a region typically characterized by lower average prices.

Sales of new, single-family homes surged 14.8% last month to a seasonally adjusted annual rate of 1,369,000 units, up from a revised rate of 1,192,000 units in April, the Commerce Department said. Sales were strongest in the South and the Northeast. Average house prices nationwide declined to $256,700 in May from $262,500 in April.

New-Home Sales

Yesterday's data may stoke fears that the housing market is at its peak, as consumers rush to buy homes before interest rates rise further. At its meeting Wednesday, the Federal Open Market Committee is widely expected to raise its short-term interest-rate target from a 46-year low of 1%, which would tend to put upward pressure on mortgage rates.

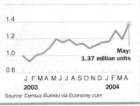

HAVE A HOUSE?

New single-family home sales, in millions of units at annual rate

May:
1.37 million units

J F M A M J J A S O N D J F M A
2003   2004

Source: Census Bureau via Economy.com

Separately, orders for durable goods fell 1.6% to $189.1 billion last month, after a decline of 2.6% in April -- revised from 2.9% -- and a gain of 5.9% in March, according to the Commerce Department. The last back-to-back declines in the indicator, which measures purchases of goods generally expected to last more than three years, were in November and December 2002, according to Insight Economics, an independent economic-research firm in Danville, Calif.

New-Home Sales—Fifth Paragraph

Sales of new, single-family homes surged 14.8% last month to a seasonally adjusted annual rate of 1,369,000 units, up from a revised rate of 1,192,000 units in April, the Commerce Department said. Sales were strongest in the South and the Northeast. Average house prices nationwide declined to $256,700 in May from $262,500 in April.

The *Journal*'s online edition also presents a number of charts that depict existing-home sales.

1. Scroll down the online edition's home page's left-hand menu-bar and click on Economy.
2. Click on Economic Chartbook under Data and Resources and then scroll down to Existing-Home Sales.
3. Click on Reports from Briefing.com under Data and Resources and then click on Existing Home Sales.

The fifth paragraph of the Friday, June 25, 2004, online article on page 112 reported the Commerce Department's announcement of 1.369 million *new-home sales* at a seasonally adjusted annual rate in May of 2004. The accompanying chart shows the rise over the previous 18 months. This report, like existing-home sales, usually appears in the last week of the month.

The *Journal*'s online edition presents a number of reports that depict new-home *sales.*

1. Scroll down the online edition's home page's left-hand menu-bar and click on Economy.
2. Click on Economic Indicators under Data and Resources and then click on New-Home Sales.
3. Click on Reports from Briefing.com under Data and Resources and then click on New Home Sales.

Charts 7–13 and 7–14 on page 114 and Chart 7–12 on page 109 illustrate the close correlation between home sales and housing starts as well as the favorable impact of falling interest rates on sales and construction through the 2001 recession and the years immediately following.

Retail Sales

The U.S. Department of Commerce's monthly release on *retail sales* appears in *The Wall Street Journal* around the second week of the month. Retail

CHART 7–13 Existing-Home Sales

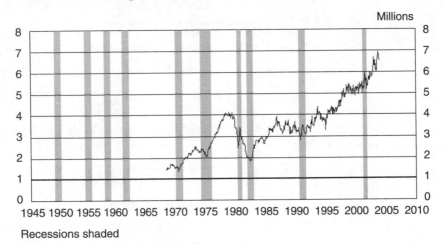

Recessions shaded

Source: National Association of Realtors.

sales are reported in current dollars and include merchandise for personal or household consumption, but do not include services (such as haircuts, dry cleaning, and restaurant meals). The second paragraph and accompanying chart of the Thursday, February 12, 2004, online edition on page 115 report that retail sales fell 0.3 percent in January 2004.

CHART 7–14 New-Home Sales

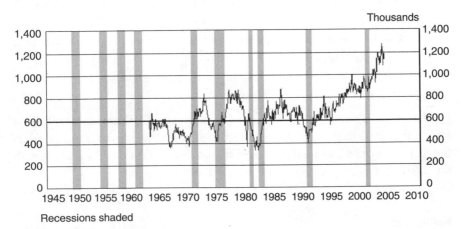

Recessions shaded

Source: U.S. Census Bureau.

The *Journal*'s online edition helps you track retail sales, as follows.

1. Scroll down the online edition's home page's left-hand menu-bar and click on Economy.

2. Click on Economic Indicators under Data and Resources and then click on Retail Sales to review the Census Bureau's latest report.

3. Click on Economic Chartbook under Data and Resources and then scroll down to the Retail Sales chart.

4. Click on Reports from Briefing.com under Data and Resources and then click on Retail Sales for up-to-date charts.

Chart 7–15 on page 117 illustrates that a historical series which employs retail sales data is not as satisfactory as using percentage changes to trace the course of the business cycle. Yet you can follow the month-to-month reports in *The Wall Street Journal* in order to track the cycle's immediate progress.

NEW ECONOMY AND OLD ECONOMY CYCLES

Autos and residential construction played a countercyclical role through the 2001 recession and the years immediately following that recession, offsetting to some extent the plunge in business capital expenditures. Business set the pace for the New Economy, not consumers. But in the Old Economy, the consumer reigned. Here's how the Old Economy cycle worked.

Retail Sales—Second Paragraph

Retail sales decreased by 0.3% to $322.87 billion, the Commerce Department reported Thursday. It was the first decline since September. Sales rose a revised 0.2% in December, after climbing 1.1% in November.

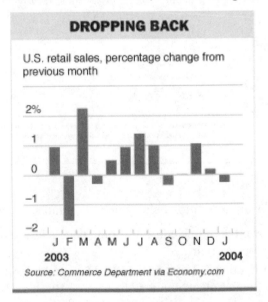

DROPPING BACK

U.S. retail sales, percentage change from previous month

Source: Commerce Department via Economy.com

CHART 7–15 Retail Sales

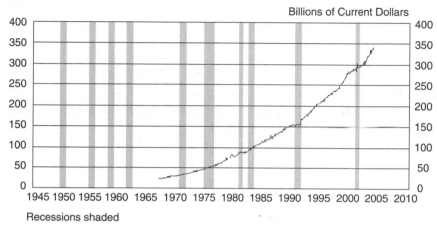

Recessions shaded

Source: U.S. Census Bureau.

Consumer debt and consumer demand provided the leading edge of the Old Economy post–World War II business cycle. Paradoxically, their strong growth led to cyclical problems with inflation, periodically choking off credit, demand, and economic expansion, and generating recession.

In summary, as the cycle moved from *peak* to *contraction*, rapidly rising inflation depressed consumer real income and consumer sentiment, bringing on a collapse in consumer demand and inevitable recession.

CPI ↑+ Employment data ↓+ Personal income ↓→
Consumer sentiment ↓→ Consumer demand ↓
(Auto sales ↓+ Consumer credit ↓+ Housing data ↓+ Retail sales↓)

Recession let the steam out of the economy, cooling inflation. The temporary reduction in the rate of inflation permitted the business cycle to resume its course after each recession. Reduced inflation encouraged consumers to indulge in a new wave of borrowing and spending, moving the cycle from *recovery* to *expansion* and launching another round of inflation.

CPI ↓+ Employment data ↑+ Personal income ↑→
Consumer sentiment ↑→ Consumer demand ↑
(Auto sales ↑+ Consumer credit ↑+ Housing data ↑+ Retail sales ↑)

There was no human villain in this drama. Blame the inanimate forces of credit and inflation, which periodically swept over the economy to leave recession's wreckage behind. There was no villain, but there were victims. There is no doubt who bore the burden of recession: the unemployed. Their loss of income was not shared by the rest of society as the economy contracted.

Old Economy unemployment hit hardest those industries that depend heavily on big-ticket consumer expenditures financed by borrowing. It was worst in construction, autos, and other durable-goods industries, and in the steel and nonferrous metal industries. Workers in communications, services, finance, and government were largely spared.

Through no fault of their own, therefore, workers (and their families) in a narrow band of industries bore most of the cycle's burden. They were not responsible for the economy's fluctuations, but they were the chief victims in every downturn. Someone must build the homes and cars and mill the lumber and steel. Yet, as if caught in a perverse game of musical chairs, those who did were always left without a seat when the music stopped.

Circumstances changed dramatically with the New Economy recession of 2001. The technology boom of the late-1990s had provided employment opportunities for a new cadre of workers in computer hardware, software, and telecommunications applications. Their ranks swelled strikingly in the upturn and shrank just as strikingly with the slump. This time white-collar rather than blue-collar workers suffered disproportionately on the leading edge of boom and bust.

Moreover, employment recovered less rapidly in the aftermath of the 2001 New Economy recession than employment had recovered from the Old Economy slumps of the 1970s. In the old days, autos and construction and the cluster of industries surrounding them laid off workers quickly as the economy plunged into recession, but just as swiftly recalled them when the economy popped back. In the technology boom of the New Economy in the late 1990s, reminiscent of the railroad booms of old, employers thought they were hiring for the long term and then were crushed in the ensuing collapse. Jobs disappeared, and the unemployed had to wait for the creation of new positions in order to rejoin the gainfully employed. The Old Economy imposed regularity on blue collar hiring and layoffs that did not apply to the New Economy's technology boom and bust. The New Economy did not reemploy the unemployed as swiftly as the Old Economy had.

But reconfigured employment patterns were not the only change brought about by the advent of the New Economy. Some now feared deflation's onset.

IN CONCLUSION: INFLATION VS. DEFLATION

As the economy struggled out of the 2001 recession and overall demand remained weak, many wondered if prices would begin to fall, inaugurating a deflationary era after decades of inflation.

That shift, from inflation to deflation, would be a momentous development should it occur. Consumer demand, driven by easy-credit conditions, had been the centerpiece of America's post–World War II Old Economy and the major origin of its inflationary bias. Here's how it worked.

Inflation is an increase in prices due to excessive spending financed by borrowing from banks. "Too many dollars chasing too few goods" is a standard way of putting it. Economists are more formal: "Inflation occurs when demand exceeds supply at current prices and prices are bid up." Both explanations conjure up the image of a gigantic auction at which customers bid for both goods and services.

Chronic inflation is a recent problem. Before the late 1940s, severe inflation was a temporary phenomenon, usually associated with war. When the federal government's wartime expenditures overshot tax revenues and the government covered the difference by selling bonds to the banking system or by printing paper money (which the federal government has not done recently), prices increased swiftly. That's how the conventional wisdom arose that government deficits cause inflation.

From 1789 until after World War II, except for war-related inflations, prices in America fell more often than they rose. As a matter of fact, prices were actually lower in 1914, on the eve of World War I, than they were in 1815, at the end of the Napoleonic Wars and the War of 1812!

Prices dropped during the 19th century because supply grew more rapidly than demand. Railroads and steamships opened new continents and made their agricultural products available throughout the world. Business mobilized the technological advances of the Industrial Revolution to produce standard items of consumption in large quantities at considerably lower cost.

Occasionally, prices rose during the upswing of the business cycle because bank borrowing financed investment expenditures or because there were temporary shortages of agricultural commodities. But these increases were more than offset in recession years, when prices tumbled as huge additions to supply came to market. Consequently, in most years *deflation* (falling prices) proved stronger than inflation.

Deflation prevailed over inflation because the institutions that, in our day, enabled and encouraged headlong private borrowing and spending had not yet evolved. A hundred years ago it wasn't easy to obtain a home mortgage. Typically, the purchase of a new home required a 50 percent down payment with interest-only mortgage payments on a seven-year loan, followed by a balloon payment of the entire principal. If you go back far enough, most of the major consumer durables that we now buy on credit were available exclusively to a small portion of the population on a cash-only basis, if they existed at all.

Only the Civil War and World Wars I and II had provided great inflationary experiences; even the period between World War I and World War II was a time of deflation (falling prices). War brought inflation, and peace brought deflation, because government borrowed and spent more massively in wartime than business borrowed and spent in peacetime. The difference was more a matter of degree than a matter of kind; peacetime investment expenditures and borrowing by farmers, railroads, and manufacturers, though substantial, were usually not large enough to boost the growth in demand beyond the increase in supply. Thus, prices fell in most years, because supply exceeded demand at current prices.

To summarize, prices fell unless there was a rapid increase in demand (spending) financed by bank borrowing or the printing press (greenbacks during the Civil War). Only when outside financing provided a boost did demand take on a life of its own and grow more rapidly than supply. It made little difference whether it was government spending for war or business spending for investment, as long as banks printed bank notes or created demand deposits or the government printed paper money. Once demand grew more rapidly than supply, and too many dollars chased too few goods, prices rose.

Following World War II rapid institutional change provided consumers with ample access to mortgage and consumer credit. These institutions served as the underpinnings of the Old Economy as it emerged in the 1960s. The 1970s illustrate the consequent impact upon the business cycle. Consumers borrowed heavily in 1972 and 1973 to make record purchases of new homes and automobiles. Business responded by adding plant and equipment to meet the demand and by stockpiling inventory to satisfy customers' orders. The sharp growth in consumer and business demand boosted prices rapidly, and the rate of inflation increased from 4 percent in 1972 to 12 percent in 1974. Interest rates moved in parallel fashion. Soon consumers became discouraged, because their incomes failed to keep pace, so their expenditures on homes, autos, and other goods plunged.

This led to a general decline in production, and, by early 1975, unemployment was at a postwar record high. The cycle was complete. The drop in demand reduced both inflation and interest rates, thereby restoring consumer confidence and spending. Recovery and expansion brought boom conditions. Rising inflation and interest rates returned in 1978, eroding consumer confidence once again. Consumer demand fell, and the 1980 recession began; another cycle had come full circle.

Recovery from the 1980 recession had barely begun when the Federal Reserve (to be fully discussed in the next chapter) strangled the credit markets in 1981–1982, ending the inflationary spiral. In the 1980s, the Federal Reserve (or Fed, as it's familiarly known) interrupted the normal course of the cycle by implementing its tight money policy of 1981–1982, and then strongly influenced the cycle through its new posture toward inflation. The Fed squashed the cycle flat and squeezed high inflation out of the system, permitting the economy to expand gradually and steadily in the middle and late 1980s.

But why didn't the 1980s repeat the experience of the 1970s? Why didn't burgeoning consumer demand, backed by exploding credit, drive inflation upward once again? Because the Federal Reserve fine-tuned demand by maintaining interest rates at relatively high levels. At the first signs of strong or weak economic conditions, the Fed adjusted its monetary policy to maintain good growth without inflation. In addition, with the advent of the New Economy in the 1990s, rising business investment put in place the facilities required for a rapidly growing supply that also held price increases in check.

And that leads to issues best covered in Chapter 8. The next chapter discusses the Federal Reserve and whether or not the Fed, so successful in combating inflation, can also prevent deflation's onset.

8

THE FEDERAL RESERVE SYSTEM: MONETARY POLICY AND INTEREST RATES

IRRATIONAL EXUBERANCE

W E RECALL ALAN GREENSPAN, the Federal Reserve's chairman, sagely warning us of the stock market's "irrational exuberance" during the millennium bubble. At the time, the Federal Reserve (or simply the Fed, as it's commonly known) was applying an Old Economy strategy despite the fact that the New Economy was upon us. The Fed drove up interest rates in the late 1990s in order to prevent the booming economy from generating a return of inflation. The Fed's Old Economy reasoning went like this: reduce bank lending, thereby reducing household and business borrowing (borrowed funds are less attractive at high rates of interest). This constriction of household and business spending financed by borrowing, on residential construction, autos, and other durable goods, as well as on plant, equipment, and inventory, would prevent demand from surging ahead of supply, and thus keep inflation in check. The Fed's Old Economy policy worked, and inflation remained modest.

But the New Economy bubble burst nonetheless. The stock market began to collapse in 2000, and recession gripped the economy by 2001. Although

GDP grew in 2002 and 2003, unemployment remained unacceptably and stubbornly high. Businesses had shed two million jobs (and employees) in their efforts to stem losses or shore up profits, as output's growth and employment's decline bolstered productivity. Output per worker rose because fewer hands were now obliged to do more work. Although rising productivity was a feature of the New Economy, not everyone saw it as a blessing.

The Fed responded to the 2001 recession by reversing course (abandoning its late 1990s restrictive policy) and driving interest rates into the basement. The Fed had demonstrated its Old Economy ability to throttle upwardly spiraling prices and squeeze inflation down to an acceptable figure. Now the Fed wanted to reduce recession's impact, spur economic recovery, and prevent deflation. Could the Fed deal with the New Economy's problems as well as it had dealt with the Old Economy's problems? Could the Fed prevent prices from spiraling downward, and thereby nip deflation in the bud, as easily as it had once held inflation in check? Pulling back on the credit reins had brought the Old Economy steed to a halt. Would dangling credit reins inspire a New Economy gallop? Or were other tactics required to spur the economy forward?

To fully comprehend these issues, and in order to gain insight into the Fed's plans for the New Economy, let's begin with an overview of the Fed's attempts to control the Old Economy.

THE FED AND THE OLD ECONOMY
From 1965 to 1980, under its initial Old Economy regime (very different from the revised Old Economy regime that emerged after 1980), the Fed attempted to stimulate demand for goods and services with liberal credit policies that pushed interest rates down and thereby depressed the cost of borrowing money. The Fed hoped to motivate households and businesses to borrow funds in order to buy homes and autos and equipment and buildings. The Fed's objective was to boost the economy higher and faster, thereby generating increased employment opportunities.

The Fed wanted supply (production) to rise and meet burgeoning demand in order to spur job growth. Unfortunately, as demand grew more rapidly than supply, prices spiraled upward. When inflation became a problem, the only solution appeared to be a periodic reversal of those liberal credit policies— which invariably helped plunge the economy into recession. These policy reversals exacerbated the business cycle so that inflation escalated during boom and unemployment rose during bust.

To repeat, in each recession the Federal Reserve depressed interest rates and demand roared ahead in short order. When demand exceeded supply at current prices, prices surged upward. At this point the Fed reversed course and employed policies designed to dampen inflation. It slammed on the brakes, raising interest rates, depressing demand temporarily, and causing recession. But as soon as the inflation rate dropped, the Fed reversed course again and helped bring on the next round of expanding demand and inflation. Prices rose throughout these years because lower inflation during recession did not offset higher inflation during expansion.

Thus began (1965–1980) the first American peacetime period with significant and continuing inflation. In all other eras, inflation had been the product of wartime government spending financed by borrowing, while peacetime had been a period of stable prices or even deflation. Consequently, almost everyone viewed government spending financed by borrowing, whether in time of war or peace, as the single source of inflation, and this mindset spilled over into the postwar world. No one comprehended that a new economic dynamic was at work in which private (consumer and business) borrowing and spending generated inflation. Ever greater waves of borrowing by the private sector (not government) now drove the inflationary cycle.

So you see that the Old Economy and its world of cyclically and secularly rising private-sector debt, spending, costs, and inflation was actually a newcomer—a fresh post–World War II world phenomenon . And the Federal Reserve's easy-credit bias had played a large role in the Old Economy's arrival.

By 1980, however, after two decades of inappropriate inflationary policies, the Federal Reserve resolved to come to grips with the problem. The spurs had to be removed, the reins taken in hand, and the runaway horse restrained. The Fed tightened up; interest rates reached the stratosphere, borrowing and spending dried up, and the economy came closer to collapsing in 1981–1982 than at any time since World War II.

After the recession of 1981–1982 throttled demand and eliminated inflation, the Fed slowly began to ease up. But the Fed was determined not to return to the errors of the past; it would not let credit become easy, or demand grow too rapidly, or inflation get out of control again. The Fed had revised its Old Economy strategy—from stimulating demand to restraining inflation.

The Fed had acted single-handedly to stretch out the business cycle and forestall recession. By squashing the cycle flat in the early 1980s, and then restraining inflation in the middle and late 1980s, the Fed had interrupted the cycle's regular and periodic oscillations. This created a period of steady expansion during which the economy did not overheat and inflation remained minimal.

Throughout the bubble economy of the late 1990s the Fed tugged gently on the economy's reins, but it did not have to pull back sharply. A little Old Economy restraint worked wonders in a New Economy world. Business's heavy investment in new capacity, especially high-technology capacity, significantly boosted supply so that swiftly growing demand could not bid prices rapidly upward. If demand must grow more rapidly than supply in order to drive up prices, the New Economy saw to it that supply would advance as swiftly as demand to hold inflation in check. Yet the Fed maintained policies appropriate for an Old Economy world and the perceived need to keep inflation under control.

After the bubble popped and the New Economy slipped into the 2001 recession, the Fed sharply reduced interest rates in order to stimulate demand. Within a few years interest rates had fallen to low levels not seen since the early 1960s. But robust demand did not swiftly reappear. The New Economy's deflationary potential in a world in which supply continually threatened to outstrip demand created the new hazard of secularly falling prices (deflation).

Now that you have an overview of the Fed's role in the birth and demise of the Old Economy, it is time for a more detailed examination of inflation's dynamic.

THE FED AND INFLATION

You have already seen that the Fed squashed the business cycle flat in the early 1980s, bringing an end to excessive inflation for the foreseeable future. Before that, during the high-inflation 1970s, business cycle fluctuations had grown more severe and inflation's pace had accelerated. *Thus, the Fed's stand against inflation in 1981–1982 was the most important turning point in our post–World War II economic history.*

The business cycle and inflation had spun out of control in the late 1960s and in the 1970s because consumers and businesses had borrowed ever more heavily to finance ever larger expenditures on homes, cars, and other durable goods, as well as plant, equipment, and inventory. As oceans of borrowing supported tidal waves of spending (i.e., demand for goods and services), supply could not keep pace, and prices rose.

To understand this phenomenon, consider a hypothetical example in which people have as much to spend at the end of a given year as at the beginning, but have increased their output of goods and services by 5 percent during that year. Prices would have to fall by 5 percent in order that the same amount of spending (demand) could absorb an additional 5 percent of goods and services (supply). And if folks continued each year to produce

5 percent more while their spending did not grow, then prices would fall by 5 percent year after year. We would have chronic deflation.

Similarly, if people's ability to spend (demand) grew by 20 percent while output (supply) grew by 5 percent, you can imagine prices being bid up by 15 percent in that year. And if their spending continued to grow by 20 percent a year while their output grew by only 5 percent, you can imagine chronic annual inflation of 15 percent. Now you understand how changing supply and demand generate deflation and inflation.

You may ask, "How is it possible for spending (demand) to grow more rapidly than the output (supply) of society? You can spend only what you have, after all." That's true. For instance, suppose you earn $100,000 a year and your income is a measure of the value of the goods and services that you produce or supply for the market. Also, suppose that your spending (demand) is limited by your income. Demand and supply ($100,000) are equal, so prices don't change.

But suppose that you have access to bank credit, so that you can borrow $500,000 to have a house built. Your demand (spending) rises to $500,000, even though your income (supply) remains at $100,000. Demand exceeds supply in this case, and if your situation is repeated often enough in others, prices rise. Whenever demand exceeds supply at current prices, a situation made possible by borrowing (credit), inflation (rising prices) occurs.

The $500,000 provided by the banks was *not* produced and saved by someone else, thereby equating earlier supply with new demand. It was created out of thin air by the banking system, and that is why your bank-financed spending is inflationary. It also illustrates the importance of understanding the banking and credit system to comprehend the reasons for the ever-escalating business cycle and inflation of 1965–1980 and inflation's subsequent demise.

Private borrowing by consumers and businesses has always been a feature of our economy, but it did not begin to reach heroic proportions and grow at an explosive pace until the late 1960s. From that point on, credit doubled every five years until the Fed slammed the door shut in the early 1980s. There was no way production could keep pace with the 1970s' demand binges, so rising inflation filled the gap.

But borrowing and spending did not grow smoothly. They surged forward periodically, generating the wave-like action of the business cycle. The rise of borrowing and spending carried inflation with it; interest rates rose too, as spiraling borrowing drove up the cost of credit. Steep increases in prices and interest rates eventually choked off the boom, discouraging consumers and businesses from continued borrowing and spending. The wave crashed and the cycle completed itself as the economy contracted into recession.

The Fed exacerbated the worst aspects of the cycle in the late 1960s and throughout the 1970s by attempting to alleviate them. Reining in credit expansion at the peak of the cycle in order to curb inflation merely contributed to the severity of the inevitable downturn and made recession worse. Easing up during recession, in order to encourage borrowing and spending and thus pull the economy out of a slump, contributed to the excesses of the next boom. And with each wave of the cycle, inflation and interest rates ratcheted higher and higher.

The Fed reversed course in 1981–1982 and brought an end to 15 years of escalating inflation and cyclical instability by applying a chokehold of high interest rates. The economy was brought to the brink of collapse. But when the Fed relaxed its grip and interest rates declined from exorbitant to merely high, the manic rounds of boom and bust had ceased. The economy set out on a healthy expansion, without excessive inflation, that lasted through the late 1980s and into the 1990s. The Fed continued to fine-tune the Old Economy, raising interest rates whenever growth seemed excessive and reducing rates when recession threatened.

The New Economy of the late 1990s made the Fed's job that much easier. Business's heavy investment in new capacity, especially high-technology capacity, held inflation in check by letting supply grow almost as rapidly as demand. After the New Economy slipped into the 2001 recession, the Fed sharply reduced interest rates in order to stimulate demand. Now observers did an about-face and wondered if demand would grow sufficiently rapidly to prevent deflation—that is, a world of continually falling prices.

Borrowing and Inflation

- Bank lending finances spending; spending generates inflation.
- The Fed controls bank lending and can thereby control inflation.
- A drop in borrowing and spending will reduce inflation and, if sufficiently sharp, will lead to recession.

What is the Fed? How does it work? What, exactly, did it (and does it) do? Let's start your investigation with a bit of background.

THE FED'S HISTORY

The United States was the last major industrial nation to establish a central bank. The modern German state commissioned a central bank in 1875; the

Bank of France was founded in 1800; and the Bank of England had entered its third century of operation when the Federal Reserve System was created in 1913.

America's tardiness was due to our traditional suspicion of centralized financial power and authority. Historically, we have felt more comfortable with small banks serving a single community. In fact, some states limited branch banking until recently. For instance, the First National Bank of Chicago became one of the nation's biggest, even though Illinois law severely constrained its branch facilities in downstate Illinois. Similarly, the big New York City banks (until after World War II) were hampered by legislation that confined them to the city and its suburbs and kept their branches out of upstate New York. On the other hand, California's liberal branch banking laws once helped Bank of America build its position as the nation's largest bank. To this day, a rational, nationwide scheme for organizing our banking institutions does not exist.

Alexander Hamilton proposed a central bank shortly after the country's founding. The two early attempts to create one failed when confronted with the nation's suspicion of the Eastern financial community. Consequently, our economy grew until the eve of World War I without benefit of coordination or control of its banking activity. Banking, like the sale of alcohol following the repeal of Prohibition, was largely subject to local option.

Under these circumstances, the banks had to fend for themselves, and the business cycle created perils for them as well as opportunities for profit. During recessions, when business income was down (usually following periods of speculative excess), banks found it difficult to collect on loans.

At the same time, nervous businesspeople and investors made large withdrawals, sometimes demanding payment in gold or silver specie. These precious metal coins composed the ultimate reserve for deposits; however, no bank possessed enough of them to secure every depositor, and the banking system functioned on the assumption that only a minority of depositors would demand their funds on any one day. When panic set in and a queue formed out the door and around the block, a bank could be wiped out in a matter of hours. As rumor spread, one bank after another failed, until only the most substantial institutions, with the greatest specie reserve, were left standing. The chain reaction damaged many people, not the least of whom were innocent depositors who could not reach their funds in time.

Congress took up the issue after the panic of 1907. In that crisis—as the story goes—J.P. Morgan kept New York's most important bankers locked up in his home overnight until they agreed to contribute a pool of specie to be lent to the weakest banks until the run subsided. It worked, but the near disaster had made it clear that the time had come to establish an American central bank that could lend to all banks in time of panic; the nation's financial system could no longer rely on the private arrangements of J.P. Morgan. Thus, Congress established the Federal Reserve System in 1913. All member banks were required to make deposits to the system, creating a pool of reserves from which financially strapped banks could borrow during a crisis.

The system was originally conceived as a lender of last resort. In times of severe economic stress, it would use the pooled reserves of the banking system to make loans to banks under stress. When conditions improved, the loans were to be repaid. As time went by, however, the Fed discovered two things: first, that the reserve requirement could be used to control banking activity; and second, that control over the banking system provided a means of influencing the business cycle.

The reasoning was straightforward. Bank lending is a key ingredient in the business cycle, driving the cyclic expansion of demand. It cannot, however, grow beyond the limits set by bank reserves; so, when the Fed wants to give the economy a boost by encouraging banks to lend more, it increases reserves. On the other hand, by decreasing reserves and thereby shrinking available credit, the Fed exerts a restraining effect on the economy.

OPEN-MARKET OPERATIONS

The mechanism used by the Fed to manipulate the banking system's reserves is astonishingly simple: It buys or sells securities on the open market. Briefly put, when the Fed buys securities, the sellers deposit the proceeds of the sale in their banks, and the banking system's reserves grow. On the other hand, when the Fed sells securities, buyers withdraw funds from their banks in order to make the purchases, and bank reserves fall.

This illustration may help you understand the process. Imagine that the Fed, a government-securities dealer, and all banks (not an individual bank) are the only players in this example. Keep in mind that there are trillions of dollars of U.S. Treasury securities outstanding and that anyone (domestic and foreign corporations; individuals; state, local, and foreign governments; private banks; and central banks) can buy them. Billions of dollars of securities are traded each day in New York City.

The Fed increases and reduces bank reserves by its actions in this market. It trades in U.S. Treasury securities rather than some other instrument because the government securities market is so broad and Federal Reserve activities have a relatively small impact on the market.

realize—the Fed is not an agency of the U.S. government, but a corporation owned by banks that have purchased shares of stock. Federally chartered banks are required to purchase this stock and be members of the Federal Reserve System; state-chartered banks may be members if they wish. All banks, however, are subject to the Fed's control.

True, the Fed does have a quasi-public character, because its affairs are managed by a Board of Governors appointed by the president of the United States with the approval of Congress. Nonetheless, once appointed, the Board of Governors is independent of the federal government and is free to pursue policies of its own choosing. New laws could, of course, change its status. That's why the chairman of the board is so frequently called upon to defend the policies of the Fed before Congress, and why Congress often reminds the Fed that it is a creature of Congress, which can enact legislation to reduce, alter, or eliminate the Fed's powers. Indeed, legislators and others do suggest from time to time that the Fed be made an agency of the U.S. government in order to remove its autonomy. So far, however, Congress has kept the Fed independent, and it is likely to remain so, exercising its best judgment in guiding the nation's banking activity.

In some ways, the Fed's control over the banking system's reserves is the most important relationship between any two institutions in the American economy. The Fed can increase or reduce bank reserves at will, making it easier or more difficult for the banks to lend, thus stimulating or restricting business and economic activity.

THE FED AND THE MONEY SUPPLY
How does that bank lending increase the supply of money? Where does the money come from? There is an astonishingly simple answer to these questions: The banks create it by crediting the checking account deposits of their borrowers. Thus, bank lending creates money (deposits).

Moreover, the only limits to the money supply are:

1. The Fed's willingness to provide the banks with reserves, so that they can lend.
2. The banks' ability to find borrowers.

It may sound strange that banks create money, but, nonetheless, it's true.

The reason so much controversy surrounds the money supply is that many people misunderstand its nature. Checking accounts (or demand deposits, as they are formally called) constitute three-quarters of the money supply, and currency and coins in circulation together make up the remaining quarter. The one-quarter of the money supply that exists as cash comes from a two-tiered source: The U.S. Treasury mints coins and prints paper money for the Fed, and the Fed distributes them.

These arrangements have an interesting and important history. Before the Civil War, with the exception of the two short-lived attempts at a central bank that were mentioned earlier, all paper money was issued by private banks and was called bank notes. These bank notes resembled modern paper currency and entered circulation when banks lent them to customers.

The banks' incentive to issue bank notes to borrowers, instead of gold and silver coins, came from the limited supply of gold and silver coins (specie). If banks wished to lend more than the specie on hand, they would have to issue bank notes. Each bank kept a specie reserve that was no more than a fraction of its outstanding bank notes. This reserve was used to satisfy those who demanded that a bank redeem its notes with specie; as long as the bank could do so, its notes were accepted at face value and were "good as gold." Bank notes and minted coins circulated together.

After the Civil War, checking accounts replaced bank notes. They were safer and more convenient, because the customer (borrower) had to sign them and could write in their exact amount. In modern times, all customers, whether depositors or borrowers, began to make use of checking accounts. The private bank note passed into history.

The U.S. Treasury first issued paper money during the Civil War, and it continued to do so until some time after World War II. During the 20th century, however, most of our paper money has been issued by the Federal Reserve System, and today the Fed has that exclusive responsibility; if you examine a piece of currency, you will see that it is a "Federal Reserve Note." Thus, ironically, bank notes constitute all of our currency today, just as they did before the Civil War, but the notes are issued by the central bank rather than by a host of private banks.

Since the Treasury prints currency at the Fed's request to meet the public's needs, the common notion that the federal government cranks out more paper money to finance its deficits has no factual basis. The amount of paper money in circulation has nothing to do with the deficits of the federal government. When the federal government runs a deficit (expenditures exceed revenue), the Treasury borrows by issuing bonds that are bought by investors; the government gets the money, and the investors get the bonds. If a bond is sold to a bank (and banks are major purchasers of U.S. Treasury securities), the bank pays for it by crediting the checking account of the U.S. Treasury, thus increasing the total volume of all checking accounts. This is called *monetizing the debt*; it enlarges the money supply but does not affect currency in circulation. (If the bond is purchased by the Fed, the transaction is also characterized as monetizing the debt, and the effect is similar to an expansionary monetary policy in which the Fed buys U.S. Treasury securities through open-market operations.)

By contrast, the Fed issues paper money in response not to the budget deficits of the *federal government*, but to the *public*'s requirements for cash. It supplies banks with currency, and the banks pay for it with a check written on their reserve account. Checks written to "cash" by bank customers then determine the amount of currency circulating outside banks. This demand for currency has no impact on the money supply because checking accounts decrease by the amount currency increases when the check is "cashed."

How then does the money supply grow? It increases in the same fashion that outstanding bank notes grew in the 19th century. When banks lend, they create demand deposits (checking accounts) or credit an existing demand deposit. The more that banks lend, the more that the money supply (which is mostly demand deposits) increases. Today, as 100 years ago, bank reserves set the only limit on bank lending and, therefore, on the money supply. The difference is that, instead of keeping specie as reserves, the banks must maintain reserves with the Fed.

Remember: Bank loans create deposits (checking accounts), not the other way around. As long as the banking system has sufficient reserves, it can make loans in the form of demand deposits (money). You must abandon the notion that depositors' funds provide the wherewithal for bank lending.

That may be true for the traditional mortgage-lending activity of a savings and loan association, but it is not true for commercial banks. After all, where would depositors get the funds if not by withdrawing them from another checking account? But this actually does not increase deposits for the entire system; it only reshuffles deposits among banks. The total is unchanged.

Thus, demand deposits (checking accounts), and with them the money supply, grow when banks lend, and it makes no difference who the borrower is. When a business borrows from its bank in order to stock goods for the Christmas season, the bank creates a deposit (money) on which the business writes checks to pay for merchandise. If you borrow from your bank to buy a car, the loan creates a demand deposit that increases the money supply. Therefore, as you can see, it is not just the federal government that "monetizes debt" when it borrows from the banking system; businesses and consumers "monetize" their debt too.

One last point must be made about the nature of bank reserves. A hundred years ago, these reserves consisted of gold and silver specie; today, they are deposits that banks maintain with the Federal Reserve System. Of what do these reserves consist, if not specie? They are merely checking accounts that the banks have on deposit with the Fed, very much like the checking account you have at your own bank.

Recall that the banks' checking accounts (reserves) increase when the Fed buys securities from a government securities dealer. In other words, banks' reserves are nothing more than accounts the banks maintain at the Fed, accounts that grow at the Fed's discretion whenever it buys securities in the open market.

If it sounds like a house of cards, or like bookkeeping entries in a computer's memory, that's because it is. Nothing "backs up" the money supply except our faith in it, expressed every time we accept or write a check. Those checking accounts, and hence the money supply, built on borrowing, *must keep growing* if the economy is to grow over the business cycle. The forward surge of the cycle, when demand grows rapidly and pulls the economy's output with it, is founded on spenders' ability and willingness to borrow and to go into debt.

This, then, is the critical significance of the money supply: It measures the increase in demand made possible by bank lending. With that in mind, it is now time to discuss the price borrowers are willing to pay for those funds.

THE FED AND INTEREST RATES

Every commodity has a price; the *interest rate* is the price of money. As with any commodity, that price fluctuates according to the laws of supply and demand.

The demand for money increases and interest rates rise during economic expansion as consumers and businesses finance increased spending. They do so by drawing on three sources of funds: current savings, liquidation of financial assets, and borrowing from banks and other financial intermediaries. It's easy to see that an increase in the demand for funds will drive up interest rates.

During recessions, however, as the economy moves from trough to recovery, cash becomes plentiful again. Savings grow, financial assets accumulate, and debt is repaid. Interest rates fall as the supply of funds exceeds the demand for funds at current rates.

The cyclical rise and fall of interest rates would occur with or without the Federal Reserve System. Yet the Fed's influence on interest rates is so pervasive that it is now time to study the Fed's actions in detail.

Begin with a summary statement of the Fed's objectives and actions that refers to neither the money supply nor interest rates, which will be developed later:

- *Expansionary policy:* If the Fed buys securities, thus increasing member bank reserves, the banks will be able to lend more, stimulating demand. Such an expansionary policy has traditionally been pursued during a period of recession, when the economy is at the bottom of the business cycle.

- *Contractionary policy:* If the Fed sells securities, and bank reserves are reduced, the banks will not be able to lend as much, which will curtail the share of demand that depends on borrowing and, hence, will reduce the total level of demand. This policy has been followed at the peak of the cycle to restrain the growth of demand and inflationary increases in prices.

These relationships can be easily summarized in the following manner: (Read ↑ as "up," ↓ as "down," and → as "leads to.")

Expansionary policy: Fed buys securities → Bank reserves ↑→ Bank lending ↑→ Demand ↑

Contractionary policy: Fed sells securities → Bank reserves ↓→ Bank lending ↓→ Demand ↓

Now include money in the analysis.

The Fed was traditionally activist, alternately pursuing "easy money" policies (supplying banks with reserves) or "tight money"policies (depriving banks of reserves), depending on the state of the business cycle. During periods of recession and through the recovery stage and the early period of expansion, the Fed's easy money policy contributed to rapid growth in the money supply (demand deposits or checking accounts), as banks lent money (demand deposits or checking accounts) freely in response to plentiful reserves. As the expansionary phase of the cycle reached its peak, the Fed switched to a tight money policy, restricting the growth of bank reserves and, hence, the money supply.

The Fed's actions with respect to the money supply may be added to the earlier set of directed arrows and summarized as shown:

Expansionary policy: Fed buys securities → Bank reserves ↑→ Bank lending ↑→ Money supply ↑→ Demand ↑

**Contractionary policy: Fed sells securities → Bank reserves ↓→
Bank lending ↓→ Money supply ↓→ Demand ↓**

As you can imagine, the Fed's actions also have an impact on interest rates. The Fed traditionally pursued an easy money policy to hold interest rates down and promote relaxed credit conditions in order to boost demand during the recovery phase of the cycle. Eventually, when the expansion was fully under way, the peak of the cycle was not far off, and credit availability was constricting on its own, the Fed switched to a tight money policy, which reduced the supply of credit even further and drove up interest rates.

The Fed's actions with respect to *interest rates* may be included with the directed arrows and summarized as follows:

**Easy money policy: Fed buys securities → Bank reserves ↑→
Interest rates ↓→ Bank lending ↑→ Money supply ↑→ Demand ↑**

**Tight money policy: Fed sells securities → Bank reserves ↓→
Interest rates ↑→ Bank lending ↓→ Money supply ↓→ Demand ↓**

THE FED AND THE POSTWAR BUSINESS CYCLE

With these principles in mind, you can examine the Fed's record of expansionary (low interest rate) and contractionary (high interest rate) monetary policies in the Old Economy (see Charts 8–1 and 8–2 on page 138). Remember that the Fed's initial (1965–1980) Old Economy objective had an inflationary bias. At the same time the Fed did try to counteract the natural swing of the cycle, stimulating demand at the trough with low interest rates, making it easy for the banks to lend, and curbing inflation at the peak with high interest, making it difficult for the banks to lend. The peaks and valleys of the cycle are reflected in these oscillations. Recessions are shaded in gray.

The economic events that began in the early 1970s clearly illustrate these ideas. Do you recall the feverish inflationary boom of 1973, when demand for autos and housing was so insistent that the United Auto Workers Union complained about compulsory overtime and there were shortages of lumber? The demand for borrowed funds was very strong, and bank lending grew apace. Accordingly, the Fed instituted a tight money policy (see Charts 8–1 and 8–2 for the years 1973 and 1974), forcing interest rates upward.

As the Fed applied the brakes and raised interest rates, the boom came to a halt. More than two million people were thrown out of work when the

CHART 8–1 Short-Term Interest Rates: The Prime Rate and the Treasury-Bill Rate

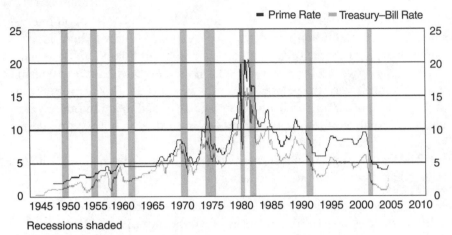

Recessions shaded

Source: Federal Reserve.

full force of recession hit in late 1974 and early 1975. So, the Fed switched to an easy money policy to stimulate the economy from 1975 through 1977, and interest rates fell. By 1977 the economy was expanding once more, and the Fed reversed itself again, adopting a tight money policy. It was 1974 all over again, except that inflation was even more severe. While the Fed pur-

CHART 8–2 Long-Term Interest Rates: Yield on New Issues of High-Grade Corporate Bonds and Yield on Long-Term Treasury Bonds

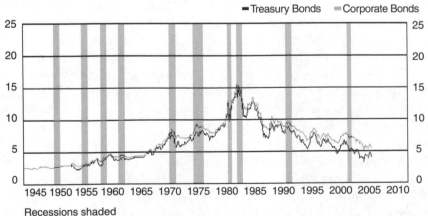

Recessions shaded

Source: Federal Reserve.

sued its traditional tight money policy, President Carter instituted voluntary wage and price controls.

President Carter reshuffled his cabinet in 1979, appointed Fed Chairman G. William Miller to the position of Secretary of the Treasury, and asked Paul Volcker, president of the Federal Reserve Bank of New York, to replace Mr. Miller. Mr. Volcker accepted the appointment and immediately rallied the members of the Federal Reserve Board of Governers to maintain the fight against inflation, obtaining a commitment from them to pursue the struggle beyond the cycle's present phase. Interest rates were at a postwar high, the cyclical peak had arrived, and a downturn was inevitable.

The 1980 downturn was so sharp that the Board of Governors set aside its inflation-fighting stance temporarily, providing banks with sufficient reserves and lowering interest rates to prevent undue hardship. Mr. Volcker's battle plan, which will be described more fully in a moment, had been postponed by the exigencies of the moment.

In summary, then, the overall aim of the Fed under its initial (1965–1980) Old Economy rules had favored full employment and erred on the side of expansion, thereby generating inflation. Secondarily, the Fed sought to reverse the extremes of the cycle: to dampen excessive inflation and to stimulate a depressed economy. After 1980 price stability (controlling inflation) became the Fed's revised Old Economy goal.

THE MONETARIST CRITIQUE
However, another look at interest rates on page 138 reveals that the Fed's policies contributed to the cycle's severity. Like an inexperienced driver with one foot on the gas and the other on the brake, attempting to achieve a steady speed but only able to surge forward after screeching to a halt, the Fed alternately stimulated and restrained the economy. Record interest rates at the cyclical peaks of the late 1960s and the middle and late 1970s provide evidence of the Fed's desperate attempts to bring inflationary expansion under control. Yet these sudden stops were partly the result of previous attempts, such as those made in 1972 and 1976, to stimulate rapid expansion by providing borrowers with low interest rates. As the economy accelerated and inflation began to go out of control, the Fed hit the brakes.

Meanwhile, the business cycle of the 1970s rose higher and higher, with inflation becoming more severe with each boom and unemployment becoming more severe with each bust. The Fed's policies had failed.

In the 1970s, a growing group of economists began to criticize the Fed's policy, accusing the Fed of contributing to the severity of the business cycle instead of reducing cyclical fluctuations. In their view, the Fed's contractionary policy, applied at the peak of the cycle, only added to the severity of the impending recession, while its expansionary policy, during the early stages of recovery, only set the stage for the subsequent inflations.

These economists, known as the *monetarist* school, believe that the rate of increase in the money supply is the single most important determinant of business cycle conditions. If the money supply grows rapidly, the economy expands; if the money supply does not grow rapidly, or even contracts, economic activity also contracts. The monetarists also believe that because other forces intrinsic to the economy will lead to normal cyclical activity and fluctuation in the rate of growth in the money supply, the Fed's best course of action is to attempt to keep the money supply's growth on an even keel, preferably at a low rate, reflecting the economy's long-range ability to increase output. According to the monetarists' view, anything beyond that rate will lead to inflation, and attempts to reduce the swings of the cycle will instead only exacerbate them.

It's as if the monetarists were saying, "If you want a comfortable temperature, set the thermostat and leave it. Don't fiddle with it by alternately raising and lowering it every time you feel a little chilly or a bit too warm, because this will just cause wide swings in temperature, which only heighten discomfort rather than reduce it."

The Road to Hell Is Paved with Good Intentions

- The effect of the Fed's policies in the 1970s was the opposite of its intentions.
- The Fed's policies increased the amplitude of the cycle's swings.
- The rate of inflation and interest rates rose over the course of the cycle.

DEBT AND THE CYCLE

Now, although the Fed was unable to control the cycle or inflation in the 1970s, it was not solely responsible for the course of events. You can see tidal waves of consumer and business borrowing (referred to earlier) in Chart 8–3 (page 141), doubling every five years: $100 billion in 1969, $200 billion in 1974, and $400 billion in 1979. This borrowing drove demand forward during the expansionary phase of the cycle, creating the inflationary conditions that provoked the Fed's tight money policy and the subsequent

CHART 8–3 Total Private Borrowing

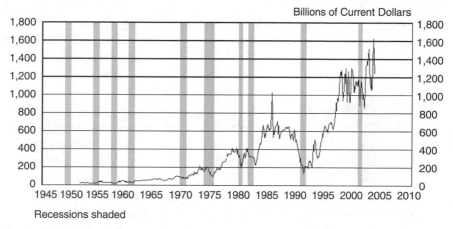

Recessions shaded

Source: Federal Reserve.

crash into recession. The downturn would have occurred in the Fed's absence; the Fed's policies just made it more severe. Unfortunately, after recession took hold, the quick shift to an easy money policy fostered the next giant wave of borrowing, spending, and inflation, and this inevitably produced (once the wave's internal energy was spent and the Fed tightened up) a major collapse.

Be sure to notice that interest rates rose over time due to the ever-escalating demand for funds and consequent ever-escalating expenditures and inflation. You saw this in Charts 8–1 and 8–2 on page 138, when consumer and business borrowing doubled every five years in the 1970s.

Since the demand for funds continuously exceeded the supply of funds at current prices, and since prices rose at ever-higher rates, interest rates (the price of borrowed money) climbed in the long run. Certainly lenders would not issue loans at a rate of interest lower than the rate of inflation. Why lend funds at rates too low to offset the decline in the real-dollar value of the amount loaned?

But you can see in Charts 8–1 and 8–2 that by the mid 1980s interest rates had fallen from their record peaks although private borrowing reached an all-time high. It is now time to examine the Fed's transition to an anti-inflationary stance in more detail.

Inflation's Engine: The 1970s

- Explosive borrowing → Explosive spending → Explosive inflation

---

THE FED'S REVOLUTION

Although the Fed may not have been entirely responsible for the debacle of the late 1970s, the monetarists' criticism of its "stop–go" policies had hit home. In October 1979, shortly after Mr. Volcker began his term of office, the Fed announced an accommodation with the monetarist position. Henceforth, Mr. Volcker said, the Fed would set targets for monetary growth that it believed were consistent with an acceptable (low) rate of inflation. In the summer of 1980, Mr. Volcker persuaded the Fed that it would have to renew immediately its commitment to halting inflation, a commitment that it had suspended briefly during the recession of the previous spring.

After earlier recessions, the Fed had always reverted to an expansionary policy of a year or two's duration (see Charts 8–1 and 8–2 on page 138). Following the 1980 slump, however, the Fed decided to prevent rapid recovery and expansion by maintaining a very tight money policy during the early phases of recovery. Mr. Volcker persuaded the Board of Governors that inflation had become so severe that the economy could not tolerate the usual easy-money-aided recovery. The rate of inflation had risen over each successive cycle and had barely declined during the 1980 recession. Rapid stimulation and recovery of demand would quickly bid prices up once again. This time, tight money was the only appropriate remedy, even if it stunted the recovery.

In consequence, the Fed's 1980, 1981, and 1982 tight money policies drove the prime rate to 21.5 percent and first-mortgage rates to 18 percent, unleashing the worst recession since World War II. For the first time, the Fed had stopped a recovery in its tracks and watched the economy slide off into back-to-back recessions. The Fed had made up its mind that restraining demand in order to control inflation was worth the price of economic contraction.

But the Fed relaxed its grip in the summer of 1982, first, because inflation had been wrung out of the economy and unemployment had reached an intolerable level; and second, because there were strong signs that Congress was losing patience with the Fed's restrictive policies. The Fed had accomplished its objective, so there was no need to further antagonize those who had the power to terminate the Fed's independent status. Yet, despite the eventual relaxation, you should realize that the Fed's 1981 policies marked a major revision in its Old Economy strategy that had significant and far-reaching consequences for our economy.

The Fed Beats Back Inflation: Early 1980s

- Restrictive policy → Bank reserves ↓→ Interest rates ↑→
  Bank lending ↓→ Money supply ↓→ Demand ↓→ Inflation ↓

The Fed's early 1980s policies were a radical departure from those of the 1960s and 1970s. The 1981–1982 recession signaled a new era, a major turning point in postwar economic history. The Fed had abandoned its initial Old Economy game plan: spurring the economy onward during slack conditions only to apply a chokehold when boom and inflation got out of hand, and then dealing with a repeat performance in the next cycle but on a new, higher plateau. General restraint over the course of the cycle was the Fed's revised Old Economy strategy.

Mr. Volcker knew that easy conditions and a pro-growth attitude had contributed to the disaster of the 1970s. He also knew that he was on a tightrope, and that the cautious attitude described above could not lapse into complacency. But by the mid-1980s, new appointees to the Board of Governors who favored an easy money policy had begun to undermine Mr. Volcker's go-slow approach. You will notice on page 138 that interest rates fell, signaling dramatically easier conditions.

Why did these new appointees to the Board of Governors pursue a policy which appeared to be such a reckless reversal of the Fed's successful approach? And why were they appointed? Because President Reagan and his advisers, who called themselves *supply-side economists,* wanted supply-siders on the Board. Supply-siders favor easy credit and low interest rates.

By 1987, at the end of Mr. Volcker's second four-year term as the board's chair, he was the only veteran of the tight money campaigns of the early 1980s. As the supply-siders pushed easier and easier conditions, Mr. Volcker informed President Reagan that he did not wish to be appointed to another term as chair—a term in which the board's policy of restraint could be undone by a new majority that favored easy money and in which easy money could once again unleash the forces of inflation upon the economy.

President Reagan appointed Alan Greenspan to succeed Mr. Volcker. Many observers were pessimistic and did not believe that Mr. Greenspan would be more successful than Mr. Volcker in controlling the supply-siders. But these fears were unfounded, because, under Mr. Greenspan, the board continued to be responsible, refusing to permit a rekindling of the inflation of the 1970s.

You can see in Chart 8–3 on page 141 that private borrowing did not increase in the late 1980s, fluctuating around $600 billion annually. Thus, the board maintained sufficient restraint to prevent the headlong expansion of private borrowing and, with it, the explosion in demand that precedes a new round of inflation.

(The big jump in borrowing in the last quarter of 1985 was due to state and local government borrowing in anticipation of tax law changes that never came about. State and local borrowing is included with these private borrowing figures, but it is usually quite small.)

The Fed Controls Inflation: Late 1980s Throughout 1990s

- Moderate restraint → Moderately high interest rates → Moderate borrowing → Moderate spending → Moderate inflation

---

Instead, Mr. Greenspan's board had to confront a new problem at the turn of the 1990s. Recession forced them to temporarily suspend the struggle against inflation. As private borrowing plunged to levels not seen since the 1970s (see Chart 8–3 on page 141), the Fed eased and short-term interest rates fell to 17-year lows, although long-term rates held steady (see Charts 8–1 and 8–2 on page 138).

The economy responded as the Fed had hoped. Borrowing and spending recovered, and the economy surged forward in 1993 and 1994. Then the Fed switched to a policy of restraint in 1994 and 1995, raising interest rates in order to create a "soft landing" following the mid-decade expansion. Again, the Fed's policy worked and the economy grew rapidly at the end of the decade while inflation remained low.

After the onset of the New Economy, the bursting of the millennium bubble, and the 2001 recession, the Fed began to sharply reduce interest rates in order to stimulate demand (see Charts 8–1 and 8–2). Within a few years interest rates had fallen to low levels not seen since the early 1960s, but the Fed remained confidant that it could fine-tune the economy back to health while avoiding chronic deflation.

FINE-TUNING AND DEREGULATION

All of this raises the issue of economic "fine-tuning." How did the Fed manage to initiate such effective policies in the 1980s and afterward, when it seemed incapable of such sensitive fine-tuning in the 1970s? A small part of the answer lies in the Fed's change in focus from stimulating demand to controlling inflation. The larger part involves a dramatic change in the regulatory climate.

In the 1970s and earlier, interest rate regulations restricted the Fed to operating a switch that was either "off" or "on." But deregulation in the late 1970s and early 1980s permitted a metamorphosis; the switch became a valve, allowing the flow of credit to be more finely calibrated.

The history of this transition deserves some explanation. Until the end of the 1970s, banks and savings-and-loan companies were not permitted to pay more than a statutory maximum of slightly more than 5 percent on consumer savings accounts. During the rapid expansions of 1968–1969 and 1973–1974, Treasury bill interest rates climbed to well above 5 percent, providing an incentive for large depositors to withdraw their funds from these financial intermediaries and invest them in Treasury bills in order to earn the higher market return.

This process was called *disintermediation* (a coinage only an economist could love), because savers bypassed the financial intermediaries to invest their funds directly in Treasury bills; S&Ls suffered severely due to their dependence on consumer savings accounts.

The upshot was that, as soon as boom conditions developed and the Fed began exercising a tight money policy, driving interest rates up, an ocean of deposits drained out of the banks and especially out of the S&Ls. The savings and loans literally ran out of money. They couldn't make mortgage loans, even if borrowers were willing to pay exorbitant rates of interest.

You can understand, then, why the Fed's tight money policies during these earlier periods did not cause credit to constrict gradually as interest rates climbed; instead, the availability of credit suddenly dried up for certain key areas of the economy (e.g., residential construction almost shut down).

Then, when the boom peaked and the economy slipped off into recession, the Fed switched to an easy money policy. As soon as Treasury bill interest rates fell below the statutory maximum that banks and S&Ls were able to pay, depositors sold their Treasury bills and redeposited the funds, propelling a tidal wave of deposits back into the financial intermediaries. As a result, S&Ls practically gave money away to finance home building.

These fund flows out of and then back into the banks and S&Ls exacerbated the business cycle. In 1969 and 1974, analysts didn't talk about tight conditions; they talked about the "credit crunch" and how it had stopped the economy in its tracks. Then, as deposits came flooding back into the system in 1970–1972 and 1975–1977, demand, fueled by cheap credit, took off like a rocket. No wonder inflation escalated and the business cycle's waves rose higher, only to plunge into deeper troughs.

By 1980, deregulation had begun to remove interest rate ceilings from consumer savings accounts. The new, flexible-rate accounts were even called "T-bill accounts" for a while, because they were pegged to the Treasury bill rate and were designed to prevent savers from defecting to the savings accounts' chief competitor, the Treasury bill, as interest rates rose.

When the Fed made its desperate stand against inflation in 1981–1982, deregulation had been partially accomplished: The T-bill accounts prevented a run on the savings-and-loan companies' deposits. These accounts required a minimum deposit of $10,000, however, so many savers were attracted by recently created money-market mutual funds that had much smaller minimum deposit requirements. The money-market funds invested in commercial paper and other short-term instruments, thus providing yields slightly higher than those of Treasury bills. Consequently, banks and S&Ls still faced a partial drain on their deposits.

But deregulation had begun to work. The S&Ls did not run out of money in 1981–1982, although they were obliged to raise mortgage rates to prohibitive levels as T-bill account interest rates went up with the yield on Treasury bills. Residential construction was, at last, constrained by the price borrowers had to pay for funds rather than by the availability of those funds.

After the Fed eased in mid-1982, and as the economy rebounded strongly in 1983, banks and S&Ls received permission to offer "money-market accounts," which competed directly with the money-market funds. Although deregulation was not 100 percent complete (as it is today), depositors now had little reason to keep their funds elsewhere, and so a large volume of funds returned to the banks and S&Ls from the money-market mutual funds.

Now that the Fed had a finely honed scalpel, it could maintain interest rates at sufficiently low levels to encourage demand, but it could easily nudge them upward whenever inflationary conditions threatened. And it would not have to fear disintermediation, the destructive flows of funds out of banks and S&Ls.

Early 1984 provided the first test; to confirm the results, review the interest rate record in Charts 8–1 and 8–2 on page 138 once again. Interest rates collapsed in late 1982, but the Fed didn't wait long before it began to tighten up again. Demand had roared ahead throughout 1983; and, by the end of the year, there were many alarming signs that inflation was about to rekindle. Although the Fed had allowed interest rates to drift upward throughout 1983, more decisive, positive action was required by early 1984.

Charts 8–1 and 8–2 show that the Fed's tight money policy in the spring of 1984 forced interest rates quickly upward, inducing a mini-slowdown in 1984. There was talk of recession, but the Fed had carefully tuned the slow-down and did not let it develop into recession. Once the danger was past, the Fed permitted interest rates to drop sharply, and demand began to grow once again.

Although deregulation became suspect in the late 1980s because of the excesses and consequent failures associated with unregulated lending prac-tices by the savings and loan industry, the deregulation of interest rates helped the Fed alter the course of America's economic history.

By the early 1990s, of course, the Fed faced a different problem. Private borrowing tumbled so steeply during the 1990–1991 recession (see Chart 8–3 on page 141) that the Fed redirected its efforts to stimulate demand with low interest rates (see Charts 8–1 and 8–2 on page 138). By 1994–1995, however, the Fed briefly bumped rates upward to prevent demand's rapid growth. Then, failing to see signs of escalating inflation, the Fed eased again and let borrowing grow through the end of the 1990s.

Although borrowing reached new heights at the end of the 1990s and into the new millennium (see Chart 8–3 on page 141), the New Economy's advent kept inflation moderate. Business had added and was adding hi-tech pro-ductive capacity at a torrid pace. As long as supply grew as rapidly as demand, inflation could not threaten. Instead, many observers worried that borrow-ing's collapse might drag down spending, too, initiating deflation's onset.

THE FED AND THE 2001 RECESSION

Consumer demand had ruled the Old Economy, generating its own business cycle dynamic:

1. Households borrowed and spent to build homes and buy cars and other durable goods.
2. Rising demand for these goods boosted output, capacity utiliza-tion, and costs, thereby igniting inflation.
3. Robust capacity utilization prompted industry to invest in new plant and equipment, contributing to boom conditions and exacer-bating inflation.
4. Rising prices and interest rates capped the boom and brought recession.

The Fed's initial Old Economy strategy of promoting robust economic conditions and full employment contributed to the business cycle's severity, as well as inflation's and interest rates' secular rise. Until 1980 the Fed chose to err on the side of ease and expansion. Then, in the early 1980s, the Fed revised its Old Economy strategy in order to curb inflation and limit the cycle's severity. Restraint, achieved by interest rate increases designed to curtail consumer expenditures, had become the Fed's overriding mission.

But the New Economy brought a changed dynamic to the business cycle. Business investment, not consumer expenditures, led the economy's 1990s expansion. The personal-computer revolution placed a PC on every office desk and in every home. That required additional investments in word processing and spreadsheet software, multimedia, the Internet, and telecommunications networks. High-technology plant and equipment expenditures erupted (see Chart 5–1 on page 72) to lead a spectacular boom.

The 1990s boom reminds us of 19th-century railway expansions. In those days, as companies built their roads west from Chicago to the Pacific, these firms hoped that growing traffic would provide revenues sufficient to sustain them until they reached the West Coast. If a railroad ran out of funds in, say, the Dakotas, because traffic failed to meet rosy projections, the corporation went through bankruptcy and construction ceased. Then, perhaps a decade later, a reorganized and refinanced corporation would complete the road to the West Coast. Only time and rising revenues could prompt another building boom.

Business decisions inaugurated the railroad age and the personal computer age. Both eras justified huge capital expenditures on grounds that they enhanced productivity and reduced costs—whether for shipping goods and people or processing and transmitting data. The railway age lowered transport costs, thereby broadening domestic and export markets for agriculture and industry. The 1990s technology boom transformed office procedures by permitting individuals at their desks to electronically manipulate and send text, data, and images. Massive business capital expenditures—not consumer demand—led the New Economy north.

When the New Economy boom fizzled—much as the 19th-century railroad booms had periodically fizzled—the Fed switched from restraint to ease. Interest rates plunged (see Charts 8–1 and 8–2 on page 138) and the Fed hoped that lower rates would stimulate borrowing and spending and thereby reinvigorate demand. The Fed's policy succeeded insofar as private borrowing remained robust throughout the recession, the first such occurrence since World War II (see Chart 8–3 on page141). Falling interest rates motivated households to borrow heavily to acquire new homes and autos and other durable goods. Residential construction and automobile production stayed strong, mitigating recession's damage.

While falling interest rates may have been sufficient to maintain the consumer sector, falling rates did little to preserve business investment in plant and equipment. Capital expenditures deteriorated sharply (see Chart 5–1 on page 72). Just as, in our earlier example, 19th-century railways waited for growing traffic to spur a new round of track construction, the New Economy would wait for more robust capacity utilization before making significant additions to plant and equipment. The leading investments had been made and the initial infrastructure was in place; low interest rates were insufficient motivation to build ahead of demand.

Moreover, returning to consumer expenditures, whereas low interest rates might sustain household activity, they could not guarantee growing consumer purchases of homes and cars. The Fed's expansionary policy and the consequent interest rate drop had maintained these expenditures throughout the 2001 recession. If interest rates had hit bottom and had nowhere to go but up, how could residential construction and automobile production exceed their already robust levels?

And that question led to a larger question. Now that the recession had been stopped, what would lead the next boom? Merely replacing worn-out hardware and software would be insufficient. The New Economy now required the next new thing. What would it be?

That unanswered question led some to fear that demand would not grow sufficiently rapidly to prevent prices from falling. Could the Fed also manage the threat of deflation in a New Economy? Or was deflation merely a passing buzzword, a temporary pause before resuscitated demand rekindled concern over rising prices?

THE FED AND DEFLATION

To come to grips with the issue of deflation, consider once again the Fed's initial Old Economy experience with inflation and the Fed's revised Old Economy struggle against inflation. Think of the economy as a frisky horse, on which the rider (the Fed) had to continually pull back on the reins (tight money) to prevent a runaway, breakneck gallop (inflation). That description summarizes the Fed's post-1980 inflation-fighting posture after the Fed had brought inflation under control.

The rider had learned a lesson the hard way during the Fed's pre-1980 (initial Old Economy) stop–go policy and its unintended consequences of escalating inflation and interest rates. By periodically letting the reins go slack and permitting the horse to break into a gallop, only to be thrown from the horse as it reared when the rider desperately yanked on the reins, the Fed had inadvertently stoked inflation's fire before 1980.

With the advent of the New Economy and the 2001 recession, however, the Fed dropped the reins again. By 2003 the Fed had depressed interest rates to levels not seen for 40 years. But interest rates can't fall below zero. Everyone wanted to know whether or not slack reins would as effectively propel the economy forward as reining in demand had succeeded in controlling inflation. The question remained: Was deflation a New Economy nemesis, or would inflation rise again? Or would the New Economy just perk along without raising concern about either?

You can put matters in perspective by recalling that deflation was more common than inflation in 19th-century America. Recall, too, that institutional rigidities limited private borrowing's growth. Businesses, and especially households, faced severe constraints on their ability to borrow and spend. There were no 30-year amortized mortgages, no credit cards, and relatively constrained—when compared with today—industrial access to the capital markets. That's why private-sector spending could seldom propel demand forward more rapidly than supply and why the private sector was rarely responsible for 19th-century inflation.

The federal government, on the other hand, had easier access to the credit markets. The federal government could borrow and spend—could even print and spend paper money—in ways that were closed to the private sector. That explains the link between war and inflation in the minds of most. Indeed, it explains why the War of 1812 and the Civil War are the 19th century's most important inflationary episodes. Only wartime federal-government borrowing and spending could noticeably propel demand forward more rapidly than supply, and drive prices significantly higher.

Since 19th-century bouts of high-powered borrowing and spending were wartime occurrences (War of 1812 and Civil War), it was relatively easy for 19th-century peacetime supply to outstrip demand. When the frontier moved west, dumping abundant supplies of cotton, grain, and beef on domestic and world markets, agricultural prices fell and pulled other prices down with them. Indeed, the opening of the American West was part of a worldwide phenomenon.

As European capital helped build railroads across the United States, Canada, Argentina, and Australia, and larger steamships plied the oceans, global commodity prices plunged and deflation spread. The Industrial Revolution and manufacturing's burgeoning output of standard items of consumption, such as flour, dressed meat, canned food, textiles, clothing, household crockery and utensils, furniture and furnishings, tools, and building materials, drove down prices for all goods comprising the everyday needs of life. As the cost of producing food, clothing, and shelter declined throughout the world economy, so did prices generally.

Now fast-forward to the 21st century and consider, once again, the global forces of supply and demand. No one knows how long the Fed must let the credit reins dangle in its attempt to prop up borrowing and spending. Meanwhile, supply is not standing still. China in particular, and the other Asian economies generally, have become manufacturing platforms, spewing industrial goods back toward the U.S. and other more-developed economies. These new manufacturing platforms remind us of the U.S., Canada, Argentina, and Australia—the 19th-century agricultural platforms that set off rounds of global deflation with their agricultural-commodity exports. If these 21st-century manufacturing nations have as large an impact on 21st-century global industrial supply as the 19th-century primary-product exporters had on 19th-century global agricultural supply, manufacturing prices may begin to decline secularly and deflation may be upon us.

But falling manufacturing prices do not guarantee deflation. We use wholesale price indexes that give heavy weight to falling commodity and industrial prices to measure 19th-century deflation because of the scarcity of historical retail-price data. Today's consumer price index includes retail goods and services prices—items missing in our 19th-century wholesale-price measures of deflation. Retail prices are less volatile than wholesale prices both downward and upward, and it would take severe deflationary pressure to reduce the price of services such as rent and medical care that play an important role in today's CPI. That is why 21st-century retail-price deflation is less likely than 19th-century wholesale-price deflation.

Nonetheless, if demand's growth remains puny while supply's growth is robust for a substantial stretch of years, the CPI could fall secularly. The Fed may be unable to stop deflation's onset because it is more difficult to stimulate demand with falling interest rates when interest rates are already low than it is to restrain demand with rising interest rates when interest rates are already high.

The future was murky as the economy emerged from the 2001 recession. By 2004 the Fed began easing rates upward as the economy gained strength and inflationary fears rekindled. China's economy grew so rapidly that its voracious appetite for and consumption of industrial raw materials such as oil, steel, and cement bid their prices rapidly upward, reinforcing fears of inflation. Asia's manufacturing platforms might drive down manufacturing prices, but their need for inputs stimulated primary-product prices. That could squeeze manufacturers' profit margins, but did it necessarily translate into falling finished-goods prices? Concerns regarding deflation seemed forgotten.

But what would the next recession bring? The Chinese bubble could burst, reversing the upward course of raw-materials prices and sending finished-goods prices downward, too. Would that depress U.S. economic conditions and prices? Or would domestic U.S. inflationary forces prevail despite recession? No one can accurately forecast all these events and circumstances.

TRACKING THE FED

You can, however, use the *Journal*'s print and online editions to track the Federal Reserve's response to these conditions. The Fed's Open Market Committee sets the Fed's monetary policy. The Committee is composed of the seven members of the Board of Governors plus five of the presidents of the district Federal Reserve banks (New York and four others on a rotating basis). This 12-member committee holds its scheduled meetings on Tuesdays, roughly every six weeks, to set the interest rate on federal funds—the rate at which the reserve banks lend to one another.

If economic activity is robust and reserves scarce, the federal funds rate will rise as banks that are short of reserves attempt to borrow reserves from banks with excess reserves. If economic activity is slack and reserves plentiful, the federal funds rate will fall as banks find little need to borrow reserves from one another.

If the Fed pursues a contractionary policy, by selling U.S. Treasury securities, in the midst of robust economic activity, the federal funds rate will rise as banks that wish to lend to households and businesses attempt to borrow reserves from other banks at a time when the total pool of reserves is shrinking. If the Fed pursues an expansionary policy, by purchasing U.S. Treasury securities, in the midst of slack economic activity, the federal funds rate will fall because few banks will attempt to borrow reserves from other banks at a time when the total pool of reserves is growing.

In 1999 and 2000 the Fed pursued a contractionary policy, and raised the federal funds rate, in an attempt to prevent surging inflation during the millennium bubble. Then, in 2001, 2002, and 2003 the Fed's expansionary pol-

Other Journal Sites

As of 5:27 p.m. EST Tuesday, March 16, 2004

Home
News ▶
Technology ▶
Markets ▶
Personal Journal ▶
Opinion ▶
Leisure/Weekend ▶

The Print Edition
Today's Edition
Past Editions
Features
Columnists
In-Depth Reports
Discussions
Company Research

Site Map
My Online Journal
Portfolio
Personalize My News
E-Mail Setup
My Account/Billing
Customer Service
The Online Journal
The Print Edition
Contact Us

THE AFTERNOON REPORT

By JOSEPH SCHUMAN

A Less Cheerful Fed Leaves Rates Alone

March 16, 2004 5:27 p.m.

The Federal Reserve today left its benchmark interest rate unchanged as expected, and offered a grimmer view of the labor market than it has in the past with no hint of new inflation worries, signaling it will keep rates at historical lows for some time to come.

The Federal Open Market Committee said it would leave its target for the federal funds rate charged on overnight loans between banks at the 46-year low of 1%. The makers of U.S. monetary policy continued to credit their own "accommodative" rates and the corresponding cheapness of borrowed money, as well as robust productivity growth, for providing needed support to the economy. But they seemed less certain about the country's economic expansion. Previously, the committee said economic data "confirms" that output is expanding briskly. Today it said the data "indicates" expansion continues apace. This may seem like a small change, but the Fed weighs these words carefully. The more drastic revision dealt with employment, addressing a labor market that keeps bucking expectations for the kind of improvement we see elsewhere in the economy. "Although job losses have slowed, new hiring has lagged," it said, dropping all previous mention of perceived improvement. And the Fed said consumer prices are expected to remain low, despite some nongovernmental surveys that suggest businesses are being squeezed by costs.

⎤
⎬ **Open Market Committee**
⎦

As it has since December, the Fed was pretty clear about these key criteria it's watching when it considers what to do with rates: "With inflation quite low and resource use slack, the Committee believes that it can be patient in removing its policy accommodation." Recent reports from the Fed and the Labor Department have shown the country's use of its factory capacity is improving but remains slack, and that the U.S. work force, too, is vastly underused. With inflation also kept at bay, in the Fed's view, there seems no reason for it to consider raising rates. Another justification for leaving them alone, but one unmentioned, may be last week's bombings in Spain. Those attacks have shaken financial markets and renewed security worries.

Open Market Committee—Second Paragraph

The Federal Open Market Committee said it would leave its target for the federal funds rate charged on overnight loans between banks at the 46-year low of 1%.

ECONOMY

Text of the Fed's Statement
March 16, 2004 3:41 p.m.

The full text of the Federal Reserve Open Market Committee's March 16 statement on interest rates:

"The Federal Open Market Committee decided today to keep its target for the federal funds rate at 1%."

"The Committee continues to believe that an accommodative stance of monetary policy, coupled with robust underlying growth in productivity, is providing important ongoing support to economic activity. The evidence accumulated over the intermeeting period indicates that output is continuing to expand at a solid pace. Although job losses have slowed, new hiring has lagged. Increases in core consumer prices are muted and expected to remain low."

"The Committee perceives the upside and downside risks to the attainment of sustainable growth for the next few quarters are roughly equal. The probability of an unwelcome fall in inflation has diminished in recent months and now appears almost equal to that of a rise in inflation. With inflation quite low and resource use slack, the Committee believes that it can be patient in removing its policy accommodation."

"Voting for the FOMC monetary policy action were: Alan Greenspan, Chairman; Timothy F. Geithner, Vice Chairman; Ben S. Bernanke; Susan·S. Bies; Roger W. Ferguson, Jr.; Edward M. Gramlich; Thomas M. Hoenig; Donald L. Kohn; Cathy E. Minehan; Mark W. Olson; Sandra Pianalto; and William Poole."

icy pushed the federal funds rate down from 6.0 percent to 1.0 percent in an attempt to stimulate economic activity.

You can use the *Journals*'s online edition (http://online.wsj.com) to track the Fed's actions. General directions for retrieving online infor-mation appear in Chapter 1 on pages 7 through 11. Appendix D on

WSJ.com THE WALL STREET JOURNAL.
ONLINE

As of 12:47 a.m. EST Thursday, March 4, 2004

BEIGE BOOK REPORT

CEOs Shift Back Into Hiring Mode, But Only Modestly

By JAMES R. HAGERTY
Staff Reporter of THE WALL STREET JOURNAL
March 4, 2004 12:47 a.m.; Page A2

Chief executives at some of the biggest U.S. companies say they are back in hiring mode, a new survey shows, but it isn't clear whether they will create jobs on a large scale anytime soon.

The Business Roundtable, an association of CEOs at big U.S. companies, said the latest quarterly survey of its members shows they expect "steady improvement in economic conditions" and "modest job growth."

For the first time since the roundtable's quarterly survey began in late 2002, the percentage of CEOs projecting that their companies will add jobs in the U.S. was larger than the percentage expecting to reduce their work forces. Among the 122 CEOs responding to the survey, conducted in the second half of February, 33% said they expected to add jobs in the U.S. in the next six months, up from 25% in the December survey and just 12% in the prior quarter. In the latest survey, 45% of the CEOs predicted steady U.S. employment for their companies in the next six months, and 22% expected a decline.

Henry McKinnell, chairman of the roundtable and chairman and chief executive of New York drug maker Pfizer Inc., said capital spending is strong, and "unprecedented" productivity gains should spur economic growth. He cautioned that the survey results don't suggest job growth will be as robust as it usually is during economic recoveries. "We're not quite that bullish at this point," Mr. McKinnell said.

A Federal Reserve report released Wednesday also showed restrained hiring. The latest "beige book," a survey of anecdotal reports from the Fed's 12 district banks, said employment generally showed only moderate increases in January and February. Wages and salaries have increased slightly in recent weeks, but employers are grumbling about big rises in employee health-care costs, the Fed reported.

Beige Book

Beige Book—Fifth Paragraph

A Federal Reserve report released Wednesday also showed restrained hiring. The latest "beige book," a survey of anecdotal reports from the Fed's 12 district banks, said employment generally showed only moderate increases in January and February. Wages and salaries have increased slightly in recent weeks, but employers are grumbling about big rises in employee health-care costs, the Fed reported.

---

page 174 also furnishes you with a quick guide to the *Journal*'s online edition.

The Tuesday, March 16, 2004, online edition carried an article on that day's Open Market Committee meeting (see page 153) as well as the full text of the Committee's press release (see page 154). The Fed held the federal funds rate at the low rate of 1.0 percent, as you can see from the reprint on page 154, because of its continuing concern about a recovery that failed to provide swift employment growth.

The Fed, of course, does not conduct policy in a vacuum. It has a large staff of economists and also relies on reports from the regional Federal Reserve banks. The Fed's "Beige Book" compiles these reports from the district banks and summarizes national economic conditions at six-week intervals. The fifth paragraph of an article in the Thursday, March 4, 2004, online edition (see page 155) discussed the previous day's report that hiring was restrained.

You can review the latest Beige Book Report and the minutes of the Fed's Open Market Committee meetings in the online edition:

1. Scroll down the online edition's home page's left-hand menu-bar and click on Economy.
2. Click on Economic Indicators under Data and Resources and then click on Beige Book Report. You can see that the Wednesday, March 3, 2004, report on page 157 was generally upbeat. (Note that separate reports are available for each Federal Reserve district.)
3. Click on Federal Reserve Monitor to track the Fed, as in the excerpt from Thursday, July 1, 2004, on page 158.

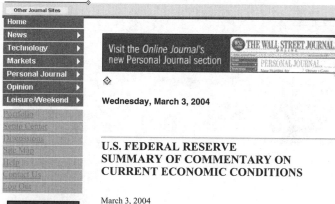

Visit the *Online Journal's* new Personal Journal section

THE WALL STREET JOURNAL
ONLINE
PERSONAL JOURNAL.

Wednesday, March 3, 2004

WSJ.com
CareerJournal.com

click here

THE WALL STREET JOURNAL
Print Editions
Customer Service

U.S. FEDERAL RESERVE SUMMARY OF COMMENTARY ON CURRENT ECONOMIC CONDITIONS

March 3, 2004

Table of Contents

Summary

Economic activity continued to expand in January and February, according to information received by Federal Reserve District Banks. Growth was variously described as moderate in Boston, Philadelphia, Cleveland, Atlanta, Chicago, St. Louis, and Kansas City, firm in Minneapolis, sound in San Francisco, and showing signs of accelerating in New York, Richmond, and Dallas.

Beige Book

Consumer spending rose in most Districts. There were gains in sales of general merchandise in January and February in all Districts except St. Louis, which reported a slight decline. In contrast to the general improvement in merchandise sales, motor vehicle sales slowed in most Districts. Tourism activity increased compared to last winter. Service sector activity has been expanding. Manufacturing output continued to rise in all Districts except Cleveland, where it has been steady. Real estate market conditions showed little change: commercial markets generally remain soft and demand for housing continues to be strong. Agricultural conditions were mixed: demand for beef appears to be recovering

Beige Book—First Paragraph

Economic activity continued to expand in January and February, according to information received by Federal Reserve District Banks. Growth was variously described as moderate in Boston, Philadelphia, Cleveland, Atlanta, Chicago, St. Louis, and Kansas City, firm in Minneapolis, sound in San Francisco, and showing signs of accelerating in New York, Richmond, and Dallas.

Home

News   Technology   Markets   Personal Journal

Freddie
Mac℠   We make home possible℠

Thursday, July 1, 2004

Federal Reserve Monitor

The Federal Open Market Committee is the policy-setting panel of the Federal
seven member of the Board of Govenors, the president of the Federal Reserve
remaining eleven Federal Reserve Bank presidents, in one-year rotations.

2004 Meeting Schedule

August 10
September 21
November 10
December 14

The FOMC, whose primary goals are to foster economic growth and job creation
and restrain inflationary pressure, controls two short-term interest rates:

Federal-Funds Rate – The interest rate banks charge each other for overnight
loans. The FOMC sets a target level for the federal-funds rate and then guides the
rate near that target by its activities in the open market. The market level of the
fed-funds rate is also influenced by demand created by banks' needs for money.

Discount Rate – On Jan. 9, 2003, the Federal Reserve adopted a new system for
lending directly to banks and other depository institutions. Three new credit rates
are now in place: primary, secondary and seasonal. The central bank often will
refer to the primary credit rate as the discount rate, which is available to banks
that are in sound financial condition. Find out more.

After each FOMC meeting the committee issues a statement indicating whether
inflation or weakness is the greater risk to the economy in the foreseeable future,
or whether the risks are balanced. Until 2000, the central bank had maintained an
official bias on rates, meant to suggest their near-term direction.

This concludes this chapter's discussion of monetary policy. Let's turn
now to Chapter 9 for a discussion of the federal government's role in the outlook for supply and demand, known as *fiscal policy*.

9

FEDERAL FISCAL POLICY

SURPLUS AND DEFICIT

THE FEDERAL BUDGET needs no introduction. It's been an issue for debate in every presidential election going back further than most folks remember.

By the late 1990s, after decades of deficit, the federal budget flipped into surplus. Some spoke of surpluses "as far as the eye could see." The focus of debate among our elected officials then switched from what to do about the funds we didn't have to what to do with the funds we did have. Some forecasts went so far as to name a year by which we would retire the outstanding federal debt or fully fund Social Security.

That didn't last long. The federal budget lapsed into deficit once again after the economy slid into the 2001 recession. Now it was deficits "as far as the eye could see," and record deficits at that. Forecasters projected that the outstanding federal debt would continue to climb and no one had a clear idea how we would fund Social Security.

This chapter will examine the reciprocal relationship between the federal budget and the economy, with special attention to the federal deficit. Here are some of the questions that will arise: Are federal deficits predominantly active or passive? That is, do they determine the level of economic activity or are they the consequence of the economy's health? How effective is fiscal policy (federal spending and taxing) in controlling economic activity? Do federal deficits generate inflation? What is the political dynamic surrounding the use of fiscal policy?

Let's begin with the issue of deficits and inflation, but not before you have examined the data.

DEFICITS AND INFLATION

The Wall Street Journal reports federal budget figures for each month in the second half of the subsequent month. See on this page, for instance, the print-edition article on October 2003's budget deficit of $69.55 billion from the Tuesday, November 18, 2003, issue. Since these monthly data are not seasonally adjusted, only the annual data reported at the end of each October for the fiscal year that concludes September 30 is useful for judging the trend of federal budget surplus and deficit. See the example from the *Journal*'s Tuesday, October 21, 2003, online edition on page 161 that reported the federal government's $374 billion budget deficit for fiscal 2003.

You can find general directions for retrieving *Wall Street Journal* online information (http://online.wsj.com) in Chapter 1 on pages 7 through 11. Appendix D on page 374 also furnishes you with a quick guide to the *Journal*'s online edition.

U.S. Budget Deficit Widened in October To $69.55 Billion

Dow Jones Newswires

Monthly Budget Deficit

WASHINGTON—The federal government posted a $69.55 billion total budget deficit in October, the first month of fiscal year 2004, widening from a $54.07 billion deficit a year earlier, the Treasury Department said.

Last month's budget gap compared with a revised surplus of $26.31 billion in September, previously reported at $26.38 billion. The October deficit was a bit narrower than analysts had expected. The Congressional Budget Office had predicted the U.S. would post a deficit of around $71 billion in October.

In its monthly statement, the Treasury said receipts totaled $135.84 billion in October, up from $124.56 billion a year earlier and down from $191.65 billion the previous month.

Outlays totaled $205.39 billion last month, up sharply from $178.63 billion a year earlier and $165.34 billion the month before. About $11 billion of the increase in October outlays was due to the fact that Nov. 1 fell on a weekend this year, shifting those outlays into October from November, CBO said.

October outlays also were boosted by $5 billion in payments to states for emergency fiscal relief, which largely wraps up the $10 billion in payments authorized earlier this year, CBO said.

As for receipts, about $8 billion of the increase was due to higher receipts of corporate income taxes, CBO said. Those receipts were boosted in part by recent legislation that allowed firms to delay until October about $5 billion in payments that otherwise would have been due in September.

The federal government racked up a record $374 billion budget deficit in fiscal year 2003 and White House officials have said they expect the budget deficit could exceed $500 billion in fiscal year 2004.

WSJ.com THE WALL STREET JOURNAL.
O N L I N E

As of Tuesday, October 21, 2003

ECONOMY

Budget Deficit
Doubles Level Hit
In Previous Year

By DEBORAH LAGOMARSINO and JOHN D. MCKINNON
Staff Reporters of THE WALL STREET JOURNAL
October 21, 2003

WASHINGTON -- The government racked up a $374 billion budget deficit in fiscal year 2003 -- more than double last year's -- and is on track to post a shortfall of more than $500 billion in the current fiscal year.

Federal Budget Deficit

The final budget numbers for 2003 -- confirming recent projections by the Congressional Budget Office -- were better than analysts expected as recently as last summer, however. They reflect an economy that is picking up steam and spinning off somewhat more tax revenue than anticipated, officials said. Lower-than-expected government spending

Still, the budget picture is likely to continue deteriorating for another year, even as the economy improves, Office of Management and Budget Director Josh Bolten said in a statement. He suggested the 2004 deficit likely will reach $500 billion. But he repeated the administration's view that "we can put the deficit on a reasonable downward path if we continue progrowth economic policies and exercise responsible spending restraint."

THE BIG PICTURE

Federal surplus/deficit as a percentage of GDP

'98 '99 '00 '01 '02 '03 '04 '05 '06 '07 '08
—Projected—

Note: Projections don't include some possible future tax breaks, or new spending items such as a Medicare prescription-drug benefit

Sources: White House Office of Management and Budget; Congressional Budget Office

Democrats were skeptical and seized the moment to step up criticism of the Bush administration's handling of the government's finances. The Treasury has seen a projected $5.6 trillion 10-year surplus disappear during the Bush administration's first three years, thanks to a combination of a weak economy, increased spending for war and homeland security, and the administration's tax cuts.

Federal Budget Deficit–First Paragraph

WASHINGTON -- The government racked up a $374 billion budget
deficit in fiscal year 2003 -- more than double last year's -- and is on track
to post a shortfall of more than $500 billion in the current fiscal year.

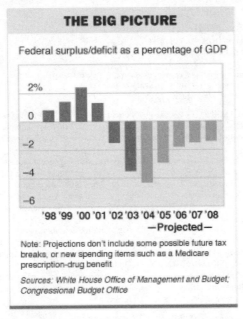

THE BIG PICTURE

Federal surplus/deficit as a percentage of GDP

'98 '99 '00 '01 '02 '03 '04 '05 '06 '07 '08
—Projected—

Note: Projections don't include some possible future tax
breaks, or new spending items such as a Medicare
prescription-drug benefit

Sources: White House Office of Management and Budget;
Congressional Budget Office

The conventional wisdom says that federal deficits cause inflation. Chart
9–1 on page 163 shows that the deficit grew dramatically in 1975 and
1981–1982 and shrank to an insignificant number in 1979. If the conventional
wisdom made sense, inflation should have jumped in 1975 and 1981–1982 with
the increase in the federal deficit and subsided in 1979 when the budget
balanced.

But that didn't happen. As a matter of fact, the opposite occurred. (See
Chart 7–1 on page 86.) Inflation narrowed in 1975 and 1981–1982 and
peaked in 1979. In other words, not only do the facts not support the conventional wisdom, they seem to indicate the opposite. Inflation fell with the
increases in the federal deficit (1975 and 1981–1982) and rose when the
deficit declined (1979). Does this mean that balanced budgets *generate* inflation, while deficits *reduce* inflation?

Now that *would* be a scoop.

To resolve the problem, you must put the federal deficit in perspective.
Chart 9–2 on page 163, which reproduces Chart 8–3, depicts private borrow-

CHART 9–1 Federal Government Expenditures, Revenues, Surplus, or Deficit

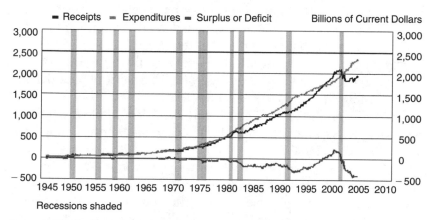

Source: U.S. Dept. of Commerce, Bureau of Economic Analysis, *National Income & Product Accounts,* Table 3.2, line 1,19,33.

ing. Compare it with the federal deficit in Chart 9–1. Recall that private borrowing includes mortgage borrowing to support residential construction, installment credit to finance the purchase of autos and other consumer durables, and business indebtedness to pay for expenditures on plant, equipment, and inventory. But it also includes (unfortunately, because it is confusing) borrowing by state and local governments, for reasons that need not be developed here.

CHART 9–2 Total Private Borrowing

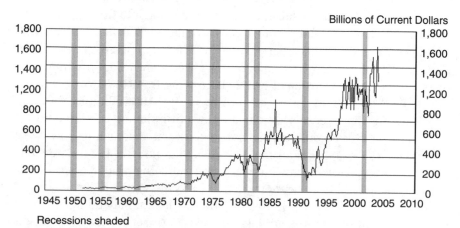

Source: Federal Reserve.

Keep in mind that both charts portray annual borrowing, not outstanding debt. By 2004, outstanding federal debt was over $7 trillion and outstanding private debt was around $35 trillion. Each year's borrowing adds to the outstanding figure, so that an annual federal deficit of $500 billion would boost the outstanding federal figure from $7 trillion to $7.5 trillion, and annual private borrowing of $1.5 trillion would lift the private total to $36.5 trillion. (Don't confuse either of these with the balance of trade deficit, to be examined in Chapter 10.)

Now compare private borrowing with the federal deficit in 1975, and note that both were approximately $100 billion. Then they move in opposite directions: The federal deficit shrinks to nothing in 1979, and private borrowing balloons to $400 billion. Total borrowing grew from $200 billion in 1975 ($100 billion of private plus $100 billion of federal) to $400 billion in 1979 (all private). This explains the burst of inflation in the late 1970s. Total borrowing doubled, financing the huge increase in demand (greater than the economy's increase in production at current prices) that drove up inflation. Thus, the growth in private borrowing in the late 1970s overwhelmed the decline in federal borrowing, generating rapid price increases.

On the other hand, if you continue to look at the record in Charts 9–1 and 9–2, you'll notice that private borrowing slumped in 1981 and 1982, dropping to almost $200 billion annually from its $400 billion peak in 1979. The federal deficit, however, popped back up from next to nothing in 1979 to about $200 billion in 1982. Once again, when you add private and federal borrowing, you see an offset: The total is $400 billion in both years ($400 billion private in 1979 with no federal deficit and $200 billion for each in 1982). When total borrowing stopped growing from 1979 through 1982, the rate of inflation subsided as demand came into line with supply.

This illustrates the fallacy in the conventional wisdom and explains why inflation seemed to behave so perversely when compared to the federal deficit. You can't ignore private borrowing when analyzing inflation. As a matter of fact, the explosion of private borrowing from 1970 to 1973 ($100 billion to $200 billion) and from 1975 to 1979 ($100 billion to $400 billion) explains that decade's two great rounds of inflation. Inflation did not grow in the 1980s because private borrowing fluctuated in a narrow range (except for 1985) and demonstrated no upward trend after 1984. By the end of the decade, private borrowing was still fluctuating around $600 billion annually, the level it had reached more than five years earlier. When it plunged to $200 billion in the early 1990s, inflation withered. Federal borrowing's growth to $400 billion was not large enough to offset private borrowing's decline.

Another development also requires clarification: the burst of private borrowing in late 1985. This burst was due to state and local governments' trying to beat an anticipated change in tax laws that never came to pass. Some Congressmen had suggested that interest paid on state and local bonds no longer be tax-exempt. Enactment of this legislation would have increased state and local interest payments, because their bonds had paid below-market rates for years due to the tax-exempt benefit to investors (i.e., bond holders were willing to receive below-market yields, provided they were tax-exempt). State and local governments moved up their borrowing in antic-ipation of the 1986 change that never came to pass.

But the main point to bear in mind is that the large federal deficits of the 1980s and early 1990s did not generate inflation, despite the attention paid them. They were overshadowed by the recessionary drop in private bor-rowing. For instance, the drop in private borrowing (see Chart 9–2 on page 163) during the 1990–1991 recession was far larger than the surge in fed-eral borrowing, keeping total borrowing—and hence, inflation—below the levels of the 1980s. By the middle 1990s the two remained below the highs of the 1980s.

But by the late 1990s private borrowing had surged to record levels (see Chart 9–2), and this time a fluke in state and local government borrowing could not be blamed. Consumers and businesses were truly borrowing and spending record amounts. Why didn't this lead to a surge of inflation? Because, as you saw in Chapters 4 and 8, the economy had sufficient excess capacity to supply all the goods demanded without any strain on productive facilities or any surge of inflation. Demand grew rapidly, but so did the econ-omy's ability to supply goods and services.

With the advent of the 2001 recession, the Federal Reserve's expan-sionary monetary policy (falling interest rates) and the federal government's expansionary fiscal policy (tax cuts) stimulated private and public borrow-ing. You can see from Chart 9–2 that private borrowing remained over a tril-lion dollars a year as record mortgage and consumer-credit borrowing off-set slumping business borrowing. At the same time, Chart 9–1 on page 163 shows that federal borrowing began to grow once more with the advent of the 2001 recession. Yet inflation remained dormant because of the econ-omy's excess capacity (see Chart 4–3 on page 47).

What about concerns about deflation now and in the future? As Chap-ter 8 explained, overall retail and service prices are not likely to fall even if manufacturing prices decline. Rising federal deficits will also moderate inflation, although they will stabilize at some point. But private borrowing could begin to fall if residential construction and automobile production dwindle because interest rates are no longer falling. A sharp drop in house-hold expenditures on homes and cars would markedly reduce private bor-rowing, especially if business capital expenditures and borrowing recover slowly, and contribute to any deflationary tendency.

That concludes a swift overview of current events and the impact of the federal budget on inflation and deflation. What about the overall relationship of the federal budget and economic activity? In order to sort out the continuing debate surrounding the federal government's taxing and spending programs and their impact on the economy, you must go back to the 19th and early 20th centuries.

ALONG CAME KEYNES

In the 19th and early 20th centuries economics was governed by an axiom known as *Say's Law*: "Supply creates its own demand." This meant that eco-nomic recession and depression and their accompanying unemployment were temporary and self-correcting phenomena. After all, capitalists pro-duce goods for market, and workers offer their labor for hire *so that they, in turn, can demand goods in the marketplace*. If the goods cannot be sold or the labor is not hired, then a lower price or wage will be asked, until price and wage cutting permit all of the goods or labor to be sold. No goods will remain chronically unsold and no labor will remain chronically unemployed as long as prices and wages remain flexible.

Using this line of reasoning, 19th-century economists argued that reces-sion and its concomitant unemployment were transitory phenomena and should generate neither a great deal of concern nor any corrective policy pre-scription by the government. Society and government ought to let well enough alone (i.e., follow the policy of laissez-faire) and let market forces prevail. The operation of the market would eventually restore full employment.

With Say's Law as their guide, no wonder economists could not under-stand the Great Depression, which began in 1929 and hit bottom in 1933. Nor could they understand why the economy's performance remained anemic for so long after 1933. After all, they reasoned, the economy should naturally return to conditions of full production and full employment as business cut prices in order to sell products and workers took wage cuts in order to find employment. If the economy continued in a slump, that was the fault not of the economists and their theories, but of employers and employees who refused to cut prices and wages.

The economists' logic did not help the businesses that were failing or the workers who were out of jobs. Prices and wages had fallen, yet conditions remained dismal; something was dreadfully wrong, and somebody had to do something about it. In America, President Franklin Delano Roosevelt was elected. He responded with massive public-works programs, which, by the way, were funded by federal deficits. The economics community was horrified, and they insisted that the federal government's efforts would merely deny resources to the private sector, and thus provide no net benefit. F.D.R. ignored economic theory. He was a practical man with a practical solution: If people were out of work, then the government would be the employer of last resort and put them to work building roads, parks, bridges, dams, and other public projects.

In 1936, an Englishman named John Maynard Keynes (rhymes with *brains*) gave intellectual credentials to F.D.R.'s practical policies by proposing that the problem was the economists' theories, not the economy. Keynes tackled Say's Law (and the economics establishment) at the knees by declaring that demand could be chronically insufficient and the economy *could* be chronically plagued with substantial excess capacity and unemployment.

Keynes scolded his fellow economists for arguing that their theories were right and that the problem lay with the practical world of business and work that was not living up to theoretical expectations. Science—even "the dismal science" of economics—dictates that a theory that does not conform to the facts must be discarded.

Keynes declared that it was ridiculous to expect price and wage cuts to solve the economy's problem. A totally new approach had to be devised. He believed the only answer was to boost demand by the use of some exogenous (outside) force. Workers could not be expected to buy more under conditions of actual and threatened unemployment, nor business to spend more on plant and equipment when excess capacity and weak profits were the rule. But if consumers and business would not spend, how could the economy pull out of its slump? Through government spending, Keynes argued, even if the government had to borrow funds. Once government began to spend on public works, the people who were employed on these projects would spend their earnings on privately produced goods and services. In a multiplier effect, the total level of demand would be lifted and full employment restored. When the pump-priming operation was over and the private economy was back on its feet, the government could gradually withdraw from the economic scene. Pump-priming by government intervention became know as *Keynesian* economics.

Keynesian theory came to dominate economics, rendering Say's Law archaic. The next generation of economists pushed Keynesian theory a bit further, reasoning that a tax cut could be as effective in priming the pump as an increase in government expenditures. Reducing taxes would increase consumers' disposable income and their consumption expenditures. The new generation believed this would be as effective as an increase in government expenditures for restoring demand to a level sufficient to ensure full employment.

Economists now argued that it didn't matter how the pump was primed, whether through expenditure increases or tax cuts. Putting more into the expenditure stream than was removed from the income stream (in the form of taxes) would always create a net boost in total demand. If government expenditures increased while tax revenues remained the same, the increase in public expenditures would boost demand. If government expenditures remained the same while taxes were cut, the increase in private consumption expenditures would boost demand. In either case, or in both together, the increased government deficit and the borrowing needed to fund that deficit made possible a net addition to total demand.

The increase in the deficit measures the increase in demand, and the government finances that deficit by borrowing from the public through the sale of U.S. Treasury securities. Now, it might seem that borrowing from the public would have the same effect as taxing the public, since it removes funds from the private sector, and would thus neutralize the spending increase. After all, if the public refrains from spending to buy government bonds, isn't the public's expenditure reduced? The answer is yes, if the bonds are purchased by private citizens; however, this is generally not the case. The largest share of bonds is sold to the banking system, which purchases them by creating a demand deposit (checking account) for the government. This is known as "monetizing" the debt, as described in Chapter 8. The fact that the government borrows from the banks permits an increase in government spending without a decrease in private spending.

The federal government's attempts to influence economic activity through its power to tax and spend is known as *fiscal policy*. Although this chapter discusses fiscal policy in the context of the need to stimulate demand in order to deal with recession, it should be clear that fiscal policy could also be employed to deal with inflation. For example, increasing taxes or reducing government expenditures, which would create a surplus, drains spending from the economy, reducing total demand and, consequently, cooling inflation.

As the discussion of fiscal policy continues, remember that it is not the same thing as *monetary policy*, which was discussed in Chapter 8. Monetary policy refers to the actions of the Federal Reserve System; *fiscal policy* refers to the actions of the federal government. Monetary policy works through its influence on the banking system, the money supply, bank lend-ing, and interest rates, whereas fiscal policy works through its direct impact on aggregate demand.

Also keep in mind that fiscal policy is the province solely of the federal government, not of state or local government. Only the federal government has the flexibility to run the necessary budget deficits or surpluses large enough to influence total demand. Most state and local governments are limited, either de facto or de jure, to operating with a balanced budget.

THE KENNEDY TAX CUT

Keynesian economics, with its emphasis on fiscal policy, had won the hearts and minds of academic economists by the early 1960s. Not everyone, how-ever, was convinced. When President Kennedy assumed office in 1961 and proposed a tax cut to stimulate the level of economic activity, Republicans and conservative Democrats in Congress attacked it as fiscally irresponsi-ble. They demanded a balanced budget and argued that tax cuts would gen-erate unacceptable deficits. President Kennedy's Keynesian reply was that the deficits would disappear as soon as the tax cut stimulated the level of demand, output, and income, providing even greater tax revenues, despite the decline in the tax rate. These arguments did not immediately persuade Congress, and the tax cut did not pass until the spring of 1964, following Pres-ident Kennedy's assassination.

The nation enjoyed full employment and a balanced budget in 1965, and Keynesian fiscal policy became an accepted method of "fine-tuning" the economy. Indeed, this technique became so legitimate that it was employed by the next two Republican presidents. President Nixon cut taxes to deal with the 1970 recession, and President Ford cut taxes to deal with the 1974–1975 recession. In each case, the Federal Reserve also pursued an easy money policy in order to stimulate demand. Conservatives joined lib-erals and Republicans agreed with Democrats that tax cuts were necessary to get the economy moving.

By the late 1970s, however, severe inflation prompted a new and grow-ing group of economists to conclude that attempts to stimulate demand with easy money and easy fiscal policies had gone awry. Escalating inflation, which reduced real income, had drawn more and more people into the labor force. The new entrants to the labor force, usually the secondary or tertiary wage earners in the family, had fewer skills and thus were more difficult to employ. Unemployment grew as inflation escalated. The economy had the worst of both worlds. Thus, this new group of economists and politicians argued that what was known as "full-employment policy," actually the Keynesian prescription of stimulating demand through easy monetary and fiscal policies, had been a failure.

Moreover, they continued, increased inflation had discouraged savings and investment. Rising prices penalized savers for their thrift, because the value of real savings fell. This encouraged personal indebtedness rather than saving, and inasmuch as saving is the ultimate source of all funds for investment, the level of investment was bound to shrink over time. These critics charged that the lack of savings and the resulting lack of investment were reflected by the low levels of business investment in new machinery and technology and by the resulting decline in productivity.

Finally, they attacked the progressive income tax, which propelled people into higher tax brackets despite a drop in real income. Higher marginal tax rates, they said, removed the incentive to work more and to work harder.

Why should businesses invest in new ideas, new products, and more efficient ways of doing things if higher taxes confiscated the profits? Why should workers put in more hours on the job if higher taxes reduced the additional pay to a meaningless figure?

SUPPLY-SIDE ECONOMICS

The views of these economists and politicians came to be called *supply-side* economics, which they developed in contrast to *demand-side*, or Keynesian, economics. The supply-siders argued that it was more important to support policies that bolstered the economy's ability to supply or produce more goods than to enhance demand. Therefore, the supply-side economists advocated drastic federal income tax reductions over a three-year period, with deficits to be avoided by a parallel reduction in federal spending. Federal expenditure programs, in their view, tended to overregulate private activity and to waste tax dollars in a variety of boondoggles and unnecessary transfer payments.

Supply-side theory claimed that a massive, across-the-board tax cut would accomplish two major objectives. First, it would provide incentives for increased work, thus boosting output. A greater supply, or output, of goods and services would dampen inflation. Second, increased disposable income would lead to increased savings, providing a pool of funds to finance investment. Once again, the supply of goods and services would be stimulated, and increased output would reduce inflation.

Supply-side economics was a total contradiction of Keynesian fiscal policy, which had prevailed for almost half a century. It was widely and correctly viewed as a device to restrict and contract the federal government, and so it was admired and promoted by conservatives and viewed with suspicion by liberals. The supply-siders began to make their voices heard during President Carter's administration, placing him in a potential quandary. He had pledged to balance the federal budget by the end of his first term in office. Rapid economic expansion and inflation had pushed revenues upward more rapidly than expenditures; consequently, his goal was in sight by late 1979. The tax cut proposed by the supply-siders would have postponed that goal, unless, of course, it was accompanied by large reductions in federal expenditures, which, as a Democrat, President Carter could not endorse.

The 1980 recession created an even sharper dilemma for him. He might have advocated a tax cut (the traditional Keynesian prescription for recession), but this would have played into the hands of the supply-siders, who would have demanded compensating spending cuts. By now the supply-siders had a presidential candidate, Ronald Reagan, as their principal spokesman. The situation was further complicated for President Carter by the fact that the supply-side tax cut favored upper-income groups, rather than the lower-income groups traditionally targeted for tax cuts by the Democrats. Thus, political circumstances precluded President Carter from trying to deal with the 1980 recession by means of tax reductions.

After his inauguration in 1981, as the economy slid into the 1981–1982 recession, President Reagan pushed for and obtained the supply-side tax cuts. What a strange historical reversal: Twenty years after President Kennedy battled Republicans and conservatives for his tax cut, President Reagan now had to battle Democrats and liberals for his. Whereas Democrats had once advocated tax cuts to stimulate the economy and the Republicans had opposed those cuts, it was now the Republicans who were advocating tax cuts over the opposition of the Democrats. The parties had done a complete about-face.

The shift of the mantle of fiscal conservatism from Republicans to Democrats is one of the most important political changes since World War II. President Reagan's supply-side tax cut of 1981–1983 accompanied the recession of 1981–1982. It generated a chaotic reduction in federal revenue, because a smaller proportion of a declining level of income was collected in taxes. Meanwhile, total expenditures continued to grow, despite reductions in the budget left by President Carter. Democrats criticized the resulting deficit and demanded that the tax cuts be rescinded. Republicans insisted that there be no tax increase, despite the deficits.

The debate occurred in the midst of recession and recovery. The Republicans contended that any tax increase would jeopardize the supply-side expansion. The Democrats countered that continued deficits and the accompanying government borrowing drove up interest rates and jeopardized the expansion. Beneath the economic details of the debate, both sides had ideological positions to defend. The Democrats realized that continued deficits put relentless pressures on domestic expenditures. Only a tax increase could generate the revenue that made these expenditure programs affordable. The Republicans were also aware that the only way to deliver a knockout punch to the domestic programs, while increasing military expenditures, was to hold taxes down and let the clamor to end the deficits force legislators to curtail domestic spending. So, the real battle was over domestic programs, not taxes, the deficit, or even supply-side economics. Indeed, there are some political analysts who believe that the whole supply-side argument was only a cynical "Trojan horse," the sole purpose of which was to decimate federal social programs and repeal the New Deal.

In the end, no compromise on these issues was attained. The Democrats held on to the social programs, the Republicans held on to the military programs, and President Reagan made it clear that he would veto any tax increase. The deficit remained. Finally, in a desperate attempt to at least seem to be doing something about the problem, Congress passed the Gramm-Rudman Balanced Budget Act in late 1985, mandating gradual elimination of deficits over a five-year period. The political fight was pushed into the future. The Democrats hoped that military expenditures would be cut and taxes raised, the Republicans and the president hoped that domestic expenditures would be cut, and they all hoped that this Procrustean bed would dismember someone else.

In any event, the Gramm-Rudman Act failed in its objective, because Congress and the president ignored it. By the early 1990s, it was a dead letter.

CROWDING OUT

Meanwhile, the argument over supply-side economics (never the real issue) was lost in the shuffle, as the political wrangling over the impact of the deficit continued. The Democrats insisted that the increased federal borrowing due to the tax cut would crowd out private borrowing (and hence capital expenditures). Ironically, Republicans had criticized President Carter's (shrinking) deficits in the late 1970s on precisely the same grounds. Yet, you have seen that private borrowing exploded in those years. The inconsistencies in the political debate provide further evidence that the real issues were not (and are not) economic.

Indeed, any fear about "crowding out" was misplaced, for it was the actions of the Federal Reserve that largely determined whether private borrowing at reasonable rates was possible. Whenever the Fed pursues a tight money policy, private borrowers must compete with the government for funds; whenever the Fed pursues a sufficiently easy policy, there is room for both private and public borrowing. The point is that difficulty or ease of credit conditions is determined largely by the Fed and not by any crowding out dynamic.

Forget about Crowding Out

- The Fed's influence on interest rates is far more important than the federal government's borrowing.

Keep in mind that the Fed's objective throughout the 1980s was to restrain the expansion rather than stimulate it, so perhaps a little crowding out, if it helped prevent credit conditions from becoming too easy, was not so unhealthy. Tight money restricted consumer borrowing more than business borrowing, allocating funds (and resources) away from consumption expenditures and toward investment expenditures in new plant and equipment.

And as the economy and tax revenues grew in the late 1980s, private borrowing held its own, while federal borrowing shrank (see Charts 9–1 and 9–2 on page 163). Then, the recession of 1990–1991 and the full impact of the S&L crisis hit, multiplying the deficit, but without crowding out private borrowing.

In order to relate this discussion of fiscal policy to the business cycle, you need to know how *not* to relate it. Please realize that the huge federal deficits were responsible for neither the 1981–1982 recession nor the subsequent recovery and expansion. The Federal Reserve's tight money policy generated the recession; the recession choked off inflation; and the stifling of inflation, along with the release of the Fed's grip, is what produced recovery and expansion in the middle and late 1980s.

Thus, President Reagan's administration should be neither blamed for the recession nor lauded for the recovery and expansion or inflation's demise. Those phenomena were created by monetary policy, not fiscal policy.

BALANCING THE BUDGET

You can see from Chart 9–1 that the federal deficit grew enormously with each recession—for two chief reasons. First, recession reduced receipts because of lower personal income tax revenues, unemployment (the unemployed paid no income tax), and lower profits-tax revenues. Second, tax cuts accompanied the recessions of 1970, 1974–1975, and 1981–1982. In addition, note that federal expenditures continued to grow during each recession despite revenue's setback, generating the budget gap. Since the deficit grew with each successive recession, closing this deficit gap became more difficult and took longer every time.

In order to close the deficit gap, receipts must grow more rapidly than expenditures. The gap began to shrink in the late 1980s until the S&L crisis and the 1990–1991 recession hit. Ross Perot made deficit reduction a central plank of his campaign platform in the 1992 presidential election. Mr. Perot's insistent message forced Republican incumbent, George H.W. Bush, and Democratic challenger, Bill Clinton, to also confront the federal-deficit issue.

Both Keynesian and supply-side advocacy and their tolerance for deficits had gone swiftly out of fashion. Ideology had been banished, and balanced-budget pragmatism was in. Bill Clinton promised to reduce the federal deficit when he took office, and he recommended a tax increase that Congress enacted.

Good fortune smiled on President Clinton's terms in office, at least as far as deficit reduction is concerned. Notice (see Chart 9–1 on page 163) federal revenues' increasingly steep trajectory in the 1990s as tax collections rose along with the New Economy's rapidly rising incomes. Expenditure growth flattened because a healthy economy curtailed the need for welfare and unemployment-assistance payments. The deficit shrank in the 1990s as a growing economy generated additional tax revenues and President Clinton's tax increases took hold.

By the end of that decade, and sooner than most analysts had forecast, revenues shot past expenditures (see Chart 9–1) and the deficit was history. Now analysts were forecasting that a new age of budgetary surplus had begun. Then the 2001 recession and tax cuts took hold. Chart 9–1 clearly portrays the sudden slump of tax revenues and the new vigor of federal expenditures. Surpluses had turned to deficits overnight.

President George W. Bush had recommended, and Congress had enacted, sharp tax cuts in order to deal with the 2001 recession. Suddenly, in a reversal reminiscent of the Kennedy and Reagan tax-cut revolutions of the early 1960s and 1980s, balanced-budget pragmatism was out and deficits were O.K. President Bush mobilized both Keynesian and supply-side arguments to press his case for tax cuts, saying that his tax cuts would stimulate both demand and supply. Some tax-cut advocates went so far as to insist that tax cuts would actually reduce the federal deficit by swiftly stimulating the economy. They argued that the percentage gain in income due to the tax cuts would exceed the percentage reduction in the tax rate, thereby boosting federal tax collections.

You can reach your own conclusion as to whether or not tax cuts will spur tax-revenue growth and balance the federal budget. For a timely update on the federal government's fiscal status, turn to the online *Journal*.

Follow these directions to Briefing.com's report:

1. Scroll down the online edition's home page's left-hand menu-bar and click on Economy.
2. Click on Reports from Briefing.com under Data and Resources and then click on Treasury Budget.

Longtime observers had seen it all before. Democrats who had advocated President Kennedy's proposed tax cuts and opposed President Reagan's tax cuts now opposed President Bush's tax cuts as well. These Democrats were now deficit hawks. Republicans who had been fiscal conservatives when that term had meant balanced-budget advocacy now had no objection to bigger federal deficits and larger federal debt. These Republicans were a curious mixture of Keynesian and supply-side advocates. Politics will do that to you.

CONCLUSION

No one could credibly forecast the course of the federal deficit in the years immediately following the 2001 recession, but the word "up" seemed as good as any other description.

Meanwhile, the federal budget was not the only deficit generating consternation among policy makers. The U.S. International Accounts deficit had also reached record size and continued to climb. Turn to Chapter 10 for a discussion of this growing cause for concern.

10

U.S. INTERNATIONAL TRANSACTIONS

POSTWAR PERSPECTIVE

THE PHRASES OF INTERNATIONAL COMMERCE are always in the news. Foreign exchange rates, devaluation, IMF, NAFTA, balance of trade, and the other terms used to discuss America's international economic relations can certainly be defined and described in the context of current events. But to understand them thoroughly, you must think back to World War II. Most of our modern international economic institutions were formed at the end of the war and immediately afterward, when the American dollar assumed the central role in the world's economy that it still plays today. Let's take the time to review postwar international economic developments before plunging into the current data and terminology.

In the summer of 1944, in the resort town of Bretton Woods, New Hampshire, well before World War II came to a close, the United States hosted a conference to plan international monetary affairs for the postwar years, since the Allies were already certain of victory. The United States knew that the war was taking a drastic toll on the rest of the world's economies, while the U.S. economy was growing stronger. Both victor and vanquished would need food, fuel, raw materials, and equipment, but only the United States could furnish these requirements. How were other nations to pay for these imports? They had very little that Americans wanted. If they sold their money for dollars in order to buy goods from us, the strong selling pressure on their currencies and their strong demand for dollars would drive their currencies down in value and the dollar up. Soon the dollar would be so expensive, in terms of foreign currency, that the rest of the world could not afford to buy the American goods necessary to rebuild.

It would have been very easy to say that this was everyone else's problem, not ours, but America's statesmen knew that it was our problem as well. This lesson had been learned the hard way in the aftermath of World War I. Following that war, the United States had washed its hands of international responsibilities; consequently, the world economy had suffered a severe dollar shortage. Many nations were forced to devalue their currencies. Other nations used gold in desperation to settle their accounts with the United States, so America ended up with most of the world's gold supply. Moreover, each nation sought shelter in shortsighted protectionist devices, shattering the world economy. Economic nationalism spilled into the diplomatic arena, where its malevolent force accelerated the world into the second global war.

Determined to avoid these mistakes the second time around, the United States convened the Bretton Woods Conference to anticipate such problems and establish institutions to handle them. The conference's principal task was to prevent runaway depreciation of other currencies after the war. It therefore created the International Monetary Fund (IMF), a pool of currencies to which all nations (but mostly the United States) contributed and from which any nation could borrow in order to shore up the value of its own currency. If a nation's currency was under selling pressure, and weak and falling in value compared to other currencies, buying pressure designed to drive its price upward could be implemented with strong currencies borrowed from the IMF. For instance, Britain could borrow dollars from the IMF to buy pounds, thus supporting the price of the pound.

The dollar was pegged to gold at $35 an ounce, and all other currencies were pegged to the dollar (e.g., a dollar was worth a fixed number of francs or pounds). At the time, the United States had most of the world's gold and other nations had hardly any, so the entire system was tied to gold through the U.S. dollar. This system of fixed exchange rates was constructed to provide stability in international economic relationships. Traders and investors knew exactly what a contract for future delivery of goods or future return on investment was worth in terms of the foreign exchange in which a contract was written. There was no incentive to speculate on shifting exchange rates, which could wipe out profit margins or generate large losses.

To draw an analogy, consider a shipment of oranges from California to New York and investments made by Californians on the New York Stock Exchange. Californians must be concerned about the price of oranges in New York and the price of a share of stock on the exchange, but they need not be concerned about fluctuations in the value of New York currency versus California currency, since both states use dollars. Now think how much more difficult selling and investing in New York would be for Californians if the exchange rate between their currencies fluctuated.

The diplomats wished to avoid precisely that problem after World War II, and that's why the Bretton Woods Conference established the IMF and a system of fixed exchange rates. Unfortunately, after the war, the U.S. balance-of-trade surplus (the amount by which the revenue from all exports exceeds the cost of all imports) created a greater dollar shortage than the conference had anticipated. Other nations were continually selling their currencies in order to buy American dollars with which to purchase American goods. Selling pressure forced down the price of other currencies despite the IMF, which was not large enough to bail them out, and many of these currencies faced runaway depreciation against the dollar.

The United States responded to this crisis with the Marshall Plan. George C. Marshall, a career soldier, had been chairman of the Joint Chiefs of Staff during the war. At the war's end, President Truman appointed him Secretary of State. Marshall understood that a shortage of essential items such as food, fuel, raw materials, and machinery and equipment hobbled Europe's recovery. Only the United States could supply Europe's needs in sufficient quantities. He further understood that the dollar shortage prevented Europe from importing what it needed from the United States. He proposed, and President Truman and Congress approved, a plan whereby the European nations drew up a list of their needs and the United States gave (not loaned) them the dollars they required to satisfy those needs. This reduced the strain on Europe's balance of payments and freed their currencies from the pressure of devaluation. American exports, of course, benefited, as our dollars bounced right back to us for purchases of American goods.

By the time of the Korean War, everyone was talking about the "economic miracle of Europe." The Marshall Plan had been extended to victor and vanquished alike, probably history's greatest example of benevolence as enlightened self-interest. The United States had learned from its mistakes following World War I. Isolationism was myopic; the United States had to play an active role in world affairs. And our generosity would be repaid many times over, as foreign markets for our goods recovered rapidly.

The Marshall Plan became a cornerstone of American foreign policy. The United States provided the rest of the world with desperately needed dollars in this and also a number of other ways, not all of them purposeful. For example, the United States began to maintain a substantial military presence overseas, and our foreign bases salted their host countries with dollars when native civilians were employed at the bases and American personnel spent their paychecks. In addition, American business firms resumed overseas investing, especially in Europe, spending dollars to purchase subsidiaries and to build facilities. Finally, Americans started to travel abroad in great numbers, seeding Europe with funds. All of these activities meant that dollars were sold for foreign exchange (foreign currency), and so they helped offset the constant sale by other nations of their currency in order to buy American goods.

Furthermore, whenever foreign banks, businesses, or individuals received more dollars than were immediately required, they were delighted to deposit those dollars in either American or foreign banks in order to hold them for a rainy day. Since dollars were in vigorous demand because of the continuing need to buy American exports, those dollars could always be sold in the future, and, meanwhile, they were a handy private reserve.

To summarize, there were four principal outflows of dollars from the United States: foreign aid (such as the Marshall Plan), foreign investment, military presence overseas, and tourism. Two principal influxes of foreign exchange offset these outflows: foreign purchase of American exports, which greatly exceeded our purchases of imports, and foreigners' willingness to hold dollars as a liquid investment. The four outflows of dollars (roughly) equaled the two influxes of foreign exchange.

By the late 1950s and early 1960s, however, some foreign banks, businesses, and individuals found that they had more dollars than they could use. They did not wish to buy American goods, and they had found making other investments more attractive than holding dollars, so they decided to sell them.

The United States did not have to rely on the IMF to support the dollar and maintain a fixed exchange rate between the dollar and other currencies. Rather, the U.S. Treasury stood ready to redeem dollars with gold whenever selling pressure on the dollar became heavy: The United States propped up the price of the dollar relative to other currencies by buying the dollar for gold. Since a foreign holder of dollars could buy gold at $35 per ounce and sell that gold for foreign exchange anywhere in the world, there was no need to sell dollars below the fixed rate of exchange. Whenever the dollar fell a little, foreigners would buy gold with their dollars and cash that gold in for other currencies at full value, which kept the dollar up. And the U.S. price of $35 per ounce of gold set the world price for gold, simply because the United States had most of the world's supply. As more and more dollars were redeemed for it, a stream of gold started to leave the United States. American holdings of gold were cut almost in half by the time increasing alarm was voiced in the early 1960s.

An alternative solution had to be found, or else the U.S. supply of gold would disappear. The foreign central banks stepped in and agreed to support the price of the dollar as part of their obligation to maintain fixed exchange rates under the Bretton Woods agreement. These official institutions had potentially limitless supplies of their own currencies. If a bank, business, or individual in another nation wanted to sell dollars, and this selling pressure tended to force the price of the dollar down in terms of that nation's currency, the foreign central bank would buy the dollars for its currency and thus support the price of the dollar.

Neither the U.S. Treasury nor the Federal Reserve System could support the dollar in this way, because neither had limitless supplies of foreign currency. As long as the foreign central banks were willing to buy and accumulate dollars, private citizens, banks, and businesses in other countries were satisfied. In this way, the system of fixed exchange rates survived.

By the late 1960s and early 1970s, however, the situation had once again become ominous. The United States no longer had a favorable balance of trade. Other nations were selling more to, and buying less from, the United States. America's favorable balance of trade had been the single big plus in its balance of payments, offsetting the outflows of dollars mentioned earlier: foreign aid (the Marshall Plan), American tourism, foreign investment, and the American military presence overseas. Now the dollar holdings of foreign central banks began to swell ever more rapidly, as their citizens liquidated dollar holdings. These central banks realized that they were acquiring an asset that ultimately would be of little value to them. Having been put in a position of continually buying dollars they would never be able to sell, they insisted that the United States do something to remedy the situation.

The French suggested that the dollar be officially devalued as a first step, because it had had a very high value in terms of other currencies ever since World War II. They reasoned that if the dollar were worth less in terms of other currencies, American exports would be cheaper for the rest of the world, imports would be more expensive in the United States, and thus the U.S. balance of trade would shift from negative to positive as the United States exported more and imported less. In addition, if foreign currencies were more expensive, Americans would be less likely to travel and invest overseas. This would partially stem the dollar hemorrhage. Others suggested that the foreign central banks stop supporting (buying) the dollar and that the dollar be allowed to float downward to a more reasonable level as foreigners sold off their holdings.

For many years, the United States resisted both devaluation and flotation, until, in a series of developments between 1971 and 1973, the U.S. ceased redeeming the dollar for gold and permitted it to float. It promptly fell, relative to other currencies, because foreign central banks no longer felt obliged to purchase it in order to support its price.

At the same time, the price of gold increased, because the United States would no longer redeem dollars with gold. The willingness of the United States to sell gold virtually without limit at $35 per ounce had kept its value from rising, but now the price of gold could increase according to the forces of private supply and demand. Consequently, it fluctuated with all other commodity prices, rising rapidly during the general inflation at the end of the 1970s and then falling with commodity prices after 1980.

The dollar fell until the summer of 1973, and then it fluctuated in value until the end of the 1970s. Although foreign central banks no longer felt an obligation to buy dollars, they occasionally did so to keep the dollar from plummeting too far or too fast. They took this action in their own interest at the suggestion of exporters, who knew that a low value for the dollar and a high value for their own currencies made it difficult to export to the United States. Nevertheless, by the end of the 1970s the dollar's value was at a postwar low.

The history of the dollar in the 1980s and 1990s was a roller-coaster ride. The dollar's value headed steeply upward in the early 1980s and rose to a new postwar high by mid-decade. After that it fell once again, so that by the late 1980s and early 1990s it had dropped beneath its low in the late 1970s. The dollar began to rise again in the mid-1990s until it climbed above its level in the late 1970s during the 2001 recession. Then the dollar's value fell again as the economy emerged from recession in 2002 and 2003. What caused these ups and downs, and what does the future hold? You can find an answer in *The Wall Street Journal*'s coverage of the U.S. current account, the U.S. balance of trade, and foreign exchange rates.

These few statistical series portraying America's international transactions have generated more confusion in public perception than perhaps any others, but you will see that they are really not difficult to grasp and follow on a regular basis. Take time to familiarize yourself with these series before becoming acquainted with the *Journal*'s coverage.

THE U.S. INTERNATIONAL ACCOUNT

In order to comprehend the *U.S. International Account*, think of yourself as representing the United States in all dealings with the rest of the world. If you wish to do business with the rest of the world, you must buy its currencies (called *foreign exchange*). Likewise, in order to do business in the United States, the rest of the world must buy dollars.

Now set up an accounting statement. The left side will include all the uses you had for all the foreign exchange you purchased. The right side of the account will include all the uses for the dollars that the rest of the world purchased. The two sides must balance: *For every dollar's worth of foreign exchange that you buy with a dollar, the rest of the world must use a dollar's worth of foreign exchange to buy that dollar.* There are no leaks. It is impossible for you to buy any amount of foreign currency without the seller of that currency buying an equivalent value of dollars. It doesn't matter what you do with the foreign exchange you bought, nor what they do with the dollars they bought (even if both of you do *nothing* with your newly purchased money). The international account merely records what both parties do with their funds.

U.S. International Account

Money going out (−)	Money coming in (+)
Uses by the United States for all foreign exchange purchased with U.S. dollars	Uses by the rest of the world for all U.S. dollars purchased with foreign exchange

Congratulations. You have just constructed an international account.

Once the accounting statement has been set up, you may add other details. Each side of the statement will have a *current account* and a *capital account*. Subdivide the current account into merchandise trade, services, and foreign aid; subdivide the capital account into private investment and central bank transactions

U.S. International Account

U.S. purchase of foreign money (debit) (−)	Foreign purchase of U.S. money (credit) (+)
Current account payments by the U.S. to rest of world	*Current account payments to the U.S. by rest of world*
Goods and services imports by the U.S.	Goods and services exports by the U.S.
Merchandise trade imports	Merchandise trade exports

Services for which the U.S. pays the rest of the world	Services the U.S. sells the rest of the world
Foreign aid payments by the U.S. to the rest of the world	Foreign aid payments by the rest of the world to the U.S.
Capital account outflows of funds from the U.S.	*Capital account inflows of funds to the U.S.*
Private investment by the U.S. in the rest of the world	Private investment by the rest of the world in the U.S.
Central bank transactions, e.g., Fed buys foreign currencies	Central bank transactions, e.g., foreign central banks buy dollars

To summarize: The left side of this account (*debit*) shows what you, representing the United States, are doing with the foreign exchange you purchased with American dollars. The right side of the account (*credit*) shows what the rest of the world is doing with the dollars it purchased with its money. Remember, *the two sides must be equal*; a transaction can take place only if things of equal worth are exchanged.

Although the *total* for each side must be equal, the individual categories need not be. You can balance one category against another in order to arrive at a merchandise trade balance, goods and services balances, and so on. Each category in the international account will be examined in turn.

The Current Account

Balance on Goods and Services

Merchandise Trade: You can use the foreign exchange you have purchased to buy foreign goods, and the rest of the world can use dollars to buy American goods. Thus, if you import goods into the United States, you have incurred a debit (−), because you have sold dollars to buy foreign currency in order to make the transaction; in other words, money has left the United States. On the other hand, if the rest of the world buys American goods, you have earned a credit (+). It is customary to talk about the balance on merchandise trade by netting imports against exports to determine whether we have an export (+) surplus or an import (−) deficit.

Services: If you use your dollars to buy foreign currency in order to travel in a foreign country, or to use a foreign air carrier, or to pay interest on a foreign debt, all this would be classified as an outflow of funds, or a debit (−). On the other hand, if the rest of the world uses the dollars it buys to travel in the United States, or to fly with an American air carrier, or to pay interest on a debt to the United States, that flow of money into the United States would be a credit (+).

When the net credit (+) or debit (−) balance on this account is added to the credit (+) or debit (−) balance of the merchandise trade account, this subtotal is referred to as the *balance on goods and services.*

Foreign Aid. If you use the foreign money you have purchased to make a gift to the rest of the world, that's a debit (−); if the rest of the world uses the dollars it has purchased to make a gift to the United States, that's a credit (+). Until the Persian Gulf war, and our request to our allies that they compensate us for Operation Desert Storm, foreign aid had always been a debit (−) entry for the U.S. But in 1991 it temporarily switched to credit (+) and, as you will see, made a big difference in our international transactions that year.

When the foreign aid transaction is combined with the balance on goods and services, it completes the *balance on current account,* which will be a debit (−) balance or a credit (+) balance, depending on whether more funds flowed out of or into the United States.

The Capital Account

Private Investments. As a private investor, you may wish to sell U.S. dollars and buy foreign exchange in order to make an investment somewhere else in the world. This could be a direct investment in the form of plant and equipment expenditures or the purchase of a foreign company, or it could be a financial asset, either long-term or short-term. (Stocks and bonds, for instance are long-term investments, while a foreign bank account or a holding in foreign currency is a short-term investment.)

Any of these transactions will be a debit (−) in the American account, because dollars have left the United States. Conversely, when a private investor in another country sells foreign exchange in order to purchase U.S. dollars to make a direct or financial investment in the United States, whether long-term or short-term, this is classified as a credit (+).

Central Bank Transactions. If, as a representative of the Federal Reserve System, you sell dollars in order to buy foreign currency, this too is a debit (−), and when foreign central banks buy dollars, it is a credit (+).

Surplus and Deficit

Consider one more point before you plow into the data. References are constantly being made to deficits or surpluses in the balances on trade, goods and services, and current account. Now and then you may encounter a comment about a deficit or a surplus in the international account, despite this chapter's assertion that it always balances. How can you explain this apparent paradox?

Trade, goods and services, and current account are easy. You already know that there can be a surplus (+) or a deficit (–) in these separate accounts. But how could anyone speak of a deficit in the total international account when it *must always balance*? Because that is the shorthand way of saying that the nation's currency is under selling pressure and that the value of the currency will fall unless some remedial action is taken.

For instance, at the time (1960s) that the foreign central banks supported the value of the dollar, their purchases of dollars constituted a "plus" (+) in the American balance of payments, because they sopped up the excess dollars that their own economies didn't need. (Had they not done so, the dollar would have fallen in value.) Obviously, if you remove a plus from an accounting system that is in balance, what remains has a negative bottom line. Since a remedial action made the account balance, and since without it the account would have been negative, reference was made to a deficit in the U.S. International Account.

Before 1971, when the United States still sold gold internationally in order to redeem the dollar, these sales were plus (+) entries in our international account. If you wonder why the loss of gold is a plus, remember that anything sold by the United States is a plus because the rest of the world must pay us for it. By removing gold sales from the international account, you assure that the remaining items net out to a negative balance. Therefore, people often referred to the size of the U.S. gold loss as the deficit in the U.S. International Account.

And now for one final tip before you look at the data: Keep your eyes on the money. That's the best way to determine whether something is a plus (+) or minus (–) in the international account. If *we* pay for it, it's a minus, because money is going out. If *they* pay for it, it's a plus.

EXAMINING THE DATA

The Wall Street Journal regularly publishes two Commerce Department reports dealing with the U.S. International Account and the balance of trade that will be useful to you.

1. *Current account* figures for the previous *quarter* appear in the third week of the last month of each quarter.
2. *Monthly balance-of-trade* figures for the previous month are also released in the third week of each month.

WSJ.com THE WALL STREET JOURNAL.
ONLINE

Other Journal Sites

As of 11:02 a.m. EST Friday, March 12, 2004

Home
News
Technology
Markets
Personal Journal
Opinion
Leisure/Weekend

The Print Edition
Today's Edition
Past Editions
Features
Columnists
In-Depth Reports
Discussions
Company Research
Markets Data Center
Site Map
My Online Journal
Portfolio
Personalize My News
E-Mail Setup
My Account/Billing
Customer Service
The Online Journal
The Print Edition
Contact Us
Help
Subscribe

BARRON'SOnline
Advertiser Links
Investor Resource
Center

Lind-Waldock -
Commodity Broker

Financial HP
Workstations at PC
Prices

Free Schwab Guide
to Investment
Advice

ECONOMY

U.S. Current-Account Deficit Narrows, Surprising Experts

DOW JONES NEWSWIRES
March 12, 2004 11:02 a.m.

WASHINGTON -- The U.S. current account deficit, the broadest gauge of the nation's global trade, unexpectedly narrowed in the fourth quarter, while U.S. business inventories posted their fifth straight monthly gain in January.

A separate report from the University of Michigan showed a slight decline in consumer confidence in March.

The trade gap, which measures goods, services and financial transactions, narrowed to $127.5 billion from October through December, the Commerce Department said Friday.

For all of 2003, the current account deficit expanded to a record $541.8 billion, up from 2002's $480.9 billion.

The narrower fourth-quarter deficit surprised economists. A Dow Jones Newswires-CNBC survey of 12 economists had predicted a deficit of $136.0 billion.

The third-quarter deficit was revised to $135.3 billion, a bit higher than the previously reported $135 billion.

The Bush administration has said the best way to handle the mushrooming deficits is to get other countries to remove trade barriers and open their markets to U.S. companies. But Democrats and other critics point to the deficits as evidence that the president's free-trade policies aren't working and are contributing to the loss of U.S. jobs.

A $122.9 billion shortfall in goods and services trade during the fourth quarter -- wider than the $121.6 billion gap in the third period -- made up the bulk of the fourth-quarter current-account deficit.

Foreign transfers, such as foreign-aid payments to international organizations, contributed $17.2 billion to the fourth quarter's current-account deficit, slightly more than the previous quarter. But the balance on investment income recorded a $13.8 billion surplus as Americans earned more on their overseas investments than foreigners did on their U.S. investments.

U.S. Current-Account Deficit

U.S. Current-Account Deficit–Third and Fourth Paragraphs

The trade gap, which measures goods, services and financial transactions, narrowed to $127.5 billion from October through December, the Commerce Department said Friday.

For all of 2003, the current account deficit expanded to a record $541.8 billion, up from 2002's $480.9 billion.

You can find general directions for retrieving *Wall Street Journal* online information (http://online.wsj.com) in Chapter 1 on pages 7 through 11. Appendix D on page **XX** also furnishes you with a quick guide to the *Journal*'s online edition. According to the third paragraph of the Friday, March 12, 2004, *Balance on Current Account* online article on page 186 and above, the U.S. current-account deficit was $127.5 billion in the last quarter of 2003. The current account set a record $541.8 billion deficit for all 2003, as reported in the last paragraph.

The U.S. Department of Commerce's Bureau of Economic Analysis quarterly report is available in the online edition:

1. Scroll down the online edition's home page's left-hand menu-bar and click on Economy.
2. Click on Economic Indicators under Data and Resources and then click on Current Account.

Use Chart 10–1 on page 188 to focus on recent international account developments, with special attention to the following. (Note that this chart displays data at quarterly, not annual, rates.)

Looking at Chart 10–1, first, note that the merchandise trade balance dropped like a stone in the early 1980s, dragging the current-account deficit with it.

Second, the merchandise-trade deficit stopped falling in the late 1980s, halting the deterioration in the current-account balance.

Third, the current-account balance moved back above zero in 1991, although the merchandise-trade balance lagged behind.

Fourth, all balances continued to deteriorate in the 1990s.

Fifth, the merchandise trade balance dragged all balances further downward after 1999, notwithstanding a brief up tick during the 2001 recession.

Service income—such as the net earnings that the United States receives from foreign investments, the sale of banking, transport, and insurance services, and foreign tourism in the United States—comprises most of the gap

CHART 10–1 U.S. International Account: Current-Account Balance, Goods and Services Balance, and Merchandise Trade Balance (Quarterly)

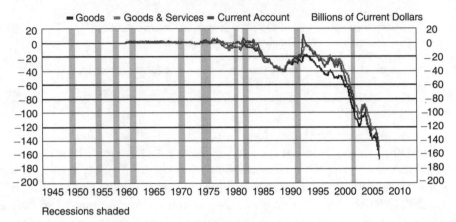

Recessions shaded

Source: U.S. Dept. of Commerce, Bureau of Economic Analysis, *U.S. International Transactions,*
Table 1, line 71,73,76.

between the current account and merchandise trade balance. Notice that, until the late 1970s and early 1980s, U.S. service earnings grew so rapidly that the balance on current account remained positive (+) despite a negative (–) merchandise trade balance.

Then, in the 1980s, the U.S. merchandise trade balance and the balance on current account dropped off the end of the world, so that by the mid-1980s both numbers exceeded $150 billion at annual rates. The following circumstances can explain this development.

1. The Fed's contractionary, anti-inflationary stand in the early 1980s drove U.S. interest rates above world-market levels. Consequently, Americans were reluctant to sell dollars (on which they received high rates of interest), and the rest of the world was eager to buy dollars (in order to enjoy high rates of interest). Strong demand for the dollar drove its price upward, reducing the value of foreign currencies, and thereby making imports relatively attractive to Americans and our goods relatively less attractive to the rest of the world.

2. Even after U.S. interest rates fell, the dollar remained an attractive haven because of President Reagan's perceived pro-business position and the fear of left-wing governments elsewhere. A strong dollar continued to hurt our balance on merchandise trade.

3. Recovery from the 1981–1982 recession proceeded earlier and more swiftly in the U.S. than in the rest of the world. Therefore, our demand for imports grew more rapidly, because American incomes grew more rapidly.

4. As the U.S. led the world out of recession, our economy attracted foreign investment, further boosting the dollar and hurting our trade and current-account balances.

At this point you should return to page 182 and review the International Account statement. If the capital account is positive because of foreign purchases of dollars, as it was all through the 1980s, then the current account must be negative. Otherwise, the international accounts cannot balance. The Japanese bought Rockefeller Center, and we used those funds to purchase Toyotas. Or, to put matters the other way around, because we bought Toyotas, they had the funds to buy Rockefeller Center.

Put it in simple terms. Suppose the rest of the world invests $1 in the U.S. (capital account positive). That provides us with $1 to spend on foreign goods and services. If, in addition, we export $2 worth of goods and services, that provides us with another $2 and a total of $3 ($1 of foreign investment funds plus $2 of export earnings) with which to purchase imports. Because they invested more in us than we invested in them, we had the wherewithal to purchase more from them than they purchased from us.

By way of contrast, the U.S. invested heavily in the rest of the world (−) for most years in the first three-quarters of the 20th century, thereby becoming the world's greatest creditor nation and running a balance-of-trade and current-account surplus (+). But after 1980 we became the world's greatest debtor nation, as the flow of foreign investment capital into the U.S. (+) generated a deficit (−) in the current account.

By the mid-1980s, President Reagan and his advisers viewed the situation with alarm. Free traders, they didn't want Congress imposing tariffs in order to reduce imports. So, we proposed that our major trading partners dump some of the dollars they had accumulated in the 1970s, thereby forcing down the dollar's value. As our export prices fell and import prices rose, the problem would take care of itself because of Americans' shrinking import purchases and foreigners' growing expenditures on our exports.

This agreement, negotiated at New York's Plaza Hotel in 1985, became known as the Plaza Accord and began to show results in 1987. You can see from Chart 10–1 on page 188 that our trade and current account balances began to improve in 1987 and that by the early 1990s these deficits had shrunk considerably. But they had help. Europe's economies broke out of their malaise in the late 1980s. As European incomes grew more rapidly, so did European imports of American goods. This helped reduced our balance of trade deficit.

In any event, you can see that even though the dollar had fallen all the way back down to its pre-1980 level, our balance-of-trade deficit persisted in the early 1990s and then continued to escalate toward the end of the decade. For a brief period, as the 2001 recession reduced America's appetite for imports, our trade deficit shrank, pulling the other current-account numbers up, too. But they all began to deteriorate as soon as economic recovery stimulated our imports in 2002 and 2003. The dollar's fall had not cured America's trade imbalance. Obviously, more was involved than the dollar's value and the relative health of other economies.

But one last point remains regarding the current account before turning to the trade data in *The Wall Street Journal*. Our balance on current account popped back up above zero briefly in 1991 because of payments made to us by our Desert Storm allies. Those payments offset the continued trade deficit and momentarily pushed the current account into the black.

You can use the *Journal* to follow the Commerce Department's monthly merchandise-trade report. The Friday, November 14, 2003, print-edition article provides data for September 2003 (see pages 191 and 192). According to the third paragraph and the statistical summary, the United States ran a $41.27 billion trade deficit in September 2003 due to exports of $86.13 billion and imports of $127.43 billion.

The online edition's Economic Chartbook and Reports from Briefing. com provide the data in chart form:

1. Scroll down the online edition's home page's left-hand menu-bar and click on Economy.

2. Click on Economic Chartbook under Data and Resources and scroll down to Trade Deficit.

3. Click on Reports from Briefing.com under Data and Resources and then click on Trade Balance.

Investor's Tip

• There is no long-run correlation between our balance of trade and the stock market's performance. If the trade figures improve, less attention will be paid to them.

U.S. Trade Deficit Swells 4.4% With Chinese Imports Surging

By NEIL KING JR.

WASHINGTON—A surge in imports widened the U.S. trade deficit in September, but American manufacturers applauded signs that shipments of U.S. goods grew strongly as well.

The tally was another sign of robust growth at the end of the third quarter; both exports and imports had been down in August.

Trade Deficit — The overall imbalance between imports and exports of goods and services grew to $41.27 billion, or 4.4%, as U.S. consumers bought $4.12 billion more in foreign goods and services in September than in August. Imports from China accounted for a quarter of that growth, and rose to a record of $14.79 billion—twice their monthly average of just four years ago.

The total trade gap came in at slightly more than most economists predicted.

But U.S. manufacturers were cheered by news that exports grew by $2.37 billion, largely on increased sales of semiconductors, computer accessories, consumer goods and bulk crops like soybeans.

"This was the largest monthly increase in exports we have seen in 39 months," said Jerry Jasinowski, president of the National Association of Manu-

facturers. "Given the sharp decline of exports in recent years, this is heartening news."

The U.S. saw exports to neighboring Canada and Mexico jump by $2.05 billion. Exports to nearly every other part of the world were flat for the month. Economists attribute the increase in exports to a weaker dollar and increased economic growth overseas.

In another historic marker, it now appears certain that China this year will outpace Mexico for the first time as the second-largest supplier of goods and services to the U.S. after Canada. This comes after China last year bumped Japan from its long-held place as America's third-largest supplier.

Mexico's exports to the U.S. in 2002 topped $134.62 billion compared with $125.19 billion from China. Through September, China's exports were $108.61 bil-

lion compared with $101.93 billion from Mexico.

China's booming sales will undoubtedly increase pressure on Beijing to loosen its tight control on the national currency. Many members of Congress and U.S. manufacturers believe China is maintaining an unfair trade advantage by keeping the yuan undervalued. There is also a growing movement among harder hit U.S. companies to seek trade protections against cheaper Chinese imports.

The September trade deficit with China, $12.69 billion, was the third monthly record in a row. U.S. exports to China in September grew by just $60 million, with totals well below the figures in March and June. At the current rate, the U.S. looks set to rack up an annual trade gap with China exceeding $120 billion, far wider than the $103 billion last year.

The overall import surge came largely on the strength of increased purchases of cars and car parts as well as televisions, VCRs, computer goods, telephones and pharmaceuticals.

Japan's exports to the U.S. grew only slightly, by $200 million, while other Pacific Rim countries also posted small increases.

Mr. Jasinowski, whose organization represents 14,000 U.S. manufacturers, said he anticipated still wider trade deficits in coming months as the world economy continued to revive. But "improving economic conditions abroad in 2004 and continued realignment of the dollar should support stronger export growth and an improving trade balance starting in the middle of next year," he said.

Widening Gap

An ever-larger share of the U.S. trade deficit is due to the imbalance between the U.S. and China. Below, monthly U.S. trade with China.

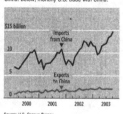

Source: U.S. Census Bureau

Statistical Summary

TRADE

Here are the Commerce Department's monthly trade figures, in billions of dollars.

	Sept. 2003	Aug. 2003-r
Total exports	**$86.16**	**$83.79**
Goods	59.83	57.68
Services	26.33	26.12
Total imports	**127.43**	**123.31**
Goods	106.31	102.40
Services	21.13	20.91
Overall trade balance	**-41.27**	**-39.52**
Goods	-46.48	-44.72
Services	5.21	5.20

r-Revised

FOREIGN EXCHANGE RATES

Each day (Monday's and Saturday's table and chart formats differ) *The Wall Street Journal* publishes several reports on foreign exchange trading activity. Start with the data on the third section's first page, under the **Markets Diary** heading. The excerpt on page 193 from the Thursday, September 21, 2005, issue is an example. The table provides a record of the dollar's value compared to the euro and Japanese yen for the previous day and the past year.

Trade Deficit—Third Paragraph

The overall imbalance between imports and exports of goods and services grew to $41.27 billion, or 4.4%, as U.S. consumers bought $4.12 billion more in foreign goods and services in September than in August. Imports from China accounted for a quarter of that growth, and rose to a record of $14.79 billion—twice their monthly average of just four years ago.

Statistical Summary

TRADE

Here are the Commerce Department's monthly trade figures, in billions of dollars.

	Sept. 2003	Aug. 2003-r
Total exports	$86.16	$83.79
Goods	59.83	57.68
Services	26.33	26.12
Total imports	127.43	123.31
Goods	106.31	102.40
Services	21.13	20.91
Overall trade balance	−41.27	−39.52
Goods	−46.48	−44.72
Services	5.21	5.20

r-Revised

The *Journal* also publishes daily a table on *Exchange Rates* (check the front-page index of the first and third sections under *Currency Trading*). The Monday, December 29, 2003, table appears on page 193. You can use it to keep abreast of the dollar's value against a wide range of currencies other than the euro, which is used by all the major nations of continental Europe. For instance, on Friday, December 26, 2003, the British (U.K.) pound was worth approximately $1.77, the Canadian dollar about $0.77, the Japanese yen about nine-tenths of a cent, and the Swiss franc approximately $0.80.

You can see that these quotations list the value of a single unit of foreign exchange in terms of the American dollar. However, foreign currencies are usually quoted in units per American dollar. Thus on December 26, 2003, the dollar was worth approximately 108 Japanese yen and 1.25 Swiss francs.

MARKETS DIARY / *Sept. 21, 2005*

For an expanded view of yesterday's markets, turn to the **Markets Lineup on page C2.**

	Close	Change	Pct. chg.	52 wks
DJ Industrial Average	10378.03	-103.49 ▼	0.99%	2.66%
Nasdaq composite	2106.64	-24.69 ▼	1.16	11.72
S&P 500	1210.20	-11.14 ▼	0.91	8.68
Russell 2000	649.94	-10.69 ▼	1.62	14.85
Nikkei Stock Average	13196.57	48.00 ▲	0.37	19.76
DJ Stoxx 600 (Europe)	291.89	-3.04 ▼	1.03	21.62
Euro (in U.S. dollars)	$1.2210	$0.0083 ▲	0.68	-0.40
Yen (per U.S. dollar)	111.32	-0.59 ▼	0.52	0.67
Gold (Comex, troy oz.)	$468.90	$2.70 ▲	0.58	15.15
Oil (Nymex, barrel)	$66.80	$0.60 ▲	0.91	38.16

	Yield	Previous	Change in pct. pts.	12-mo return
10-year Treasury	4.18%	4.26% ▼	0.07	*2.97%
3-mo. Treasury	3.40	3.60 ▼	0.20	*2.07
DJ Corporate Bond	5.12	5.17 ▼	0.05	3.16

*Total return via Ryan Labs

Exchange Rates   December 26, 2003

The foreign exchange mid-range rates below apply to trading among banks in amounts of $1 million and more, as quoted at 4 p.m. Eastern time by Reuters and other sources. Retail transactions provide fewer units of foreign currency per dollar.

	U.S. $ EQUIVALENT		CURRENCY PER U.S. $	
Country	Fri	Wed	Fri	Wed
Argentina (Peso)-y	.3387	.3384	2.9525	2.9551
Australia (Dollar)	.7410	.7419	1.3495	1.3479
Bahrain (Dinar)	2.6525	2.6525	.3770	.3770
Brazil (Real)	.3447	.3438	2.9011	2.9087
Canada (Dollar)	.7652	.7644	1.3068	1.3082
1-month forward	.7641	.7633	1.3087	1.3101
3-months forward	.7621	.7614	1.3122	1.3134
6-months forward	.7596	.7588	1.3165	1.3179
Chile (Peso)	.001679	.001683	595.59	594.18
China (Renminbi)	.1208	.1208	8.2781	8.2781
Colombia (Peso)	.0003582	.0003579	2791.74	2794.08
Czech. Rep. (Koruna)				
Commercial rate	.03813	.03821	26.226	26.171
Denmark (Krone)	.1672	.1673	5.9809	5.9773
Ecuador (US Dollar)	1.0000	1.0000	1.0000	1.0000
Egypt (Pound)-y	.1623	.1623	6.1599	6.1599
Hong Kong (Dollar)	.1288	.1288	7.7640	7.7640
Hungary (Forint)	.004780	.004766	209.21	209.82
India (Rupee)	.02200	.02199	45.455	45.475
Indonesia (Rupiah)	.0001177	.0001177	8496	8496
Israel (Shekel)	.2289	.2296	4.3687	4.3554
Japan (Yen)	.009301	.009316	107.52	107.34
1-month forward	.009310	.009326	107.41	107.23
3-months forward	.009328	.009343	107.20	107.03
6-months forward	.009358	.009373	106.86	106.69
Jordan (Dinar)	1.4104	1.4104	.7090	.7090
Kuwait (Dinar)	3.3931	3.3948	.2947	.2946
Lebanon (Pound)	.0006605	.0006605	1514.00	1514.00

	Fri	Wed	Fri	Wed
Malaysia (Ringgit)-b	.2632	.2632	3.7994	3.7994
Malta (Lira)	2.8852	2.8904	.3466	.3460
Mexico (Peso)				
Floating rate	.0889	.0887	11.2461	11.2740
New Zealand (Dollar)	.6475	.6474	1.5444	1.5446
Norway (Krone)	.1472	.1482	6.7935	6.7476
Pakistan (Rupee)	.01740	.01747	57.471	57.241
Peru (new Sol)	.2883	.2887	3.4686	3.4638
Philippines (Peso)	.01801	.01802	55.525	55.494
Poland (Zloty)	.2676	.2675	3.7369	3.7383
Russia (Ruble)-a	.03407	.03420	29.351	29.240
Saudi Arabia (Riyal)	.2666	.2666	3.7509	3.7509
Singapore (Dollar)	.5861	.5862	1.7062	1.7059
Slovak Rep. (Koruna)	.03020	.03027	33.113	33.036
South Africa (Rand)	.1495	.1496	6.6890	6.6845
South Korea (Won)	.0008334	.0008337	1199.90	1199.47
Sweden (Krona)	.1364	.1374	7.3314	7.2780
Switzerland (Franc)	.7973	.8015	1.2542	1.2477
1-month forward	.7979	.8021	1.2533	1.2467
3-months forward	.7991	.8033	1.2514	1.2449
6-months forward	.8008	.8049	1.2488	1.2424
Taiwan (Dollar)	.02941	.02941	34.002	34.002
Thailand (Baht)	.02527	.02524	39.573	39.620
Turkey (Lira)	.00000071	.00000070	1408451	1428571
U.K. (Pound)	1.7704	1.7745	.5648	.5635
1-month forward	1.7662	1.7703	.5662	.5649
3-months forward	1.7579	1.7620	.5689	.5675
6-months forward	1.7450	1.7492	.5731	.5717
United Arab (Dirham)	.2723	.2723	3.6724	3.6724
Uruguay (Peso)				
Financial	.03420	.03420	29.240	29.240
Venezuela (Bolivar)	.000626	.000626	1597.44	1597.44
SDR	1.4751	1.4751	.6779	.6779
Euro	1.2429	1.2452	.8046	.8031

Special Drawing Rights (SDR) are based on exchange rates for the U.S., British, and Japanese currencies. Source: International Monetary Fund.

a-Russian Central Bank rate. b-Government rate. y-Floating rate.

World Value of the Dollar

The table below, based on foreign-exchange quotations from Reuters, gives the rates of exchange for the U.S. dollar against various currencies as of Friday, September 23, 2005. Unless otherwise noted, all rates listed are middle rates of interbank bid and asked quotes, and are expressed in foreign currency units per one U.S. Dollar.

Country (Currency)	Value 09/23	Value 09/16	Country (Currency)	Value 09/23	Value 09/16	Country (Currency)	Value 09/23	Value 09/16
Albania (Lek)	102.160	101.055	Ghana (Cedi)	9025	9075	Paraguay (Guarani) d	6123	6128
Algeria (Dinar)	72.5950	72.5500	Gibraltar (Pound)	0.5597	0.5521	Peru (Nuevo Sol) d	3.3124	3.2927
Angola (New Kwanza)	89.2022	89.2073	Greenland			Philippines (Peso)	56.2430	56.2114
Angola			(Danish Krone)	6.1932	6.0960	Pitcairn Island		
(Readj Kwanza)	89.2022	89.2073	Grenada			(NZ $)	1.4530	1.4203
Antigua			(East Caribbean $)	2.6700	2.6900	Poland (Zloty) o	3.2145	3.1762
(East Caribbean $)	2.6700	2.6900	Guadeloupe (Euro)	0.8301	0.8174	Puerto Rico (US $)	1.0000	1.0000
Argentina (Peso)	2.9087	2.9112	Guam (US $)	1.0000	1.0000	Qatar (Rial)	3.6386	3.6386
Armenia (Dram)	448.500	463.500	Guatemala (Quetzal)	7.6400	7.6175	Reunion, Ile de la		
Aruba (Florin)	1.7900	1.7900	Guinea Bissau			(Euro)	0.8301	0.8174
Australia (Dollar)	1.3205	1.3028	(CFA Franc)	544.34	532.41	Romania (New Leu)	2.9607	2.8423
Azerbaijan (Manat)	4593.0	4506.0	Guinea Rep (Franc)	3925.0	3935.0	Russia (Ruble) m, b	28.4738	28.3768
Bahamas (Dollar)	1.0000	1.0000	Guyana (Dollar)	190.000	190.000	Rwanda (Franc)	542.75	542.75
Bahrain (Dinar)	0.3770	0.3770	Haiti (Gourde)	41.9000	41.4000	Saint Christopher		
Bangladesh (Taka)	65.7325	65.7350	Honduras Rep			(East Caribbean $)	2.6700	2.6900
Barbados (Dollar)	1.9900	1.9888	(Lempira)	18.8600	18.8600	Saint Helena (Pound)	0.5597	0.5521
Belarus (Ruble)	2152.0	2153.5	Hong Kong (Dollar)	7.7588	7.7610	Saint Lucia		
Belize (Dollar)	1.9600	1.9700	Hungary (Forint)	206.101	201.126	(East Caribbean $)	2.6700	2.6900
Benin (CFA Franc)	544.34	532.41	Iceland (Krona)	62.2050	61.8350	Saint Pierre (Euro)	0.8301	0.8174
Bermuda (Dollar)	0.9700	0.9600	India (Rupee) m	43.8596	43.8404	Saint Vincent		
Bhutan (Ngultrum)	43.8300	43.8000	Indonesia (Rupiah)	10225	10152	(East Caribbean $)	2.6700	2.6900
Bolivia			Iran (Rial) o	9013	9015	Samoa, American		
(Boliviano) f	8.0375	8.0375	Israel (Shekel)	4.6019	4.5393	(US $)	1.0000	1.0000
Bosnia & Herzeg.			Ivory Coast			Samoa, Western		
(Convertible Mark)	1.6096	1.5912	(CFA Franc)	544.34	532.41	(Tala)	2.6525	2.6972
Botswana (Pula)	5.3792	5.4054	Jamaica (Dollar) o	62.5250	62.5250	Sao Tome and Principe		
Bouvet Island			Japan (Yen)	112.423	111.359	(Dobra)	7830	7883
(Krone)	6.4778	6.3712	Jordan (Dinar)	0.7085	0.7081	Saudi Arabia (Riyal)	3.7509	3.7495
Brazil (Real)	2.2650	2.2989	Kazakhstan (Tenge)	134.175	134.045	Senegal (CFA Franc)	544.34	532.41
Brunei (Dollar)	1.6844	1.6789	Kenya (Shilling)	72.9000	73.5500	Seychelles (Rupee)	5.4175	5.4175
Bulgaria (Lev)	1.6233	1.5986	Kiribati			Sierra Leone (Leone)	2355.0	2355.0
Burkina Faso			(Australia $)	1.3205	1.3028	Singapore (Dollar)	1.6849	1.6818
(CFA Franc)	544.34	532.41	Korea, North (Won)	2.0000	2.0000	Slovakia (Koruna)	32.0616	31.3283
Burundi (Franc)	1036.0	1036.0	Korea, South (Won)	1030.5	1030.5	Slovenia (Tolar)	198.755	195.740
Cambodia (Riel)	4115.0	4105.0	Kuwait (Dinar)	0.2920	0.2921	Solomon Islands		
Cameroon (CFA Franc)	544.34	532.41	Laos, People DR			(Dollar)	7.1556	7.4627
Canada (Dollar)	1.1712	1.1787	(Kip)	10400	10400	Somalia (Shilling) d	2132.5	2172.0
Cape Verde Isl			Latvia (Lat)	0.5776	0.5689	South Africa		
(Escudo)	91.7500	90.4500	Lebanon (Pound)	1503.1	1503.5	(Rand) c	6.3735	6.3857
Cayman Islands			Lesotho (Maloti)	6.3725	6.2750	Sri Lanka (Rupee)	101.420	101.450
(Dollar)	0.8200	0.8200	Liberia (US $)	1.0000	1.0000	Sudan (Dinar) c	250.715	250.715
Central African Rep			Libya (Dinar)	1.3150	1.3140	Sudan Rep (Pound)	2507.2	2507.2
(CFA Franc)	544.34	532.41	Liechtenstein			Suriname (Guilder)	2515.0	2515.0
Chad (CFA Franc)	544.34	532.41	(Swiss Franc)	1.2921	1.2695	Swaziland		
Chile (Peso)	537.63	535.62	Lithuania (Lita)	2.8656	2.8220	(Lilangeni)	6.3725	6.2750
China (Yuan)	8.0881	8.0887	Macau (Pataca)	8.0061	8.0061	Sweden (Krona)	7.7882	7.6453
Colombia (Peso) o	2288.9	2299.9	Macedonia (Denar)	47.8500	47.8500	Switzerland (Franc)	1.2922	1.2695
Comoros (Franc)	405.500	402.500	Madagascar DR			Syria (Pound)	52.2100	52.2100
Congo Dem Rep			(Malagasy Ariary)	2064.5	2055.9	Taiwan (Dollar) o	33.1785	32.9381
(CFA Franc)	544.34	532.41	Malawi (Kwacha)	124.300	124.160	Tanzania (Shilling)	1139.0	1136.3
Congo, People Rep			Malaysia (Ringgit) e	3.7685	3.7695	Thailand (Baht)	41.1015	41.0172
(CFA Franc)	544.34	532.41	Maldives (Rufiyaa)	12.7800	12.8200	Togo, Rep		
Costa Rica (Colon)	486.700	485.600	Mali Rep (CFA Franc)	544.34	532.41	(CFA Franc)	544.34	532.41
Croatia (Kuna)	6.1626	6.0880	Malta (Lira)	0.3521	0.3507	Tonga Islands		
Cuba (Peso)	1.0000	1.0000	Martinique (Euro)	0.8301	0.8174	(Pa'anga)	1.9675	1.9531
Cyprus (Pound)	0.4755	0.4681	Mauritania (Ouguiya)	268.170	268.170	Trinidad & Tobago		
Czech Republic			Mauritius (Rupee)	29.6800	29.6000	(Dollar)	6.2581	6.2768
(Koruna)	24.4499	23.7699	Mexico (Peso)	10.8366	10.8425	Tunisia (Dinar)	1.3375	1.3202
Denmark (Krone)	6.1920	6.0976	Moldova (Leu)	12.5900	12.5500	Turkey (New Lira)	1.3495	1.3425
Djibouti (Franc)	174.250	172.700	Mongolia (Tugrik) m	1193.0	1193.0	Turks & Caicos		
Dominica			Montserrat			(US $)	1.0000	1.0000
(East Caribbean $)	2.6700	2.6900	(East Caribbean $)	2.6700	2.6900	Uganda (Shilling)	1859.5	1852.8
Dominican Rep (Peso)	30.8500	30.7500	Morocco (Dirham)	9.1172	9.0053	Ukraine (Hryvnia)	5.0238	5.0100
Ecuador (US $) g	1.0000	1.0000	Mozambique (Metical)	24750	24450	United Arab Emir.		
Egypt (Pound)	5.7600	5.7670	Myanmar (Kyat)	6.4200	6.4200	(Dirham)	3.6730	3.6730
El Salvador			Namibia (Dollar)	6.3725	6.3440	United Kingdom		
(Colon) d	8.7520	8.7520	Nauru Island			(Pound Sterling)	0.5625	0.5531
Equatorial Guinea			(Australia $)	1.3205	1.3028	Uruguay (Peso) m	24.0385	24.0964
(CFA Franc)	544.34	532.41	Nepal (Rupee)	69.7500	69.7500	Vanuatu (Vatu)	110.800	110.150
Estonia (Kroon)	12.9430	12.7884	Netherlands Antilles			Venezuela		
Ethiopia (Birr) o	8.7157	8.7157	(Guilder)	1.7800	1.7800	(Bolivar) d	2145.9	2145.9
European Union			New Zealand (Dollar)	1.4533	1.4203	Vietnam (Dong) o	15875	15885
(Euro)	0.8301	0.8174	Nicaragua			Virgin Islands		
Faeroe Islands			(Cordoba Oro)	16.3700	16.3700	(US $)	1.0000	1.0000
(Danish Krone)	6.1932	6.0960	Nigeria (Naira) m	132.300	131.800	Yemen (Rial) a	182.500	182.750
Falkland Islands			Norway (Krone)	6.4767	6.3694	Yugoslavia		
(Pound)	0.6269	0.6269	Oman (Sul Rial)	0.3850	0.3850	(New Dinar)	70.6150	68.8921
Fiji (Dollar)	1.6955	1.6863	Pakistan (Rupee)	59.8444	59.8444	Zambia (Kwacha)	4355.0	4325.0
French Guiana (Euro)	0.8301	0.8174	Panama (Balboa)	1.0000	1.0000	Zimbabwe (Dollar)	26003	26002
Gabon (CFA Franc)	544.34	532.41	Papua New Guinea					
Gambia (Dalasi)	28.2250	27.8500	(Kina)	2.9630	3.0143			

*US $ per national currency unit. a-parallel. b-Russian Central Bank rate. c-commercial. d-freemarket. e-Government rate. f-financial. h-Floating rate as of 2/22/01. m-market. o-official.

The online edition also provides exchange-rate data:

1. Scroll down the online edition's home page's left-hand menu-bar and click on Markets and Markets Data Center.

2. Scroll down to Currencies in the right-side list and click on Exchange Rates.

Most foreign-exchange trading is conducted by banks on behalf of their customers. Banks will also provide future delivery of foreign exchange for customers who want a guaranteed price in order to plan their operations and limit risk due to exchange-rate fluctuation. The price for future delivery is known as the *forward rate,* and you can see forward quotes for the major currencies immediately beneath the current rate.

Every day (Monday's table and chart format differs) the *Journal* also provides exchange rates for major currencies in terms of each other's value and on Saturdays publishes a weekly comparison of the dollar's value against almost every currency in the world. See **World Value of the Dollar** from the Saturday, September 24, 2005, issue on page 194.

You can also obtain these data from the online edition:

1. Scroll down the online edition's home page's left-hand menu-bar and click on Markets and Markets Data Center.

2. Scroll down to Currencies in the right-side list and click on Key Cross Rates and World Value of Dollar.

The example of *Key Currency Cross Rates* on page 196 is drawn from the Thursday, April 8, 2004, online edition.

Recall the earlier outline of the dollar's postwar history (see pages 187–190). Chart 10–2 on page 197 provides graphic evidence of the dollar's value in terms of the most important foreign currencies. The dollar fell to its post–World War II low (at the time) against most currencies in the late 1970s because of severe inflation here at home and its impact on our trade balance. The merchandise-trade balance sank dramatically, as rising prices impeded our ability to sell and whetted our appetite for imports (see Chart 10–1 on page 188). Since people in the rest of the world needed fewer dollars (because they weren't buying as many of our goods) and we needed more foreign exchange (because we were buying more of their goods), the dollar's value plunged.

The dollar's rally in the early 1980s was a two-phase process. The first phase in 1981–1982 had two major causes.

First, high interest rates strengthened the dollar. When interest rates in the United States are higher than interest rates elsewhere, foreign exchange

News   Technology   Markets   Personal Journal

MARKETS DATA
SECTION INDEX ⊕

Key Currency Cross Rates
For late New York Trading Thursday, April 8, 2004

The New York foreign exchange selling rates below apply to trading among banks in amounts of $1 million and more, as quoted at 4 p.m. Eastern time by Dow Jones and other sources. Retail transactions provide fewer units of foreign currency per dollar.

REUTERS ◗

	Dollar	Euro	Pound	SFranc	Peso	Yen	CdnDlr
Canada	1.3271	1.6032	2.4340	1.0342	0.1185	0.0125	....
Japan	106.28	128.39	194.92	82.825	9.4899	....	80.083
Mexico	11.200	13.529	20.540	8.7277	....	0.1054	8.4388
Switzerland	1.2832	1.5501	2.3534	....	0.1146	0.0121	0.9669
U.K.	0.5453	0.6587	....	0.4249	0.0487	0.0051	0.4109
Euro	0.8278	....	1.5182	0.6451	0.0739	0.0078	0.6238
U.S.	....	1.2080	1.8340	0.7793	0.0893	0.0094	0.7535

Source: Reuters

is sold for dollars, and the capital accounts will show a net flow of private investment into the United States. The Fed's tight money policy pushed interest rates in the United States higher than those in Europe and Japan, prompting heavy dollar purchases by foreign investors who wished to enjoy the high interest rates available here. (See the list of reasons on page 188 for the U.S. current-account deficit in the early 1980s.)

Second, the U.S. balance on current account improved dramatically until late 1982 because of rapidly growing service income and despite a sharply negative balance of trade. This positive element in the U.S. international accounts not only generated a flow of dollars into the United States but also encouraged private businesses and individuals in the rest of the world to invest in dollars, because they believed that the dollar would remain strong in the future.

The second phase in 1983–1984 is somewhat more complex. The interest rate differential between the United States and the rest of the world had narrowed since mid-1982, while the balance on current account deteriorated rapidly due to the plunge in our merchandise trade balance (see Chart 10–1).

Under these circumstances, the dollar's value should have fallen. Nev-

CHART 10–2 Foreign Exchange Rates

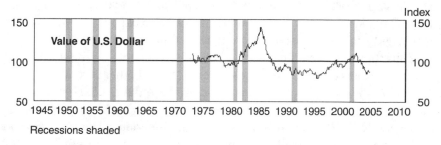

Recessions shaded

Source: The Conference Board, *Business Cycle Indicators,* Series U0M750.

Recessions shaded

Source: The Conference Board, *Business Cycle Indicators,* Series U0M758.

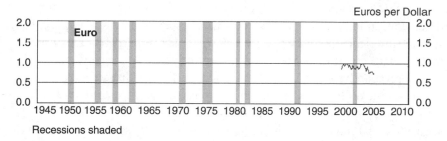

Recessions shaded

Source: Federal Reserve.

ertheless, it improved because of the continuing flow of investment dollars into the United States and the continuing reduced flow of our investment dollars to the rest of the world. The rest of the world believed America to be the safest, most profitable home for its funds. To foreigners (indeed, to many Americans), President Reagan symbolized America's protection of, and concern for, business interests. Certainly, the United States was a secure haven: Investments would not be expropriated, nor would their return be subject to confiscatory taxation. And the return was good; even if the interest rate differential between here and abroad had narrowed, U.S. rates were still higher than those in most other countries. Moreover, profits had been strong, and the stock market reflected this. Foreign investors who built a stake in our stock market and American business were rewarded handsomely.

Thus, the dollar remained strong because the huge net capital flow into the United States bid the dollar's price up and forced other currencies down. The rise in the dollar's value, together with the quicker economic expansion here than abroad, depressed our exports and stimulated our imports. Consequently, the deterioration in our merchandise trade balance in 1983 and 1984 was a result of the dollar's appreciation, not a cause of it.

But by 1985 the U.S. began to pressure our major trading partners, requesting their assistance in reducing our trade deficit by driving the dollar's value down. They (i.e., their central banks) complied by agreeing to the Plaza Accord and sold dollars, contributing to the dollar's slide. As a result, by the late 1980s, the dollar had lost most of the increase of the early 1980s.

The dollar stopped falling by the end of the 1980s for a variety of reasons. Rapid export growth halted the surge in our balance-of-trade deficit. American interest rates rose. Foreign central banks actively supported the dollar once again because they were no longer willing to let the dollar fall in order to protect our markets from their exports. These developments stimulated dollar purchases and helped halt the dollar's decline.

The dollar remained low throughout the 1990s, depressed by renewed deterioration in America's balance of trade (see Chart 10–1 on page 188). As the American economy operated at higher levels and grew faster than its trading partners, it drew vast quantities of imports. Americans sold dollars in order to purchase foreign goods, and the dollar's value stayed depressed.

Then the dollar began to climb again as foreign investors poured funds into the U.S. stock market. They bought dollars in order to purchase U.S. securities, and that bid the dollar upward. The dollar's value grew with the expansion of the millennium bubble. When the bubble burst in the 2001 recession, foreign investors' enthusiasm for U.S. stocks cooled and they repatriated their funds. The dollar's value slid as foreign investors dumped stocks and sold dollars in order to purchase their own currencies.

Chart 10–2 on page 197 shows that the dollar continued to fall through 2003. A number of forces worked to depress the dollar's value. First, American economic recovery stimulated our demand for imports and, hence, sales of the dollar to purchase other currencies. The continued deterioration of the current account symbolized U.S. demand for foreign exchange to buy foreign goods and services. Second, the rest of the world's enthusiasm for American investments deteriorated after the bursting of the millennium bubble. As we eagerly consumed foreign products and the rest of the world less eagerly invested here, our demand for foreign exchange grew more rapidly than foreign demand for dollars. Consequently the dollar's value fell.

Investor's Tip

- This brief history should warn you how difficult it is to predict the dollar's value and the course of international economic events. That's why foreign exchange speculation is not for amateurs. Even some pros go broke doing it.

CONCLUSION

The continued fall of the dollar, as outlined in the previous paragraph, raised the following concern: If foreign investors became increasingly leery of investing in the U.S. and, worse yet, began liquidating their holdings of U.S. investments, the dollar would fall. If American demand for imports remained strong nonetheless, the dollar's value would deteriorate even further. As the dollar's value cascaded downward, foreign holders of American investments would preemptively liquidate those investments to avoid a capital loss. (For a foreigner, the value of dollar-denominated investments falls with the dollar's value.) Moreover, the sale of dollar-denominated investments, such as U.S. Treasury securities, would depress their price and raise U.S. interest rates. A sharp interest-rate jump could engender recession.

The preceding scenario showcases the fear of many that America's rising international indebtedness could contribute to domestic economic instability.

The next chapter introduces the composite index of leading economic indicators, designed and devised to forecast the economic and business developments we've discussed thus far.

11

LEADING ECONOMIC INDICATORS

ECONOMIST'S BAROMETER

NOW THAT YOU HAVE EXAMINED THE BUSINESS CYCLE in detail and learned to use *The Wall Street Journal*'s statistical series, you may be looking for a device to make analysis somewhat easier. Perhaps, while wading through the stream of data, you felt the need for a single indicator that could predict changes in the business cycle.

You want something akin to the meteorologist's barometer, to inform you of rain or shine without a detailed examination of cloud formations. Unfortunately, economists have never agreed on a single economic indicator to predict the future. Some indicators are better than others, but none is consistently accurate; all give a false signal on occasion. To deal with this, economists have devised a composite, or combination, of statistical series drawn from a broad spectrum of economic activity, each of which tends to move up or down ahead of the general trend of the business cycle.

These series are referred to as leading indicators because of their predictive quality. Ten have been combined into the *composite index of leading economic indicators* by The Conference Board, a New York research organization.

The components of the index are:

1. Average weekly hours, manufacturing.
2. Average weekly initial claims for unemployment insurance.
3. Manufacturers' new orders in 1992 dollars, consumer goods and materials industries.
4. Vendor performance—slower deliveries diffusion index.
5. Manufacturers' new orders in 1992 dollars, nondefense capital goods industries.
6. New private housing units authorized by local building permits.
7. Stock prices, 500 common stocks (S&P 500).
8. Money supply—M2—in 2000 dollars.
9. Interest rate spread, 10-year Treasury bonds less federal funds rate.
10. University of Michigan index of consumer expectations.

There are three general criteria for inclusion in the index. First, each series must accurately lead the business cycle. Second, the various series should provide comprehensive coverage of the economy by representing a wide and diverse range of economic activity. And, third, each series must be available monthly, with only a brief lag until publication, and must be free from large subsequent revisions.

The leading indicators meet these criteria, and weaving these series into a composite provides a statistic that is more reliable and less erratic than any individual component by itself.

Finally, the component indicators measure activity in physical units, current dollars, constant dollars, percentages, interest rates, and index form. This variety of measurements is reduced to an index with 1996 assigned a base value of 100. All other months and years are expressed as a percentage of the base year.

The report in the Thursday, January 22, 2004, online edition (see page 202) of *The Wall Street Journal*, is representative. (You can find general directions for retrieving *Wall Street Journal* online information (http://online.wsj.com) in Chapter 1 on pages 7 through 11. Appendix D on page 374 also furnishes you with a quick guide to the *Journal*'s online edition.) This statistic usually appears in the fourth week of the month. According to the January 22, 2004, online edition's third paragraph (see page 203), the index had risen to 114.3 (1996 = 100) by December 2003.

WSJ.com THE WALL STREET JOURNAL.
ONLINE

Other Journal Sites

As of 11:06 p.m. EST Thursday, January 22, 2004

Home
News
Technology
Markets
Personal Journal
Opinion
Leisure/Weekend

The Print Edition
Today's Edition
Past Editions
Features
Columnists
In-Depth Reports
Discussions
Company Research
Markets Data Center
Site Map
My Online Journal
Portfolio
Personalize My News
E-Mail Setup
My Account/Billing
Customer Service
The Online Journal
The Print Edition
Contact Us
Help
Subscribe

BARRON'S Online

Advertiser Links
Investor Resource
Center

Lind-Waldock -
Commodity Broker

Financial HP
Workstations at PC
Prices

Free Schwab Guide
to Investment
Advice

ECONOMY

Leading Index, Jobless Report Show U.S. Economy Is Growing

A WALL STREET JOURNAL ONLINE NEWS ROUNDUP
January 22, 2004 11:06 p.m.

Leading economic indicators rose in December and pointed to job growth in early 2004.

Indeed, layoffs appeared to be subsiding as initial jobless claims dropped last week and the four-week moving average hit another three-year low.

The Conference Board reported Thursday that its composite index of leading indicators climbed 0.2% in December to 114.3, after a revised 0.2% gain a month earlier. The index was equal to 100 in 1996.

Leading Indicators

The private research group attributed much of the positive December reading to financial and labor market developments.

"All indicators point to continued economic growth," Conference Board economist Ken Goldstein said in a press release. "More job gains than in November and December are in store for the early months of 2004," along with continued robust consumer spending and an uptick in business investment, he said.

Seven out of 10 indicators in the index rose in December. The biggest positive contributors to the index were vendor performance, stock prices, building permits and falling claims for unemployment insurance. The biggest drag was a drop in money supply.

Meanwhile, initial jobless claims fell by 1,000 in the week ending Saturday to a seasonally adjusted 341,000, the Labor Department reported Thursday. The four-week moving average, which smooths out weekly fluctuations, fell by 3,250 to 344,500. The last time claims were lower was in the week ending Jan. 27, 2001, when they dropped to 338,000.

Economists had expected claims to rise by 2,000, according to a survey by Dow Jones and CNBC. A Labor Department statistician said "no special factors" caused the drop.

Claims for the previous week, ended Jan. 10, were revised downward by 1,000 to 342,000. That was the first downward revision in roughly one and a half years.

Economists believe the labor market is recovering, albeit gradually, from a three-year slump. Jobless claims have held below 400,000 for 16 consecutive weeks. Anything below that level is widely seen as an indication of an improving labor market.

Leading Indicators–Third Paragraph

The Conference Board reported Thursday that its composite index of leading indicators climbed 0.2% in December to 114.3, after a revised 0.2% gain a month earlier. The index was equal to 100 in 1996.

The online edition's Economic Indicators and Reports from Briefing.com provide the Conference Board's latest bulletin as well as data in chart form:

1. Scroll down the online edition's home page's left-hand menu-bar and click on Economy.
2. Click on Economic Indicators under Data and Resources and then click on Leading Indicators.
3. Click on Reports from Briefing.com under Data and Resources and then click on Leading Indicators.

You can see from Chart 11–1 below that the index did a good job of forecasting recession except in 1981–1982 and 1990–1991. For all other instances, the index forecast of the downturn seems clear. In 1981–1982

CHART 11–1 Composite Index of 10 Leading Indicators

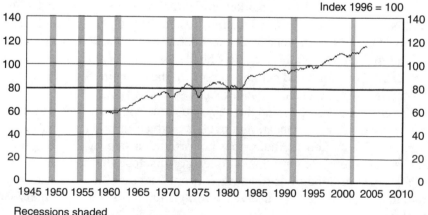

Recessions shaded

Source: The Conference Board, *Business Cycle Indicators,* Series GOM 910.

you should observe that lead-time presents a difficult call because the index double-clutched just prior to the recession's start. The first pump on the clutch is at least a half-year before the downturn begins. The index sloped downward ever so slightly before the 1990–1991 recession, following a lethargic performance in the late 1980s. This lends credence to the observation made earlier that there might have been no recession in 1990–1991 had it not been for the Persian Gulf crisis.

But you can also see the false alarms of 1962, 1966, 1984, and 1987. In each case the index fell for at least three consecutive months, although no recession followed.

The 1962 decline followed on the heels of President Kennedy's forced rollback of Big Steel's price increase. The stock market went into shock and business activity slowed, but you can see that the setback was brief. This decline was clearly a random event and of no cyclical significance.

The indicators' 1966 setback was more like developments in the 1980s. The Vietnam War had begun, and inflation was climbing. The Fed tightened in response, in order to raise interest rates and curb consumer and business demand. Housing starts crashed, and it was "nip-and-tuck" for a while, but the Fed quickly eased when alarm spread so that recession never took hold.

The Fed faced similar conditions and tightened in 1984 as the cycle came roaring back from the 1981–1982 recession. The economy went into the doldrums temporarily, and the leading indicators fell, but once again the Fed eased as soon as inflation subsided, and the economy emerged with only a scratch.

The October 1987 stock market crash was as severe as 1962's decline, but this time the market's own dynamic created the problem, rather than the actions of the president. Nonetheless, fears of recession swirled about for several months, and the composite index headed south. Soon, however, everyone realized the crash had nothing to do with the economy's fundamentals, and concern evaporated as the index snapped back.

To conclude, keep in mind that this statistic is not an analytical tool that permits you to probe beneath the cycle's surface in order to analyze its dynamic. The composite index does not provide a step-by-step diagnosis that reveals the cycle's rhythm. It does not disclose the forces that lead from one set of conditions to another. It only averages a number of convenient series that are themselves leading indicators, but are otherwise unrelated.

This series is of interest solely because it provides an omen of future events. You need all the statistical reports appearing in the *Journal* in order to build an understanding of the timing, direction, and strength of the business cycle. After all, a meteorologist needs more than a barometer, and most Americans who make decisions in the business community, or wish to be fully informed of current economic events, need far more than a crude, general directional signal to guide their long-range planning.

Investor's Tip

- The composite index of leading economic indicators is not the square root of the universe. There is no single index or formula that provides all the answers to the problem of business forecasting.

You are now ready for a detailed investigation of stocks, bonds, commodities, and other investment vehicles. Before turning to it, peruse the next chapter's summary and prospect of Old and New Economies.

12

OLD ECONOMY AND NEW ECONOMY: SUMMARY AND PROSPECT

T HE 2001 RECESSION TAUGHT A BITTER LESSON to the New Economy's advocates. You can't repeal the business cycle. It's part and parcel of any capitalist economy. The substantial productivity improvements that accompanied the PC revolution could not prevent the rising labor costs that burst the millennium bubble. For a while—in the late 1990s—it seemed as if we had tamed both inflation and the business cycle. Unemployment and the CPI were remarkably low. The Old Economy's constraints and the business cycle's roller-coaster ride appeared to be relics of the past, confined to the years 1965 through 1980.

The early 1960s followed the Eisenhower years, which President Kennedy and his advisers criticized severely for sluggish economic performance and too many recessions. They excoriated the fiscal policy of President Eisenhower's administration and the monetary policy of the Federal Reserve for excessive concern with inflation and complacency about slow economic growth and unemployment. These critics charged that, because of the attempt to restrain demand in order to combat "creeping inflation," the economy's growth rate had fallen and recovery from frequent recessions in the 1950s had been weak.

The Kennedy and Johnson administrations pursued an expansionary fiscal policy and persuaded the Federal Reserve to pursue an expansionary monetary policy. Consequently, the economy rapidly gained steam in the middle and late 1960s. The low level of inflation (inherited from the Eisenhower years) and the Fed's easy money policy (in response to Kennedy-administration requests) were the most important ingredients in the rapid economic expansion that began in the 1960s.

The expansion's relaxed and easy progress was its most important early feature. The problems began in the late 1960s, when the Fed did not exercise enough restraint on the boom. Its half-hearted measures were too little and too late. Private borrowing and spending on residential construction, autos, and other consumer durables and business capital expenditures—not federal borrowing and spending on the Vietnam War—generated the inflation of the late 1960s. The Fed's attempts to deal with inflation remained inadequate throughout the 1970s, so that its stop-and-go policies only exacerbated inflation over the course of the cycle. Secularly rising inflation and unemployment were the hallmarks of the Old Economy.

It was not until Paul Volcker persuaded the Fed to take a stand in the early 1980s with a policy of continued restraint that inflation was brought under control and stability ensured for the rest of the decade. By the end of the 1980s, with Alan Greenspan now running the Fed, Americans enjoyed better economic conditions than at any time since the early 1960s. The Fed had tamed the Old Economy's excesses, but the New Economy did not yet predominate.

The 1990s brought sustained expansion. The Fed's firm reins kept inflation low, so that production, employment, and profits improved in a climate of low inflation. The New Economy gained strength as the PC revolution motivated corporate America to invest heavily in new hardware and software. This time, unlike the 1970s, business capital expenditures—not household purchases of homes and autos—led the boom. These investments rewarded business with growing productivity and profits until rising wages stifled the boom in the late 1990s and led to the 2001 recession.

Interestingly and ironically the Fed reintroduced a little of the Old Economy with its expansionary response to the 2001 recession. Residential construction and auto sales responded positively to the Fed's low interest rate policy. Neither had faltered during recession, and both contributed importantly to recovery. Yet inflation remained tame during recovery because of low capacity utilization, the availability of imports, and the New Economy's continued productivity improvements—this time in a milieu of higher unemployment that restrained wages as well as prices.

But the Fed's easy-money policy did not swiftly restore the booming New Economy capital expenditures of the late 1990s. These remained below their previous peak, and robust economic conditions awaited their return. Industry did not wish to invest substantially in new capacity when so much old capacity remained idle.

Similarly, the stock market recovered some of the ground lost during the 2001 recession, but did not break through to new highs. Earnings had recovered because productivity gains continued, but it would take the promise of renewed and sustained boom conditions to convince investors that earnings prospects were sufficiently rosy to justify still-higher share prices. The New Economy was not dead, but it could no longer promise exuberant economic growth, corporate earnings, or stock-market gains.

You should now be ready to venture on to Part II, "Your Choice of Investments." It shows you how to use *The Wall Street Journal* to track the stock, bond, and money markets, and how to follow the markets for futures, options, and commodities.

YOUR CHOICE
OF INVESTMENTS

CHAPTER 13

THE STOCK MARKET

A FIRST GLANCE: MARKETS DIARY

THE STOCK MARKET IS A GOOD BAROMETER OF ECONOMIC ACTIVITY, because it reflects the value of owning the businesses responsible for most of our economy's output. The Dow Jones Industrial Average (DJIA) is the most popular indicator of stock-market performance, although the S&P 500 provides broader market coverage.

The Dow represents share prices of 30 blue-chip industrial corporations, chosen because their operations cover the broad spectrum of industrial America, although you can see from the list presented on page 211 that not all of these firms are literally "industrials" (e.g., American Express, Verizon, Disney, McDonald's, and Wal-Mart are in financial services, communications, entertainment, fast food, and retailing). (Dow Jones publishes separate indexes for public utilities and transportation companies.)

There are broader stock-market barometers than the Dow that include more corporations, but the Dow Industrials remains the most closely watched average because it was the first barometer and, more significantly, because its handful of blue-chip companies reflect stock-market activity with surprising precision. Other measures of the stock market's performance will be mentioned shortly.

You probably already know a fair bit of the information in the next several pages, but the material provides a basis for some more complex ideas presented later in this chapter.

The majority of the following discussion uses examples from the print edition of the *The Wall Street Journal*, but *The Wall Street Journal Online* also provides this data. (You can find general directions for retrieving *Wall Street Journal* online information [http://online.wsj.com] in Chapter 1 on pages 7 through 11. Appendix D on page 374 also furnishes you with a quick guide to the *Journal*'s online edition.) Scroll down the home page's left-hand menu-bar and click on Markets and Markets Data Center. Home page and Markets Data Center (also called Markets Data Index) examples from the Tuesday, July 6, 2004, *The Wall Street Journal Online* appear on pages 212 and 213.

Every day (Monday's and Saturday's table and chart format differ) in the print edition, at the bottom of the first page of the third section (C1), *The Wall Street Journal* publishes a stock-market summary under **Markets Diary.** See the excerpt from the Thursday, September 21, 2005, issue on page 214.

The online edition also provides a good first look at the day's stock-market activity when you click on Markets in the home page's left-hand menu-bar and then click on Markets Main. See the Markets excerpt from the Thursday, November 4, 2004, edition on page 215.

Returning to the print edition (see page 214), **Markets Diary** features the following domestic stock-market averages: the Dow Jones Industrial

The 30 Stocks in the Dow Jones Industrial Average (April 16, 2004)

Alcoa	Honeywell
Altria Group	Intel
American Express	IBM
American International Group	JP Morgan Chase
Boeing	Johnson & Johnson
Caterpillar	McDonald's
Citigroup	Merck
Coca Cola	Microsoft
Disney	Pfizer
Du Pont	Procter & Gamble
Exxon Mobil	SBC Communications
General Electric	3M
General Motors	United Technologies
Hewlett Packard	Verizon
Home Depot	Wal-Mart

WSJ.com **THE WALL STREET JOURNAL.**
O N L I N E

Other Journal Sites | As of 8:17 p.m. EDT Tuesday, July 6, 2004 | Online Journal

Home

News ▶

Home:>U.S.< | **EUROPE** ASIA   Set my Home page

News Main
U.S. Business
Europe Business
Asia Business
Americas Business
World News
Economy
Politics & Policy
Earnings
Media & Marketing
Health Edition
News by Industry

Technology ▶

Markets → **Markets** ▶

Personal Journal ▶

Opinion ▶

Leisure/Weekend ▶

The Print Edition
Today's Edition
Past Editions
Features
Columnists
In-Depth Reports
Discussions
Company Research
Markets Data Center
Site Map
My Online Journal
Portfolio
Personalize My News
E-Mail Setup
My Account/Billing
Customer Service
The Online Journal
The Print Edition
Contact Us
Help
Subscribe

BARRON'S Online

What's News
* * *

MICROSOFT'S CEO SENT employees a memo issuing prescriptions to problems that include sinking morale and a stagnant stock price. Steve Ballmer's 4,900-word memo lays out $1 billion in cost cuts and calls for stepping up innovation to drive revenue and profit higher. 8:16 p.m.
* * *

Kerry named Edwards as his running mate, raising the stakes in his campaign's bet that the economy and youth appeal are the keys to Democrats' hopes for taking back the White House. (Complete coverage 7:45 p.m.

• **Al Hunt:** Choice Reshapes Electoral Map

• **Issues:** How They Compare | **Bio:** John Edwards
* * *

Major stock indexes fell on surging oil prices and profit warnings. The Dow industrials dropped 63.49 points to 10219.34. 7:33 p.m.
* * *

The U.S. service sector expanded in June, albeit at a slower pace than in the previous month. Hiring and new orders climbed, suggesting a pickup in the sector may be ahead.
* * *

The U.S. proposed tariffs on shrimp from China and Vietnam, saying exporters from those countries have been dumping shrimp in the American market at artificially low prices.
* * *

The defense for Belnick argued that Tyco's former top lawyer took onetime CEO Kozlowski at his word that millions of dollars of compensation had been properly approved. (Complete coverage) 7:28 p.m.
* * *

A car bomb killed 14 people in a town near Baghdad. Insurgents say they have kidnapped an Egyptian man. Three U.S. Marines were killed in western Iraq. U.S. airstrikes hit a purported militant safehouse in Fallujah, killing at least 10. (Complete coverage) 5:55 p.m.
* * *

HIV infected a growing number of people despite a huge push to fight the virus in developing countries, according to new data published by the UNAIDS program. (Report summary)
* * *

News   Technology   Markets   Personal Journal   Opinion

Markets Data Index

Data Bank
- Data Bank
- Closing Stock Diary
- Closing Stock Data Bank

U.S. Stocks
Market Wrap
- Quotes Search
- Most Actives - Summary
- Leaders - Summary
- Losers - Summary
- Volume Pctg Leaders - Summary
- Most Actives - Top 100
- Leaders - Top 100
- Losers - Top 100
- Volume Pctg Leaders - Top 100
- NYSE Highs/Lows
- NMS Highs/Lows
- AMEX Highs/Lows
- OTC Bulletin Board Most Actives
- DJIA Hour by Hour
- Index Charts
- Closing Stock Tables
After Hours
- Most Actives: 4-6:35 p.m.
- Leaders/Losers: 4-6:35 p.m.
Statistics
- Dividends
- Index Components
- Money Flow - Summary
- Money Flow - Top Gainers
- Money Flow - Top Decliners
- New Securities Issues
- New Stock Listings

- Odd Lot Trading
- Short Interest
- Stock Splits
- Yields On Dow Stocks
Historical Index Data
Dow Jones Industrial Average
- One-Day Gains/Losses, All Time
- One-Day Gains/Losses, 2004
- One-Day Gains/Losses, 2003

Corporate Earnings
- Digest of Earnings
- Earnings Calendar
- Earnings Restatements
- Earnings Surprises
- Going-Concern Statements
Industry Earnings
- 2nd Quarter 2004
- 1st Quarter 2004
- 4th Quarter 2003
- 3rd Quarter 2003
Company Earnings
- 2nd Quarter 2004
- 1st Quarter 2004
- 4th Quarter 2003
- 3rd Quarter 2003

Global Indexes
- DJ Global Indexes
- World Leading Groups
- World Lagging Groups
- Americas Groups
- Asian Groups
- European Groups
- U.S. Leading & Lagging Groups
- DJ Global Portfolio Indexes
- DJ Industry Group Center

Bond Markets
- Bond Indexes
- Bond Yields
- Bond Diaries
- Federal Reserve Data
- Federal Reserve Monitor

- Guaranteed Investment Contracts
- International Government Bonds
- Returns on International Gov't Bonds
- Key Rates
- Money Rates
- Mortgage- Backed Securities & CMOs
- Treasury Quotes
- Tax-Exempt Bonds
- Mortgage & Banking Rate Center

MARKETS DIARY / *Sept. 21, 2005*

For an expanded view of yesterday's markets,
turn to the **Markets Lineup on page C2.**

	Close	Change	Pct. chg.	52 wks
DJ Industrial Average	10378.03	−103.49 ▼	0.99%	2.66%
Nasdaq composite	2106.64	−24.69 ▼	1.16	11.72
S&P 500	1210.20	−11.14 ▼	0.91	8.68
Russell 2000	649.94	−10.69 ▼	1.62	14.85
Nikkei Stock Average	13196.57	48.00 ▲	0.37	19.76
DJ Stoxx 600 (Europe)	291.89	−3.04 ▼	1.03	21.62
Euro (in U.S. dollars)	$1.2210	$0.0083 ▲	0.68	−0.40
Yen (per U.S. dollar)	111.32	−0.59 ▼	0.52	0.67
Gold (Comex, troy oz.)	$468.90	$2.70 ▲	0.58	15.15
Oil (Nymex, barrel)	$66.80	$0.60 ▲	0.91	38.16

	Yield	Previous	Change in pct. pts.	12-mo return
10-year Treasury	4.18%	4.26% ▼	0.07	*2.97%
3-mo. Treasury	3.40	3.60 ▼	0.20	*2.07
DJ Corporate Bond	5.12	5.17 ▼	0.05	3.16

*Total return via Ryan Labs

Average, the Nasdaq Composite, the S&P 500, and the Russell 2000. The table provides the previous trading day's closing value, the change in absolute and percentage terms, and the percentage change over the prior year.

Now let's take the time to consider the Dow Industrials in more detail.

CALCULATING THE DOW

Each day in the print edition's **Markets Lineup** section (the second page of the third section, C2) the *Journal* publishes in chart form a detailed summary of the Dow Jones Industrial Average (see the example from the Friday, April 16, 2004, *Journal* on page 217). Six-month summaries of the Dow Jones Transportation Average (20 stocks) and the Dow Jones Utility Average (15 stocks) are provided separately below the Industrial Average.

The Wall Street Journal Online also provides six-month charts. Scroll down the home page's left-hand menu-bar, click on Markets and Markets Data Center, then Index Charts under U.S. Stocks—Market Wrap.

After glancing at the print edition's top chart of the Dow Jones Averages, your first question—once you know what this index signifies—probably is,

THE WALL STREET JOURNAL.
WSJ.com
ONLINE

Home
News ▶
Markets Main
Today's Markets
Market Movers
Tech Stocks
Markets Data Center
Europe Markets
Asia Markets
Americas Markets
Deals & Deal Makers
Commodities
Credit Markets
Foreign Exchange
Heard on the Street
Personal Journal ▶
Opinion ▶
Leisure/Weekend ▶

ADVERTISEMENTS

DEALS

Go To Deals Search
Add to Personalized
Home Page

The Print Edition
Today's Edition
Past Editions
Features
Columnists
In-Depth Reports
Discussions
Company Research
Markets Data Center
Site Map
My Online Journal
Portfolio
Personalize My News
E-Mail Setup
My Account/Billing
Customer Service
The Online Journal
The Print Edition
Contact Us
Help
Subscribe

BARRON'SOnline

After a Slow Start, Stocks Get Their Wheels Turning

It's back to business as usual on Wall Street.

Stocks waffled early but shot up about 11 a.m. Eastern and haven't looked back as investors, moving past the postelection relief rally, are revisiting major hot-button issues of economy -- jobs and spending -- and so far like what they see.

Investors yesterday, considering the impact of another four years of a Bush administration on big industries such as health-care, defense and financials, ramped up buying, though some of the gains disappeared by the day's end. FULL STORY

◇

ACE fired two executives, including the president of its ACE Casualty Risk unit, and suspended three others while announcing new steps to improve business practices amid Spitzer's investigation of alleged bid-rigging in the insurance industry.
• Marsh Dismisses 4 Executives Amid Probe

* * *

Gold rocketed to 16-year highs, fueled by a weak U. S. currency, while oil plunged $2 a barrel. The dollar fell to its lowest level against the euro since hitting an all-time low in February.

* * *

Wachovia will pay $37 million to settle SEC charges over improper disclosures of stock purchases during its 2001 merger with First Union.

* * *

Fremont Investment Advisors agreed to pay $2.1 million in restitution and $2 million in civil penalties to end a mutual-fund market-timing case brought by Spitzer and the SEC.

* * *

Viacom intends to submit a bid to buy MarketWatch, according to an SEC filing. Viacom already owns a stake in the financial-information company.

* * *

A jury found four former Merrill bankers and an ex-Enron executive guilty of conspiracy and fraud in connection with a scheme to inflate the energy firm's 1999 earnings.

* * *

Calculating the Dow

Company	Price: April 15, 2004
Alcoa	33.00
Altria Group	55.59
American Express	49.75
American International Group	74.68
Boeing	41.53
Caterpillar	80.80
Citigroup	49.92
Coca Cola	51.20
Disney	24.70
Du Pont	45.07
Exxon Mobil	43.68
General Electric	30.76
General Motors	45.39
Hewlett Packard	21.89
Home Depot	35.86
Honeywell	34.50
IBM	93.97
Intel	26.66
Johnson & Johnson	54.52
JP Morgan Chase	38.77
McDonald's	26.93
Merck	46.98
Microsoft	25.22
Pfizer	37.34
Procter & Gamble	106.12
SBC Communications	24.36
3M	82.85
United Technologies	88.14
Verizon	37.06
Wal-Mart	57.79
Total	**1,465.03**

$$\text{DJIA} = \frac{\text{Sum of Stock Prices}}{\text{Divisor}} = \frac{1,465.03}{0.14090166} = 10,397.54$$

MARKETS LINEUP
STOCKS

Dow Jones Industrial Average

Daily High, Low and Close, and 90-Day Moving Average

Close: 10397.46 ▲ +19.51
Divisor: 0.14090166
Market Cap: $3.706 trillion

Dow Divisor on April 15, 2004: 0.14090166

High
Close
Low

10500
10000
9500
9000

Nov.   Dec.   Jan.   Feb.   Mar.   Apr.
2003   2004

DJIA, 5 Minute

10410
10380
10350
10320

9:30   9:30   4:00
Apr. 14 Apr. 15

Hour by Hour

APR 15	INDEX	VOLUME
Open	10377.95	71,425
10 a.m.	10400.52	28,193,384
11 a.m.	10361.69	69,582,574
12 noon	10387.04	106,497,260
1 p.m.	10398.46	140,448,453
2 p.m.	10358.64	167,660,928
3 p.m.	10378.94	202,919,065
Close	10397.46	259,690,396
Change	+ 19.51	
% Change	+ 0.19	

	THEORETICAL	ACTUAL
High	10481.21	10430.62
Low	10279.37	10322.16

Yearly Range

YEAR	HIGH	LOW
1998	9374.27	7539.07
1999	11497.12	9120.67
2000	11722.98	9796.03
2001	11337.92	8235.81
2002	10635.25	7286.27
2003	10453.92	7524.06
YTD	10737.70	10048.23

P/E Ratio[†] and Yield

	P/E RATIO	DIV YIELD
4/15/2004	20.19	1.94
Year ago	28.54	2.36

Dow 30 Components Primary market net point change

Alcoa	−0.02	Citigroup	−1.03	GenMotor	−0.57	JohnsJohns	+1.92	ProctGam	+0.31
AltriaGp	+0.01	CocaCola	+0.01	HewlettPk	−0.10	JPMorgChas	−0.50	SBC Comm	+0.20
AmExprss	−0.05	Disney	−0.30	HomeDpt	+0.04	McDonalds	−0.07	3M	+0.19
AmIntlGp	−0.37	DuPont	+0.07	Honeywell	+0.02	Merck	+1.56	UnitedTech	−0.03
Boeing	−0.04	ExxnMobl	+0.38	IBM	+0.27	Microsoft☆	−0.33	Verizon	−0.02
Caterpillar	−0.23	GenElec	+0.28	Intel☆	−0.75	Pfizer	+1.53	WalMart	+0.37

Dow Jones Transportation Average

Close: 2913.94 ▲ +4.59
Divisor: 0.22477839
Volume: 26,494,779

Daily Close

3000
2900
2800
2700

O N D J F M A
2003   2004

P/E Ratio[†] and Yield

	P/E RATIO	DIV YIELD
4/15/04	33.88	1.16
Year ago	nil	1.30

Components

AMR	−0.22
AlxBldwn☆	+0.07
BurlNthSF	−0.15
CH Robin☆	+0.05
CNF	+0.34
ContlAirln B	−0.11
CSX	−0.14
DeltaAir	−0.72
ExpditrInt☆	+0.63
FedExCp	+0.19
GATX	+0.44
JBHunt☆	+0.24
NorflkSo	+0.23
NowestAir☆	+0.14
RyderSys	+0.37
SowestAir	−0.23
UnPacific	unch
USF Cp☆	−0.22
UtdParcel B	+0.49
YellowCp☆	−0.37

Dow Jones Utility Average

Close: 271.98 ▲ +2.11
Divisor: 1.71492630
Volume: 32,978,500

Daily Close

290
270
250
230

O N D J F M A
2003   2004

P/E Ratio[†] and Yield

	P/E RATIO	DIV YIELD
4/15/04	26.12	3.60
Year ago	nil	5.03

Components

AEP	+0.42
AES Cp	−0.29
CentptEngy	+0.08
ConEd	+0.29
DominRes	+0.90
DukeEngy	−0.01
EdisonInt	+0.10
Exelon	−0.05
FstEngy	+0.33
NiSource	+0.11
PG&E	+0.07
PubSvcEnt	+0.72
SouthernCo	+0.19
TXU	+0.43
WillmsCos	+0.34

☆ Trades on Nasdaq † Trailing 12 months

How can an average of stock-market prices be over $10,000? I don't know of *a single* stock that trades that high, much less 30 of them.

The answer involves the manner in which the Dow deals with "stock splits." Companies split their stock (say, two for one) to prevent the stock from becoming too expensive. Shareholders receive two shares for each share they own, and the stock's price is halved; thus, the total value of the shares remains the same.

These splits usually occur when the price of a "round lot" (100 shares) climbs too high. Round-lot transactions are popular with large investors because of the lower commission per share, and it's much easier to buy a round lot at $50 than at $100 a share. Most companies would rather split their stock than see it become too expensive and discourage investors' purchases.

Here's how this applies to the Dow Jones Industrial Average. Suppose you are calculating the average of a group of 30 stocks (such as the Dow) by adding the share prices of all of them and dividing by 30. If (to make the arithmetic simple and the point clear) each of the 30 were selling at $100, obviously the average would be $100 ($3,000 ÷ 30). However, if each of the 30 happened to split two for one, then each would be worth $50, per share; that is, the average price per share of these 30 stocks would suddenly be $50, not $100. Clearly, it makes no sense to reduce the average because of such splits, since someone who owns the stock has exactly as much equity (ownership value) after a split as before it.

Reducing the divisor from 30 to 15 is one solution: 30 shares at $50 each ($1,500) divided by 15 (not 30) keeps the average at 100. Future stock splits can be handled in a similar fashion with an appropriate adjustment in the divisor.

Another, though less important, reason for changing the divisor is that occasionally Dow Jones replaces one of the 30 industrial stocks with another. Here, too, it wouldn't make sense to change the average; just because one stock is substituted for another doesn't mean the market, itself, has changed. Therefore, the divisor is adjusted at the same time, to keep the average constant. See, for example, the excerpts from the Friday, April 2, 2004, print issue of *The Wall Street Journal* on page 219 and 220 that discuss changes in the Dow.

Now consider a real-life example (see page 216) using the Dow on April 15, 2004. Add the share prices for all 30 companies in the Dow. The total for April 15, 2004, is $1,465.03, and when you divide that by a divisor of 0.14090166 (see page 217) you get $10,397.54—the Dow average for April 15, 2004.

Dow Jones Shakes Up Index

AIG, Pfizer, Verizon Supplant
AT&T, Kodak, International Paper;
Blue Chips Rise and Bonds Fall

By E.S. Browning

THE DOW JONES Industrial Average will change its makeup for the first time in more than four years, by deleting three stocks that were members when Eisenhower was president.

The 30-stock average is adding insurance company **American International Group** Inc., drug maker **Pfizer** Inc. and telephone-service provider **Verizon Communications** Inc. Those stocks replace AT&T Corp., **Eastman Kodak** Co. and International Paper Co.

The three departing stocks had been Dow stalwarts for decades. AT&T was in the industrial average from Oct. 4, 1916, to Oct. 1, 1928; it re-entered on March 14, 1939. Kodak has been a component of the Dow since July 18, 1930, and International Paper since July 3, 1956.

THURSDAY'S MARKETS

The changes to the average, which tracks the prices of blue-chip stocks, take effect when trading begins on April 8.

The changes won't directly affect the value of the Dow, as the math used to calculate it will be adjusted to reflect the prices of the stocks concerned. However, the stock market yesterday began the new quarter with a small gain, partly as a result of a much stronger-than-expected report on March manufacturing activity, and partly in response to the news of the Dow's new look.

Despite declines by the three departing stocks, the industrial average rose 15.63 points, or 0.15%, to 10373.33, leaving it still down 0.77% for the year so far. The Nasdaq Composite Index, whose many technology stocks would be among the beneficiaries of a stronger economy, jumped 1.04%, or 20.79 points, to 2015.01. It once again is in positive territory for the year so far, up 0.6%.

Gold continued its recent advance, rising 50 cents to another 15-year high of $427.80, while the dollar continued to sag against the yen, hitting a four-year low of 103.76 yen to the dollar.

The revisions to the Dow industrials weren't provoked by any specific event, said Paul E. Steiger, managing editor of The Wall Street Journal, who oversees the makeup of the Dow Jones Industrial Average.

"None of these changes was triggered by an event such as an imminent merger, which was the case in the past three instances of changes dating back to the early 1990s," Mr. Steiger said. "Rather, they recognize trends within the U.S. stock market, including the continued growth of the financial and health-care sectors and the diminishing relative weight of basic-materials stocks."

The 107-year-old Dow last changed composition

on Nov. 1, 1999, when **Home Depot** Inc., **Intel** Corp., **Microsoft** Corp. and **SBC Communications** Inc. replaced Chevron Corp., **Goodyear Tire & Rubber** Co., Sears, Roebuck & Co. and Union Carbide Corp.

The performance of the four new component stocks since then suggests that being added to the widely followed barometer doesn't necessarily herald a lasting price increase for the stocks concerned.

Since the 1999 adjustment, the Dow industrials overall have fallen only about 3% in value, but all four of the new stocks have fallen harder.

As of Wednesday's close, Home Depot had de-
Please Turn to Page C3, Column 4

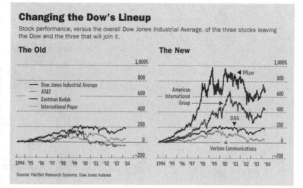

Changing the Dow's Lineup

Stock performance, versus the overall Dow Jones Industrial Average, of the three stocks leaving the Dow and the three that will join it.

The Old
— Dow Jones Industrial Average
— AT&T
— Eastman Kodak
— International Paper

The New
American International Group
Pfizer
DJIA
Verizon Communications

Source: FactSet Research Systems; Dow Jones Indexes

The figures used on page 216 to compute the Dow are the closing prices for the New York Stock Exchange (NYSE) and the NASDAQ. NYSE *Composite Transactions* prices (to be discussed below) vary slightly from the prices used here. Why the discrepancy? Because the composite includes closing prices of stocks traded on other exchanges such as the Pacific Stock Exchange, which continues its operations for half an hour after the New York Exchange closes. If you wish to calculate the Dow on your own, you must obtain the New York Exchange and NASDAQ closing prices, rather than the Composite prices. See, for instance, **Yields on Dow Components** for February 27, 2004, from the Monday, March 1, 2004, *Journal*'s print edition on page 221. It carried the New York City and NASDAQ closing prices.

So much for the Dow; you are now ready to move on to a more detailed analysis of the other stock-market indicators of stock-market performance.

Elements of the Dow

Below, the 30 current members of the Dow Jones Industrial Average, and the three stocks that will replace three others before the start of April 8 trading.

CONSUMER CYCLICALS

| | | | | | | | | **INDUSTRIALS** |

$258.33
WMT
Wal-Mart

TELECOM

TECHNOLOGY **FINANCIAL** **HEALTH CARE** **ENERGY**

$307.60
GE
General Electric

$85.00
HD
Home Depot

$81.24
SBC
SBC Communications

Market capitalization, in billions
Stock symbol
Company

$269.54
MSFT
Microsoft

$267.07
C
Citigroup

$150.54
JNJ
Johnson & Johnson

$273.16
XOM
Exxon Mobil

$64.16
MMM
3M

$51.17
DIS
Walt Disney

$15.50
T
AT&T

BASIC MATERIALS

CONSUMER NON CYCLICALS

$176.36
INTC
Intel

$86.34
JPM
J.P. Morgan Chase

$98.32
MRK
Merck

$44.50
UTX
United Technologies

$36.26
MCD
McDonald's

VZ

$42.08
DD
DuPont

$135.55
PG
Procter & Gamble

$158.00
IBM
IBM

$66.58
AXP
American Express

PFE

$32.86
BA
Boeing

$26.41
GM
General Motors

$30.13
AA
Alcoa

$123.00
KO
Coca-Cola

$69.68
HPQ
Hewlett-Packard

AIG

$29.18
HON
Honeywell

$7.50
EK
Eastman Kodak

$20.30
IP
International Paper

$110.60
MO
Altria Group

$27.00
CAT
Caterpillar

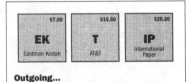

$7.50
EK
Eastman Kodak

$15.50
T
AT&T

$20.30
IP
International Paper

Outgoing...
These three stocks are leaving the Dow. They originally joined in 1930, 1928, and 1956 respectively.

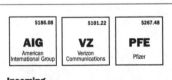

$186.08
AIG
American International Group

$101.22
VZ
Verizon Communications

$267.48
PFE
Pfizer

Incoming...
These three stocks are joining the Dow, in the first changes to the Dow since 1999.

'Hey Charlie, Buy Me Some American Cotton Oil!'

At the beginning, the Dow Jones Industrial Average included such stocks as American Cotton Oil and Tennessee Coal. In fact, there were only 12 original Dow stocks when the average of industrial shares was started in 1896. The one surviving original stock is General Electric Co. (though it dropped out of the average twice, in the years after the average's launch). The index's inventor was Charles Dow (left), who had started Dow Jones & Co., publisher of The Wall Street Journal, along with Edward Jones and Charles Bergstresser in 1882.

The Original 12 Dow Companies
March 1896. Dow's point level was 40.94

- American Cotton Oil
- American Sugar Refining Co.
- American Tobacco
- Chicago Gas
- Distilling & Cattle Feeding Co.
- General Electric Co.
- Laclede Gas Light Co.
- National Lead
- North American Co.
- Tennessee Coal, Iron & Railroad
- U.S. Leather
- U.S. Rubber Co

Sources: Dow Jones Indexes; FactSet Research Systems; WSJ reporting

Yields on Dow Components

February 27, 2004

Components of the Dow Jones Averages, ranked by dividend yield based on recent price and annualized dividend amount.

COMPANY	INDICATED YIELD %	IND ANN DIVIDEND	PRICE 2/27/04	CHG FROM 2/13/04
Industrials				
SBC Commun	5.21	1.25	24.01	−1.04
AT&T	4.74	0.95	20.03	+0.03
Altria Group	4.73	2.72	57.55	+2.89
General Motors	4.16	2.00	48.12	−0.76
J.P. Morgan Chase	3.32	1.36	41.02	+0.86
Citigroup	3.18	1.60	50.26	+0.77
Du Pont	3.10	1.40	45.09	+0.63
Merck	3.08	1.48	48.08	−0.80
General Electric	2.46	0.80	32.52	−0.20
Exxon-Mobil	2.37	1.00	42.17	+0.26
Int'l Paper	2.26	1.00	44.26	+0.86
Honeywell Int'l	2.14	0.75	35.05	−1.36
Coca-Cola	2.00	1.00	49.96	−1.18
Caterpillar	1.95	1.48	75.75	−1.67
3M	1.85	1.44	78.02	−1.66
Johnson & Johnson	1.78	0.96	53.91	−0.32
Procter & Gamble	1.78	1.82	102.51	+0.46
Eastman Kodak	1.75	0.50	28.54	−0.49
Alcoa	1.60	0.60	37.47	+0.46
Boeing	1.57	0.68	43.37	−1.08
United Tech	1.52	1.40	92.11	−2.52
McDonald's	1.41	0.40	28.30	+1.67
Hewlett-Packard	1.41	0.32	22.71	−0.30
Walt Disney	0.79	0.21	26.53	−0.39
Home Depot	0.77	0.28	36.31	+0.14
American Express	0.75	0.40	53.42	−0.23
IBM	0.66	0.64	96.50	−3.21
Wal-Mart Stores	0.60	0.36	59.56	+3.24
Microsoft	0.60	0.16	26.50	−0.08
Intel	0.55	0.16	29.23	−0.91
Transportations				
GATX Corp	3.40	0.80	23.52	+0.54
Alex & Baldwin	2.65	0.90	33.95	−0.05
Union Pacific	1.89	1.20	63.64	−1.20
Burl North SF	1.86	0.60	32.18	−0.22
Ryder System	1.63	0.60	36.84	+0.59
United Parcel Sv B	1.59	1.12	70.63	−0.19
Norfol Southern	1.44	0.32	22.16	−0.14
CSX	1.27	0.40	31.53	−0.07
C.H. Robinson	1.21	0.48	39.61	−0.17
CNF	1.20	0.40	33.25	+2.12
USF	1.05	0.37	35.35	+0.20
Expeditors Intl	0.42	0.16	38.48	−0.81
FedEx Corp	0.35	0.24	68.68	−0.23
Southwest Airlines	0.14	0.02	13.81	−0.74
AMR	...	...	15.20	−0.01
Cont'l Airlines B	...	...	14.65	+0.02
Delta Air Lines	...	...	8.98	−0.81
JB Hunt	...	...	27.40	−0.66
Northwest Airlines	...	...	10.84	−0.30
Yellow	...	...	31.59	−1.16
Utilities				
Consol Ed	5.12	2.26	44.17	+0.83
Duke Energy	5.01	1.10	21.96	+0.65
Public Serv Ent.	4.67	2.20	47.14	+1.49
Southern	4.62	1.40	30.32	+0.82
NiSource	4.24	0.92	21.71	+0.26
Domin Resources	4.11	2.58	62.83	−0.19
Amer El Power	4.06	1.40	34.50	+1.05
FirstEnergy	3.88	1.50	38.63	+1.12
CenterPoint Energy	3.82	0.40	10.46	+0.14
Exelon	3.28	2.20	67.14	+1.57
TXU	1.78	0.50	28.13	+3.77
Edison Int'l	0.87	0.20	23.09	+1.26
Williams	0.42	0.04	9.47	−0.67
AES	...	...	9.06	−0.06
PG&E	...	...	28.17	+0.55

MARKETS LINEUP AND MARKETS SCORECARD

As already stated, the **Markets Lineup** section appears on the second page of the third section of the *Journal*'s print edition. It provides a comprehensive summary of stock-market activity in the following tables: **Major Stock Indexes, Most Active Issues,** and **Price Percentage Gainers and Losers**. See pages 217, 222, 223, and 224 for an example from the Friday, April 16, 2004, *Wall Street Journal*. Examine **Markets Lineup** after you have looked at the **Markets Diary** on page C1 in order to get a more detailed view of the previous day's trading activity.

The Wall Street Journal Online also provides this information. Scroll down the home page's left-hand menu-bar and click on Markets and Markets Data Center. Under U.S. Stocks—Market Wrap you will find *Most Active Issues (Summary and Top 100), Price Percentage Leaders (Summary and Top 100), Price Percentage Losers (Summary and Top 100), Volume Percentage Leaders (Summary and Top 100), NYSE, AMEX,* and *NMS*

MARKETS LINEUP
STOCKS

Nasdaq Composite

Nasdaq 100 P/E ratio†:   57
Nasdaq 100 est. P/E ratio: 32
Nasdaq 100 dividend yield: .18%

Daily Close and 90-Day Moving Average   Close: 2002.17 ▼ –22.68   **Nasdaq Composite, 5 Minute**

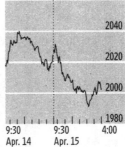

S&P 500 Index

P/E ratio†:   23
Est. P/E ratio: 18
Dividend yield: 1.61%

Daily Close and 90-Day Moving Average   Close: 1128.84 ▲ +0.67   **S&P 500, 5 Minute**

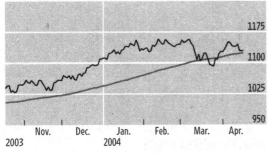
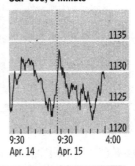

Russell 2000

P/E ratio†:   96
Est. P/E ratio: 28
Dividend yield: 1.01%

Daily Close and 90-Day Moving Average   Close: 580.30 ▼ –1.72   **Russell 2000, 5 Minute**

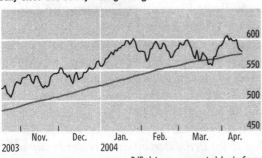
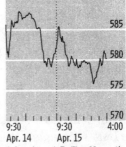

P/E data on as-reported basis from Birinyi Associates † Trailing 12 months

Major Stock Indexes

Dow Jones Averages	DAILY					52-WEEK			YTD
	HIGH	LOW	CLOSE	NET CHG	% CHG	HIGH	LOW	% CHG	% CHG
30 Industrials	10430.62	10322.16	10397.46	+ 19.51	+0.19	10737.70	8306.35	+24.70	-0.54
20 Transportations	2930.54	2893.11	2913.94	+ 4.59	+0.16	3080.32	2297.85	+25.27	-3.10
15 Utilities	273.74	269.92	271.98	+ 2.11	+0.78	282.87	217.19	+25.23	+1.90
65 Composite	2990.62	2957.13	2977.75	+ 8.53	+0.29	3062.38	2374.15	+24.96	-0.77
Dow Jones Indexes									
US Total Market	268.62	265.36	267.25	+ 0.08	+0.03	274.54	207.28	+28.82	+1.74
US Large-Cap	245.09	242.30	244.04	+ 0.15	+0.06	250.84	196.33	+24.04	+1.09
US Mid-Cap	326.26	321.72	323.98	- 0.15	-0.05	334.64	230.56	+40.52	+3.53
US Small-Cap	373.32	367.52	370.14	- 0.45	-0.12	386.09	247.46	+49.58	+3.48
US Growth	1051.10	1037.57	1044.81	- 0.95	-0.09	1069.37	817.06	+27.77	+2.27
US Value	1370.70	1355.35	1365.65	+ 2.94	+0.22	1422.20	1069.84	+27.49	+1.19
Global Titans 50	185.34	183.79	184.86	+ 0.84	+0.46	191.85	150.78	+22.30	+0.04
Asian Titans 50	115.53	113.00	113.69	- 1.06	-0.92	118.74	71.25	+54.53	+7.67
DJ STOXX 50	2757.05	2730.96	2746.70	+ 5.29	+0.19	2804.06	2243.17	+18.28	+3.25
Nasdaq Stock Market									
Composite	2031.84	1989.21	2002.17	- 22.68	-1.12	2153.83	1424.37	+40.45	-0.06
Nasdaq 100	1481.77	1449.40	1459.45	- 16.21	-1.10	1553.66	1081.04	+34.69	-0.58
Biotech	792.43	783.66	790.20	+ 2.67	+0.34	816.20	522.58	+51.21	+9.12
Computer	909.80	884.27	891.00	- 16.39	-1.81	1012.13	663.75	+33.75	-4.70
Telecommunications	188.95	184.18	185.38	- 2.78	-1.48	204.89	123.06	+50.64	+0.99
Standard & Poor's Indexes									
500 Index	1134.08	1120.75	1128.84	+ 0.67	+0.06	1157.76	892.01	+26.33	+1.52
MidCap 400	602.11	593.14	597.45	- 1.07	-0.18	616.70	422.65	+41.36	+3.72
SmallCap 600	285.64	281.40	283.12	- 0.59	-0.21	293.64	192.75	+46.88	+4.70
SuperComp 1500	253.06	250.05	251.83	+ 0.08	+0.03	258.20	196.24	+28.17	+1.83
New York Stock Exchange									
Composite	6582.90	6531.31	6569.46	+ 18.29	+0.28	6780.03	5004.98	+31.22	+2.01
Financial	6758.19	6663.38	6712.64	- 28.45	-0.42	7109.18	5108.05	+31.34	+0.54
Health Care	6094.05	5953.21	6089.50	+136.21	+2.29	6227.42	4996.77	+21.87	+2.76
Others									
Russell 2000	586.02	575.81	580.30	- 1.72	-0.30	606.39	383.70	+51.24	+4.20
Wilshire 5000	11081.42	10948.04	11024.00	+ 1.08	+0.01	11314.42	8459.72	+30.20	+2.08
Value Line	377.26	371.94	374.17	- 0.85	-0.23	386.84	257.57	+45.27	+3.17
Amex Composite	1238.45	1230.74	1232.88	- 0.94	-0.08	1275.96	842.89	+46.27	+5.06

Source: Reuters

Highs/Lows, OTC Most Actives, DJIA Hour by Hour, Index Charts, and *Closing Stock Tables* (the latter listed as an Adobe Acrobat file).

Returning to the print edition, the **Nasdaq Composite**, **S&P 500 Index,** and **Russell 2000** charts appear to the right of the **Dow Jones Industrial Average** charts under **Markets Lineup** and will be described in greater detail later. Just below these charts you will find the **Major Stock Indexes** table. **Major Stock Indexes** lists the **Dow Jones Averages** as well as a variety of other domestic indexes in greater detail than provided in the **Markets Diary** on the first page of the third section (C1). These statistics permit you

Most Active Issues

Top 10 from the New York Stock Exchange with market caps over $500 million.

38 millions shares of Pfizer traded on April 15, 2004 →

STOCK	VOLUME	CLOSE	CHG
LucentTch	45,778,800	4.22	-0.05
Pfizer	38,067,900	37.34	+1.53
AdvMicro	24,810,700	16.22	-0.90
GenElec	24,536,900	30.76	+0.28
Nokia	23,534,100	16.05	-0.53
Citigroup	22,516,900	49.92	-1.03
TX Instr	20,033,600	28.02	-0.66
NortelNtwks	19,884,900	5.63	-0.08
JohnsJohns	18,880,300	54.52	+1.92
EMC Cp	18,540,100	13.02	-0.18

Top 10 from the Nasdaq and Amex exchanges with market caps over $500 million.

STOCK (EXCHANGE)	VOLUME	CLOSE	CHG
Nasdaq 100 (A)	119,139,600	36.15	-0.66
Intel (Nq)	89,488,945	26.66	-0.71
CiscoSys (Nq)	72,933,332	22.82	-0.44
Microsoft (Nq)	67,341,653	25.22	-0.30
SPDR (A)	60,421,000	112.96	-0.43
OracleCp (Nq)	40,664,071	12.08	-0.29
ApldMatl (Nq)	40,015,953	21.47	-0.93
SiriusSat (Nq)	32,510,997	3.78	+0.03
SunMicrsys (Nq)	32,104,370	4.42	-0.14
JDS Uniphs (Nq)	31,634,258	4.09	-0.16

Price Percentage Gainers...

Top 10 from the NYSE, Nasdaq, and Amex exchanges with market caps over $500 million.

Big dollar and percentage gain →

Big percentage but small dollar gain →

STOCK (EXCHANGE)	CLOSE	CHANGE	% CHG
TomBrown (N)	47.72	+8.95	+23.1
NtlProc (N)	22.21	+3.20	+16.8
TrexCo (N)	39.51	+5.26	+15.4
IvanhoeMn (Nq)	6.31	+0.68	+12.1
CooperT&R (N)	22.99	+2.48	+12.1
EvergrnRes (N)	39.01	+3.98	+11.4
Quicksilver (N)	45.49	+4.51	+11.0
WhlngPitts (Nq)	21.41	+2.11	+10.9
AppleCptr (Nq)	29.30	+2.66	+10.0
WestGasRes (N)	54.90	+4.42	+ 8.8

And Losers

STOCK (EXCHANGE)	CLOSE	CHANGE	% CHG
C-COR.net (Nq)	11.30	- 2.85	-20.1
CNET Ntwrks (Nq)	10.31	- 1.91	-15.6
SanDisk (Nq)	27.91	- 4.60	-14.1
CyprsSemi (N)	17.75	- 2.60	-12.8
Rambus (Nq)	25.29	- 3.14	-11.0
RedbackNtwk (Nq)	6.24	- 0.73	-10.5
Nelnet A (N)	22.00	- 2.50	-10.2
Provalis ADS (Nq)	3.95	- 0.44	-10.0
LexarMedia (Nq)	15.45	- 1.60	- 9.4
DeltaAir (N)	6.98	- 0.72	- 9.4

to compare the performance of your own investments with the broadest gauges of stock-market activity.

Dow Jones Indexes, under **Dow Jones Averages**, divides the stock market into *U.S. Total Market, U.S Large-Cap, U.S Mid-Cap, U.S Small-Cap, U.S Growth, U.S Value, Global Titans 50, Asian Titans 50,* and *DJ STOXX 50* categories. These labels are virtually self-explanatory. *Cap* stands for capitalization, a measure of company size. The *DJ STOXX 50* are large-cap European issues.

NASDAQ (National Association of Securities Dealers Automated Quotations) stocks are traded electronically (over-the-counter), not on an organized exchange, and typically represent high-tech issues as well as ownership of smaller and less widely held companies.

The Standard and Poor's 500 (S&P 500), which is a composite, includes some stocks not listed on the New York Exchange. Since it weights (measures the importance of) its constituent companies by their market value (share price multiplied by the number of share outstanding), unlike the Dow, which weights by price alone, and since it includes far more companies than the Dow, most professional observers prefer this index to the Dow.

The **New York Stock Exchange** tracks the movements of all stocks listed on that exchange. Notice that this composite, like most others, is broken out into a number of components.

Since this index includes all stocks listed (about 3,000), rather than a sample like the Dow, you may wonder why it isn't preferred to the Dow or S&P 500. Because most investors aren't interested in all the stocks listed, just the most important ones.

The category **Others** includes the *Russell 2000*, the *Wilshire 5000*, the *Value-Line* composite, and the *Amex Composite* indexes.

The *Russell 2000* tracks stocks issued by small companies.

The *Wilshire 5000* measures all the 5,000 or so stocks that are actively traded on the two major exchanges as well as on the NASDAQ. This excludes several thousand stocks that are not actively traded.

The *Value-Line* composite is prepared by the investment service of the same name. It contains about 1,700 stocks traded on the two major exchanges as well as over-the-counter.

The *AMEX* index measures all the stocks (about 1,000) traded on the American Stock Exchange. Most of these companies were traditionally between the New York and NASDAQ (over-the-counter) companies in size, but this distinction has evaporated with the rapid growth of many of the NASDAQ companies. This exchange was once known as the Curb Exchange, because its business was conducted in the street and it had no premises.

Most Active Issues, to the left of **Major Stock Indexes** in the print edition, lists the day's 10 most heavily traded stocks on the three major markets that have market capitalizations over $500 million (see page 224): the NYSE, the NASDAQ system, and the AMEX. For instance, you can see that over 38 million shares of Pfizer changed hands on Thursday, April 15, 2004.

As an investor, you want to know the percentage performance of your stocks. A $1 rise in the price of a stock that you purchased at $100 a share is an event to note, but if you had paid $2 a share for the stock, the same $1 rise is a cause for celebration. In the first case, your investment increased by 1 percent, in the second, by 50 percent.

Price Percentage Gainers and Losers tracks the top 10 percentage gainers and losers with market capitalizations over $500 million (see page 224). On April 15, 2004, Tom Brown, Inc, an independent energy company, gained 23.1 percent in value. This is quite a leap. If, at that time, you had typed Tom Brown Inc. into Article Search at *The Wall Street Journal Online* Web site, a number of recent articles would have informed you that Calgary-based Encana had acquired Tom Brown Inc. on April 15, thus accounting for the large leap in value. Note that Ivanhoe Mine Ltd's large percentage gain was last in dollar terms ($0.68) because the other stocks traded at higher prices.

Turn now to **Markets Scorecard** (see page **227**) in the print edition, usually located toward the middle of the third section (check the third-section index), which provides additional stock-market data. **Price Percentage Gainers and Losers**, **Most Active Issues,** and **Volume Percentage Leaders** supplement the **Markets Lineup** report with information for smaller companies. **Markets Scorecard's Diaries** provides other important measures of the day's trading activity: *advances versus declines, new highs versus new lows*, and the *trading volume of stocks advancing and declining*. On April 22, 2004, 2,465 issues advanced and 839 declined on the New York Exchange (see page 228).

The online edition also provides information on the NYSE, AMEX, and NASDAQ. Click on the home page's Markets and Markets Data Center in the left-hand menu-bar, and then click on Closing Stock Diary under Data Bank. See the example on page 231 from the Tuesday, July 6, 2004, edition. It may cement your understanding if you analyze the data from the online edition on page 231 in accordance with the following description of the same listings in the print edition.

The measures in the **Diaries** can confirm the strength or weakness of the day's trading. For example, on April 22, 2004 (see page 228), more NYSE

MARKETS SCORECARD

Thursday, April 22, 2004 4 p.m. ET

Price Percentage Gainers...   And Losers

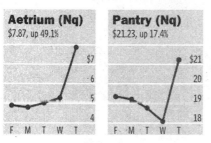

Aetrium (Nq)
$7.87, up 49.1%

Pantry (Nq)
$21.23, up 17.4%

Arris Gp (Nq)
$6.55, down 25.4%

Maxtor (N)
$6.69, down 12.0%

ISSUE (EXCH)	VOLUME	CLOSE	CHG	% CHG	ISSUE (EXCH)	VOLUME	CLOSE	CHG	% CHG
AllAmSemi (Nq)	978,115	8.67	+3.12	+56.2	BroadVisn (Nq)	3,405,617	4.28	-2.02	-32.1
Aetrium (Nq)	2,267,255	7.87	+2.59	+49.1	ArrisGp (Nq)	23,926,679	6.55	-2.23	-25.4
NtwkEngns (Nq)	6,728,714	4.36	+1.07	+32.5	AscentialSftwr (Nq)	6,823,691	18.11	-4.94	-21.4
EpicorSftwr (Nq)	1,122,837	15.30	+2.82	+22.6	GrafTech (N)	10,452,000	11.25	-3.01	-21.1
AdvMedOp (N)	4,283,400	30.45	+5.53	+22.2	MagalSec (Nq)	6,305,170	25.06	-3.57	-12.5
SurModics (Nq)	1,707,732	22.98	+3.92	+20.6	WstnDgtl (N)	18,335,000	8.98	-1.27	-12.4
JacoElec (Nq)	130,088	6.70	+1.08	+19.2	MaceSecurity (Nq)	4,452,577	4.80	-0.67	-12.2
KVH Ind (Nq)	1,600,419	15.81	+2.48	+18.6	BisysGp (N)	5,891,400	13.69	-1.89	-12.1
Laserscope (Nq)	2,647,461	31.97	+4.97	+18.4	LJ Int (Nq)	288,929	3.50	-0.48	-12.1
UtdRentals (N)	2,271,900	19.87	+3.02	+17.9	VitriaTch (Nq)	811,447	3.73	-0.51	-12.0
Pantry (Nq)	433,615	21.23	+3.15	+17.4	Maxtor (N)	16,887,600	6.69	-0.91	-12.0
GtLakesChm (N)	1,578,100	26.75	+3.88	+17.0	GSE Sys (A)	29,300	1.81	-0.24	-11.7
Fiserv (Nq)	11,736,395	40.85	+5.79	+16.5	KeyTch (Nq)	130,447	14.38	-1.82	-11.2
StckYale (Nq)	11,452,587	3.68	+0.51	+16.1	CabotMicro (Nq)	4,502,053	33.36	-4.20	-11.2
SonestaHtl (Nq)	8,100	6.10	+0.80	+15.1	CompTch (A)	33,000	4.38	-0.52	-10.6
Servotrnics (A)	5,700	4.40	+0.57	+14.9	Skechers A (N)	523,700	12.54	-1.41	-10.1
Unifi (N)	2,854,600	3.05	+0.38	+14.2	Conmed (Nq)	594,996	27.14	-3.01	-10.0
Airgate (Nq)	384,597	20.30	+2.45	+13.7	AlignTech (Nq)	2,041,117	19.20	-2.04	-9.6
AskJeeves (Nq)	6,677,234	41.32	+4.91	+13.5	Sanfilipo (Nq)	915,218	33.72	-3.57	-9.6
DraxisHlth (Nq)	561,213	4.32	+0.51	+13.4	CircorInt (N)	231,900	21.90	-2.25	-9.3

stocks advanced than declined. Moreover, the advancers were more actively traded: 1,463,709 to 355,936. These figures confirm the overall strength among NYSE stocks that day.

Closing tick and *Closing Arms (trin)* are even finer measures of stock-market strength or weakness.

A *tick* is a measure of movement in closing stock prices; a positive (+) tick means prices were rising at the end of the day, and a negative (−) tick indicates falling prices. The closing tick nets all stocks whose last trade was higher than the previous trade (+) on the NYSE against all stocks whose last trade was lower (−); a "+" closing tick means that more stocks were rising than falling, and a "−" closing tick means that more stocks were falling

Most Active Issues

ISSUE (EXCH)	VOLUME	CLOSE	CHG
Nasdaq 100 (A)	133,403,500	36.92	+0.93
Microsoft (Nq)	84,028,729	25.95	+0.50
CiscoSys (Nq)	71,565,492	23.15	+0.78
Intel (Nq)	63,882,405	26.52	+0.25
SPDR (A)	59,767,400	114.25	+1.58
ApldMatl (Nq)	57,620,277	19.73	-0.50
SiriusSat (Nq)	55,658,805	3.62	+0.15
Motorola (N)	51,328,600	20.72	+1.42
LucentTch (N)	48,353,900	3.90	-0.06
OracleCp (Nq)	46,737,424	12.37	+0.30
SunMicrsys (Nq)	43,173,835	4.27	+0.11
GenElec (N)	35,003,900	30.85	+0.15

Volume Percentage Leaders

ISSUE (EXCH)	VOLUME	% DIF*	CLOSE	CHG
AllAmSemi (Nq)	978,115	6918.6	8.67	+3.12
Aetrium (Nq)	2,267,255	4189.9	7.87	+2.59
RushEnt B (Nq)	474,739	2553.8	12.50	+0.78
RushEnt A (Nq)	500,822	2261.9	12.50	+0.63
BHPBilton PLC (N)	279,500	1834.7	16.98	+0.19
NwHrznWld (Nq)	131,902	1485.6	6.05	-0.10
AdvMedOp (N)	4,283,400	1475.5	30.45	+5.53
LeucdaNat (N)	1,960,400	1445.4	50.74	-2.26
MercryCptr (Nq)	2,271,719	1331.2	23.24	+0.85
ButlrMfg (N)	590,300	1121.4	24.37	+1.37
Reebok (N)	7,866,900	1036.7	38.11	-3.86
AscentialSftwr (Nq)	6,823,691	1014.7	18.11	-4.94
Selectica (Nq)	1,838,991	983.2	5.14	+0.13

*Common stocks of $5 a share or more with average volume over 65 trading days of at least 5,000 shares. a-has traded fewer than 65 days

Diaries

	NYSE	NASDAQ	AMEX	
Issues traded	3,440	3,325	965	Fewer issues declined than advanced.
Advances	2,465	2,092	562	
Declines	839	1,077	305	
Unchanged	136	156	98	New lows fell short of new highs.
New highs	178	136	20	
New lows	87	25	29	
zAdv vol (000s)	1,463,709	1,487,253	64,160	Advance volume greater than decline volume.
zDecl vol (000s)	355,936	564,575	11,815	
zTotal vol (000s)	1,825,620	2,082,370	80,047	
Closing Tick	+714	+29	+122	Positive tick indicates more stocks advanced than declined on last trade.
Closing Arms[1] (trin)	.71	.74	.34	
zBlock trades	27,170	p12,059	p1,523	

Breakdown of Trading

BY MARKET	NYSE	NASDAQ	AMEX	
NYSE volume → New York	1,825,619,790	...	14,692,100	Arms index of less than one indicates buying pressure.
Chicago	63,708,670	7,754,949	13,938,650	
CBOE	...	...	131,000	
ArcaEx	20,115,100	417,659,600	69,786,300	
Nasdaq InterMkt	261,147,920	938,481,498	132,366,130	
NASD ADF†	...	2,171,200	...	
Phila	10,207,600	...	4,600,100	
Amex	...	153,900	80,046,865	
Boston	22,659,200	198,663,706	5,249,300	
National	22,991,100	517,485,072	62,965,600	
Composite volume → Composite	2,226,449,380	2,082,369,925	383,776,045	

NYSE first crossing 13,100 shares, value n.a.
Second (basket) 9,718,488 shares, value 344,381,070
[1]A comparison of the number of advancing and declining issues with the volume of shares rising and falling. Generally, an Arms of less than 1.00 indicates buying demand; above 1.00 indicates selling pressure. p-previous day. z-primary market NYSE & Amex only. † Alternate Display Facility

than rising. On April 22, 2004, more stocks were rising than falling at their last trade, and so the closing tick for the day was +714.

The *Arms index (trin)*, named for Richard W. Arms, Jr., its creator, measures market strength. A trin greater than one indicates money flowing out of stocks (bearish sign). While a trin of less than one indicates money flow-

Late-Trading Snapshot

04/22/04 4 p.m. - 6:30 p.m. ET

Late Price Percentage Gainers   ...And Losers

ISSUE (EXCH)	VOL (000s)	LAST	CHG	% CHG	ISSUE (EXCH)	VOL (000s)	LAST	CHG	% CHG
EncoreWire (Nq)	11.0	41.95	+5.10	+13.8	OxfordHlth (N)	372.7	50.01	-5.14	-9.3
Ramtron (Nq)	11.7	4.65	+0.55	+13.4	Cutera (Nq)	55.0	14.15	-1.29	-8.4
NeoMagic (Nq)	50.8	4.44	+0.43	+10.7	Emulex (N)	278.1	18.26	-1.33	-6.8
Celestica (N)	309.3	18.35	+1.60	+9.6	VitesseSemi (Nq)	1,005.6	5.35	-0.35	-6.1
Corning (N)	1,039.4	11.20	+0.95	+9.3	ATP Oil&Gas (Nq)	75.3	6.76	-0.44	-6.1
FormFactor (Nq)	22.2	21.00	+1.54	+7.9	TripathTch (Nq)	9.4	4.11	-0.25	-5.7
GileadSci (Nq)	537.0	63.50	+4.28	+7.2	iPass (Nq)	30.1	11.70	-0.69	-5.6
SciAtlanta (N)	85.9	35.90	+2.35	+7.0	SeaChange (Nq)	15.8	12.30	-0.61	-4.7
Benthos (SC)	21.0	8.53	+0.54	+6.8	Polycom (Nq)	110.3	22.20	-1.00	-4.3
MicrochpTch (Nq)	174.8	30.20	+1.87	+6.6	aaiPharma (Nq)	15.4	7.70	-0.29	-3.6

Late Most Active Issues

ISSUE (EXCH)	VOL (000s)	LAST	CHG	% CHG	ISSUE (EXCH)	VOL (000s)	LAST	CHG	% CHG
Microsoft (Nq)	16,170.2	27.20	+1.25	+4.8	Corning (N)	1,039.4	11.20	+0.95	+9.3
MylanLabs (N)	14,145.7	24.33	...	...	MltmedGm (Nq)	1,028.8	25.57	...	...
Nasdaq 100 (A)	4,449.5	37.17	+0.25	+0.7	CiscoSys (Nq)	1,013.4	23.35	+0.20	+0.9
PacSunwear (Nq)	4,185.3	23.06	...	...	VitesseSemi (Nq)	1,005.6	5.35	-0.35	-6.1
Amazon.com (Nq)	2,506.5	47.50	-1.36	-2.8	NortelNtwks (N)	877.2	5.76	+0.07	+1.2
SPDR (A)	2,375.4	114.50	+0.25	+0.2	EverestCp Trll (N)	711.8	22.85	...	...
Amgen (Nq)	1,623.2	58.32	+1.19	+2.1	Xilinx (Nq)	690.5	36.86	-0.93	-2.5
Intel (Nq)	1,331.5	26.77	+0.25	+0.9	Maxtor (N)	650.8	6.76	+0.07	+1.0
Broadcom A (Nq)	1,187.2	43.00	+2.20	+5.4	SemiConHldrs (A)	645.3	38.47	+0.24	+0.6
OracleCp (Nq)	1,178.0	12.55	+0.18	+1.5	SprintPCS (N)	629.7	9.53	-0.03	-0.3

Late-Trading Activity

	THURSDAY	WEDNESDAY	TUESDAY	MONDAY	FRIDAY
Issues Traded	3,550	2,878	3,554	3,390	3,018
Advances	723	672	1,167	637	758
Declines	575	779	502	880	730
Unchanged	2,252	1,427	1,885	1,873	1,530
Advancing Volume	51,100,652	21,497,253	61,941,844	22,789,274	15,366,809
Declining Volume	16,126,297	30,298,915	7,682,458	24,165,743	16,868,117
Total Volume	113,192,462	64,274,767	83,343,156	61,392,550	47,984,653

The Late-Trading Snapshot reflects trading activity in NYSE and Amex issues reported by electronic trading services, securities dealers and regional exchanges between 4 p.m. and 6:30 p.m. Eastern time, and in Nasdaq NMS issues between 4 p.m. and 6:30 p.m., with a minimum price of $3 and volume of 5,000. The primary market is indicated for each issue. N-NYSE A-Amex Nq-Nasdaq SC-Nasdaq SmallCap

Money Flows

April 22, 2004 4 p.m. ET

Total money flows (in millions of dollars)

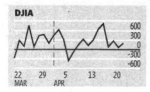

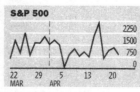

Uptick vs. Downtick Trading by Dollar Volume

MARKET	MONEY FLOW (IN MILLIONS)	MONEY FLOW PREV DAY	UP/DN RATIO	MARKET	MONEY FLOW (IN MILLIONS)	MONEY FLOW PREV DAY	UP/DN RATIO
DJIA*	+235.6	+58.2	113/100	S&P 500*	+877.7	+667.7	109/100
Blocks	−35.4	+8.9	97/100	Blocks	+7.9	+668.0	100/100
DJ US Total Mkt*	+1,204.6	+917.6	109/100	Russell 2000*	+139.3	+133.7	106/100
Blocks	+126.1	+772.6	102/100	Blocks	−107.2	−55.6	86/100

Issue Gainers

...And Losers

ISSUE (EXCH)	CLOSE	MONEY FLOW (IN MILLIONS)	UP/DN RATIO	ISSUE (EXCH)	CLOSE	MONEY FLOW (IN MILLIONS)	UP/DN RATIO
Motorola (N)	20.72	+105.1	147/100	SPDR (A)	114.25	−543.3	75/100
SBC Comm (N)	25.40	+80.7	207/100	Nasdaq 100 (A)	36.92	−156.4	86/100
SPDR Fncl (A)	28.77	+73.8	286/100	SemiConHldrs (A)	38.23	−103.4	67/100
FstData (N)	46.45	+46.5	166/100	CapOneFnl (N)	70.65	−64.6	62/100
ImCloneSys (Nq)	71.84	+38.4	144/100	Pfizer (N)	36.54	−52.7	80/100
FordMotor (N)	15.77	+37.8	139/100	CiscoSys (Nq)	23.15	−44.0	75/100
Inco (N)	33.34	+34.5	339/100	UnibncoBra (N)	21.80	−37.7	15/100
TycoInt (N)	29.40	+34.4	173/100	KohlsCp (N)	41.30	−37.5	76/100
Caterpillar (N)	84.10	+33.6	131/100	ArchCoal (N)	32.10	−34.6	21/100
SprintFON (N)	19.09	+33.2	251/100	AT&T (N)	18.03	−34.4	55/100
UtilHldrs (A)	79.78	+33.1	324/100	BEA Sys (Nq)	12.30	−32.7	26/100
HewlettPk (N)	21.81	+29.9	163/100	Dell (Nq)	35.40	−31.3	66/100
CocaCola (N)	51.46	+28.7	129/100	Nextel (Nq)	25.50	−31.2	73/100
EliLilly (N)	74.02	+26.9	154/100	GenElec (N)	30.85	−30.9	89/100
GoldmanSachs (N)	101.80	+25.5	131/100	WstnDgtl (N)	8.98	−30.5	52/100

Source: WSJ Market Data Group *without block trades.
Money flow figures are the dollar value of composite uptick trades minus the dollar value of downtick trades. The up/down ratio reflects the value of uptick trades relative to the value of downtick trades.

Dow Jones Global Sector Titans

April 22, 2004

INDEX/COMPONENT	PRICE/CLOSE	% CHG	INDEX/COMPONENT	PRICE/CLOSE	% CHG
Automobile	251.45	+1.89	Health Care	274.93	+0.48
FordMotor(US)	15.77	+5.56	Aventis(FR)	65.80	+4.86
ToyotaMotor(JP)	4120.00	+3.00	AbbottLab(US)	44.25	+2.62
Banks	110.13	+0.60	Industrial Goods/Svcs.	191.83	+1.69
JPMorganChase(US)	38.38	+1.86	3MCo(US)	86.95	+3.61
BankAm(US)	81.39	+1.01	TycoInt(US)	29.40	+2.58
Basic Resources	143.59	+0.85	Insurance	219.99	+0.87
IntPaper(US)	43.02	+4.44	PrudentialFin(US)	44.75	+4.02
Alcoa(US)	33.11	+4.32	Allstate(US)	46.69	+1.50
Chemicals	185.59	+0.83	Media	255.07	+0.44
DowChem(US)	41.86	+2.45	Vivendi(FR)	22.05	+3.04
DuPont(US)	44.83	+1.43	LibertyMed A(US)	11.34	+1.89
Construction	118.82	+1.07	Noncyclical Goods/Svcs.	282.24	+1.69
Lafarge(FR)	70.65	+2.84	eBay(US)	82.59	+10.43
StGobain(FR)	43.36	+1.90	InteractiveCorp(US)	34.44	+5.84
Cyclical Goods/Svcs.	195.48	+1.21	Retail	244.83	+0.99
YumBrandsI(US)	39.50	+9.42	Lowes Cos(US)	53.29	+2.38
Starbucks(US)	39.23	+5.88	HomeDepot(US)	36.35	+2.28
Energy	253.99	+0.81	Technology	466.61	+1.46
Schlumberger(US)	63.84	+3.27	Motorola(US)	20.72	+7.36
ChevronTexaco(US)	91.80	+2.15	CiscoSys(US)	23.15	+3.49
Financial Services	299.15	+1.17	Telecommunications	190.84	+0.28
MerillLynch(US)	57.25	+2.80	Nextel A(US)	25.63	+3.35
AmExpress(US)	50.78	+1.80	SBC Comm(US)	25.40	+2.54
Food & Beverage	224.19	+0.87	Utilities	90.48	+0.66
SaraLee(US)	22.99	+3.33	Exelon(US)	66.21	+1.69
Danone(FR)	143.50	+2.14	E.ON(GR)	57.66	+1.16

WSJ.com THE WALL STREET JOURNAL. ONLINE

Closing Stock Market Diaries
Tuesday, July 6, 2004

For Market Close of July 06, 2004

NYSE Market Diary	Latest Close	Previous Close	Week Ago
Issues Traded	3,411	3,405	3,439
Advances	1,262	2,128	1,713
Declines	2,007	1,160	1,587
Unchanged	142	117	139
New Highs	92	86	114
New Lows	33	16	37
Advancing Volume	271,979,160	412,807,820	758,107,980
Declining Volume	978,346,050	656,194,410	602,264,880
Volume Traded	1,262,067,640	1,082,196,410	1,374,839,540
Closing Tick	+ 161	+ 639	+ 148
Closing Arms (trin)	2.26	2.92	0.86
Block Trades	19,425	14,333	17,934
Nasdaq Market Diary	Latest Close	Previous Close	Week Ago
Issues Traded	3,235	3,181	3,262
Advances	781	1,455	1,834
Declines	2,322	1,552	1,261
Unchanged	132	174	167
New Highs	48	42	87
New Lows	77	40	16
Advancing Volume	143,018,895	326,959,165	1,108,480,701
Declining Volume	1,705,847,375	822,608,711	405,037,445
Volume Traded	1,861,144,817	1,176,018,104	1,520,122,376
Block Trades	n.a.	7,730	9,893
Amex Market Diary	Latest Close	Previous Close	Week Ago
Issues Traded	962	928	960
Advances	297	469	434
Declines	572	364	428
Unchanged	93	95	98
New Highs	19	17	21
New Lows	12	10	15
Advancing Volume	9,220,360	20,463,150	31,249,000
Declining Volume	43,577,800	25,460,605	17,964,190
Volume Traded	54,185,810	48,219,755	53,993,450
Block Trades	n.a.	815	882

Closing Tick = The net difference of the number of stocks closing higher than their previous trade from those closing lower; NYSE trading only.

ing into stocks (bullish sign), as the trin of 0.71 from our example on April 22, 2004, shows.

The Arms index is computed by dividing two ratios:

$$\text{Arms index} = \frac{\dfrac{\text{Advance}}{\text{Declines}}}{\dfrac{\text{Advance volume}}{\text{Decline volume}}} = \frac{\dfrac{2,465}{839}}{\dfrac{1,463,709}{355,936}} = \frac{2.938}{4.112} = 0.714 = 0.71$$

In this example, a trin of less than one indicates that the (denominator) ratio of the volume of advancing stocks to declining stocks (1,463,709/355,936) was greater than the (numerator) ratio of advancing stocks to declining stocks (2,465/839) *and therefore, a disproportionate share of the trading volume was in advancing stocks (a bullish sign)*. A trin of more than one would indicate the opposite, a bearish sign.

The above example, drawn from the April 23, 2004, *Journal*, is complex because it employs the actual trading data for April 22, 2004. Consider instead the following simple hypothetical examples. The first illustrates a bull (rising) market, the second a bear (falling) market.

Use hypothetical numbers of your own to create additional examples. This will establish your understanding of the Arms index.

Bull Market

$$\frac{\dfrac{\text{Advances}}{\text{Declines}}}{\dfrac{\text{Advance volume}}{\text{Decline volume}}} = \frac{\dfrac{1}{1}}{\dfrac{2}{1}} = \frac{1}{2} = 0.5$$

Although advances and declines were equal, advance volume was twice decline volume, and, therefore, a trin of 0.5 is a bullish sign.

$$\frac{\dfrac{\text{Advances}}{\text{Declines}}}{\dfrac{\text{Advance volume}}{\text{Decline volume}}} = \frac{\dfrac{1}{2}}{\dfrac{1}{1}} = \frac{1}{2} = 0.5$$

Although declines exceeded advances, advance volume equaled decline volume, and a trin of 0.5 remained a bullish sign.

Bear Market

$$\frac{\dfrac{\text{Advances}}{\text{Declines}}}{\dfrac{\text{Advance volume}}{\text{Decline volume}}} = \frac{\dfrac{1}{1}}{\dfrac{1}{2}} = 2$$

Although advances and declines were equal, decline volume was twice advance volume, and, therefore, a trin of 2 is a bearish sign.

$$\dfrac{\dfrac{\text{Advances}}{\text{Declines}}}{\dfrac{\text{Advance volume}}{\text{Decline volume}}} = \dfrac{\dfrac{2}{1}}{\dfrac{1}{1}} = 2$$

Although advances exceeded declines, decline volume equaled advance volume, and a trin of 2 remained a bearish sign.

The last row of the **Diaries** section lists the number of block trades (trades of 10,000 shares of stock). On Thursday, April 22, 2004, 27,170 block trades occurred on the New York Stock Exchange.

Finally, the **Diaries** component of **Markets Scorecard** on page 228 lists the number of stocks that hit new highs and lows for the NYSE, NASDAQ, and AMEX (i.e., the number that closed higher or lower than at any time in the past 52 weeks). On Thursday, April 22, 2004, 178 stocks reached new highs and 87 reached new lows on the New York Stock Exchange.

NYSE Highs & Lows (in the front page indexes of the first and third sections) lists these stocks by name. Consider the example on page 234 from the Friday, April 23, 2004, *Journal*.

Returning to **Markets Scorecard** in the print edition (on page 228), **Breakdown of Trading** provides trading volume on all stock exchanges of securities listed on the NYSE, NASDAQ, and AMEX. As mentioned earlier, shares listed on the NYSE trade on a variety of exchanges as well as electronically and, therefore, the composite volume of all trades will be greater than the New York volume. Taking the NYSE as our example, trading of all NYSE stocks on all exchanges reached a composite volume of 2,226,449,380 shares on Thursday, April 22, 2004. Note that New York trading of these shares was around 1.8 billion and that 400 million shares of NYSE-listed stocks traded on other exchanges that day.

The **Late-Trading Snapshot** on page 229, which includes **Late Price Percentage Gainers and Losers**, **Late Most Active Issues**, and **Late-Trading Activity**, provides information on trading activity between 4:00 p.m. and 6:30 p.m. Eastern time. The online edition lists this feature under After Hours below U.S. Stocks when you click on Markets and Markets Data Center on the home page's left-hand menu-bar. See the example on page 235 from Tuesday, July 6, 2004.

Money Flows on page 229 reflect the dollar value of composite uptick trades (a trade that generated a price increase) less the value of downtick trades. **Uptick vs. Downtick Trading by Dollar Volume** on page 230 presents money flows for key stock-market indicators, while **Issue Gainers and Losers** (page 230) does the same for individual stocks. The online edition lists Money Flow—Summary, as well as Gainers and Decliners, under

NYSE Highs & Lows

April 22, 2004 4 p.m. ET

New 52-Week Highs — 178

ABM Ind	18.85	BlackDeck	61.25	DeRigo ADS	6.10	IL Tool	89.40	NtlProc	26.22	ThermoElec	30.63
AaronRent s	26.17	BlountInt	12.33	Deere	74.93	ImpTob ADS	46.41	NtwrkAssoc	19.75	3M s	87.18
AdvanceAuto s	44.41	BocaRsrts A	18.25	Dimon	7.63	IntShiphld	17.10	NewfldExpl	53.15	TimberInd	65.30
AdvMedOp	30.45	BiseCascCp	53.23	DuqsnLt pfH n	50.30	JacuzziBrnd	9.99	Nucor	67.25	TitanInt	6.75
AlbertoCl s	47.58	BordersGrp	25.24	EagleMat s	62.80	JardenCp s	39.97	PMI Gp	44.81	TomBrown	47.87
Allergan	90.95	BoydGaming	25.70	EagleMat B n	61.10	JoAnnStrs	30.15	PMI Gp Hits n	28.93	TytaMtr ADS	76.55
Allete	36.15	BriggsStrat	73.13	EmanChm	44.00	Kellogg	42.41	PaxarCp	15.75	TransatlHldg	93.35
AllianceData	38.10	Brinks	29.81	Ecolab s	29.20	KenCole A	37.39	PediatrixMed	71.62	TysonFood A	19.32
AlliantTech	61.57	BrownShoe	39.95	Elan ADS	23.20	KimbClark	65.75	PepBoys	29.38	UST Inc	39.00
Amdocs	30.09	ButlrMfg	24.80	EncoreAcq	29.95	KineticCnpts n	49.30	PhlpLngDst	20.36	UtdIndl	21.65
AmRE Ptnrs	17.47	CNF	37.86	Engelhard	30.87	KnghtRidder	79.50	PilgrmPr	23.96	UnvlCp	53.72
AmTower A	13.80	CNF Tr Tecons	52.93	ESCO Tech	49.36	LafargeNoAm	44.49	PitneyBws	44.40	ValeroEngy	62.25
Anthem	95.20	CNH Global*	20.84	FMC	44.84	LeeEnt	48.11	ProgrsvCp	91.97	Valspar	51.00
AnthmEq un	110.42	CSS Ind s	34.85	FstData	46.80	EliLilly	74.76	RPC	13.29	VarianMed	92.98
ApogentTch	33.10	CVS Cp	39.45	FisherSci	59.60	MGIC Inv	74.18	RemtnO&G	21.96	VoltInfoSci	27.20
AppldIndTch	26.81	CabotO&G	35.55	FleetwdEnt	16.06	MarriottInt A	48.21	RobHalfIntl	26.95	WsteConn	40.85
Aramark	29.04	CaesarsEnt	14.60	Flowserve	22.98	McCrmkCo	34.00	RogersCp	61.70	Watsco	30.88
ArchChem	29.99	CardnlHlth	73.91	Genentech	119.30	McCrmkCo Vtg	33.72	SantdrBcp	29.30	WatsonWyatt A	26.64
ArgosyGamng	37.87	CaremarkRx	34.84	GA Gulf	32.91	MediaGen A	70.90	SaraLee	23.00	WattsWater A	24.77
ArmorHldg	35.97	ChpkeEn6.0pf n	76.20	GA Pac	37.26	MedicisPhrm s	44.97	SelectMedCp s	18.57	WelptHlth	118.50
ArrowElec	28.70	ChoiceHtl	47.43	GlbIPymts	51.13	MichaelStr	52.57	Skyline	45.39	WstCstHspty	6.87
AveryDensn	64.97	Coach s	45.33	GrphPack n	5.40	Millennium	17.41	SmthNphADS s	53.70	Weyerhsr	68.05
AztarCp	26.18	ConAgraFoods	29.36	Gtech	64.95	MolinaHlthcr n	33.97	SonocoPdt	25.99	WlvrinWrld	27.38
BKF CapGp	28.00	Cooper	59.16	HarmanInt s	87.25	MonacCoach	30.88	SpectraSite n	41.47	WldFuelSvc	43.00
Ball Cp	71.30	CrnPdtsInt	44.32	HarteHanks	24.10	Mtrola Un	54.84	StanleyWks	45.56	Wrigley	60.98
Bancol ADS	8.10	CorrCorp	38.00	HarvstNatRes	15.80	Motorola	20.77	StationCno	49.63	YorkInt	42.20
Bard CR	110.88	Covance	36.20	Hilton	17.95	MuellerInd	36.93	SterisCp	27.70	Yum!Brands	40.16
BeckmnCoultr	58.14	Crane	34.40	HormelFood	30.86	MVC Captl	9.03	Stryker Cp	100.65	ZenithNtl	43.75
BectonDksn	54.10	CrownCastl	15.80	ITT Ind	80.25	NBTY	39.05	Supervalu	31.15	Zimmer	85.25
Bemis s	28.45	Cummins	66.66	IDEX Cp	47.00	NCI Bldg	32.00				

New 52-Week Lows — 87

AL Pwr pfA h	24.70	EmpDistFlc pfD	26.30	CBTCS 03-16 n	24.35	NRG Engy n	20.69	PfdCpIncStr n	21.75	SlBrEmrgDbt n	16.90
AlIncWrld	11.49	EntPropTr	25.90	CBTCS 04-1 n	24.40	NuvCA Inv	13.95	PfdIncoStrat	21.83	SlBrWldInco	14.27
ASBCCap pf	26.05	EqResdntl pfB	26.65	MBIACpClyFd n	14.41	NuvCT Prm	14.38	PPlus GSG-1	23.00	ScudderMuni	11.06
BRE Prop pfC n	23.90	FstRpBnk pfA n	24.75	Metlife nts33 n	23.00	NuvInsCA	14.39	PblcStorg pfA n	22.60	SeligQual	12.20
BAm5.5Sbnts n	23.49	GAPwrPINES n	23.15	MS QtyInc	13.27	NuvInsQual	14.82	PblcStorg pfF	26.50	SimonProp pfF	26.40
BlkRkAdvTr	11.03	GdnSrlCorts n	23.40	MS IMInc	'13.52	NuvNY TxF	13.09	PblcStrg pfW n	24.11	SntcScDmnRs n	22.80
BlkRkFL Muni	13.44	HnckJ PfdIncoll	23.18	MS IMB	13.68	NuvSelTxF2	12.75	PblcStorg pfX n	23.70	TVA Parrs	24.30
Citigroup pfM	49.51	HnckJPfdIncIlln	21.95	MS QtySec	13.50	NuvSelTxF	13.18	PblcStorg pfZ n	22.81	VnKmCAInc	15.23
ColonIInvMun	9.69	HnckJ TxAdv n	17.10	MS QtyInv	13.34	NuvTX Qual	13.75	PutnmMgdMun	6.97	VnKmOpII	13.17
CpAsBdCabco n	23.00	INGGrp6.2Scs n	24.20	MS IMT	13.47	OGE Engy pf	25.50	PutnmMstInco	6.21	VnKmNYInc	14.35
DreyfStrMuni	8.66	IBMII7.125Corts	25.81	MSGldnSch4-4n	22.60	ONB Cap	26.02	PutnmTxF	11.80	VnKmFL	15.10
DufPhlpsBnd	12.90	iStarFnl pfG n	24.85	MSGdnSch4-2n	22.20	ONBCap Tr	26.17	RMKStrIncFd n	14.73	VnKmGrCA	14.37
DukeRlty pfJ n	23.61	KohlsCp	39.59	MuniHldgInsll	12.52	PartnerRe pfT	25.80	RyceFcs pfA n	24.31	VrznMDCorts n	23.50
DukeRlty pfK n	23.10	CBTCS 01-23	26.02	MuniyldCAInFd	13.08	PIMCO NY	12.85	SLGrnRltypfC n	24.62	WtCtHsTrups n	25.20
1838BondFd	17.90	CBTCS 01-1	26.00	MuniyldFL Fd	13.15						

Statistics below U.S. Stocks when you click on Markets and Markets Data Center on the home page's left-hand menu-bar. See the example on page 236 from Tuesday, July 6, 2004. **Dow Jones Global Sector Titans** (page 230) presents trading results for some of the world's largest corporations.

Finally, the online edition enables you to check industry performance and then move on to specific firms within an industry. Click on Markets and Markets Data Center (from the home page's left-hand menu-bar) and Industry Groups/Sectors, and then look at DJ Industry Group Center.

THE ODD-LOT TRADER

So far this discussion has proceeded without regard to the magnitude of individual investments, except for the observation that companies split their

WSJ.com **THE WALL STREET JOURNAL.**
                    O N L I N E

Most Active Issues

Tuesday, July 6, 2004 , 4 p.m. to 6:35 p.m.

The Late-Trading Snapshot reflects trading activity after regular trading hours in NYSE and Amex issues reported by electronic trading services, securities dealers and regional exchanges between 4 p.m. and 6:35 p.m. Eastern time, and in Nasdaq NMS issues between 4 p.m. and 6:30 p.m., with a minimum price of $3 and volume of 5,000. The primary market is indicated for each issue. N-NYSE A-Amex Nq-Nasdaq SC-Nasdaq SmallCap

Late-Trading Activity					
	Tuesday	Monday	Friday	Thursday	Wednesday
Issues Traded	2,938	2,720	3,072	3,399	3,452
Advances	1,359	522	701	444	540
Declines	448	647	441	464	513
Unchanged	1,131	1,551	1,930	2,491	2,399
Advancing Volume	32,549,337	9,276,742	14,656,329	22,338,660	25,368,823
Declining Volume	14,832,820	7,477,032	17,179,816	45,608,831	17,720,916
Total Volume	87,533,728	27,478,470	64,678,275	133,943,884	80,383,881

Late Most Active Issues					
Issue	**Exchange**	**Volume**	**Last**	**Change**	**% Chg**
Nasdaq 100	A	3,194.8	36.02	-0.01	...
Microsoft	Nq	1,921.9	28.02	...	...
SunMicrsys	Nq	1,858.4	3.91	+0.03	+0.8
Intel	Nq	1,654.3	26.14	+0.03	+0.1
PepsiCo	N	1,577.4	53.50	...	...
CiscoSys	Nq	1,355.2	22.39	+0.02	+0.1
Level3Comm	Nq	1,352.7	3.12	+0.02	+0.6
OracleCp	Nq	1,300.5	11.22	+0.02	+0.2
VeritasSftwr	Nq	1,092.7	16.97	-0.03	-0.2
OcciPete	N	981.5	48.86	...	...
Micromuse	Nq	819.2	5.30	+0.13	+2.5
AutDataProc	N	817.0	40.77	...	...
AscentialSftwr	Nq	781.4	11.30	-2.72	-19.4
ApldMatl	Nq	759.9	17.93	-0.08	-0.4
Dell	Nq	704.0	35.07	+0.14	+0.4
Alltel	N	687.7	49.65	...	...
Elan ADS	N	660.0	25.25	...	...
SPDR	A	656.0	111.89	...	...
RobHalfIntl	N	640.0	28.79	...	...
HewlettPk	N	625.9	20.00	-0.04	-0.2
GenElec	N	619.6	31.83	...	...
Tellabs	Nq	572.6	8.11	-0.03	-0.4
NSTAR	N	569.4	47.68	...	...
SemiConHldrs	A	471.1	34.62	+0.04	+0.1
Yahoo	Nq	457.8	33.38	+0.16	+0.5
Pfizer	N	447.9	33.87	...	...
Wachovia	N	428.9	44.11	...	...
JohnsCtrl	N	425.5	51.52	...	...
TibcoSftwr	Nq	425.5	7.34	...	...
SecureCmptg	Nq	424.1	6.70	-3.23	-32.5

Home

THE FUTURE OF ADVERTISING
ONLINE — THE WALL STREET JOURNAL ONLINE
NO. 6 IN A SERIES: TM ADVERTISING / AMERICAN AIRLINES

Money Flows
Uptick vs. Downtick Trading by Dollar Volume
For Tuesday, July 6, 2004 - 6:00 p.m. Eastern Time

Money flow figures are the dollar value of composite uptick trades minus the dollar value of downtick trades. The up/down ratio reflects the value of uptick trades relative to the value of downtick trades. Money flow figures for nonblock and block trades are presented separately for indexes. View a more detailed explanation here.

Market	Money Flow (in Millions)	Up/Down Ratio
Dow Jones Industrial Average	36.43	103/100
Block Trades	-65.52	90/100
Dow Jones Total Market Index - US	502.96	105/100
Block Trades	337.99	110/100
S & P 500	413.62	106/100
Block Trades	158.52	106/100
Russell 2000	86.91	105/100
Block Trades	88.86	126/100

Gainers and Decliners

View an expanded list of the Top 100 Gainers

Gainers	Last Price	% Change	Money Flow (in Millions)	Up/Down Ratio
Nasdaq 100	36.04	-0.78	200.45	124/100
Anthem	86.40	-1.90	93.08	224/100
TycoInt	32.14	-0.29	60.39	254/100
iShrRu2000	114.12	-2.08	58.46	131/100
SPDR	111.89	-0.99	47.94	107/100
UtdHlthGp	60.08	-0.87	40.08	194/100
OracleCp	11.20	-0.45	34.19	180/100
RetailHldrs	89.88	-0.12	34.18	200/100
Wachovia	44.11	-0.03	30.49	236/100
WelptHlth	108.40	-2.57	27.06	119/100
ChevronTex	93.39	0.14	25.51	140/100
BiotchHldrs	143.25	-2.05	23.19	213/100
GenMotor	44.55	-0.69	22.62	166/100
SBC Comm	24.13	0.02	22.22	165/100

stock chiefly in order to keep its price within the small investor's reach. Remember that round lots are trades of 100 shares whose commission per share is lower than that on *odd-lot* (less than 100 shares) transactions. Yet many small investors still trade in odd lots because they cannot afford to deal in round lots. For instance, Genentech closed at $118.22 on Friday, April 23, 2004, putting the cost of a round-lot purchase at $11,822 ($118.22 multiplied by 100) and out of the reach of a large number of small investors.

Many market analysts used to believe that odd-lot transactions were a contrary (negative) indicator, because they saw the small investor as a market follower who buys more as the market peaks and sells more as it bottoms out (the opposite of the savvy, big-time trader who gets in at the bottom and out at the top). Therefore, according to this wisdom, a high ratio of odd-lot buying to selling is a sign of a market peak (time to sell), while the opposite indicates a market trough (time to buy). However, since a great many small investors in recent years have abandoned odd-lot trading in favor of mutual funds, this omen has become less significant to analysts.

The Journal provides a daily record of **Odd-Lot Trading** for the day preceding the previous trading day, usually at the bottom of the second page of the NYSE Listings. See the example below from the Friday, April 23, 2004, print issue that indicated sales of 12,237,088 shares and purchases of 10,626,393 shares on Wednesday, April 21, 2004. According to the contrarian wisdom outlined above, this was a *buy* signal for the savvy investor.

A more detailed report appears on Saturdays. For example, see **Odd-Lot Trading** from the Saturday, September 24, 2005, *Wall Street Journal* on page 238. Odd-lot purchases (19,053,644 shares) exceeded odd-lot sales (15,681,172 shares) on Thursday, September 22, 2005, in NYSE trading by odd-lot specialists, and orders to buy (56,197,806) by all NYSE member firms for the week ended September 9, 2005, exceeded orders to sell plus short sales (48,854,193 + 6,507,010 = 55,361,203).

Odd-Lot Trading

NEW YORK - The New York Stock Exchange specialists reported the following odd-lot transactions (in shares)

	CUSTOMER PURCHASES	SHORT SALES	OTHER SALES	TOTAL SALES	
April 21, 2004	10,626,393	987,249	11,249,839	12,237,088 ◄—	Odd-lot sales exceeded purchases on April 21, 2004.

Odd-Lot Trading

NEW YORK - The New York Stock Exchange specialists reported the following odd-lot transactions (in shares)

	CUSTOMER PURCHASES	SHORT SALES	OTHER SALES	TOTAL SALES
September 22, 2005	19,053,644	2,657,201	13,023,971	15,681,172

New York Stock Exchange odd-lot trading for all member firms dealing in odd-lots, for the week ended September 9, 2005:

	SHARES	VALUES
Customers' Orders to Buy	56,197,806	$2,557,271,819
Customers' Orders to Sell	48,854,193	$2,275,985,551
Customers' Short Sales	6,507,010	$223,794,892

Round-Lot transactions (in shares) for the week ended September 9, 2005:

	PURCHASES	SALES (INC SHORT SALES)	SHORT SALES
Total	6,028,950,730	6,028,950,730	860,703,380
For Member Accounts:			
As Specialists	515,697,030	517,645,200	137,893,910
As Floor Traders	285,600	399,900	164,900
Others	1,393,047,316	1,327,241,317	231,403,350

American Stock Exchange round-lot and odd-lot trading statistics for the week ended September 9, 2005:

	PURCHASES	SALES (INC SHORT SALES)	SHORT SALES
Total	318,503,630	318,503,630	28,942,100
For Member Accounts:			
As Specialists	45,289,530	59,845,963	5,217,611
As Floor Traders	25,500	29,900	22,800
Others	19,130,862	20,910,976	6,919,683
Customer odd-lots	1,306,458	2,089,430	

Odd-lot purchases exceeded sales on September 22, 2005, but odd-lot orders to sell exceeded buy orders for the week ended September 9, 2005.

FOLLOW YOUR STOCK

Suppose, now that you have studied the various stock-market indicators and indexes, you decide that the time is right to get into the market, and do so. You will want to follow the progress of your investment. Here's how you do it. If you own shares of AMR (American Airlines), you can follow the stock's daily performance in *The Wall Street Journal* print edition by turning to **New York Stock Exchange Composite Transactions** (see page 239). Recall that this composite report includes a small amount of trading activity on regional exchanges. You'll find a reference to all exchanges in the index on the front pages of the first (A1) and third (C1) sections.

You can follow your stock in the online edition by typing the ticker symbol (AMR) or full name into the Quotes and Research field at the home page. This link provides extensive information about the company in addition to stock quotes. A copy of the results of your search on Thursday, July 15, 2004, appears on page 241. It may cement your understanding to

NEW YORK STOCK EXCHANGE
COMPOSITE TRANSACTIONS

A

YTD %CHG	52-WEEK HI	LO	STOCK (SYM)	DIV	YLD %	PE	VOL 100s	CLOSE	NET CHG
-22.1	16.87	3.70	AAR AIR		...	dd	2878	11.64	-0.45
6.4	18.85	13.03	ABM Ind ABM	.40	2.2	10	832	18.52	-0.23
-5.9	25.35	15.95	ABN Am ADS ABN	1.11e	5.0	...	1799	22.10	-0.05
4.1	45.98	30.30♦	ACE Ltd ACE	.76	1.8	9	12150	43.10	-0.40
-16.6	10.85	4.92♦	AES Cp AES		...	dd	15482	7.87	-0.06
15.2	42.57	28	AFLAC AFL	.38f	.9	27	6510	41.68	-0.13
4.0	22.80	15.25	AGCO Cp AG		...	21	7892	20.94	-0.52
-3.1	30.63	24.50	AGL Res ATG	1.12	4.0	13	737	28.20	-0.18
10.8	6.87	1.74♦	AK Steel AKS		...	dd	10612	5.65	-0.17
-5.6	37.30	26.38♦	AMB Prop AMB	1.70f	5.5	21	2516	31.05	-0.55
-4.2	25.12	5.81	Amcol ACO	.28f	1.4	27	1542	19.45	-0.48
-1.9	29	21.99	AMLI Rsdntl AML	1.92	7.3	29	449	26.30	-0.13
-0.5	17.65	3.59	AMR AMR		...	dd	28363	12.88	-0.37
-23.1	4.60	1.19	APT Satelt ATS		...		911	1.83	0.11
75.2	14.10	6.39	AT&T Wrls AWE		...		88155510	14	0.06
-9.7	23.18	16	AT&T T	.95	5.2	9	106467	18.34	0.31
-4.2	19.12	9.67	AVX Cp AVX	.15	.9	dd	2735	15.93	0.12
2.0	24.37	13.44♦	AXA ADS AXA	.52e	2.4	...	1830	21.91	0.01
21.3	17.30	9	AZZ AZZ		...		5	16.20	0.05
26.3	26.17	14.47	AaronRent RNT s	.04f	.2	23	832	25.42	-0.75
16.8	22.40	13.00	AaronRent A RNTA s	.04f	.2	20	2	21.60	-0.15
19.9	6.55	2.30	ABB ADS ABB s	1.23e	20.2	dd	1399	6.09	-0.01
-5.8	47.25	37.65	AbbottLab ABT		...	25	37189	43.90	-0.35
0.8	41.26	40	AbbottLab wi n		...		10	41.20	0.65
32.7	36.38	23.07	Abercrombie A ANF	.13p	...	16	8008	32.80	-0.28
-7.2	8.46	6.10	Abitibi ABY	.10g	...	...	4806	7.53	0.01
0.7	15	8.17♦	AcadiaRlty AKR	.64	5.1	42	1018	12.59	0.21
-6.4	26.95	15.26	Accenture ACN		...	23	45848	24.64	0.42
-19.4	27.71	12.58	ActionPerf ATN	.20	1.3	20	2225	15.80	-0.07
2.1	43.10	17.48	Actuant A ATU s		...	31	667	36.96	-0.09
-1.0	26.44	14.11	Acuity Br AYI	.60	2.4	21	3076	25.53	0.23
-21.4	17.10	8.56	Adecco ADO	.11e	.9	...	666	12.67	0.60
3.8	18.45	5.90	Administaff ASF		...	38	1565	18.04	0.04
8.7	44.41	24.12	AdvanceAuto AAP s		...	27	5474	44.23	-0.10
-9.0	14.24	9.35	AdvMktg MKT	.04	.4	19	215	10.37	0.08
57.0	30.45	13.70	AdvMedOp AVO		...		16955	30.85	0.40
9.8	18.50	5.80	AdvMicro AMD		...	dd	73991	16.36	-0.10
1.8	6.04	2.27	AdSemEg ADS ASX s	stk	...	...	1115	5.14	0.11
5.9	22.40	7.90	Advntst ADS ATE	.09e	.4	...	318	21.05	0.33
1.0	34.20	25.13	ADVO AD s	.33e	1.0	19	804	32.08	-0.11
-7.4	16.23	8.65♦	Aegon AEG	.47e	3.4	11	2045	13.70	0.07
24.0	37.80	16.17	Aeropostale ARO		...	24	4206	34	0.20
33.7	95.09	47.90	Aetna AET	.04	...	15	7554	90.36	-0.99
-10.2	57.96	42.10♦	AffilCmptr A ACS		...	13	34413	48.90	0.48
8.3	58.89	29.59	AffilMangr AMG s		...	27	5332	50.23	-1.07
-11.8	19.25	16.27	AffRsdntlComm ARC n	.15p	...	...	787	16.76	-0.14
-16.1	4.14	1.58	AgereSys A AGRA		...	dd	84303	2.56	0.03
-14.5	3.88	1.51	AgereSys B AGRB		...	dd	76381	2.48	0.04
0.9	38.80	15.44	AgilentTch A		...	dd	23999	29.50	0.13
3.6	15.07	9.72♦	AgnicoEgl AEM	.03g	.2	dd	6090	12.51	-0.24
-12.3	33.42	20.30	AgreeRlty ADC	1.94	7.8	...	343	24.81	-0.86
-22.8	16.96	10.36	Agrium AGU	.11g	.9	dd	2585	12.71	-0.11
2.1	9.59	3.52	Ahold ADS AHO	.70e	8.8	...	4328	7.92	-0.12
0.1	55.40	40.50	AirProduct APD	.92	1.7	30	6344	52.87	0.08
2.0	24.95	16.55	Airgas ARG	.16	.7	21	2780	21.90	-0.10
22.7	5.18	2.05	AirnetSys ANS		...	17	124	4.60	0.11
3.4	20.84	6.80	AirTranHldg AAI		...	10	9756	12.30	0.19
11.2	18.70	11.65	AlamoGp ALG	.24	1.4	21	116	16.97	...
27.5	23	8.65	AlarisMed AMI		...	dd	2392	19.40	-0.29
-7.9	31.86	17	AlaskaAir ALK		...	79	4991	25.13	-1.58
-13.7	35.08	22.70♦	AlbanyInt AIN	.28	1.0	18	700	29.26	-0.46
-0.9	30.75	25.10	Albemarle ALB	.58	2.0	20	1226	29.70	-0.20

(AMR → points to the AMR AMR row)

YTD %CHG	52-WEEK HI	LO	STOCK (SYM)	DIV	YLD %	PE	VOL 100s	CLOSE	NET CHG
-13.9	39.44	21.75	Alcoa AA	.60	1.8	25	50576	32.71	-0.40
22.1	76	40	Alcon ACL	.35e	.5	35	5407	73.94	0.05
22.1	164.65	68.51	Alexanders ALX		...	dd	7	152.22	0.92
-1.5	65.20	41.85	AlexREEq ARE	2.40f	4.2	22	837	57.05	-0.70
21.3	269.25	163.97	Allghny Y	stk	...	12	53	264.52	-2.58
13.0	15.35	7	AllghnyEngy AYE		...	...	7490	14.42	-0.17
-14.1	14	3.75	AllghnyTch ATI	.24	2.1	dd	3472	11.35	-0.47
17.6	90.95	69.50	Allergan AGN	.36	.4	dd	4358	90.35	-0.29
17.1	36.15	22.28	Allete ALE	1.13	3.2	12	2137	35.82	-0.18
4.2	39.25	29.47	AllncCapMgt AC	1.45e	4.1	35	1494	35.17	0.19
35.2	38.10	20	♦AllianceData ADS		...	37	7853	37.43	0.21
11.0	34.16	14.60	AllncGamg AGI		...	52	7650	27.37	-1.00
5.4	6	2.70	Alliance AIQ		...	dd	248	3.90	-0.06
2.8	26.55	17.05	AlliantEngy LNT	1.00	3.9	14	2384	25.59	-0.30
7.4	61.57	46.50	AlliantTech ATK		...	17	3721	62.02	0.45
-13.1	14.26	6.17	Allianz ADS AZ s	1.36e	12.3	...	2394	11.06	0.02
-7.0	31.12	19.70♦	AlldCap ALD	2.28	8.8	14	5554	25.94	-0.44
3.5	34.99	20.45	AlldDomq ADS AED	.92e	2.8	...	212	32.69	-0.98
-4.9	35.10	27.05	AldIrhBk ADS AIB	1.31e	4.3	...	741	30.19	0.30
-4.2	14.44	7.67	AlldWaste AW		...	dd	11533	13.30	-0.19
13.4	38.32	14.78	AllmericaFnl AFC		...	21	2591	34.88	-0.49
8.1	48.16	34.54	Allstate ALL	1.12f	2.4	10	20649	46.50	-0.19
4.1	55.36	46.90♦	Alltel un AYZ	3.88	7.5	...	2408	51.74	0.46
11.0	53.28	43.75♦	Alltel AT	1.48	2.9	13	20637	51.70	0.89
3.5	23.97	16.85	Alpharma A ALO	.18	.9	80	2012	20.81	-0.18
28.0	3.31	1.39	Alstom ADS ALS s	.26e	12.0	...	1307	2.15	-0.02
5.0	69.75	47.20	AltanaAG AAA	1.87e	3.0	...	40	63.31	0.60
2.7	58.96	30.20	AltriaGp MO	2.72	4.9	12	40926	55.90	-0.60
-24.0	21.16	10.50	Alumina ADS AWC	.57e	3.7	...	113	15.23	0.03
-9.9	92.25	16.25	AluCpChina ACH	1.70e	2.4	...	2243	69.39	-0.35
5.1	79.76	55.80	AmbacFnl ABK	.44	.6	12	3932	72.90	-0.07
33.5	30.09	16.40	Amdocs DOX		...	32	20109	30	0.57
26.3	67.48	44.23♦	AmerHess AHC	1.20	1.8	10	8097	67.13	-0.21
-5.4	48.34	40.35	Ameren AEE	2.54	5.8	14	4666	43.51	-0.06
39.0	40.12	16.14	AmMovil ADS AMX	.11e	.3	...	14469	37.99	0.34
-12.3	16	2.80	AmWstHldg B AWA		...	4	7680	10.88	-0.10
-1.4	42.10	22.97	AmerAxle AXL		...	11	2973	39.86	0.02
0.9	35.10	24.70	AEP AEP	1.40	4.5	dd	14369	30.77	-0.19
-1.4	49.70	39.75	AmElecPwr un	4.63	10.3	...	199	44.92	-0.19
26.4	13.15	8.55	AmEqtyLf AEL n	.01p	...	...	1712	12.60	0.14
4.2	53.98	36	AmExpress AXP	.40	.8	21	45948	50.27	-0.51
13.9	31	21.27	AmFnl AFG	.50	1.7	7	914	30.13	-0.15
-10.0	18.62	13.40♦	AmFnlRlty AFR n	.75e	4.9	...	2621	15.35	-0.13
-1.3	23.45	14.12	AmGreetgs AM		...	16	3436	21.59	-0.23
7.9	29.15	11.30	AmHmMrtg AHH	2.20a	9.3	6	3259	23.77	-0.07
11.6	77.36	54.20	AmIntlGp AIG	.26	.4	19	42332	73.96	0.26
-18.1	47.28	32.34	AIPC PLB	.19p	...	15	1440	34.30	0.21
-2.8	22.52	15.83	AmLandLse AML	1.00	5.2	16	77	19.40	-0.09
22.2	27.90	15.20	AmMedSecGp AMZ		...	13	387	27.40	0.56
0.3	17.47	10.51	AmRE Ptnrs ACP		...	16	44	17.05	-0.05
-12.5	13.10	7.58	AmRltyInv ARL		...	10	5	7.99	0.04
58.1	6.12	1.65	AmRetire ACR		...	dd	637	5.06	0.04
26.3	18.30	6.18	AmSftyIns ASI		...	11	224	16.56	-0.24
7.8	115.63	69.70	AmStandard ASD		...	19	3918	108.55	-0.58
-2.1	28.95	23.01	AmStWtr AWR	.88	3.6	31	226	24.47	0.18
24.3	13.80	5.80	AmTower A AMT		...	dd	29335	13.45	-0.27
13.0	19.83	5.50♦	AmeriCredit ACF		...	37	23848	18	-0.30
-0.3	30.19	22.50	Amerigas APU	2.20	7.9	19	573	27.92	0.42
-1.0	51.60	34.70	AmeriGp AGP		...	15	2051	44.71	-0.56
3.4	73.44	50.40♦	AmeriSrcBrg ABC	.10	.2	15	9636	58	-0.02
-6.3	40.47	28.25	AmeronInt AMN s	.80	2.5	11	250	32.50	-0.06
12.8	41.73	24.53	AmerUsGp A AMH	.40	1.0	10	1142	39.45	-0.45
14.5	28.90	17.52	Ametek AME s	.24f	.9	20	3579	27.62	-0.08
5.8	21.56	8.90	AMN Hlthcare AHS		...	20	2093	18.15	-0.17
-3.8	15.38	10.25	AmpcoPgh AP	.40	3.0	dd	46	13.15	0.19
6.4	34.70	21.50	Amphenol APH s		...	26	12976	34	-0.13

analyze the data from the online edition in accordance with the following description of the listings in the print edition.

In the accompanying excerpts from the Monday, April 26, 2004, print edition of the *Journal* (above and page 240), the first column gives the year-to-date (YTD) percentage change of the stock price. The second and third

15.2	42.57	28	AFLAC **AFL**	.38f	.9	27	6510	41.68	−0.13
4.0	22.80	15.25	AGCO Cp **AG**	...		21	7892	20.94	−0.52
−3.1	30.63	24.50	AGL Res **ATG**	1.12	4.0	13	737	28.20	−0.18
10.8	6.87	1.74✦AK Steel **AKS**		...		dd	10612	5.65	−0.17
−5.6	37.30	26.38✦AMB Prop **AMB**		1.70f	5.5	21	2516	31.05	−0.55
−4.2	25.12	5.81	Amcol **ACO**	.28f	1.4	27	1542	19.45	−0.48
−1.9	29	21.99	AMLI Rsdntl **AML**	1.92	7.3	29	449	26.30	−0.13
−0.5	17.65	3.59	AMR **AMR**	...		dd	28363	12.88	−0.37
−23.1	4.60	1.19	APT Satelt **ATS**	...	...		911	1.83	0.11
75.2	14.10	6.39	AT&T Wrls **AWE**	...		88	155510	14	0.06
−9.7	23.18	16	AT&T **T**	.95	5.2	9	106467	18.34	0.31
−4.2	19.12	9.67	AVX Cp **AVX**	.15	.9	dd	2735	15.93	0.12
2.0	24.37	13.44✦AXA ADS **AXA**		.52e	2.4	...	1830	21.91	0.01
21.3	17.30	9	AZZ **AZZ**	...		21	5	16.20	0.05
26.3	26.17	14.47	AaronRent **RNT** s	.04f	.2	23	832	25.42	−0.75

AMR (American Airlines) →

columns tell you the highest and lowest value of one share of the stock in the past 52 weeks expressed in dollars and fractions of a dollar. AMR (American Airlines) stock was as low as $3.59 (ouch!) and as high as $17.65 in the year preceding Friday, April 23, 2004.

Footnotes and symbols, including arrows and underlining, are fully explained in the box on the upper left of the first page of the Composite listings.

The fourth column gives the company name and stock ticker symbol (AMR).

The fifth column of data reports the latest annual cash dividend. As you can see, American Airlines paid no dividends in the latest quarter. The dividend is expressed as a percentage of the closing price in the next column.

The seventh column shows the price-earnings (P/E) ratio, which is obtained by dividing the price of the stock by its earnings per share. (This important statistic is discussed in detail in Chapter 3.) On April 23, 2004, American Airlines had losses (negative earnings, not profits), so the code "dd" appears to indicate a negative number.

The eighth column informs you of the number of shares traded that day, expressed in hundreds of shares: 2,836,300 shares of American Airlines traded on April 23, 2004. If a z appears before the number in this column, the figure represents the actual number (not hundreds) of shares traded.

The ninth column reveals the stock's closing (last) price for the trading day. On Friday, April 23, 2004, American Airlines closed at $12.88.

The last column provides the change in the closing price of the stock from the price at the close of the previous day. You can see that this stock closed 37 cents lower than the previous closing price.

WSJ.com THE WALL STREET JOURNAL ONLINE | DOW JONES INDUSTRY GROUP CENTER | Article Search

▶ DOW JONES GLOBAL INDEXES

HOME | NEWS | TECHNOLOGY | MARKETS | PERSONAL JOURNAL | OPINION | LEISURE/WEEKEND | PORTFOLIO

QUOTES & NEWS
Quote
Valuations and Ratios
Stock Charting
Industry Comparison
News
Press Releases

COMPANY PROFILE
Key Facts
Executives
Insider Holdings
Insider Transactions
Institutional Holdings

FINANCIALS
Quarterly Earnings
Quarterly Cash Flow
Quarterly Balance Sheet
Annual Earnings
Annual Cash Flow
Annual Balance Sheet
Margins and Returns

ANALYST RATINGS
Earnings Estimates

RESEARCH REPORTS

Free & Premium
Research

WEB RESOURCES

SEC Filings
AMR Web Site
Annual Reports

Find Litigation
Information on
this company at

FindLaw

⚠ZACKS

MEDIA PARTNER TO
E-WORLD 2004

Portfolio
Setup Center
Discussions
Site Map

COMPANY RESEARCH

Help   Print

QUOTE AMR Corp. (AMR)

Go to Stock Charting page

07/15/04   2:27 p.m. EDT   NYSE

Last 9.25	Change 0.01	% Change 0.11%
Open 9.40	High 9.45	Low 9.00
Bid N/A	Ask N/A	Prior Day's Close 9.24
Volume 3,837,900	Avg. Vol. 10 Day 4,188,900	Avg. Monthly Vol.* 103,173,000
Prior Day's Volume 6,431,700	52-Week High 17.65 (01/27/04)	52-Week Low 7.90 (08/04/03)

10 Day (Hourly)

After Hours Trading
Real-Time Quotes

U.S. stock prices on NYSE and AMEX are delayed 20 minutes or more, Nasdaq prices are delayed 15 minutes or more.
* 3 months

News more

11:05 a.m. Fulcrum Starts AMR Corp. At Buy

July 14   Why Some Airlines Tack On Fees For Kids Flying by Themselves

July 14   Delta to Record $1.65 Billion In Noncash Charges for Quarter

Historical Quotes
*Find a Security's closing price on any day after 1/2/1970
(1/2/1970)

Symbol: [   ]   Date: [   ]   [Go]   Help ⍰

Ratings & Estimates
Mean Recommendation   1.80 **Earning Consensus**
(1= Strong Buy, 5=Strong Sell)   **Estimate**

Stock Data, Short Interest and Ratings & Estimates tables reflect U.S. exchange data.

TRADING CENTER

Stock Data

Market Cap (Mil)	$1,828
P/E Ratio	n.a.
Dividend Yield	n.a.%
Latest Dividend	$n.a.
Date of Last Dividend	n.a.
Last Stock Split	100% stock div.
Date of Last Split	06/10/98
Shares Outstanding (Mil)	160
Public Float(Mil)	

All data updated daily
Source: Reuters

NYSE Volume Breakdown

	VOLUME		VOLUME
9:30 to 10:00	177,140,000	1:00 to 1:30	60,183,730
10:00 to 10:30	139,385,640	1:30 to 2:00	70,786,270
10:30 to 11:00	109,864,360	2:00 to 2:30	73,076,040
11:00 to 11:30	101,969,060	2:30 to 3:00	117,543,960
11:30 to 12:00	81,110,940	3:00 to 3:30	138,587,540
12:00 to 12:30	75,153,300	3:30 to 4:00	295,456,180
12:30 to 1:00	65,816,700	Total	1,506,073,720

PREFERRED STOCK LISTINGS

Monday, February 23, 2004

AMEX

STOCK	DIV	YLD	CLOSE	NET CHG
ABC Trups	.90	7.9	11.40	0.20
Alcoa pf	3.75	4.5	83.60	-1.40
AllgntCapTr	.99	9.4	10.50	0.04
AmCoinTrl pf	1.15	12.9	8.90	-0.15
Baylake Trups	1.00	9.2	10.90	-0.15
BrkshrInco pfA	2.25	8.5	26.50	-0.25
Citi DJIA nts	.20	1.8	10.97	-0.01
Citi Eq nts			8.43	-0.02
CIrdoBus pf	1.00	9.1	10.99	-0.01
CTBI Pfd Tr	.83	7.6	10.85	0.23
EasyGrdnProd pf	2.35	10.4	22.65	-0.15
FCB/NC CapTrII	2.10	7.6	27.60	0.15
FidBkCap	.85	8.3	10.30	
FstWstCap9 3/8	.94	9.2	10.27	0.10
GlcrWtrTr pf	2.27	9.0	25.15	
GoldmanSachs nts			10.93	
GWB Cap pfB	.98	8.8	11.10	-0.02
HrtldFnl pf	2.40	9.1	26.50	-0.10
Hillman	2.90	11.1	26.15	-0.35
MBHI Cap pf	2.50	9.1	27.50	-0.10
MerLynSel10 7-06			10.22	0.07
MerLynSel10 5-06			10	-0.02
MerLynOil nts			10.81	-0.08
MerLynPfizer nts			26.94	-0.10
MerLynSemi nts			9.67	-0.23
MerLynInd15 2-07			10.86	0.16
MerLynSel10 5-07			10.18	-0.09
MerLynAmxBtc nts			10.65	-0.02
MerLynQualcomm	.50p		25.97	0.04
MerLynTxInstr	2.38	7.9	30.15	-1.35
MerLynCiscoSys	.44p		25.36	
MerLynInd15 6-06			11.51	-0.02
MerLynAmexDef			10.41	-0.03
MerLynInd15 8-07			10.92	0.28
MerLynBoeing	2.73	6.2	44.04	-0.94
MerLynSel10 11-06			11.72	0.13
MerLynAdobe	3.31	8.9	37.06	-1.60
MerLynIntel			24.75	-0.06
MerLynCitiGp nts			25.35	0.03
MerLynSel10 9-07			12.30	-0.11
MerLynSR4 nts			9.03	0.01
MerLynIH nts			9.33	0.14
MerLynBio 2-07			9.86	-0.05
MerLynMicron	.51p		25.55	-0.17
MerLynEuro50			11.50	-0.30
MerLynApMtls	3.79	8.9	42.35	-1.30
MerLynInd15 5-07			10.61	-0.04

STOCK	DIV	YLD	CLOSE	NET CHG
MS Eqty nts			10.84	-0.03
NHTB Cap	.93	9.0	10.35	-0.15
NPBCap Tr	1.96	7.1	27.53	0.21
Old2ndCapTr			11	0.10
OzarkCap	.90	8.3	10.85	0.35
Popular 6.70pf	1.67	6.5	25.60	0.01
Popular pfA	1.59	6.3	25.10	-0.30
PriceLegcy pf	1.40	8.7	16.10	-0.30
ProFac pfA	1.72	8.7	19.74	0.03
PrvdntTr 10%			27.15	0.05
◆R&G Fncl pfC	1.90	7.1	26.67	-0.03
RBI Cap pf	.91	8.9	10.19	
R&G Fncl pfD	1.81	6.9	26.07	0.07
RpublcCapTrl	2.15	7.9	27.25	-0.30
SndySprgCap	2.34	8.6	27.10	0.10
SeaCoast Tr	2.13	7.7	27.68	0.08
ScndBcpTrl	.90	8.0	11.25	-0.09
◆SnclrBdct pfD	3.00	6.3	47.53	-0.27
SMAN CapTr			10	
SmurfitStn A	1.75	7.0	25.01	0.30
SterlingBcshII	2.30	8.3	27.74	0.24
SVB CapII pf			25	
TAYCCp Tr	2.44	8.6	28.44	
TeamFnCpl	.95	8.7	10.90	-0.09
TelbncCapII	2.25	8.9	25.36	-0.04
W Hldg pfD	1.85	7.2	25.80	-0.55
W Hldg pfB	1.81	7.1	25.50	-0.41
W Hldg pfC	1.90	7.2	26.35	-0.25
W Hldg pfF	1.67	6.7	25.03	0.03
W Hldg pfG	1.73	6.8	25.40	0.10
W Hldg pfE	1.72	6.8	25.20	-0.01
WebstCap pfB	.86	8.2	10.44	0.03
WintrstCap pf	2.25	8.6	26.06	-0.65

NYSE

STOCK	DIV	YLD	CLOSE	NET CHG
ABN Am pfF	.39p		25.56	-0.04
ABN Am pfB	1.78	7.0	25.39	-0.01
ABN Am pfE	1.48	6.0	24.74	0.10
ACE CapTr	2.22	8.4	26.52	0.05
◆ACE pfC	1.95	7.0	27.90	0.08
AES Tr	3.38	8.0	42.50	
AGL Cap Trups	2.00	7.4	27.20	0.16
◆AMB Prop pfM	.23p		25.23	0.17
AMR Pines	1.97	9.4	20.85	-0.75
AbbeyNtl	1.75	6.9	25.36	0.01
AbeyNtl ADS	1.84	6.7	27.62	-0.04
AbeyNtl 7 1/4%	1.81	7.1	25.65	-0.02
AbeyNtl nts	1.81	6.8	26.70	-0.16

STOCK	DIV	YLD	CLOSE	NET CHG
Citigroup pfR	.38p		25.75	-0.05
Citigroup pfS	1.50	5.9	25.34	0.04
Citigroup pfV	1.78	6.7	26.75	
Citigroup pfX	1.72	6.8	25.15	0.02
Citigroup pfZ	1.74	6.5	26.84	0.01
CtznUtil Tr	2.50	4.9	51.20	0.20
ClevelandElec	2.25	8.1	27.84	-0.13
ClvdElec pf	7.40	7.2	103	-0.50
CslFnl Toprs	2.09	9.6	21.72	0.22
ColonlCpTrIII	2.08	7.7	27	
ColonlCpTrIV	.57p		27.10	0.09
◆ColonlProp pfD	2.03	7.6	26.74	-0.10
◆ColonlProp pfC	2.31	8.4	27.35	-0.03
ComcastHldg	1.43	3.8	37.50	0.25
ComercaCap pfZ	1.90	7.0	27.26	0.03
◆ComrclRlty pf	2.25	8.2	27.60	-0.35
ConAgraCap pfB	1.25	5.0	25.20	-0.05
ConEd Pines	1.81	6.6	27.37	-0.09
ConEd 7.35Pines	1.84	7.1	25.79	0.04
ConEd pf	5.00	5.3	94.20	0.40
ConEd pfC	4.65	5.1	91	-0.25
ConEd41 Pines	1.88	6.9	27.29	-0.09
ConstBrnds pfA	.84e	2.7	31.05	-0.42
CnsmrEngylll Toprs	2.31	8.9	25.95	-0.05
CnsmrEngy Trups	2.25	8.3	26.96	-0.03
CnsmrEngyl Toprs	2.09	8.2	25.42	0.02
CnsmrEngyII Toprs	2.05	8.1	25.26	0.04
CnsmrEngy pfB	4.50	5.6	80.75	
Converium nts	2.06	7.4	27.72	-0.16
◆CpOffcProp pfG	2.00	7.6	26.37	-0.03
◆CpOffcProp pfH			25.75	
◆CpOffcProp pfB	2.50	9.7	25.80	0.05
CorrCorp pfA	2.00a	7.9	25.20	
CorrCorp pfB	.73p		25.50	-0.03
Cntrywd Trups	1.69	6.5	26.17	0.07
CousnProp pfA	1.94	7.4	26.25	0.55
CrdtAstTrKey	1.88	7.0	27.01	0.02
◆Crescent pfB	2.38	8.3	28.55	0.40
◆CrescentRE pfA	1.69	7.5	22.60	-0.19
CriimiMae pfG	1.50	14.3	10.51	
DQE Pines	2.09	8.0	26.04	0.09
DTEEngy pfB	2.19	8.5	25.76	-0.07
Decs TrIX	2.13	17.6	12.10	-0.26
DelmarPL pfA	2.03	7.8	25.90	0.35
◆DelphiFnl 33nts	2.00	7.5	26.81	-0.12
DelphiTr Trups	.44p		26.80	-0.03
DeltaAir nts	2.03	10.8	18.85	0.10
DetEd 7 3/8	1.84	7.2	25.48	0.08
DetEd 7 5/8	1.91	7.4	25.72	0.15
DetEd Quids Jr	1.89	7.4	25.51	0.06

You can also follow the volume of trading throughout the previous day by consulting the **NYSE Volume Breakdown**, which appears at the end of NYSE Composite Transactions and provides New York Stock Exchange trading volume by half hours. The copy on page 242 was drawn from the Wednesday, April 21, 2004, print edition and covers the previous day's trading.

Over-the-counter (OTC) stocks, as they were once known, are not traded on an exchange, as mentioned earlier. Instead, dealers have established a market for them using a computer network referred to as NASDAQ (National Association of Securities Dealers Automated Quotations). You can follow this market in **NASDAQ National Market Issues**, which is similar in form to **NYSE Composite Transactions**, as are **American Stock Exchange** listings.

Smaller companies with smaller capitalizations are listed as **NASDAQ Small-Cap Issues** and show trading volume, closing price, and price change only. The same information is provided for an intermediate range of firms under the heading **NASDAQ NM Issues Under $100 Million Market Cap**. With this information, you can track the performance of any share of stock traded on the New York or American exchange or the NASDAQ.

Finally, *The Wall Street Journal* publishes **Preferred Stock Listings** daily (check the third-section index). Owners of preferred stock receive dividends before owners of common stock. (That's why they're "preferred.") Consequently, investors have traditionally viewed these issues as more akin to bonds—upon which a company is obliged to pay interest—than common stock. See the example from the Tuesday, February 24, 2004, print *Journal* on page 242.

MUTUAL FUNDS

At this point you may wonder if you can get into the stock market without purchasing a particular stock.

Mutual funds provide a way to invest in the stock market indirectly. Investment companies establish mutual funds to pool the resources of many investors and thus create a large, shared portfolio of investments. Individuals invest in mutual funds by purchasing shares in the fund from the investment company. These mutual funds are open-ended, which means the investment companies are always willing to sell more shares to the public and to redeem outstanding shares. Therefore, the pool of capital, the number of investors, and the number of shares outstanding can expand or contract.

The value of the fund's assets divided by the number of shares outstanding determines the value of each share. Any gain in the fund's portfolio is passed through to the individual investors. Purchases of additional shares by new investors do not reduce the value of existing shares because the purchaser makes a cash contribution equal to the value of the share.

This raises an important point: Mutual fund shares are not traded on the open market. They are purchased from, and sold back to, the investment company.

Mutual funds are popular with individual investors because they permit diversification in a wide variety of securities with a very small capital outlay. In addition, a mutual fund lets you take advantage of the professional management skills of the investment company.

When you purchase a mutual fund share, you own a fraction of the total assets in the portfolio. The price of that share is equal to its net asset value (net value of assets held by the fund divided by the number of mutual fund shares outstanding plus any sales commission). As with any pooled investment in common stock, price appreciation and dividends earned will determine the gain in net asset value.

A **Mutual Funds** listing of the major funds available to investors appears every day (check the indexes in the first and third sections). The following example provides excerpts from the Friday, January 9, 2004, print edition of the *Journal* and reports figures for Thursday, January 8, 2004.

Mutual funds are classified according to whether or not they charge a sales commission called a *load. No-Load (NL) Funds* don't require a commission to purchase or sell the shares of the fund. There is, however, a "management fee" charged on the assets of NL as well as loan funds, which is generally less than 1 percent of the investment. Net asset values are calculated after management takes its fee.

Front-End Loaded Funds charge a one-time admission or sales fee to purchasers of their shares, as well as the management fee levied by all funds. This "sales" or commission fee can be as high as 8 percent, which will effectively reduce your overall rate of return, depending on how long you hold the fund. A *p* after the fund's name indicates there is a distribution charge (sales commission), or front-load, on the fund.

Back-End Loaded Funds levy a fee of up to 8 percent when the shares are sold back to the investment company. An *r* indicates this *redemption* charge. Some back-loaded funds vary their fees according to the length of time the shares are held. If you sell your shares after one year, the fee may be as high as 8 percent. But if you hold the shares for a long time (say, 30 years), no fee may be charged. (Remember that *all* funds have built-in management fees in addition to any loads.)

MUTUAL FUNDS

Explanatory Notes

Mutual-funds listings for Nasdaq-published share classes with net assets of at least $100 million each. **NAV** is net asset value. Percentage performance figures are total returns, assuming reinvestment of all distributions and after subtracting annual expenses. Figures don't reflect sales charges ("loads") or redemption fees. **NET CHG** is change in NAV from previous trading day. **YTD%RET** is year-to-date return. **3-YR%RET** is trailing three-year return annualized.

e-Ex-distribution. **f**-Previous day's quotation. **g**-Footnotes x and s apply. **j**-Footnotes e and s apply. **k**-Recalculated by Lipper, using updated data. **p**-Distribution costs apply, 12b-1. **r**-Redemption charge may apply. **s**-Stock split or dividend. **t**-Footnotes p and r apply. **v**-Footnotes x and e apply. **x**-Ex-dividend. **z**-Footnote x, e and s apply. **NA**-Not available due to incomplete price, performance or cost data. **NE**-Not released by Lipper; data under review. **NN**-Fund not tracked. **NS**-Fund didn't exist at start of period.

Source: Lipper

Thursday, January 8, 2004

A

FUND	NAV	NET CHG	YTD %RET	3-YR %RET
AAL Mutual A				
Balance p	11.85	0.03	1.1	0.4
Bond p	10.30	-0.01	0.3	6.5
CGrowth p	29.77	0.13	1.6	-5.4
EqInc p	12.68	0.06	1.2	-2.8
HiYBdA	6.81	0.01	1.5	8.0
Intl p	9.07	0.12	3.3	-7.4
MidCap p	14.05	0.02	1.2	0.6
MuniBd	11.59	...	0.3	5.9
SmCap	16.27	0.10	2.3	9.1
AAL Mutual Inst				
Balance	11.84	0.03	1.1	0.8
AARP Invst				
Balanced	16.98	0.04	1.3	-1.1
CapGr	41.35	0.10	1.7	-9.3
GNMA	15.26	...	0.3	5.5
GroInc	20.55	0.10	1.9	-3.7
Income	12.95	...	0.4	5.8
MgdMuni	9.40	...	0.3	6.1
ShtTmBd	10.55	...	0.1	4.4
ABN AMRO Funds				
BalancedN p	11.52	0.05	1.4	0.3
Bond N	10.12	...	0.3	5.7
Bond I	10.12	...	0.3	6.0
Growth I	22.61	0.12	1.9	-3.3
GrowthN	22.39	0.12	1.9	-3.6
M&C BalanN	16.16	0.01	0.6	-1.9
M&C Gro N	21.99	0.04	0.9	-6.4
MidCapN p	22.32	0.49	5.2	11.4
Value	10.51	0.04	0.8	-1.3
VeredAggGro N	15.80	0.03	1.5	-7.9
AHA Funds				
LtdMatI	10.82	...	0.1	4.8
AIM Investments A				
Agrsv p	9.47	0.05	1.7	-6.4
Bal p	24.14	0.05	0.9	-4.4
BasicVal p	29.64	0.07	1.4	2.6
BlChp p	11.41	0.05	1.9	-9.2

FUND	NAV	NET CHG	YTD %RET	3-YR %RET
CorEqi p	11.67	0.10	2.3	-3.3
Dynm p	15.19	0.11	3.1	-10.7
Enrgy p	20.56	0.07	0.9	1.6
FinSvc p	30.01	0.17	1.7	1.4
Gold&Prec p	3.95	0.03	1.8	41.7
HlthSc p	48.56	-0.07	0.6	-1.6
Leisure p	42.05	0.28	1.3	4.4
S&P500 t	11.93	0.06	1.8	-3.7
SmCoGth p	11.61	0.11	4.4	-5.0
Tech p	26.40	0.59	7.3	-21.7
TotRtn p	24.30	0.12	1.5	0.9
AMF Funds				
AdjMtg	9.88	...	-0.1	3.4
IntMtg	9.64	...	0.1	4.4
ShtUSGv	10.69	...	...	4.3
UltraShrt p	9.93	...	...	NS
USGvMtg	10.61	...	0.2	5.0
AXA Rosenberg				
US SmCp	13.30	0.06	2.9	16.2
USSmCpInv t	13.15	0.06	3.0	15.8
AcadnEm	16.45	0.04	4.7	24.0
Accessor Fd				
Mortg	12.73	...	0.3	5.8
SmMidCp	21.43	0.06	2.0	5.3
Activa				
IntmdBd	10.30	...	0.3	6.4
Value p	7.14	0.03	1.1	0.8
Advance Capital I				
Balanc p	18.64	0.05	1.1	4.3
Bond p	10.12	0.01	0.5	8.2
Equity p	24.97	0.09	2.3	-0.2
RetInc p	10.10	0.01	0.5	8.4
AegisValueFd	16.94	0.04	1.0	24.1
Alger American O				
Balanced	13.42	0.06	2.0	1.9
Growth	34.37	0.27	3.2	-5.1
LevAll	29.17	0.21	3.8	-6.2
MidCpGr	19.30	0.26	4.9	3.6
SmCap	18.09	0.15	4.1	-3.8
Alger Funds A				
CapApr	8.26	0.07	4.0	-7.4

FUND	NAV	NET CHG	YTD %RET	3-YR %RET
IntDivMuC p	14.37	...	0.3	NS
MuCA C t	10.87	...	0.4	4.7
PremGrC t	15.83	0.12	2.6	-14.4
TechC t	53.10	1.14	6.9	-13.7
USGovtC	7.18	...	0.1	3.9
AllianceBernstein I				
QuasInstlI	8.31	0.07	4.3	2.8
ReEInvI	10.48	0.03	-0.5	15.9
Alpine Funds				
RealInc&Gr	17.40	-0.04	-0.5	19.7
Am Skandia Adv Fds A				
MarCpGrA p	13.37	0.04	1.0	-2.9
TotRtBdA p	10.67	...	0.3	6.6
Am Skandia Adv Fds B				
AllGrIncB p	12.56	0.05	1.2	-0.4
FHiYdBB t	7.44	0.02	1.1	7.2
GoSachCGB	10.29	0.05	1.9	-14.9
MarCpGrB p	13.02	0.03	0.9	-3.4
TotRtBdB p	10.56	...	0.3	6.1
Am Skandia Adv Fds C				
MarCpGrC p	13.01	0.04	1.0	-3.3
Amer AAdvant AMR				
BalAmr	13.16	0.03	0.8	7.2
IntBdAmr	10.33	...	0.3	6.6
IntlAmr	17.11	0.16	3.0	2.0
LgCapAmr	16.79	0.07	1.1	6.2
SmCapAmr	17.31	0.06	1.9	22.8
Amer AAdvant Inst				
HiYldBdInst	10.87	0.02	1.0	11.7
HiYldBdPlan	10.87	0.02	1.0	NS
IntlInst	17.04	0.15	3.0	1.8
S&PInst	15.38	0.07	1.9	-3.1
Amer AAdvant Plan				
IntlPlan	16.94	0.16	3.0	1.7
American Century Adv				
EqGro p	19.91	0.01	1.6	-1.5
EqInc p	7.82	0.01	0.5	9.9
IncGro p	28.23	0.11	2.0	-0.4
IntlGr p	8.25	0.13	4.0	-7.8
SmCpVal p	9.40	-0.09	2.4	17.4
StrAgg p	7.13	0.04	2.3	1.3
StrMod p	6.45	0.02	1.7	2.8
Ultra p	26.81	0.02	1.6	-4.8
Value p	7.56	0.03	0.9	8.8
American Century Inv				
✦Balanced	15.48	0.01	1.1	2.1
CaHYMu	9.93	0.01	0.3	6.3
✦CaIntTF	11.55	...	0.3	5.1
✦CaLgTF	11.81	...	0.3	5.4
✦CaLtdTF	10.84	0.01	0.3	4.3
DivBnd	10.36	...	0.3	NS
✦EqGro	19.92	0.01	1.6	-12
✦EqInc	7.82	0.01	0.5	10.2
✦EqIndex	4.57	0.02	1.8	-3.4
Gift	14.56	0.08	2.5	-10.5
✦GinnieMae	10.63	...	0.3	5.5
✦Gl Grwth	6.99	0.06	3.1	-5.0
✦GlGold r	13.31	0.04	1.1	51.3
✦GovtBd	10.81	...	...	6.0
✦Grwth	18.44	0.14	2.8	-6.7
✦Heritage	11.28	0.06	1.9	-5.0

FUND	NAV	NET CHG	YTD %RET	3-YR %RET
SDGovt	4.88	...	...	4.1
SelectA	8.68	...	0.3	3.8
SmCapAdv p	6.65	0.07	4.6	9.0
SmCapGrA p	4.50	0.02	3.9	NS
SmColA	7.51	0.03	2.3	9.4
StockA	18.64	0.07	1.2	-3.7
StrAgA	11.09	0.05	1.6	-13.2
TE BdA	3.93	...	0.3	4.7
USGrtMtgA p	5.12	...	0.3	NS
UtilitiesA	6.56	0.02	0.9	-8.5
American Express B				
BluCpB t	7.71	0.03	1.3	-5.8
DivrBd t	4.87	...	0.2	4.7
DivrEqB t	9.69	0.05	1.7	5.5
EqSelB t	11.33	0.02	2.1	0.9
EqValB t	9.19	0.06	2.1	-2.4
GlBdB t	NA	...	NA	NA
GloEqB t	4.75	0.01	2.4	-8.9
GwthB t	23.03	0.03	1.2	-14.0
HiYdB t	4.49	...	0.3	4.6
HiYldBd t	2.86	0.01	1.5	6.1
MgdAllB t	8.67	0.03	1.9	0.2
MutiB t	9.16	0.03	1.1	-4.1
NwDB t	22.89	0.09	1.6	-5.6
SDGovt	4.88	-0.01	...	3.4
SelectB t	8.67	...	0.2	2.9
SmCapAdv t	6.41	0.06	4.6	8.1
SmColB t	7.04	0.03	2.3	8.6
StockB t	18.47	0.08	1.3	-4.5
StrAgB t	9.96	0.05	1.5	-13.9
USGrtMtgB t	5.12	...	0.2	NS
UtilitiesB t	6.52	0.03	1.1	-9.1
American Express Y				
BiuCpY	7.94	0.03	1.3	-4.9
DivrBd	4.87	...	0.3	5.6
EqSel	12.30	0.02	2.2	1.9
GrwthY	25.13	0.03	1.2	-13.1
MutlY	9.23	0.04	1.2	-3.2
NwDY	24.25	0.09	1.5	-4.7
SDGovt	4.88	...	...	4.3
SelectY	8.67	...	0.2	3.9
StockY	18.64	0.07	1.2	-3.6
AmerExpS&P500E	4.39	0.02	1.6	-3.3
American Funds Cl A				
BalA p	17.49	0.05	1.2	8.1
AmcpA p	17.14	0.02	1.7	1.2
AMutlA p	24.67	0.10	1.2	5.4
BondA p	13.57	0.01	0.5	8.1
CapIBA p	48.49	0.19	1.4	9.3
CapWA p	19.12	0.10	1.7	12.1
CapWGrA	30.74	0.23	2.9	7.9
EupacA p	31.25	0.33	3.4	1.2
FdInvA p	29.41	0.19	1.9	0.6
GovtA p	13.73	-0.01	0.1	5.3
GwthA p	25.14	0.14	2.4	-1.5
HI TrA p	12.50	0.02	1.5	6.9
HiInMuniA	15.41	0.02	0.4	6.2
ICAA p	29.30	0.17	1.6	1.9
IncoA p	17.42	0.06	1.5	8.7
IntBdA p	13.85	...	...	5.1
LtdTEBdA	15.66	0.01	0.4	5.5

When both redemption and distribution fees are charged, the fund is identified by a *t* after the fund's name.

The absence of the letters *p, r,* and *t* after the fund name indicates a no-load fund.

Loaded funds are sold through brokers, which explains the commission fee. The investment company contracts with the broker to act as the fund's marketer.

Since no-load funds are directly marketed and have no outside sales force, there is no commission fee. In order to invest in a no-load fund, you must select the fund (e.g., in response to a newspaper ad or direct-mail solicitation) and contact the investment company directly. A broker customarily will not act for you in the purchase of no-load funds, because he or she will not receive a commission fee of any kind.

Some companies and organizations offer many funds, each with its own special objective. Take the AARP (American Association of Retired Persons) CaGr (Capital Growth) fund shown on page 245 and below, for example. The first column provides the fund's name. The second column reveals the fund's net asset value of $41.35. As you recall, this is calculated by totaling the market value of all securities owned by the fund and then dividing by the number of fund shares outstanding. In short, net asset value (NAV) equals a dollar value of the pool per mutual fund share. The third column reveals the increase or decrease in net asset value. In this case, AARP's capital growth fund increased by 10 cents a share. The fourth column reveals that the fund's shares had gained 1.7 percent for the year. The last column tracks the percent return per annum over the past three years, during which AARP's capital growth fund fell by 9.3 percent annually.

Markets Lineup provides a snapshot of **Mutual Funds** performance in the lower right of page C2 (see page 247). The top table, **How the Largest Mutual Funds Did**, is split into *Stock* and *Bond Funds*. Below these are the **Lipper Indexes**, which show large funds' performances grouped by investment objective (see page 247). For instance, the excerpt from the Friday, January 9, 2004, print *Journal* on page 247 reveals that Fidelity's Magellan Fund had a year-to-date return of 1.7 percent while an index of core large-cap stocks had a return of 1.78 percent.

On Mondays *The Wall Street Journal* print edition publishes **Mutual-Fund Performance Yardsticks.** See page 248 for an example from the September 26, 2005, edition. This table provides more detail than the daily Lip-

	AARP Invst			
	Balanced	16.98	0.04	1.3	−1.1
AARP Investments →	CapGr	41.35	0.10	1.7	−9.3
(Capital Growth)	GNMA	15.26	...	0.3	5.5
	GroInc	20.55	0.10	1.9	−3.7
	Income	12.95	...	0.4	5.8
	MgdMuni	9.40	...	0.3	6.1
	ShtTmBd	10.55	...	0.1	4.4

═══{ MUTUAL FUNDS }═══

How the Largest Mutual Funds Did

Stock Funds	NET CHANGE	YTD RETURN	52-WK RETURN
Vanguard 500	+0.52	+1.8	+26.5
Fidelity Magellan	+0.45	+1.7	+23.4
American ICAA	+0.17	+1.6	+24.9
American WshA	+0.10	+1.4	+23.1
American GrwthA	+0.14	+2.4	+32.1
Fidelity Contrafd	+0.09	+1.1	+28.5
American IncomeA	+0.06	+1.5	+24.7
Fidelity GwthInc	+0.14	+1.4	+17.7
Vanguard Inst Index	+0.51	+1.8	+26.6
American EupacA	+0.33	+3.4	+35.8
Bond Funds			
Pimco Inst TotRet	−0.01	+0.3	+ 5.8
Vanguard GNMA	−0.01	+0.3	+ 2.7
Vanguard TotBroad	...	+0.3	+ 4.5
Pimco Admin TotRet	−0.01	+0.3	+ 5.6
American America	+0.01	+0.6	+12.3

Fidelity's Magellan Fund → Fidelity Magellan

Lipper Indexes

Stock-Fund Indexes	PRELIM CLOSE	PERCENT CHANGE FROM		
		PREVIOUS CLOSE	WEEK AGO	DEC 31
Large-Cap Growth	3046.79	+0.51	+2.32	+2.32
Large-Cap Core	2221.00	+0.45	+1.78	+1.78
Large-Cap Value	9532.18	+0.47	+1.46	+1.46
Multi-Cap Growth	2625.66	+0.62	+2.86	+2.86
Multi-Cap Core	6902.36	+0.50	+2.08	+2.08
Multi-Cap Value	4079.65	+0.47	+1.67	+1.67
Mid-Cap Growth	637.39	+0.54	+2.68	+2.68
Mid-Cap Core	636.26	+0.43	+2.09	+2.09
Mid-Cap Value	950.23	+0.58	+2.07	+2.07
Small-Cap Growth	540.62	+0.75	+4.01	+4.01
Small-Cap Core	383.82	+0.62	+2.81	+2.81
Small-Cap Value	611.18	+0.61	+2.46	+2.46
Equity Income Fd	4105.68	+0.44	+1.27	+1.27
Science and Tech Fd	675.95	+1.71	+6.35	+6.35
International Fund	782.36	+1.20	+3.10	+3.10
Balanced Fund	4971.29	+0.37	+1.28	+1.28
Bond-Fund Indexes				
Short Inv Grade	253.47	...	+0.12	+0.12
Intmdt Inv Grade	301.18	+0.02	+0.34	+0.34
US Government	397.42	...	+0.16	+0.16
GNMA	433.57	...	+0.31	+0.31
Corp A-Rated Debt	1071.06	+0.03	+0.28	+0.28

Large-Cap Core Funds → Large-Cap Core

Indexes are based on the largest funds within the same investment objective and do not include multiple share classes of similar funds.

Source: Lipper Inc.

Mutual-Fund Performance Yardsticks

Mutual-fund categories and their benchmarks ranked by one-year total return

Investment objective	TOTAL RETURN			ANNUALIZED	
	Four-week	Year-to-date	One-year	Three-year	Five-year
Utility	0.03%	14.93%	31.72%	19.79%	1.29%
European Region	0.05	7.89	30.62	21.00	3.55
International	0.87	6.34	25.18	17.81	0.76
Vanguard Small Co. Index	-2.28	5.38	25.12	21.90	6.54
Midcap Growth	-1.53	5.17	24.12	16.12	-5.47
Small-Cap Growth	-2.21	2.74	24.02	16.99	-3.60
Small-Cap Core	-2.02	4.56	23.73	20.17	8.14
Midcap Value	-1.41	6.81	23.52	19.12	11.98
Midcap Core	-1.46	6.45	23.35	17.34	3.64
Small-Cap Value	-1.96	4.88	23.09	20.79	14.20
Multicap Growth	-1.56	4.15	21.39	16.11	-11.86
Global	-0.42	5.15	21.33	15.91	-0.79
Science & Technology	-2.07	-0.43	21.32	18.29	-18.97
Multicap Value	-0.97	4.44	18.25	16.37	4.39
Multicap Core	-1.47	4.31	17.76	16.25	7.44
Health & Biotechnology	-0.72				
Large-Cap Value	-0.61				
Equity Income	-1.43	3.58	14.33	12.30	4.08

Short-Term → Bond Funds

Investment objective	TOTAL RETURN			ANNUALIZED	
	Four-week	Year-to-date	One-year	Three-year	Five-year
S&P 500, reinvested daily	-1.80%	1.94%	12.56%	12.03%	-2.71%
Large-Cap Growth	-2.23	0.25	12.54	8.00	-11.82
Balanced	-0.52	2.69	10.59	9.26	1.56
Stock & Bond	-0.38	2.45	10.44	10.15	2.27
Large-Cap Core	-2.07	-0.17	8.66	7.29	-3.50
High Yield Taxable Bond	0.47	2.37	8.05	13.21	5.65
	0.83	2.22	7.25	9.77	7.15
← Mid-Cap Value Funds	-1.73	-1.26	5.39	8.99	0.70
	1.11	3.02	4.73	4.47	5.51
Single State Muni Debt	1.09	3.00	4.68	4.32	5.44
L-T Inv Grade Corp Bond	1.27	2.64	4.56	6.03	6.82
L-T US Treas/Govt Bond	1.55	3.36	4.36	3.69	6.03
Interm Inv Grade Corp Bond	1.18	2.37	3.71	4.74	6.32
Interm US Treas/Govt Bond	1.67	2.13	3.67	3.72	5.96
Lipper L-T Govt Bond Index	1.25	2.88	3.67	3.46	5.93
Mortgage	0.77	1.98	2.88	3.16	5.42
Interm Municipal Debt	0.99	1.58	2.50	3.20	4.71
S-T Inv Grade Corp Bond	0.63	1.36	1.78	2.65	4.40

Note: Returns are as of Sept. 23; N.A. means not available.

Source: Lipper

per Indexes, and summarizes the performance of all funds within categories, not just large funds. Monday's **Mutual-Fund Performance Yardsticks** also provides key indexes with which investors can compare their fund's performance.

Lipper Leaders, which appears under **Mutual-Fund Performance Yardsticks** (see page 248), compares fund performance based on various investment objectives. Looking at the Monday, September 26, 2005, report, you can see reports on mutual funds that invest in public utilities, European stocks, and international stocks. These are top-performing funds, and you can see that all provided substantial returns over the past year. The report also ranks each fund according to its historic return, the consistency of returns, capital preservation, tax efficiency, and expense minimization. For instance, you can see that Eaton Vance utilities provided great returns compared to other funds, but had a weak record for expense minimization. That's a trade-off that most investors would probably find agreeable. Fidelity Nordic, on the other hand, had high but inconsistent returns. Some investors might not like that. Note that no fund was tops in every performance category. Investors must select their objectives.

If you are a hedge-fund investor, you can compare your fund's performance with **Dow Jones Hedge Benchmark,** which illustrates performance for a variety of hedge-fund classifications: *Convertible Arbitrage, Merger Arbitrage, Event Driven, Distressed Securities, Equity Market Neutral.* The example below is an example from the Friday, January 23, 2004, *Journal.*

To compare mutual fund performance online, click on Scorecards under Mutual Funds in the right column after going to Markets and Markets Data Center (from the home page's left-hand menu-bar). **Mutual Fund Scorecards** enables you to research fund performance by selecting appropriate criteria.

For the broadest possible coverage, you can invest in the overall stock market by selecting an *index fund* that places your capital in one of the better-known stock-market barometers. For instance, returning to the **Mutual**

Dow Jones Hedge Benchmarks

	CLOSE	NET CHG	% CHG	YTD % CHG	52-WK CHG
Convertible Arbitrage	125.13	−0.19	−0.15	1.0	13.0
Merger Arbitrage	108.34	0.34	0.31	1.4	9.5
Event Driven	109.35	0.14	0.13	2.1	20.5
Distressed Securities	127.78	0.10	0.08	3.0	27.2
Equity Market Neutral	99.97	0.12	0.12	0.6	0.0

previous day's values, after fees; www.djindexes.com

VANGUARD INDEX FDS					
♣500	105.30	0.72	2.6	−3.5	← Vanguard 500
♣Balanced	18.69	0.07	2.3	2.2	Net Asset
♣CalSoc	7.77	0.06	3.3	−4.6	Value $105.30
♣DevMkt	7.96	−0.03	1.9	−1.7	
♣EmerMkt r	12.30	0.01	3.8	11.7	
♣Europe	22.40	−0.14	1.8	−2.0	
♣Extnd	27.87	0.24	4.5	3.0	
♣Growth	25.70	0.20	3.1	−4.6	
♣ITBond	10.85	−0.03	1.7	9.1	
♣LTBond	11.79	−0.03	2.7	10.3	
♣MidCp	13.60	0.15	3.6	6.3	
♣Pacific	8.20	0.03	2.1	−0.9	
♣SmCap	23.80	0.19	5.3	7.4	
♣SmGth	14.06	0.20	7.5	9.7	
♣SmVal	11.85	0.02	3.1	9.7	
♣STBond	10.32	−0.01	0.5	6.0	
♣TotBd	10.42	−0.01	1.3	7.1	
♣TotIntl	10.86	−0.04	2.1	−0.5	
♣TotSt	26.76	0.19	3.0	−1.9	
♣Value	19.34	0.12	2.1	−2.5	

Funds listing of all funds, *Vanguard Group* has an index fund, called the *500* (see above), that places all of its resources in the S&P 500. On Friday, January 18, 2004, Vanguard's Index 500 had a net asset value of $105.30.

At the beginning of each month, in its own section of the *Journal*'s print edition, the **Monthly Review of Mutual Funds** (for the previous month) provides the investment objectives of each fund, the total return and ranking for the past 10 years, the maximum initial sales commission, and annual expenses. **The Review** includes **Mutual Funds Monthly Review** (see page 251) and a reference guide, *How to Read the Monthly Performance Tables*, in the first couple of pages of the report.

Some other highlights (not replicated on these pages) of the **Monthly Review of Mutual Funds** are **How the Largest Funds Fared, Leaders and Laggards, Category Kings in 16 Realms,** and **Mutual Fund Yardstick: How Fund Categories Stack Up.**

CLOSED-END FUNDS

The mutual funds described above are open-ended because they continually issue new shares in order to expand their pool of capital. They sell their shares to investors and buy them back. *Closed-end funds,* on the other hand, do not issue additional shares after their initial offering and do not buy them back. Shares of close-end funds trade on an organized exchange or over-the-counter, and appreciate or depreciate with investor demand like any

MUTUAL FUNDS MONTHLY REVIEW

A

NAV$ 1/30	FUND NAME	INV OBJ	JAN	YR	3 YR	5 YR	10 YR	MAX INIT CHRG	EXP RAT
AAL Mutual A									
11.88	Balance p	BL	1.4	17.8 E	0.0 C	2.2 C	NS ..	5.50	1.05
10.34	Bond px	IB	0.9	6.7 A	6.8 C	6.0 C	5.7 D	4.50	0.85
29.78	CGrowth p	LC	1.7	25.6 E	-6.2 C	-1.1 B	10.3 B	5.50	1.02
12.70	EqInc p	EI	1.4	32.0 B	-3.7 E	0.4 E	NS ..	5.50	1.06
6.75	HiYBdA x	HC	1.0	24.6 C	6.8 C	3.0 D	NS ..	4.50	0.93
8.85	Intl p	IL	0.8	37.4 E	-8.7 E	-3.3 E	NS ..	5.50	1.71
14.15	MidCap p	MC	1.9	37.2 D	-1.6 E	6.1 D	8.9 E	5.50	1.30
11.57	MuniBd x	GM	0.4	5.7 D	6.1 B	4.7 B	5.5 A	4.50	0.79
16.45	SmCap	SC	3.4	48.9 D	5.3 D	10.4 C	NS ..	5.50	1.47
AAL Mutual Inst									
11.87	Balance	BL	1.4	18.3 E	0.4 C	2.7 C	NS ..	0.00	0.56
AARP Invst									
17.02	Balanced	BL	1.6	20.5 D	-1.9 D	NS ..	NS ..	0.00	0.78
41.37	CapGr	LG	1.7	30.6 C	-11.0 C	-3.4 B	7.6 C	0.00	0.97
15.25	GNMA	MT	0.5	2.4 C	5.5 C	5.7 B	5.8 C	0.00	0.70
20.53	GroInc	LC	1.8	32.8 B	-4.7 B	NS ..	NS ..	0.00	0.80
12.97	Income	AB	0.9	5.8 C	5.8 E	NS ..	NS ..	0.00	0.83
9.35	MgdMuni	GM	0.1	6.3 B	6.1 B	NS ..	NS ..	0.00	0.56
10.54	ShtTmBd	SB	0.3	3.0 C	4.4 D	NS ..	NS ..	0.00	0.75
ABN AMRO Funds									
11.52	BalancedN p	BL	1.4	19.9 D	-0.6 C	2.8 C	NS ..	0.00	1.07
10.15	Bond N x	IB	1.0	4.8 C	5.7 E	5.7 D	6.2 C	0.00	0.74
10.15	Bond I x	IB	1.0	5.0 C	6.0 D	NS ..	NS ..	0.00	0.49
22.56	Growth I	LG	1.7	28.4 D	-4.6 A	NS ..	NS ..	0.00	0.83
22.33	GrowthN	LG	1.6	28.0 D	-4.9 A	0.9 A	12.0 A	0.00	1.11
16.15	M&C BalanN	BL	0.5	14.2 E	-1.8 D	0.0 E	NS ..	0.00	1.15
21.90	M&C Gro N	LG	0.5	20.9 E	-6.7 A	-3.3 B	NS ..	0.00	1.06
22.41	MidCapN p	MV	5.7	49.6 B	8.0 C	15.6 B	NS ..	0.00	1.30
10.56	Value	LV	1.2	30.4 E	-2.6 D	0.4 D	8.5 D	0.00	0.96
16.09	VeredAggGro N	SG	3.4	53.4 C	-8.9 E	13.6 A	NS ..	0.00	1.46
AHA Funds									
10.82	LtdMatl x	SB	0.2	2.0 D	4.7 C	5.4 B	5.6 B	0.00	0.85
AIM Institutional									
23.60	Const I	XG	1.9	36.1 D	-9.8 C	-0.2 B	7.7 C	0.00	0.75
26.76	SmCpGrl p	SG	3.3	48.5 D	NS ..	NS ..	NS ..	0.00	0.89
AIM Investments A									
9.57	Agrsv p	MG	2.8	33.8 E	-9.4 C	2.2 C	9.2 B	5.50	1.30
13.25	AsianPac p	PR	3.0	51.4 B	5.3 B	11.6 B	NS ..	5.50	2.25
24.36	Bal p	BL	1.8	21.3 C	-5.5 E	-0.7 E	7.4 C	4.75	1.06
29.69	BasicVal p	XV	1.5	38.9 B	0.8 C	10.2 A	NS ..	5.50	1.33
11.32	BlChp p	LC	1.1	30.3 C	-11.0 E	-4.6 E	9.0 C	5.50	1.47
17.59	CapDev p	MC	2.7	41.5 C	-1.0 E	7.2 D	NS ..	5.50	1.53
12.01	Chart p	LC	1.0	29.6 D	-8.2 D	-2.6 C	8.2 C	5.50	1.30
21.91	Const p	XG	1.9	35.4 D	-10.2 C	-0.7 C	7.1 D	5.50	1.29
8.28	DentTred p	XG	3.6	42.3 C	-14.5 D	NS ..	NS ..	5.50	2.01
11.64	DevMkt p	EM	4.4	61.5 C	8.5 C	9.8 D	-0.4 E	4.75	2.00
23.31	EuroGrow p	EU	4.2	55.2 A	0.8 B	9.0 A	NS ..	5.50	2.01
15.96	GlAgGr p	GL	3.8	47.6 B	-5.6 D	3.1 C	NS ..	4.75	2.10
16.00	GlGr p	GL	1.5	32.8 E	-9.9 E	-3.8 E	NS ..	4.75	2.04
27.03	GlHltCr p	HB	3.3	27.5 D	1.9 B	9.5 C	12.7 B	4.75	1.94
13.92	GlTrend p	GL	2.8	42.8 B	3.3 A	7.5 B	NS ..	4.75	2.00
4.49	HiYld p	HC	2.5	29.8 A	2.2 E	-2.4 E	2.1 E	4.75	1.16
6.72	Inco p	AB	1.1	10.8 A	4.8 E	2.2 E	4.8 E	4.75	1.02
9.22	IntGov p	IG	0.5	2.2 E	5.6 D	4.9 E	5.5 C	4.75	0.89
16.83	IntlGrow p	IL	3.2	37.1 E	-4.7 D	0.0 D	4.5 C	5.50	1.74
10.33	LimM p	SU	0.1	1.5 C	4.2 D	4.6 D	5.0 C	1.00	0.53
12.62	LrgCpBV p	LV	2.0	38.8 A	0.6 B	NS ..	NS ..	5.50	1.42
9.30	LrgCpGr t	LG	1.9	34.4 B	-13.7 D	NS ..	NS ..	5.50	1.82
27.44	MdCpCEq p	MC	1.9	32.8 E	4.0 B	13.4 B	12.8 B	5.50	1.43
9.73	MidCpGr p	MG	3.3	47.2 B	-8.8 C	NS ..	NS ..	5.50	1.90
8.22	Muni p	GM	0.7	6.1 C	5.8 C	4.5 C	4.7 D	4.75	0.82
14.89	Oppl p	SG	5.2	51.0 C	-0.7 B	16.9 A	NS ..	5.50	1.33
9.48	PremEqty p	LC	1.1	29.2 D	-10.4 E	-4.6 E	7.6 D	5.50	1.17
20.67	RealEst p	SE	3.7	47.2 A	20.4 A	17.5 A	NS ..	4.75	1.72
15.84	SelEqty p	XC	2.2	36.3 B	-11.7 E	-1.8 E	7.6 E	5.50	1.32
12.37	SmCpEq p	SG	2.8	54.4 C	8.0 A	NS ..	NS ..	5.50	1.67
26.55	SmCpGr p	SG	3.3	47.8 D	-5.0 D	10.2 B	NS ..	5.50	1.35
9.99	Summit I p	XG	2.3	40.1 C	-13.7 D	-5.1 D	7.5 D	8.50	0.99
11.70	TF Int p	IM	0.3	4.6 D	5.7 B	5.1 A	5.1 B	1.00	0.38
12.38	Weing p	LG	2.5	36.5 A	-14.9 E	-9.3 E	5.1 E	5.50	1.47
AIM Investments B									
9.16	Agrsv t	MG	2.8	32.9 E	-10.0 D	NS ..	NS ..	0.00	2.05
24.30	Bal t	BL	1.8	20.4 D	-6.2 E	-1.4 E	6.5 E	0.00	1.81
28.21	BasicVal t	XV	1.5	38.1 B	0.1 D	9.4 A	NS ..	0.00	1.98
10.81	BlChp t	LC	1.0	29.3 D	-11.6 E	-5.3 E	NS ..	0.00	2.12
16.62	CapDev t	MC	2.7	40.6 C	-1.6 E	6.5 D	NS ..	0.00	2.18
11.53	Chart t	LC	1.1	28.8 D	-8.8 D	-3.3 D	NS ..	0.00	2.00
20.66	Const t	XG	1.8	34.5 E	-10.8 C	-1.5 C	NS ..	0.00	1.99
8.03	DentTred t	XG	3.6	41.4 C	-15.1 D	NS ..	NS ..	0.00	2.66
22.36	EuroGrow t	EU	4.2	54.3 B	0.2 B	8.3 A	NS ..	0.00	2.66
15.01	GlAgGr t	GL	3.7	46.9 B	-6.1 D	2.6 C	NS ..	0.00	2.60
15.20	GlGr t	GL	1.5	32.2 E	-10.4 E	-4.3 E	NS ..	0.00	2.54
24.76	GlHltCr t	HB	3.2	26.8 D	1.4 B	9.0 C	12.2 C	0.00	2.44
4.51	HYld t	HC	2.4	29.1 A	1.5 E	-3.1 E	1.4 E	0.00	1.91
6.72	Inco t	AB	0.9	9.8 A	4.0 E	1.4 E	4.0 E	0.00	1.77
9.25	IntGov t	IG	0.4	1.4 E	4.8 E	4.1 E	4.7 E	0.00	1.64
15.82	IntlGrow t	IL	3.1	36.1 E	-5.4 D	-0.7 D	NS ..	0.00	2.44
9.00	LrgCpGr t	LG	1.7	33.5 B	-14.3 D	NS ..	NS ..	0.00	2.47
25.00	MdCpCEq t	MC	1.9	31.9 E	3.3 C	12.7 B	12.1 C	0.00	2.08
14.13	Oppl t	SG	5.1	50.0 D	-1.4 B	16.1 A	NS ..	0.00	1.98
8.84	PremEqty t	LC	1.0	28.1 D	-11.1 E	-5.3 E	6.8 E	0.00	1.92
20.73	RealEst t	SE	3.5	46.2 B	19.6 A	16.7 A	NS ..	0.00	2.37
14.25	SelEqty t	XC	2.1	35.2 C	-12.4 E	-2.5 E	6.7 E	0.00	2.07
12.10	SmCpEq t	SG	2.8	53.6 C	7.3 A	NS ..	NS ..	0.00	2.32
24.93	SmCpGr t	SG	3.2	46.6 D	-5.7 D	9.4 B	NS ..	0.00	2.08
11.42	Weing t	LG	2.3	35.5 A	-15.5 E	-10.0 E	NS ..	0.00	2.17
AIM Investments C									
24.33	Bal t	BL	1.8	20.4 D	-6.2 E	-1.4 E	NS ..	0.00	1.81
28.20	BasicVal t	XV	1.5	38.0 B	0.1 D	NS ..	NS ..	0.00	1.98
10.81	BlChp t	LC	1.0	29.5 D	-11.6 E	-5.3 E	NS ..	0.00	2.12
11.56	Chart t	LC	1.0	28.7 D	-8.8 D	-3.3 D	NS ..	0.00	2.00
20.65	Const t	XG	1.8	34.4 E	-10.8 C	-1.5 C	NS ..	0.00	1.99
9.21	IntGov t	IG	0.4	1.4 E	4.7 E	4.1 E	NS ..	0.00	1.64
15.83	IntlGrow t	IL	3.1	36.1 E	-5.4 D	-0.7 D	NS ..	0.00	2.44
24.98	MdCpCEq t	MC	1.9	31.9 E	3.3 C	NS ..	NS ..	0.00	2.08
8.85	PremEqty t	LC	1.0	28.3 D	-11.1 E	-5.3 E	NS ..	0.00	1.92
10.09	ShortTerm t	SB	0.4	3.2 B	NS ..	NS ..	NS ..	0.00	1.20
AIM Investor Class									
23.27	EuroGrow p	EU	4.3	NS ..	NS ..	NS ..	NS ..	0.00	NA
NA	Hyld p	HC	NA	NS ..	NS ..	NS ..	NS ..	0.00	NA
6.73	Inco p	AB	1.1	NS ..	NS ..	NS ..	NS ..	0.00	NA
9.31	LrgCpGr p	LG	1.9	NS ..	NS ..	NS ..	NS ..	0.00	NA
8.22	Muni p	GM	0.7	NS ..	NS ..	NS ..	NS ..	0.00	NA
AIM / INVESCO A									
14.63	AdvHeaA p	HB	4.3	31.6 D	-4.3 D	0.3 E	10.8 E	5.50	1.65
30.46	FinSvc p	SE	3.6	36.5 D	NS ..	NS ..	NS ..	5.50	1.38
25.80	Tech p	TK	3.9	50.8 D	NS ..	NS ..	NS ..	5.50	1.47
9.96	Utilities p	UT	1.3	23.6 D	NS ..	NS ..	NS ..	5.50	1.41
AIM / INVESCO B									
25.39	Tech t	TK	3.9	49.4 D	NS ..	NS ..	NS ..	0.00	2.15
AIM / INVESCO K									
41.51	Leisure p	SE	0.8	33.6 E	NS ..	NS ..	NS ..	0.00	1.87
11.65	SmCoGth p	SG	4.9	43.8 E	NS ..	NS ..	NS ..	0.00	1.70
AIM / INVESCO Inst									
26.43	Tech	TK	4.0	51.5 D	-26.0 E	-5.5 C	NS ..	0.00	0.90
AIM / INVESCO Inv									
11.52	CorEqi p	LC	1.0	27.6 D	-4.7 B	0.4 A	7.6 D	0.00	1.08
15.12	Dynm p	MG	2.6	42.5 C	-14.9 D	-0.9 D	8.8 C	0.00	1.21
20.63	Enrgy p	NR	1.3	26.8 E	0.9 D	19.1 B	11.0 C	0.00	1.69
30.58	FinSvc p	SE	3.6	36.4 D	1.5 E	5.4 E	13.5 B	0.00	1.40
3.54	Gold&Prec p	AU	-8.8	33.0 D	36.3 C	15.4 E	-2.7 E	0.00	1.88
49.97	HlthSc p	HB	3.6	33.2 C	-1.7 C	1.0 E	11.9 C	0.00	1.44
41.85	Leisure p	SE	0.9	34.3 E	1.7 E	10.3 D	13.5 B	0.00	1.50
11.90	S&P500 t	SP	1.8	33.6 D	-5.3 D	-1.8 D	NS ..	0.00	0.65
11.67	SmCoGth p	SG	4.9	44.1 E	-9.0 E	3.7 D	8.6 C	0.00	1.50
25.58	Tech p	TK	3.9	50.1 D	-26.6 E	-6.1 C	7.7 D	0.00	1.77
24.15	TotRtn p	BL	0.9	20.0 D	0.0 C	-0.6 E	7.1 D	0.00	1.26
AMF Funds									
9.88	AdjMtg x	MT	0.1	1.5 E	3.3 E	4.4 E	5.1 E	0.00	0.44

other share of stock. Meanwhile, the investment company has its initial (fixed) pool of capital with which to make investments.

The success of the fund's investments determines the net asset value of the fund's shares (a fluctuating numerator to be divided by a fixed denominator), which can differ from their market value (stock price) as determined by supply and demand. The stock price may be above net asset value, trading at a premium, or below, trading at a discount. Either way, the fund's management takes its fee for administering the fund.

Why would fund managers choose to be confined by a closed-end fund rather than grow with a conventional open-end mutual fund? Because their pool of capital is not subject to the volatile swings generated by purchases and redemptions.

The Wall Street Journal publishes a daily report on **Closed-End Funds**. You can find it in the index on page C1. The following example is taken from the Tuesday, January 13, 2004, issue.

CLOSED-END FUNDS

Monday, January 12, 2004

AMEX

STOCK (SYM)	DIV	LAST	NET CHG
◆Abrdn AP IncFd FAX	.42	6.50	0.10
◆AbrdnAusEq IAF	.17e	9.49	0.03
EqInc AT&T Fd ATF	2.72f	88.02	0.32
◆BancroftFd BCV	.71e	19.20	0.13
↓ Bexil BXL	.60	22.65	2.55
BlkRkBIG Tr BCT	.90a	16.10	0.10
BlkRkCA Tr RAA	.85a	14.01	0.09
BlkRkCA Tr2 BCL	.98	13.78	-0.06
BlkRkFL IQM Tr RFA	.85a	15.58	-0.04
BlkRkMD Muni BZM	.86	15.25	0.27
BlkRkManInco Tr2 RLE	1.01	14.12	-0.07
BlkRkNJ Muni BLJ	.94a	14.90	0.25
BlkRkNY IQM Tr RNY	.88	14.42	-0.03
BlkRkNY Mil Tr2 BFY	.95	13.95	-0.01
BlkRkPA Tr BPS	.89	15.33	-0.10
BlkRkVA Muni BHV	.87	16.29	0.02
CIM HiYld CIM	.45a	4.88	0.06
◆CastleFd CVF	.76a	23.20	...
◆CntIFdCan CEF	.01g	5.54	-0.01
CntlSec CET	1.40e	21.52	0.11
◆ColCAInsMun CCA	1.00	15.53	0.07
◆CollnsMun CFX	1.04	15.84	0.26
↓ CornstnStrat CLM	1.04	9.40	0.30
CornstnTtlRtn Fd CRF	2.11	18.09	0.05
DE AZ Mun Fd VAZ	.96a	16.10	-0.04
DE CO InsFd VCF	.96a	16.47	-0.06
DE FL MunFd VFL	1.02a	16.60	0.05
DE MN Fdll VMM	1.02	16.35	-0.05
↓ DE MN Fd III VYM	.90	15.65	0.15
DE MN Fd VMN	.96a	16	0.16
DreyfCAMunFd DCG	.46m	8.16	0.06
DreyfMunInc DMF	.72	10.27	0.04
DreyfNYMun DNM	.41	8	-0.05
EtnVncCA MIT CEV	1.02	15.50	0.10
EtnVncFL MIT FEV	1.03	15.65	...
EtnVncCA EVM	.90a	13.97	-0.02
EtnVncCA II EIA	.95	14.53	-0.01
EtnVncFL EIF	.93a	14.89	...
EtnVncMA MAB	.95a	15.69	0.04
EtnVncMuni EIM	.94	14.36	0.12
EtnVncMuni II EIV	1.00a	15.09	-0.02
EtnVncNJ EMJ	.96a	15.74	-0.01
EtnVncNY ENX	.96	14.15	0.15
EtnVncNY II NYH	.96a	14.90	0.05
EtnVncOH EIO	.93a	15.91	-0.06
EtnVncPA EIP	.94a	15.99	-0.01
EtnVncLtdFd EVV n	1.61	19.09	0.11
EtnVncMA MIT MMV	1.02	15.86	0.30
EtnVncMi MIT EMI	1.03	16.20	...
EtnVncNJ MIT EVJ	1.07	15.98	0.03
EtnVncNY MIT EVY	1.04	15.75	-0.05
EtnVncOH MIT EVO	1.01	15.95	0.12
EtnVncPA MIT EVP	1.00	16.38	0.03
◆Elsworth Fd ECF	.32e	8.20	-0.07
Engex EGX		10.20	0.10
EvrgrnIncoFd EAD n	1.65	16.15	0.22
EvrgrnMgdFd ERK n	1.57a	19.42	0.07
FstInlMMMuniFd MXN	.80a	14.47	-0.07
↓ FstTrVal100Fd FVL n		16.75	-0.04
FstTrValDivFd FVD n	.23y	14.55	-0.07
FstTri4CnrsFd FCM n	.18e	19.78	...
Foxby FXX		2.49	-0.01
FrkInCap FKL		1.15	-0.18
◆FrkInTmpltaTr FTF n	1.19	14.86	-0.12
◆GlblIncoFd GIF	.32	5.07	0.05
IndonesiaFd IF n	.02e	5.06	-0.03
ING ClrnRlEst IIA n	.41	14.83	0.08
IntrmMuniFd SBI	.61	10.26	-0.02
MA HlthEdu MHE	.87	14.96	-0.02
MN MunInco MXA	.94a	15.88	-0.12
MunInsFd MIF	.50e	9.91	0.06
MuninvestFd MVF	.64	9.28	0.03
Nasd01-8 Tiers		9.86	0.14
NeubrgrBrmCA NBW	.75	13.50	0.10
NeubrgrbxoOpp NOX n	1.27	14.97	0.02
NeubrgrBrm NBH	.80	13.87	0.09
NeubrgrBrmNY NBO	.78	13.60	0.05
NubrgrRlEstSec NRO n	.40e	14.95	0.06
◆NuvAZ NFZ	.92a	26.59	0.01
◆NuvAZ Fd2 NKR	.86a	14.75	0.01
◆NuvAZ Fd3 NXE	.80	13.78	0.11
◆NuvCA Fd2 NVX	.91	14.27	0.07
◆NuvCA Fd3 NZH	.86	13.56	0.06
◆NuvCA Prm NCU	.88	13.78	0.07
◆NuvCT Fd2 NGK	.88a	16.45	0.09
◆NuvCT NFC	.89	16.10	0.04
◆NuvCT Fd3 NGO	.78	14.19	0.01
◆NuvDivAdv2 NXZ	1.83a	15.65	0.03
◆NuvDivAdv 3 NZF	.97	14.78	0.11
◆NuvGA NZX	.88a	16.10	0.24
◆NuvGA Fd2 NKG	.80a	14.51	0.29
◆NuvGA Prm NPG	.91a	17.05	-0.03
◆NuvCA InsDivAdv NKL	.91a	14.88	0.05
◆NuvCA Muni NKX	.91	14.60	0.05
◆NuvInsDivAdv NVG	.93a	15.65	0.24
◆NuvFL Muni NWF	.86	16.10	0.04
◆NuvMA Muni NGX	.86a	16.75	-0.02
◆NuvNY InsDivAdv NXO	.89a	15	0.03
◆NuvNY Muni NRK	.87	14.93	...
◆NuvMuni NEA	.93a	15.26	0.05
◆NuvMD NFM	.94	16.67	-0.08
◆NuvMD Fd2 NZR	.88a	15.81	0.04
◆NuvMD Fd3 NWI	.79	14.17	-0.04
◆NuvMI NZW	.89	15.59	0.17
◆NuvMO Prm NOM	.88	17	-0.04
NuvMuniInsOpp NMZ n	.09y	15.25	0.16
↓ ◆NuvNJ NXJ	.94	15.80	0.14
◆NuvNJ Fd2 NUJ	.92a	15.39	-0.03
◆NuvNY Fd2 NXK	.95a	15.24	0.13
◆NuvNC NRB	.92a	16.80	...
◆NuvNC Fd2 NNO	.86a	16.02	0.12
◆NuvNC Fd3 NII	.80a	15.05	0.10
◆NuvOH Fd2 NBJ	.92	15.83	0.08
◆NuvOH Fd3 NVJ	.88a	16.01	...
◆NuvPA NXM	.97a	16.30	-0.19
◆NuvPA Fd2 NVY	.92a	15.99	-0.01
◆NuveenRlEst JRS	1.38a	18.88	0.13
◆NuvVA NGB	.94	17.75	0.26
◆NuvVA Fd2 NNB	.89a	17.60	-0.15
PMC Cap PMC	.48	5.60	0.08
◆PachldrHI PHF	.90	9.38	0.06
PrgrssvReEFd PGF	3.38	30.40	1.05
PutnamCA Inv PCA	.74	13.71	0.17
PutnmNYInv PMN	.68	12.52	0.04
RMR RIEstFd RMR n		14.91	-0.06
SAL Tr Trups	2.44	26.20	-0.06
ScudderRE II SRO n	1.20	15.50	0.10
◆ScudderRE SRQ	1.44	19.37	0.13
Tuxis TUX	.67e	7.87	...
↓ ◆VnKmAdvIl VKI	.96	15.66	0.11
◆VnKmCA VKC	.60a	10.20	-0.02
◆VnKmMAInc VMV	.97	17.30	0.20
◆VnKmOHInc VOV	.89	15.71	-0.05
◆VnKmSelect VKL	.85	13.13	0.02
VestaurSec VES	1.14e	13.27	0.02

NASDAQ

STOCK (SYM)	DIV	LAST	NET CHG
BrntlyCap BBDC	.69e	10.34	0.11
◆HnckJ Fnl JHFT	.74e	16	-0.15
↓ RensCap RENN	1.25e	14.43	-0.06
RoyceFocus FUND	.62e	9.09	0.10
S&P 500 Fd PEFX	.02e	8.89	0.05

NYSE

STOCK (SYM)	DIV	LAST	NET CHG
ACM OppFd AOF	.72	9.19	0.05
ACM IncFd ACG	.81	8.70	0.04
ACM MgdDir ADF	.81	8.48	0.04
ACM Mgdinco AMF	.42m	4.80	-0.03
ACM MuniSec AMU	.87	11.92	0.05
◆ASA ASA	.60a	45.45	-0.52
◆AbrdnGlobInc Fd FCO	.72	14.22	-0.03
◆AdamsExp ADX	.83e	12.63	0.06
◆AdvntCymrFd AVK n	2.06a	27.15	0.25
◆AimSelREIF RRE	1.24	16.58	0.04
AllncAll ACM	1.67e	15.13	0.07
AllianceCal AKP	.96	14.15	-0.04
AllianceNa AFB	1.00	14.30	0.11
AllianceNY AYN	.92	13.67	-0.04
AllncWrld II AWF	1.11	13.21	0.06
AllncWrld AWG	1.08	13.99	0.24
AllmrST ALM	.65f	9.81	0.11
AmIncmFd MRF	.66	8.79	0.05
AmMuninco XAA	.94a	14.84	0.05
AmSelPort SLA	1.05	14	0.04
AmStrat ASP	.87	13.20	-0.09
AmStratII BSP	1.14	14.06	0.03
AmStratII CSP	1.05a	13.30	0.05
ApexMunFd APX	.56a	8.57	0.01
◆AsiaPacFd APB	.18e	14.46	-0.16
◆AsiaTigers GRR	.07e	11.41	0.06
BlkRkAdvTr BAT	.70	11.30	0.04
BlkRkTrmTr BFC	.77a	17.13	0.14
◆BlkRkInco Tr BCX	.90a	14.21	0.03
BlkRkCA MT Tr BJZ	.74	13.86	0.09
BlkRkCA Muni BZA	.96a	14.03	0.01
BlkRkCA Mi Tr BFZ	.91	13.72	0.10
BlkRkCB Tr BHK	1.05a	13.58	0.01
BlkRkDivAch Tr BDV n		15.18	0.03
BlkRkFL08 Tr BRM	.75a	16.47	0.08
BlkRkFL Muni2 BFO n	.90	15.41	-0.06
BlkRkFL Muni BIE	.93a	14.85	-0.03
BlkRkFL Mi Tr BBF	.90	14.44	0.14
BlkRkHiYld Tr BHY	1.01	10.95	0.07
BlkRkIncoOpp Tr BNA	.84	11.39	0.06
BlkRkInco Tr BKT	.61a	7.74	0.09
BlkRkInsFL Tr BAF	.96a	14.74	0.13
BlkRk Tr BYM	.94	14.54	0.06
BlkRkM08 Tr BRM	.80a	17.41	0.02
BlkRkInsNY Tr BSE	.90	14.29	0.04
BlkRkIQM Tr BKN	.91	14.88	0.07
BlkRkInv Tr BQT	.03	-9.65	0.04
BlkRkbxInco Tr BLN n	1.50	19.20	...
↓ BlkRkMT Tr BPK	.78	14.87	-0.01
BlkRkMuni20 BKX n	.94	15.48	0.17
BlkRkMuniB8 Tr BBX	1.04	14.83	-0.01
BlkRkMunilnco Tr BFK	.97	14.47	0.13
BlkRkMTT Tr BMN	.58a	10.99	-0.01
BlkRkNJ Mi Tr BNJ	.90	14.83	0.08
BlkRkNY Tr BLN	.75a	16.99	0.04
BlkRkNY Mi Tr BLH	.74	14.78	-0.02
BlkRkNY Muni	.93	14.43	0.08
BlkRkNY Mi Tr BNY	.90	14.21	0.06
BlkRkPfOppTr BPP n	2.00	24.90	0.02
BlkRkStrBsl Tr BHD	1.56a	16.45	0.02
BlkRkStrMuni Tr BSD	.96	15.02	0.19
◆BlueChipVal BLU	.63e	6.25	0.02
BoulderGro BIF	.03m	6.08	0.04
BoulderTotR BTF	.03m	15.54	-0.04
◆BrazilEqty BZL	.41e	7.96	0.19
↓ ◆BrazilFd BZF	.63e	26.59	0.78
CignaHilnco HIS	.28a	2.93	0.04
CignaInv IIS	.92a	17.20	0.08
CalamsConvFd CHY n	1.46	17	0.24
Calamos CHI	1.80a	21.19	0.50
CotlEurRus Fd CEE	.22e	25.13	-0.28
ChrtwlDvdInco CWF	1.00	10.18	0.07
◆ChileFd CH	.47e	15.50	0.72
◆ChinaFund CHN	1.78e	41.30	-2.00
CitigrpInvLnFd TLI	.72	15.20	0.11
◆ChnStrAdvInco RLF	1.38a	18.60	0.14
◆ChnStrPrInco RPF	1.38a	18.64	0.28
◆ChnStrQuInco RQI	1.32a	17.56	-0.07
◆ChnStrPfInco RNP n	2.04	25.88	0.09
◆ChnStrTR RFI	1.02a	18	-0.09
◆ColonIHilnco CXE	.48	6.68	0.11
◆ColonIIntmk CMK	.65a	9.03	0.09
◆ColonialIntr CIF	.32	3.74	0.03
◆ColonInvMun CXH	.67	10.60	0.03
◆ColonMuni CMU	.42	5.83	0.03
CpHiYld CIYE	1.00e	9.03	-0.03
CpHiYld COY	1.08e	9.86	-0.02
CpHiYld V HYV	1.38e	16.05	0.02
CpHiYld III HYI	1.82e	15	0.02
CrSuisIncoo CIK	.42m	4.56	0.04
CrSuisHighYld DHY	.17	5.55	0.09
DebtStratFd DSU	.88e	7.28	0.09
DE InpDivInco DDF	.96	12.41	0.04
DE InGlbDiv DGF	.96	12.62	0.01
DNP SelInc DNP	.78a	11.20	0.01

EXCHANGE-TRADED PORTFOLIOS

Monday, February 23, 2004
Includes Exchange-Traded Funds and HOLDRs

AMEX

YTD %CHG	HI	LO	STOCK (SYM)	DIV	YLD %	VOL 100s	CLOSE	NET CHG
1.6	107.92	74.31	Diamond DIA	2.20e	2.1	73320	106.23	-0.19
2.8	89.82	68.15	PharmaHldrs PPH	1.62e	2.0	1271	81.72	-0.40
4.1	94.94	63.25	RetailHldrs RTH	.65e	.7	8529	94	-0.48
4.0	3.65	1.91	B2BHldrs BHH		...	764	2.88	-0.10
4.7	146.17	85.42	BiotchHldrs BBH	.04e	...	9692	141.70	-1.35
24.0	17.30	7.47	BrdBndHldrs BDH	.06e	.4	5860	16.68	-0.04
3.4	66.08	35.96	Europe01Hldrs EKH	1.18e	1.9	42	63.05	-0.50
0.5	40.16	24.39	IntArchHldrs IAH	.15e	.4	373	36.19	-0.71
-1.1	54.41	25.35	IntrntHldrs HHH	.10e	.2	3040	49.66	-1.40
11.9	4.61	2.10	IntInfrHldrs IIH	.08e	1.9	687	4.23	-0.16
2.3	56.60	39.80	Mkt2000Hldrs MKH	1.16e	2.1	73	55.38	-0.22
2.2	136.70	91.33	RegBkHldrs RKH	4.00e	3.0	1575	135.50	0.06
14.1	72.59	52.76	OilSvcHldrs OIH	.42e	.6	6564	70.75	-0.21
-2.5	45.78	21.80	SemiConHldrs SMH	.08e	...	2217329	40.45	-1.10
-2.9	40.20	25.05	SftwreHldrs SWH	.65e	1.8	8583	36.93	-0.69
1.6	29.15	20.78	TelecomHldrs TTH	1.01e	3.6	1448	27.93	-0.06
1.6	81.01	58.10	UtilHldrs UTH	3.10e	3.9	425	79.62	0.26
20.0	59.06	30	WirlsHldrs WMH	.52e	.9	198	57.92	-0.10
4.9	52.20	37.70	iShrDJUSEn IYE	.90e	1.7	410	51.88	0.57
-5.3	55.21	50.33	iShrDJTA IYT	.38p	...	30	50.98	-0.65
-1.1	46.23	29.13	iShrDJUSBM IYM	.68e	1.5	1028	45.10	-0.07
1.3	57.30	37.18	iShrDJUSCCy IYC	.13e	.2	196	56.14	-0.45
5.0	51	36.61	iShrDJUSCNC IYK	.94e	1.9	449	50.71	0.03
4.1	109.01	69.15	iShrDJUSFin IYG	2.07e	1.9	135	107.50	-0.24
3.9	60.67	45.33	iShrDJUSHlth IYH	.53e	.9	1129	59.20	-0.45
0.7	51.12	32.31	iShrDJUSInd IYJ	.39e	.8	282	49.41	-0.13
5.3	106.40	72.86	iShrDJUSRE IYR	6.43e	6.2	782	104.51	0.04
2.6	55.20	36.84	iShrDJUSTot IYY	.86e	1.6	307	54.10	-0.35
1.7	59.70	43	iShrDJUSUtil IDU	1.80e	3.1	482	58.58	-0.02
5.2	94.13	59.80	iShrDJUSFI IYF	1.86e	2.0	131	92.60	-0.18
4.9	22.75	15.33	iShrDJUStc IYZ	.50e	2.3	697	22.08	-0.10
-0.5	53.54	30.34	iShrDJTch IYW		...	1340	48.26	-0.99
3.0	117.30	70.21	iShrSP400V IJJ	1.36e	1.2	465	113.71	-1.13
3.0	79.25	52.26	iShrRu3000V IWW	1.78e	2.3	64	78	-0.26
4.4	65.68	35.96	iShrMSEMU EZU	.79e	1.2	185	63.95	-0.05
3.1	171.60	100.15	iShrRu2000V IWN	2.71e	1.6	4521	165.45	-1.46
2.4	39.62	26.58	iShrRu3000G IWZ	.33e	.9	139	38.70	-0.37
5.7	69.20	39.52	iShrSPEu350 IEV	1.11e	1.6	680	67.80	-0.02
2.3	94.86	58	iShrSP600G IJT	.36e	.4	635	90.80	-1.34
2.0	106.30	62.59	iShrSP600V IJS	.96e	.9	540	102.59	-1.21
3.4	14.32	8.62	iShrMSAusy EWA	.43e	3.1	563	13.81	-0.02
16.6	15.90	8.49	iShrMSAus EWO	.17e	1.1	1044	15.56	0.04
11.6	14.88	7.36	iShrMSBlg EWK	1.01e	7.0	239	14.45	0.04
-6.2	18.81	7.19	iShrMSBra EWZ	.27e	1.7	2268	15.95	-0.15
0.4	15	9.54	iShrMSCan EWC	.20e	1.4	2544	14.31	-0.09
3.9	177.91	99.70	iShrMSCIEmrgMkt EEM	.81e	.5	1520	170.30	-1.50
4.6	21.78	10.66	iShrMSFra EWQ	.28e	1.3	39	21.32	-0.03
1.7	17.25	8.07	iShrMSGer EWG	.20e	1.2	669	16.47	-0.04
5.0	22.90	13	iShrMSIta EWI	.61e	2.9	369	20.71	0.26
-0.7	10.30	6.19	iShrMSJpn EWJ	.00e	...	54057	9.57	0.06
8.7	28.50	14.70	iShrMSSK EWY	.24e	.9	719	27.21	-0.19
9.0	7.05	4.82	iShrMSMay EWM	.10e	1.4	7455	7.03	-0.02
12.6	20.47	11.26	iShrMSMex EWW	.21e	1.1	4514	19.24	-0.32
4.8	17.50	9.55	iShrMSNth EWN	.37e	2.2	52	17.14	0.03
6.7	7.40	3.89	iShrMSSng EWS	.12e	1.9	2592	6.40	-0.01
6.9	30.48	16.90	iShrMSEsp EWP	.27e	.9	295	29.51	0.02
4.0	16.03	9.11	iShrMSSwl EWL	.05e	.3	251	15.33	0.03
4.4	16.59	10.16	iShrMSUK EWU	.48e	3.0	493	16.27	0.04
5.9	79.52	48.59	iShrMSCI Pac EPP	1.51e	2.0	527	76.79	-0.10
4.0	60.09	35.93	iShrMSSoAfr EZA	1.36p	...	477	58.50	0.30
11.3	18.08	8.71	iShrMSSwe EWD	.25e	1.4	399	17.37	0.17
1.1	103.79	100.55	iShrLehAggBd AGG	.93e	.9	243	103.23	0.28
1.3	109.90	76.17	iShrGldSach IGE	1.79e	1.7	176	108.23	0.17
19.4	36.46	13.52	iShrGSNetwkng IGN		...	8394	32.97	-0.68
0.3	70.67	32.91	iShrGSSmcdtor IGW	.00p	...	1618	62.95	-1.99
-0.1	41.10	24.04	iShrGSSftwr IGV		...	1236	37.73	-1.00
0.5	50.80	28	iShrGSchsTch IGM		...	1232	46.10	-1.10
1.8	117.96	105.77	iShrGSInvst LQD	5.93e	5.3	336	112.56	0.31
0.3	83.04	81.82	iShrLeh1-3 SHY	1.43e	1.7	1335	82.75	0.08
2.8	97.66	80.91	iShrLeh20+ TLT	4.61e	5.2	5025	87.88	0.54
1.8	90.80	82.15	iShrLeh7-10 IEF	3.48e	4.0	2302	86.22	0.28
3.7	144.72	85.63	iShrMSCI EAFE EFA	1.57e	1.1	4236	141.90	0.40
11.0	11.60	6.55	iShrMSHK EWH	.15e	1.4	5428	11.10	-0.17
11.7	12.71	7.34	iShrMSTaiwn EWT	.02e	.2	1590	12.55	0.05
5.4	79.84	45.97	iShrNasBlotch IBB		...	4020	75.80	-1.40
2.8	62.30	42.05	iShrRu1000 IWB	1.09e	1.8	794	61.27	-0.22
3.1	60.96	40.52	iShrRu1000V IWD	1.42e	2.4	3474	60.16	-0.02
2.5	65	35.97	iShrRu2000G IWO	.20e	.3	8956	60.74	-1.26
3.3	78.88	47.64	iShrRuMidGrth IWP	.17e	.2	495	76.15	-1.00
3.1	71.05	43.98	iShrRuMid IWR	.91e	1.3	226	69.17	-0.73
3.3	98.35	61.68	iShrRuMidVlu IWS	1.89e	2.0	540	96.36	-0.49
2.1	49.11	33.32	iShrRu1000G IWF	.48e	1.0	17093	47.80	-0.45
2.7	66	44	iShrRu3000 IWV	1.09e	1.7	1002	64.64	-0.27
2.7	120.06	68.23	iShrRu2000 IWM	1.30e	1.1	61024	113.81	-1.74
0.0	86.95	54.26	iShrSP/Tpx ITF	.24e	.3	23	83.62	0.27
2.8	122.33	76.31	iShrSP400 IJH	1.00e	.8	586	118.29	-1.19
0.2	101.77	98.71	iShrSP1500 ISI		...	43	100.07	-0.61
2.7	58.01	41.25	iShrSP500G IVW	.76e	1.3	1660	57.08	-0.28
3.4	58.18	37.44	iShrSP500V IVE	1.13e	2.0	2396	57.23	-0.14
6.0	49.59	31.05	iShrSPGblTele IXP	.65e	1.3	51	48.28	-0.21
3.0	55.97	32.01	iShrSPGbl IT IXN		...	16	52.20	-0.89
3.1	116.48	79.06	iShrSP500 IVV	2.06e	1.8	2077	114.67	-0.33
2.4	50.99	36.93	iShrSPHlthcr IXJ	.30e	.6	169	48.84	-0.13
1.9	60.24	42.55	iShrSPGbl GE IXC	.62e	1.0	189	59.98	0.44
2.0	125.64	81.71	iShrSP400G IJK	.51e	.4	223	121.12	-1.59
4.9	62.74	37.25	iShrSPGblFnl IXG	1.31e	2.1	130	61.20	0.08
2.3	142.47	85.54	iShrSP600 IJR	1.01e	.7	12355	137.10	-1.58
2.4	64.20	32.81	iShrTr40 ILF	.74e	1.2	278	60.28	0.27
5.5	114.05	78.18	iShrCohenSt ICF	6.37e	5.7	925	111.96	0.16
0.0	39	23.54	Nasdaq 100 QQQ	.01e	...	f12353	36.45	-0.41
0.9	43.85	28.30	PwrShsDynOTC PWO		...	154	40.30	-0.70
3.8	36.55	26.81	PwrShsDynMkt PWC	.25e	.7	459	35.61	-0.46
3.1	142.90	100.67	RydexSP500 ETF RSP	1.00e	.7	148	139.60	-0.89
3.0	116.60	79.38	SPDR SPY	1.63e	1.4	3580939	114.59	-0.29
0.1	32.34	20.65	SPDR ConsDiscr XLY	.19e	.6	2901	31.51	-0.23
5.6	22.91	17.82	SPDR ConStpl XLP	.36e	1.6	8090	23	0.13
6.1	29.39	21.45	SPDR Engy XLE	.48e	1.6	6055	29.22	0.23
5.8	30.16	19.15	SPDR Fncl XLF	.52e	1.7	13970	29.77	...
3.7	31.98	24.88	SPDR Hlthcare XLV	.35e	1.1	3317	31.26	-0.06
0.5	27.95	17.85	SPDR Indu XLI	.34e	1.3	15507	26.89	-0.10
-0.6	27.10	17.01	SPDR Materials XLB	.48e	1.8	9309	26.54	0.01
1.0	22.24	13.42	SPDR Tch XLK	.14e	.7	10662	20.59	-0.28
1.7	24.14	17.39	SPDR Utls XLU	.80e	3.4	3211	23.73	0.09
2.7	111.90	70.10	SP400 Spdrs MDY	.86e	.8	17828	108.24	-0.91
2.7	63.77	44.87	sTrackDJGlTltn DGT	1.24e	2.0	45	62.85	-0.11
1.8	48.67	33.53	sTrackDJLCapG ELG	.93e	2.0	83	47.51	-0.37
3.3	129.05	89.69	sTrackDJLCapV ELV	2.58e	2.0	66	127.80	0.15
2.3	70.80	39.96	sTrackDJSCapG DSG	.14e	.2	79	67.82	-1.00
3.2	173.80	106.30	sTrackDJSCapV DSV	8.07e	4.8	18	167.89	-3.21
2.6	82.50	57.25	sTrackFort500 FFF	1.41e	1.7	46	81.25	-0.33
2.5	52.28	27.19	sTrackMSHTch35 MTK		...	211	48.68	-1.17
2.2	170.12		sTrackWlshREIT RWR	8.14e	5.2	51	156.13	-0.47
-4.8	49.24	47.35	VangdInfoTch VGT		...	13	46.73	-1.01
1.7	50.63	49.03	VangdValue VTV		...	112	50.10	-0.04
-0.9	50.65	48.05	VangdSmCap VB		...	16	48.58	-0.86
0.7	50.75	49.15	VangdLgCap VV		...	58	49.82	-0.22
-2.3	50.40	47.75	VangdSmCapGrth VBK		...	19	47.85	-0.60
0.2	50.87	49.33	VangdGrowth VUG		...	9	49.68	-0.17
5.2	53.01	50.65	VangdCnsmrStpls VDC		...	16	53.27	0.32
2.0	50.28	48.10	VangdCnsmrDiscr VCR		...	2	49.50	-0.05
3.2	51.92	48.30	VangdMatrls VAW		...	9	50.81	0.12
-0.1	50.45	49.05	VangdUtil VPU		...	6	49.77	0.07
0.5	50.92	48.96	VangdMdCap VO		...	27	49.59	-0.41
2.3	51.46	49.4	VangdFnl VFH		...	24	51	-0.14
0.7	50.85	48.40	VangdSmCapValue VBR		...	21	49.56	-0.59
0.5	51.50	49.75	VangdHlthCr VHT		...	52	50.31	-0.26
3.1	112.09	74.39	VangdVipersTot VTI	1.38e	1.3	1123	109.81	-0.74
2.9	75.50	44.83	VangdVipersExt VXF	.61e	.8	200	72.75	-0.80

NASDAQ

YTD %CHG	HI	LO	STOCK (SYM)	DIV	YLD %	VOL 100s	CLOSE	NET CHG
-0.9	69.97	42.25	BldrsAsia50 ADRA	.68e	1.0	6	64.89	-0.06
-0.2	78	43.98	BldrsEmg50 ADRE	3.35e	4.5	z4865	74.32	-0.66
4.5	65.29	36.25	BldrsEur100 ADRU	1.13e	1.8	z341	62.68	0.22
0.3	86.24	71.75	FdltyNasCompFd ONEQ	.07p	...	1354	80.05	-1.38

NYSE

YTD %CHG	HI	LO	STOCK (SYM)	DIV	YLD %	VOL 100s	CLOSE	NET CHG
4.3	37.46	20.25	FrescoDJSEuro50 FEZ	.66e	1.8	218	36.63	0.06
3.1	35.58	21.15	FrescoDJS50 FEU	.75e	2.1	1234	35.03	0.11
3.7	56.30	49.75	iShrDJSelDiv DVY	.29p	...	3598	55.83	0.07
3.4	60.44	39.23	iShrSP100Gbl IOO	.65e	1.1	154	59.34	-0.01
2.1	104.29	101.08	iShrTIPSBdFd TIP	.12p	...	1135	103.88	0.33

CBOE

YTD %CHG	HI	LO	STOCK (SYM)	DIV	YLD %	VOL 100s	CLOSE	NET CHG
2.8	57.60	40.15	iShrSP100 OEF		...	1352	56.66	-0.12

MITTS

Monday, February 23, 2004		

Market Index Target-Term Securities feature principal protection while offering the potential to capture gains in the composite price performance of an underlying index.

AMEX

STOCK (SYM)		VOL 100s	CLOSE	NET CHG
MerLynBdbnd	BDM	12	8.81	-0.04
MerLynDJIAM		63	10.05	0.04
MerLyEngy06	ESM	5	11.91	-0.04
MerLynNik 6-07	NML	10	9.43	0.12
MerLynS&P6-09	MLW	74	10.09	-0.01
MerLynS&P5-09	MCP	10	9.96	-0.04
MerLynRssl	RRM	21	10.14	0.13
MerLynNsdq	MNM	11	9	-0.01
MerLynMjr11	EUM	22	9.50	-0.09
MerLynEFO6	EFM	40	11.17	...
MerLynTpTen	MTT	39	16.56	-0.15
MerLynSPDR06	GWM	26	9.49	0.03
MerLynSPDR	CSM	5	9.54	0.08
MerLynDJ	MDJ	18	9.64	-0.02
MerLynNik 3-07	MLJ	10	9.12	0.10
MerLynEngy	ESY	8	9.80	0.04

STOCK (SYM)		VOL 100s	CLOSE	NET CHG
MerLynNik06	NKM	7	9.24	-0.06
MerLynNik 3-09	MNK	36	10.75	0.06
TargetsMerLyn	RSM	48	10.95	0.05
MerLynNik05	MLN	120	9.67	-0.07
MerLynS&P9-09	MKP	63	10.15	0.02
MerLynMITTS05	EUF	2	10.95	0.04
MerLynRssl04	RUM	245	11.63	-0.13
MerLynSP7-05	MLF	317	9.97	-0.08
MerLynSP06	FML	157	9.38	-0.08

NASDAQ

STOCK (SYM)		VOL 100s	CLOSE	NET CHG
MerLynNik 3-11		236	9.95	0.35
MerLynSP Mktlndx	MTSP	z15932	9.15	0.04
MerLynMITTS	MTDB	10	9.31	-0.01
MerLynDJIA10		20	9.25	-0.15
MerLynS&P7-10	z1481		9.95	...
MerLynSP500	MITT	1	8.95	-0.09
MerLynNik 9-10	z24060		9.60	0.20
MerLynDJIA		141	10.19	0.02

NYSE

STOCK (SYM)		VOL 100s	CLOSE	NET CHG
MerLynSP9-05	MIJ	3	10	0.02

You can also track closed-end funds in the online edition by going to Mutual Funds in the Markets and Markets Data Center (from the home page's left-hand menu-bar) and clicking on Closed-End Funds.

Turn to page 253 for an example from the Tuesday, February 24, 2004, *Journal* of the daily listing of **Exchange-Traded Portfolios.** These are closed-end funds arranged for convenience by exchange (primarily AMEX) so that you can avoid the lengthier closed-end fund listing.

MITTS—Market Index Target-Term Securities—are a Merrill Lynch product akin to closed-end funds. Above is an example of the daily listing from the Tuesday, February 24, 2004, *Journal*.

RISKY BUSINESS

Margin and Option Trading

If you are confident a stock will rise, you may purchase it and realize your gain if your prediction proves true. But there are a number of ways you can *leverage* your purchase in order to increase your gain (i.e., you can capture the increase on a larger number of shares of stock than you can currently afford to purchase). Your *leverage* is the ratio between the value of the shares you control (and from which you will reap a profit) and the amount of capital (money) you have invested. The smaller your investment and the larger the value of the shares you control, the greater your leverage.

For instance, under current regulations set by the Fed, you may borrow from your broker up to half the initial value of the shares of stock you purchase, which provides leverage of two to one. It's called *buying on margin*. If you buy $200 worth of stock from your broker, with a margin (your capital) of $100 (50 percent margin) and a $100 loan from the broker, and the stock doubles in value (from $200 to $400), you have made $200 on a $100 investment (less interest and brokerage costs) instead of $100 on a $100 investment that was not margined. That's leverage.

Options provide another opportunity to leverage your investment. They give you the right (option) to buy or sell stock at a stated price for future delivery at a premium (cost to buy the option). People do this for the same reason they buy or sell any stock: They think it's going up or down in value. Only in this case, they believe the market price of the stock will be higher or lower than the price at which they agreed to buy or sell it. Investors stand to gain if they can buy a stock below its market price (and can then sell it at the market price), or can sell it above market price (after having purchased it below market price).

For instance, suppose you had the option to buy a share of stock for $25 in a few months' time that currently trades at 23.50 and you were convinced the stock would be trading at 28 by then. Wouldn't you pay a premium for the right to buy a $28 stock for $25? That's a good deal, as long as the premium is smaller than the spread between $25 and the $28 price at which you think the stock will trade. Conversely, if you were convinced that a stock, currently trading at 23.50, would fall to 18, wouldn't you pay a fee (premium) for the right to sell it at $20, knowing you could obtain it at $18?

The excerpt from the Monday, March 8, 2004, print *Journal* on page 256 provides an example of **Most Active Listed Options**. This report appears daily, and you can find it in the front-page indexes of the first (A1) and third (C1) sections under Index/Listed Options. The excerpt on page 256 takes Apple Computer as an example (AAPL, listed as AppleC in **Most Active Listed Options**).

The online edition provides option information when you click on Markets and Markets Data Center from the home page's left-hand menu-bar, then go down the left side to Listed Options below Options/Futures under U.S. Stocks. See the Wednesday, July 14, 2004, excerpt on page 257 for American Express, drawn from the Thursday, July 15, 2004, online edition.

MOST ACTIVE LISTED OPTIONS

Friday, March 5, 2004

Composite volume and close for actively traded equity and LEAPS, or long-term options, with results for the corresponding put or call contract. Volume figures are unofficial. Open interest is total outstanding for all exchanges and reflects previous trading day. Close when possible is shown for the underlying stock or primary market. **XC**-Composite. **p**-Put. **o**-Strike price adjusted for split.

OPTION/STRIKE			VOL	EXCH	LAST	NET CHG	CLOSE	OPEN INT	OPTION/STRIKE			VOL	EXCH	LAST	NET CHG	CLOSE	OPEN INT
RJ Reyn	Jan 05	25	107,468	XC	36.20	1.90	61.08	9,002	Gen El	Apr	32.50 p	15,053	XC	0.70	...	32.77	25,268
RJ Reyn	Jan 05	35	106,782	XC	26.20	-2.00	61.08	13,590	RJReyn	Mar	45	14,904	XC	16.30	-1.90	61.08	1,301
RJ Reyn	Jan 06	5	79,268	XC	56.30	-1.90	61.08	4,534	Amgen	Apr	65	13,995	XC	1.40	0.20	63.25	19,588
RJ Reyn	Jan 06	30	74,726	XC	31.20	-2.00	61.08	9,104	CompAsc	Mar	25 p	13,626	XC	0.20	-0.10	26.84	17,559
RJ Reyn	Jan 06	25	70,230	XC	36.30	-1.90	61.08	7,851	RJReyn	Mar	55	13,040	XC	6.30	-0.30	61.08	1,212
Intel	Mar	30	55,399	XC	0.30	-0.45	28.95	131,360	Citigrp	Mar	50	12,587	XC	0.80	0.15	50	79,664
Nasd100Tr	Mar	36 p	47,770	XC	0.30	-0.05	36.63	278,909	ATT Wrls	Jan 05	12.50	12,210	XC	2.05	-0.05	13.56	84,877
Nasd100Tr	Mar	37	38,001	XC	0.40	-0.10	36.63	289,447	SemiHTr	Apr	40 p	11,631	XC	1.25	0.05	41.25	16,575
Nasd100Tr	Mar	37 p	31,879	XC	0.75	...	36.63	283,506	AppleC	Apr	25	11,554	XC	2.65	1.15	26.74	35,189
RJ Reyn	Jan 05	30	29,724	XC	31.30	-1.90	61.08	2,419	SemiHTr	Mar	42.50 p	11,341	XC	1.65	...	41.25	37,618
Nasd100Tr	Mar	36	24,567	XC	0.95	-0.15	36.63	148,355	Transocn	Mar	30	11,192	XC	1.25	-0.50	30.77	13,783
Nasd100Tr	Apr	36 p	23,880	XC	0.75	-0.05	36.63	133,370	BostSc	Mar	45	11,177	XC	0.45	-0.05	43.53	8,113
Oracle	Mar	12.50	20,725	XC	0.55	-0.15	12.71	56,915	RJ Reyn	Jan 06	35	11,004	XC	26.30	-1.90	61.08	4,210
RJReyn	Mar	50	20,704	XC	11.30	-1.90	61.08	2,000	BostSc	Mar	42.50	10,720	XC	1.60	-0.75	43.53	37,717
Nasd100Tr	Mar	35 p	18,996	XC	0.15	...	36.63	207,599	Nokia	Jan 05	15	10,361	XC	8.30	0.60	23.22	22,643
Gen El	Mar	32.50 p	17,684	XC	0.25	-0.05	32.77	58,051	Nasd100Tr	Mar	40 p	10,270	XC	3.30	0.10	36.63	14,349
MStewrt	Mar	12.50 p	17,517	XC	2.40	1.60	10.86	9,695	Cisco	Mar	22.50 p	10,242	XC	0.35	0.05	22.89	34,557
Nasd100Tr	Mar	38	16,493	XC	0.10	-0.05	36.63	192,032	Nasd100Tr	Apr	30 p	10,225	XC	0.05	...	36.63	27,097
Nasd100Tr	Apr	37 p	15,481	XC	1.20	...	36.63	76,150	Nasd100Tr	Apr	37	10,135	XC	0.90	-0.15	36.63	67,855
									Nasd100Tr	Mar	41	10,001	XC	4.20	0.10	36.63	10,736

Apple Computer call option at $2.65 on March 5, 2004

Turning to the examples on this page, the first column lists the option. The second column provides the month—on the third Friday—that your option expires. The third column gives the strike price—$25—at which you have the option of buying (call) or selling (put) the stock. (A *p* in the fourth column indicates a put; otherwise the option is a call.) Think of the strike price as the price at which you strike a deal.

The next five columns list trading volume, the exchange on which the option is traded (see the notes above the data), the premium you must pay per share to purchase the option, the premium's change at the end of the day, and the underlying stock's closing price. Take Apple as an example. You could purchase an option at a strike price of $25.00. On March 8, 2004, you had to pay a premium of $2.65 for the right (option) to buy a share of Apple stock at $25.00 by the close of trading on Friday, April 16, 2004 (third Friday of April). Once the deal was struck, the seller (writer) of the option would be bound to deliver the stock to you at that price at any time before

---

Apple Computer call option at $2.65 on March 5, 2004

						NET		OPEN
ATT Wrls	Jan 05	12.50		12,210	XC	2.05	-0.05	13.56	84,877
SemiHTr	Apr	40	p	11,631	XC	1.25	0.05	41.25	16,575
AppleC	Apr	25		11,554	XC	2.65	1.15	26.74	35,189
SemiHTr	Mar	42.50	p	11,341	XC	1.65	...	41.25	37,618
Transocn	Mar	30		11,192	XC	1.25	-0.50	30.77	13,783

THE WALL STREET JOURNAL.
O N L I N E

News   Technology   Markets   Personal Journal   Opinion   Leisure/Weekend

0-9 I A I B I C I D I E I F I G I H I I I J-K I L I M I N I O I P I Q-R I S I T I U-V I W-Z I

LEAPS ▶   Index Options ▶

AmExpr (AXP)							Underlying
			Call				Put
Expiration	Strike	Last	Volume	Open Interest	Last	Volume	
Jan	35.00	...	...	59	0.25	300	
Jul	45.00	4.20	4	280	0.05	10	
Aug	45.00	...	...	30	0.20	10	
Oct	45.00	...	...	226	0.70	110	
Jan	45.00	...	...	5708	1.40	16	
Aug	47.50	2.20	232	122	0.45	26	
Oct	47.50	3.00	30	754	1.40	124	
Jan	47.50	4.00	30	57	2.10	3	
Jul	50.00	0.05	297	18239	0.90	2016	
Aug	50.00	0.90	70	2652	1.70	36	
Oct	50.00	1.55	263	2508	2.45	20	
Jan	50.00	2.60	1187	14349	3.20	900	
Aug	55.00	0.05	130	872	...	...	
Oct	55.00	0.25	11	3572	...	...	
Jan	55.00	0.75	474	9468	6.30	10	
Jan	60.00	0.25	350	10798	...	...	

*Underlying stock price represents listed exchange price only. It may not match the composite clo

the close of business on April 16, 2004, *at your option.* The decision to purchase is up to you. You can take it or leave it once you have paid the premium.

Why would you buy such a contract? Because you were convinced that Apple would trade at more than $27.65 (strike price of $25 plus premium of $2.65) plus commissions at any time before the third Friday in April of 2004. Then you would have the option to buy it at $25.00 (the strike price) from the option writer and sell it at the higher market price. When the call price rises above the strike price, an option is said to be *in the money*.

Trading is done in round lots of 100 shares. Thus, on Monday March 8, 2004, when Apple was $26.74, you could have purchased an options contract for $265 (100 × $2.65) to buy 100 shares at $25.00 by the close of business on Friday, April 16, 2004. How would you have done?

Not bad. Apple traded at $29.30 on Thursday, April 15, 2004, just one day before the option expired. Back in March you paid a $265 premium

(100 × $2.65) for the option to call (buy) 100 shares at $25.00. By April 13, 2004, those shares were worth $2,930 (100 × $29.30) on the market. Thus, by exercising your option you could have purchased (called) $2,930 worth of securities for $2,500 (100 × $25.00), less your premium of $265, for a gain of $166 ($2,930 – $2,500 – $265 = $166 exclusive of brokerage fees) on your $265 investment in only a month's time. That's leverage!

Notice that purchasing the option provided you with a much higher return than buying Apple stock at $26.74 on March 8, 2004. By April 16, 2004, Apple stock had appreciated by 9.5 percent ($29.30 – $26.74 = $2.56, a return of 9.5 percent on a $26.74 investment), considerably less than the 63 percent gain on the option ($166 return on a $265 investment). But also notice that the option carried considerably greater risk. When a stock does not appreciate, you at least preserve your capital (you still have the stock). When an option expires, your money's gone (you have nothing).

You should know, however, that you need not purchase a stock underlying an option in order to realize your gain. You can sell the option instead and enjoy the premium's increased value. When a stock rises and the spread between its value and the strike price grows, the premium's value will rise, too, as options purchasers seek to claim this spread. (The bigger the spread, the bigger the premium.) Since you are the option holder, you keep the premium's gain in value—the difference between the premium's value when you purchased the option and when you sold it. As a matter of fact, most investors never intend to buy the underlying stock. Instead, they hope to sell their option at a profit, i.e., the premium's increased value.

Thus, if you buy a call, you're speculating that the stock's price will rise sufficiently to earn you a return (spread) over and above the premium you must pay to buy the option. But suppose it doesn't? Suppose the stock rises only a little, or even falls in value, so that you have the option to buy a stock at a price greater than market value? What then? Would you have to buy the stock from the option writer at the strike price? No, because you have only purchased an option to buy. There's no requirement to do so. You can let the option expire without exercising it, and you have only lost your premium.

A rising market motivates investors to buy calls. They hope the price of their stock will shoot up and they will be able to exercise their option and recover their premium, and then some. This does not necessarily mean that option writers (people who sell the option) are counting on the market to stay flat or even fall. The call writer may have decided to sell a stock if it reaches a certain target level (i.e., take his or her gain after the stock rises a certain number of points). If it does rise, the call writer will receive the increment

MOST ACTIVE LISTED OPTIONS

Tuesday, February 17, 2004

Composite volume and close for actively traded equity and LEAPS, or long-term options, with results for the corresponding put or call contract. Volume figures are unofficial. Open interest is total outstanding for all exchanges and reflects previous trading day. Close when possible is shown for the underlying stock or primary market. XC-Composite. **p**-Put. **o**-Strike price adjusted for split.

Nasdaq 100 put option at $0.80 on February 17, 2004 →

OPTION/STRIKE				VOL	EXCH	LAST	NET CHG	CLOSE	OPEN INT	OPTION/STRIKE				VOL	EXCH	LAST	NET CHG	CLOSE	OPEN INT
Nasd100Tr	Mar	34	p	97,544	XC	0.15	−0.10	37.44	326,166	GreenptFn	Mar	40		19,998	XC	5.20	−1.70	45.25	6,968
ConocPhil	Feb	65		78,568	XC	4.50	0.70	69.37	9,462	CoxCom	Jan 05	5	p	19,600	XC	0.05	...	33.24	58,674
Nasd100Tr	Feb	37	p	58,360	XC	0.15	−0.30	37.44	284,054	ATT Wrls	Jul	12.50		19,466	XC	1.50	1.05	13.78	82,998
ATT Wrls	Jan 05	12.50	p	52,336	XC	0.55	−0.70	13.78	6,590	GreenptFn	Feb	40		19,353	XC	5.20	−1.60	45.25	3,215
ATT Wrls	Mar	14		49,668	XC	0.20	0.10	13.78	33,874	ATT Wrls	Jan 06	12.50		17,654	XC	2.10	1.10	13.78	22,089
ConocPhil	Feb	60		44,966	XC	9.40	1.00	69.37	4,082	NortelNwk	Feb	8		17,573	XC	0.45	0.15	8.39	24,403
ATT Wrls	Jan 05	10	p	44,482	XC	0.25	−0.15	13.78	49,159	ConocPhil	Feb	55		17,311	XC	14.40	0.90	69.37	1,987
Nasd100Tr	Feb	38		41,598	XC	0.15	0.10	37.44	226,507	ATT Wrls	Apr	14	p	17,262	XC	0.40	−1.75	13.78	234
Nasd100Tr	Mar	37	p	37,429	XC	0.80	−0.30	37.44	155,928	GlaxoSKln	Feb	40		16,372	XC	2.90	0.30	42.85	5,208
Nasd100Tr	Mar	35	p	35,609	XC	0.30	−0.10	37.44	139,473	Nasd100Tr	Mar	36	p	16,340	XC	0.50	−0.20	37.44	169,286
ATT Wrls	Mar	14	p	32,302	XC	0.35	−2.40	13.78	430	ATT Wrls	Jul	10		15,483	XC	0.10	−0.20	13.78	88,961
ATT Wrls	Jan 05	12.50		30,209	XC	1.95	1.35	13.78	36,963	Nasd100Tr	Mar	37		15,094	XC	1.25	0.20	37.44	154,116
Nasd100Tr	Feb	37		29,937	XC	0.60	0.70	37.44	191,054	FstillHn	Feb	20	p	15,015	XC	0.05	−1.20	21.12	7,895
ATT Wrls	Apr	14		29,920	XC	0.25	0.15	13.78	3,440	SemiHTr	Feb	47.50		14,387	XC	0.50	0.10	42.52	48,953
Nasd100Tr	Feb	38	p	25,306	XC	0.65	−0.45	37.44	214,481	ATT Wrls	Jul	10		14,020	XC	3.80	1.75	13.78	83,119
ATT Wrls	Feb	12.50		25,257	XC	1.25	1.10	13.78	99,850	Microsft	Apr	30		13,951	XC	0.15	...	26.99	107,105
BP PLC	Feb	45		22,907	XC	3.70	1.05	48.72	2,338	ATT Wrls	Jan 06	15		13,905	XC	0.15	−0.20	13.78	12,452
Gen El	Jun	30	p	22,577	XC	0.55	−0.10	33.05	28,082	Nasd100Tr	Mar	38		13,673	XC	0.70	0.15	37.44	103,626
ATT Wrls	Mar	12.50		22,353	XC	1.35	1.05	13.78	167,771	Rambus	Feb	30		12,380	XC	1.40	0.30	25.84	28,701
Nasd100Tr	Mar	38	p	20,172	XC	1.30	−0.35	37.44	89,256	Microsft	Mar	27.50		12,090	XC	0.40	...	26.99	23,803

Volume & Open Interest Summaries

AMERICAN				CHICAGO BOARD				PHILADELPHIA			
Call Vol:	480,659	Open Int:	50,801,272	Call Vol:	830,958	Open Int:	66,925,202	Call Vol:	584,836	Open Int:	48,381,553
Put Vol:	369,314	Open Int:	37,933,135	Put Vol:	730,243	Open Int:	54,587,656	Put Vol:	287,430	Open Int:	37,204,274
BOSTON				INTL SECURITIES				PACIFIC			
Call Vol:	8,994	Open Int:		Call Vol:	827,295	Open Int:	58,075,709	Call Vol:	365,278	Open Int:	61,009,433
Put Vol:	7,165	Open Int:		Put Vol:	534,486	Open Int:	46,384,426	Put Vol:	184,251	Open Int:	47,890,097
								TOTAL			
								Call Vol:	3,098,020		
								Put Vol:	2,112,889		

and the premium; even if it doesn't, he or she will still receive the premium. Thus, income is the primary motive for writing the option. Instead of waiting for the stock to move up to the target level, the seller writes a call. If it doesn't move up to that price, he or she will still have earned the premium. If it does, he or she will get premium plus capital gain.

Now consider the other kind of option and turn to the Wednesday, February 18, 2004, issue of the *Journal* (see this page), using the Nasdaq 100 index as our example. Suppose you had believed on Tuesday, February 17, 2004, that the index would fall substantially below its current market value of $37.44 and had purchased a put contract. The option writer would have been obliged to buy the stock from you at the strike price regardless of current market value. Your option to sell at the strike price would give you an

Nasdaq 100 put option at $0.80 on February 17, 2004 —

ATT Wrls	Jan 05	10	p	44,482	XC	0.25	−0.15	13.78	49,159
Nasd100Tr	Feb	38		41,598	XC	0.15	0.10	37.44	226,507
Nasd100Tr	Mar	37	p	37,429	XC	0.80	−0.30	37.44	155,928
Nasd100Tr	Mar	35	p	35,609	XC	0.30	−0.10	37.44	139,473
ATT Wrls	Mar	14	p	32,302	XC	0.35	−2.40	13.78	430
ATT Wrls	Jan 05	12.50		30,209	XC	1.95	1.35	13.78	36,963

opportunity to buy at the lower market value (assuming your forecast was correct) and sell at the strike price to profit on the difference.

Notice the $0.80 premium for the March contract at a strike price of $37.00. If the Nasdaq 100 fell below $36.20 (strike price less premium, or $37.00 − $0.80) before the March expiration date, you could buy the stock at the (lower) market price and sell (put) it to the option writer at the (higher) contract price of $37.00. The difference, less the premium and any brokerage fees, would be your profit.

By Thursday, March 18 (one day before the contract expired), the Nasdaq 100 had fallen to $35.34. You could have purchased the Nasdaq 100 at the market price of $35.34 and sold it to the option writer for $37.00, for a gain of $1.66 a share, less the $0.80 premium and brokerage fees.

To be precise, your premium would have been $80.00 (100 × $0.80). When the Nasdaq 100 fell to $35.34, you could have purchased 100 shares at $3,534 (100 × $35.34) in the market and exercised your option to sell for $3,700 (100 × $37.00), for a gain of $86.00 ($166 of gain on the stock less $80 of premium) on an initial investment of $80.00. Again, you must subtract the broker's fee from your profit.

To repeat, be aware that most options buyers do not exercise their options. They sell them if they show a profit or let them expire if they do not. The premium's value will grow as the underlying stock's price falls and you, as the option holder, will realize the premium's gain in value.

If you guessed wrong and the Nasdaq 100 rose, so that the market price exceeded the strike price, you wouldn't want to exercise your option to sell at a price below market. Instead, you would permit your option to expire without exercising it. Your loss would be only the premium you paid.

Why would someone write a put? Because he or she is prepared to buy a stock if it should drop to a particular price. The writer earns the premium whether or not the option is exercised. If he or she believes the stock will rise in price, then the writer has little concern that an option holder will put it to him or her at less than the market price. And the writer has collected the premium. But if the market does fall, and falls sufficiently that the contract comes in the money, the writer will have to buy the stock at the contract price, which will be above market. That's not necessarily bad, since the writer had already planned to buy the stock if it fell to the strike price, and he or she has collected a premium, too.

In addition to simply playing the options market for profit, investors can use options to hedge against price fluctuations of their investment in the underlying security. For instance, you can write (sell) call options against a stock you own. If the stock falls in value, you at least get to keep the premium. If it rises above the strike price, you keep the premium and realize a gain on the stock.

On the other hand, if you like a stock but think it will fall in value, write (sell) a put instead of buying the stock. If it doesn't fall, you collect the premium anyway. If it does fall, you still collect the premium and purchase the stock at a lower price.

These strategies involve *covered* options, i.e., options in stock you own or intend to buy. You can write *naked* options on stock you don't own and do not intend to buy. It seems like an easy way to collect a premium. But suppose you've written a call option thinking the stock couldn't possibly rise that far, and it does. You'll have to buy that stock at the market price if the option is exercised and then sell it at the lower strike price. That could hurt.

Conversely, you can write naked put options and collect your premium if you believe a stock could never fall *that* far. But if there's another crash like the one accompanying the 2001 recession, and the market collapses, you may find yourself in the embarrassing position of having to buy stock at prices substantially above market in order to meet your obligation to sell the stock at the much lower market price. Where will you obtain the funds to cover the difference between the high price at which you purchased the stock and the low price at which you must sell it?

That's one of the reasons options are risky business.

One more comment about leverage. You can minimize risk if you buy options whose strike price is close to the market price, but you also reduce your relative gain. Leverage increases as the strike price increasingly deviates from the market price. That is, not surprisingly, risk and reward move together.

You can spread the risk of options investing by purchasing *index options* (see page 262) in the entire market rather than an option on an individual stock. Instead of buying all the stocks in one of the stock-market averages (or buying an index mutual fund), you can buy a put or call on an index option (such as the Nasdaq 100 in the examples on pages 259 and 262), just as you can invest in options on individual stocks.

Index Options, appearing daily in the print edition, on the *Dow Jones Industrial Average*, the *NASDAQ*, and the *S&P 500,* permits you to speculate on changes in the broad market without purchasing a large number of stocks. But the index options on the *S&P 100* are the most widely traded.

Index Options listings are available online, too. Click on Markets and Markets Data Center in the left-hand menu of the home page, then go down the left side to Listed Options below Options/Futures under U.S. Stocks.

THE WALL STREET JOURNAL.
O N L I N E

News   Technology   Markets   Your Money   Opinion

Options ▶ LEAPS ▶

			Prices at close July 14, 2004		
Nasdaq 100 (NDX)					
Underlying Index	High	Low	Close	Net Change	Fr Dec
Nasdaq 100	1433.61	1411.52	1416,05	−12.63	
	Strike			**Volume**	**Last**
Jul	1200.00 put			130	0.05
Jul	1235.00 put			10	0.10
Jul	1250.00 put			8	0.05
Jul	1300.00 put			152	0.05
Jul	1325.00 put			381	0.20
Jul	1350.00 put			109	0.10
Jul	1375.00 put			396	0.65
Jul	1400.00 put			2,017	2.60
Jul	1400.00 put			217	20.00
Jul	1425.00 put			2,996	12.00
Jul	1425.00 call			1,664	4.50
Jul	1450.00 put			2,273	0.60
Jul	1450.00 put			484	35.00
Jul	1475.00 call			57	57.00
Jul	1475.00 put			1,058	26.50
Jul	1500.00 call			46	0.15
Jul	1500.00 put			83	86.00
Jul	1525.00 call			47	0.10
Jul	1525.00 call			12	
Jul	1550.00 call			120	0.05
Jul	1575.00 put			3	0.05
Jul	1650.00 put			8	0.05
Aug	1025.00 put			110	0.30
Aug	1075.00 put			10	0.50
Aug	1150.00 put			118	1.00
Aug	1175.00 put			63	1.50
Aug	1200.00 put			37	2.10

July 2004 "put" option →

You will find Index Options two lines above Listed Options. An excerpt from the Wednesday, July 14, 2004, edition illustrating **Index Options** and the **Nasdaq 100** appears above. Note the July 2004 put at a price of $1,500.00 with a $86.00 (in the money) premium. That option was written at a time when the Nasdaq 100 traded at more than $86.00 over its July 14, 2004, $1,416.05 price. Someone did very well betting on the market's decline.

Finally, the investor can purchase longer-term options on some stocks. *The Journal* publishes a daily print listing of **Leaps–Long-Term Options**.

Home

News   Technology   Markets   Personal Journal   Opinion   Leisure/Weekend

MARKETS DATA   0-9 I A I B I C I D I E I F I G I H I I I J-K I L I M I N I O I P I Q-R I S I T I U-V I W-Z I
SECTION INDEX ▶
Index Options ▶

Leaps – Long-Term Options

Leaps quotations, updated once a day at 9 p.m. Eastern time, are organized alphabetically by company name. Click the name of a company at the left to see end-of-day quotes for that company. Click a letter above to view a list of companies for that letter.

These pages display composite volume, close and open interest for Leaps as of the end of the previous trading day, with results for the corresponding put or call contract. Volume figures are unofficial. Open interest is total outstanding for all exchanges and reflects the previous trading day. Close when possible is shown for the underlying stock on primary market.

Company names followed the word "old" denote contracts on stocks before a stock split or spinoff.

Please note: Options quotations are only displayed for contracts traded that day. If no contracts traded for a company, that company will not be listed.

← American Express

News   Technology   Markets   Personal Journal   Opinion   Leisure/Weekend

0-9 I A I B I C I D I E I F I G I H I I I J-K I L I M I N I O I P I Q-R I S I T I U-V I W-Z I
Index Options ▶

Prices at close July 14, 2004

AmExpr (AXP)					Underlying stock price*: 49.25			
			Call			Put		
Expiration	Strike	Last	Volume	Open Interest	Last	Volume	Open Interest	
Jan 06	60.00	1.75	20	8961	...	...	811	

Underlying stock price represents listed exchange price only. It may not match the composite closing price.

To find **Leaps–Long-Term Options** online, click on Markets and Markets Data Center from the home page's left-hand menu-bar, then go down the left side to Leaps, which appears below Options/Futures under U.S. Stocks. Excerpts for Leaps and American Express from the Thursday, July 15, 2004, edition are on page 263.

Many of these possibilities sound intriguing, easy, and potentially profitable. Keep in mind, however, that there are substantial commission costs. Furthermore, as in any leveraged situation, the potential for considerable loss exists. Options are not for novices, and even buying on margin exposes you to up to twice the risk of simply buying a stock with your own money. With leverage you can move a big rock with a small stick—but the stick can also break off in your hands, and the rock can roll back over your feet.

In fact, the whole options game is tricky and multifaceted. Consequently, before you can invest in options, your broker will evaluate your past investment experience and your current financial position. It will not be easy to qualify.

Short Interest

Instead of speculating on a price increase, some investors borrow stock from their broker in the hope of a price *decrease*. They sell the stock and leave the proceeds of the sale with their broker. If the stock falls, the borrower buys it back at the lower price and returns it to the broker, at which time the broker returns the funds from the original sale to the borrower. The advantage to the borrower is obvious: Borrowers pocket the difference between the high price when they borrowed and sold the stock and the low price when they bought and returned the stock.

For example, if you borrow a $2 stock from your broker and sell it, you have $2. If it falls to $1, you can buy it on the market and return the stock to the broker and you keep the other dollar. This is called *selling short*. But what advantage does the broker gain? Brokers lend stocks because you have to leave the cash from your sale of the stock with them as collateral for the borrowed stock, and they can then lend (or invest) the cash at interest.

If you borrow a $2 stock from your broker in the hope that if falls to $1, you can easily return the stock to your broker if the market heads south. But what happens if you guess wrong and the stock rises to $3? You have only $2 and, therefore, cannot repurchase the stock for $3 in order to return it to your broker. How can brokers protect themselves?

Your broker will insist that you maintain a substantial deposit (margin) at the brokerage firm in order to cover that risk, and, if the stock does appreciate, you will be required to deposit additional margin. This risk can be appreciably reduced if you have a buy-stop order with your broker that instructs the broker to repurchase the stock for your account as soon as it rises to a level slightly higher than the price at which you borrowed it. Your loss will be held to a minimum.

Toward the end of each month, *The Wall Street Journal* print edition reports **NYSE and AmEx Short Selling Highlights** for stocks traded on the New York and American stock exchanges. The *Journal* publishes **NASDAQ Short Selling Highlights** approximately one week later (check the index of the third section under NY/AMEX or NASDAQ Short Sales). The Thursday, April 22, 2004, and Tuesday, April 27, 2004, *Journal* excerpts (see below and pages 266, 267, and 268) serve as examples. You can also use these reports to trace the short-interest position in individual stocks.

Short interest is the number of borrowed shares that have not been returned to the lender. A great deal of short interest in a stock indicates wide-

---

Short Interest On the NYSE Advances 2.1%

Some of the Bearish Bets Might Have Bitten Skeptics Since the Market Rose

By PETER A. McKAY

NEW YORK—The level of short-selling on the New York Stock Exchange rose in the latest monthly tally, despite a stock-market rally over the period.

For the month through April 15, the number of short-selling positions not yet closed out rose 2.1% to 7,498,770,107 shares, up from 7,347,296,852 in mid-March.

The short ratio, or number of days' average volume represented by the outstanding short positions, rose to 5.3, compared with 5.1.

SHORT SELLING

Investors who sell securities "short" borrow stock and sell it, betting the stock's price will fall, and they will be able to buy the shares back later at a lower price for return to the lender. Short interest often is considered an indication of the level of skepticism in the market.

Short interest reflects the number of shares that have yet to be repurchased to give back to lenders. In general, the higher the short interest, the more people are expecting a downturn. Short positions rise in value as stocks fall, and vice versa.

Over the period covered by the latest short-interest report, the Dow Jones Industrial Average rose 2.9%—a trend that would have hurt the value of many short positions.

The next NYSE short-interest report is scheduled to appear in The Wall Street Journal on May 21.

NYSE AND AMEX SHORT SELLING HIGHLIGHTS

LARGEST SHORT POSITIONS

RANK	APR 15	MAR 15	CHANGE
NYSE			
1 Lucent Technol	285,242,695	276,804,016	8,438,679
2 Calpine Corp	106,983,187	106,577,514	405,673
3 Sprint Corp-PCS Gp	104,953,122	109,152,416	-4,199,294
4 Ford Motor Co	90,492,905	87,367,940	3,124,965
5 Gen'l Electric	77,659,198	28,806,050	48,853,148
6 Time Warner	58,700,099	59,663,421	-963,322
7 Tyco Int'l	56,180,037	51,939,740	4,240,297
8 AMR Corp	52,594,496	47,644,633	4,949,863
9 Nortel Networks	51,789,124	53,531,853	-1,742,729
10 Xerox Corp	49,436,043	49,510,929	-74,886
11 Pfizer Inc	49,327,678	37,805,502	11,522,176
12 Silicon Graphics	48,511,990	47,710,174	801,816
13 Gen'l Mtr	47,284,722	46,184,220	1,100,502
14 Advanced Micro Dev	47,268,591	43,760,307	3,508,284
15 Micron Technol	46,218,899	41,812,896	4,406,003
16 Manulife Fin'l	42,770,312	37,260,235	5,510,077
17 Delta Air Lines	41,687,428	30,944,318	10,743,110
18 Viacom Inc B	41,146,527	13,309,648	27,836,879
19 Motorola Inc	39,895,447	37,495,536	2,399,911
20 JPMrgnChs	39,646,940	42,519,484	-2,872,544
AMEX			
1 Nasdaq-100 Trust r	292,865,070	386,221,035	-93,355,965
2 SPDR 500 SPY r	87,983,701	122,533,770	-34,550,069
3 Semi Holdrs SMH r	37,191,848	37,397,661	-205,813
4 iShrRus2000Idx IWM	31,853,978	27,264,475	4,589,503
5 Wheaton River	31,302,979	16,427,704	14,875,275
6 SPDR Fin'l Sel Sct XLF r	28,868,086	21,785,084	7,083,002
7 iShrMSCIJapan EWJ r	19,869,759	16,109,526	3,760,233
8 Diamond Tr r	15,725,736	20,822,955	-5,097,219
9 iShrLehmn20+Bd TLT r	14,492,014	13,948,469	543,545
10 Grey Wolf Inc	11,999,865	11,515,041	484,824

LARGEST CHANGES

RANK	APR 15	MAR 15	CHANGE
NYSE			
INCREASES (in shares)			
1 Gen'l Electric	77,659,198	28,806,050	48,853,148
2 Viacom Inc B	41,146,527	13,309,648	27,836,879
3 Pfizer Inc	49,327,678	37,805,502	11,522,176
4 Delta Air Lines	41,687,428	30,944,318	10,743,110
5 Lucent Technol	285,242,695	276,804,016	8,438,679
6 Affiliated Mgrs s	11,213,548	4,025,783	7,187,765
7 Nat'l Semicondctr	11,453,979	4,361,554	7,092,425
8 Banco Bilbao Viz	8,168,906	1,600,641	6,568,265
9 Providian Fin'l	10,981,445	5,308,152	5,673,293
10 Solectron Corp	31,909,569	26,323,228	5,586,341
11 Manulife Fin'l	42,770,312	37,260,235	5,510,077
12 Citigroup Inc	32,767,992	27,306,721	5,461,271
13 Lyondell Chemical	20,340,145	15,221,622	5,118,523
14 Fisher Scientific	7,585,322	2,558,742	5,026,580
15 AMR Corp	52,594,496	47,644,633	4,949,863
DECREASES (in shares)			
1 Caremark Rx Inc	14,947,095	51,401,226	-36,454,131
2 Bank of America	23,482,473	50,610,495	-27,128,022
3 Agere Systems A	17,162,896	35,111,426	-17,948,530
4 Novartis AG ADS	2,085,288	12,562,396	-10,477,108
5 SBC Comm	24,315,157	33,470,628	-9,155,471
6 VeriznCommunic	15,478,063	23,697,254	-8,219,191
7 EMC Corp	18,511,441	24,728,488	-6,217,047
8 Fleetwood Entrprs	8,537,034	14,372,940	-5,835,906
9 Fst Data Corp	12,002,867	17,241,349	-5,238,482
10 Revlon Inc A	3,636,344	8,696,366	-5,060,022
11 BellSouth Corp	12,281,983	17,128,640	-4,846,657
12 Nokia Cp ADS	10,158,524	14,899,114	-4,740,590
13 Petroleo Brasil A	1,876,555	6,142,777	-4,266,222
14 Sprint Corp-PCS Gp	104,953,122	109,152,416	-4,199,294
15 Meridian Resource	6,195,260	10,297,359	-4,102,099
AMEX			
INCREASES (in shares)			
1 Wheaton River	31,302,979	16,427,704	14,875,275
2 IamGold Corp	10,512,492	441,631	10,070,861
3 SPDR Fin'l Sel Sct XLF r	28,868,086	21,785,084	7,083,002
4 iShrRus2000Idx IWM	31,853,978	27,264,475	4,589,503
5 iShrMSCIJapan EWJ r	19,869,759	16,109,526	3,760,233
6 Golden Star Resrcs r	6,400,765	2,817,635	3,583,130
7 SPDR Energy Sel XLE	8,327,415	6,379,014	1,948,401
8 iShrS&P500Ind IVV r	4,048,507	2,251,813	1,796,694
9 Apex Silver Mines r	3,763,939	2,235,026	1,528,913
10 Eagle Broadbrand	7,175,708	5,662,036	1,513,672
DECREASES (in shares)			
1 Nasdaq-100 Trust r	292,865,070	386,221,035	-93,355,965
2 SPDR 500 SPY r	87,983,701	122,533,770	-34,550,069
3 Diamond Tr r	15,725,736	20,822,955	-5,097,219
4 SPDR Cons Staple XLP	1,477,698	3,936,456	-2,458,758
5 iShrLehmnBd IEF	3,543,352	5,043,822	-1,500,470
6 Avanir Pharma	705,355	1,881,462	-1,176,107
7 Harken Energy	2,929,784	3,939,871	-1,010,087
8 iShrGS$Investop LQD r	1,158,563	1,775,345	-616,782
9 iShrMSCIEAFE EFA	651,666	1,252,216	-600,550
10 streetTracksWilshr	313,206	863,283	-550,077

NYSE Short Interest

Billions of shares

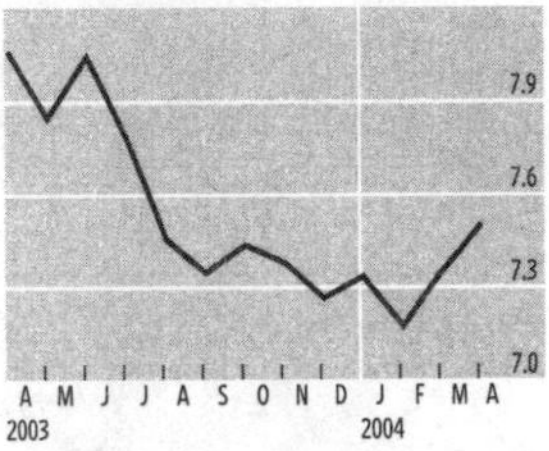

7.9
7.6
7.3
7.0
A M J J A S O N D J F M A
2003
2004

Short Interest Ratio

Short Interest Ratio (5.3) is the number of trading days at average daily volume required to cover total short interest position.

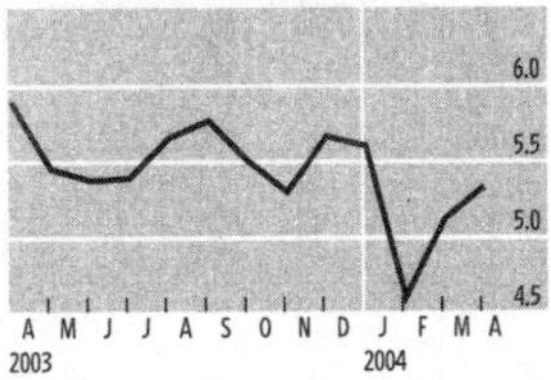

6.0
5.5
5.0
4.5
A M J J A S O N D J F M A
2003
2004

LARGEST SHORT INTEREST RATIOS

The short interest ratio is the number of days it would take to cover the short interest if trading continued at the average daily volume for the month.

RANK	APR 15 SHORT INT	AVG DLY VOL-a	DAYS TO COVER
NYSE			
1 Pre-Paid Legal Svc	8,302,458	93,255	89
2 Quebecor World	2,331,313	28,677	81
3 NiSource Inc Sails	3,688,203	55,132	67
4 Fairfax Financial	1,493,572	24,945	60
5 Manulife Fin'l	42,770,312	770,745	55
6 CryoLife Inc	6,210,955	146,700	42
7 Trinity Industries	9,139,094	221,173	41
8 Banco Bilbao Viz	8,168,906	209,327	39
9 ProQuest Co	4,226,759	117,432	36
10 Coachmen Indus	1,407,614	44,032	32
11 Fed'l Agric Mtg	1,482,040	49,359	30
12 Affiliated Mgrs s	11,213,548	377,973	30
13 Phoenix Cos	7,748,020	291,523	27
14 Great Atl&Pc	4,398,504	166,286	26
15 BT Group ADS	1,874,211	71,405	26
16 Triarc Cos B	2,996,466	116,895	26
17 Administaff Inc	6,128,375	240,568	25
18 MSC Software Corp	4,552,222	180,541	25
19 Trex Co	3,231,662	130,255	25
20 Fresh Del Monte	4,930,037	199,914	25
AMEX			
1 Rewards Networks Inc r	2,903,521	117,050	25
2 Interpharm Hldgs r	2,003,785	82,631	24
3 Questcor Pharma	1,510,539	76,304	20
4 Bentley Pharma	1,723,626	89,259	19
5 iShrS&P00 OEF	1,365,253	70,716	19

Issues that split in the latest month are excluded.
The largest percentage increase and decrease sections are limited to issues with previously established short positions in both months.

LARGEST % INCREASES

RANK	APR 15	MAR 15	%
NYSE			
1 Sunoco Logistics	595,301	15,135	3,833.
2 Syngenta AG ADS	2,211,334	265,323	733.
3 Vale Rio Doce A	3,260,014	620,871	425.
4 Banco Bilbao Viz	8,168,906	1,600,641	410.
5 Wellchoice Inc	2,072,827	473,142	338.
6 MasTec Inc	1,564,741	425,523	267.
7 Viacom Inc B	41,146,527	13,309,648	209.
8 Fisher Scientific	7,585,322	2,558,742	196.
9 Plains Exploration	2,802,832	964,554	190.
10 Georgia Gulf	1,622,171	577,763	180.
11 Affiliated Mgrs s	11,213,548	4,025,783	178.
12 Gen'l Electric	77,659,198	28,806,050	169.
13 Nat'l Semicondctr	11,453,979	4,361,554	162.
14 Commscope Inc	3,730,338	1,446,736	157.
15 Nomura Hldgs ADS	952,203	380,245	150.
16 ABN Amro Hldg ADS	1,518,532	630,844	140.
17 MFA Mtge Invest	997,655	420,898	137.
18 Titan Corp	7,402,793	3,124,516	136.
19 Suncor Energy	1,970,831	838,807	135.
20 Serono ADS	1,129,259	488,479	131.
21 Vale Rio Doce	3,590,029	1,570,933	128.
22 Philips Electron	1,948,871	865,502	125.
23 Ambac Fin'l	1,088,949	492,919	120.
24 DPL Inc	3,562,125	1,645,987	116.
25 Westar Energy	1,053,173	488,559	115.
26 Bay View Cap	1,174,899	557,156	110.
27 Providian Fin'l	10,981,445	5,308,152	106.
28 Kennametal Inc	1,143,051	554,442	106.
29 Rockwell Automatn	1,918,320	934,426	105.
30 Total S.A. ADS	1,680,597	837,437	100.
AMEX			
1 IamGold Corp	10,512,492	441,631	2,280.
2 DHB Industries Inc r	1,489,879	377,847	294.
3 iShrMSCIUK EWU	1,979,659	615,336	221.
4 Provident Engy r	1,110,488	428,753	159.
5 Golden Star Resrcs r	6,400,765	2,817,635	127.
6 iShrS&PMidcp400 IJH	1,214,131	561,493	116.
7 iShrDJUSRIEst IYR	1,692,937	852,465	98.
8 Wheaton River	31,302,979	16,427,704	90.
9 iShrS&P500Ind IVV r	4,048,507	2,251,813	79.
10 Apex Silver Mines r	3,763,939	2,235,026	68.

LARGEST % DECREASES

RANK	APR 15	MAR 15	%
NYSE			
1 Highland Hospital	17,921	1,013,006	-98.
2 Endesa S.A. ADS	71,284	717,339	-90.
3 ENI S.p.A. ADS	117,685	892,560	-86.
4 Novartis AG ADS	2,085,288	12,562,396	-83.
5 Caremark Rx Inc	14,947,095	51,401,226	-70.
6 AmBev ADS	932,140	3,193,981	-70.
7 Petroleo Brasil A	1,876,555	6,142,777	-69.
8 RPM Int'l	1,630,793	4,448,927	-63.
9 TXU Corp Equity	397,420	1,076,313	-63.
10 UIL Hldgs	495,773	1,278,110	-61.
11 NSTAR	745,472	1,888,723	-60.
12 Heinz (HJ) Co	1,958,425	4,877,291	-59.
13 Glenboro Rlty	551,217	1,327,658	-58.5
14 Revlon Inc A	3,636,344	8,696,366	-58.
15 Lloyds TSB Gp ADS	976,675	2,157,513	-54.
16 Bank of America	23,482,473	50,610,495	-53.
17 AmSouth Bancorp	2,582,438	5,498,825	-53.
18 Int'l Flav & Frag	591,388	1,247,639	-52.
19 Ashland Inc	586,993	1,211,967	-51.
20 Fst Amer Corp	1,755,703	3,619,209	-51.5
21 Agere Systems A	17,162,896	35,111,426	-51.1
22 Peabody Energy	803,284	1,624,320	-50.5
23 Telecom Brasil ADS	1,066,030	2,008,239	-46.
24 Ahold Koninklijke	1,108,996	2,086,781	-46.
25 Thermo Electron	1,135,759	2,136,450	-46.
26 Petroleo Bras ADS	4,230,087	7,952,603	-46.
27 Checkpoint System	1,048,554	1,953,590	-46.3
28 Ameren Corp	3,947,026	6,928,297	-43.
29 Allianz AG ADS	1,670,264	2,915,799	-42.7
30 Amer Axle & Mfg	1,044,298	1,805,816	-42.2
AMEX			
1 streetTracksWilshr	313,206	863,283	-63.7
2 Avanir Pharma	705,355	1,881,462	-62.5
3 SPDR Cons Staple XLP	1,477,698	3,936,456	-62.5
4 iShrMSCIEAFE EFA	651,666	1,252,216	-48.
5 iShrMSCICanada EWC	642,940	1,183,551	-45.7
6 iShrGS$Investop LQD r	1,158,563	1,775,345	-34.7
7 iShrLehmnBd IEF	3,543,352	5,043,822	-29.7
8 SPDR 500 SPY r	87,983,701	122,533,770	-28.2
9 Harken Energy	2,929,784	3,939,871	-25.6
10 Palatin Technolog	1,409,302	1,881,002	-25.1

spread speculation that a stock will fall. Remember, however, that these shares must be repaid, and that those who owe stock must buy it in order to repay it. Their stock purchases could bid the stock up.

This ambivalence illustrates the difficulty in using short-interest data as an analytical tool. For instance, the charts included with **NYSE and AmEx**

Short Interest Grows as Market Bets on Rate Rise

*Portfolio Losses Slow,
Down 2.5% This Year;
Sellers Pin Hopes on Fed*

By PETER A. McKAY

NEW YORK—Short interest rose at the Nasdaq Stock Market this month, as sellers began to anticipate an interest-rate increase by the Federal Reserve.

For the month through April 15, the number of short-selling positions not yet closed out rose 2.8% to 4,993,345,137 shares, up from 4,855,579,913 in mid-March.

The short ratio, or number of days' average volume represented by the outstanding short positions, rose to 2.9 from 2.6 a month earlier.

Investors who sell securities "short" borrow stock and sell it, betting the stock's price will fall, and they will be able to buy the shares

**SHORT
SELLING**

back later at a lower price for return to the lender. Short interest often is considered an indication of the level of skepticism in the market. Short interest reflects the number of shares that have yet to be repurchased to give back to lenders. In general, the higher the short interest, the more people are expecting a downturn. Short positions rise in value as stocks fall, and vice versa.

Over the period covered by the latest short-interest report, the Nasdaq Composite Index rose 3%—a trend that would have hurt the value of many short positions.

Nevertheless, short sellers are becoming emboldened, after taking a prolonged beating, said Harry Strunk, managing director of Aspen Grove Capital Management, which tracks short sales.

He said the average short portfolio is down about 2.5% for the year, including a 0.5% decline in March. While that performance isn't great, short sellers are at least happy to see their losses are slowing, compared with a 28.2% drop in the average portfolio in 2003, the worst annual performance in 12 years.

At this point, Mr. Strunk said, shorts increasingly believe their losing streak is running out of steam, and will reverse course if the Federal Reserve begins raising interests rates, as many observers expect this summer.

Short Selling Highlights for New York Stock Exchange issues (see page 266) indicate approximately 7.5 billion shares had not yet been returned to brokers (NYSE Short Interest) and that this was approximately 5.3 times recent trading volume (*Short Interest Ratio*). Despite the fact that this indicates considerable sentiment that stocks will fall, a short-interest ratio of over 2

NASDAQ SHORT SELLING HIGHLIGHTS

LARGEST SHORT POSITIONS

RANK		APR 15	MAR 15	CHANGE
1	Microsoft Corp	164,410,145	143,129,838	21,280,307
2	Level 3 Communicat	76,392,086	69,794,255	6,597,831
3	Juniper Networks	68,569,100	62,219,089	6,350,011
4	Sirius Satellite	66,641,372	58,576,268	8,065,104
5	Intel Corp	59,326,969	62,328,895	-3,001,926
6	Cisco Systems	52,750,761	55,641,604	-2,090,843
7	Nextel Comm	51,827,126	51,504,379	322,747
8	Yahoo! Inc	51,726,382	47,985,787	3,740,595
9	InterActiveCorp	49,186,780	49,051,787	134,993
10	JDS Uniphase	46,153,191	52,627,650	-6,474,459
11	XM Satellite Radio	43,140,986	41,830,496	1,310,490
12	Charter Comm A	41,285,837	38,736,985	2,548,852
13	Oracle Corp	40,011,235	40,953,307	-942,072
14	Dell Inc	35,737,612	30,520,223	5,217,389
15	Amazon.com	35,320,650	28,051,233	7,269,417
16	Applied Materials	32,271,982	31,875,890	396,092
17	eBay Inc	29,585,986	29,702,125	-116,139
18	Corvis Corp	27,868,872	28,737,546	-868,674
19	Comcast Corp A	26,252,807	35,053,445	-8,800,638
20	Sun Microsystems	25,987,196	38,289,870	-12,302,674
21	Sandisk Corp	25,629,539	24,699,633	929,906
22	Ariba Inc	25,196,240	22,979,675	2,216,565
23	WebMD Corp	24,043,498	23,118,406	925,092
24	Qualcomm Inc	23,414,984	20,612,367	2,802,617
25	ADC Telecommun	21,733,257	25,395,170	-3,661,913
26	Biogen Idec Inc	21,316,435	17,983,670	3,332,765
27	Comcast Corp A Spl	20,420,037	20,373,237	46,800
28	Flextronics Int'l	20,245,501	19,116,463	1,129,038
29	Ciena Corp	20,224,598	22,053,499	-1,828,901
30	RF Micro Devices	19,434,310	18,299,545	1,134,765

LARGEST CHANGES

RANK		APR 15	MAR 15	CHANGE
INCREASES (in shares)				
1	Microsoft Corp	164,410,145	143,129,838	21,280,307
2	Sirius Satellite	66,641,372	58,576,268	8,065,104
3	Amazon.com	35,320,650	28,051,233	7,269,417
4	Level 3 Communicat	76,392,086	69,794,255	6,597,831
5	Juniper Networks	68,569,100	62,219,089	6,350,011
6	Genta Inc	17,438,816	11,999,401	5,439,415
7	Dell Inc	35,737,612	30,520,223	5,217,389
8	Marvell Technology	8,893,174	4,405,324	4,487,850
9	Credence Systems	10,400,984	6,619,384	3,781,600
10	Yahoo! Inc	51,726,382	47,985,787	3,740,595
11	Transmeta Corp	10,922,193	7,523,245	3,398,948
12	Biogen Idec Inc	21,316,435	17,983,670	3,332,765
13	IPIX Corp	3,483,703	294,540	3,189,163
14	Alios Therapeutics	5,714,012	2,824,166	2,889,846
15	Broadcom Corp A	13,214,549	10,390,881	2,823,668
16	Qualcomm Inc	23,414,984	20,612,367	2,802,617
17	U.S.I. Hldgs	3,905,324	1,125,809	2,779,515
18	Tibco Software Inc	5,731,062	3,048,538	2,682,524
19	Medarex Inc	8,008,721	5,363,527	2,645,194
20	Charter Comm A	41,285,837	38,736,985	2,548,852
DECREASES (in shares)				
1	Sun Microsystems	25,987,196	38,289,870	-12,302,674
2	Bookham Tech ADS	5,966,363	17,398,486	-11,432,123
3	Comcast Corp A	26,252,807	35,053,445	-8,800,638
4	Gemstar-TV Guide	4,124,255	11,620,684	-7,496,429
5	JDS Uniphase	46,153,191	52,627,650	-6,474,459
6	Sonus Networks	7,834,293	13,144,486	-5,310,193
7	3Com Corp	8,861,821	13,654,525	-4,792,704
8	Andrew Corp	11,258,791	15,582,650	-4,323,859
9	Avanex Corp	6,574,601	10,712,432	-4,137,831
10	Manugistics Group	1,239,726	5,015,292	-3,775,566
11	ADC Telecommun	21,733,257	25,395,170	-3,661,913
12	Finisar Corp	14,281,335	17,328,107	-3,046,772
13	Intel Corp	59,326,969	62,328,895	-3,001,926
14	Cisco Systems	52,750,761	55,641,604	-2,890,843
15	Hollywood Entrmnt	4,626,904	7,479,268	-2,852,364
16	ASML Hldg N.V.	3,746,556	6,280,657	-2,534,101
17	Powerwave Technol	12,404,368	14,639,936	-2,235,568
18	US Oncology	1,429,105	3,624,976	-2,195,871
19	Extreme Networks	7,975,595	9,897,077	-1,921,522
20	Express Scripts	2,729,309	4,648,246	-1,918,937
21	Ciena Corp	20,224,598	22,053,499	-1,828,901
22	SafeNet Inc	984,464	2,809,705	-1,825,241
23	Martek Biosciences	4,019,424	5,795,706	-1,776,282
24	Nektar Therapeut	4,522,986	6,287,458	-1,764,472
25	Cray Inc	5,670,554	7,433,021	-1,762,467

Nasdaq Short Interest

Billions of shares

Short Interest Ratio

Short Interest Ratio (2.9) is the number of trading days at average daily volume required to cover total short interest position.

LARGEST SHORT INTEREST RATIOS

The short interest ratio is the number of days it would take to cover the short interest if trading continued at the average daily volume for the month.

RANK		APR 15 SHORT INT	AVG DLY VOL-a	DAYS TO COVER
1	Renaissance Learng	2,227,027	37,341	60
2	Aksys Ltd	5,497,229	94,357	58
3	ParkerVision Inc	1,697,098	31,182	54
4	Commerce One	8,666,599	164,333	53
5	FPIC Insurance Grp	2,012,988	39,745	51
6	Mair Holdings Inc	1,354,790	28,631	47
7	BUCA Inc	2,152,342	45,840	47
8	BriteSmile Inc	1,010,420	21,527	47
9	1-800 Contacts	1,113,400	24,185	46
10	Zi Corp	1,077,975	23,815	45
11	Foamex Int'l Inc	3,796,271	93,350	41
12	Research Frontiers	1,618,316	40,622	40
13	Med-Design Corp	1,106,146	29,672	37
14	Medis Technol	1,905,296	54,271	35
15	ICU Medical Inc	4,609,271	132,288	35
16	LML Payment Sys	1,078,354	31,180	35
17	Crown Media Hldgs	1,330,449	38,741	34
18	Integrated Alarm	7,861,814	229,390	34
19	West Corp	2,474,789	72,420	34
20	Conceptus Inc	7,447,003	230,302	32

Issues that split in the latest month are excluded.

LARGEST % INCREASES

RANK		APR 15	MAR 15	%
1	Sento Corp	541,931	5	10,838,520.0
2	Sunterra Corp	1,737,708	1,667	104,141.6
3	Digital Recorders	823,745	1,737	47,323.4
4	Royal Olympic Cru	179,775	500	35,855.0
5	Mace Sec Int'l	695,564	2,768	25,028.8
6	Magal Security Sys	517,123	4,154	12,348.8
7	Amer Dental Prtnrs	178,221	1,857	9,497.3
8	Amer Bldg Cntrl	456,273	5,995	7,510.9
9	Media Services Grp	208,446	5,264	3,859.8
10	Metrocall Hldgs	288,379	15,803	1,724.8
11	Hauppauge Digital	217,499	12,518	1,637.5
12	IPIX Corp	3,483,703	294,540	1,082.8
13	Futuremedia PLC	195,509	16,621	1,076.3
14	Cosi Inc	402,641	35,006	1,050.2
15	Avatar Hldgs	364,519	37,349	876.0
16	Corio Inc	229,552	24,353	842.6
17	Focus Enhancements	433,609	61,593	604.0
18	Chindex Int'l Inc	269,994	40,930	559.6
19	Vascular Solutions	688,371	138,166	398.2
20	EVCI Career Collg	764,854	173,739	340.2
21	Tegal Corp	871,103	216,207	302.9
22	Escalon Medical	1,014,794	256,504	295.6
23	Noble Int'l Ltd	500,493	136,574	266.5
24	Trico Marine Svcs	1,066,234	306,098	248.3
25	U.S.I. Hldgs	3,905,324	1,125,809	246.9
26	Nissan Motor ADS	893,160	259,856	243.7
27	Large Scale Bio	608,308	178,787	240.2
28	Lipid Science Inc	1,376,520	424,422	224.3
29	Yak Communications	417,274	130,426	219.9
30	Arch Wireless Inc A	307,993	97,217	216.8
31	Stolt Offshore ADS	2,006,224	646,208	210.5
32	SCM Microsystems	299,774	97,562	207.3
33	Aastrom Bioscience	1,451,791	475,687	205.2
34	ITC Deltacom	304,714	101,436	200.4
35	Sanderson Farms	513,202	176,507	190.8

LARGEST % DECREASES

RANK		APR 15	MAR 15	%
1	Dynabazaar Inc	2,593	627,390	-99.6
2	Envoy Comm	3,028	212,424	-98.6
3	Aware Inc	117,340	1,846,174	-93.6
4	Senetek PLC ADS	27,429	399,888	-93.1
5	AirNet Comm	19,737	284,016	-93.1
6	Makita Corp ADS	18,311	261,251	-93.0
7	Genaissance Pharm	126,747	1,136,369	-88.8
8	Randgold & Expl	24,058	192,211	-87.5
9	Cmwwlth Biotechnol	28,720	199,100	-85.6
10	VIA Net.Works	33,580	221,665	-84.9
11	Parallel Petroleum	48,963	308,573	-84.1
12	AEterna Labs	40,550	246,411	-83.5
13	Price Legacy	63,161	366,296	-82.8
14	Oscient Pharmaceuticals	315,415	1,656,482	-81.0
15	Versant Corp	192,339	795,878	-75.8
16	Manugistics Group	1,239,726	5,015,292	-75.3
17	Heidrick & Struggl	373,198	1,341,450	-72.2
18	Cardima Inc	99,176	344,007	-71.2
19	Insmed Inc	217,151	645,539	-66.4
20	Inter Parfums Inc	184,244	543,226	-66.1
21	Bookham Tech ADS	5,966,363	17,398,486	-65.7
22	SafeNet Inc	984,464	2,809,705	-65.0
23	Gemstar-TV Guide	4,124,255	11,620,684	-64.5
24	Keynote Systems	279,981	759,885	-63.2
25	US Oncology	1,429,105	3,624,976	-60.6
26	Tularik Inc	953,569	2,391,924	-60.1
27	icad Inc	380,549	934,347	-59.3
28	E X F O Electro-Optic	402,528	958,580	-58.0
29	Bon-Ton Stores	129,329	299,834	-56.9
30	Telesystem Int'l	420,592	971,052	-56.7
31	Lynx Therapeutics	334,714	730,313	-54.2
32	Avocent Corp	457,053	982,150	-53.5
33	Pinnacle Airlines	157,361	335,844	-53.1
34	Answerthink Inc	164,343	347,193	-52.7
35	SSP Solutions	332,630	690,451	-51.8

The largest percentage increase and decrease sections are limited to issues with previously established short positions in both months.

has been a rule of thumb that stocks will rise, because these borrowed stocks must be repurchased to be repaid. Now you can see why it is difficult to find meaning in the ratio.

Nonetheless, this does not mean that you should remain unconcerned if there is a substantial short-interest increase in an individual stock in your portfolio. The forces that move the entire market may not be the same as those that move an individual stock. What does the smart money know about your stock that you don't? It's an important question, and one that you should ask. So follow this report each month in the *Journal*.

Foreign Markets

Finally, you can buy shares on stock exchanges throughout the world. The front page of the third section of the print edition (Monday's and Saturday's table and chart formats differ), under **Markets Diary,** summarizes the previous day's performance of the Nikkei (Japan) and the DJ Stoxx 600 (Europe). See the example below from the Thursday, September 21, 2005, *Journal.*

The *Journal* provides daily listings of foreign issues, and you can find a reference to them on the front-page indexes of the first and third sections under **World Stock Markets** (and periodically under **International Stocks and Indexes**). A representative sample from the Tuesday, May 4, 2004, *Journal* appears on page 270.

MARKETS DIARY / Sept. 21, 2005

For an expanded view of yesterday's markets, turn to the **Markets Lineup on page C2.**

	Close	Change	Pct. chg.	52 wks
DJ Industrial Average	10378.03	−103.49 ▼	0.99%	2.66%
Nasdaq composite	2106.64	−24.69 ▼	1.16	11.72
S&P 500	1210.20	−11.14 ▼	0.91	8.68
Russell 2000	649.94	−10.69 ▼	1.62	14.85
Nikkei Stock Average	13196.57	48.00 ▲	0.37	19.76
DJ Stoxx 600 (Europe)	291.89	−3.04 ▼	1.03	21.62
Euro (in U.S. dollars)	$1.2210	$0.0083 ▲	0.68	−0.40
Yen (per U.S. dollar)	111.32	−0.59 ▼	0.52	0.67
Gold (Comex, troy oz.)	$468.90	$2.70 ▲	0.58	15.15
Oil (Nymex, barrel)	$66.80	$0.60 ▲	0.91	38.16

	Yield	Previous	Change in pct. pts.	12-mo return
10-year Treasury	4.18%	4.26% ▼	0.07	*2.97%
3-mo. Treasury	3.40	3.60 ▼	0.20	*2.07
DJ Corporate Bond	5.12	5.17 ▼	0.05	3.16

*Total return via Ryan Labs

INTERNATIONAL STOCKS & INDEXES

Monday, May 3, 2004

Americas

	CLOSE	NET CHG
TORONTO in Canadian dollars		
ATI Techs	20.25	0.30
AbitibiConsld	9.64	0.04
Alcan	55.63	0.51
Aliant	28.44	−0.06
BCE	27.10	−0.49
BankMontreal	51.90	...
BankNvaSctia	34.95	−0.20
BarrickGold	26.23	0.10
Bombardier B	5.97	−0.07
Brascan A	48.31	1.81
Brookfield Props	38.80	0.46
CanImpBnkCmrc	68.09	0.90
CanNtlRlwy	52.00	0.30
CanNtrlRsrcs	77.47	2.07
CanPacRlwy	30.60	0.10
EnCana Corp	55.51	1.71
Enbridge	50.88	0.73
Falconbridge	29.75	0.25
GreatWestLifeco	49.65	−0.71
HuskyEnergy	25.80	0.55
ImperialOil	61.15	1.00
Inco	40.15	0.91
Investors Group	33.75	−0.84
Loblaw Cos	59.22	0.47
MagnaIntl A	108.11	−0.68
ManulifeFin	50.90	0.19
NatlBnkCan	44.71	0.23
Nexen	50.93	0.78
Noranda	20.02	0.38
NortelNtwrks	4.60	−0.59
PetroCanada	61.90	1.28
PlacerDome	19.10	0.10
Potash	111.91	0.05
PowerCan	54.09	−0.16
PowerFin	55.65	−0.15
RogersComm B	23.65	−0.01
RsrchMotion	122.79	3.09
RylBnkCan	60.98	0.03
ShawComm B	22.41	−0.47
ShellCan	65.00	0.50
Shoppers Drug	30.75	0.35
SunLifeFin	36.85	0.50
SuncorEnergy	34.01	1.31
TELUS Corp	23.80	0.55
TalismanEngy	80.99	3.02
TeckCominco	20.65	0.30
Thomson	43.56	−0.09
TorontoDomBnk	44.60	0.12
TransCanada	27.12	−0.03
Weston (George)	91.33	−0.34
MEXICO CITY in pesos		
America Movil L	20.11	0.81
BBVA Bancomer B	12.00	...
Carso Telecom A1	17.48	0.45
Cemex CPO	67.37	0.53
Femsa Un	50.00	0.30
GpoTelevisa	25.37	0.57
GrpoCarso A	44.67	2.95
Grupo Fin Inb O	14.73	0.44
TelefonosMex	19.79	0.31
WalMartMex	34.00	0.69
BRAZIL in real		
BcoBrasil(BZ)	18.85	−0.25
PetroleoBras or	86.50	2.00
PetroleoBras pf	75.40	0.70
Vale do Rio ord	131.00	0.69
ValeRioDoce A	114.70	0.70
CHILE in pesos		
Antarchile A	5850.00	−99.00
BancoSntChile	15.00	...
Empresas CMPC	11499.00	−291.00
Falabella	1120.00	−20.00
PetroChile	4380.00	−20.00
VENEZUELA in bolivars		
ElecCaracas	415.05	−14.95
MercanServFin	2400.00	...
MercantilSer B	2201.00	−99.00
NacTelfVen	8280.00	5.00
Sivensa	25.85	0.10

Europe

	CLOSE	NET CHG
RylDutchPetro	40.95	0.38
Unilever	56.00	1.05
BRUSSELS in euros		
Almanij	49.34	0.04
DelhaizeGrp	40.25	−0.25
Dexia	13.80	0.08
Electrabel	275.80	1.90
GrpeBruxLam	51.00	0.80
InterBrew	25.00	−0.06
KBC Bank	x46.12	0.46
RTL Group	51.10	0.10
Solvay	69.80	−0.10
UCB	33.50	0.12
FRANKFURT in euros		
Allianz	88.25	−0.26
BASF	42.90	−0.14
BMW	36.45	0.48
BayerHypVerein	14.49	0.01
Bayer	22.20	−0.53
Commerzbank	14.30	−0.08
DaimlerChrysler	37.90	0.51
Deutsche Bank	69.22	0.47
Deutsche Post	18.75	0.36
Deutsche Tel	14.36	−0.04
EON AG	55.29	−0.01
Infineon Tech	10.95	0.26
Metro	37.09	0.10
Munchen Ruck	89.62	−0.59
RWE	36.64	0.43
SAP	127.60	1.10
Siemens	61.50	1.25
T-Online Intl	9.20	0.13
ThyssKrup	14.54	0.06
Volkswagen	37.36	0.61
LONDON closed		
MADRID in euros		
BancoBilVizAr	11.16	0.15
BancoPoplrEsp	46.44	0.41
BancoSantHisp	8.99	0.10
Endesa	15.40	0.11
GasNatural	20.81	0.34
Iberdrola	16.66	0.21
Inditex	18.22	0.08
Repsol	17.68	0.11
Telefonica Mov	8.98	0.16
Telefonica	12.47	0.06
MILAN in euros		
BancaIntesa	2.77	0.01
ENI	17.12	0.17
Enel	6.72	0.07
Generali	21.95	−0.05
Mediaset	9.32	0.16
SanpaoloIMI	9.80	0.07
TelecmItalMob	4.77	0.02
TelecmItalia	2.71	0.04
TelecomItRNC	1.97	0.02
Unicrdtoltly	3.95	0.05
PARIS in euros		
AGF	50.80	−0.15
AXA	x17.53	0.34
Accor	35.33	0.21
Alcatel	12.79	0.36
Arcelor	13.85	−0.01
Autoroutes Sud	32.11	−0.32
Aventis	63.25	−0.30
BNP Paribas	50.65	0.55
Bouygues	28.78	0.29
CNP Assurances	49.08	−0.42
CapGemini	29.60	0.08
Carrefour	38.92	0.21
Casino Guichard	74.25	...
Christian Dior	52.50	0.10
Credit Agricole	20.99	0.41
EADS	21.63	0.53
EssilorIntl	49.01	0.20
Finaxa	57.00	0.50
FranceTelecm	20.18	0.05
GrpeDanone	141.00	1.20
Hermes Intl	167.70	1.50
JCDecaux(FR)	17.34	−0.16
L'AirLiquide	147.60	1.50
LOreal	63.35	0.45
LVMH Moet	58.85	0.05
Lafarge	70.95	1.45
LagardereGrp	51.05	0.80
Michelin	40.00	0.96
SanofiSynth	52.80	−0.20
SchneiderElec	56.30	0.10
Societe Generale	70.60	1.10
SodexhoAllnc	23.40	0.39
Tele Francaise1	26.11	0.34
Thales	31.27	0.28
Thomson	16.32	0.22
Total	156.70	2.40
Unibail(FR)	79.00	0.20
Veolia Environ	22.21	0.02
Vinci	83.00	1.80
VivendiUniv	21.17	0.18
Wanadoo	8.26	0.16
RUSSIA closed		
STOCKHOLM in krona		
ForeningsSpar	142.50	...
HnnesMaurtz B	188.00	1.00
LM Ericsson B	21.10	0.40
Nordea	52.00	0.50
Sandvik	249.00	0.50
SkanEnskIda A	111.50	0.50
Svenska Hand A	147.50	...
SvenskaCell B	300.00	0.50
TeliaSonera	31.20	−0.20
Volvo B	262.50	1.00
SWITZERLAND in Swiss francs		
ABB	7	...
Adecco	61	3
CibaSpcltyChm	90	...
Credit Suisse	46	1
FinRichemont	33	...
HolcimReg	68	1
Nestle	332	4
Novartis	58	...
PargesaHldg	3455	5
RocheHldg ctf	135	−2
RocheHldg	189	−3
SGS	691	11
SeronoB	795	18
SwatchGrp	175	2
SwissReins	86	1
Swisscom	401	−2
Syngenta	104	...
SynthesStratec	1430	21
UBS	94	2
ZurichFinSvc	205	...

Africa

	CLOSE	NET CHG
JOHANNESBURG in rand		
AngloAmPlatnm	241.00	1.00
AngloGoldAshnti	223.00	2.00
MTNGroupSA)	28.69	−0.41
Sasol	105.00	0.60
Standard Bank	40.42	0.29

Asia

	CLOSE	NET CHG
HONG KONG in H.K. dollars		
BOC Hong Kong	13.25	−0.05
CLPHldgs	41.40	−0.10
CNOOC	2.85	0.03
CathayPacAir	14.15	...
CheungKngInfr	18.65	...
CheungKong	59.75	...
China Unicom	5.95	−0.10
ChinaMobile	21.00	0.40
CiticPacific	19.50	0.40
EspritHldgs(HK)	32.00	...
HKChinaGas	13.25	−0.15
HangSengBnk	99.25	0.25
HendrsnLndDev	34.60	−0.40
HongKongElec	34.10	−0.20
Hutchison Whamp	52.50	...
MTR Corp	11.85	...
SunHngKaiPr	67.00	...
SwirePac A	51.50	0.50
WharfHldgs	21.85	0.45
Yue Yuen Indl	21.00	−0.05
TAIWAN in new Taiwan dollars		
AsustekCptr	73.50	2.50
Au Optronics	64.50	−3.50
CathayFnl	59.00	...
Chi Mei Opto	66.50	−5.10
China Developmt	17.60	−0.60
Mega Financial	21.80	−0.50
NanYaPlastics	44.40	−0.20
QuantaCptr	69.50	−0.50
Taiwan Cell	31.00	0.50
TaiwanSemiMfg	58.00	0.50
United Microelec	29.50	−0.30
INDONESIA closed		
KOREA in won		
HyundaiMtr	45450	700
KT Corp	41700	800
Kookmin Bk	45000	1200
KoreaElecPwr	19800	600
LG Electronics	71200	...
POSCO	138000	−5500
SKTelecom	202000	2000
SamsngElectro	556000	−1000
Samsung SDI	148000	−2000
Shinhan Fin	21300	850
SingaporeTech	1.95	0.06
SngprPress	21.30	0.30
SngprTelecm	2.37	0.03
UntdOvrseas	13.50	−0.20
TOKYO closed		

Pacific

	CLOSE	NET CHG
NEW ZEALAND in N.Z. $		
CarterHolt	2.06	−0.04
ContactEnrgy	5.78	−0.02
IndepNewsppr	5.00	−0.05
SkyNetwork	5.45	−0.05
TelecomNZ	5.60	−0.06
SYDNEY in Australian dollars		
AMP	5.72	−0.05
AXA AsiaPac	3.08	−0.07
CmwlthBkAust	31.46	0.21
CocaColaAmtl	6.83	−0.06
ColesMyer	8.37	...
FostersGrp	4.82	−0.07
GenPropTr	3.02	0.01
HardieJmsInd	6.65	−0.05
InsuranceAU	4.81	−0.05
LendLease	10.61	−0.06
Lion Nathan	6.19	−0.06
MacquarieBnk	34.21	−0.44
Mirvac Group	4.17	−0.03
NatAustBnk	29.45	−0.02
NewcrestMng	11.26	−0.14
NewsCp pf	11.61	−0.24
NewsCp	12.60	−0.17
Orica	14.16	−0.61
Origin Energy	5.67	−0.03
PatrickCorp(AU)	5.00	−0.10
ProminaGrp	3.73	−0.02
PublgBrdcast	12.05	−0.13
QBE Ins		
QantasA		
RinkerGr		
RioTinto		
Santos		
StGeorg		
Stocklan		
SuncpMe		
Tabcorp		
Telstra		
TollHldg		
WMCRe:		
Wesfarn		
Westfld'		
Westpac		
Woodsid		
Woolwo		
WstfldA		
WstfldH		

x = Ex-

Dow Jones Country Indexes

May 3, 200

In U.S. dollar terms

COUNTRY	INDEX	CHG	% CHG	YTD % CHG
Australia	214.95	−2.07	−0.95	−1.44
Austria	192.21	−0.15	−0.08	+16.35
Belgium	222.41	−0.36	−0.16	+2.36
Brazil	324.35	+1.07	+0.33	−13.06
Canada	226.59	+0.58	+0.26	−5.07
Chile	204.45	−1.72	−0.83	−5.47
Denmark	243.17	−0.08	−0.03	+1.73
Finland	704.94	+2.01	+0.29	−10.54
France	212.55	+1.07	+0.51	−0.65
Germany	173.05	+0.37	+0.21	−4.34
Greece	150.66	+1.47	+0.99	+8.67
Hong Kong	212.99	+0.16	+0.08	−1.76
Indonesia	61.27	−0.03	−0.05	+11.41
Ireland	352.10	−0.98	−0.28	+3.13
Italy	172.88	+0.59	+0.34	+1.12
Japan	86.16	−0.04	−0.05	+10.91
Malaysia	114.88	...	...	+5.77

COUNTRY	INDEX	CHG
Mexico	198.95	+4.17
Netherlands	240.87	+0.92
New Zealand	180.33	−1.41
Norway	163.65	−0.48
Philippines	70.88	+0.58
Portugal	172.59	+0.88
Singapore	137.01	−0.52
South Africa	135.60	+0.01
South Korea	118.41	+0.56
Spain	220.98	+1.02
Sweden	276.11	+1.56
Switzerland	350.57	+1.79
Taiwan	117.62	−1.77
Thailand	67.05	+0.07
U.K.	177.80	+0.13
U.S.	264.17	+2.47
Venezuela	33.75	−1.26

International Stock Market Indexes

COUNTRY	INDEX	5/3/04 CLOSE	NET CHG	% CHG	YTD NET CHG
World	DJ World Index	189.30	+1.02	+0.54	+2.35
Argentina	Merval	1074.20	−3.73	−0.35	+2.25
Australia	All Ordinaries	3388.00	−19.70	−0.58	+82.00
Belgium	Bel-20	2451.26	+11.65	+0.48	+207.08
Brazil	Sao Paulo Bovespa	19708.58	+101.35	+0.52	−2527.81
Canada	Toronto 300 Composite	8257.60	+13.63	+0.17	+36.71
Chile	Santiago IPSA	1415.36	−15.24	−1.07	−69.44
China	Dow Jones China 88	135.37	Closed	...	−0.36
China	Dow Jones Shanghai	179.16	Closed	...	+9.75
China	Dow Jones Shenzhen	163.98	Closed	...	+8.24
Europe	DJ STOXX 600	240.39	+1.34	+0.56	+11.08
Europe	DJ STOXX 50	2722.97	+15.28	+0.56	+62.60
Euro Zone	DJ Euro STOXX	251.27	+1.65	+0.66	+8.06
Euro Zone	DJ Euro STOXX 50	2806.46	+18.98	+0.68	+45.80
France	Paris CAC 40	3705.48	+31.20	+0.85	+147.58
Germany	Frankfurt Xetra DAX	4007.65	+22.44	+0.56	+42.49
Hong Kong	Hang Seng	11950.62	+7.66	+0.06	−625.32
India	Bombay Sensex	5584.99	−70.10	−1.24	−253.97
Israel	Tel Aviv 25	528.13	+0.93	+0.18	+23.98
Italy	Milan MIBtel	21122.00	+112.00	+0.53	+1200.00
Japan	Tokyo Nikkei 225	11761.79	Closed	...	+1085.15
Japan	Tokyo Nikkei 300	227.38	Closed	...	+23.84
Japan	Tokyo Topix Index	1186.31	Closed	...	+142.62
Mexico	I.P.C. All-Share	10191.52	+243.39	+2.45	+1396.24
Netherlands	Amsterdam AEX	343.62	+2.21	+0.65	+5.97
Russia	DJ Russia Titans 10	2486.60	Closed	...	+311.83
Singapore	Straits Times	1839.23	−2.80	−0.15	+74.71
South Africa	Johannesburg All Share	10400.18	+14.38	+0.14	+12.96
South Korea	KOSPI	866.11	+3.27	+0.38	+55.40
Spain	IBEX 35	8170.60	+61.10	+0.75	+433.40
Sweden	SX All Share	210.65	+1.19	+0.57	+16.48
Switzerland	Zurich Swiss Market	5816.90	+42.50	+0.74	+329.10
Taiwan	Weighted	6029.77	−88.04	−1.44	+139.08
Turkey	Istanbul National 100	17678.25	−344.44	−1.91	−946.77
U.K.	London FTSE 100-share	4489.70	Closed	...	+12.80
U.K.	London FTSE 250-share	6210.70	Closed	...	+408.40

THE WALL STREET JOURNAL.
ONLINE

Tuesday, July 6, 2004

Dow Jones Global Indexes
For July 6 at 6:00 p.m. EDT

(All index values based on U.S. dollars unless noted)

	Index	Net Change	Percent Change
World	189.91	-1.27	-0.66
World (ex. U.S.)	148.72	-0.57	-0.38
Americas	261.36	-2.35	-0.89
Latin America	209.22	-2.75	-1.30
Europe	209.97	-1.07	-0.51
Euro Zone	206.77	-1.58	-0.76
Europe (ex. U.K.)	225.11	-1.63	-0.72
Pacific	97.62	-0.13	-0.13
Pacific (ex. Japan)	176.64	1.67	0.95

	Local Currency Index	Net Chg	Pct Chg	Dollar Index	Net Chg	Pct Chg
Brazil	2618293	-44202	-1.66	339.34	-6.29	-1.82
Canada	276.62	-0.11	-0.04	240.58	-0.43	-0.18
Chile	353.70	1.03	0.29	209.01	-0.38	-0.18
Mexico	735.73	-5.43	-0.73	196.39	-2.42	-1.22
U.S.	264.28	-2.46	-0.92	264.28	-2.46	-0.92
Venezuela	1562.08	-1.44	-0.09	37.56	-0.03	-0.08
Austria	213.73	-2.24	-1.04	204.30	-2.15	-1.04
Belgium	240.78	-0.60	-0.25	230.29	-0.56	-0.24
Denmark	270.45	-0.01	0.00	264.15	0.06	0.02
Finland	837.97	-7.60	-0.90	716.41	-6.50	-0.90
France	222.85	-1.58	-0.70	215.91	-1.54	-0.71
Germany	182.46	-2.33	-1.26	173.87	-2.21	-1.26
Greece	203.46	1.37	0.68	143.56	0.97	0.68
Ireland	393.84	-0.75	-0.19	367.78	-0.70	-0.19
Italy	223.59	-1.10	-0.49	175.60	-0.86	-0.49
Netherlands	255.78	-2.29	-0.89	243.87	-2.17	-0.88
Norway	203.46	0.43	0.21	176.95	1.17	0.67
Portugal	203.88	-0.34	-0.17	169.20	-0.28	-0.17
Spain	310.38	-1.52	-0.49	223.01	-1.09	-0.49
Sweden	358.04	-3.51	-0.97	281.90	-2.82	-0.99
Switzerland	321.72	-2.25	-0.69	352.88	-2.25	-0.63
U.K.	182.59	-1.41	-0.77	179.67	-0.24	-0.13
S. Africa	341.36	-1.52	-0.44	149.39	-2.77	-1.82

International Stocks & Indexes, on page 270, informs you of the most important firms on the most important exchanges around the world. **Dow Jones Country Indexes** and **International Stock Market Indexes** are also in this section. These indexes provide additional important data by country.

The online edition lists International Stocks below U.S. Stocks. Click on Markets and Markets Data Center from the home page's left-hand menu-bar, then scroll down the left side.

For **Dow Jones Global Indexes** online, scroll down the home page's left side and click on Markets and Markets Data Center from the home page's left-hand menu-bar. You'll find the link in the upper right, as in the excerpt on page 27 from the Tuesday, July 6, 2004, edition.

Foreign investing can be risky for Americans, as the events of 1997 and 1998 made abundantly clear. Remember, when you invest in foreign markets, you must be concerned with the fluctuation of foreign currency values as well as the value of the shares you purchase. A rise in the dollar's value against the currency in which your shares are denominated can wipe out your gain, while a fall in the dollar's value could accentuate that gain. In addition, information on foreign stocks is often not as complete and accurate as on U.S. stocks. Let the buyer beware.

If the risks of international investing alarm you, there is a way you can invest in foreign companies while keeping your money in dollars and in the United States. *American Depository Receipts* (ADRs) are negotiable instruments representing foreign securities that trade like U.S stocks. They are listed each day in the print *Journal* at the end of **NASDAQ Small-Cap Issues**. For instance, see the listing of **ADRS** on page 273 from the Tuesday, May 4, 2004, edition.

Dow Jones Specialty Indexes (check the third-section index, although this table occasionally appears in the second section) present closing prices and percent changes on a broad variety of international indexes (see page 273).

The **MSCI** (Morgan Stanley Capital International) **Indexes**, which present indexes of stock-market activity in key foreign countries, can be located by checking the first and third section's index under Currency Trading. The example from the Monday, May 3, 2004, print *Journal* is on page 274.

EARNINGS AND DIVIDENDS

Many investors focus so heavily on the potential capital gain (increase in price) of their stock that they ignore the dividends it pays. These dividends can be an important part of a stock's total return, so take a moment to consider corporate earnings and dividends.

ADRS

Monday, May 3, 2004

AngloAm ADS	**AAUK**	1719	20.48	0.10
AtlasPac ADS	**APCFY**	43	2.76	−0.25
Daiei	**DAIEY**	z671	8.31	−0.39
DankaBus	**DANKY**	z61325	4.14	0.07
FujiPhoto ADS	**FUJIY**	z50539	32.60	0.73
Ftrmdia	**FMDAY**	19848	1.34	0.02
HighvldSt! ADS	**HSVLY**	z19734	2.66	−0.26
KirinBrew ADS	**KNBWY**	z24568	9.93	−0.09
Nissan ADS	**NSANY**	1311	22.03	0.12
RankGp ADS	**RANKY**	z1015	11.50	−0.49
Rexam ADS	**REXMY**	z4832	41.65	0.75
Santos ADS	**STOSY**	z3752	18.81	−0.08
Sanyo ADS	**SANYY**	1	23.05	0.40
Senetek ADS	**SNTK**	5255	0.65	−0.05
TelMex	**TFONY**	z1152	34.25	−0.84
TrintyBio	**TRIB**	3576	3.02	...

Dow Jones Specialty Indexes

Monday, May 3, 2004

	CLOSE	NET CHG	% CHG	YTD % CHG	YLD
Composite Internet	70.86	+1.27	+1.82	+2.43	...
Internet Commerce	101.00	+2.12	+2.14	+10.21	...
Internet Services	39.18	+0.74	+1.93	+0.33	...
Equity REIT	175.51	+2.72	+1.57	−4.36	6.23
Equity REIT*	488.40	+7.56	+1.57	−2.69	...
Composite REIT	156.44	+2.29	+1.49	−4.82	5.91
Composite REIT*	454.53	+6.77	+1.51	−3.14	...
Islamic Market	1528.08	+10.64	+0.70	−0.23	...
Islamic Tech	1983.01	+9.06	+0.46	−8.80	...
Islamic U.S.	1718.86	+18.40	+1.08	+0.25	...
Australia 30 -c	3002.18	−7.46	−0.25	+2.72	...
Canada 40 -c	1196.67	+2.71	+0.23	+0.25	...
France 30 -c	241.70	+1.84	+0.77	+3.82	...
Germany 30 -c	237.14	+1.10	+0.47	−0.41	...
Hong Kong 30 -c	3788.09	+7.43	+0.20	−1.30	...
Japan 100 -c	2460.04	Closed	...	+12.13	...
Switzerland 30 -c	311.44	+2.17	+0.70	+6.25	...
U.K. 50 -c	186.70	Closed	...	−0.65	...
Sustainability	878.21	+4.49	+0.51	−1.56	...
CBOT Treasury	127.69	0.00	0.00	−0.62	...
100% U.S. Portfolio Index*	150.92	+1.42	+0.95	+1.76	...
80% U.S. Portfolio Index*	153.96	+1.18	+0.77	+1.44.	...
60% U.S. Portfolio Index*	157.07	+0.93	+0.60	+1.11	...
40% U.S. Portfolio Index*	158.38	+0.64	+0.41	+0.77	...
20% U.S. Portfolio Index*	154.41	+0.24	+0.16	+0.34	...
100% Global Portfolio Index*	321.79	+2.06	+0.64	+2.00	...
80% Global Portfolio Index*	299.80	+1.55	+0.52	+1.52	...
60% Global Portfolio Index*	278.90	+1.09	+0.39	+0.99	...
40% Global Portfolio Index*	254.57	+0.64	+0.25	+0.44	...
20% Global Portfolio Index*	224.49	+0.19	+0.08	−0.33	...

MSCI Indexes

	APR 30	APR 29	% CHG FROM 12/03
U.S.	1038.5	1044.6	-0.7
Britain	1357.7	1367.0	+0.7
Canada	1017.8	1017.2	-0.2
Japan	711.3	725.1	+11.6
France	1207.0	1213.3	+3.5
Germany	491.7	495.4	-0.1
Hong Kong	6404.8	6407.5	+1.0
Switzerland	755.9	757.1	+5.8
Australia	676.1	676.2	+3.1
World Index	1035.7	1042.9	-0.1
EAFE MSCI	1302.9	1314.2	+1.1

As calculated by Morgan Stanley Capital International Perspective, Geneva. Each index, calculated in local currencies, is based on the close of 1969 equaling 100.

Corporations issue stock to raise capital; investors buy these shares so as to participate in the growth of the business, to earn dividends, and to enjoy possible capital gains. The ability of a corporation to pay dividends and the potential for increase in the value of a share of stock depend directly on the profits earned by the corporation: The greater the flow of profit (and anticipated profit), the higher the price investors will pay for that share of stock.

The ownership value of any asset depends on the income it can generate. The value of farmland reflects profits that can be reaped by raising crops on it, and the value of an apartment building reflects rent that can be collected. Similarly, the value of a share in the ownership of a corporation ultimately depends on the ability of that corporation to create profits. Note that the value of an asset depends not only on the income it currently earns, but also on its potential for greater earnings and on investors' willingness to pay for these actual and potential earnings.

A corporation's profit is one of the most important measures of its success. Profit indicates the effectiveness and efficiency with which its assets are managed and employed. Profits calibrate the ability of a firm to make and sell its product or service for more than the cost of production. Profit means that the firm has efficiently combined the labor, material, and capital necessary to produce and market its product at a price that people will pay and that will provide the owners with the financial incentive to expand the operation. When costs exceed revenues and the firm takes a loss, the amount that the public is willing pay for the firm's product no longer justifies the cost of producing it.

DIGEST OF CORPORATE EARNINGS REPORTS

COMPANY	PERIOD	REV (mill)	% CHG	INC CT OP (mill)	NET (mill)	% CHG	PER SHARE CURR	PER SHARE PREV	% CHG
Abbott Labs	Q12/31	5,531	14	...	a944.4	51	.60	.40	50
ABT (N) ↓ Yr		19,681	11	...	a2,753	-1.4	1.75	1.78	-1.7

a-Includes net nonrecurring charges of $78,614,000, or five cents a diluted share in the quarter and $725.817,000, or 46 cents a diluted share in the year.

COMPANY	PERIOD	REV (mill)	% CHG	INC CT OP (mill)	NET (mill)	% CHG	PER SHARE CURR	PER SHARE PREV	% CHG
Advanced Magnetics	Q12/31	0.63	-59	...	(0.94)	...	(.12)	(.05)	...
AVM (A)									
Coastal Bncp	Q12/31	...	...	...	3.25	-48	.60	1.05	-43
CBSA (Nq) ↑ Yr		...	...	...	13.5	-32	2.22	2.99	-26
Community Bcshr-SC	Q12/31	...	...	...	1.30	-11	.29	.33	-12
SCB (A) Yr		...	...	...	5.64	4.4	1.27	1.38	-8.0
Crescent Fin'l	Q12/31	...	...	...	0.50	24	.16	.16	...
CRFN (Sc) Yr		...	...	...	1.66	35	.61	.61	...
Downey Fin'l	Q12/31	...	...	...	23.8	-41	.85	1.43	-41
DSL (N) ↑ Yr		...	...	...	101.7	-9.4	3.64	3.99	-8.8
Eastern VA Bncshrs	Q12/31	...	...	...	1.85	14	.38	.33	15
EVBS (Sc) Yr		...	...	...	7.08	6.5	1.46	1.36	7.4
Environ Tectonics	13wk11/28	7.12	-41	...	(0.70)	...	(.10)	.06	...
ETC (A) L 39 wk		18.0	-48	...	(1.26)	...	(.18)	.23	...
FFLC Bancorp Inc	Q12/31	...	...	...	2.13	-4.6	.39	.40	-2.5
FFLC (Nq) Yr		...	...	...	9.15	3.5	1.67	1.61	3.7
First Bancorp-IN	Q12/31	...	...	...	0.36	-11	.22	.26	-15
FBEI (Nq) 6 mo		...	...	...	0.61	-24	.38	.51	-25
First Finl Bkshrs	Q12/31	...	...	...	8.52	-0.4	.55	.55	...
FFIN (Nq) Yr		...	...	...	35.3	4.0	2.27	2.19	3.7
First Fin'l Hldgs	Q12/31	...	...	...	5.25	-22	.41	.50	-18
FFCH (Nq)									
First M&F Corp	Q12/31	...	...	...	2.81	2.9	.61	.59	3.4
FMFC (Nq) Yr		...	...	...	10.9	6.4	2.35	2.22	5.9
Fst Nat'l Corp-SC	Q12/31	...	...	...	3.67	-3.5	.47	.49	-4.1
FNC (A) Yr		...	...	...	14.8	6.9	1.91	1.79	6.7
Gen'l Electric	Q12/31	36,964	4.1	...	4,560	47	.45	.31	45
GE (N) ↓ Yr		134,187	1.5	15,589	15,002	6.3	1.49	1.41	5.7
Guaranty Fed Bcsh	Q12/31	...	...	...	0.92	6.3	.32	.30	6.7
GFED (Nq) 6 mo		...	...	...	2.00	13	.69	.62	11

GE → (Gen'l Electric)

Company is changing from a fiscal year ending June 30 to a calendar year.

COMPANY	PERIOD	REV (mill)	% CHG	INC CT OP (mill)	NET (mill)	% CHG	PER SHARE CURR	PER SHARE PREV	% CHG
Hancock Hldg	Q12/31	...	...	...	15.2	11	.91	.82	11
HBHC (Nq) Yr		...	...	...	55.0	7.7	3.29	3.00	9.7
Huntington Bncshrs	Q12/31	...	...	...	a93.3	35	.40	.29	38
HBAN (Nq) ↓ Yr		...	...	a385.7	372.4	15	1.61	1.33	21

a-Includes nonrecurring gains of $351,000 in the quarter and $19,778,000 in the year.

COMPANY	PERIOD	REV (mill)	% CHG	INC CT OP (mill)	NET (mill)	% CHG	PER SHARE CURR	PER SHARE PREV	% CHG
KeyCorp	Q12/31	...	...	...	234.0	-4.5	.55	.57	-3.5
KEY (N) Yr		...	...	...	903.0	-7.5	2.12	2.27	-6.6
LSB Corp	Q12/31	...	...	...	a2.30	198	.52	.17	206
LSBX (Nq) ↓ Yr		...	...	...	a4.14	33	.94	.69	36

a-Includes a pretax gain of $1,996,000 related to litigation.

EXPLANATORY NOTES

Revenue, income and net figures are in millions, except * indicates full amount. INC CT OP figure is income from continuing operations, if applicable; otherwise it is income before extraordinary items or accounting adjustments. PREV under per share indicates year-earlier period. Figures in parentheses are losses.

▲ indicates net income increase of 25% or more. ▼ indicates net income decrease of 25% or more. P-Profit in latest period vs. year-earlier loss. L-Loss in latest period vs. year-earlier profit.

(N)-New York Stock Exchange (A)-American Stock Exchange (Pa)-Pacific
(Nq)-Nasdaq National Market (Sc)-Nasdaq Small Cap (C)-Chicago
(P)-Philadelphia (B)-Boston (T)-Toronto (F)-Foreign

WSJ.com subscribers can get more detailed earnings reports at WSJ.com. Five-day archive available

If you are a stock owner, then, in addition to following the market indexes, you will need to monitor the earnings of particular stocks. You can do so by using *The Wall Street Journal*'s **Digest of Corporate Earnings Reports**, listed as Earnings Digest in the front-page index of the first and third sections.

The print edition carried a report on General Electric in the Monday, January 19, 2004, issue (see page 275 and below). The statement reports earnings for the quarter ending December 31, 2003 (Q12/31), and compares them with the figures for the same period one year earlier. Typical comparisons include the first six months of the year (reported between 6/01 and 8/31) or nine months to a year (reported between 9/01 and 12/31). Look for revenues (REV), percent change in revenues from year before (% CHG), operating income (INC CT OP), net income (NET), percent change in net income (% CHG), net income per share for the current and previous periods (i.e., total earnings divided by total shares of stock outstanding), and the percent change in net income per share from the previous to the current period. As you can see, General Electric's performance improved very strongly in 2003.

For the online report, go to the home page and scroll down the left-hand menu-bar to Markets and Markets Data Center. The Digest of Earnings appears under Corporate Earnings at the top of the right column.

Improved earnings are important, because (among other things) they permit corporations to pay dividends, an important source of income for many stockholders. The stock pages list current annual dividends. You can also use the *Journal*'s daily **Corporate Dividend News** (see the Thursday, January 22, 2004, print excerpt on page 277), listed in the front-page index of the first and third sections under Dividend News, to be informed of future dividend payments.

To find dividend information in the online edition, type a company's name or stock symbol in the Quotes and Research field of the home page.

The January 22, 2004, print report provides dividend news for January 21, 2004. The companies listed under the heading **Regular** will pay regular cash dividends on the payable date to all those who were stockholders

	COMPANY	PERIOD	REV (mill)	% CHG	INC CT OP (mill)	NET (mill)	% CHG	PER SHARE CURR	PREV	% CHG
General	Gen'l Electric............	Q12/31	36,964	4.1	...	4,560	47	.45	.31	45
Electric	GE (N) ↓	Yr	134,187	1.5	15,589	15,002	6.3	1.49	1.41	5.7

Corporate Dividend News

Intel Doubles Quarterly Payout

SANTA CLARA, Calif.—Intel Corp., a week after reporting better-than-expected fourth-quarter earnings, doubled its quarterly dividend to four cents.

The semiconductor manufacturer said the dividend is payable March 1 to stock of record Feb. 7.

Last week, Intel said its fourth-quarter profit more than doubled on a 22% rise in revenue, leading to increased speculation that the technology market is recovering.

The company's 2003 cash-dividend payments totaled $524 million.

Dividends Reported Jan. 21

COMPANY	PERIOD	AMT	PAYABLE DATE	RECORD DATE
REGULAR				
Airgas Inc	Q	.04	3-31-04	3-15
AmeriSourceBergn	Q	.025	3-01-04	2-16
AptarGroup Inc	Q	.07	2-26-04	2-04
Bowne & Co	Q	.055	2-20-04	2-06
Briggs & Stratton	Q	.33	4-01-04	3-01
Brown & Brown	Q	.07	2-18-04	2-04
Burlington Resrcs	Q	.15	4-09-04	3-10
Century Bncp A-MA	Q	.12	2-13-04	1-30
Citigp pfF	Q	.795625	3-01-04	2-13
Citigp pfG	Q	.776625	3-01-04	2-13
Citigp pfH	Q	.778875	5-01-04	4-15
Citigp pfM	Q	.733	5-01-04	4-15
Comm Bancorp Inc	Q	.22	4-01-04	3-15
Dow Jones & Co	Q	.25	3-01-04	2-02
East West Bncp-CA	Q	.10	2-11-04	1-28
FSF Fin'l	Q	.35	2-16-04	1-30
Fst Community	Q	.05	2-16-04	2-02
Fst Fed'l Bnksh	Q	.09	2-27-04	2-13
Fst Tennesee Nat'l	Q	.40	4-01-04	3-12
FstEnergy Corp	Q	.375	3-01-04	2-06
Goldcorp Inc	M	.015	2-17-04	2-05
Hawaiian Elc	Q	.62	3-10-04	2-11
Hemlock Fedl Fin'l	Q	.17	2-10-04	1-30
Jefferies Grp	Q	.08	3-15-04	2-17
LSI Industries	Q	.072	2-10-04	2-03
Newhall Land&Farm	Q	.10	3-05-04	2-06
Newmil Bancorp	Q	.15	2-18-04	2-03
Ohio Valley Banc	Q	.18	2-10-04	1-30
Overseas Shiphldg	Q	.175	3-09-04	2-20
Park Nat'l Corp	Q	.88	3-10-04	2-23
Penford Corp	Q	.06	3-05-04	2-13
Pinnacle West Cap	Q	.45	3-01-04	2-02
Polymedica Corp	Q	.15	2-16-04	2-05
Roanoke Elec Steel	Q	.05	2-25-04	2-06
Schwab (Charles)	Q	.014	2-19-04	2-05
Sensient Technol	Q	.15	3-01-04	2-09
Southern Fin'l Bcp	Q	.17	2-20-04	2-06
Southwest Gas	Q	.205	3-01-04	2-17
Susquehanna Bncshs	Q	.22	2-20-04	2-02
TC PipeLines	Q	.55	2-13-04	1-30
Titan Corp $1pf	Q	.25	3-05-04	2-06
VA Fin'l Grp	Q	.19	2-23-04	1-30
Warwick Comm Bncp	Q	.15	2-13-04	2-01
IRREGULAR				
Adtran Inc	Q	.08	2-17-04	2-03
Belmont Bancorp	Q	.03	2-13-04	2-02
Boyd Gaming Corp	Q	.075	3-02-04	2-13
Enterra Energy	~	b.10	2-15-04	1-31
Regionl Hldrs RKH	~	.0224	2-18-04	1-30
Regionl Hldrs RKH	~	.148088	4-05-04	3-12
Util Hldrs UTH	~	.055	4-02-04	3-08
Republic Bncshr-FL	A	.30	2-06-04	1-23
Sea Containers A	Q	.025	2-20-04	2-05
Sea Containers B	Q	.0225	2-20-04	2-05
Traffix Inc	Q	.08	2-10-04	2-01
FUNDS, REITS, INVESTMENT COS, LPS				
Amer Ins Mtge-'85		m1.145	5-03-04	1-31
m-Reflects $.02 regular and $1.125 from mortgage proceeds.				
Apex Municipal Fd	M	.048	2-26-04	2-13
Capital Auto	Q	.4165	2-19-04	2-09
First Tr/4Corners	M	.0883	2-17-04	2-04

COMPANY	PERIOD	AMT	PAYABLE DATE	RECORD DATE
Genesis Energy	Q	.15	2-13-04	1-30
GulfTerra Energy	Q	.71	2-13-04	1-30
Health Care Reit	Q	.585	2-20-04	1-30
Hugoton Rlty Tr	M	.134306	2-13-04	1-30
Kinder Morgan Engy	Q	.68	2-13-04	1-30
Meredith Entprs	Q	.25	2-18-04	2-04
Mesa Royalty Tr	M	.392802	4-30-04	1-27
Mesabi Trust	Q	.30	2-20-04	1-30
Mid-Amer Apt pfF	M	.1927	2-13-04	2-01
Muni IntermDur	M	.072	2-26-04	2-13
Muni NY 'IntermDur	M	.06	2-26-04	2-13
MuniAssets Fund	M	.066	2-26-04	2-13
MuniEnhanced Fd	M	.061	2-26-04	2-13
MuniHldgs CAIns	M	.079	2-26-04	2-13
MuniHldgs FLIns	M	.086	2-26-04	2-13
MuniHldgs Fd	M	.096	2-26-04	2-13
MuniHldgs FdII	M	.087	2-26-04	2-13
MuniHldgs InsII	M	.073	2-26-04	2-13
MuniHldgs Ins	M	.076	2-26-04	2-13
MuniHldgs NJIns	M	.079	2-26-04	2-13
MuniHldgs NYIns	M	.079	2-26-04	2-13
MuniInsd Fd	M	.038634	2-26-04	2-13
MuniVest FdII	M	.092	2-26-04	2-13
MuniVest Fd	M	.056	2-26-04	2-13
MuniYld AZ Fd	M	.077	2-26-04	2-13
MuniYld CA Fd	M	.081	2-26-04	2-13
MuniYld CA Ins	M	.073	2-26-04	2-13
MuniYld FL Fd	M	.077	2-26-04	2-13
MuniYld FL Insd	M	.078	2-26-04	2-13
MuniYld Fd	M	.081	2-26-04	2-13
MuniYld Insd	M	.081	2-26-04	2-13
MuniYld MI InsII	M	.078	2-26-04	2-13
MuniYld MI Insd	M	.084	2-26-04	2-13
MuniYld NJ Fund	M	.00	2-28-04	2-13
MuniYld NJ Insd	M	.078	2-26-04	2-13
MuniYld NY Insd	M	.07	2-26-04	2-13
MuniYld PAIns	M	.083	2-26-04	2-13
MuniYld Qlty	M	.081	2-26-04	2-13
MuniYld QltyII	M	.072	2-26-04	2-13
Pacific Energy	Q	.4875	2-13-04	1-30
PermianBasin Rylty	M	.064598	2-13-04	1-30
SalomonBros Emerg	M	h.15	2-27-04	2-18
STOCKS				
Amcon Distributing		s	–	–
s-1-for-6 reverse stock split pending shrhldr approval 03/11/04.				
Burlington Resrcs		s	6-01-04	5-05
s-2-for-1 stock split.				
Community Bk Sys		s	4-12-04	3-17
s-2-for-1 stock split.				
Eaton Corp		s	2-23-04	2-09	← Eaton
s-2-for-1 stock split.				
Nat'l Instruments		s	2-20-04	2-06
s-3-for-2 stock split.				
OmniVision Technol		s	2-17-04	1-30
s-2-for-1 stock split.				
Sandisk Corp		s	2-18-04	2-03
s-2-for-1 stock split.				
FOREIGN				
Knightsbridge Tnkr	Q	t.80	2-10-04	1-27
INCREASED				

	AMOUNTS			
	NEW	OLD		
Bank of the Ozarks	Q	.07	.065	2-06-04	1-30
Bank One Corp	Q	c.44875	.25	4-01-04	3-12
c-Incorrectly appeared as a regular dividend in 01/20 column.				
Colonial Bancorp	Q	.145	.14	2-13-04	1-30
Connecticut Bncshr	Q	.20	.18	2-17-04	2-03
Eaton Corp	Q	.54	.48	2-27-04	2-09
Intel Corp	Q	.04	.02	3-01-04	2-07
Kinder Morgan Mgt	Q	.68	.66	2-13-04	1-30
Massbank Corp	Q	.25	.23	2-18-04	2-02
Provident Bkshs	Q	.245	.24	2-13-04	2-02
Sabre Hldgs A	Q	.075	.07	2-17-04	1-30
SouthTrust Corp	Q	.24	.21	4-01-04	2-20
INITIAL				
Amer Bank	A	.10	3-01-04	2-16
First Potomac Rlty	~	.10	2-10-04	1-30

A-Annual. M-Monthly. Q-Quarterly. S-Semi-annual.
b-Payable in Canadian funds. c-Corrected. h-From income. k-From capital gains.
r-Revised. t-Approximate U.S. dollar amount per American Depositary Receipt/Share before adjustment for foreign taxes.

Stocks Ex-Dividend Jan. 23

COMPANY	AMOUNT	COMPANY	AMOUNT
Citigp Inv Corp Ln	.0575	MS 6%Sparqs 04	.443625
Goldman Sachs Grp	.25	MS 7%BstBuySparqs	.375375
High Inco Oppy	.05	Municipal High Inc	.0465
Intermediate Muni	.051	Real Estate Inco	.109
Managed HiIncoPort	.05	Zenix Income Fd	.0325
Managed Municipals	.058	t-Approximate U.S. dollar amount per American Depositary Receipt/Share before adjustment for foreign taxes.	
ML 6% Strides BDQ	.49845		
Mesa Royalty Tr	.392802		

	COMPANY	PERIOD	AMT	PAYABLE DATE	RECORD DATE
	REGULAR				
	Roanoke Elec Steel	Q	.05	2-25-04	2-06
Schwab →	Schwab (Charles)	Q	.014	2-19-04	2-05
	Sensient Technol	Q	.15	3-01-04	2-09

STOCKS

Amcon Distributing............................	s	–	–
s-1-for-6 reverse stock split pending shrhldr approval 03/11/04.			
Burlington Resrcs...............................	s	6-01-04	5-05
s-2-for-1 stock split.			
Community Bk Sys............................	s	4-12-04	3-17
s-2-for-1 stock split.			
Eaton Corp.......................................	s	2-23-04	2-09 ←— Eaton Corp.
s-2-for-1 stock split.			
Nat'l Instruments	s	2-20-04	2-05
s-3-for-2 stock split.			
OmniVision Technol...........................	s	2-17-04	1-30
s-2-for-1 stock split.			
Sandisk Corp	s	2-18-04	2-03
s-2-for-1 stock split.			

on the record date. For instance, the January 22, 2004, excerpt on page 277 reports that Charles Schwab announced a quarterly dividend of $0.014 per share payable on February 19, 2004, to all stockholders of record on February 5, 2004.

Some companies prefer to pay dividends in extra stock rather than cash. Returning to the report, you can see above that Eaton Corporation announced a two-for-one stock split effective February 23, 2004, for all holders of record on February 9, 2004. That is, each shareholder received an additional amount of stock equal to the number of shares in his or her current holdings, thereby reducing each share's value by half. As noted earlier, companies split their stock in this fashion in order to reduce its price and make round-lot purchases of 100 shares more accessible to more investors.

Finally, you can compare the dividend performance of your stocks with the **Yields on Dow Components**. See page 279 from the October 29, 2004, print *Journal*. This table, referred to earlier, lists the 30 Dow industrials in rank order according to their dividend yield (dividend payment as a percentage of stock price).

INDUSTRY GROUPS

Each day the *Journal* displays the stock market's performance by industry in the **Market by the Slice** section, which usually appears within **New York Stock Exchange Composite Transactions** (see the Monday, January 19, 2004, print example on page 280). The graphic ranks the 10 economic sectors by percentage change in the previous day's stock-market trading, and also reports the performance of two leaders in each sector.

For the online edition, go to the home page and scroll down the left-

Yields on Dow Components

October 29, 2004
Components of the Dow Jones Averages, ranked by dividend yield based on recent price and annualized dividend amount.

COMPANY	INDICATED YIELD %	IND ANN DIVIDEND	PRICE 10/29/2004	CHG FROM 10/15/2004
Industrials				
Altria Group	6.03	2.92	48.46	+1.10
General Motors	5.19	2.00	38.55	−0.40
SBC Commun	4.95	1.25	25.26	−1.42
Merck	4.85	1.52	31.31	+0.81
Verizon	3.94	1.54	39.10	−1.77
Citigroup	3.61	1.60	44.37	+0.43
JPMorgan Chase	3.52	1.36	38.60	−0.14
DuPont	3.27	1.40	42.87	+0.11
Coca-Cola	2.46	1.00	40.66	+1.46
Pfizer	2.35	0.68	28.95	+0.45
General Electric	2.34	0.80	34.12	+0.57
Honeywell Int'l	2.23	0.75	33.68	−1.32
Exxon-Mobil	2.19	1.08	49.22	+0.20
Caterpillar	2.04	1.64	80.54	−0.55
Procter & Gamble	1.95	1.00	51.18	−2.51
Johnson & Johnson	1.95	1.14	58.38	+1.80
McDonald's	1.89	0.55	29.15	+0.16
3M	1.86	1.44	77.57	−0.41
Alcoa	1.85	0.60	32.50	−0.07
Hewlett-Packard	1.71	0.32	18.66	+0.45
Boeing	1.60	0.80	49.90	−0.29
United Tech	1.51	1.40	92.82	+1.15
Microsoft	1.14	0.32	27.99	...
Wal-Mart Stores	0.96	0.52	53.92	+1.39
American Express	0.90	0.48	53.07	+0.57
Walt Disney	0.83	0.21	25.22	+0.31
Home Depot	0.83	0.34	41.08	+1.27
IBM	0.80	0.72	89.75	+4.90
Intel	0.72	0.16	22.26	+1.65
AIG	0.49	0.30	60.71	+2.86

COMPANY	INDICATED YIELD %	IND ANN DIVIDEND	PRICE 10/29/2004	CHG FROM 10/15/2004
Transportations				
GATX Corp	2.93	0.80	27.28	+0.73
Alex & Baldwin	2.46	0.90	36.66	+2.28
Union Pacific	1.91	1.20	62.97	+2.48
Burl North SF	1.63	0.68	41.81	+2.09
United Parcel Sv B	1.41	1.12	79.18	+1.44
Ryder System	1.20	0.60	50.10	+2.46
Norfolk Southern	1.18	0.40	33.95	+2.68
CSX	1.10	0.40	36.50	+1.76
USF	1.03	0.37	35.84	−1.90
CNF	0.91	0.40	43.78	−3.27
C.H. Robinson	0.89	0.48	53.94	+6.64
Expeditors Int'l	0.39	0.22	57.10	+2.60
FedEx Corp	0.31	0.28	91.12	+4.92
J.B. Hunt	0.29	0.12	40.86	+2.70
Southwest Airlines	0.13	0.02	15.77	+1.39
AMR	...	...	7.72	+0.73
Cont'l Airlines B	...	...	9.28	+0.64
Delta Air Lines	...	...	5.45	+2.03
Northwest Airlines	...	...	8.85	+0.50
Yellow	...	...	47.99	−0.36
Utilities				
Consol Ed	5.20	2.26	43.45	+0.20
Public Serv Ent	5.17	2.20	42.59	+0.90
Southern	4.53	1.43	31.59	+1.30
Duke Energy	4.48	1.10	24.53	+0.79
NiSource	4.29	0.92	21.45	+0.20
Amer El Power	4.25	1.40	32.93	+0.70
Domin Resources	4.14	2.66	64.32	−0.87
Exelon	4.04	1.60	39.62	+1.73
CenterPoint Energy	3.81	0.40	10.51	−0.17
TXU	3.68	2.25	61.22	+11.73
FirstEnergy	3.63	1.50	41.33	−0.34
Edison Int'l	2.62	0.80	30.50	+1.62
Williams	0.32	0.04	12.51	−0.07
AES	...	...	10.90	−0.18
PG&E	...	...	32.04	+1.13

hand side to Markets and Markets Data Center. See the variety of reports under Corporate Earnings at the top of the right column. Page 281 provides **Industry-by-Industry Quarterly Earnings** for companies reporting as of Wednesday July 14, 2004.

INSIDER TRADING

Finally, if you want to see what the officers and directors of the company in which you own stock are doing, you can follow **Insider Trading Spotlight** daily in the *Wall Street Journal*. An example from the Monday, April 19, 2004, print issue appears on page 282.

It may be worth your while to know whether your company's key exec-

Market by the Slice

Performance of Dow Jones U.S. Economic Sectors, ranked by percentage change

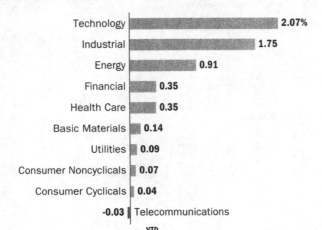

SECTOR	INDEX/PRICE	CHG	% CHG	YTD % CHG	SECTOR	INDEX/PRICE	CHG	% CHG	YTD % CHG
Basic Materials	176.99	+0.24	+0.14	-2.26	**Health Care**	290.66	+1.02	+0.35	+1.62
NewmtMin	43.08	+0.49	+1.15	-11.38	Zimmer	76.15	+5.49	+7.77	+8.17
DowChem	41.11	+0.42	+1.03	-1.11	Pfizer	35.00	+0.18	+0.52	-0.93
Consumer Cyclicals	280.80	+0.12	+0.04	+0.83	**Industrial**	245.03	+4.21	+1.75	+3.96
HughesElectro	17.23	+0.46	+2.74	+4.11	GenElec	33.35	+1.35	+4.22	+7.65
Carnival	43.65	+0.78	+1.82	+9.87	TycoInt	28.30	+0.70	+2.54	+6.79
Consumer Noncyclicals	241.64	+0.17	+0.07	-0.45	**Technology**	538.80	+10.91	+2.07	+9.29
InterActvCp	34.88	+0.88	+2.59	+2.80	CiscoSys	29.22	+2.06	+7.58	+20.59
Gillette	36.54	+0.47	+1.30	-0.52	Microsoft	27.88	+0.33	+1.20	+1.86
Energy	246.08	+2.23	+0.91	unch	**Telecommunications**	124.84	-0.04	-0.03	+4.80
Schlumbgr	53.89	+1.20	+2.28	-1.52	Nextel	26.53	-0.47	-1.74	-5.45
ExxnMobl	40.50	+0.22	+0.55	-1.22	SBC Comm	26.47	-0.27	-1.01	+1.53
Financial	455.72	+1.61	+0.35	+2.19	**Utilities**	114.53	+0.10	+0.09	-0.01
MerLyn	60.57	+0.98	+1.64	+3.27	Calpine	5.63	+0.24	+4.45	+17.05
WellsFargo	57.19	+0.69	+1.22	-2.89	FstEngy	37.00	+0.31	+0.84	+5.11

indexes.dowjones.com

utives and members of its board of directors have purchased or sold its stock recently. Are they playing with their own money, or have they bailed out? In the example on page 282, there was more selling than buying during the week preceding April 19, 2004. Chairman Charles Schwab sold 321,000 shares of Charles Schwab stock worth $3,623,000 on the 12th and 13th of April (the *I* after CB indicates that this was an indirect transaction through a trust or family members). Oracle's CEO sold a million shares totaling over $12 million on April 14, 2004.

For online information, click on the home page's Markets and Markets Data Center in the left-hand menu-bar. You'll find the Insider Trading Spot-

THE WALL STREET JOURNAL.
O N L I N E

Thursday, July 15, 2004

Industry-by-Industry Quarterly Earnings
Companies reporting as of July 14, 2004

The columns below show, by industries, earnings reported for the second quarter of 2004 and those for the like quarter of 2003, with percentage changes. Where individual company reports cover three-month periods other than calendar quarters, the nearest comparable periods have been used. For all dollar figures, "000"s have been omitted. The table reflects the fact that many companies have closed down facilities, sold off assets or otherwise restructured operations. The "net income" columns include both income from operations and the gains or losses associated with such moves. The "net on continuing operations" columns, insofar as possible, exclude such gains and losses. In cases where the after-tax gains or losses haven't been reported, they are retained in "net on continuing operations". The intent is to show how each industry would have fared if its companies throughout the quarter had been structured as they were at the end of the period. Percent changes are not provided for periods containing net losses. Updated Fridays, with daily updates during peak earnings releases. Download a comma delimited version of this page.

No. of cos.		Net on Continuing Operations			Net Income		
		2nd Qtr. 2004	2nd Qtr. 2003	% Chg	2nd Qtr. 2004	2nd Qtr. 2003	% Chg
Basic Materials							
1	Chemicals, Commodity	12,921	2,380	+443	12,921	2,380	+443
3	Chemicals, Specialty	56,858	47,732	+19	56,858	47,732	+19
1	Aluminum	404,000	217,000	+86	404,000	216,000	+87
1	Steel	39,423	15,615	+152	39,423	15,615	+152
6	Total	513,202	282,727	+82	513,202	281,727	+82
Consumer Cyclicals							
3	Casinos	169,953	105,700	+61	169,953	105,700	+61
6	Recreational Products	618,607	316,745	+95	618,024	316,802	+95
1	Toys	-14,576	14,623		-14,576	14,623	
8	Restaurants	352,519	293,537	+20	318,234	293,537	+8
3	Furnishings & Appliances	-20,631	9,009		-28,455	10,409	
5	Home Construction	528,995	389,816	+36	528,995	389,816	+36
2	Broadcasting	-80,983	3,171		-81,473	3,134	
6	Publishing	477,615	456,641	+5	477,615	456,908	+5
12	Retailers, Broadline	3,309,412	2,644,448	+25	3,232,280	2,715,046	+19
26	Retailers, Specialty	2,384,601	1,807,471	+32	2,383,311	1,696,047	+41
3	Retailers, Drug-based	417,180	263,111	+59	417,180	263,111	+59
27	Retailers, Apparel	1,283,769	907,436	+41	1,284,630	906,278	+42
3	Clothing & Fabric	54,422	41,600	+31	54,422	41,305	+32
4	Footwear	333,709	270,037	+24	333,709	270,037	+24
109	Total	9,814,592	7,523,345	+30	9,693,849	7,482,753	+30
Consumer Noncyclicals							

light under Other Stats at the bottom of the right column. See the Tuesday, July 6, 2004, **Insider Spotlight** excerpt on page 283.

INITIAL PUBLIC OFFERINGS
Every Thursday *The Wall Street Journal*'s **IPO Scorecard** presents a listing of current initial public stock offerings (IPOs). These are privately held com-

Insider Trading Spotlight

Biggest Individual Trades

(Based on reports received by Thomson Financial on April 15)

COMPANY NAME	SYMBOL	INSIDER'S NAME	TITLE	$ VALUE (000)	NO. OF SHRS IN TRANS (000)	RANGE OF SHR VALUES	TRANS DATES
Buyers							
Gabelli Dividend Income	GDV	M. Gabelli	CII	1,620	87	18.02-18.74	4/13-14/04
Stewart Stevenson	SVC	M. Lukens	CEO	402	25	16.04-16.10	4/14/04
Stewart Stevenson	SVC	H. Wolf	CB	174	11	15.79-15.84	4/14/04
Public Storage	PSAA	D. Angeloff	DI	140	5	28.00	4/13/04
Tarrant Apparel	TAGS	G. Guez	CEO	95	52	1.69-1.98	4/12-14/04
RMK High Income Fund	RMH	J. Kelsoe	OE	79	5	15.80	4/14/04
Newalliance Bancshares	NABC	S. Flanagan	D	73	5	14.66-14.68	4/08/04
Newalliance Bancshares	NABC	J. Zaccagnino	D	70	5	14.00	4/13/04
AXM Pharma	AXJ	D. Maclellan	DI	52	10	5.08	4/13/04
Flaherty Clay Tot Ret	FLC	D. Crumrine	CEO	49	2	24.68	4/14/04
Sellers							
American Dental Partners	ADPI	M. Mannion	DI	35,899	2,362	15.20	4/13/04
Price Legacy	PLRE	M. Galinson	DI	16,300	1,000	16.30	4/13/04
Price Legacy	PLRE	J. Mcgrory	CEOI	16,300	1,000	16.30	4/13/04
Oracle Corp	ORCL	L. Ellison	CEO	12,356	1,000	12.25-12.45	4/14/04
Genentech	DNA	A. Levinson	CEO	8,363	75	111.50	4/12/04
Performance Food Group	PFGC	C. Gray	FO	6,293	188	33.54	4/14/04
Valero Energy	VLO	W. Greehey	CEO	5,696	95	60.11	4/13/04
Cintas Corp	CTAS	R. Farmer	CBI	3,693	80	45.99-46.33	4/13-14/04
Charles Schwab	SCH	C. Schwab	CBI	3,623	321	10.95-11.49	4/12-13/04
Pall Corp	PLL	M. Kachur	CEO	2,882	120	23.90-24.07	4/13/04

*-Half of the transactions were indirect. B-beneficial owner of more than 10% of a security class. CB-chairman. CEO-chief executive officer. CFO-chief financial officer. CI-chief investment officer. CO-chief operating officer. D-director. DO-director and beneficial owner. FO-former executive. H-officer, director and beneficial owner. I-indirect transaction filed through a trust, insider spouse, minor child or other. O-officer. OD-officer and director. OE-other executive. P-president. UT-unknown. VP-vice president. Includes transactions related to stock option exercises.

Source: Thomson Financial

panies that are selling their shares to the public for the first time. See the example from the Thursday, January 22, 2004, print *Journal* on page 284.

For online information, click on the home page's Markets and Markets Data Center in the left-hand menu-bar. See the extensive initial public offering information under IPOs near the bottom of the right column. The example on page 285 shows the Latest Initial Public Offerings as of Tuesday, July 6, 2004.

GREED VERSUS FEAR

Perhaps this chapter has made clear to you how complex the stock market can be, and how many ways there are to invest in stocks. No wonder that even

Home

News   Technology   Markets   Personal Journal   Opinion   Leisure Weekend

Tuesday, July 6, 2004

Insider Spotlight

Insider Activity for the week ending July 02, 2004

Here's a rundown of insider trading activity for the most recent week. An insider is any officer, director or owner of 10% or more of a class of the company's securities. The table shows purchases and sales which must be reported to the SEC and other regulators by the 10th of the month following the month of the trade, includes both open-market and private transactions involving direct and indirect holdings. Excludes stock valued at less that $2 per share, acquisitions through options and companies being acquired. Included are purchases, sales and stock registered for sale for individual officers, companies, and sectors. Source: Thomson Financial.

Insider Buying

Top ten individual insiders making insider purchases.   Notes>>

Rank	Company	Name	Title*	Start Date	End Date	High Price	Low Price	Number of Shares	Market Value	Avg. 6-month Buy Return
1	Midway Games Inc	Redstone, Sumner	B	June 25 2004 12:00 AM	June 25 2004 12:00 AM	12.26	12.50	325,500	4,043,213	-0.05
2	Valence Technology Inc	Berg, Carl	DO	June 28 2004 12:00 AM	June 28 2004 12:00 AM	3.42	3.42	877,193	3,000,000	0.69
3	Sei Investments Co	Zimmer, Kenneth	O	June 29 2004 12:00 AM	June 29 2004 12:00 AM	29.22	29.32	100,000	2,923,880	...
4	Elizabeth Arden Inc Fl	Thomas, Jw	D	June 23 2004 12:00 AM	June 23 2004 12:00 AM	20.55	20.55	137,425	2,824,084	1.07
5	Midway Games Inc	Redstone, Sumner	B	June 24 2004 12:00 AM	June 24 2004 12:00 AM	12.30	12.47	146,600	1,816,257	-0.05
6	Chesapeake Energy Corp	Mcclendon, Aubrey	CEO	June 24 2004 12:00 AM	June 24 2004 12:00 AM	14.82	15.05	100,000	1,496,282	0.70
7	Chesapeake Energy Corp	Ward, Tom	P	June 24 2004 12:00 AM	June 24 2004 12:00 AM	14.73	15.05	100,000	1,493,770	0.60
8	Midway Games Inc	Redstone, Sumner	B	June 28 2004 12:00 AM	June 28 2004 12:00 AM	12.00	12.87	117,000	1,460,385	-0.05
9	Healthextras Inc	Hooks, Kevin	O	June 24 2004 12:00 AM	June 24 2004 12:00 AM	15.85	15.85	74,250	1,176,863	...
10	Sei Investments Co	Zimmer, Kenneth	O	June 29 2004 12:00 AM	June 29 2004 12:00 AM	29.25	29.25	28,868	844,389	...

Ranked by market value in U.S. $.

IPO Scorecard/*Update on New Stock Issues*

The market for initial public offerings of stock is still scuffling to get going in 2004. Only two IPOs have hit the market so far, though several are in the near-term pipeline.

COMPANY	SYMBOL	OFFER PRICE	YESTERDAY'S CLOSE	——— % CHANGE FROM ——— OFFER PRICE	FIRST-DAY CLOSE	IPO DATE*
Crosstex Energy	XTXI	19.50	25.25	+29.5%	– 0.6%	Jan. 13
K-Sea Transport	KSP	23.50	27.51	+17.1	+ 1.6	Jan. 9
Kintera	KNTA	7.00	10.50	+50.0	+ 1.9	Dec. 19
Luminent Mortgage Capital	LUM	13.00	14.10	+ 8.5	+ 4.0	Dec. 19
Franklin Bank	FBTX	14.50	18.96	+30.8	+ 6.5	Dec. 18
Knology	KNOL	9.00	10.41	+15.7	+11.0	Dec. 18
Marshall Edwards	MSHL	7.50	12.15	+62.0	+62.0	Dec. 18
Tempur-Pedic International	TPX	14.00	16.00	+14.3	+ 3.2	Dec. 18
China Life Insurance	LFC	18.68	30.56	+63.6	+28.8	Dec. 17
Falcon Fin. Invstmt Trust	FLCN	9.00	9.65	+ 7.2%	+ 6.6	Dec. 17
Orbitz	ORBZ	26.00	22.81	-12.3%	– 8.7	Dec. 17
Provide Commerce	PRVD	15.00	18.17	+21.1%	+39.8	Dec. 17
Universal Technical Inst.	UTI	20.50	29.10	+42.0%	+10.4	Dec. 17
Highland Hospitality	HIH	10.00	12.15	+21.5%	+14.1	Dec. 16

*First trading day   Sources: WSJ Market Data Group; Dow Jones Newswires

major investors feel they need an expert's advice before they venture their capital.

There is a saying, "Greed and fear drive the stock market." For example, greedy investors fueled the late 1990s blaze of speculative gains before the crash of the 2001 recession, while fear held the market back after the crash.

So far, there has been no discussion of investors' psychological dynamics, the herd instinct created by greed and fear. Instead, these chapters treated the fundamentals of investing and then applied that analysis to a variety of stock-market indicators. Here is a brief summary of these approaches.

Fundamental analysis tries to determine the intrinsic value of stocks by discovering their future earnings potential within the context of the business environment, and then concludes whether their present market value accurately reflects that intrinsic value.

This book's version of fundamental analysis began with a review of

Search   Quotes & Research

•Advanced Search   Symbol   Name
• Help

U.S. Markets

Home

News   Technology   Markets   Personal Journal   Opinion   Leisure Weekend

Tuesday, July 6, 2004

Latest Initial Public Offerings

IPOs for the following companies were launched between July 2003 and June 2004. Companies are listed under the date when the IPO price was set for their offerings. Source: Dow Jones Newswires.

June

Wednesday, June 30

> **Design Within Reach**Inc. (DWRI) -- An initial offering of 4.1 million shares was priced at $12.00 per share, in the expected range of $10.00 to $12.00 a share. The offering was led by CIBC World Markets. The company, based in San Francisco, California, sells home and commercial furnishings. Web site: http://www.dwr.com/

> **Life Time Fitness**(LTM) -- An initial offering of 9.9 million shares was priced at $18.50 per share, in the expected range of $17.00 to $19.00 a share. The offering was led by CS First Boston. The company, based in Eden Prairie, Minnesota, is a fitness-center operator. Web site: http://www.lifetimefitness.com/

> **WellCare Group**(WCG) -- An initial offering of 5.6 million shares was priced at $17.00 per share, above the expected range of $14.00 to $16.00 a share. The offering was led by Morgan Stanley. The company, based in Tampa, Florida, provides Medicaid and Medicare managed care. Web site: http://www.wellcare.com/

Friday, June 25

> **Cabela's**Inc. (CAB) -- An initial offering of 7.8 million shares was priced at $20.00 per share, above the expected range of $15.00 to $17.00 a share. The offering was led by CS First Boston. The company, based in Sidney, Nebraska, sells hunting, fishing and camping merchandise. Web site: http://www.cabelas.com/

> **Motive**(MOTV) -- An initial offering of 5.0 million shares was priced at $10.00 per share, below the expected range of $11.00 to $13.00 a share. The offering was led by J.P. Morgan. The company, based in Austin, Texas, licenses self-management software. Web site: http://www.motive.com/

> **Multi-Fineline Electronix**(MFLX) -- An initial offering of 5.6 million shares was priced at $10.00 per share, below the expected range of $12.00 to $14.00 a share. The offering was led by Needham &Co. The company, based in Anaheim, California, manufactures circuit boards for portable devices. Web site: http://www.mflex.com/

Thursday, June 24

> **Gol Intelligent Airlines**(GOL) -- An initial offering of 16.5 million shares was priced at $17.00 per share, in the expected range of $15.00 to $17.00 a share. The offering was led by Morgan Stanley. The company, based in Sao Paulo, Brazil, is a low-fare Brazilian passenger airline. Web site: http://www.voegol.com.br/

business cycle conditions and inflation's outlook and the impact of monetary and fiscal policy on them. From there, the analysis proceeded to a discussion of profits under a variety of cyclical and inflationary settings, and delved into the importance of these settings. At the same time, it dealt with the importance of the price-earnings ratio and the importance of current stock-market valuation as a determinant of potential appreciation.

This chapter provided some additional assistance in the fundamental analysis of a particular stock. You learned how to compare that stock's performance to its industry's performance and then compare the industry to the overall market. A company's earnings and its price-earnings ratio are also ingredients in fundamental analysis. Final steps include an appraisal of a company's management and a forecast of future prospects founded upon its marketing and technological outlook and the ability to control costs.

If that makes sense, you must nonetheless keep in mind that *technical analysis*, a school with a number of passionate advocates, takes a different approach. It studies the historical price trend of the stock market, a group of stocks, or a single stock to forecast future trends. Technical analysis makes extensive use of charts to comprehend historical developments and thereby predict price movements. This reduces an understanding of the psychology of the market and the forces of greed and fear to an analysis of charts of past price movements. For instance, if stock prices (or the price of a stock) rise and then fall back, only to rise again above the previous high, one school of technical analysis views this as a sign of market strength. On the other hand, failure of the stock to surpass its earlier peak is viewed as a sign of weakness.

CONCLUSION

You can make money in the stock market if you have the time and expertise required to study it closely. But as you know from Chapters 2 and 3, timing is crucial. You have to know when to get in and when to get out, because it's very difficult to find a stock that will buck the market's trend for long. Just remember that, by investing in an index fund, you can invest in that trend without investing in an individual stock.

Turn now to a discussion of commodities and futures contracts as investment vehicles.

Investor's Tip

- To avoid greed and fear, take the long-run view developed in these chapters.

C H A P T E R

14

COMMODITIES AND PRECIOUS METALS

HISTORICAL BACKGROUND

I<small>T'S NOW TIME TO TURN TO COMMODITIES AND PRECIOUS METALS</small> as investment opportunities. But before you do, let's take a historical step backward to gain a little perspective on commodity and commodity futures markets, where gold (among other things) is traded for delivery and payment at a later date.

Drastic price fluctuations plagued the farmers and producers of commodities throughout our nineteenth-century westward expansion. After a period of rapid western settlement, new farms and ranches flooded the market with their output. Prices plummeted, devastating farmers and ranchers who had hoped for higher prices to cover their debts. Only after the market absorbed the excess capacity did prices firm and rise again, instigating a new round of price increases and cyclical expansion. Changing seasons and changes in the weather created additional uncertainties for commodity producers. An abundant harvest could glut the market while drought might generate near-famine conditions.

Wildly fluctuating prices for cotton, grain, and meat hurt the farmer and rancher as well as the textile manufacturer, flour miller, and meat packer. In order to protect themselves from unpredictable swings in market prices, these "producers" and "consumers" began contracting to buy and sell output (*commodities*) at predetermined prices for future delivery (*forward contracts*). That way both parties could more accurately forecast revenues and costs and remove some of the uncertainty and risk from their operations.

The contracting parties custom tailored the quantity, quality, delivery date, and other conditions of the forward contracts. Soon, buyers and sellers felt the need for greater flexibility. Suppose either party wanted to get out of the deal, for whatever reason. Who would take the cotton, hogs, or cattle? As a result, commodity producers and users established exchanges to trade these commodities, just as stock exchanges had been established to trade ownership in corporations. And just as a share of stock became a standardized unit of corporate ownership to be exchanged on the open market, commodity contracts were standardized with respect to quantity, quality (grade), delivery date, and price so that they could be traded, too. That established the modern *futures* contract, which can be bought and sold anonymously without any special reference to initial producer or ultimate user.

The futures contract is settled at the price initially agreed to when the contract is entered into, regardless of the commodity's market price (cash or spot price) at the time of future delivery and payment, and regardless of any subsequent change in the value of the contract due to changes in the market price. In this way, producers, such as farmers and ranchers, who contract to sell their output for future delivery, protect themselves from potentially lower spot (cash) prices, while forgoing the possibility that the actual cash prices might be higher at the time of delivery. Conversely, manufacturers, millers, meat packers, and other commodity processors who contract to buy goods for future delivery forgo potentially low spot prices at the time of delivery to avoid the possible risk of higher prices later. Futures contracts limit both the potential risk and the potential reward of the cash market for producers and consumers; the price risk is hedged.

For instance, if you are a wheat farmer and wheat's spot and future price is $4 a bushel, you can contract to sell it for the $4 futures price. If the spot price falls to $3, you have protected yourself by hedging (hemming in) your risk. You will have sold your wheat for $1 more than the spot price. Should the price rise to $5, you will not be able to take advantage of that opportunity, although you will have protected yourself (hedged) against the downside risk. In other words, hedging permits you to guarantee a good price while forgoing the risk and reward of extreme prices. The miller may have the same motivation to lock in $4 with a futures contract and forgo either high or low prices.

The futures market protects buyers and sellers of commodities, but it also provides a market for speculative trading. Speculators do not produce or consume the commodities they trade; they hope to profit from fluctuations in commodity prices. The possibility for speculative profits arises as futures prices fluctuate with spot prices.

If wheat sells for $4 a bushel in spot and futures markets, farmers and millers will contract for future delivery of the crop at that price. But if you are smart enough to correctly forecast that wheat will rise to $6 a bushel by the time of future delivery, you may wish to also contract to buy wheat for future delivery at $4 a bushel. Why? Because if you are right, the wheat you bought for delivery at $4 can be resold for $6 on the spot market at a gain of $2 when the day of future delivery arrives.

Moreover, you won't have to take delivery of the wheat, because as the spot price starts to rise, the price of futures contracts will also rise. After all, other speculators will begin to buy futures contracts when they see the spot price rise, bidding its price up. Therefore, when the price of the futures contract for which you paid $4 reaches $5, you can offset it by contracting for a futures sale at $5. You earn $1 by selling a bushel of wheat for $5 for which you paid only $4.

Conversely, if wheat is $6 a bushel and you correctly forecast that it will fall to $4, you can enter into a contract to sell wheat for future delivery at $6 and then fulfill your obligation on that date by purchasing wheat in the spot market for $4 and reselling it for $6 at a gain of $2. As the futures price falls to $5 with the spot price, you can make $1 with a $5 purchase of a contract for future delivery by using it to discharge your obligation to sell a contract for $6.

Speculation is important to the futures market because it provides liquidity by increasing sales and purchases of futures contracts. Speculative buying and selling broadens and deepens the market for producers and processors. As a result, fewer than 5 percent of futures contracts are held for actual delivery. The business of the exchange is conducted by traders who make a market for others and buy and sell on their own account.

The responsibilities of the commodity exchanges include collecting and maintaining margin moneys (to be discussed below), regulating delivery, reporting trade data, settling trading accounts at the end of every day, and clearing trades. The exchanges rely upon insurance, lines of credit, and member backing to guarantee that all trades are honored. These safeguards, as well as standardization of quality (grade) and quantity, enable traders to conduct their business anonymously without knowing from which farm or mine their goods originated.

LONG POSITION
Miller and manufacturer enter into futures contracts to buy commodities for future delivery at a set price. This is called a *long* position.

Investors also take long positions (i.e., purchase futures contracts that enable them to buy commodities at a stipulated price for future delivery) when they expect market prices at the time of delivery to be higher than the present futures price. If the investors' forecast of future cash prices is accurate, they will profit by selling at a high spot price the commodity they purchased for a low futures price. For instance, if you expect gold prices to be higher in October than the current October gold futures contract, you will buy that contract. If you are correct, and in October the spot prices *are* higher than the October futures contract price, your gain will be the difference between the low futures price at which you purchased the gold and the high spot price at which you sell it.

In practice, however, fewer than 5 percent of all futures contracts are actually held to delivery; investors rarely trade the actual commodity. An investor who has taken a long position (i.e., bought a contract for future delivery) can sell the contract before the delivery date. Again, as above, if you are correct, and gold prices are rising, the October contract will have risen as well, because market forces push future prices toward spot prices as the date of delivery approaches. You will be able to sell your contract to buy gold to someone else at a higher price than you paid for it.

SHORT POSITION

Farmers, ranchers, and miners enter into futures contracts to sell commodities for future delivery at an agreed upon price. This is known as a *short* position.

Investors take short positions when they anticipate that spot prices will be lower than present futures prices. If, for example, you anticipate falling gold prices and feel that spot prices will be lower than present futures contract prices, you can take a short position in gold and thereby contract to sell gold at favorable futures prices. If you wait until the time of delivery, you can buy gold in the cash market at the low spot price and then complete or perform the contract to sell the gold at the higher contract futures price.

But as you learned earlier, futures contracts are rarely performed; they are generally offset with an opposing trade. As gold prices fall, and therefore futures prices with them, you can buy a contract at the new low price and discharge your obligation to sell a contract at the old high price. Your gain is the difference between the two prices.

MARGIN

Whether you buy (long position) or sell (short position) a futures contract, your broker will ask you for a percentage of the value of the contract (between 10 and 20 percent) as a good-faith deposit. For example, suppose you buy a contract for 5,000 bushels of wheat at $10 a bushel and your broker requires a 10 percent margin deposit. Since the total value of the contract is $50,000, your broker will ask for a $5,000 margin deposit.

There are two kinds of margin, initial margin and maintenance margin. *Initial margin* is the amount of money you must have in your trading account before you can buy a contract. The $5,000 mentioned earlier is an example. *Maintenance margin* is the amount of money you must keep in your account in order to hold a futures position. It becomes an issue when your broker subtracts trading losses from your initial margin. The broker will demand additional margin in order to maintain a minimum margin in the event you incur more losses that your broker will also subtract from your margin account. But if prices move in your favor, your profits will accrue in your account.

The following examples illustrate the role of initial and maintenance margins in a series of simulated trades.

A HYPOTHETICAL EXAMPLE

There are five players in this hypothetical example: the mining company that produces gold, brokerage A that keeps an account for the mining company, a speculator who trades gold futures, brokerage B that keeps an account for the speculator, and the exchange or clearinghouse.

On September 30, 2002, the mining company fears that the price of gold will decline and decides to pre-sell some of its future production. At the same time, the speculator believes that the price of gold will rise. Both parties execute a transaction for 1,000 ounces of gold. The mining company informs brokerage A that it wishes to sell (short position) 1,000 ounces of gold for December 2003 delivery. Brokerage A then sends an order on the floor of the Comex, a division of the New York Mercantile Exchange, to sell 10 December 2003 gold contracts (each standard contract for gold contains 100 ounces). At the same time, the speculator instructs brokerage B to buy (long position) 1,000 ounces of gold for delivery December 2003. The two floor brokers, both representing their respective clients, then execute the transactions at $329 per ounce. Let's assume the initial margin requirement for the mining company at broker A is 10 percent while the initial margin requirement for the speculator at broker B is 20 percent.

Initial margin requirements are higher for speculators than producers. Producers, such as miners and farmers, remain in the commodity that they trade because they are the ones who physically produce it. This is very different from speculators, who move their money whenever and wherever they wish, creating additional risk and cost for brokers and exchanges.

The mining company posts a margin of $32,900 (10 percent of $329 per ounce × 1,000 ounces) at broker A, and the speculator posts a margin of $65,800 (20 percent of $329 per ounce × 1,000 ounces) at broker B.

Here is how the account looks in the beginning:

Date	Mining Company's Margin	Future Price	Speculator's Margin
9/30/02	$32,900	$329.00	$65,800

If the December 2003 price falls from $329 to $326 on October 1, 2002, the mining company that sold at $329 has a $3 per-ounce profit, while the speculator that bought at $329 has a $3 per-ounce loss. There is a profit for the mining company because it can buy (long position) a December 2003 contract for 1,000 ounces of gold at $326 per ounce and use that position to discharge its obligation to sell (short position) 1,000 ounces at $329 per ounce—for a gain of $3 per ounce, or $3,000 total. To repeat, the mining company buys gold at a low price ($326 per ounce) to discharge its obligation to sell at a high price ($329 an ounce) for a gain of $3 per ounce. It's like buying at a low price and selling at a high price.

There is a loss for the speculator, who can only get $326 per ounce for the gold the speculator is obligated to buy at $329 per ounce. *At the end of each and every day, the loser must pay the winner because the exchanges require daily settlement of all accounts.* If you're a seller (short position) and the price falls, you win. If you're a buyer (long position) and the price falls, you lose.

The buyer (speculator) must pay the mining company $3 per ounce, or $3,000. Broker B subtracts the $3,000 from the speculator's margin account and forwards the money to the exchange. The exchange passes the $3,000 to broker A, who credits the mining company's margin account.

At the end of October 1, 2002, the accounts read:

Date	Mining Company's Margin	Future Price	Speculator's Margin
9/30/02	$32,900	$329.00	$65,800
10/1/02	$35,900	$326.00	$62,800

Jumping to March 3, 2003, you see that December 2003 gold is now $351.80 per ounce:

Date	Mining Company's Margin	Future Price	Speculator's Margin
9/30/02	$32,900	$329.00	$65,800
10/1/02	$35,900	$326.00	$62,800
3/3/03	$13,100	$351.80	$88,600

Suppose each trader must maintain the following minimum margins (maintenance margin) in his or her account: 5 percent of the starting contract, or $16,450, for the mining company and 10 percent, or $32,900, for the speculator. If either of the traders loses 50 percent of the margin deposit (for the mining company $16,450, and for the speculator $32,900), the exchange issues a margin call to demand the deposit of additional funds into the account.

That clearly occurred on March 3, 2003, when gold's price reversed course and rose to $351.80. Now the mining company, which had attempted to hedge (limit) its exposure to falling prices, faced the reality of buying at $351.80 in order to sell at $329 for a loss of $22,800 ($351.80 − $329.00 = $22.80 × 1,000 ounces = $22,800). The $22,800 loss reduced the mining company's margin to $13,100 ($35,900 − $22,800 = $13,100), $3,350 less than the $16,450 minimum ($16,450 − $13,100 = $3,350) maintenance requirement. Under these circumstances the exchange requires the mining company to add $3,350 to its account to keep a balance of at least $16,450 ($13,100 + $3,350 = $16,450).

If the speculator wishes to close out his or her position on March 3, 2003, the speculator tells broker B to sell a contract for delivery of 1,000 ounces of gold at $351.80 per ounce to offset the initial contract to buy at $329 an ounce. (Revenue from the sale liquidates the expense of the purchase.) That would provide a gain of $22,800 ($351.80 − $329.00 = $22.80 × 1,000 ounces = $22,800). Note that the speculator's gain equals the mining company's loss.

All gains and losses are reflected in the respective margin accounts. The speculator bought at $329.00 an ounce and sold at $351.80 an ounce for a profit of $22.80 per ounce. For 1,000 ounces that is a gain of $22,800. Notice that on March 3, 2003, the speculator's margin account has $88,600 in it, which is exactly $22,800 (the profits from 1,000 ounces of gold purchased for $329,000 and sold for $351,800) more than the initial margin amount of $65,800.

Be aware that you can lose more than your initial investment because of the margin system. Suppose gold had fallen in value, not risen, and the

March 3, 2003, transaction had not occurred. Suppose further that by October 2, 2003, the price of December 2003 gold had fallen to $250 per ounce and the speculator had not sold his or her initial position. In this event, here's how the accounts would look:

Time	Mining Company's Margin	Future Price	Speculator's Margin
9/30/02	$32,900	$329.00	$65,800
10/1/02	$35,900	$326.00	$62,800
10/2/03	$111,900	$250.00	–$13,200

Because of the $76 per ounce drop in price (from $326 per ounce on October 1, 2002, to $250 per ounce on October 2, 2003) for the 1,000 ounces, a total of $76,000 would transfer from the speculator's margin account to the mining company's margin account. Since the speculator had only $62,800 in his or her account, the speculator must deposit an additional $13,200 ($76,000 less $62,800) to satisfy the loss. If the speculator now cuts his or her losses and sells a contract for December 2003 gold at the price of $250 per ounce to close out the position, the speculator has lost $13,200 in addition to the loss of the initial margin deposit of $65,800. Ouch!

Now consider a real-life example taken from *The Wall Street Journal*.

INVESTING SHORT

The Wall Street Journal reports commodity prices on a daily basis (see the first or third section's index). The excerpt from the Tuesday, March 4, 2003, print edition *Wall Street Journal* on page 295 is an example. **Futures** provides quotes for future delivery of specified amounts of each commodity. The line in boldface across the top tells you the name of the commodity, the exchange where it is traded, the size of a contract, and the unit in which the price is quoted.

The majority of the following discussion refers to *The Wall Street Journal*'s print edition, but *The Wall Street Journal Online* also provides this data. (You can find general directions for retrieving *Wall Street Journal* online information [http://online.wsj.com] in Chapter 1 on pages 7 through 11. Appendix D on page 374 also furnishes you with a quick guide to the *Journal*'s online edition.) Scroll down the online home page's left-hand menu-bar to Markets and click on Commodities, as in the example from the Wednesday, July 7, 2004, edition on page 296. There you will see the

FUTURES

Exchange Abbreviations

For commodity futures and futures options

CBT-Chicago Board of Trade;
CME-Chicago Mercantile Exchange;
CSCE-Coffee, Sugar & Cocoa Exchange, New York;
CMX-COMEX (Div. of New York Mercantile Exchange);
EUREX-European Exchange;
FINEX-Financial Exchange (Div. of New York Cotton Exchange);
IPE-International Petroleum Exchange;
KC-Kansas City Board of Trade;
LIFFE-London International Financial Futures Exchange;
MATIF-Marche a Terme International de France;
ME-Montreal Exchange;
MPLS-Minneapolis Grain Exchange;
NQLX-Nasdaq Liffe
NYCE-New York Cotton Exchange;
NYFE-New York Futures Exchange (Sub. of New York Cotton Exchange);
NYM-New York Mercantile Exchange;
ONE-OneChicago
SFE-Sydney Futures Exchange;
SGX-Singapore Exchange Ltd.;

Futures prices reflect day and overnight trading
Open interest reflects previous day's trading

Monday, March 3, 2003

Grain and Oilseed Futures

	OPEN	HIGH	LOW	SETTLE	CHG	LIFETIME HIGH	LOW	OPEN INT
Corn (CBT)-5,000 bu.; cents per bu.								
Mar	231.75	234.25	231.75	233.50	1.75	301.50	224.00	25,429
May	234.00	235.75	233.75	234.50	1.25	301.00	229.25	175,382
July	235.50	238.00	235.50	236.75	1.25	297.25	233.75	134,519
Sept	238.00	239.50	237.50	237.50	.50	276.00	233.00	31,700
Dec	238.25	240.00	238.25	238.75	.75	269.00	235.00	79,362
Mr04	243.00	245.00	243.00	244.00	.75	264.00	242.00	5,805
May	248.75	248.75	248.75	248.00	.75	255.50	246.00	538
July	249.75	249.75	249.75	249.50	1.00	264.50	246.50	2,145
Dec	240.50	240.50	240.50	240.50	-1.25	260.00	232.50	1,824

Est vol 40,806; Fri 76,540; open int 456,705, -3,013.

	OPEN	HIGH	LOW	SETTLE	CHG	LIFETIME HIGH	LOW	OPEN INT
Oats (CBT)-5,000 bu.; cents per bu.								
Mar	223.00	224.00	222.00	223.00	2.00	225.50	130.00	675
May	206.25	206.75	204.00	203.25	-.50	221.00	167.00	4,622
July	189.00	189.75	186.50	186.75	-1.25	197.00	175.00	903
Dec	158.25	158.50	158.25	158.50	-.50	163.50	154.00	302

Est vol 902; Fri 1,226; open int 6,616, -24.

	OPEN	HIGH	LOW	SETTLE	CHG	LIFETIME HIGH	LOW	OPEN INT
Soybeans (CBT)-5,000 bu.; cents per bu.								
Mar	576.75	581.00	575.00	576.50	-.50	593.00	449.00	11,913
May	577.00	580.25	574.25	576.75	1.75	588.00	461.00	114,916
July	576.25	579.00	573.25	576.00	1.75	586.50	450.00	49,197
Aug	567.50	568.00	564.50	564.75	2.25	580.00	510.00	6,904
Nov	523.00	529.00	523.00	528.25	5.50	543.00	484.00	43,607
Ja04	526.50	529.50	526.50	529.50	5.00	545.00	507.00	1,921
Mar	530.00	530.00	530.00	531.50	4.50	538.00	508.00	433

Est vol 52,288; Fri 58,405; open int 234,073, -417.

	OPEN	HIGH	LOW	SETTLE	CHG	LIFETIME HIGH	LOW	OPEN INT
Soybean Meal (CBT)-100 tons; $ per ton.								
Mar	179.00	179.30	176.20	178.20	.30	187.20	145.50	10,380
May	176.90	177.70	175.30	176.70	.50	185.50	146.00	63,434
July	175.50	176.00	173.80	174.80	.30	184.50	147.00	37,304
Aug	169.50	170.60	169.20	169.40	1.10	181.30	148.00	18,000
Sept	165.30	165.40	163.80	164.70	.20	178.00	148.00	8,645
Oct	157.30	158.70	157.30	158.00	1.60	170.00	148.10	5,911
Dec	156.50	157.50	155.70	156.90	1.30	168.50	148.00	23,085
Ja04	156.60	157.50	156.30	156.80	1.20	159.50	151.00	3,237
Mar	158.00	158.00	158.00	157.50	.50	159.50	152.50	1,079
May	158.50	158.50	158.50	158.00	.50	160.00	153.00	817

Est vol 26,450; Fri 32,427; open int 172,332, -1,523.

	OPEN	HIGH	LOW	SETTLE	CHG	LIFETIME HIGH	LOW	OPEN INT
Soybean Oil (CBT)-60,000 lbs.; cents per lb.								
Mar	20.82	20.88	20.52	20.56	-.21	22.92	16.70	7,108
May	20.92	21.05	20.67	20.72	-.20	22.45	16.80	63,634
July	21.10	21.10	20.76	20.84	-.18	22.15	16.95	31,461
Aug	20.85	20.95	20.75	20.76	-.14	21.65	19.32	8,682
Sept	20.72	20.75	20.60	20.63	-.07	21.30	19.20	4,963
Oct	20.24	20.25	20.15	20.17	.02	20.95	18.95	2,782
Dec	20.05	20.10	19.97	20.02	.03	21.00	18.90	14,532
Ja04	20.05	20.10	19.95	20.00	.07	20.18	19.35	1,553

Est vol 19,221; Fri 24,186; open int 136,449, +325.

	OPEN	HIGH	LOW	SETTLE	CHG	LIFETIME HIGH	LOW	OPEN INT
Wheat (CBT)-5,000 bu.; cents per bu.								
Mar	313.75	319.50	313.75	318.25	5.75	448.50	288.50	3,630
May	310.50	318.00	310.50	316.00	5.75	422.00	287.00	40,172
July	307.00	312.50	306.50	310.50	5.75	380.00	280.50	32,860
Sept	312.50	316.50	312.50	314.50	5.25	382.00	303.00	3,937
Dec	320.00	327.00	320.00	325.00	5.50	385.00	291.00	9,048

Est vol 18,315; Fri 25,566; open int 89,950, +47.

	OPEN	HIGH	LOW	SETTLE	CHG	LIFETIME HIGH	LOW	OPEN INT
Wheat (KC)-5,000 bu.; cents per bu.								
Mar	343.00	348.00	343.00	346.50	5.50	486.50	297.50	3,630
May	335.50	340.00	335.50	337.50	4.50	458.25	299.50	19,824
July	329.00	332.25	329.00	331.00	5.00	408.00	302.00	15,515
Sept	333.50	335.75	333.50	335.25	5.25	405.00	321.00	4,982
Dec	344.00	344.50	342.75	344.25	3.50	408.00	331.50	2,403

Est vol 5,478; Fri 6,727; open int 46,597, -908.

	OPEN	HIGH	LOW	SETTLE	CHG	LIFETIME HIGH	LOW	OPEN INT
Wheat (MPLS)-5,000 bu.; cents per bu.								
Mar	386.75	392.50	386.75	391.25	9.50	522.00	311.00	1,947
May	373.00	379.00	372.00	378.00	7.00	492.00	313.00	10,717
July	360.50	366.00	360.00	364.00	4.75	460.00	314.50	6,442
Sept	356.50	362.00	356.00	360.00	7.00	422.00	318.00	2,322
Dec	360.00	363.50	360.00	361.25	5.25	425.00	325.50	1,798

Est vol 3,792; Fri 5,654; open int 23,239, +129.

Livestock Futures

	OPEN	HIGH	LOW	SETTLE	CHG	LIFETIME HIGH	LOW	OPEN INT
Cattle-Feeder (CME)-50,000 lbs.; cents per lb.								
Mar	76.10	76.50	75.70	76.12	-.02	83.95	72.40	3,347
Apr	75.85	76.45	75.65	76.10	.12	83.50	74.20	4,774
May	77.20	77.60	76.75	77.30	.02	83.75	74.65	4,077
Aug	80.50	80.85	80.07	80.40	-.17	85.70	77.25	2,513
Sept	80.80	80.80	80.15	80.25	-.27	85.35	77.65	363
Oct	80.60	80.80	80.15	80.25	-.35	85.30	79.50	218

Est vol 1,951; vol Fri 2,895; open int 15,380, +242.

	OPEN	HIGH	LOW	SETTLE	CHG	LIFETIME HIGH	LOW	OPEN INT
Cattle-Live (CME)-40,000 lbs.; cents per lb.								
Apr	76.00	76.15	74.65	74.95	-.87	80.15	66.60	51,083
June	70.40	70.75	69.40	69.75	-.65	73.00	65.15	24,272
Aug	67.50	67.80	66.87	67.05	-.30	71.40	65.40	9,550
Oct	69.65	69.82	69.10	69.35	-.27	72.70	68.55	6,702
Dec	70.75	70.95	70.35	70.37	-.22	73.25	69.75	3,284
Fb04	72.20	72.32	72.00	72.05	-.15	74.00	71.70	1,093

Est vol 22,592; vol Fri 20,291; open int 96,200, -1,389.

	OPEN	HIGH	LOW	SETTLE	CHG	LIFETIME HIGH	LOW	OPEN INT
Hogs-Lean (CME)-40,000 lbs.; cents per lb.								
Apr	54.40	54.55	53.82	54.37	-.17	60.47	40.00	18,729
May	60.10	60.22	59.55	59.95	-.42	64.45	43.05	2,510
June	63.25	63.40	62.70	63.32		66.90	50.40	10,217
July	61.25	61.37	60.85	61.32	.05	63.80	56.20	3,283
Aug	59.90	60.10	59.55	60.02		61.20	54.50	3,084
Oct	51.90	51.90	51.55	51.75	-.10	54.70	49.05	1,203
Dec	50.90	50.90	50.70	50.82	-.10	53.45	48.72	484

Est vol 7,133; vol Fri 10,155; open int 39,616, -63.

	OPEN	HIGH	LOW	SETTLE	CHG	LIFETIME HIGH	LOW	OPEN INT
Pork Bellies (CME)-40,000 lbs.; cents per lb.								
Mar	87.72	88.15	86.20	87.20	-.52	89.60	57.87	724
May	89.15	89.35	87.30	88.50	-.65	90.55	59.30	1,541
July	89.70	89.80	87.55	89.20	-.50	90.35	61.37	455

Est vol 680; vol Fri 662; open int 2,746, +34.

THE WALL STREET JOURNAL.
O N L I N E

As of Wednesday, July 7, 2004

COMMODITIES

Crude-Oil Prices Jump on Worries About Supply From Three Nations

By LEAH MCGRATH GOODMAN
DOW JONES NEWSWIRES
July 7, 2004

NEW YORK -- Crude-oil futures in New York settled 3.3% higher, reaching their highest point in more than a month as supply concerns in Nigeria, Russia and Iraq prompted speculators to snap up contracts.

A production shutdown by a major oil company in Nigeria, a pipeline attack in Iraq and word that Russia's biggest oil company soon may face insolvency ignited the rally.

"With the resumption of the uptrend, you're probably going to have more buying," said Kyle Cooper, an energy analyst in Houston for Citigroup Inc.

Crude futures set for August delivery on the New York Mercantile Exchange rose $1.26 to $39.65 a barrel, marking the highest settlement in a front month since crude ended at $39.96 on June 2.

The rally lifted August heating-oil futures on Nymex to a high of $1.1060 a gallon, up 3.33 cents, or 3.1%. The price marked a summertime high for heating-oil contracts, reflecting concerns of tight supplies heading into the winter. The rise also marked the highest price posted for a front-month contract since heating oil reached $1.1300 a gallon March 10, 2003, shortly before the U.S.-led war in Iraq.

Nymex gasoline futures set for August delivery climbed to a high of $1.2815 a gallon, up 3.71 cents, or 3%.

In Nigeria, French oil giant   Total SA shut down production after oil workers at the company threatened to strike over company reorganization plans. The labor dispute dashed Total's efforts yesterday to restart oil- and natural-gas production that had been halted Friday. Total provides 10% of Nigeria's roughly 2.3 million barrels a day of oil.

Mobil Producing Nigeria Unlimited, a unit of   Exxon Mobil Corp. and Nigeria's second-largest oil producer, also faced strike threats by its oil workers.

lead commodity story of the day. Then return to Markets and click on Markets Data Center and scroll down the right column to Commodities, where you will find listings for both Futures and Spot prices.

Returning to the March 4, 2003, print edition, examine the listing for **Crude Oil** (see below) as an illustration. This commodity trades on the New York Mercantile Exchange (NYM) in contracts of 1,000 barrels at prices quoted in dollars per barrel. The quotations are for delivery in April through December of 2003, January through June of 2004, as well as December 2004 and 2005.

Using September 2003 as an example drawn from the Tuesday, March 4, 2003, issue (see below), *The Wall Street Journal* provides the following information by column (note the column headings on page 295):

Open—opening price: $29.85 per barrel for September 2003 delivery

High—highest price for trading day: $30.00

Low—lowest price for trading day: $29.80

Settle—settlement price or closing price for the trading day: $30.05

Change—difference between the latest settlement price and that of the previous trading day: a decrease of $0.13 (minus $0.13) for September 2003 delivery

Lifetime High—highest price ever for the September 2003 contract: $30.57

Petroleum Futures

Crude Oil, Light Sweet (NYM)-1,000 bbls.; $ per bbl.

September 2003 crude oil contract → $30.05 per barrel

Crude oil futures on March 3, 2003

	Open	High	Low	Settle	Change	Lifetime High	Lifetime Low	Open Interest
Apr	36.45	36.45	35.36	35.88	-0.72	39.99	20.55	173,661
May	34.75	34.78	33.80	34.24	-0.59	36.25	20.70	75,639
June	33.28	33.30	32.40	32.85	-0.43	34.20	19.82	81,656
July	31.98	32.00	31.40	31.68	-0.30	32.80	20.76	40,291
Aug	30.66	30.77	30.50	30.76	-0.22	31.75	21.16	31,803
Sept	29.85	30.00	29.80	30.05	-0.13	30.57	21.05	31,569
Oct	29.50	29.50	29.50	29.51	-0.07	30.02	20.55	25,977
Nov	28.80	28.80	28.70	29.05	-0.02	29.65	20.70	15,059
Dec	28.55	28.89	28.35	28.65	0.02	29.15	15.92	49,351
Ja04	27.95	28.10	27.95	28.14	0.04	28.57	20.35	13,756
Feb	27.45	27.61	27.45	27.67	0.06	28.10	20.35	5,394
Mar	26.95	27.14	26.95	27.22	0.08	27.40	20.35	4,993
Apr	26.75	26.75	26.65	26.77	0.09	26.96	20.35	3,578
May	26.10	26.10	26.10	26.32	0.10	26.48	20.35	3,348
June	25.70	25.80	25.70	25.91	0.11	26.10	20.53	16,078
Dec	24.25	24.30	24.25	24.43	0.20	24.50	16.35	15,820
Dc05	23.85	23.90	23.85	23.93	0.20	24.00	17.00	12,173

Est vol 156,202; vol Fri 225,617; open int 637,041, -6,278.

Petroleum Futures

Crude Oil, Light Sweet (NYM)-1,000 bbls.; $ per bbl.

May	30.24	31.25	30.07	31.04	0.88	36.87	20.70	131,673
June	28.70	29.50	28.40	29.19	0.83	34.90	19.82	77,841
July	27.77	28.25	27.65	28.22	0.78	33.39	20.76	41,539
Aug	27.27	27.60	27.15	27.64	0.71	32.35	21.16	27,356
Sept	26.98	27.35	26.81	27.24	0.69	31.53	21.05	26,852
Oct	26.69	26.70	26.67	26.94	0.67	30.93	20.55	22,514
Nov	26.38	26.50	26.38	26.66	0.64	30.40	20.70	15,226
Dec	26.05	26.34	26.00	26.38	0.61	29.96	15.92	34,562
Ja04	25.90	25.90	25.89	26.11	0.59	29.40	20.35	14,033
Feb	25.60	25.60	25.60	25.84	0.57	28.70	20.35	5,639
June	24.75	24.75	24.75	24.95	0.49	26.63	20.53	16,296
Dec	24.00	24.00	23.90	24.23	0.43	25.00	16.35	19,932
Dc06	23.50	23.50	23.50	23.95	0.43	24.25	19.10	7,521
Dc08	23.80	23.80	23.80	23.99	0.43	24.20	19.75	6,279

Est vol 96,591; vol Fri 149,424; open int 503,681, +6,329.

(Margin left) September 2003 crude oil contract, $27.24 per barrel →

(Margin right) Crude oil futures on March 31, 2003

Lifetime Low—lowest price ever for the September 2003 contract: $21.05

Open Interest—number of contracts outstanding for September 2003 delivery (for previous trading day): 31,569 contracts have not been offset by an opposing trade or fulfilled by delivery

The bottom line (see examples on page 295) provides the estimated volume (number of contracts) for the day (56,202) as well as the actual volume for the prior trading day (225,617). Finally, the total open interest is given for all crude oil contracts (637,041) along with the change in the open interest from the previous trading day (–6,278).

Recall that you sell (short) futures contracts when you expect commodity prices to fall, because you anticipate a lower spot price than the futures contract price for which you are obligated. If you held the contract to maturity, you could buy at the (lower) spot price and sell at the (higher) contract price. But you also recall that contracts are usually not held to maturity. If your forecast of falling prices proves accurate, you can offset your short position to sell (*at the contract price that has remained unchanged*) with an offsetting purchase of a lower-priced long position to buy. The price difference is your profit per barrel. Follow the step-by-step example below in order to sharpen your understanding.

1. Turn to page 297 (top panel) and note once again (from the excerpt of the Tuesday, March 4, 2003, *Wall Street Journal*) the $30.05 price on March 3, 2003, for the September 2003 crude-oil contract. Suppose at that time you sold short one September 2003 crude-oil futures contract (1 contract is for 1,000 barrels) because you believed crude oil prices would fall. Your broker

would adjust your account—upward—by $30,050 ($30.05 × 1,000 barrels) to reflect the sale and ask for a margin of 20 percent ($6,010).

2. By Monday, March 31, 2003 (see the Tuesday, April 1, 2003, *Journal* excerpt on page 298), your forecast proved accurate, as the September 2003 crude-oil contract price dropped to $27.24 a barrel. You then instructed your broker to purchase a long position to buy crude oil for September 2003 delivery at the March price of $27.24 in order to offset your obligation to sell at $30.05. In other words, you *bought* a contract in order to meet your need to *sell* a contract.

3. In that way, you realize the difference ($2.81) between the initial high futures price at which you sold ($30.05) and the present low price ($27.24) at which you bought. Your net gain on Monday March 31, 2003, after about 1 month, is $2,810 ($2.81 per barrel × 1,000 barrels), reflecting the difference between the contract's original value of $30,050 (see number 1 above) and its current value of $27,240 ($27.24 × 1,000 barrels).

Keep in mind that you need never take possession of the commodity or actually buy or sell it. All of your gain (or loss) is reflected in your margin account, which rises or falls daily with the futures prices of the commodity in which you have taken a position. You need not sell to know your profit or loss. Your broker handles all transactions and maintains a running record of your gain or loss.

Return for a moment to your margin deposit of $6,010. This is a performance bond or good-faith money, not a down payment. It says you are prepared to meet your contractual obligation to sell crude oil at the contract price. But remember that you must first buy the crude oil in order to sell it. Since you agreed to deliver crude oil at $30.05 a barrel, a higher spot price would have placed you in the embarrassing position of buying high in order to sell low. Had crude oil increased rather than fallen in value, your broker would have asked you to deposit additional "maintenance margin" to cover the difference in price.

For instance, if the spot and futures price rises to $40.05 a barrel, how does your broker know that you will be able to meet the $10,000 difference ($10.00 × 1,000 barrels) between the $34.05 you will pay for crude oil and the $30.05 at which you must deliver it? Your margin deposit of $6,010 does not cover the loss, and your broker does not wish to be responsible for it. Your broker will demand a bigger margin (deposit) from you as crude oil prices increase.

Livestock Futures

September 2003 contract →

Cattle-Feeder (CME)-50,000 lbs.; cents per lb.

Mar	76.10	76.50	75.70	76.12	-.02	83.95	72.40	3,347
Apr	75.85	76.45	75.65	76.10	.12	83.50	74.20	4,774
May	77.20	77.60	76.75	77.30	.02	83.75	74.65	4,077
Aug	80.50	80.85	80.07	80.40	-.17	85.70	77.25	2,513
Sept	80.60	80.80	80.15	80.25	-.27	85.35	77.65	363
Oct	80.60	80.80	80.15	80.25	-.35	85.30	79.50	218

Est vol 1,951; vol Fri 2,895; open int 15,380, +242.

Cattle futures on March 3, 2003

Should the price surge suddenly and unexpectedly before you can respond to your broker's call for more margin, your broker will liquidate your position to cover the difference and protect his or her own position. After all, your broker is liable for orders exercised on your behalf. You will lose your margin before the broker takes a loss on your behalf. Commodities trading is risky. However, as noted on page 291, your broker will add profits to your account whenever petroleum prices fall.

INVESTING LONG

Commodity prices do not always march in lock step. Cattle prices rose at the same time that crude-oil prices fell in the examples above. Use the excerpts from the same issue of the *Journal* (see page 295) to track cattle futures on the first and last dates.

Test your understanding of these concepts by answering these questions:

1. What were the prices for the September 2003, contracts (from the March 4, 2003, and April 1, 2003, excerpts shown above and below) and how much did they change?

2. How could an investor have profited from these price movements by purchasing long contracts? By how much would the investor have profited in each case? Note that prices are quoted in cents per pound and that a contract is 50,000 pounds.

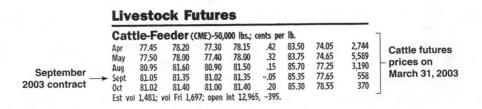

Livestock Futures

September 2003 contract →

Cattle-Feeder (CME)-50,000 lbs.; cents per lb.

Apr	77.45	78.20	77.30	78.15	.42	83.50	74.05	2,744
May	77.50	78.00	77.40	78.00	.32	83.75	74.65	5,589
Aug	80.95	81.60	80.90	81.50	.15	85.70	77.25	3,190
Sept	81.05	81.35	81.02	81.35	-.05	85.35	77.65	558
Oct	81.02	81.40	81.00	81.40	.20	85.30	78.55	370

Est vol 1,481; vol Fri 1,697; open int 12,965, -395.

Cattle futures prices on March 31, 2003

WSJ.com THE WALL STREET JOURNAL.
O N L I N E

DJIA Comp. - cbot

Data retrieved at 07/14/04 16:52:41 • All quotes are in exchange local time • Data provided by FutureSource

Contract	Month	Last	Change	Open	High	Low	Volume	Openint	Exch	C
Dow Jones Indus.-$10	Sep '04	10196y						43324	CBOT	07/
Dow Jones Indus.-$10	Dec '04	10192y						51	CBOT	07/
Dow Jones Indus.-$10	Mar '05	10197y							CBOT	07/
Dow Jones Indus.-$10	Jun '05	10211y							CBOT	07/
Dow Jones Indus.-$10	Dec '05	10217y							CBOT	07/
Dow Jones Indus.-$10	Dec '06	10089y							CBOT	07/

FutureSource Click here for Real-time data

OTHER FUTURES

You can purchase futures contracts on investments other than commodities and track them in the print edition's **Futures** table. For instance, futures contracts are available on **Treasury Bonds**, **Eurodollars**, the **S & P 500**, the **NYSE Composite Index,** and the **Dow Jones Industrial Average**. Whereas futures began with commodities like wheat, trading activity is now far heavier for instruments like Treasury bonds.

In the online edition, click on Markets and Markets Data Center in the home page's left-hand menu-bar. You will find Index (such as the Dow Jones Industrial Average) and Interest Rate futures under Futures and currency futures under Other when you scroll down the right column to Commodities. An example of index futures—for the Dow Jones Industrial Average—from the Wednesday, July 14, 2004, edition is shown above.

Financial futures, relatively new types of contracts first introduced in the early 1970s, are classified into *Interest Rate, Currency,* and *Index* futures.

TRACKING COMMODITIES

The Wall Street Journal print edition carries a commodities article daily (check the first and third section indexes). This report includes the **Commodities Indexes**, which gives the close, net change, and year change for the *Dow Jones-AIG Futures*, the *Dow-Jones AIG Spot*, the *Reuters U.K.,* and the *Reuters CRB Futures* indexes. On Mondays it includes a graph of the fluctuations in the *Dow Jones Commodity Indexes* over the past year. A sample from the April, 26, 2004, *Journal* is on page 302. (Recall that page 296 carried an example of the Wednesday, July 7, 2004, online edition's **Commodities** page.)

Wheat Prices Extend Losses By Sinking to Five-Week Lows

By TOM SELLEN

OsterDowJones Commodity News

CHICAGO—U.S. wheat prices fell to five-week lows Friday, extending their downtrend to three straight days of lower prices.

Beneficial rains over areas of the U.S. hard red winter wheat belt prompted large commodity funds to sell out of previous bets that prices would rise, which also encouraged lo-

COMMODITIES REPORT

cal traders to sell, sources said.

Chicago Board of Trade wheat futures for July delivery fell 4.25 cents to $3.8275 a bushel. On the Kansas City Board of Trade, where hard red winter wheat is traded, the July contract fell 6.25 cents to $3.9025 a bushel.

"Wheat is going to struggle unless we can find added demand or we can tighten up the balance sheet, either through greater demand or through lower production," said Shawn McCambridge, senior grains analyst at Prudential. CBOT July wheat futures have lost nearly 24 cents in the last four trading sessions alone, and some traders and analysts said the sell-off could further pressure prices toward major technical support around $3.64 a bushel.

In other commodity markets:

SOYOIL: Futures rose on the CBOT, lifted by an unconfirmed rumor that Ag

Commodity Prices

The commodity-price indexes are often considered indicators of the direction of inflation. The futures index is based on prices five months in the future and the spot, on immediate-delivery prices. Daily closes over the past 52 weeks.

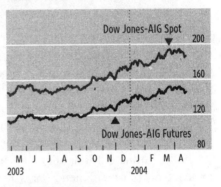

Source: WSJ Market Data Group

Processing Inc. bought 700 soyoil receipts from **Archer Daniels Midland**. Strength in the South American market and a lack of farmer selling also supported the market. July soyoil rose 1.24 cents to 32.68 cents a pound.

COPPER: Prices rose on the Comex division of the New York Mercantile Exchange, recouping some of the week's losses as traders bought to cover earlier bets, analysts said. May futures rose 1.75 cents to $1.2430 a pound.

Futures listings appear on page C10.

Commodity Indexes	CLOSE	Friday, April 23, 2004 NET CHG	YR AGO
Dow Jones-AIG Futures............	145.485	+0.332	112.624
Dow Jones-AIG Spot................	186.591	+0.426	144.797
Reuters U.K...........................	1710.96	+1.02	1443.56
Reuters C R B Futures.............	270.12	+0.57	234.03

Home

| News | Technology | Markets | Personal Journal | Opinion | Leisure Weekend |

Cash Prices

(Closing Market Quotations)

Tuesday, July 6, 2004

	Tuesday		Monday	Year Ago
	Low	Hi		
Grains and Feeds				
Barley, top-quality Mpls., bu	u2.8	sp	z	3.75
Bran, wheat middlings, KC ton	u45	50	51.5	46.5
Corn, No. 2 yel. Cent. Ill. bu	bpu2.455	sp	2.48	2.265
Corn Gluten Feed, Midwest, ton	65	76	71.5	62
Cottonseed Meal, Clksdle, Miss. ton	180	sp	182	135
Hominy Feed, Cent. Ill. ton	95	sp	z	66.25
Meat-Bonemeal, 50% pro Ill. ton	280	290	z	183
Oats, No. 2 milling, Mpls., bu	u1.565	1.585	z	1.5675
Sorghum, (Milo) No. 2 Gulf cwt	u4.46	4.79	4.745	4.18
Soybean Meal, Cent. Ill., 44% protein-ton	uz	z	z	z
Soybean Meal, Cent. Ill., 48% protein-ton	u352.5	367.5	328.5	189.5
Soybeans, No. 1 yel Cent. Ill., bu	bpu9.465	sp	9.195	6.045
Wheat, Spring 14%-pro Mpls bu.	u4.325	4.505	z	3.9175
Wheat, No. 2 sft red, St.Lou. bu	bpu3.505	sp	3.445	2.835
Wheat, hard, KC, bu	3.87	sp	3.9175	c2.98
Wheat, No. 1 sft wht, del Port Ore	u4.05	sp	4.02	3.44
Foods				
Beef, Carcass Equiv. Index Value,choice 1-3,600-700 lbs.	u131.57	sp	z	118.72
Beef, Carcass Equiv. Index Value,select 1-3,600-700 lbs.	u128.54	sp	z	109.86
Broilers, Dressed A lb.	ux0.8591	sp	z	0.6268
Broilers, 12-Cty Comp Wtd Av	u0.8344	sp	z	0.6244
Butter, AA Chgo., lb	u1.895	sp	1.895	1.1475
Cheddar Cheese, barrels, Chgo lb.	n138.25	sp	138.25	148
Cheddar Cheese, blocks, Chgo lb.	n137	sp	141	151
Milk, Non-fat Dry, Chgo	92	sp	92	84
Cocoa, Ivory Coast, ton	1563	sp	c1547	1925
Coffee, Brazilian, NY lb.	nz	z	0.6325	0.49
Coffee, Colombian, NY lb	nz	z	0.82	0.68
Eggs, Lge white, Chgo doz.	u0.61	0.64	z	0.71

The Wall Street Journal print edition reports **Cash Prices** for immediate delivery on a wide variety of commodities on a daily basis.

All of the print edition's commodity news can be located using the indexes on the front pages of the first and third sections. The online edition's cash prices may be found by clicking on Markets and Markets Data Center in the home page's left-hand menu-bar and then scrolling down the right side to the Commodities section under Spot Prices. You'll find a sample for Tuesday, July 6, 2004, on page 303.

CONCLUSION

Commodities and futures investing are far riskier than stock market investing, because positions are highly leveraged. You can lose your entire investment if prices move the wrong way. Moreover, individual commodities and futures contracts can be drastically affected by random events—droughts, floods, wars, and political upheavals. It also is possible to lose more than your initial investment because of the margin system. Yet these markets also present tremendous opportunities for those who can accurately forecast price trends. But most of us cannot do this. So consider bonds—the next chapter's topic—for a far safer investment vehicle.

15

LONG-TERM
INTEREST RATES

INTRODUCTION

THIS CHAPTER WILL EXAMINE LONG-TERM DEBT INSTRUMENTS. You will discover why they, like stocks, appreciate when prices are stable but become poor investments when inflation turns severe. Let's begin our investigation with a general discussion of the origin of these investments.

Governments and businesses turn to the credit markets and issue long-term debt instruments to raise large sums whenever their internally generated funds, such as tax revenues or profits, fall short of their current or capital expenditures. The federal government, for instance, borrowed hundreds of billions of dollars in the capital markets in 2001, 2002, and 2003 because recession and tax cuts suppressed revenue growth while expenditures continued to climb.

Corporations, on the other hand, issue debt (i.e., sell bonds that are redeemed after a long period throughout which they pay interest) in order to finance the purchase of new plants and equipment. Take public utilities, for example. Profits cannot cover the cost of new generating and switching stations, satellites, and transmission lines, so the difference has to be made up by borrowing. Since the projects of public utility companies are long-term and generate income for these companies over several decades of useful life, it's appropriate that the financing be long-term too. The stretch-out in earnings on these assets will provide for the regular payment of interest and principal.

You already know that corporations can raise funds by selling shares via the stock market (see Chapter 13). In that process, the ownership of a corporation is subdivided by the issue of new stock. The situation is very different when corporations borrow funds in the credit markets. Ownership does not change hands, although, of course, the debt burden increases.

New credit market debt, whether sold by government or business, is subdivided into discrete units called notes or bonds and is issued for a specified length of time. At the conclusion of that period, the issuer redeems the note or bond and repays the initial purchase price. Notes are medium-term debt instruments that are redeemed in 1 to 10 years, whereas bonds are issued with maturities of more than 10 years. (Chapter 16 discusses debt instruments with maturities of less than a year.)

Notes and bonds are sold or auctioned in the *primary* (initial issue) market and then traded on the *secondary* market until they mature (redeemed by the issuer). They have a specific face or *par value* (such as $1,000) and pay a specified annual, semiannual, or quarterly amount, known as *coupon interest*.

When you purchase a bond, expect to receive an interest return (called the *current* or *true* yield) determined by the relationship between the fluctuating market price of the bond (more, less, or equal to its fixed $1,000 par value) and the fixed periodic payment of coupon interest. If you hold the bond to maturity (i.e., until it is redeemed by the issuer), you will also receive back its par value.

But you need not hold the note or bond to maturity, because there is a secondary market for notes and bonds that is separate from the initial-issue market. The existence of this secondary or resale market makes it much easier for government and business to sell bonds in the initial primary market. If note and bond buyers could not sell and resell these instruments over and over again, it would be very difficult for government and businesses to issue them in the first place. These instruments are issued in discrete units (such as $1,000) for convenient trading.

Trading on the secondary market determines the market prices of all notes and bonds and thereby determines their current yields. The secondary market dog wags the primary market tail. Not only are primary market auction or issue prices determined by secondary market trading, but primary market coupon rates will quickly reflect true yields established in the secondary market.

There are three principal issuers of bonds: the United States government and its agencies, corporations, and state and local governments. Let's examine each of their issues in turn.

TREASURY AND AGENCY ISSUES

Both the U.S. Treasury and a variety of federal agencies issue long-term debt instruments. The Treasury issues notes with durations of 1 to 10 years and bonds with maturities over 10 years in $1,000 denominations and pays a stated coupon interest payment semiannually. In October of 2001 the Treasury stopped issuing 30-year bonds. (Seasoned 30-year bonds remain outstanding.) Chapter 16 will discuss Treasury bills, which have maturities of a year and less.

Treasury bills, bonds, and notes are referred to collectively as *Treasury securities*. These securities are the safest of all debt instruments because they are backed by the full taxing power of the U.S. government.

The government sells Treasury securities when it needs funds. These primary-market sales are made at auction to securities dealers. Dealers then resell them on the secondary market to investors, where they are traded freely until maturity. The value of daily trading in the secondary market (an over-the-counter market) far exceeds the value of the daily trades on the New York Stock Exchange. *The Wall Street Journal* print edition reports activity in the primary and secondary markets for long-term Treasury securities in its daily **Credit Markets** (see page 308) article in the third (C) section (see first and third section indexes).

Here are typical and usual schedule dates for Treasury-security auctions. The Treasury announces its auction of two-year notes once a month. The auction takes place during the last full week of the month, and the notes are issued shortly thereafter (around the last day of the month). Five-year and 10-year notes are auctioned and issued in the beginning of the month. The Treasury generally auctions three-year notes quarterly, during the second week of February, May, August, and November and issues them shortly afterward, around the 15th of the same month.

Bonds and notes are almost always issued in denominations of $1,000, which is referred to as the *par value* of the bond. Each bond has a coupon rate indicating the dollar amount the security will pay annually until maturity. Interestingly, bonds are seldom auctioned at precisely their par value, because market conditions will influence buyers' bids at the auction.

The Treasury entertains bids at the primary auction and arrays them from highest to lowest. The Treasury accepts bids starting at the highest price and works down until it has accepted a sufficient number of bids to realize its target funding. The par value and coupon interest rate is established before the auction begins, but the true yield is determined by the price established at the auction. It can be higher or lower than the $1,000 par value. If higher, the true yield will be less than the coupon rate. If lower, the true yield will be more than the coupon rate.

Foreign Central Banks Bid Large

Weak Dollar Draws Buying, As Market Absorbs Securities To the Tune of $56 Billion

By Michael Mackenzie
Dow Jones Newswires

NEW YORK—The weak dollar was manna from heaven for primary dealers bidding for new Treasurys this week.

The market smoothly absorbed $56 billion in securities, thanks in no small part to massive buying by foreign central banks, which took down nearly half. Comments by Federal Reserve Chairman Alan Greenspan also provided support.

CREDIT

MARKETS

"The refunding has been pretty successful, and the market is assuming a lot of the recent currency intervention by central banks has been placed in the auctions," said Rick Klingman, head of government trading at ABN Amro, New York.

Asian central banks led by the Bank of Japan have been heavy presences in foreign-exchange markets in a bid to stem the slide of the dollar and protect their competitiveness on global markets. In January, the Bank of Japan, on behalf of Japan's government, intervened in record amounts, buying $67 billion against the yen.

The Treasury auctions ended yesterday with $16 billion in 10-year notes. They also included $24 billion in three-year notes Tuesday and $16 billion in five-year notes Wednesday. The amount of "indirect bidders," a category that includes foreign central banks, was sharply above that in previous sales, ranging from 43% in the five-year auction to a peak of 46% for the three-year. But the 45% figure in the 10-year sale stood out, because Asian central banks are believed to prefer shorter-dated maturities.

Analysts also pointed to Mr. Greenspan's semiannual testimony on monetary policy and the economy before Congress Wednesday and yesterday, which hit home the message that interest-rate increases are nowhere on the horizon.

Throw foreign demand into the mix and ice it with a dose of Greenspan, and it was no surprise that results were still good, even as the 10-year when-issued yield—where the security was trading prior to its official sale—fell sharply toward the lower end its 4.21% to 4.02% range before yesterday's sale. The new note was sold at a high rate of 4.06%,

below its preauction deadline when-issued yield of 4.065% and with a solid bid-to-cover ratio of 2.00.

At the December reopening of the previous 10-year note, the bid-to-cover was 1.78. More importantly the indirect bid was only around 23.9%.

Most Treasury issues ended lower. At

Yield Comparisons

Based on Merrill Lynch Bond Indexes, priced as of midafternoon Eastern time.

	2/12	2/11	52-WEEK HIGH	52-WEEK LOW
Corp. Govt. Master	3.46%	3.44%	4.02%	2.81%
Treasury				
1-10 yr	2.33	2.31	2.70	1.57
10+ yr	4.72	4.68	5.28	3.86
Agencies				
1-10 yr	2.60	2.61	3.18	1.77
10+ yr	5.14	5.08	5.75	4.24
Corporate				
1-10 yr High Quality	3.16	3.14	3.75	2.47
Medium Quality	3.80	3.77	4.74	3.38
10+ yr High Quality	5.57	5.53	6.24	4.79
Medium Quality	5.94	5.89	6.86	5.36
Yankee bonds (1)	3.83	3.81	4.34	3.21
Current-coupon mortgages (2)				
GNMA 6.50% (3)	4.89	4.87	5.81	3.70
FNMA 6.50%	4.92	4.90	6.11	3.99
FHLMC 6.50%	4.98	4.95	6.16	4.10
High-yield corporates	7.28	7.35	11.53	6.88
Tax-Exempt Bonds				
7-12 yr G.O. (AA)	3.24	3.27	4.12	2.82
12-22 yr G.O. (AA)	4.05	4.07	4.97	3.79
22+ yr revenue (A)	4.50	4.52	5.32	4.32

Note: High quality rated AAA-AA; medium quality A-BBB/Baa; high yield, BB/Ba-C.
(1) Dollar-denominated, SEC-registered bonds of foreign issuers sold in the U.S. (2) Reflects the 52-week high and low of mortgage-backed securities indexes rather than the individual securities shown. (3) Government guaranteed.

4 p.m., the 10-year note maturing Nov. 15, 2113 was down 7/32 point, or $2.19 per $1,000 face value, at 101 18/32. Its yield rose to 4.052% from 4.025% Wednesday, as yields move inversely to prices. The 30-year bond was down 19/32 point at 106 16/32 to yield 4.937%, up from 4.899% Wednesday.

Corporate and High-Yield Bonds

Trump Hotels & Casino Resorts Inc. bonds gained on news that DLJ Merchant Banking arm of Credit Suisse Group's Credit Suisse First Boston would make a $400 million cash investment to sponsor a recapitalization. Bonds of the Trump Atlantic City Associates unit, the 11¼% issue due 2006, were quoted about eight points higher at 84½ bid.

Elsewhere, debt of Revlon Inc. rose after it said an agreement with an institutional investor and Ronald O. Perelman's MacAndrews & Forbes Holdings Inc. will allow the company to cut debt by about 50%. Its 8⅛% notes due 2006 were bid at 100½, up from 77½ Wednesday.

—Liz Rappaport contributed to this article.

If you wish to purchase a Treasury note directly from the Treasury, visit www.treasurydirect.gov for instructions. You will pay the noncompetitive price in accordance with the next paragraph.

Look at the Friday, February 13, 2004, print *Journal* excerpt (see below) from the **Credit Markets** article (see the first and third section indexes) that reports on the previous day's 4.06 percent five-year note issue. Noncompetitive bids totaled $133 million. These small bidders took the market (average) price established at the auction. Notice that (on the average) successful bidders paid 99.511 percent of par ($1,000), so that a $1,000 five-year note cost $995.11 (on the average), which is $4.89 less than par. The coupon rate (interest rate) was 4.0 percent, or $40.00 annually, per $1,000 note. But since successful bidders paid only $995.11 on the average, the true yield was a slightly higher 4.06 percent. Therefore, the 4.06 percent true yield on these five-year notes was slightly higher than the coupon rate of 4.0 percent.

The majority of this chapter's discussion refers to *The Wall Street Journal*'s print edition, but *The Wall Street Journal Online* also provides this data. (You can find general directions for retrieving *Wall Street Journal* online information [http://online.wsj.com] in Chapter 1 on pages 7 through 11. Appendix D on page 374 also furnishes you with a quick guide to the *Journal*'s online edition.) Scroll down the online home page's left-hand menu-bar to Markets and then click on Credit Markets. Auction results (on the days auctions occur) appear to the right of the **Credit Markets** article.

Major financial institutions, not individuals, bid in the primary market for Treasury securities, but your bank or broker can act as your agent if you wish to purchase a Treasury note or bond in the secondary (resale) market. This market is very liquid, which means that you should have no trouble buying or selling securities on any business day. *The Wall Street Journal* print edition reports trading on the secondary market for Treasury notes and bonds on a daily basis under **Treasury Bonds, Notes & Bills**. See the report on pages 310 and 312–315

AUCTION RESULTS

Here are results of yesterday's Treasury auction of five-year notes. All bids are awarded at a single price at the market-clearing yield. Rates are determined by the difference between that price and the face value.

Applications	$31,980,856,000
Accepted bids	$16,000,060,000
Bids at market-clearing yield accepted	85.61%
Accepted noncompetitively	$133,629,000
" foreign noncompetitively	$0
Auction price (Rate)	99.511 (4.060%)
Interest rate	4.00%
Cusip number	912828CA6

On February 12, 2004, the Treasury auctioned five-year notes in the primary market for a yield of 4.06%. →

The notes are dated Feb. 15, and mature Feb. 15, 2014.

Treasury Bonds, Notes and Bills

February 17, 2004

Explanatory Notes

Representative Over-the-Counter quotation based on transactions of $1 million or more. Treasury bond, note and bill quotes are as of mid-afternoon. Colons in bid-and-asked quotes represent 32nds; 101:01 means 101 1/32. Net changes in 32nds. n-Treasury note. i-Inflation-Indexed issue. Treasury bill quotes in hundredths, quoted on terms of a rate of discount. Days to maturity calculated from settlement date. All yields are to maturity and based on the asked quote. Latest 13-week and 26-week bills are boldfaced. For bonds callable prior to maturity, yields are computed to the earliest call date for issues quoted above par and to the maturity date for issues below par. *When issued.

Source: eSpeed/Cantor Fitzgerald

U.S. Treasury strips as of 3 p.m. Eastern time, also based on transactions of $1 million or more. Colons in bid and asked quotes represent 32nds; 99:01 means 99 1/32. Net changes in 32nds. Yields calculated on the asked quotation. ci-stripped coupon interest. bp-Treasury bond, stripped principal. np-Treasury note, stripped principal. For bonds callable prior to maturity, yields are computed to the earliest call date for issues quoted above par and to the maturity date for issues below par.

Source: Bear, Steams & Co. via Street Software Technology Inc.

Government Bonds & Notes

RATE	MATURITY MO/YR	BID	ASKED	CHG	ASK YLD
3.000	Feb 04n	100:01	100:02	...	0.15
3.625	Mar 04n	100:09	100:10	...	0.68
3.375	Apr 04n	100:15	100:16	...	0.80
5.250	May 04n	101:00	101:01	...	0.80
7.250	May 04n	101:16	101:17	...	0.74
12.375	May 04	102:23	102:24	...	0.69
3.250	May 04n	100:20	100:21	...	0.88
2.875	Jun 04n	100:22	100:23	...	0.88
2.250	Jul 04n	100:17	100:18	...	0.95
2.125	Aug 04n	100:18	100:19	-1	0.96
6.000	Aug 04n	102:14	102:15	...	0.93
7.250	Aug 04n	103:01	103:02	-1	0.93
13.750	Aug 04	106:07	106:08	...	0.91
1.875	Sep 04n	100:16	100:17	...	0.98
2.125	Oct 04n	100:23	100:24	...	1.04
5.875	Nov 04n	103:16	103:17	...	1.05
7.875	Nov 04n	105:00	105:00	-1	1.02
11.625	Nov 04	107:22	107:23	-1	1.07
2.000	Nov 04n	100:22	100:23	...	1.05
1.750	Dec 04n	100:17	100:18	...	1.07
1.625	Jan 05n	100:14	100:15	...	1.11
7.500	Feb 05n	106:07	106:08	-1	1.11
1.500	Feb 05n	100:11	100:12	...	1.12
1.625	Mar 05n	100:15	100:16	...	1.16
1.625	Apr 05n	100:14	100:15	...	1.23
6.500	May 05n	106:13	106:14	-1	1.22
6.750	May 05n	106:23	106:24	...	1.22
12.000	May 05	113:08	113:09	...	1.15
1.250	May 05n	100:00	100:00	...	1.24
1.125	Jun 05n	99:24	99:25	...	1.28
1.500	Jul 05n	100:06	100:07	...	1.34
6.500	Aug 05n	107:17	107:18	...	1.34
10.750	Aug 05	113:26	113:27	1	1.32
2.000	Aug 05n	100:28	100:29	...	1.39
1.625	Sep 05n	100:09	100:10	...	1.43
1.625	Oct 05n	100:06	100:07	...	1.48
5.750	Nov 05n	107:07	107:08	...	1.50
5.875	Nov 05n	107:14	107:15	...	1.50
1.875	Nov 05n	100:18	100:19	...	1.53
1.875	Dec 05n	100:15	100:16	...	1.59
1.875	**Jan 06n**	**100:12**	**100:13**	**1**	**1.66**
5.625	Feb 06n	107:24	107:25	-1	1.63
9.375	Feb 06	115:01	115:02	-1	1.64
2.000	May 06n	100:14	100:15	...	1.78
4.625	May 06n	106:05	106:06	...	1.78
6.875	May 06n	111:02	111:03	-1	1.78
7.000	Jul 06n	112:00	112:00	...	1.87
2.375	Aug 06n	101:03	101:04	...	1.91
6.500	Oct 06n	111:17	111:18	...	2.00
2.625	Nov 06n	101:16	101:17	...	2.05
3.500	Nov 06n	103:27	103:28	1	2.04
3.375	Jan 07i	109:14	109:15	2	0.10
2.250	Feb 07n	100:05	100:06	...	2.18
6.250	Feb 07n	111:26	111:27	1	2.14
6.625	May 07n	113:16	113:17	...	2.26
4.375	May 07n	106:16	106:17	1	2.27
3.250	Aug 07n	102:27	102:28	1	2.39
6.125	Aug 07n	112:14	112:15	...	2.38
3.000	Nov 07n	101:26	101:27	1	2.48
3.625	Jan 08i	112:02	112:03	...	0.49
3.000	Feb 08n	101:13	101:14	...	2.61
5.500	Feb 08n	111:00	111:01	...	2.57
2.625	May 08n	99:20	99:21	...	2.71
5.625	May 08n	111:20	111:21	...	2.69
3.250	Aug 08n	101:25	101:26	...	2.82
3.125	Sep 08n	101:04	101:05	1	2.85
3.125	Oct 08n	101:00	101:01	...	2.88
3.375	Nov 08n	102:00	102:00	...	2.92
4.750	Nov 08n	108:06	108:07	1	2.88
3.375	Dec 08n	101:28	101:29	...	2.94
3.250	Jan 09n	101:08	101:09	1	2.97
3.875	Jan 09i	114:22	114:23	...	0.81
3.000	**Feb 09n**	**100:00**	**100:00**	**2**	**3.00**
5.500	May 09n	112:07	112:08	1	2.96
9.125	May 09	102:04	102:05	...	0.00
6.000	Aug 09n	114:15	114:16	1	3.10
10.375	Nov 09	106:28	106:29	...	0.94
4.250	Jan 10i	118:08	118:09	-1	1.05
6.500	Feb 10n	117:17	117:18	2	3.25
11.750	Feb 10	110:09	110:10	...	1.21
10.000	May 10	110:20	110:21	...	1.27
5.750	Aug 10n	113:20	113:21	2	3.39
12.750	Nov 10	119:02	119:03	-2	1.56
3.500	Jan 11i	114:20	114:21	-4	1.28
5.000	Feb 11n	109:02	109:03	1	3.52
13.875	May 11	126:09	126:10	...	1.81
5.000	Aug 11n	108:26	108:27	1	3.64
14.000	Nov 11	131:19	131:20	...	2.05

MATURITY	TYPE	BID	ASKED	CHG	ASK YLD
3.375	Jan 12i	114:08	114:09	-2	1.46
4.875	Feb 12n	107:23	107:24	1	3.74
3.000	Jul 12i	111:12	111:13	-3	1.55
4.375	Aug 12n	103:29	103:30	2	3.83
4.000	Nov 12n	101:00	101:00	2	3.86
10.375	Nov 12	127:25	127:26	-3	2.53
3.875	Feb 13n	99:25	99:26	1	3.90
3.625	May 13n	98:00	98:00	2	3.88
1.875	Jul 13i	101:21	101:22	-4	1.68
4.250	Aug 13n	102:02	102:03	1	3.98
12.000	Aug 13	138:12	138:13	-1	2.83
4.250	Nov 13n	101:28	101:29	3	4.01
2.000	Jan 14i	102:12	102:13	-3	1.73
4.000	**Feb 14n**	**99:22**	**99:23**	**2**	**4.03**
13.250	May 14	149:02	149:03	-3	3.03
12.500	Aug 14	146:28	146:29	-4	3.13
11.750	Nov 14	144:15	144:16	...	3.20
11.250	Feb 15	162:15	162:16	3	4.12
10.625	Aug 15	158:05	158:06	2	4.19
9.875	Nov 15	151:19	151:20	2	4.24
9.250	Feb 16	146:01	146:02	2	4.29
7.250	May 16	127:06	127:07	2	4.36
7.500	Nov 16	129:26	129:27	...	4.41
8.750	May 17	142:28	142:29	2	4.43
8.875	Aug 17	144:13	144:14	3	4.46
9.125	May 18	148:01	148:02	3	4.51
9.000	Nov 18	147:09	147:10	3	4.55
8.875	Feb 19	146:01	146:02	3	4.59
8.125	Aug 19	138:04	138:05	2	4.64
8.500	Feb 20	142:23	142:24	4	4.67
8.750	May 20	145:28	145:29	3	4.68
8.750	Aug 20	146:03	146:04	2	4.70
7.875	Feb 21	136:03	136:04	1	4.75
8.125	May 21	139:11	139:12	2	4.75
8.125	Aug 21	139:14	139:15	1	4.77
8.000	Nov 21	138:05	138:06	2	4.78
7.250	Aug 22	129:07	129:08	1	4.84
7.625	Nov 22	134:03	134:04	1	4.83
7.125	Feb 23	127:27	127:28	2	4.86
6.250	Aug 23	116:27	116:28	2	4.90
7.500	Nov 24	133:21	133:22	2	4.89
7.625	Feb 25	135:13	135:14	2	4.90
6.875	Aug 25	125:18	125:19	2	4.93
6.000	Feb 26	113:28	113:29	2	4.95
6.750	Aug 26	124:07	124:08	3	4.95
6.500	Nov 26	120:25	120:26	2	4.96
6.625	Feb 27	122.19	122:20	4	4.96
6.375	Aug 27	119:07	119:08	3	4.98
6.125	Nov 27	115:25	115:26	4	4.98
3.625	Apr 28i	127:00	127:01	-2	2.18
5.500	Aug 28	107:00	107:01	4	5.00
5.250	Nov 28	103:17	103:18	4	5.00
5.250	Feb 29	103:20	103:21	4	4.99
3.875	Apr 29i	132:30	132:31	-1	2.17
6.125	Aug 29	116:09	116:10	5	4.99
6.250	May 30	118:11	118:12	4	4.99
5.375	**Feb 31**	**106:28**	**106:29**	**3**	**4.91**
3.375	Apr 32i	127:00	127:01	-2	2.10

U.S. Treasury Strips

MATURITY	TYPE	BID	ASKED	CHG	ASK YLD
May 04	ci	99:25	99:25	...	0.93
May 04	np	99:25	99:25	...	0.93
Jul 04	ci	99:19	99:20	-1	0.96
Aug 04	ci	99:18	99:18	-1	0.88
Aug 04	np	99:16	99:17	-2	0.98
Nov 04	ci	99:07	99:07	-1	1.06
Nov 04	bp	99:08	99:08	...	1.01
Nov 04	np	99:08	99:08	...	1.01
Jan 05	ci	99:12	99:12	...	0.69
Feb 05	ci	98:30	98:31	...	1.05
Feb 05	np	98:28	98:29	...	1.13
May 05	ci	98:19	98:20	-1	1.12
May 05	bp	98:18	98:19	-1	1.15
May 05	np	98:17	98:17	-1	1.19
May 05	np	98:16	98:17	-1	1.21
Jul 05	ci	98:22	98:23	-1	0.93
Aug 05	ci	98:02	98:03	-1	1.29
Aug 05	bp	97:31	98:00	-1	1.35
Aug 05	np	98:00	98:01	-1	1.34
Nov 05	ci	97:13	97:14	-1	1.50
Nov 05	np	97:12	97:13	-1	1.52
Nov 05	np	97:12	97:13	-1	1.51
Jan 06	ci	97:16	97:17	-1	1.32
Feb 06	ci	96:23	96:24	-1	1.66
Feb 06	bp	96:24	96:25	-1	1.65
Feb 06	np	96:25	96:26	-1	1.63
May 06	ci	96:03	96:04	-1	1.77
May 06	np	96:01	96:02	-1	1.80
Jul 06	ci	96:09	96:10	-1	1.57
Jul 06	np	95:17	95:19	-1	1.89
Aug 06	ci	95:11	95:12	-1	1.91
Oct 06	np	94:26	94:28	...	2.00
Nov 06	ci	94:15	94:17	-1	2.07
Nov 06	np	94:16	94:18	-1	2.06
Feb 07	ci	93:17	93:18	...	2.23
Feb 07	np	93:21	93:22	...	2.19
May 07	ci	92:22	92:24	...	2.34
May 07	np	92:24	92:26	...	2.32
Aug 07	np	91:27	91:29	-1	2.43
Aug 07	ci	91:23	91:25	...	2.48
Aug 07	np	91:26	91:28	...	2.44
Nov 07	ci	91:00	91:02	-1	2.52
Nov 07	np	91:01	91:03	-1	2.51
Feb 08	ci	89:26	89:28	...	2.70
Feb 08	np	90:00	90:02	-1	2.64
May 08	ci	88:21	88:24	-1	2.84
May 08	np	88:30	89:00	-1	2.77
Aug 08	ci	87:28	87:30	-1	2.88
Nov 08	ci	86:24	86:27	-1	3.00
Nov 08	np	86:30	87:01	-1	2.96
Feb 09	ci	85:20	85:22	-1	3.12
May 09	ci	84:19	84:22	-1	3.20
May 09	np	85:11	85:13	-1	3.03
Aug 09	ci	83:22	83:25	-1	3.25
Aug 09	np	83:27	83:30	-1	3.21
Nov 09	ci	83:01	83:04	-1	3.25
Nov 09	bp	82:00	82:02	1	3.47
Feb 10	ci	81:10	81:13	1	3.46
Feb 10	np	81:24	81:27	1	3.37
May 10	ci	80:11	80:14	1	3.52
Aug 10	ci	79:12	79:15	1	3.57
Aug 10	np	79:22	79:26	1	3.51
Nov 10	ci	78:24	78:27	1	3.56
Feb 11	ci	77:03	77:07	1	3.74
Feb 11	np	77:19	77:22	1	3.64
May 11	ci	76:03	76:07	1	3.79
Aug 11	ci	75:05	75:09	1	3.83
Aug 11	np	75:15	75:19	1	3.77
Nov 11	ci	74:10	74:14	1	3.85
Feb 12	ci	72:27	72:31	1	3.98
Feb 12	np	73:13	73:16	1	3.89
May 12	ci	71:22	71:26	1	4.06
Aug 12	ci	70:22	70:25	1	4.11
Aug 12	np	71:18	71:22	1	3.96
Nov 12	ci	69:20	69:24	-1	4.16
Nov 12	np	70:23	70:27	1	3.98
Feb 13	ci	68:21	68:25	1	4.21
May 13	ci	67:20	67:24	1	4.26
Aug 13	ci	66:21	66:25	1	4.30
Nov 13	ci	65:22	65:26	1	4.34
Feb 14	ci	64:26	64:30	1	4.37
May 14	ci	63:25	63:29	1	4.42
Aug 14	ci	62:28	63:00	1	4.45
Nov 14	ci	61:29	62:02	1	4.49

Treasury Bills

MATURITY	DAYS TO MAT	BID	ASKED	CHG	ASK YLD
Feb 19 04	1	0.77	0.76	...	0.77
Feb 26 04	8	0.87	0.86	0.04	0.87
Mar 04 04	15	0.87	0.86	0.02	0.87
Mar 11 04	22	0.89	0.88	0.01	0.89
Mar 18 04	29	0.88	0.87	0.04	0.88
Mar 25 04	36	0.85	0.84	0.02	0.85
Apr 01 04	43	0.86	0.85	0.02	0.86
Apr 08 04	50	0.85	0.84	0.01	0.85
Apr 15 04	57	0.88	0.87	0.01	0.88
Apr 22 04	64	0.87	0.86	0.01	0.87
Apr 29 04	71	0.88	0.87	...	0.88
May 06 04	78	0.90	0.89	...	0.90
May 13 04	**85**	**0.90**	**0.89**	**...**	**0.90**
May 20 04	92	0.90	0.89	...	0.90
May 27 04	99	0.90	0.89	0.03	0.90
Jun 03 04	106	0.90	0.89	0.01	0.90
Jun 10 04	113	0.90	0.89	0.01	0.90
Jun 17 04	120	0.87	0.86	0.01	0.87
Jun 24 04	127	0.91	0.90	-0.01	0.92
Jul 01 04	134	0.92	0.91	...	0.93
Jul 08 04	141	0.93	0.92	0.01	0.94
Jul 15 04	148	0.94	0.93	...	0.95
Jul 22 04	155	0.95	0.94	...	0.96
Jul 29 04	162	0.95	0.94	...	0.96
Aug 05 04	169	0.96	0.95	...	0.97
Aug 12 04	**176**	**0.97**	**0.96**	**0.01**	**0.98**

Inflation-Indexed Treasury Securities

RATE	MAT	BID/ASKED	CHG	*YLD	ACCR PRIN
3.375	01/07	109-14/15	2	0.114	1164
3.625	01/08	112-02/03	...	0.497	1141
3.875	01/09	114-22/23	...	0.811	1124
4.250	01/10	118-08/09	-1	1.051	1096
3.500	01/11	114-20/21	-4	1.277	1059
3.375	01/12	114-08/09	-2	1.457	1038
3.000	07/12	111-12/13	-3	1.548	1026
1.875	07/13	101-21/22	-4	1.680	1004
2.000	01/14	102-12/13	-3	1.735	1000
3.625	04/28	127-00/01	-2	2.180	1140
3.875	04/29	132-30/31	-1	2.168	1122
3.375	04/32	127-00/01	-2	2.099	1039

*Yield to maturity on accrued principal.

Bellwether 10-year T-note

November 2018 T-note

June 2005 T-note

February 2021 T-bond

May 2021 T-bond

Bellwether strip

for Tuesday, February 17, 2004, in the Wednesday, February 18, *Journal*. You can locate it using the front-page index of the first or third section under Treasury/Agency Issues.

These data are also available online. From the *Journal*'s home page, scroll down the left-hand menu-bar and click on Markets and Markets Data Center. Then scroll down to Bond Markets in the right column and click on Treasury Quotes. The example below is from Tuesday, July 6, 2004.

WSJ.com THE WALL STREET JOURNAL. ONLINE

Search   Quotes & Research

•Advanced Search   Symbol   Name
•Help   U.S. Markets

Home

News   Technology   Markets   Personal Journal   Opinion   Leisure Weekend

Treasury Quotes

Tuesday, July 6, 2004

U.S. Government Bonds and Notes

Representative Over-the-Counter quotation based on transactions of $1 million or more. Treasury bond, note and bill quotes are from midafternoon. Colons in bond and note bid-and-asked quotes represent 32nds; 101:01 means 101 1/32. Net change in 32nds. n-Treasury Note. i-Inflation-indexed issue. Treasury bill quotes in hundredths, quoted in terms of a rate of discount. Days to maturity calculated from settlement date. All yields are to maturity and based on the asked quote. For bonds callable prior to maturity, yields are computed to the earliest call date for issues quoted above par and to the maturity date for issues quoted below par. *-When issued. Daily change expressed in basis points.

Rate	Maturity Mo/Yr	Bid	Asked	Chg	Asked Yield
2 1/4	Jul 04 n	100:01	100:02	....	1.17
2 1/8	Aug 04 n	100:03	100:04	....	1.17
6	Aug 04 n	100:15	100:16	-1	1.15
7 1/4	Aug 04 n	100:20	100:21	....	1.09
13 3/4	Aug 04	101:10	101:11	-2	1.00
1 7/8	Sep 04 n	100:03	100:04	....	1.28
2 1/8	Oct 04 n	100:05	100:06	....	1.47
5 7/8	Nov 04 n	101:16	101:17	....	1.50
7 7/8	Nov 04 n	102:06	102:07	-1	1.51
11 5/8	Nov 04	103:17	103:18	-2	1.48
2	Nov 04 n	100:04	100:05	-1	1.53
1 3/4	Dec 04 n	100:01	100:02	....	1.60
1 5/8	Jan 05 n	99:30	99:31	....	1.66
7 1/2	Feb 05 n	103:14	103:15	-1	1.71
1 1/2	Feb 05 n	99:26	99:27	....	1.71
1 5/8	Mar 05 n	99:27	99:28	....	1.80
1 5/8	Apr 05 n	99:24	99:25	-1	1.87
6 1/2	May 05 n	103:26	103:27	-2	1.92
6 3/4	May 05 n	104:01	104:02	-1	1.92

The first column (in the print edition) of **Treasury Bonds, Notes & Bills** begins with figures headed **Government Bonds & Notes**. Turn to the *bellwether* (named after the lead sheep in the flock that wears a bell) 10-year Treasury note on page 310 and in the blowup below. The bellwether is the most recently issued bill, note, or bond with a particular (e.g., 2-year, 5-year, 10-year) maturity. Notice in the example on page 310 that the 2-, 5-, and 10-year notes are in boldface.

The first two columns describe the bond or note in question (the bellwether in this case). Begin with the coupon rate in the first column (*Rate*). Since it is 4.0, a $1,000 note or bond will pay $40.00 annually (4.0 percent of $1,000). The second column, titled *Maturity-Mo/Yr* (maturation date), provides the year and month of maturity: February 2014.

The letter *n* following the date indicates that the security is a note. All other issues are bonds. You will notice in the example on page 310 that there are no *n*'s after February 2014, because there are no notes with maturities greater than 10 years. A letter *i* following the date indicates that the security is inflation indexed. Bond issues (securities with initial maturities exceeding 10 years) that mature in less than 10 years (those with no letter following the month) are seasoned issues, sold sometime in the past, that are now approaching maturity.

The third (*Bid*) and fourth (*Asked*) columns in the example below represent the prices buyers bid or offered and sellers asked. The price quoted is a percentage of par ($1,000) value, with a number after the colon representing 32nds. Thus, a price of 99:22 for the February 2014 (bellwether) bond means that on February 17, 2004, buyers were willing to pay 99 22/32 percent of the par ($1,000) value, or $996.875 (99 + 0.6875 of par, or $1,000 × 0.996875). Whenever the price exceeds par value, the security trades at a *premium*; securities below par trade at a *discount*. Thus the bellwether bond traded at a discount on February 17, 2004.

The second-to-last column (*Chg*) is the change in bid price, expressed in 32nds, from the previous trading day. The bellwether bond below rose by

	Rate	Maturity Mo/Yr	Bid	Asked	Chg	Ask Yld
	12.000	Aug 13	138:12	138:13	−1	2.83
	4.250	Nov 13n	101:28	101:29	3	4.01
Bellwether T-note	2.000	Jan 14i	102:12	102:13	−3	1.73
$996.875 price →	4.000	Feb 14n	99:22	99:23	2	4.03
	13.250	May 14	149:02	149:03	−3	3.03
	12.500	Aug 14	146:28	146:29	−4	3.13
	11.750	Nov 14	144:15	144:16	...	3.20

2/32nds ($6.25) on February 17, 2004 (2/32 of 1 percent of $1,000 equals $6.25).

The last column (*Ask Yld*) is the yield to maturity of 4.03 percent, which is slightly more than the coupon rate of 4.0 percent because the bond traded at $996.875, somewhat below its $1,000 par. (See Chapter 16, pages 342 through 344, for additional discussion of the price-yield relationship.)

Here's a rough-and-ready way to approximate the yield:

$$\text{Approximate yield} = \frac{\text{Coupon rate}}{\text{Market price}} = \frac{\$40.00}{\$996.875} = 4.04\%$$

In this particular example, the approximate yield to maturity of 4.04 percent does not equal the actual yield to maturity of 4.03 percent, but it nonetheless offers a good approximation.

Why do securities sell at premiums (prices above the $1,000 par value) and discounts (prices below par)? Once again, market forces provide the answer. If the economy is awash in cash and, therefore, demand for Treasury securities (the next best thing to cash) is strong on the part of those who desire an interest return, securities buyers will bid their price up. Since the coupon rate—the numerator in the yield fraction—is fixed, a higher market price—the denominator in the yield fraction—will reduce the yield (see the approximate yield example above). Conversely, a cash shortage will prompt sales of securities on the part of those who need cash, reducing their price and increasing yields.

To illustrate this, note from the example below that two Treasury bonds with similar maturities can have different coupon rates although they have the same yields. For example, the 7.875 percent ($78.75 annually) February 2021 bond yields 4.75 percent, whereas the 8.125 percent ($81.25 annually) May 2021 bond also yields 4.75 percent. Why is there no difference in the yield when there is a $2.50 ($81.25 − $78.75) difference in the coupon

February 2021 T-bond, $78.75 annual coupon payment, $1,360.94 price, 4.75% yield	8.750	Aug 20	146:03	146:04	2	4.70
	7.875	Feb 21	136:03	136:04	1	4.75
May 2021 T-bond, $81.25 annual coupon payment, $1,393.44 price, 4.75% yield	8.125	May 21	139:11	139:12	2	4.75
	8.125	Aug 21	139:14	139:15	1	4.77

	12.000	May 05	113:08	113:09	...	1.15
June 2005 T-note,	1.250	May 05n	100:00	100:00	...	1.24
$997.50 price	1.125	Jun 05n	99:24	99:25	...	1.28
($2.50 below par)	1.500	Jul 05n	100:06 .	100:07	...	1.34
	6.500	Aug 05n	107:17	107:18	...	1.34

payment? Because these securities have different prices. The February bond's bid price is 136 3/32, or $1,360.94, while the May bond's price is 139 11/32, or $1,393.44. In other words, the $2.50 coupon difference is offset by a $32.50 ($1,393.44 − $1,360.94) difference in market price. Thus, differing prices will ensure that Treasury bonds and notes with similar maturity dates and features will have similar yields, whether the coupon is different or not.

Treasury bonds are almost risk-free when held to maturity. Yet their value will fall when interest rates rise, and you will suffer a loss if you must sell your bonds before they mature. For instance, the 1.125 percent June 2005 note traded at $997.50 on February 17, 2004 (see above), or $2.50 below par, because interest rates had increased somewhat since its issue in 2003. If you had purchased it at par when issued, and had been obliged to sell it on February 17, 2004, you would have suffered a slight loss.

On the other hand, looking at the 9 percent November 2018 bond in the example below, you see that its price had risen to $1,472.81 ($472.81 above par) since its 1988 issue at high interest rates. Substantial capital gains can be earned in low-risk Treasuries while enjoying a comfortable yield (9 percent at issue, or $90 annually in this case).

Bond prices converge on par and fluctuate very little as the maturity date approaches. Thus, bonds with the longest time to maturity offer the greatest opportunities for speculation, the greatest risk of loss, and (usually) the highest yields.

Finally, examine the data on pages 310 and 315 under **U.S. Treasury Strips**. You can purchase Treasuries in the secondary market that pay no annual interest but are offered at a deep discount so that you receive the equivalent of interest as the price appreciates. For instance, turning to the February 18, 2004, publication of the February 17 data, you can see that the

9.125	May 18	148:01	148:02	3	4.51	November 2018 T-note,
9.000	Nov 18	147:09	147:10	3	4.55	$1,472.81 price
8.875	Feb 19	146:01	146:02	3	4.59	($472.81 above par)

May	14	ci	63:25	63:29	1	4.42
Aug	14	ci	62:28	63:00	1	4.45
Nov	14	ci	61:29	62:02	1	4.49

Bellwether Strip, $619.06 price → (points to Nov 14 row)

Treasury Bills

MATURITY	DAYS TO MAT	BID	ASKED	CHG	ASK YLD
Feb 19 04	1	0.77	0.76	...	0.77
Feb 26 04	8	0.87	0.86	0.04	0.87

most recently issued (bellwether) bond traded at $619.06 (61 29/32). If you had purchased it that day, you could count on it appreciating more than 50 percent by the time it matured in November 2014. Many investors purchase these securities in order to accumulate a nest egg for a special purpose, such as a child's college education.

Investor's Tip

- Bonds are a good investment in low-inflation times because falling interest rates send bond prices upward.
- Unload your bonds when inflation threatens, because rising interest rates will depress bond prices.

Since fluctuations in market interest rates are crucial in determining the value of your investment, make a habit of tracking **Key Interest Rates** in Tuesday's *Wall Street Journal* print edition (check the third section's index). This information is available online by clicking on Markets and Markets Data Center in the left-hand menu-bar of the *Journal*'s home page. Then click on Key Rates under Bond Markets in the right column. Take a look at the Tuesday, July 6, 2004, example on page 316.

The Treasury is not the only government agency that issues long-term debt. The *Journal* publishes a **Government Agency & Similar Issues** report daily, which you can find using the front-page index of the first or third section under Agency Issues. The Monday, March 8, 2004, print edition (see page 317) covered Friday, March 5, 2004, trading activity for these agencies: **Fannie Mae (Federal National Mortgage Association), Freddie Mac (Federal Home Loan Mortgage Corporation), Federal Farm Credit Bank, Federal Home Loan Bank, GNMA Mtge. Issues (Government National Mortgage Association),** and the **Tennessee Valley Authority.**

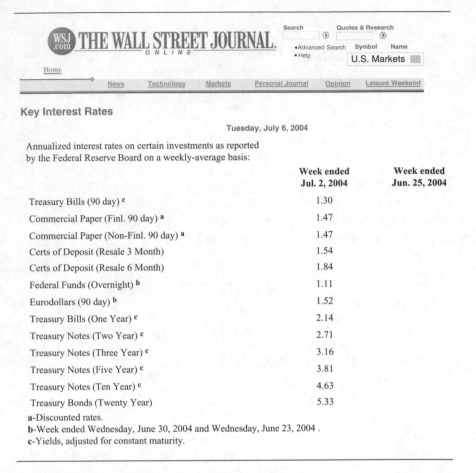

The columns read *Rate, Mat. Bid, Asked,* and *Yld*, and provide the same information as Treasury securities. The discussion below deals with some of these issues.

Fannie Mae stands for the **Federal National Mortgage Association**, a publicly owned corporation sponsored by the federal government and established to provide a liquid market for mortgage investors. Fannie Mae buys mortgages from mortgage bankers and other mortgage writers, earns the interest payments made by homeowners, and pays for these mortgages with the sale of bonds (debentures) to investors in $10,000 and $5,000 denominations. Pension funds, insurance companies, mutual funds, and other large institutional investors are the principal purchasers of these bonds, which are called *Fannie Maes*.

Government Agency & Similar Issues

Over-the-Counter mid-afternoon quotations based on large transactions, usually $1 million or more. Colons in bid and asked quotes represent 32nds; 101:01 means 101 1/32.

All yields are calculated to maturity, and based on the asked quote.

*Callable issue, maturity date shown. For issues callable prior to maturity, yields are computed to the earliest call date for issues quoted above par, or 100, and to the maturity date for issues below par.

Source: Bear, Stearns & Co. via Street Software Technology Inc.

Fannie Mae Issues

RATE	MAT	BID	ASKED	YLD
3.63	4-04	100:10	100:12	...
5.63	5-04	100:30	101:00	0.15
3.00	6-04	100:18	100:20	0.66
6.50	8-04	102:15	102:17	0.66
3.50	9-04	101:09	101:11	0.87
1.88	12-04	100:18	100:20	1.05
7.13	2-05	105:20	105:22	0.97
3.88	3-05	102:24	102:26	1.07
5.75	6-05	105:22	105:24	1.15
7.00	7-05	107:19	107:21	1.27
2.88	10-05	102:07	102:09	1.42
6.00	12-05	107:22	107:24	1.53
5.50	2-06	107:07	107:09	1.66
2.13	4-06	100:22	100:24	1.76
5.50	5-06	107:15	107:17	1.91
2.25	5-06	100:29	100:31	1.79
5.25	6-06	107:15	107:15	1.86
4.38	10-06	105:28	105:30	2.02
2.63	11-06	101:11	101:14	2.08
4.75	1-07	106:19	106:21	2.29
5.00	1-07	107:23	107:25	2.17
7.13	3-07	114:03	114:05	2.25
5.25	3-07*	100:05	100:07	...
5.25	4-07	108:24	108:26	2.28
5.00	5-07*	101:03	101:05	...
4.25	7-07	105:27	105:29	2.40
6.63	10-07	114:00	114:02	2.52
3.50	10-07*	100:30	101:00	1.80
3.25	11-07	102:12	102:14	2.55
3.25	1-08	102:04	102:06	2.65
3.50	1-08*	100:29	100:31	2.39
5.75	2-08	111:11	111:13	2.67
6.00	5-08	112:19	112:21	2.77
5.25	1-09	109:26	109:28	3.05
6.38	6-09	115:08	115:10	3.19
6.63	9-09	116:22	116:24	3.28
7.25	1-10	120:09	120:11	3.39
7.13	6-10	120:05	120:07	3.50
6.63	11-10	117:20	117:22	3.62
6.25	2-11	113:24	.113:26	3.94
5.50	3-11	110:28	110:30	3.71
6.00	5-11	113:29	113:31	3.76
6.25	7-11*	101:29	101:31	0.74
5.50	10-11*	102:15	102:17	1.30
5.38	11-11	109:26	109:28	3.88
5.00	11-11*	102:24	102:26	0.86
6.00	12-11*	103:13	103:15	1.51
6.00	1-12*	103:11	103:13	1.95
6.13	3-12	114:25	114:27	3.95
6.25	3-12*	104:22	104:24	1.61
5.50	7-12*	103:31	104:01	2.46
5.25	8-12	106:10	106:12	4.33
4.38	9-12	102:13	102:15	4.03
4.75	2-13*	101:19	101:21	3.86
4.63	5-13	101:08	101:10	4.45
6.25	5-29	114:00	114:04	5.23
7.13	1-30	126:13	126:17	5.24
7.25	5-30	128:11	128:15	5.24
6.63	11-30	119:19	119:23	5.24

Freddie Mac

RATE	MAT	BID	ASKED	YLD
3.75	4-04	100:10	100:12	...
5.00	5-04	100:26	100:28	0.25
6.25	7-04	101:29	101:31	0.58
3.00	7-04	100:23	100:25	0.77
4.50	8-04	101:17	101:19	0.77
3.25	11-04	101:15	101:17	0.99
6.88	1-05	104:29	104:31	0.96
1.88	1-05	100:19	100:21	1.09
3.88	2-05	102:17	102:19	1.07
1.75	5-05	100:21	100:23	1.14
4.25	6-05	103:25	103:27	1.18
7.00	7-05	107:18	107:20	1.28
2.88	9-05	102:05	102:07	1.38
2.13	11-05	100:31	101:01	1.50
5.25	1-06	106:17	106:19	1.61
1.88	2-06	100:10	100:12	1.68
2.38	4-06	101:06	101:08	1.76
5.50	7-06	108:04	108:06	1.92
2.75	8-06	101:27	101:29	1.95
4.88	3-07	107:18	107:20	2.25
4.50	7-07*	101:04	101:06	1.33
3.50	9-07	103:09	103:11	2.50
3.25	2-08*	100:07	100:09	2.94
2.75	3-08	100:04	100:06	2.70
3.50	4-08*	100:24	100:26	2.73
5.75	4-08	111:19	111:21	2.73
5.13	10-08	109:09	109:11	2.93
5.75	3-09	112:05	112:07	3.10
5.75	4-09*	100:21	100:23	0.60
4.75	8-09*	101:21	101:23	0.72
6.63	9-09	116:22	116:24	3.28
7.00	3-10	119:05	119:07	3.44
6.88	9-10	118:31	119:01	3.57
5.63	3-11	111:20	111:22	3.71
5.88	3-11	111:17	111:19	3.97
6.00	6-11	113:29	113:31	3.78
6.38	8-11*	108:09	108:11	2.74
5.50	9-11	110:23	110:25	3.84
5.75	1-12	112:07	112:09	3.92
6.25	3-12*	109:06	109:08	2.99
6.00	5-12*	101:01	101:03	0.73
5.13	7-12	107:24	107:26	4.01
5.13	8-12*	101:14	101:16	1.76
4.75	10-12*	101:11	101:13	3.83
5.25	11-12*	104:07	104:09	3.98
4.50	1-13	102:27	102:29	4.10
4.38	3-13	101:30	102:00	4.11
4.75	5-13*	100:00	100:02	4.74
6.75	9-29	120:27	120:31	5.25
6.75	3-31	121:16	121:20	5.24
6.25	7-32	114:23	114:27	5.24

Federal Farm Credit Bank

RATE	MAT	BID	ASKED	YLD
2.38	10-04	100:23	100:25	0.96
3.88	12-04	102:03	102:06	1.02
3.88	2-05	102:14	102:16	1.06
4.38	4-05	103:18	103:20	1.05
2.13	8-05	101:03	101:05	1.31
2.50	11-05	101:20	101:22	1.48
2.63	12-05	101:27	101:29	1.52
2.50	3-06	101:16	101:18	1.70
2.25	9-06	100:20	100:22	1.97
3.00	4-08*	100:31	101:01	2.73

Federal Home Loan Bank

RATE	MAT	BID	ASKED	YLD
4.88	4-04	100:15	100:17	...
3.63	10-04	101:17	101:19	0.95
4.13	11-04	102:02	102:04	0.98
4.38	2-05	103:00	103:02	1.08
6.88	8-05	107:25	107:27	1.33
2.50	12-05	101:19	101:21	1.54
5.13	3-06	106:20	106:22	1.70
2.50	3-06	101:12	101:14	1.76
5.38	5-06	107:13	107:15	1.86
2.25	5-06	100:28	100:30	1.81
4.88	11-06	107:04	107:06	2.11
4.88	2-07	107:12	107:14	2.24
5.38	2-07	108:24	108:26	2.26
2.75	3-08	100:04	100:06	2.70
5.80	8-05	111:29	111:31	2.93
6.00	5-11	110:04	110:06	4.33
5.63	11-11	111:03	111:05	3.93
5.75	5-12	112:05	112:07	3.98
4.50	11-12	103:04	103:06	4.06

GNMA Mtge. Issues

RATE	MAT	BID	ASKED	YLD
4.00	30Yr	94:09	94:11	4.90
4.50	30Yr	98:09	98:11	4.81
5.00	30Yr	101:01	101:03	4.80
5.50	30Yr	103:05	103:07	4.67
6.00	30Yr	104:23	104:25	4.05
6.50	30Yr	105:20	105:22	3.30
7.00	30Yr	106:18	106:20	3.06
7.50	30Yr	107:14	107:16	3.38
8.00	30Yr	108:27	108:29	3.49
8.50	30Yr	108:24	108:26	4.17

Tennessee Valley Authority

RATE	MAT	BID	ASKED	YLD
4.75	7-04	101:12	101:14	0.61
6.38	6-05	106:13	106:15	1.22
5.38	11-08	110:11	110:13	2.97
5.63	1-11	111:22	111:24	3.67
6.75	11-25	120:25	120:28	5.14
7.13	5-30	126:10	126:14	5.25

Freddie Mac stands for the **Federal Home Loan Mortgage Corporation** and is another publicly owned corporation that is sponsored by the federal government. Freddie Mac purchases single-family and multifamily residential mortgages and then bundles them into mortgage pass-through securities and debt instruments which it sells in the capital markets.

The **Federal Farm Credit Bank** assists farmers by helping financial institutions, such as small commercial banks and S&Ls, provide credit to farmers for the purchase and sale of commodities and the financing of buildings and new equipment. It is an independent agency of the U.S. government primarily funded by short-term debt, although it also issues longer-term notes that trade in the secondary market and are listed in the report.

The **Federal Home Loan Bank** (FHLB) is a federally chartered, privately owned company charged with regulating the S&L industry. The FHLB borrows by issuing bonds in $10,000 denominations to provide funds to weaker S&Ls with temporary liquidity problems.

GNMA Mtge Issues are offered by the Government National Mortgage Association, a government-owned corporation that purchases, packages, and resells mortgages and mortgage purchase commitments in the form of mortgage-backed securities called *Ginnie Maes*. Each Ginnie Mae bond is backed by a package of residential mortgages, and the holder of a GNMA bond thereby owns a portion of these underlying mortgages. New GNMA bonds cost $25,000, but older, partially repaid GNMAs can cost as little as $5,000.

Mortgage payments of interest and principal are "passed through" to the Ginnie Mae holders. Thus, unlike holders of Treasuries, who receive their principal at maturity, investors in Ginnie Maes are paid interest and principal each month.

Ginnie Maes don't have stated maturity dates, because the bond's flow of income depends on the repayment of the underlying mortgages. If all homeowners pay their mortgages regularly for the mortgage's life, with no prepayments, the Ginnie Mae holder receives regular monthly checks for 30 years. However, a homeowner may choose to pay off his or her mortgage prior to maturity, sell the home, or refinance the mortgage, or may pay additional principal in some months. Any prepayment or excess principal payments are passed through to the Ginnie Mae holder, who receives a larger monthly check. This prepayment reduces the subsequent monthly payments and the Ginnie Mae's par value.

Ginnie Maes offer higher rates than Treasury bonds because of the unpredictable nature of interest and principal payments. The U.S. Treasury backs these government bonds to remove the risk of homeowner default.

Finally, you can see the mortgage interest rates associated with the various Ginnie Mae pools, as well as the range of prices that determine these bonds' yields.

You can find online examples of these instruments by clicking on Markets Data Center and then clicking on Mortgage-Backed Securities and CMOs under Bond Markets.

The **Tennessee Valley Authority** (TVA) was established by Congress in 1933 to develop the resources of the Tennessee Valley. The TVA is a federally owned corporate agency that sells bonds to finance its activities. Revenues generated from the sales of electric power pay the interest and principal of these bonds.

CORPORATE BONDS

Corporations are the second principal issuer of long-term debt, and they, like the government and government agencies, issue credit instruments in order to finance long-term needs. Most bonds are exchanged over-the-counter, like Treasury securities, by large investment banking firms on behalf of institutional investors.

Corporate Bonds (see the third-section index) lists the 40 most actively traded corporate bonds and provides the *Coupon, Maturity, Last Price, Last Yield, Estimated Spread, Comparable US Treasury Issue,* and the *Estimated $ Volume.* An example from the Wednesday, April 7, 2004, print *Journal* appears below.

You can follow the performance of a particular bond, as in the illustra-

---

Corporate Bonds

Tuesday, April 6, 2004

Forty most active fixed-coupon corporate bonds

COMPANY (TICKER)	COUPON	MATURITY	LAST PRICE	LAST YIELD	*EST SPREAD	UST†	EST $ VOL (000's)
Morgan Stanley (MWD)	4.750	Apr 14, 2014	96.103	5.257	110	10	177,904
GlaxoSmithKline Capital PLC (GSK)	4.375	Apr 15, 2014	97.341	4.711	56	10	161,115
General Motors (GM)	8.375	Jul 15, 2033	112.108	7.360	236	30	114,614
AT&T Wireless Services (AWE)	7.875	Mar 01, 2011	117.420	4.866	71	10	100,700
Pacific Gas and Electric (PCG)	6.050	Mar 01, 2034	98.654	6.149	115	30	96,338
J.P. Morgan Chase (JPM)	3.500	Mar 15, 2009	99.042	3.714	58	5	78,756
Halliburton (HAL)-c	3.125	Jul 15, 2023	110.042	0.726	n.a.	n.a.	78,402
General Electric Capital (GE)	4.250	Jan 15, 2008	103.892	3.143	1	5	76,530
Sprint Capital (FON)	8.750	Mar 15, 2032	123.940	6.820	182	30	75,075
Goldman Sachs Capital I (GS)	6.345	Feb 15, 2034	100.728	6.290	129	30	74,240
Citigroup (C)	6.000	Feb 21, 2012	110.488	4.405	25	10	68,024
Comcast Cable Communications Holdings (CMCSA)	8.375	Mar 15, 2013	121.963	5.259	109	10	64,107
Wachovia (WB)	4.875	Feb 15, 2014	99.467	4.943	78	10	60,615
General Motors Acceptance (GMAC)	8.000	Nov 01, 2031	108.492	7.281	226	30	60,250
Liberty Media (L)	5.700	May 15, 2013	102.858	5.299	111	10	59,624
Pacific Gas and Electric (PCG)	4.800	Mar 01, 2014	98.325	5.017	86	10	58,030
Carnival (CCL)-c	1.132	Apr 29, 2033	79.948	0.109	n.a.	n.a.	57,500
General Motors Acceptance (GMAC)	7.750	Jan 19, 2010	111.919	5.321	219	5	56,695
Verizon Global Funding (VZ)	6.125	Jun 15, 2007	109.617	2.929	66	3	54,450
Sprint Capital (FON)	6.900	May 01, 2019	107.411	6.138	197	10	51,390
Bank of America (BAC)	5.250	Dec 01, 2015	100.746	5.163	101	10	50,550
Citigroup (C)	3.500	Feb 01, 2008	101.095	3.191	4	5	50,072
DaimlerChrysler North America Holding (DCX)	8.500	Jan 18, 2031	120.347	6.832	183	30	47,931
Ford Motor (F)	7.450	Jul 16, 2031	98.823	7.551	255	30	47,442
Time Warner (TWX)	7.700	May 01, 2032	116.399	6.430	143	30	46,531
Citizens Communications (CZN)	9.250	May 15, 2011	108.000	7.760	361	10	43,950
Ford Motor Credit (F)	6.500	Jan 25, 2007	106.492	4.011	175	3	43,932
General Electric Capital (GE)	3.125	Apr 01, 2009	98.006	3.566	43	5	41,417
General Electric Capital (GE)	3.500	May 01, 2008	100.911	3.258	12	5	40,792
Anheuser-Busch Companies (BUD)	5.050	Oct 15, 2016	100.691	4.975	79	10	40,227
Bank One (ONE)	5.500	Mar 26, 2007	107.701	2.768	48	3	40,000
Sprint Capital (FON)	8.375	Mar 15, 2012	119.761	5.289	113	10	39,589
Time Warner Entertainment , L.P. (TWX)	8.875	Oct 01, 2012	125.737	5.095	94	10	39,059
Lehman Brothers Holdings (LEH)	4.800	Mar 13, 2014	97.973	5.061	87	10	38,940
Altria Group (MO)	7.000	Nov 04, 2013	108.577	5.817	167	10	37,685
Schering-Plough (SGP)	5.300	Dec 01, 2013	102.334	4.991	84	10	37,646
GlaxoSmithKline Capital Inc (GSK)	5.375	Apr 15, 2034	96.142	5.643	64	30	36,615
Time Warner (TWX)	7.625	Apr 15, 2031	115.263	6.427	142	30	34,420
Ford Motor Credit (F)	7.000	Oct 01, 2013	104.216	6.399	225	10	34,323
Ford Motor Credit (F)	6.875	Feb 01, 2006	106.206	3.297	146	2	34,304
Morgan Stanley (MWD)	5.800	Apr 01, 2007	108.401	2.830	56	3	33,904

Volume represents total volume for each issue; price/yield data are for trades of $1 million and greater. * Estimated spreads, in basis points (100 basis points is one percentage point), over the 2, 3, 5, 10 or 30-year hot run Treasury note/bond. 2-year: 1.500 03/06; 3-year: 2.250 02/07; 5-year: 2.625 03/09; 10-year: 4.000 02/14; 30-year: 5.375 02/31. †Comparable U.S. Treasury issue. c-Convertible bond.

Source: MarketAxess Corporate BondTicker

(left margin annotation pointing to AT&T Wireless Services row:) **AT&T Wireless →**

tion on page 319. A key to all footnotes appears under **Explanatory Notes** at the bottom of the listing.

In the case of the AT&T bond shown on page 319, the coupon rate at issue per $1,000 bond (7.875 percent) and the date of maturity (March 1, 2011, the year the bond is due for redemption) follow the company name.

Corporate bonds are issued in denominations of $1,000, and this bond originally paid an annual fixed-dollar interest return of $78.75 (7.875 percent of $1,000). Thus, AT&T promised to pay the bearer $78.75 a year until the bearer redeemed the bond at maturity on March 1, 2011, for its face value of $1,000.

You can see from the next two columns that the last price was 117.420 and that the last yield was 4.866 percent. Since bonds are issued in denominations of $1,000, the reported prices are a percentage of the face value of $1,000. Thus, 117.420 means this bond traded at a price of $1,174.20 (117.420 percent of $1,000) at the day's close.

Estimated spread and UST (comparable US Treasury issue in years) are followed by reported volume in thousands of dollars. The AT&T bond had a yield of 71 basis points (100 basis points = 1 percent) above the comparable 10-year Treasury note.

If you bought this bond on Tuesday, April 6, 2004, your yield would be 4.866 percent, significantly less than the coupon rate of 7.875 percent, because on April 6 the bond had a value of $1,174.20, more than its par value of $1,000. An annual payment of $78.75 on an investment of $1,174.20 provides a lower yield than a payment of $78.75 on an investment of $1,000.

If the current yield on securities of similar risk and maturity as the AT&T bond falls below the coupon rate of 7.875 percent (as it has here), an investor will pay more than the par value for the bond. When commentators speak of the bond market rising and falling, they mean the price of the bond, not the interest rate. Bondholders want interest rates to fall so that the value of their bonds will rise. You can see that the AT&T bond went from $1,000 to $1,174.20 as its yield fell from 7.875 percent to 4.866 percent.

Investor's Tip

• Rising inflation, or fear of inflation, which drives interest rates up, hurts corporate bonds as well as Treasuries. Bond prices fall as interest rates rise.

Not only interest rates but also the relative strength of the issuing company will affect the price of its bonds. "Junk" bonds offer higher rates of interest because of their inherently risky nature. They are issued by companies that have high debt-to-equity ratios and high debt-to-cash-flow ratios and must therefore pay high interest rates to attract investors' money. Any fluctuation in the business of the issuing corporation could affect the timely payment of interest and the repayment of principal on the bonds.

Junk, or high-yield bonds, have been around for a long time and should be distinguished from their well-heeled cousins, the investment-grade bonds issued by financially secure corporations. Interest in junk bonds, especially on the part of institutions such as insurance companies and S&Ls, grew in the early 1980s, when falling interest rates boosted the prices of all bonds.

Investors used the proceeds from the sale of junk bonds to purchase the stock of corporations, particularly conglomerates that had fallen on hard times. These new owners often hoped to service their junk-bond debt by selling off divisions of the company they had purchased. Sometimes the company was worth more dead than alive and was dismembered so that the total value of the pieces exceeded the purchase price of the corporation. Sometimes top management bought a company from stockholders (called "going private") and then shrank it down to a profitable base. Often, however, the highly leveraged surviving company was burdened with a huge, high-yield debt. Many companies failed and defaulted on their bonds, so that by the end of the 1980s, and especially during the 1990–1991 recession, junk bonds fell out of favor and their prices sank and their yields soared. But the 1992 recovery and falling interest rates resuscitated many of these bonds, so that some investors realized strong capital gains as their prices climbed.

A dozen years later in 2004 junk bonds no longer offered deep-discount

High-Yield Bonds

Tuesday, January 20, 2004

Ten most active fixed-coupon high-yield, or "junk", corporate bonds

COMPANY (TICKER)	COUPON	MATURITY	LAST PRICE	LAST YIELD	*EST SPREAD	UST†	EST VOL (000's)
American Tower (AMT)	9.375	Feb 01, 2009	107.000	6.681	363	5	29,100
Nextel Communications (NXTL)	7.375	Aug 01, 2015	110.750	5.389	134	10	22,460
Nortel Networks Limited (NT)	6.125	Feb 15, 2006	104.500	3.826	217	2	17,882
Tyco International Group SA (TYC)-c	2.750	Jan 15, 2018	133.531	0.373	n.a.	n.a.	16,172
R.J. Reynolds Tobacco Holdings (RJR)	7.750	May 15, 2006	107.125	4.466	280	2	15,158
Millennium America (MCH)	9.250	Jun 15, 2008	111.500	6.216	316	5	13,500
Chesapeake Energy (CHK)	8.125	Apr 01, 2011	112.500	3.903	n.a.	n.a.	12,506
United Rentals (North America) (URI)	10.750	Apr 15, 2008	115.250	2.404	n.a.	n.a.	10,504
XTO Energy (XTO)	6.250	Apr 15, 2013	109.427	4.963	91	10	10,130
Edison Mission Energy (EIX)	9.875	Apr 15, 2011	107.000	8.552	449	10	7,500

Volume represents total volume for the market; price/yield data are for trades of $250,000 and greater. * Estimated spreads, in basis points (100 basis points is one percentage point), over the 2, 3, 5, 10 or 30-year hot run Treasury note/bond. 2-year: 1.875 12/05; 3-year: 2.625 11/06; 5-year: 3.250 01/09; 10-year: 4.250 11/13; 30-year: 5.375 02/31. †Comparable U.S. Treasury issue. c-Convertible bond.

Source: MarketAxess Corporate BondTicker

opportunities. For example, look at the Tuesday, January 20, 2004, example on page 321 of **High-Yield Bonds** from the January 21 print edition. You will notice that High-Yield Bonds lists a number of companies that have issued junk bonds, but none offer the deep discounts of yesteryear.

You can also follow **New Securities Issues** daily in the *Journal* (check the index in the first and third sections). It lists all new corporate, municipal, government agency, and foreign bonds issued on the previous day and provides pertinent information regarding these securities, including their ratings. (See the excerpt from the Wednesday, January 21, 2004, print *Journal* below.)

New Securities Issues

The following were among yesterday's offerings and pricings in U.S. and non-U.S. capital markets, with terms and syndicate manager, based on information provided by Dow Jones Newswires and Factiva. (A basis point is one-hundredth of a percentage point; 100 basis points equal a percentage point.)

CORPORATE

Developers Diversified Realty Corp.—$275 million, increased from $200 million, of notes was priced via joint lead managers Deutsche Bank Securities and J.P. Morgan Chase & Co., according to people familiar with the offering. Terms: maturity: Jan. 30, 2009; coupon: 3.875%; price: 99.584; yield: 3.967%; spread: 93 basis points above Treasurys; call: make-whole call at Treasurys plus 15 basis points; settlement: Jan. 23, 2004; ratings: Baa3 (Moody's Investors Service Inc.), triple-B (Standard & Poor's Ratings Group).

Jefferson-Pilot Corp.—$300 million, increased from $250 million, of notes was priced via bookrunner Morgan Stanley, according to people familiar with the offering. Terms: maturity: Jan. 30, 2014; coupon: 4.75%; price: 99.873; yield: 4.766%; spread: 74 basis points above Treasurys; call: make-whole call at Treasurys plus 15 basis points; settlement: Jan. 27, 2004; ratings: double-A (S&P), AA- (Fitch Inc.).

GLOBAL

Aktiebolaget Spintab—€250 million of Eurobonds was priced with the following terms, lead manager Barclays Capital said: maturity: July 27, 2005; coupon: three-month euro interbank offered rate; price: 100.05; reoffer: 100.05; payment: Jan. 26, 2004; ratings: Aa3 (Moody's), AA- (Fitch); listing: London; interest: quarterly.

Allgemeine Hypothekenbank Rheinboden AG—€1.5 billion of pfandbrief bonds was priced via lead managers Dresdner Kleinwort Wasserstein, Deutsche Bank and Hypovereinsbank. Terms: maturity: Feb. 22, 2009; coupon: 3.5%; price: 99.673; reoffer: 99.503; payment: Jan. 27, 2004; spread: seven basis points above midswaps or 24 basis points above Jan. 2009 bundesobligation; fees: 0.25%; ratings: A1 (Moody's), triple-A (S&P), AA+ (Fitch); listing: Frankfurt.

Bank Nederlandse Gemeenten—£350 million, increased by £100 million, of bonds was priced with the following terms, lead manager Royal Bank of Scotland said: maturity: Dec. 7, 2006; coupon: 4.625%; reoffer: 99.843; payment: Feb. 3, 2004; spread: 21 basis points above gilts; yield: 4.626%; fees: 0.05%; ratings: Aaa (Moody's), triple-A (S&P); listing: Luxembourg, Amsterdam; interest: annual.

Caja Granada International Finance—€150 million of bonds was priced in two tranches via lead manager Crédit Agricole Indosuez-Crédit Lyonnais with the following terms, IFR Credit said: **Class A:** €100 million; coupon: 25 basis points above three-month euribor; price: 100.032; reoffer: 100.032. **Class B:** €50 million; coupon: 3.75%; price: 100.018; reoffer: 100.018. **Common terms:** maturity: Jan. 29, 2009; payment: Jan. 29, 2004; guarantor: Caja Granada; fees: 0.175%; ratings: A- (Fitch); listing: Luxembourg.

Carrefour SA—€500 million of Eurobonds was priced with the following terms, lead managers Barclays Capital and Natexis Banques Populaires said: maturity: Dec. 17, 2008; coupon: 3.625%; price: 99.963; reoffer: 99.963; payment: Feb. 3, 2004; ratings: A1 (Moody's), single-A-plus (S&P); listing: Luxembourg.

Eurofima—$500 million of bonds was priced with the following terms, lead managers RBC Capital Markets and Daiwa Securities SMBC Europe said: maturity: Feb. 4, 2014; coupon: 4.25%; price: 100.691; reoffer: 99.016; payment: Feb. 4, 2004; fees: 2%; ratings: Aaa (Moody's), triple-A (S&P); listing: London; interest: annual.

Euronext NV—£250 million of bonds was priced with the following terms, lead manager HSBC Bank PLC said: maturity: June 16, 2009; coupon: 5.125%; price: 99.776; reoffer: 99.776; payment: Feb. 9, 2004; spread: 52 basis points above gilts; fees: 0.25%; listing: London; interest: annual.

Hypothekenbank in Essen AG—€600 million of floating-rate notes was priced via lead manager Credit Suisse First Boston with the following terms, IFR Credit said: maturity: July 27, 2005; coupon: six-month euribor; price: 100.05; payment: Jan. 27, 2004; fees: 0.05%; ratings: Aa1 (Moody's), triple-A (S&P), AAA (Fitch); listing: Düsseldorf.

Landesbank Rheinland-Pfalz Girozentrale—€200 million of floating-rate notes was priced with the following terms, lead manager Royal Bank of Scotland said: maturity: Feb. 9, 2015; coupon: five basis points above three-month euribor for the first three years and nine basis points above three-month euribor thereafter; price: 99.883; payment: Feb. 9, 2004; ratings: Aa1 (Moody's), double-A (S&P), AAA (Fitch); listing: Luxembourg; interest: quarterly.

Rabobank Australia Ltd.—200 million Australian dollars of bonds was priced with the following terms, lead managers TD Securities and Rabobank International said: maturity: Feb. 29, 2009; coupon: 6%; price: 101.275; payment: Feb. 25, 2004; guarantor: Rabobank Nederland; fees: 1.875%; ratings: Aaa (Moody's), triple-A (S&P); listing: Luxembourg; interest: annual.

Württembergische Hypothekenbank AG—€100 million of bonds was priced with the following terms, lead manager DZ Bank AG Deutsche Zentral-Genossenschaftsbank said: maturity: Jan. 26, 2007; coupon: 3%; price: 100; payment: Jan. 26, 2004; ratings: A3 (Moody's), single-A-minus (S&P); listing: Stuttgart.

Finally, Monday's **Public and Private Borrowing** (see the excerpt from the Monday, September 26, 2005, print edition below and on page 324) provides information on the week's new issues.

For an online (in Adobe Acrobat) Securities Offering Calendar, go to the online *Journal*'s home page, scroll down the left-hand menu-bar, click on Markets and Markets Data Center, and then scroll down the right column to Calendars.

MUNICIPAL BONDS

You may wish to purchase municipal (state and local government) bonds, or tax-exempt bonds, as they are sometimes called, because earnings from these bonds are not subject to federal income tax and may not be subject to income tax in your state. These bonds were granted tax exemption in order to reduce the borrowing cost of the states, cities, and local districts that issue them. Investors purchase them knowing their return is not taxable, and they will therefore be satisfied with a yield below that of comparable federal or corporate bonds. State and local governments save billions in interest costs as a result of this indirect subsidy.

Each Wednesday, the *Journal* publishes a **Municipal Bond Index** prepared by Merrill Lynch (see the third section's index). The excerpt from the

NEW TO THE MARKET

Public Offerings of Stock

IPOs in the U.S. Market — Initial public offerings of stock expected this week; might include some offerings, U.S. and foreign, open to institutional investors only via the Rule 144a market; deal amounts are for the U.S. market only.

EXPECTED (week ending)	FILED	ISSUER/BUSINESS	SYMBOL	HEADQUARTERS	AMOUNT, in millions	PRICING RANGE Low/High	PRIMARY EXCHANGE	BOOKRUNNER(S)
Sept. 26	May 9	**TRX** Online travel industry	TRXI	Atlanta, Ga.	**$6.8**	$11.00/ $13.00	Nq	CSFB
Sept. 28	March 31 (2004)	**Taleo** Staffing mgmt. solutions	TLEO	San Francisco, Calif.	6.7	14.00/ 16.00	Nq	Citigroup, Merrill, J.P. Morgan
Sept. 28	July 15	**WebMD Health** Health information services	WBMD	New York, N.Y.	6.9	13.50/ 15.50	Nq	Morgan Stanley, Citigroup, Goldman
Sept. 28	July 19	**Caribou Coffee Company** Coffeehouse chain	CBOU	Minneapolis, Minn.	5.4	13.00/ 15.00	Nq	Merrill, T. Weisel Partners
Sept. 29	June 3	**VistaPrint** Graphic design services	VPRT	Hamilton, Bermuda	10.0	9.00/ 11.00	Nq	Goldman, Bear Stearns
Sept. 30	March 2	**Horizon Lines** Freight transportation	HRZ	Charlotte, N.C.	12.5	10.00/ 12.00	N	Goldman, UBS

Lockup Expirations

Below, companies whose officers and other insiders will become eligible to sell shares in their newly public companies for the first time. Such sales can move the stock's price.

LOCK-UP EXPIRATION	ISSUE DATE	ISSUER	SYMBOL	OFFER PRICE	OFFER AMOUNT, in millions	SHARE PERFORMANCE THROUGH FRIDAY	LOCK-UP PROVISION
Sept. 27	March 31, '05	**Fastclick**	FSTC	$12.00	$78.0	Up 2.3%	180 days

Sources: Dealogic; WSJ Market Data Group

Public and Private Borrowing

Treasurys

Monday, Sept. 26

Auction of 13-week and 26-week bills; announced on Sept. 22; settles Sept. 29

Tuesday, Sept. 27

Auction of four-week bill; announced on Sept. 26; settles Sept. 29

Wednesday, Sept. 28

Auction of two-year note; announced on Sept. 26 settles Sept. 30

Public and Municipal Finance   Deals of $150 million or more expected this week

SALE	FINAL MATURITY	ISSUER	TOTAL, in millions	Fitch	RATING Moody's	S&P	BOOKRUNNER/BOND COUNSEL(S)
Sept. 23	prelim.	**Puerto Rico Highway & Transportation Authority**	$2,000.0	–	Baa2	BBB+	Citigroup/–
Sept. 23	prelim.	**Virginia Transportation Board**	250.0	AA	–	AA	Citigroup/–
Sept. 30	prelim.	**California State University Trustees**	544.2	–	–	–	UBS Financial/–
Sept. 30	prelim.	**Los Angeles Harbor Department**	203.2	AA	Aa2	AA	Citigroup/–
Sept. 30	prelim.	**NYC Municipal Water Finance Authority**	500.0	–	–	–	Merrill/–
Sept. 30	prelim.	**New York Liberty Development**	1400.0	AA-	Aa3	A+	Goldman/Mintz Levin Cohn Ferris

Source: i-Deal LLC/Thomson Financial

Corporate Debt   Expected this week

EXPECTED (week ending)	ISSUER/BUSINESS	YEARS TO MATURITY	DEAL VALUE, in millions	RATING Moody's	S&P	HIGH-YIELD	BOOKRUNNER(S)
Sept. 30	**Affinion Group** Package enchancement services	2-part	**$750.0**	Caa1	B-	✔	CSFB, Deutsche Bank
Sept. 30	**Neiman Marcus Group** Specialty apparel retailer	3-part	**2750.0**	B3	B-	✔	CSFB, Deutsche Bank, BoA, Goldman
Sept. 30	**Pregis Group** Manufactures padded mailers	7.5	**150.0**	Caa1	CCC+	✔	CSFB, Lehman
Sept. 30	**Whiting Petroleum** Oil & natural gas exploration	8.5	**250.0**	B2	B-	✔	Merrill, J.P. Morgan, Lehman

Source: Dealogic

Municipal Bond Index

Merrill Lynch Muni Master   Week ended December 16, 2003

The following index is based on major municipal issuers having bonds with amounts outstanding at least $50 million, an investment grade rating and issuance within the last five years. The chart shown displays the market weighted average yield to worst* of each index. The index is calculated by Merrill Lynch, based on pricing obtained from Standard & Poor's Securities Evaluation.

	12/16	CHANGE IN WEEK
MUNI MASTER BOND INDEX	4.35	–0.07
REVENUE BONDS		
Sub-Index	4.74	–0.07
22-52 YEAR REVENUE BONDS		
AAA-Guaranteed	4.37	–0.08
Airport	4.68	–0.06
Power	4.59	–0.07
Hospital	4.81	–0.07
Housing		
Single-Family	4.85	–0.01
Multi-Family	5.06	–0.02
Pollution Control/Ind. Dev.	4.70	–0.06
Transportation	4.45	–0.07
Water	4.14	–0.08
Advance Refunded	2.91	–0.06
12-22 YEAR GENERAL OBLIGATIONS		
Sub-Index	4.35	–0.07
Cities	3.77	–0.07
States	4.41	–0.08

The transportation category excludes airports; other districts include school and special districts. *assuming the least advantageous maturity for each issue.

Wednesday, December 17, 2003, print *Journal,* which appears above, serves as an example. In addition to an overall index, this report presents the latest yield on a variety of municipal bond categories.

Before deciding on the purchase of a tax-exempt municipal bond, an investor must weigh four considerations: the yield available on the municipal bond, the yield on a taxable bond with the same maturity, the investor's tax bracket, and whether the bond is callable. If, for example, you are in a 28 percent tax bracket, use the "equivalent tax-exempt yield formula" to calculate your after-tax yield on a security whose income is taxable. This will be the minimum yield a municipal bond must pay you to be of equivalent value to the taxable bond.

Here's an example using a 10 percent yield on the security whose interest is taxable:

$$\text{Equivalent tax-exempt yield} = (1 - \text{Tax bracket}) \times \text{Taxable yield}$$

$$= (1 - 0.28) \times 0.10$$

$$= 0.072$$

$$= 7.2 \text{ percent}$$

Thus, in your 28 percent tax bracket, a 7.2 percent tax-exempt yield is the equivalent of a 10 percent taxable yield. Therefore, if you had the opportunity, you would purchase an 8 percent tax-exempt bond rather than a 10 percent taxable bond with similar maturity and credit-worthiness.

Municipal bond buyers should always determine if the issuing agency can call (redeem) the bond before maturity. It may wish to do so when interest rates are low in order to issue new debt at lower rates. Meanwhile, the purchaser is forced to find another investment at a disadvantageous time. Therefore, an investor who plans to hold a bond until maturity should not purchase a bond that is callable before that date.

MUTUAL FUNDS

If you recall the discussion of mutual funds in Chapter 13, you will remember that mutual funds often specialize in particular types of investments. Bond funds are mutual funds that invest primarily in debt instruments, permitting you to diversity your bond investments without venturing a large sum of capital. For example, new Ginnie Mae issues require a $25,000 minimum investment, which would be out of the reach of the small investor. Mutual funds pool large sums of money in order to invest in instruments like Ginnie Maes, from which small individual investors can then benefit.

Recall as well the description in Chapter 13 of two types of mutual funds. Open-end funds issue shares as needed, while the shares of closed-end funds are limited and fixed. Once all the shares are sold, no more shares are issued.

Go to the *Journal*'s online edition for a report that includes a variety of bonds. After clicking on Markets and Markets Data Center in the left-hand menu-bar of the *Journal*'s home page, click on Closed-End Funds under Mutual Funds after scrolling down the right side. An example from Wednesday, July 14, 2004, appears on page 327.

Search   Quotes & Research

•Advanced Search   Symbol   Name
• Help
                                    U.S. Markets

Home

        News   Technology   Markets   Personal Journal   Opinion   Leisure Weekend

Closed-End Funds

These pages include market prices, net asset value and premium/discount figures for all closed-end funds tracked by Lipper, Inc. All pages are updated daily. Some funds provide NAVs weekly only. See more information about closed-end funds and how to read these tables.

Major Categories

Select a major category of funds, or see below to refine your search.

General Equity Funds

Specialized Equity Funds

Preferred Stock Funds

Convertible Securities Funds

World Equity Funds

U.S. Government Bond Funds

U.S. Mortgage Bond Funds

Investment Grade Bond Funds

Loan Participation Funds

High Yield Bond Funds

Other Domestic Taxable Funds

World Income

National Muni Bond Funds

Single State Funds

Expanded Categories

Refine your search using Lipper's full universe of fund categories.

General Equity Funds
Growth Funds
Core Funds
Value Funds

Specialized Equity Funds
Sector Equity Funds

Preferred Stock Funds
Income & Pref Stock Fds

Convertible Securities Funds
Convertible Sec Funds

World Equity Funds
Eastern European Funds
Emerging Markets Funds
Global Funds
Latin American Funds
Pacific Ex Japan Funds
Pacific Region Funds
Western European Funds
Misc Country/Region Fds

Investment Grade Bond Funds
Corp Debt BBB Rated Fds

Loan Participation Funds
Loan Participation Funds

High Yield Bond Funds
Hi Yld Muni Debt Funds
High Yield Fds Leveraged

Other Domestic Taxable Funds
General Bond Funds
Flexible Income Funds

World Income
Global Income Funds
Emerging Mkts Debt Funds

National Muni Bond Funds
Gen & Ins Unleveraged
General Muni Leveraged
Hi Yld Muni Debt Funds
Insured Muni Leveraged

TRACKING THE BOND MARKET

It's now time to wrap up this discussion by detailing how you can use the *Journal* every day (Monday's and Saturday's table and chart formats differ) to follow the bond market. You should begin your daily analysis of bond-market activity with a glance at the **Markets Diary** report on the first page of the *Journal*'s third section (see the excerpt below from the Thursday, September 21, 2005, edition), which tracks Treasury and corporate bonds.

The **Bond Market Data Bank** (find it in the front page index of the first and third sections) appears daily in the *Journal*'s print edition. In addition to **High Yield Bond** listings (at the bottom), the data bank thoroughly covers the bond market for the preceding trading day and contains more information than you may ever want to know.

You can also compare the yield on a variety of long-term instruments by using the **Yield Comparisons** table that appears daily with the **Credit Markets** article. See the example from the Wednesday, January 21, 2004, print edition on page 329.

MARKETS DIARY / *Sept. 21, 2005*

For an expanded view of yesterday's markets, turn to the **Markets Lineup on page C2.**

	Close	Change		Pct. chg.	52 wks
DJ Industrial Average	10378.03	−103.49	▼	0.99%	2.66%
Nasdaq composite	2106.64	−24.69	▼	1.16	11.72
S&P 500	1210.20	−11.14	▼	0.91	8.68
Russell 2000	649.94	−10.69	▼	1.62	14.85
Nikkei Stock Average	13196.57	48.00	▲	0.37	19.76
DJ Stoxx 600 (Europe)	291.89	−3.04	▼	1.03	21.62
Euro (in U.S. dollars)	$1.2210	$0.0083	▲	0.68	−0.40
Yen (per U.S. dollar)	111.32	−0.59	▼	0.52	0.67
Gold (Comex, troy oz.)	$468.90	$2.70	▲	0.58	15.15
Oil (Nymex, barrel)	$66.80	$0.60	▲	0.91	38.16

	Yield	Previous		Change in pct. pts.	12-mo return
10-year Treasury	4.18%	4.26%	▼	0.07	*2.97%
3-mo. Treasury	3.40	3.60	▼	0.20	*2.07
DJ Corporate Bond	5.12	5.17	▼	0.05	3.16

*Total return via Ryan Labs

Yield Comparisons

Based on Merrill Lynch Bond Indexes, priced as of midafternoon Eastern time.

	1/20	1/16	52-WEEK HIGH	52-WEEK LOW
Corp. Govt. Master	3.44%	3.42%	4.02%	2.81%
Treasury				
1-10 yr	2.30	2.28	2.70	1.57
10+ yr	4.72	4.67	5.28	3.86
Agencies				
1-10 yr	2.60	2.59	3.18	1.77
10+ yr	5.09	5.04	5.75	4.24
Corporate				
1-10 yr High Quality	3.15	3.14	3.75	2.47
Medium Quality	3.76	3.74	4.83	3.38
10+ yr High Quality	5.54	5.50	6.24	4.79
Medium Quality	5.87	5.82	6.86	5.36
Yankee bonds (1)	3.77	3.75	4.36	3.21
Current-coupon mortgages (2)				
GNMA 6.50% (3)	4.92	4.88	5.81	3.70
FNMA 6.50%	4.95	4.92	6.11	3.99
FHLMC 6.50%	5.01	4.97	6.16	4.10
High-yield corporates	6.95	6.97	11.53	6.95
Tax-Exempt Bonds				
7-12 yr G.O. (AA)	3.18	3.12	4.12	2.82
12-22 yr G.O. (AA)	4.06	4.00	4.97	3.79
22+ yr revenue (A)	4.51	4.48	5.32	4.32

Note: High quality rated AAA-AA; medium quality A-BBB/Baa; high yield, BB/Ba-C.
(1) Dollar-denominated, SEC-registered bonds of foreign issuers sold in the U.S. (2) Reflects the 52-week high and low of mortgage-backed securities indexes rather than the individual securities shown. (3) Government guaranteed.

The **Interest Rates & Bonds** section, at the bottom of **Markets Lineup** on page C2, provides additional information (see the excerpt from the Wednesday, January 21, 2004, issue on page 330). The **Treasury Yield Curve** allows you to check the yield on the entire range of Treasury securities. Notice the normal shape of the yield curve: Yields increase with length of maturity.

You can track bond yields online, too, by going to Bond Indexes under Bond Markets (right side) after clicking on Markets and Markets Data Center in the *Journal*'s home page's left-hand menu-bar. The Tuesday, July 6, 2004, edition appears on page 331.

Finally, the **Global Government Bond Index** table appears in Monday's print edition and lists international government bonds in local cur-

═══════════[INTEREST RATES & BONDS]═══════════

Consumer Rates

Benchmark personal borrowing rate vs. Federal-funds target rate, the interest rate on overnight loans between banks.

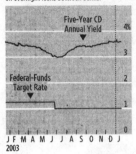

J F M A M J J A S O N D J
2003

	NAT'L AVG	WK'S CHG
Credit card	12.93%	...
Money market ann. yield	1.37	...
Five-year CD ann. yield	3.58	...
New-car loan	5.40	–0.02
30-yr. fixed-rate mortgage	5.27	–0.08
15-yr. fixed-rate mortgage	4.59	–0.10
Jumbo mortgages*	5.54	–0.07
One-year ARM	3.23	–0.03
Home-equity loan	6.84	–0.01

*Over $333,700

Most Competitive Rates

Five-year CD ann. yield

Capital One, FSB	4.29% APY
McLean, VA, 800-564-7426	
ING DIRECT	4.25%
Wilmington, DE, 877-469-0232	
Principal Bank..................................	4.21%
Des Moines, IA, 800-672-3343	
Advanta Bank Corp.	4.20%
Draper, UT, 800-788-2632	
Bank of Internet USA....................	4.16%
San Diego, CA, 877-541-2634	

Source: Bankrate.com

Treasury Yield Curve

Yield to maturity of current bills, notes and bonds.

1   3   6   2   5   10   30
month(s)   years
──────── maturity ────────
Source: Reuters

Major Bond Indexes

U.S. Treasury Securities				52-WEEK			YTD
Lehman Brothers	CLOSE	NET CHG	% CHG	HIGH	LOW	% CHG	% CHG
Intermediate	7604.04	–7.92	–0.10	7621.59	7295.23	+4.23	+1.46
Long-term	12182.60	–50.93	–0.42	12893.22	11198.53	+6.18	+2.37
Composite	8627.65	–17.27	–0.20	8775.94	8201.40	+4.90	+1.74

Broad Market Lehman Brothers (preliminary)

U.S. Aggregate	1070.83	–1.35	–0.12	1073.71	1010.55	+5.62	+1.07
U.S. Gov't/Credit	1243.99	–2.18	–0.16	1259.24	1162.61	+6.72	+1.29

U.S. Corporate Debt Issues Merrill Lynch

Corporate Master	1459.81	–2.22	–0.15	1464.57	1327.04	+9.87	+1.47
High Yield	667.93	+0.87	+0.13	667.93	523.56	+26.32	+2.29
Yankee Bonds	1062.90	–1.40	–0.13	1069.83	984.91	+7.91	+1.27

Mortgage-Backed Securities current coupon; Merrill Lynch: Dec. 31, 1986=100

Ginnie Mae	427.14	–0.29	–0.07	435.97	403.02	+1.70	+1.40
Fannie Mae	430.04	–0.37	–0.09	435.53	405.41	+4.31	+1.22
Freddie Mac	262.90	–0.30	–0.11	265.63	247.47	+4.49	+1.34

Tax-Exempt Securities Merrill Lynch; Dec. 22, 1999

6% Bond Buyer Muni	113.63	–0.19	–0.16	118.91	105.84	+4.81	+1.22
7-12 Yr G.O.	198.93	–0.69	–0.35	199.62	183.43	+8.45	+1.69
12-22 Yr G.O.	210.06	–0.77	–0.37	210.83	192.11	+9.16	+1.41
22+ Yr Revenue	199.26	–0.21	–0.11	199.47	181.89	+9.20	+1.56

Libor/Swap Curve

Counterparty receives (mid-market) semi-annual swap rates for 2 to 30 years and pays floating 3-month Libor.

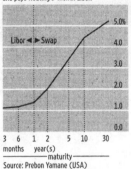

3   6   1   2   5   10   30
months   year(s)
──────── maturity ────────
Source: Prebon Yamane (USA)

rencies and the U.S. dollar. Click on Markets and Markets Data Center in the online *Journal*'s home page's left-hand menu-bar and locate International Government Bonds under Bond Markets in the right column. The Tuesday, July 6, 2004, edition appears on page 332. Notice the extremely low rates prevailing in Japan.

Major Bond Indexes

For Close of July 06, 2004   Tuesday, July 6, 2004

| 12 Month | | Index | Close | Chg. | % Chg. | 12 Month | | From 12/31 | |
High	Low					Chg.	% Chg.	Chg.	% Chg.
U.S. Treasury Securities		Lehman Brothers							
1387.68	1302.49	**Composite** (Price)	1327.99	-1.08	-0.08	-51.08	-3.70	-13.34	-0.99
8852.48	8201.40	**Composite** (Total Return)	8587.79	-2.82	-0.03	61.20	0.72	108.10	1.27
1253.02	1196.70	**Intermediate** (Price)	1213.65	-0.63	-0.05	-31.31	-2.51	-10.14	-0.83
7734.54	7323.99	**Intermediate** (Total Return)	7580.75	-0.71	-0.01	104.46	1.40	86.08	1.15
1830.07	1637.13	**Long-Term** (Price)	1699.63	-2.72	-0.16	-116.24	-6.40	-27.15	-1.57
12758.67	11198.53	**Long-Term** (Total Return)	12067.22	-11.51	-0.10	-98.87	-0.81	167.06	1.40
Broad Market	Lehman Brothers								
1275.99	1175.53	**U.S. Government/Credit**	1234.38	-0.39	-0.03	11.19	0.53	7.56	0.57
1094.87	1016.47	**U.S. Aggregate Bond**	1068.42	-0.38	-0.03	18.79	1.37	9.98	0.86
U.S. Corporate Debt Issues		Merrill Lynch							
1227.62	1059.11	**10+ Year Maturities**	1164.13			24.99	2.19	4.94	0.43
1066.67	990.34	**1-10 Year Maturities**	1040.78			20.67	2.03	7.52	0.73
1494.43	1363.44	**Corporate Master**	1448.04			29.30	2.07	9.34	0.65
670.46	583.00	**High Yield**	665.59			62.75	10.41	12.62	1.93
1088.87	1007.29	**Yankee Bonds**	1055.61			13.58	1.30	6.06	0.58
Tax-Exempt Securities		Bond Buyer Muni Index, from Dec. 22, 1999							
133.88	104.94	**Bond Buyer 6% Muni**	108.56	0.00	unch	-3.84	-3.42	-3.69	-3.29
216.41	192.11	**12-22 Year General Obligation**	207.99			6.93	3.45	0.86	0.42
202.96	183.46	**7-12 Year General Obligation**	196.16			4.47	2.33	0.54	0.28
203.97	181.89	**22+ Year Revenue**	195.17			4.66	2.45	-1.03	-0.52
Mortgage-Backed Securities		Current coupon; Merrill Lynch: Dec.31, 1986 = 100							
439.19	405.41	**Fannie Mae** (FNMA)	429.49			2.49	0.58	4.64	1.09
268.83	247.47	**Freddie Mac** (FHLMC)	262.80			1.95	0.75	3.37	1.30
436.04	403.02	**Ginnie Mae** (GNMA)	429.66			-0.63	-0.15	8.41	2.00
1108.58	1040.97	**Lehman Bros. Fixed MBS**	1099.25	-0.47	-0.04	36.03	2.93	16.61	1.40

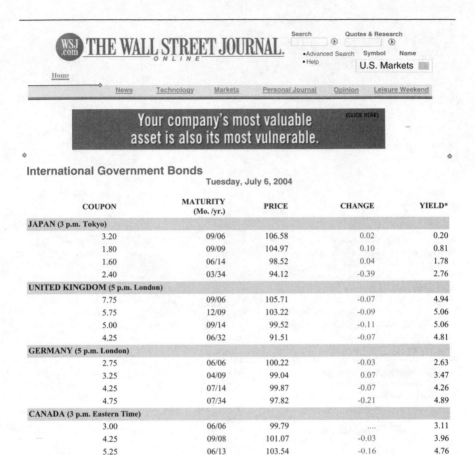

International Government Bonds
Tuesday, July 6, 2004

	COUPON	MATURITY (Mo. /yr.)	PRICE	CHANGE	YIELD*
JAPAN (3 p.m. Tokyo)					
	3.20	09/06	106.58	0.02	0.20
	1.80	09/09	104.97	0.10	0.81
	1.60	06/14	98.52	0.04	1.78
	2.40	03/34	94.12	-0.39	2.76
UNITED KINGDOM (5 p.m. London)					
	7.75	09/06	105.71	-0.07	4.94
	5.75	12/09	103.22	-0.09	5.06
	5.00	09/14	99.52	-0.11	5.06
	4.25	06/32	91.51	-0.07	4.81
GERMANY (5 p.m. London)					
	2.75	06/06	100.22	-0.03	2.63
	3.25	04/09	99.04	0.07	3.47
	4.25	07/14	99.87	-0.07	4.26
	4.75	07/34	97.82	-0.21	4.89
CANADA (3 p.m. Eastern Time)					
	3.00	06/06	99.79	....	3.11
	4.25	09/08	101.07	-0.03	3.96
	5.25	06/13	103.54	-0.16	4.76
	5.75	06/29	106.20	-0.46	5.30

*Equivalent to semi-annual compounded yields to maturity

CONCLUSION

If all this detail has set your head swimming, regain your perspective by recalling that the values of stocks and bonds should move together in the long haul and that both are paper investments that thrive in low inflation.

But short-term financial investments—the next chapter's topic—are safer still and may merit your consideration.

CHAPTER 16

MONEY-MARKET INVESTMENTS

SHORT TERM AND LIQUID

MAYBE THE RISK AND BOTHER OF INVESTING IN STOCKS, BONDS, AND COMMODITIES INHIBIT YOU. If that's so, you may be satisfied with an investment whose yield just covers the rate of inflation, provided that you can readily convert it to cash. In other words, you want your money's purchasing power to be unchanged a year or two from now, and you want the assurance that you can get your hands on your money at will.

Many circumstances might justify this point of view. Everyone's future involves some degree of uncertainty. If you are retired, your nest egg may have to meet unexpected medical bills. You don't want to be penalized for cashing out in a hurry. And investors of every age may wish to park their money for brief periods in anticipation of other planned uses of their funds. Whatever the situation, you might have a number of good reasons not to tie up your funds in riskier investments, even if they offer higher returns.

If you wish to make a short-term investment that is relatively risk-free and can be quickly converted to cash, the money market offers a variety of selections that range from one day to one year and may be obtained for large or small amounts. Most of these are probably familiar to you: bank savings accounts, interest-bearing checking accounts (money-market checking accounts), certificates of deposit, money-market mutual funds, and Treasury bills (T-bills). Market forces determine their yields, and the markets for all are interrelated.

As a general rule, the greater the liquidity (ease with which it is converted into cash) and safety of an investment, the lower the yield. A smaller investment commitment and a shorter maturity also reduce the yield.

This chapter describes the money-market investments available to individual investors and shows you how to track those investments in *The Wall Street Journal.*

CONSUMER SAVINGS AND INTEREST-EARNING CHECKING ACCOUNTS

Your interest-earning checking account or savings account at the bank or savings and loan company (S&L) is a short-term liquid investment, because you can withdraw your funds quickly and easily with relatively few restrictions. Moreover, these accounts are insured up to $100,000 by the Federal Deposit Insurance Corporation (FDIC). In the hierarchy of short-term interest rate yields, consumer checking and savings rates tend to be on the bottom because of their liquidity and safety and because of the inertia that prevents many savers from shopping for the higher yields available on alternative investments.

CERTIFICATES OF DEPOSIT

Certificates of deposit (CDs) are like savings accounts for which you receive a "certificate of deposit" from the bank or savings and loan company. Banks and S&Ls issue certificates of deposit to compete with Treasury bills and commercial paper for the investor's dollar. CDs that have maturities of one year or less are part of the money market.

CDs offer higher rates than bank money-market accounts, but you pay a price in penalties for early withdrawal of funds. Jumbo ($90,000–$100,000) certificates purchased through a broker are the only exception, and then only if the broker can sell the CD to another investor. When you tie up your funds until maturity, the CD becomes a nonliquid asset. This disadvantage is offset to some extent by FDIC deposit insurance.

You can often get a higher CD rate from your broker than your local bank or S&L, because your broker can shop nationally for the highest CD rate. You won't pay a fee for this service, because the bank pays the broker.

BANK MONEY-MARKET ACCOUNTS

You can open a money-market account with a minimum daily balance ranging from $500 to $5,000, depending on the bank. This is a highly liquid investment, because you can withdraw from the account at any time simply by writing a check, although most banks have restrictions regarding the number and frequency of checks written. These accounts offer relatively low yields because of their check-writing privileges, although the yields do tend to be a little higher than on savings accounts due to higher required minimum balances. They are also insured up to $100,000 by the FDIC.

Every day on page C2 *The Wall Street Journal* publishes **Consumer Rates** under **Interest Rates & Bonds** in the bottom left-hand corner of **Markets Line-up**. This is a listing prepared by Bankrate.com that reports on the average rate paid and charged by 100 banks on the previous day for a variety of accounts: *Credit card, Money market, Five-year CD, New-car loan, 30-year fixed-rate mortgage, 15-year fixed-rate mortgage, Jumbo mortgages* (over $333,700), *One-year ARM* (adjustable rate mortgage), and *home-equity loans*. See the excerpt below from the Thursday, January 15, 2004, *Journal*.

Consumer Rates

Benchmark personal borrowing rate vs. Federal-funds target rate, the interest rate on overnight loans between banks.

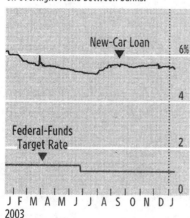

J F M A M J J A S O N D J
2003

	NAT'L AVG	WK'S CHG
Credit card	12.93%	−0.17
Money market ann. yield	1.33	−0.04
Five-year CD ann. yield	3.58	...
New-car loan	5.41	−0.10
30-yr. fixed-rate mortgage	5.32	−0.19
15-yr. fixed-rate mortgage	4.67	−0.15
Jumbo mortgages*	5.60	−0.14
One-year ARM	3.26	−0.13
Home-equity loan	6.85	−0.04

*Over $333,700

Most Competitive Rates

New-car loan

Ohio Central Savings.....................3.45%
Baltimore, MD, 800-678-6228

Pentagon Federal Credit Union..... 3.49%
Alexandria, VA, 800-247-5626

Telephone Credit Union of N.H......3.74%
Manchester, NH, 800-669-3381

The Grange Bank...........................3.88%
Columbus, OH, 800-270-8062

North Houston Bank......................4.00%
Houston, TX, 281-449-8282

Source: Bankrate.com

According to this report, *Money Market* accounts averaged 1.33 percent on Wednesday, January 14, 2004, and new-car loans averaged 5.41 percent.

On Wednesday of each week, in the *Journal*'s third section (check the index under Bankrate.com CDs), you can follow **Bankrate.com Money Markets and CDs** (see the excerpts below and on pages 337 and 338 from

BANKRATE.COM® Money Markets and CDs
Tuesday, February 24, 2004

Average Yields of Major Banks

Type	MMA	1-MO	2-MO	3-MO	6-MO	1-YR	2-YR	2.5-YR	5-YR
NEW YORK									
Savings	0.50	0.91	0.93	0.78	0.90	1.08	1.68	1.85	3.16
Jumbos	0.85	0.89	0.90	0.89	0.98	1.22	1.70	1.85	3.18
CALIFORNIA									
Savings	0.50	0.73	0.73	0.81	0.89	1.06	1.70	1.69	2.96
Jumbos	0.97	0.86	0.87	0.92	1.02	1.18	1.90	1.92	3.31
PENNSYLVANIA									
Savings	0.38	0.47	0.65	0.73	0.81	1.04	1.58	1.72	2.83
Jumbos	1.01	0.78	0.94	0.86	0.93	1.17	1.68	1.81	2.91
ILLINOIS									
Savings	0.51	0.60	0.60	0.75	0.88	1.08	1.62	1.83	3.18
Jumbos	0.81	0.75	0.75	0.85	0.97	1.19	1.86	2.08	3.36
TEXAS									
Savings	0.40	0.69	0.70	0.78	0.86	1.08	1.74	1.79	3.23
Jumbos	1.06	0.74	0.75	0.82	0.90	1.16	1.81	1.85	3.25
FLORIDA									
Savings	0.38	0.79	0.80	0.85	0.95	1.19	1.70	1.76	3.12
Jumbos	0.99	0.86	0.87	0.92	1.01	1.21	1.80	1.88	3.24
National Average									
Savings	0.44	0.70	0.71	0.79	0.91	1.14	1.72	1.81	3.07
Jumbos	0.92	0.80	0.82	0.88	1.00	1.23	1.83	1.92	3.21
WEEKLY CHANGE									
Savings	0.00	-0.01	-0.01	0.00	0.00	-0.01	-0.01	-0.01	-0.02
Jumbos	0.00	0.00	0.00	0.00	0.00	-0.01	0.00	-0.01	-0.01

The average three-month CD account earned → 0.79% in the week ending February 24, 2004.

High Yield Savings

	Phone	Min $ to Open	Ann % Yld		Phone	Min $ to Open	Ann % Yld
Money Market Account (MMA)				**6-Month CD**			
VirtualBank (3)	(877) 998-2265	$100	2.15	Stonebridge Bank (3)	(800) 807-1666	$500	2.00
Bank of Internet USA (4)	(877) 541-2634	$1,500	2.11	Nexity Bank (4)	(877) 738-6391	$1,000	1.95
National InterBank Inc (4)	(888) 580-0043	$1	2.05	IndyMac Bank, FSB (3)	(800) 734-6063	$5,000	1.90
MetLife Bank, NA (3)	(866) 226-5638	$5,000	2.01	Ascencia Bank (4)	(877) 369-2265	$500	1.86
Capital One, FSB (4)	(800) 603-1424	$10,000	2.00	New South Fed Svgs (3)	(866) 450-RATE	$5,000	1.85
1-Month CD				**1-Year CD**			
FirstBank of Puerto Rico (3)	(866) 822-8201	$10,000	1.30	Nexity Bank (4)	(877) 738-6391	$1,000	2.25
New South Fed Svgs (3)	(866) 450-RATE	$5,000	1.25	ING DIRECT (4)	(877) 469-0232	$1	2.22
Beal Bank (4)	(469) 467-5214	$25,000	1.25	Ascencia Bank (4)	(877) 369-2265	$500	2.21
Capital Crossing Bk (3)	(877) 976-7722	$2,500	1.21	Countrywide Bank (4)	(800) 479-4221	$10,000	2.21
Bank of Internet USA (4)	(877) 541-2634	$1,000	1.16	New South Fed Svgs (3)	(866) 450-RATE	$5,000	2.20
2-Month CD				**2-Year CD**			
FirstBank of Puerto Rico (3)	(866) 822-8201	$10,000	1.35	Countrywide Bank (4)	(800) 479-4221	$10,000	2.75
Beal Bank (4)	(469) 467-5214	$25,000	1.35	IndyMac Bank, FSB (3)	(800) 734-6063	$5,000	2.65
New South Fed Svgs (3)	(866) 450-RATE	$5,000	1.30	Bank of Internet USA (4)	(877) 541-2634	$1,000	2.63
Capital Crossing Bk (3)	(877) 976-7722	$2,500	1.21	Advanta Bank Corp. (4)	(800) 788-2632	$10,000	2.63
Capital One, FSB (4)	(800) 603-1424	$10,000	1.16	Capital One, FSB (4)	(800) 603-1424	$10,000	2.63
3-Month CD				**5-Year CD**			
Imperial Capital Bank (4)	(877) 906-4852	$2,000	1.76	Capital One, FSB (4)	(800) 603-1424	$10,000	4.25
IndyMac Bank, FSB (3)	(800) 734-6063	$5,000	1.75	Principal Bank (3)	(800) 672-3343	$1,000	4.21
FirstBank of Puerto Rico (3)	(866) 822-8201	$10,000	1.50	Advanta Bank Corp. (4)	(800) 788-2632	$10,000	4.17
State Farm Bank (2)	(877) 734-2265	$500	1.50	Bank of Internet USA (4)	(877) 541-2634	$1,000	4.16
Beal Bank (4)	(469) 467-5214	$1,000	1.50	Intervest Natl Bk (4)	(212) 218-8383	$2,500	4.10

Imperial Capital Bank → (pointing to Imperial Capital Bank)

the Wednesday, February 25, 2004, print *Journal*). This report lets you compare yields on a variety of money-market accounts and certificate-of-deposit (CD) accounts at different maturities with the average earned nationally (*National Average*) and in six key states: New York, California, Pennsylvania, Illinois, Texas, and Florida. You can also find the weekly change in the national average. In the week ended Tuesday, February 24, 2004, for instance, the average short-term three-month CD account earned 0.79 percent and was unchanged from the previous week. **High Yield Savings** figures represent the rates available at individual institutions for accounts requiring a small minimum balance (some as low as a dollar), and **High Yield Jumbos** are rates offered with $100,000 minimum balances. For instance, as you can see on pages 336 and 338, although 0.79 percent was the national average for three-month CDs, Imperial Capital Bank paid 1.76 percent.

Every Wednesday, accompanying the **Bankrate.com Money Markets and CDs** report, *The Wall Street Journal* publishes a brief article summarizing

High Yield Jumbos

	Phone	Min $ to Open	Ann % Yld		Phone	Min $ to Open	Ann % Yld
Money Market Account (MMA)				**6-Month CD**			
National InterBank Inc (4)	(888) 580-0043	$100,000	2.05	Nexity Bank (4)	(877) 738-6391	$100,000	1.95
Corus Bank (4)	(800) 989-5101	$100,000	2.01	IndyMac Bank, FSB (3)	(800) 734-6063	$100,000	1.90
MetLife Bank, NA (3)	(866) 226-5638	$100,000	2.01	Ascencia Bank (4)	(877) 369-2265	$100,000	1.86
Capital One, FSB (4)	(800) 603-1424	$100,000	2.00	New South Fed Svgs (3)	(866) 450-RATE	$100,000	1.85
GMAC Bank (4)	(866) 246-2265	$100,000	2.00	Capital One Bank (4)	(800) 603-1424	$100,000	1.83
1-Month CD				**1-Year CD**			
FirstBank of Puerto Rico (3)	(866) 822-8201	$100,000	1.30	Countrywide Bank (4)	(800) 479-4221	$100,000	2.31
Beal Bank (4)	(469) 467-5214	$100,000	1.25	Nexity Bank (4)	(877) 738-6391	$100,000	2.25
New South Fed Svgs (3)	(866) 450-RATE	$100,000	1.25	ING DIRECT (4)	(877) 469-0232	$100,000	2.22
Capital Crossing Bk (3)	(877) 976-7722	$100,000	1.21	Capital One Bank (4)	(800) 603-1424	$100,000	2.21
First Trade Union Bk (3)	(800) 242-0272	$100,000	1.20	Ascencia Bank (4)	(877) 369-2265	$100,000	2.21
2-Month CD				**2-Year CD**			
FirstBank of Puerto Rico (3)	(866) 822-8201	$100,000	1.35	Countrywide Bank (4)	(800) 479-4221	$100,000	2.85
Beal Bank (4)	(469) 467-5214	$100,000	1.35	Capital One Bank (4)	(800) 603-1424	$100,000	2.65
New South Fed Svgs (3)	(866) 450-RATE	$100,000	1.30	IndyMac Bank, FSB (3)	(800) 734-6063	$100,000	2.65
Capital One Bank (4)	(800) 603-1424	$100,000	1.21	State Farm Bank (2)	(877) 734-2265	$100,000	2.65
Capital Crossing Bk (3)	(877) 976-7722	$100,000	1.21	Bank of Internet USA (4)	(877) 541-2634	$100,000	2.63
3-Month CD				**5-Year CD**			
IndyMac Bank, FSB (3)	(800) 734-6063	$100,000	1.75	Capital One Bank (4)	(800) 603-1424	$100,000	4.29
State Farm Bank (2)	(877) 734-2265	$100,000	1.60	Countrywide Bank (4)	(800) 479-4221	$100,000	4.20
FirstBank of Puerto Rico (3)	(866) 822-8201	$100,000	1.50	Bank of Internet USA (4)	(877) 541-2634	$100,000	4.16
Capital One Bank (4)	(800) 603-1424	$100,000	1.50	MBNA America Bank (5)	(877) 229-5565	$100,000	4.10
Beal Bank (4)	(469) 467-5214	$100,000	1.50	Intervest Natl Bk (4)	(212) 218-8383	$100,000	4.10

Accounts are federally insured up to $100,000 per person. Yields are based on method of compounding and rate stated for the lowest required opening deposit to earn interest. CD figures are for fixed rates only. **MMA:** Allows 6 third party transfers per month, 3 of which may be checks. Rates are subject to change.

Explanation of Ratings: Safe & Sound℠, (561) 627-7330 ext. 1410, evaluates the financial condition of federally insured institutions and assigns a rank of 1 - 5 (number in parentheses) based on 3rd quarter 2003 data from federal regulators. Information is believed to be reliable, but not guaranteed. A rank of 5 indicates the most desirable performance. A "U" rating indicates that an institution is too new to rate and is not an indication of financial strength or weakness.

Source: Bankrate.com®, a publication of Bankrate, Inc., North Palm Beach, FL 33408 Internet: www.bankrate.com

Imperial Capital Bank paid 1.76% on its three-month CDs in the week ending February 24, 2004.

3-Month CD			
Imperial Capital Bank (4)	(877) 906-4852	$2,000	1.76
IndyMac Bank, FSB (3)	(800) 734-6063	$5,000	1.75
FirstBank of Puerto Rico (3)	(866) 822-8201	$10,000	1.50
State Farm Bank (2)	(877) 734-2265	$500	1.50
Beal Bank (4)	(469) 467-5214	$1,000	1.50

certificate of deposit yields for the week. See the example below from the February 25, 2005, article.

Banks and S&Ls created the money-market accounts to stem withdrawals of funds lost to competing money-market mutual funds offering higher rates than savings accounts. Although interest paid by the money-market accounts fluctuates with short-term market rates, these accounts do not enjoy yields as high as those paid by money-market mutual funds. Your account will, however, be insured by the FDIC, which is not the case with money-market mutual funds. Remember: The smaller the risk, the smaller the reward.

CD Yields Were Lower Or Unchanged in Week

NEW YORK—Yields on certificates of deposit were unchanged or lower in the latest week. The average yield on six-month "jumbo" CDs, which typically require deposits of $95,000 or more, was unchanged at 1%, according to Bankrate. com. The yield on five-year jumbos was 3.22%, down from 3.24%, the information service said.

The average yields on small-denomination "savings" CDs were lower. The average six-month yield was unchanged at 0.91%, Bankrate.com said. The average two-year CD yield was unchanged at 1.71%, and the average five-year yield was 3.09%, down from 3.10%.

MONEY-MARKET MUTUAL FUNDS

Investment companies establish mutual funds to pool the capital of many investors and thus create a large shared portfolio of investments. (Recall the earlier discussions of mutual funds in Chapter 13.) Individuals invest in mutual funds by purchasing shares in the fund, and the return on the portfolio is passed through to the investor according to the number of shares held. An enormous variety of mutual funds are available, designed for different types of investors and bearing a wide variety of yields.

Money-market mutual funds invest principally in short-term investment instruments such as Treasury bills, commercial paper, bank certificates of deposit, bankers' acceptances, and other liquid assets denominated in large amounts and therefore unavailable to the small investor. A money-market mutual fund permits you to participate in the return on a variety of short-term investments and enjoy the benefits of diversification without employing large sums of your own capital. You also take advantage of the professional management skills of the investment company.

Most money-market mutual funds are *no-load funds*. They do not charge a sales commission fee, because they are directly marketed by the investment company. However, "management" fees are subtracted from the yield you receive. Money-market mutual funds are issued and trade at a par value of one dollar. The dividends you receive are expressed as percentage yield.

Although money-market funds sell their shares for a dollar each, most have minimum investment requirements ranging from $1,000 to $25,000. As an incentive, many money-market funds also have check-writing privileges. Despite the fact that these funds are not insured by the federal government, they are safe and liquid investments whose yields tend to be higher than the yields on bank money-market accounts.

In the early 1980s, when the Federal Reserve applied a chokehold on the economy and interest rates climbed to the sky, money-market mutual funds became popular among investors and savers. Since banks and S&Ls were, at the time, prohibited from offering above-passbook rates to small depositors, huge sums poured into the money-market funds as their yields climbed above the legal passbook minimums. When the interest rate ceilings were removed from small denomination accounts at banks and S&Ls, and these accounts began to offer rates that moved with market conditions (and thus competed with the money-market mutual funds), some investors deserted the money-market funds. Once again, however, money-market fund (not insured) rates generally outdo those at the banks (insured) and consequently remain very popular.

Money-Market Funds Increase

NEW YORK—Money-market mutual-fund assets rose $15.27 billion to $2.039 trillion, up from a revised $2.024 trillion, in the week ended Wednesday, according to the Investment Company Institute.

Assets of the 1,003 retail-class shares decreased $462.2 million to $874.3 billion, the institute said. Among retail-class shares, assets of the 653 taxable shares fell by $2.21 billion to $679.82 billion, while assets of the 350 tax-exempt shares increased $1.74 billion to $194.48 billion.

Assets of the 1,092 institutional-class shares increased by $15.73 billion to $1.165 trillion. Among institutional-class shares, assets of the 858 taxable shares grew $12.36 billion to $1.056 trillion, while

Money-Market Funds

Assets, in trillions of dollars

Monthly average / Weekly

$2.200 / $2.06
2.150 / 2.05
2.100 / 2.04
2.050 / 2.03
2.000 / 2.02

2003   2004   10 17 24 31 7
                        March   April

Source: Investment Company Institute

assets of the 234 tax-exempt shares increased $3.37 billion to $108.41 billion.

Each Friday in the third section, *The Wall Street Journal* publishes an article on *money-fund assets*. The report from the Friday, April 9, 2004, print *Journal* (see above) informs you that money-fund assets rose in the latest week.

Money-Market Mutual Funds, published every Thursday in the *Journal*, lists the most popular money-market mutual funds (see Money Market Funds listed in the index on page C1) and provides several statistics for each: the average maturity (in days) of the investments in the fund, the 7-day yield for the week (average yield), and the total assets in millions of dollars as of the previous day. See the example from the Thursday, April 8, 2004, print *Journal* on page 341. You can track the performance of your money-market mutual fund and most others with this report.

TREASURY BILLS

Treasury bills (T-bills) constitute about a quarter of the total national debt (see Chapter 15's discussion of Treasury bonds), and this huge dollar volume makes Treasury bills one of the most important short-term investment instruments. The U.S. Treasury borrows by selling bills at auction (primary market) every Monday in New York, and in the following day's *Journal* you will find a summary of the auction's activity at the end of the **Credit Markets** article (see the indexes at the front of the first and third sections). An

MONEY MARKET MUTUAL FUNDS

EXPLANATORY NOTES

The following quotations, collected by the National Association of Securities Dealers Inc., represent the average of annualized yields and dollar-weighted portfolio maturities ending Wednesday, April 7, 2004. Yields don't include capital gains or losses.
a-Actual return to shareholders may vary due to capital gain or losses.
b-Account size varies due to fixed charges. c-Primarily federally tax-exempt securities. f-As of previous day. z-Unavailable.

FUND	AVG. MAT.	7 DAY YIELD	ASSETS
AAGovSel	57	.96	138
AAL MnyMktInstl	57	.54	121
AALMny	57	.24	270
AAdMileP	53	.05	430
AAdvGovP	57	.10	7
AAdvMMPlat	8	.10	3
ABN AmroGvtS	59	.42	41
ABN Amro Gvtl	59	.74	409
ABN AmroMMS	43	.34	140
ABN AmroPrY	63	.91	2019
ABN AmroPrYS	63	.66	41
ABN Amro Trsl	57	.60	376
ABN AmroInvN	48	.55	216
AIM MMCshRes	41	.55	742
AIMMMInv	41	.80	377
AXPCshMgdB p	63	.06	194
AXPCshMgtY	63	.44	219
AXPCashMgtA	63	.31	3828
AZMunCTIns	19	.51	80
AccUSGov	79	.61	1087
ActAsInsGv	44	.94	312
ActivaMM	63	.30	31
ActAsInst	50	.89	813
ActiveAstGv	48	.47	1227
ActiveAstMny	55	.67	22616
AlgerMM	52	.21	93
AllBrExRsvA	61	.01	287
AlBerExRsAd	61	.45	309
AllBrnExRsC	61	.01	43
AllBerCpRes	73	.13	11131
AllBernGvRs	78	.08	7015
AllBerMuPA	22	.06	82
AllBerTrRes	53	.05	506
AllialRGovA	56	.87	426
AllialRGovB	56	.77	333
AllialRGovC p	56	.62	180
AllialRPrimA	71	.89	1117
AllialRPrimB	71	.79	1126
AllialRPriC p	71	.64	452
AllialRTresA	70	.84	55
AllialRTreasB	70	.74	45
AllialRTreasC p	70	.59	39
AllialResTrstA	11	.61	1135
AllBrMnyRes	57	.09	2075
AmPerTrsl	20	.75	185
AmAAdMMI	53	.87	92
AAMMktCM	57	.89	23
AmPerCsh	65	.52	687
AmPerTrs	27	.30	609
AmSouthPrHl p	46	.33	56
ASOTrResA	38	.25	91
ASOTrResT	38	.30	110
Ambassador	37	.74	266
AmAAdGvP	57	.56	26
AmAAdMMP	53	.59	112
AmAAdGvM	57	.44	12
AmAAdMMM	53	.59	49
AmC CapPr	77	.55	2930
AmC GvAg	67	.63	490
AmCPrMM	65	.68	489
AmC Prime	68	.53	2175
AmIndMonyMk S	58	.52	69
AAMMktSel	53	.99	5081
AmSkmmC	54	...	39
AmSkmmA p	54	.50	96
AmSkmmB	54	...	90

FUND	AVG. MAT.	7 DAY YIELD	ASSETS
CIGNA MMF Inst	26	.60	226
CIGNA MMF Ret	26	.10	272
CNICATxExIns	27	.42	123
CNIGovtA p	31	.22	1866
CNIGvtMMS p	31	.12	203
CNI GvtMMI	31	.44	50
CNIPrMMA p	38	.22	164
CNIPrMMS p	38	.12	101
CNIPrimeInst	38	.44	304
CS CashResMM	81	.65	69
CS MuniMoney	45	.20	13
CS US Govt	71	.32	13
CadreAffMM	59	.41	29
CadreAffUS	56	.36	11
CadreLiqMM	59	.55	22
CadreResMM	59	.91	64
CadreResUS	56	.83	169
CalvCshRInstPr	45	.92	235
CalvFtGv	56	.28	180
CalvSoc	53	.29	172
CashAcctIns	71	.90	136
CashAcct Prem	71	.16	2973
CashMgtA	25	.67	7297
CashMgtB t	25	.10	131
CashEqv	61	.28	724
CshEqGv	72	.13	373
CshTrGv	49	.05	462
CshTrPr	52	.11	4437
CshTrTreas	44	.04	362
CshTrIl	46	.21	257
CdMny	34	...	...
CentnGv	61	.34	1515
Centen	46	.39	22175
CitiFndPUST	55	.50	525
CitFInsCshRsS p	50	.75	468
CitFInsCashRs	50	.90	627
CitFCashRs	49	.40	1973
CitFInstLiq	49	.94	20358
CitFUSTr	55	.70	972
CitFPrmLq	49	.70	1093
CitFUSTrs	55	.25	280
CitiznSelPrB	44	.62	263
CitiznSelPrC p	44	.37	44
CitiznSelTreA	51	.76	76
CitiznSelTreB	51	.51	201
CitizenSelPrA	44	.87	67
ClassCshMgt	51	.86	2478
ClassUSGv	48	.82	984
ClassicUSTr	5	.69	411
ColDin f	50	.30	723
ColumbMMA	50	.38	237
ColumbMMB	50	.10	82
ColumbMMC t	50	.10	12
ColumbMMZ	50	.38	248
ColumMuniZ	29	.48	80
CCMTrOSrv p	44	.26	725
CCMGovAd p	41	.28	45
CCMGovInst	41	.53	126
CG CapGov	57	.43	105
CortIdGn	78	.15	1253
CortIdUS	65	.06	188
CS Gov C	86	.67	28
CS GovA	86	.92	22
CS PrimeC	53	.66	98
CS PrimeB	53	.81	347
CSInstPrmeA	53	.91	247

FUND	AVG. MAT.	7 DAY YIELD	ASSETS
FITPrMMII	47	.49	43
FLMunincB	51	.35	58
FedTreasObSS	43	.59	4956
FdShtUS	46	.62	153
FedMstr	64	.67	166
FedMIMuCshIS	40	.73	52
FldAdvTreasC	53	.11	188
FldAdvTreasC	53	.11	108
FidGvRes	85	.76	2118
FidPrimeDlyl	57	.44	4626
FidRetGov	85	.69	4874
FidRetMM	82	.75	15739
FidSpGov	83	.68	594
FidSpMM	84	.76	5698
FidSpUSTr	84	.61	2217
FidTryDlyl	53	.37	1185
FidSelMM	84	.79	629
FidTryCR	53	.13	851
FThrdUSTrSl	48	.74	85
FThrdUSTrTr	48	.57	137
FTInsGovl	56	.86	244
FThrdUSTrPf	48	.67	1145
FThrInsGvPf	56	.71	295
FThrdInsGv	56	.61	81
FInvTrUSGvl	51	.85	258
FInvTrUSTrs	48	.66	43
FinSqFed	50	.84	7279
FinSq Gov	51	.90	3648
FinSq POF	54	.92	26941
FinSqTrsy	54	.76	1204
FinSq TOF	43	.85	3752
FinSq MMF	54	.92	9819
FITPrMonMktl	47	.89	112
FstAmGvObD	47	.49	804
FstAmGvObY	47	.64	1939
FstAmTrObD	38	.46	5406
FstAmGvObA p	47	.34	145
FstAmPrObA	54	.36	1272
FstAmPrObY	54	.66	5704
FstAmPrObD	54	.51	729
FstAmTrObA p	38	.31	1255
FstAmPrObY	38	.61	3402
FirstCshRsvl	71	.84	30
FirstCshRsvC	71	.59	209
FtInvCs	68	.39	173
First Muni I	47	.81	51
First USGv	55	.85	128
FlexInst	82	.92	34
FlexFd	82	.78	173
FrnkIFT	60	.73	3407
FrkMnyC	60	.04	61
FrkIFTGS f	38	.69	54
FrkFdl bf	38	.22	103
FremntMM	79	.66	576
FrkMny	60	.43	1639
FstAmGvObZ	47	.89	38
FstAmPrObZ	54	.94	2720
FstAmPrObl	54	.74	1477
FstAmTreResA	37	.12	1773
GEMnyMktA	53	.69	237
GabelliUST	70	.67	973
GalaxyGvRes p	73	.08	185
GalaxyGvR	36	.41	302
GalaxyGvTr	36	.55	247
GalaxyInUSTr	51	.78	3705
GalaxyInstMM	49	.94	4316
GalaxyMM R	48	.46	531
GalaxyMM T	48	.70	1108
GalaxyPRes p	60	.11	3900
GalaxTrR	49	.36	495
GalaxyTrsTr	49	.51	268
GartmrMMPr	72	.52	431
GartmrMMInst	72	.58	1140
GnGvSec	86	.32	524
GeneralB p	89	.15	5734

FUND	AVG. MAT.	7 DAY YIELD	ASSETS
JPMorganFed	48	.34	282
JPMorFedAgcy	48	.78	364
JPMorgFedPr	48	.59	1218
JPMorgGovt	49	.50	2842
JPMorgGvtAg	49	.83	3738
JPMorgGvtPr	49	.64	562
JPMPrCshMgt	51	.15	78
JPMorgPrm	51	.53	3877
JPMorgPrAgcy	51	.86	12575
JPMorgPrmPr	51	.67	5595
JPMorgTrPlus	55	.45	769
JPMorgTrPlAg	55	.79	1033
JPMorgTrPls	55	.59	1091
JPMFedInst	48	.84	1479
JPMPrinst	51	.92	26226
JPMPrRsv	51	.42	210
JPMPrSel	51	.68	707
JPMTrPlusIns	55	.84	566
JPMTrPlRsv	55	.34	219
JanusGovt	33	.51	248
JanusGvtInst	33	.95	562
JansInstCshRs	54	1.03	2153
Janus MM	27	.57	1755
JanusMMInst	27	.99	6900
JHan MMB	36	.11	87
JHanMMA	36	.16	211
LIR PremMM	24	.16	1154
LeaderMoneyMkt	62	.61	123
LEADER Swp	62	.36	12
LeadrMMInA	62	.11	87
LegMUS	61	.37	494
LegMCR f	58	.41	2203
LgcyFedMonyTr	56	.57	84
LibtyUSB	47	.01	96
LibtyUS	47	.17	337
Liq Ins Gv	1	.69	117
LiqInstSec	1	.66	110
LiqCshTr	2	.89	176
LordAbUSGB	31	.20	26
LordAbbUS A	31	.21	283
LuthBroMMA	58	.45	467
MFS CashA	52	.68	98
MFSCashC p	52	.05	93
MFSGovMonA	27	.66	120
MFSMonMkA	43	.71	837
MTBInsPrMM	52	.66	257
MTB MM S p	49	.16	55
MTB MM A	49	.37	969
MTB MM I	49	.66	622
MTB MM II	49	.59	383
MTB TrMMA	50	.30	145
MTB TrsMMI	50	.43	282
MTB TrsMMII	50	.36	376
MTB TrsMM S	50	.20	13
MTB USGvII	54	.60	938
MTB USGvA	54	.44	...
MTB USGvI	54	.67	1264
MainStay A	66	.40	179
MainStay B	66	.40	347
MainstyCsRsl	70	.61	209
ManagersMM	51	.52	38
Marshall A	49	.37	94
Marshall I	49	.92	1119
Marshall Y	49	.67	2081
MassMutIMMA	55	.10	76
MassMutIMML	55	.29	56
MassMutIMMS	55	.54	247
MassMutIMMY	55	.44	82
McMorPrin Pres	80	.84	138
MellonMMkM	47	.74	408
MerrUSGvPr	79	.97	148
MercantIGvt	52	.67	429
MercantIPrim	53	.70	680
ML CBAMon	71	.28	181
ML CMAGv	63	.47	666
ML CMAMn	68	.55	10815

example drawn from the Tuesday, January 27, 2004, print edition of the *Journal* appears below.

Treasury bills are sold on a discount basis. Buyers pay less than the $10,000 face value (par value), the amount they will receive when the bill matures and is redeemed by the U.S. Treasury. If bidding is strong and the price is high, the effective rate of interest will be low, and vice versa.

To understand how this works, place yourself in the role of a buyer and study the example below. If you pay $9,750 for a bill maturing in 91 days (about a quarter of a year), your effective annual yield is approximately 10 percent. Remember, $250 in a quarter-year is the equivalent of $1,000 in a year, or 10 percent of a $10,000 base. (Use $10,000 as the base for calculating the discount rate, rather than $9,750, because Treasury bills' yields are usually quoted on a discount basis; that is, the discount—$250—is measured against face value—$10,000.) If strong bidding drives the price to $9,875, your yield falls to 5 percent. If weak bidding or selling pressure permits the price to fall to $9,500, the effective yield rises to 20 percent. The more you pay for the Treasury bill, the lower your yield, and vice versa.

Face (redemption) value	$10,000	$10,000	$10,000
Selling price *Note: prices falling*	$9,875	$9,750	$9,500
Discount (difference)	$125	$250	$500
Approximate yield (discount rate) *Note: yield rising*	5%	10%	20%

Take a moment to review the method used to compute the discount rate in the bottom row of the above table. The following calculations show how the 10 percent rate was obtained. Discount rate (yield) = Discount divided

---

On Monday January 26, 2004, the U.S. Treasury auctioned 13-week bills in the primary market at a price of $9,977.50 and a discount of $22.50 for a discount rate of 0.890% and a coupon equivalent of 0.907%.

AUCTION RESULTS

Here are the results of the Treasury auction of 13-week and 26-week bills; All bids are awarded at a single price at the market-clearing yield. Rates are determined by the difference between that price and the face value.

	13-Week	26-Week
Applications	$33,553,128,000	$33,566,970,000
Accepted bids	$18,000,028,000	$16,000,150,000
Accepted noncomp	$1,377,319,000	$1,135,879,000
Accepted frgn non	$459,500,000	$858,200,000
Auction price (Rate)	99.775 (0.890%)	99.517 (0.955%)
Coupon equivalent	0.907%	0.976%
Bids at market yield	54.90%	69.42%
Cusip number	912795PW5	912795QV6

Both issues are dated Jan 29. The 13-week bills mature April 29, 2004, and the 26-week bills mature July 29, 2004.

by par value × Time factor multiplier (which is needed to generate the annual rate).

$$\begin{matrix} \text{Approximate} \\ \text{discount rate} \\ \text{(yield)} \end{matrix} = \frac{\text{Discount}}{\text{Face or par value}} \times 4 \quad \begin{matrix} \text{(Because 91 days} \\ \text{are about a quarter} \\ \text{of a 365-day year)} \end{matrix}$$

$$= \frac{\$250}{\$10,000} \times 4 = 2.5\% \times 4 = 10\%$$

The true discount-rate formula is very close to this approximation. The "time factor multiplier" is somewhat different, because the "year" is 360 days. Returning to the example, the discount rate would be calculated as follows:

$$\text{Discount rate} = \frac{\text{Discount}}{\text{Par value}} \times \text{Time multiplier}$$

$$= \frac{\$250}{\$10,000} \times \frac{360}{91}$$

$$= 0.0989$$

$$= 9.89\%$$

You can see that the true discount rate of 9.89 is less than the 10 percent approximation calculated above, because the time multiplier (360/91) is less than 4.

The discount rate is only an approximation of the true yield to maturity or coupon equivalent. In the first place, the purchase price of the T-bill was $9,750, not $10,000. In the fraction below, $9,750 replaces $10,000. And second, a year is 365 days, not 360. Thus, the correct time multiplier is 365/91.

Now calculate the actual yield or coupon equivalent, called the investment yield to maturity, for the same example.

$$\text{Yield to maturity} = \frac{\text{Discount}}{\text{Purchase price}} \times \text{Time factor}$$

$$= \frac{\$250}{\$9,750} \times \frac{365}{91}$$

$$= 0.1029$$

$$= 10.29\%$$

You can see that the discount rate of 9.89 percent is less than the true yield of 10.29 percent, because the discount is expressed as a percentage of the purchase price rather than par, and the year is calculated at 365 rather than 360 days.

Why are T-bills quoted on a discount rather than true-yield basis? Because the arithmetic is much easier to deal with, and that was important years ago before the advent of data-processing equipment.

Now that you understand the relationship between the discount rate and the yield to maturity (coupon equivalent), look again at the illustration on page 342 from the Tuesday, January 27, 2004, *Journal*. Potential buyers submitted $33,553,128,000 in bids, of which the Treasury accepted $18,000,028,000. The auction provided $9,977.50 (99.775 percent of face value) for each $10,000 bill auctioned on Monday, January 26, 2004, for a discount of $22.50, a discount rate of 0.89 percent, and a coupon-equivalent yield of 0.907 percent. Note that the Treasury accepted 54.90 percent of the bids for the 13-week bill. (The remaining bids fell below the $9,977.50 price and were not accepted.) Also, $1,377,319,000 worth of domestic bids were accepted noncompetitively, meaning the buyers were willing to accept whatever price the auction generated. Finally, the Treasury accepted $459,500,000 of foreign noncompetitive bids.

Here is how you calculate the discount rate using the Treasury-auction figures on page 342.

$$\text{Discount rate} = \frac{\text{Discount}}{\text{Par value}} \times \text{Time multiplier}$$

$$= \frac{\$22.50 \text{ (i.e. } \$10,000 - \$9977.50)}{\$10,000} \times \frac{360}{91}$$

$$= .008901 = 0.89\%$$

You can also compute the true (coupon-equivalent) yield as follows:

$$\text{Yield to maturity} = \frac{\text{Discount}}{\text{Purchase price}} \times \text{Time factor}$$

$$= \frac{\$22.50}{\$9977.50} \times \frac{366 \text{ (leap year!)}}{91}$$

$$= 0.009069854 = 0.907\%$$

Your motivation for buying Treasury bills is probably quite simple: You have idle cash on which you wish to earn an interest return. If you and all other bidders for Treasury bills have ample funds and are eager to buy, you will drive the price close to $10,000 and earn a low rate of return. If you and all other bidders do not have ample funds, you can be enticed only by a very low price for the right to receive $10,000 in 91 days, and you will earn a high rate of return.

Now, this discussion has been presented as if you could participate in the bidding for Treasury bills. Well, you can't. The auction is conducted in New York by the Fed, acting as the Treasury's agent, and bidding is conducted by large firms that deal in, and make a market for, Treasury bills. They bid for the bills at the weekly Monday auction (primary market), so they can resell them at a markup on any business day (secondary market).

You *can* purchase Treasury bills online by visiting www.treasury direct.gov, but you'll have to bid noncompetitively at the average rate (discount) established at the New York auction (for instance, the 0.89 percent discount rate and 0.907 yield in the example on page 342). Note that the Treasury accepted $1,377,319,000 of domestic bids noncompetitively (and $459,500,000 of foreign noncompetitive bids) on Monday, January 26, 2004. These were bids made directly to the Fed and Treasury by individuals and small institutions who could not participate in the auction.

If you purchase a Treasury bill from the Treasury, you must hold it to maturity, which is not the case if you have purchased it from your bank or broker in the secondary market. Your bank or broker can sell it on the open or secondary market for you at any time, but be prepared to pay a flat fee of $25 to $50 per transaction. In order to gain clients with large assets, however, some brokerage houses do not charge a fee if an investor purchases more than $100,000 of Treasury bills.

The Wall Street Journal reports on activity in the secondary market each day, under the heading **Treasury Bonds, Notes & Bills**. Find this table by using the front-page index or the index on the first page of Section C.

Look at the excerpts from the Monday, February 2, 2004, print edition on pages 346 and 347. The data represents quotations for Friday, January 30, 2004. Keep in mind that these bills are auctioned on Mondays, issued on Thursdays, and mature 13 weeks later (also on a Thursday). Thus, using the report in the February 2, 2004, *Journal*, you know that the latest (bellwether) 91-day bill included in the report was auctioned on Monday, January 26, 2004, and issued on Thursday, January 29, 2004. It matured 13 weeks later on April 29, 2004. (Note the boldface type for the 13- and 26-week maturity dates.)

On January 30, 2004, that bill carried a discount rate (bid) of 0.90 percent. This figure is located in the third column, headed *Bid*. Buyers (bid-

Treasury Bonds, Notes and Bills

January 30, 2004

Explanatory Notes

Representative Over-the-Counter quotation based on transactions of $1 million or more. Treasury bond, note and bill quotes are as of mid-afternoon. Colons in bid-and-asked quotes represent 32nds; 101:01 means 101 1/32. Net changes in 32nds. n-Treasury note. i-Inflation-Indexed issue. Treasury bill quotes in hundredths, quoted on terms of a rate of discount. Days to maturity calculated from settlement date. All yields are to maturity and based on the asked quote. Latest 13-week and 26-week bills are boldfaced. For bonds callable prior to maturity, yields are computed to the earliest call date for issues quoted above par and to the maturity date for issues below par. *When issued.

Source: eSpeed/Cantor Fitzgerald

U.S. Treasury strips as of 3 p.m. Eastern time, also based on transactions of $1 million or more. Colons in bid and asked quotes represent 32nds; 99:01 means 99 1/32. Net changes in 32nds. Yields calculated on the asked quotation. ci-stripped coupon interest. bp-Treasury bond, stripped principal. np-Treasury note, stripped principal. For bonds callable prior to maturity, yields are computed to the earliest call date for issues quoted above par and to the maturity date for issues below par.

Source: Bear, Steams & Co. via Street Software Technology Inc.

Government Bonds & Notes

RATE	MATURITY MO/YR	BID	ASKED	CHG	ASK YLD
4.750	Feb 04n	100:03	100:04	-2	0.75
5.875	Feb 04n	100:05	100:06	-1	0.55
3.000	Feb 04n	100:04	100:05	-1	0.67
3.625	Mar 04n	100:13	100:14	-1	0.85
3.375	Apr 04n	100:18	100:19	-1	0.91
5.250	May 04n	101:06	101:07	-1	0.92
7.250	May 04n	101:24	101:25	-1	0.92
12.375	May 04	103:06	103:07	-3	0.94
3.250	May 04n	100:23	100:24	...	0.88
2.875	Jun 04n	100:24	100:25	...	0.96
2.250	Jul 04n	100:18	100:19	-1	1.01
2.125	Aug 04n	100:19	100:20	...	1.03
6.000	Aug 04n	102:19	102:20	-2	1.04
7.250	Aug 04n	103:08	103:09	-2	1.06
13.750	Aug 04	106:23	106:24	-3	1.04
1.875	Sep 04n	100:16	100:17	...	1.06
2.125	Oct 04n	100:22	100:23	-1	1.13
5.875	Nov 04n	103:20	103:21	-1	1.15
7.875	Nov 04n	105:06	105:07	-2	1.14
11.625	Nov 04	108:03	108:04	-3	1.15
2.000	Nov 04n	100:21	100:22	...	1.16
1.750	Dec 04n	100:15	100:16	...	1.18
1.625	Jan 05n	100:12	100:13	-1	1.20
7.500	Feb 05n	106:13	106:14	-2	1.21
1.500	Feb 05n	100:08	100:09	...	1.22
1.625	Mar 05n	100:11	100:12	-1	1.28
1.625	Apr 05n	100:10	100:11	...	1.33
6.500	May 05n	106:15	106:16	-1	1.36
6.750	May 05n	106:25	106:26	-1	1.36
12.000	May 05	113:17	113:18	...	1.29
1.250	May 05n	99:25	99:26	...	1.38
1.125	Jun 05n	99:18	99:19	1	1.42
1.500	Jul 05n	100:00	100:01	1	1.48
6.500	Aug 05n	107:16	107:17	...	1.51
10.750	Aug 05	114:00	114:00	...	1.49
2.000	Aug 05n	100:21	100:22	...	1.55
1.625	Sep 05n	100:01	100:02	1	1.59
1.625	Oct 05n	99:30	99:31	1	1.63
5.750	Nov 05n	107:04	107:05	...	1.66
5.875	Nov 05n	107:11	107:12	...	1.66
1.875	Nov 05n	100:09	100:10	1	1.69
[illegible]	Dec 05n	100:06	100:07	2	1.76
1.87[illegible]	**Jan 06n**	**100:02**	**100:03**	**6**	**1.82**
5.625	Feb 06n	107:19	107:20	1	1.79
9.375	Feb 06	115:02	115:03	...	1.79
2.000	May 06n	100:03	100:04	2	1.94
4.625	May 06n	105:29	105:30	2	1.95
6.875	May 06n	110:29	110:30	1	1.95
7.000	Jul 06n	111:24	111:25	2	2.05
2.375	Aug 06n	100:21	100:22	2	2.09
6.500	Oct 06n	111:07	111:08	2	2.18
2.625	Nov 06n	101:00	101:01	2	2.23
3.500	Nov 06n	103:12	103:13	2	2.22
3.375	Jan 07i	108:25	108:26	3	0.37
6.250	Feb 07n	111:12	111:13	3	2.34
6.625	May 07n	113:01	113:02	2	2.45
4.375	May 07n	105:30	105:31	3	2.47
3.250	Aug 07n	102:06	102:07	3	2.58
6.125	Aug 07n	111:30	111:31	4	2.56
3.000	Nov 07n	101:04	101:05	5	2.68
3.625	Jan 08i	111:08	111:09	5	0.72
3.000	Feb 08n	100:24	100:25	5	2.79
5.500	Feb 08n	110:12	110:13	4	2.76
2.625	May 08n	98:28	98:29	5	2.89
5.625	May 08n	111:00	111:00	5	2.88
3.250	Aug 08n	101:00	101:01	5	3.00
3.125	Sep 08n	100:11	100:12	6	3.04
3.125	Oct 08n	100:07	100:08	5	3.06
3.375	Nov 08n	101:07	101:08	6	3.09
4.750	Nov 08n	107:13	107:14	5	3.07
3.375	Dec 08n	101:03	101:04	5	3.12
3.250	**Jan 09n**	**100:14**	**100:15**	**6**	**3.15**
3.875	Jan 09i	113:28	113:29	7	0.99
5.500	May 09n	111:12	111:13	6	3.14
9.125	May 09	102:08	102:09	-1	1.02
6.000	Aug 09n	113:19	113:20	6	3.28
10.375	Nov 09	107:02	107:03	-1	1.24
4.250	Jan 10i	117:11	117:12	8	1.21
6.500	Feb 10n	116:19	116:20	7	3.43
11.750	Feb 10	110:24	110:25	...	1.22
10.000	May 10	110:26	110:27	...	1.42
5.750	Aug 10n	112:22	112:23	9	3.55
12.750	Nov 10	119:06	119:07	...	1.74
3.500	Jan 11i	113:24	113:25	9	1.41
5.000	Feb 11n	108:02	108:03	10	3.68
13.875	May 11	126:12	126:13	...	1.98
5.000	Aug 11n	107:25	107:26	11	3.80
14.000	Nov 11	131:19	131:20	5	2.21
3.375	Jan 12i	113:10	113:11	13	1.58
4.875	Feb 12n	106:22	106:23	13	3.89
3.000	Jul 12i	110:14	110:15	12	1.67
4.375	Aug 12n	102:28	102:29	11	3.97
4.000	Nov 12n	100:00	100:00	12	4.00
10.375	Nov 12	127:13	127:14	4	2.69
3.875	Feb 13n	98:26	98:27	12	4.03
3.625	May 13n	97:01	97:02	10	4.01
1.875	Jul 13i	100:22	100:23	12	1.79
4.250	Aug 13n	101:05	101:06	13	4.10
12.000	Aug 13	137:29	137:30	1	2.99
4.250	**Nov 13n**	**100:29**	**100:30**	**12**	**4.13**
2.000	Jan 14i	101:13	101:14	14	1.84
13.250	May 14	148:23	148:24	6	3.15
12.500	Aug 14	146:15	146:16	9	3.25
11.750	Nov 14	143:26	143:27	9	3.34
11.250	Feb 15	161:09	161:10	19	4.24
10.625	Aug 15	157:00	157:00	20	4.30
9.875	Nov 15	150:13	150:14	20	4.36
9.250	Feb 16	144:26	144:27	18	4.41
7.250	May 16	126:01	126:02	17	4.47
7.500	Nov 16	128:21	128:22	19	4.52
8.750	May 17	141:19	141:20	21	4.54
8.875	Aug 17	143:03	143:04	21	4.57
9.125	May 18	146:20	146:21	22	4.62
9.000	Nov 18	145:28	145:29	22	4.67
8.875	Feb 19	144:21	144:22	23	4.70
8.125	Aug 19	136:22	136:23	20	4.75
8.500	Feb 20	141:11	141:12	23	4.78
8.750	May 20	144:17	144:18	25	4.78
8.750	Aug 20	144:24	144:25	24	4.80
7.875	Feb 21	134:24	134:25	23	4.85
8.125	May 21	138:00	138:00	24	4.85
8.125	Aug 21	138:04	138:05	24	4.86
8.000	Nov 21	136:26	136:27	24	4.88
7.250	Aug 22	127:29	127:30	25	4.93
7.625	Nov 22	132:24	132:25	24	4.93
7.125	Feb 23	126:16	126:17	25	4.96
6.250	Aug 23	115:18	115:19	21	4.99
7.500	Nov 24	132:08	132:09	24	4.99
7.625	Feb 25	133:30	133:31	24	5.00
6.875	Aug 25	124:06	124:07	24	5.02
6.000	Feb 26	112:19	112:20	21	5.04
6.750	Aug 26	122:27	122:28	23	5.04
6.500	Nov 26	119:15	119:16	23	5.05
6.625	Feb 27	121:10	121:11	23	5.05
6.375	Aug 27	118:00	118:01	24	5.06
6.125	Nov 27	114:19	114:20	23	5.06
3.625	Apr 28i	126:00	126:01	36	2.23
5.500	Aug 28	105:30	105:31	22	5.07
5.250	Nov 28	102:15	102:16	22	5.07
5.250	Feb 29	102:18	102:19	20	5.07
3.875	Apr 29i	131:27	131:28	39	2.22
6.125	Aug 29	115:06	115:07	24	5.06
6.250	May 30	117:09	117:10	22	5.05
5.375	**Feb 31**	**106:02**	**106:03**	**22**	**4.96**
3.375	Apr 32i	125:27	125:28	41	2.15

U.S. Treasury Strips

MATURITY		TYPE	BID	ASKED	CHG	ASK YLD
Feb	04	ci	99:31	99:31	...	0.97
Feb	04	np	99:31	99:31	...	1.06
May	04	ci	99:23	99:23	...	0.97
May	04	np	99:23	99:23	...	0.97
Jul	04	ci	99:17	99:17	1	1.04
Aug	04	ci	99:15	99:15	1	0.98
Aug	04	np	99:14	99:14	...	1.05
Nov	04	ci	99:04	99:04	1	1.12
Nov	04	bp	99:03	99:03	...	1.15
Nov	04	np	99:03	99:03	...	1.15
Jan	05	ci	99:06	99:07	1	0.85
Feb	05	ci	98:24	98:24	1	1.21
Feb	05	np	98:24	98:24	...	1.21
May	05	ci	98:12	98:12	2	1.27
May	05	bp	98:10	98:11	2	1.30
May	05	np	98:09	98:09	2	1.35
May	05	np	98:08	98:09	2	1.37
Jul	05	ci	98:13	98:14	2	1.08
Aug	05	ci	97:25	97:26	2	1.45
Aug	05	bp	97:22	97:23	2	1.51
Aug	05	np	97:23	97:24	2	1.50
Nov	05	ci	97:02	97:03	2	1.66
Nov	05	np	97:01	97:02	2	1.68
Nov	05	np	97:02	97:03	2	1.67
Jan	06	ci	97:03	97:04	3	1.50
Feb	06	ci	96:10	96:11	3	1.84
Feb	06	bp	96:10	96:12	3	1.83
Feb	06	np	96:12	96:13	3	1.81
May	06	ci	95:20	95:21	3	1.96
May	06	np	95:18	95:19	3	1.98
Jul	06	ci	95:25	95:26	4	1.75
Jul	06	np	95:01	95:03	4	2.07
Aug	06	ci	94:26	94:28	4	2.09
Oct	06	np	94:09	94:11	5	2.17
Nov	06	ci	93:30	93:31	4	2.25
Nov	06	np	93:30	94:00	4	2.24
Feb	07	ci	92:30	93:00	5	2.41
Feb	07	np	93:02	93:04	5	2.37
May	07	ci	92:02	92:04	5	2.51
May	07	np	92:04	92:06	5	2.50
Aug	07	np	91:06	91:08	6	2.61
Aug	07	ci	91:02	91:04	6	2.65
Aug	07	np	91:05	91:07	6	2.62
Nov	07	ci	90:10	90:12	6	2.69
Nov	07	np	90:10	90:13	6	2.69
Feb	08	ci	89:02	89:04	6	2.87
Feb	08	np	89:09	89:11	6	2.81
May	08	ci	87:29	87:31	7	3.02
May	08	np	88:05	88:08	7	2.94
Aug	08	ci	87:06	87:08	7	3.03
Nov	08	ci	85:30	86:00	7	3.18
Nov	08	np	86:04	86:06	7	3.13
Feb	09	ci	84:24	84:27	8	3.29
May	09	ci	83:23	83:26	8	3.37
May	09	np	84:14	84:17	8	3.21
Aug	09	ci	82:25	82:28	8	3.42
Aug	09	np	82:30	83:01	8	3.39
Nov	09	ci	82:03	82:06	8	3.42
Nov	09	bp	81:04	81:07	9	3.63
Feb	10	ci	80:15	80:18	10	3.62
Feb	10	np	80:25	80:28	9	3.55
May	10	ci	79:14	79:18	10	3.68
Aug	10	ci	78:15	78:18	10	3.73
Aug	10	np	78:22	78:25	10	3.68
Nov	10	ci	77:26	77:30	10	3.71
Feb	11	ci	76:06	76:09	10	3.88
Feb	11	np	76:19	76:23	11	3.81
May	11	ci	75:05	75:09	11	3.94
Aug	11	ci	74:07	74:11	11	3.98
Aug	11	np	74:14	74:18	11	3.94
Nov	11	ci	73:11	73:15	11	4.00
Feb	12	ci	72:00	72:04	11	4.11
Feb	12	np	72:15	72:19	11	4.03
May	12	ci	70:27	70:31	11	4.19
Aug	12	ci	69:29	70:00	12	4.22
Aug	12	np	70:20	70:24	12	4.10
Nov	12	ci	68:29	69:01	12	4.27
Nov	12	np	69:25	69:28	12	4.12
Feb	13	ci	67:26	67:30	12	4.33
May	13	ci	66:27	66:30	12	4.37
Aug	13	ci	65:26	65:30	12	4.42
Nov	13	ci	64:27	64:30	12	4.46
Feb	14	ci	63:30	64:02	12	4.49
May	14	ci	62:29	63:01	13	4.54
Aug	14	ci	62:00	62:04	13	4.57
Nov	14	ci	61:01	61:05	13	4.61

Treasury Bills

MATURITY	DAYS TO MAT	BID	ASKED	CHG	ASK YLD
Feb 05 04	3	0.73	0.72	-0.10	0.73
Feb 12 04	10	0.70	0.69	-0.12	0.70
Feb 19 04	17	0.80	0.79	-0.04	0.80
Feb 26 04	24	0.83	0.82	-0.02	0.83
Mar 04 04	31	0.82	0.81	-0.03	0.82
Mar 11 04	38	0.82	0.81	-0.01	0.82
Mar 18 04	45	0.82	0.81	-0.01	0.82
Mar 25 04	52	0.84	0.83	-0.02	0.84
Apr 01 04	59	0.87	0.86	-0.02	0.87
Apr 08 04	66	0.87	0.86	-0.02	0.87
Apr 15 04	73	0.90	0.89	-0.02	0.90
Apr 22 04	80	0.90	0.89	-0.01	0.90
Apr 29 04	**87**	**0.90**	**0.89**	**-0.02**	**0.90**
May 06 04	94	0.91	0.90	-0.01	0.91
May 13 04	101	0.91	0.90	-0.01	0.91
May 20 04	108	0.91	0.90	-0.01	0.91
May 27 04	115	0.88	0.87	-0.03	0.88
Jun 03 04	122	0.92	0.91	...	0.93
Jun 10 04	129	0.91	0.90	-0.02	0.92
Jun 17 04	136	0.91	0.90	-0.02	0.92
Jun 24 04	143	0.94	0.93	-0.01	0.95
Jul 01 04	150	0.95	0.94	-0.01	0.96
Jul 08 04	157	0.96	0.95	-0.01	0.97
Jul 15 04	164	0.98	0.97	...	0.99
Jul 22 04	171	0.97	0.96	-0.02	0.98
Jul 29 04	**178**	**0.99**	**0.98**	**-0.01**	**1.00**

← **91- day T - bill** (Apr 29 04)

Inflation-Indexed Treasury Securities

RATE	MAT	BID/ASKED	CHG	*YLD	ACCR PRIN
3.375	01/07	108-25/26	3	0.377	1167
3.625	01/08	111-08/09	5	0.729	1145
3.875	01/09	113-28/29	7	0.994	1128
4.250	01/10	117-11/12	8	1.218	1099
3.500	01/11	113-24/25	9	1.414	1062
3.375	01/12	113-10/11	13	1.584	1041
3.000	07/12	110-14/15	12	1.668	1028
1.875	07/13	100-22/23	12	1.792	1007
2.000	01/14	101-13/14	14	1.841	1000
3.625	04/28	126-00/01	36	2.228	1143
3.875	04/29	131-27/28	39	2.217	1125
3.375	04/32	125-27/28	41	2.147	1042

*Yield to maturity on accrued principal.

Treasury Bills

MATURITY	DAYS TO MAT	BID	ASKED	CHG	ASK YLD
Feb 05 04	3	0.73	0.72	−0.10	0.73
Feb 12 04	10	0.70	0.69	−0.12	0.70
Feb 19 04	17	0.80	0.79	−0.04	0.80
Feb 26 04	24	0.83	0.82	−0.02	0.83
Mar 04 04	31	0.82	0.81	−0.03	0.82
Mar 11 04	38	0.82	0.81	−0.01	0.82
Mar 18 04	45	0.82	0.81	−0.01	0.82
Mar 25 04	52	0.84	0.83	−0.02	0.84
Apr 01 04	59	0.87	0.86	−0.02	0.87
Apr 08 04	66	0.87	0.86	−0.02	0.87
Apr 15 04	73	0.90	0.89	−0.02	0.90
Apr 22 04	80	0.90	0.89	−0.01	0.90
Apr 29 04	87	0.90	0.89	−0.02	0.90 ←
May 06 04	94	0.91	0.90	−0.01	0.91
May 13 04	101	0.91	0.90	−0.01	0.91
May 20 04	108	0.91	0.90	−0.01	0.91
May 27 04	115	0.88	0.87	−0.03	0.88
Jun 03 04	122	0.92	0.91	...	0.93
Jun 10 04	129	0.91	0.90	−0.02	0.92
Jun 17 04	136	0.91	0.90	−0.02	0.92
Jun 24 04	143	0.94	0.93	−0.01	0.95
Jul 01 04	150	0.95	0.94	−0.01	0.96
Jul 08 04	157	0.96	0.95	−0.01	0.97
Jul 15 04	164	0.98	0.97	...	0.99
Jul 22 04	171	0.97	0.96	−0.02	0.98
Jul 29 04	178	0.99	0.98	−0.01	1.00

On Friday, January 30, 2004, the 91-day T-bill rate on the open (secondary) market was 0.90% for bills auctioned on Monday, January 26, 2004, to be issued on Thursday, January 29, 2004, and maturing 13 weeks later on Thursday, April 29, 2004.

ders) paid a price (less than $10,000) that would yield 0.90 percent if the Treasury bill were held to maturity and cashed in for $10,000. Sellers on January 30, 2004, were asking a higher price (lower interest rate), equivalent to 0.89 percent. The last column gives a true yield of 0.90 percent. (The other maturity dates are for older bills and for bills with maturities of more than 91 days.)

These data are also available online. (You can find general directions for retrieving *Wall Street Journal* online information [http://online.wsj.com] in Chapter 1 on pages 7 through 11. Appendix D on page 374 also furnishes you with a guide to the *Journal*'s online edition.) Scroll down the online home page's left-hand menu-bar to Markets and then click on Markets Data Center. Then scroll down to Bond Markets in the right column and click on Treasury Quotes. The Treasury Bills table is at the bottom. The Tuesday, July 6, 2004, excerpt is on pages 348 and 349. Note the Treasury-bill listing at the bottom.

It is now time to complete this discussion of short-term interest rates with a description of how you can track the yield on your own interest-earning investments and compare them with market rates.

Treasury Quotes
Tuesday, July 6, 2004

U.S. Government Bonds and Notes

Representative Over-the-Counter quotation based on transactions of $1 million or more.
Treasury bond, note and bill quotes are from midafternoon. Colons in bond and note bid-and-asked quotes represent 32nds;
101:01 means 101 1/32. Net change in 32nds. n-Treasury Note. i-Inflation-indexed issue. Treasury bill quotes in
hundredths, quoted in terms of a rate of discount. Days to maturity calculated from settlement date. All yields are to
maturity and based on the asked quote. For bonds callable prior to maturity, yields are computed to the earliest call date for
issues quoted above par and to the maturity date for issues quoted below par.
*-When issued. Daily change expressed in basis points.

Rate	Maturity Mo/Yr	Bid	Asked	Chg	Asked Yield
2 1/4	Jul 04 n	100:01	100:02	....	1.17
2 1/8	Aug 04 n	100:03	100:04	....	1.17
6	Aug 04 n	100:15	100:16	-1	1.15
7 1/4	Aug 04 n	100:20	100:21	....	1.09
13 3/4	Aug 04	101:10	101:11	-2	1.00
1 7/8	Sep 04 n	100:03	100:04	....	1.28
2 1/8	Oct 04 n	100:05	100:06	....	1.47
5 7/8	Nov 04 n	101:16	101:17	....	1.50
7 7/8	Nov 04 n	102:06	102:07	-1	1.51
11 5/8	Nov 04	103:17	103:18	-2	1.48
2	Nov 04 n	100:04	100:05	-1	1.53
1 3/4	Dec 04 n	100:01	100:02	....	1.60
1 5/8	Jan 05 n	99:30	99:31	....	1.66
7 1/2	Feb 05 n	103:14	103:15	-1	1.71
1 1/2	Feb 05 n	99:26	99:27	....	1.71
1 5/8	Mar 05 n	99:27	99:28	....	1.80
1 5/8	Apr 05 n	99:24	99:25	-1	1.87
6 1/2	May 05 n	103:26	103:27	-2	1.92
6 3/4	May 05 n	104:01	104:02	-1	1.92
7 1/2	Nov 24	128:05	128:06	-10	5.23
7 5/8	Feb 25	129:28	129:29	-8	5.24
6 7/8	Aug 25	120:12	120:13	-9	5.26
6	Feb 26	109:03	109:04	-8	5.29
6 3/4	Aug 26	119:00	119:00	-9	5.28
6 1/2	Nov 26	115:24	115:25	-7	5.29
6 5/8	Feb 27	117:14	117:15	-9	5.29
6 3/8	Aug 27	114:08	114:09	-8	5.29
6 1/8	Nov 27	111:00	111:00	-7	5.30

Treasury Bills

Maturity	Days to Mat.	Bid	Asked	Chg	Ask Yield
Jul 08 04	1	1.20	1.20	+0.20	1.22
Jul 15 04	8	1.18	1.18	+0.03	1.20
Jul 22 04	15	1.06	1.06	+0.01	1.08
Jul 29 04	22	1.07	1.06	+0.08	1.08
Aug 05 04	29	1.14	1.14	+0.05	1.16
Aug 12 04	36	1.13	1.12	+0.03	1.14
Aug 19 04	43	1.15	1.15	+0.02	1.17
Aug 26 04	50	1.18	1.17	+0.01	1.19
Sep 02 04	57	1.18	1.18	+0.01	1.20
Sep 09 04	64	1.19	1.18	....	1.20
Sep 16 04	71	1.20	1.20	-0.01	1.21
Sep 23 04	78	1.23	1.22	-0.01	1.24
Sep 30 04	85	1.25	1.25	....	1.27
Oct 07 04	92	1.30	1.30	+0.02	1.32
Oct 14 04	99	1.29	1.29	+0.01	1.32
Oct 21 04	106	1.35	1.35	....	1.37
Oct 28 04	113	1.39	1.39	....	1.42
Nov 04 04	120	1.44	1.44	+0.01	1.47
Nov 12 04	128	1.45	1.45	....	1.47
Nov 18 04	134	1.47	1.47	....	1.50
Nov 26 04	142	1.49	1.48	+0.01	1.51
Dec 02 04	148	1.51	1.51	+0.01	1.54
Dec 09 04	155	1.53	1.53	+0.01	1.56
Dec 16 04	162	1.55	1.55	+0.01	1.59
Dec 23 04	169	1.57	1.57	....	1.60
Dec 30 04	176	1.58	1.57	+0.02	1.60

Source: eSpeed/Cantor Fitzgerald

TRACKING SHORT-TERM INTEREST RATES

Every day (Monday's and Saturday's table and chart formats differ) you can use the **Markets Diary** report at the bottom of the first page of the *Journal*'s third section (C1) to follow Treasury bills. Consult the excerpt from the Thursday, September 21, 2005, edition on page 350. The 10-year Treasury rate was 4.18 percent and the 3-month Treasury bill rate was 3.40 percent.

You can follow an even larger array of interest rates each day in **Money Rates**, a report that lists the current yields on most of the major money-market interest-rate instruments. Look for it in the front-page index of the first and third sections. The example from the Monday, February 2, 2004, print *Journal* on page 35 reports the rates for Friday, January 30, 2004.

This information is also available online by clicking on Markets and Markets Data Center from the left-hand menu-bar on the home page, and then scrolling down the right column to Bond Markets and clicking on Money Rates. A copy of the posting for Tuesday, July 6, 2004, is on page 351.

Money Rates tracks the following domestic rates: *Prime Rate* (the rate banks charge their corporate customers), *Discount Rate* (the rate the Federal Reserve charges its member banks), *Federal Funds*, *Call Money* (rates banks charge brokers), *Commercial Paper* (short-term marketable paper issued by major corporations), *Dealer Commercial Paper* (commercial paper sold

---

MARKETS DIARY / Sept. 21, 2005

For an expanded view of yesterday's markets, turn to the **Markets Lineup on page C2.**

	Close	Change	Pct. chg.	52 wks
DJ Industrial Average	10378.03	−103.49 ▼	0.99%	2.66%
Nasdaq composite	2106.64	−24.69 ▼	1.16	11.72
S&P 500	1210.20	−11.14 ▼	0.91	8.68
Russell 2000	649.94	−10.69 ▼	1.62	14.85
Nikkei Stock Average	13196.57	48.00 ▲	0.37	19.76
DJ Stoxx 600 (Europe)	291.89	−3.04 ▼	1.03	21.62
Euro (in U.S. dollars)	$1.2210	$0.0083 ▲	0.68	−0.40
Yen (per U.S. dollar)	111.32	−0.59 ▼	0.52	0.67
Gold (Comex, troy oz.)	$468.90	$2.70 ▲	0.58	15.15
Oil (Nymex, barrel)	$66.80	$0.60 ▲	0.91	38.16

	Yield	Previous	Change in pct. pts.	12-mo return
10-year Treasury	4.18%	4.26% ▼	0.07	*2.97%
3-mo. Treasury	3.40	3.60 ▼	0.20	*2.07
DJ Corporate Bond	5.12	5.17 ▼	0.05	3.16

*Total return via Ryan Labs

Money Rates

Friday, January 30, 2004

The key U. S. and foreign annual interest rates below are a guide to general levels but don't always represent actual transactions.

Commercial Paper

Yields paid by corporations for short-term financing, typically for daily operation

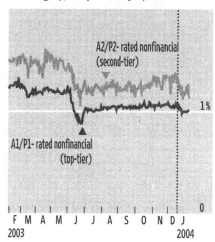

A2/P2- rated nonfinancial (second-tier)

1%

A1/P1- rated nonfinancial (top-tier)

0

F M A M J J A S O N D J
2003   2004

Source: Federal Reserve

Prime Rate: 4.00% (effective 06/27/03). The base rate on corporate loans posted by at least 75% of the nation's 30 largest banks.

Discount Rate (Primary): 2.00% (effective 06/25/03).

Federal Funds: 1.063% high, 0.875% low, 0.938% near closing bid, 0.969% offered. Effective rate: 1.02%. Source: Prebon Yamane (USA) Inc. Federal-funds target rate: 1.000% (effective 06/25/03).

Call Money: 2.75% (effective 06/30/03).

Commercial Paper: Placed directly by General Electric Capital Corp.: 1.02% 30 to 54 days; 0.80% 55 to 65 days; 1.03% 66 to 94 days; 1.04% 95 to 123 days; 1.05% 124 to 145 days; 0.80% 146 to 159 days; 1.08% 160 to 185 days; 1.11% 186 to 220 days; 1.14% 221 to 270 days.

Euro Commercial Paper: Placed directly by General Electric

Capital Corp.: 2.04% 30 days; 2.05% two months; 2.06% three months; 2.08% four months; 2.09% five months; 2.10% six months.

Dealer Commercial Paper: High-grade unsecured notes sold through dealers by major corporations: 1.03% 30 days; 1.03% 60 days; 1.05% 90 days.

Certificates of Deposit: 1.04% one month; 1.06% three months; 1.13% six months.

Bankers Acceptances: 1.02% 30 days; 1.03% 60 days; 1.04% 90 days; 1.06% 120 days; 1.10% 150 days; 1.11% 180 days. Source: Prebon Yamane (USA) Inc.

Eurodollars: 1.03% - 1.00% one month; 1.06% - 1.03% two months; 1.07% - 1.04% three months; 1.09% - 1.05% four months; 1.12% - 1.09% five months; 1.14% - 1.10% six months. Source: Prebon Yamane (USA) Inc.

London Interbank Offered Rates (Libor): 1.1000% one month; 1.1300% three months; 1.21375% six months; 1.47625% one year. Effective rate for contracts entered into two days from date appearing at top of this column.

Euro Libor: 2.07175% one month; 2.09288% three months; 2.13400% six months; 2.26038% one year. Effective rate for contracts entered into two days from date appearing at top of this column.

Euro Interbank Offered Rates (Euribor): 2.074% one month; 2.093% three months; 2.137% six months; 2.263% one year. Source: Reuters.

Foreign Prime Rates: Canada 4.25%; European Central Bank 2.00%; Japan 1.375%; Switzerland 2.25%; Britain 3.75%.

Treasury Bills: Results of the Monday, January 26, 2004, auction of short-term U.S. government bills, sold at a discount from face value in units of $1,000 to $1 million: 0.890% 13 weeks; 0.955% 26 weeks. Tuesday, January 27, 2004 auction: 0.860% 4 weeks.

Overnight Repurchase Rate: 1.00%. Source: Garban Intercapital.

Freddie Mac: Posted yields on 30-year mortgage commitments. Delivery within 30 days 5.45%, 60 days 5.51%, standard conventional fixed-rate mortgages: 3.375%, 2% rate capped one-year adjustable rate mortgages.

Fannie Mae: Posted yields on 30 year mortgage commitments (priced at par) for delivery within 30 days 5.54%, 60 days 5.61%, standard conventional fixed-rate mortgages; 3.00%, 6/2 rate capped one-year adjustable rate mortgages. Constant Maturity Debt Index: 1.036% three months; 1.101% six months; 1.380% one year.

Merrill Lynch Ready Assets Trust: 0.52%.

Consumer Price Index: December, 184.3, up 1.9% from a year ago. Bureau of Labor Statistics.

Money Rates

Tuesday, July 6, 2004

Prime Rate:	Rate	Effective Date
The base rate on corporate loans posted by at least 75% of the nation's 30 largest banks.	4.25 %	07/01/04

Discount Rate:	Rate	Effective Date
The charge on loans to depository institutions by the Federal Reserve Banks.	2.25 %	06/30/04

Federal Funds:	Rate	
Reserves traded among commercial banks for overnight use in amounts of $1 million or more. FOMC target rate effective 06/30/04.	1.2500 %	FOMC target rate
	1.3750 %	High
	1.2500 %	Low
	1.3125 %	Near Closing Bid
	1.3750 %	Offered

Source: Prebon Yamane (U.S.A)Inc.

Call Money:	Rate	Effective Date
The charge on loans to brokers on stock exchange collateral.	3.00 %	06/30/04

Source: Reuters

Commercial Paper:	Rate	Period
Commercial paper placed directly by General Electric Capital Corp.	1.28 %	30 to 59 days
	1.39 %	60 to 89 days
	1.50 %	90 to 119 days
	1.58 %	120 to 149 days
	1.68 %	150 to 179 days
	1.77 %	180 to 209 days
	1.83 %	210 to 239 days
	1.90 %	240 to 270 days

Euro Commercial Paper:	Rate	Period
Commercial paper placed directly by General Electric Capital Corp.	2.04 %	30 days
	2.06 %	Two Months
	2.08 %	Three Months
	2.09 %	Four Months
	2.10 %	Five Months
	2.13 %	Six Months

through dealers), *Certificates of Deposit, Bankers Acceptances* (rates on bank-backed business credit used to finance international trade), *Eurodollars, Treasury Bills, Overnight Repurchase Rate* (the dealer financing rate for overnight sale and repurchase of Treasury securities), *Federal Home Loan Mortgage Corp.* (Freddie Mac) and *Federal National Mortgage Association* (Fannie Mae) yields on a variety of mortgages, and *Merrill Lynch Ready Assets Trust* (a money-market mutual fund), and it provides the *Consumer Price Index.* **Money Rates** also tracks foreign money-market rates, including: *Euro Commercial Paper* (European commercial paper), *London Interbank Offered Rates (LIBOR), Euro LIBOR* (similar to LIBOR), *Euro Interbank Offered Rates* (similar to LIBOR), and *Foreign Prime Rates.* These interest rates are discussed more thoroughly below.

Federal Funds Rate

Banks lend reserves to one another overnight at the federal funds rate. This practice is profitable for lender banks, because they earn interest on funds ($1 million or more) that would otherwise be idle, and it is profitable for the borrower banks, because they acquire reserves that enable them to make additional loans and still meet their reserve requirement.

Notice that under *Federal Funds* in the **Money Rates** column on page 351, six different percentages are listed: 1.063 percent high, 0.875 percent low, 0.938 percent near closing bid, 0.969 percent offered, 1.02 percent effective, and 1.000 percent target rate.

These numbers show that, during trading on Friday, January 30, 2004, 1.063 percent was the highest interest rate proposed by a potential lender bank, and 0.875 percent was the lowest interest rate proposed by a prospective borrower. The next two percentages describe the state of trading near the end of the day: lender banks were offering 0.969 percent, and borrower banks were bidding 0.938 percent. Use the closing bid (0.938 percent) when following this interest rate. Finally, the table also lists the effective rate (1.02 percent) and the federally targeted rate (1.000 percent).

The federal funds rate is closely watched as an indicator of Federal Reserve monetary policy. A rising federal-funds rate is a sign that the Fed is draining reserves from the banks via its open market operations, forcing some banks to borrow excess reserves from other banks and thereby driving up the federal funds rate. A falling rate would indicate an easy money policy. But beware: Sharp fluctuations occur from day to day. This is such a short-term market that the rate changes on an "as needed" basis. (Chapter 8 discusses the Federal Reserve.)

Investor's Tip

- Follow the Federal-Funds Target Rate under **Bonds & Interest** in the Markets Diary on page C1, because it presents a weekly average that smooths out sharp daily movements.

Commercial Paper

Money Rates on page 351 lists 1.03 percent as the going rate for 66- to 94-day commercial paper on Friday, January 30, 2004. Commercial paper is short-term, unsecured debt issued by the very largest corporations. It is the equivalent of the Treasury bill, so in order to attract investors its rate of interest has to be higher.

Corporations issue commercial paper to avoid the higher interest rate (prime rate) levied by banks on business borrowers, and it is issued for maturities up to 270 days. There are very large minimums set on commercial paper purchases (often in excess of $1 million), and this instrument is very popular with money-market funds.

Prime Rate

This is the rate that large commercial banks charge their best corporate customers. Although it does not change as frequently as other market rates, it is an important indicator of supply and demand in the capital markets. Banks raise the prime rate whenever they have difficulty meeting the current demand for funds or when the Federal Reserve drains away their reserves through its open market operations.

Bankers Acceptances

Bankers acceptances are used to finance international trade. Large institutions, investment companies, and money-market mutual funds purchase bankers acceptances because they offer high yields for relatively short periods of time. Individual investors benefit from the higher yields when they invest in funds that include these instruments.

Call Rates

The call rate is the rate that banks charge brokers, who generally add 1 percent on loans to their clients.

Key Interest Rates

Annualized interest rates on certain investments as reported by the Federal Reserve Board on a weekly-average basis:

	WEEK ENDED:	
	Jan. 23, 2004	Jan. 16, 2004
Treasury bills (90 day)-a	0.87	0.87
Commrcl paper (Finl., 90 day)-a	1.03	1.03
Commrcl paper (Non-Finl., 90 day)-a	1.00	1.01
Certfs of Deposit (Resale, 3 month)	1.05	1.05
Certfs of Deposit (Resale, 6 month)	1.10	1.10
Federal funds (Overnight)-b	1.00	0.99
Eurodollars (90 day)-b	1.04	1.05
Treasury bills (one year)-c	1.20	1.19
Treasury notes (two year)-c	1.69	1.67
Treasury notes (three year)-c	2.19	2.16
Treasury notes (five year)-c	3.02	3.00
Treasury notes (ten year)-c	4.05	4.04
Treasury bonds (25+ year)-c	4.97	4.98

a-Discounted rates. b-Week ended Wednesday, January 21, 2004 and Wednesday, January 14, 2004 c-Yields, adjusted for constant maturity.

KEY INTEREST RATES

Every Tuesday, under the heading **Key Interest Rates**, the *Journal* reports the weekly average of most important interest rates, including long-term rates. The print-edition example above is from the Tuesday, January 27, 2004, *Journal*. In the week ended Friday, January 23, 2004, *Treasury bills* averaged 0.87 percent; *Commercial paper*, 1.03 percent; *Certificates of Deposit*, 1.05 percent; and *Federal funds*, 1.00 percent. Once again, notice the interest rate hierarchy.

This information is also available online by clicking on Markets and Markets Data Center from the left-hand menu-bar on the home page, and then scrolling down the right column to Bond Markets and clicking on Key Rates. A copy of the posting for Tuesday, July 6, 2004, is on page 356.

TREASURY YIELD CURVE

The yield curve charts the relationship between interest rates and length of maturity for all debt instruments at a particular time. A normal yield curve slopes upward, so that longer-term investments have higher yields. Thus,

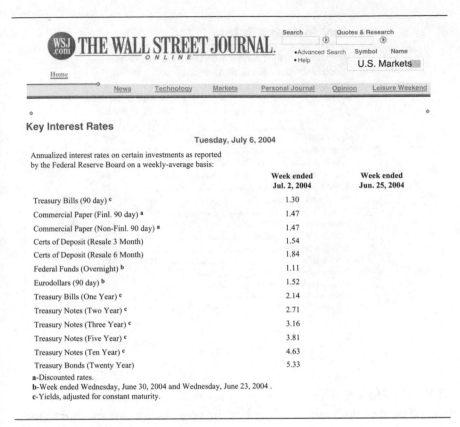

short-term Treasury bill rates are usually lower than long-term Treasury bond rates. Abnormal yield curves can be flat, inverted, or peaked in the middle (higher short-term rates than long-term rates).

The Wall Street Journal publishes a **Treasury Yield Curve** chart daily under **Interest Rates & Bonds** at the bottom of the **Markets Lineup** section on the second page of the third section (C2). See the excerpt from the Thursday, January 29, 2004, print edition on page 357. You can see the normal pattern of rising rates associated with longer maturities.

Finally, you can evaluate the yields on a variety of long- and short-term debt instruments by looking at the **Yield Comparisons** table published with the daily **Credit Markets** article (consult the first and third sections index under Credit Markets). A copy of the table from Thursday, January 29, 2004, is on page 357.

Treasury Yield Curve

Yield to maturity of current bills, notes and bonds.

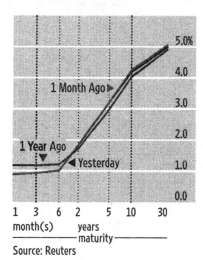

Source: Reuters

Yield Comparisons

Based on Merrill Lynch Bond Indexes, priced as of midafternoon Eastern time.

	1/28	1/27	52-WEEK HIGH	LOW
Corp. Govt. Master	3.57%	3.45%	4.02%	2.81%
Treasury				
1-10 yr	2.44	2.30	2.70	1.57
10+ yr	4.84	4.75	5.28	3.86
Agencies				
1-10 yr	2.75	2.61	3.18	1.77
10+ yr	5.22	5.12	5.75	4.24
Corporate				
1-10 yr High Quality	3.29	3.16	3.75	2.47
Medium Quality	3.89	3.76	4.83	3.38
10+ yr High Quality	5.65	5.56	6.24	4.79
Medium Quality	6.00	5.90	6.86	5.36
Yankee bonds (1)	3.90	3.79	4.34	3.21
Current-coupon mortgages (2)				
GNMA 6.50% (3)	5.12	4.99	5.81	3.70
FNMA 6.50%	5.15	5.01	6.11	3.99
FHLMC 6.50%	5.20	5.06	6.16	4.10
High-yield corporates	7.03	6.96	11.53	6.88
Tax-Exempt Bonds				
7-12 yr G.O. (AA)	3.39	3.32	4.12	2.82
12-22 yr G.O. (AA)	4.25	4.16	4.97	3.79
22+ yr revenue (A)	4.66	4.58	5.32	4.32

Note: High quality rated AAA-AA; medium quality A-BBB/Baa; high yield, BB/Ba-C.

(1) Dollar-denominated, SEC-registered bonds of foreign issuers sold in the U.S. (2) Reflects the 52-week high and low of mortgage-backed securities indexes rather than the individual securities shown. (3) Government guaranteed.

CONCLUSION

If the risk and bother of investing in stocks, bonds, and commodities seems excessive to you, a wide variety of relatively risk-free and highly liquid money-market instruments are available to you. Use *The Wall Street Journal*'s data services to check the hierarchy of rates, and then choose the instrument that's right for you.

STATISTICAL SERIES PUBLISHED IN *THE WALL STREET JOURNAL* IN ALPHABETICAL ORDER

Chapter (Page)	Series Description	Publication Schedule
13 (272)	ADRs	Daily
13 (225)	American Stock Exchange (AMEX)	Daily
10 (190)	Balance of trade	Monthly
10 (187)	Balance on current account	Quarterly
16 (336)	Bankrate.com money markets and CDs	Weekly
13 (249)	Benchmarks for mutual fund investors	Weekly
15, 16 (328, 340)	Bonds and interest	Daily
15 (328)	Bond-market data bank	Daily
13 (233)	Breakdown of trading	Daily
4 (41)	Capacity utilization	Monthly
14 (304)	Cash prices (commodities)	Daily
16 (337)	Certificate of deposit yields	Weekly
13, 15 (250, 326)	Closed-end funds (stocks & bonds)	Daily

Chapter (Page)	Series Description	Publication Schedule
14 (296)	Commodities (article)	Daily
14 (301)	Commodities indexes	Daily
7 (95)	Consumer confidence	Monthly
7 (105)	Consumer credit	Monthly
7 (83)	Consumer-price index	Monthly
16 (335)	Consumer rates	Daily
15 (319)	Corporate bonds	Daily
13 (276)	Corporate-dividend news	Daily
3 (25)	Corporate profits (Commerce Department)	Quarterly
3 (26)	Corporate profits (*The Wall Street Journal* survey)	Quarterly
15, 16 (309, 340)	Credit markets (article)	Daily
10 (195)	Currency trading	Daily
13 (276)	Digest of corporate-earnings report	Daily
13 (210, 323)	Dow Jones averages	Daily
13 (272)	Dow Jones country indexes	Daily
13 (234)	Dow Jones global sector titans	Daily
13 (249)	Dow Jones hedge benchmark	Daily
13 (225)	Dow Jones indexes	Daily
13 (272)	Dow Jones specialty indexes	Daily
5 (68)	Durable-goods orders	Monthly
7 (87)	Employment	Monthly
13 (254)	Exchange-traded portfolios	Daily
7 (111)	Existing-home sales	Monthly
9 (159)	Federal budget	Monthly
10 (191)	Foreign exchange	Daily
13 (249)	Fund leaders and laggards	Weekly
14 (294)	Future prices	Daily
13 (226)	Gainers and losers	Daily
15 (329)	Global government-bond index	Weekly
4 (34)	GDP	Quarterly

Chapter (Page)	Series Description	Publication Schedule
13 (269)	Global stocks	Daily
15 (315)	Government agency & similar issues	Daily
15 (332)	High-yield bonds	Daily
7 (107)	Housing starts	Monthly
13 (249)	How fund categories stack up	Daily
13 (246)	How the largest mutual funds did	Daily
13 (261)	Index options	Daily
4 (41)	Industrial production	Monthly
13 (280)	Insider-trading spotlight	Weekly
15, 16 (329, 335)	Interest rates & bonds	Daily
13 (269)	International stocks and indexes	Daily
13 (272)	International stock market indexes	Daily
6 (282)	Inventories	Monthly
13 (282)	IPO scorecard	Weekly
7 (89)	Jobless claims	Weekly
10 (195)	Key-currency cross rates	Daily
15, 16 (315, 355)	Key interest rates	Weekly
13 (249)	Largest stock and bond funds	Weekly
13 (233)	Late-trading snapshot	Daily
11 (200)	Leading indicators	Monthly
13 (262)	Leaps—long-term options	Daily
13 (246)	Lipper indexes	Daily
13 (221)	Major stock indexes	Daily
5 (70)	Manufacturers' orders	Monthly
13 (278)	Market by the slice	Daily
13–16 (211)	Markets diary	Daily
13–16 (214)	Markets lineup	Daily
13 (226)	Markets scorecard	Daily
13 (226)	Markets scorecard's diaries	Daily
13 (254)	MITTS—market index target-term securities	Daily

Chapter (Page)	Series Description	Publication Schedule
13 (233)	Money flows	Daily
16 (340)	Money-market mutual funds	Weekly
16 (350)	Money rates	Daily
13 (250)	Monthly review of mutual funds	Monthly
13 (226)	Most-active issues	Daily
13 (255)	Most-active listed options	Daily
13 (272)	MSCI indexes	Daily
15 (323)	Municipal-bond index	Weekly
13 (243)	Mutual funds	Daily
13 (249)	Mutual-fund scorecard	Daily
13 (225)	NASDAQ	Daily
13 (243)	NASDAQ national-market issues	Daily
13 (243)	NASDAQ NM issues under $100 million market cap	Daily
13 (265)	NASDAQ short-selling highlights	Monthly
13 (243)	NASDAQ small-cap issues	Daily
7 (113)	New-home sales	Monthly
15 (322)	New-securities issues	Daily
7 (101)	New-vehicle sales	Monthly
13 (225)	New York Stock Exchange	Daily
13 (238)	NYSE composite transactions	Daily
13 (233)	NYSE highs/lows	Daily
13 (265)	NYSE and AmEx short-selling highlights	Monthly
13 (234)	Odd-lot trading	Daily
13 (246)	Performance yardsticks	Weekly
7 (89)	Personal income	Monthly
15 (323)	The pipeline/securities-offering calendar	Weekly
3, 13 (22, 217, 222)	P/E ratio	Daily
13 (24)	Preferred-stock listings	Daily
13 (221, 226)	Price percentage gainers and losers	Daily

Chapter (Page)	Series Description	Publication Schedule
4 (58)	Producer-price index	Monthly
4 (51)	Productivity	Quarterly
4 (49)	Purchasing-managers' index	Monthly
7 (113)	Retail sales	Monthly
13 (225)	Russell 2000	Daily
1, 13 (2, 225)	S&P 500	Daily
15, 16 (312, 345)	Treasury bonds, notes, and bills	Daily
15 16 (329, 355)	Treasury yield curve	Daily
13 (233)	Uptick vs. downtick trading by dollar volume	Daily
13 (211)	U.S. stocks	Daily
13 (226)	Volume percentage leaders	Daily
13 (269)	World stock markets	Daily
10 (195)	World value of the dollar	Weekly
15, 16 (328, 356)	Yield comparisons	Daily
13 (219, 278)	Yields on Dow components	Weekly

B

STATISTICAL SERIES PUBLISHED IN *THE WALL STREET JOURNAL* IN CHAPTER ORDER

Chapter (Page)	Series Description	Publication Schedule
1 (2)	S&P 500	Daily
3 (25)	Corporate profits (Commerce Department)	Quarterly
3 (26)	Corporate profits (*The Wall Street Journal* survey)	Quarterly
3, 13 (22, 217, 222)	P/E ratio	Daily
4 (41)	Capacity utilization	Monthly
4 (34)	GDP	Quarterly
4 (41)	Industrial production	Monthly
4 (58)	Producer-price index	Monthly
4 (51)	Productivity	Quarterly
4 (49)	Purchasing-managers' index	Monthly
5 (68)	Durable-goods orders	Monthly
5 (70)	Manufacturers' orders	Monthly
6 (74)	Inventories	Monthly

Chapter (Page)	Series Description	Publication Schedule
7 (95)	Consumer confidence	Monthly
7 (105)	Consumer credit	Monthly
7 (83)	Consumer-price index	Monthly
7 (87)	Employment	Monthly
7 (111)	Existing-home sales	Monthly
7 (107)	Housing starts	Monthly
7 (89)	Jobless claims	Weekly
7 (113)	New-home sales	Monthly
7 (101)	New-vehicle sales	Monthly
7 (89)	Personal income	Monthly
7 (113)	Retail sales	Monthly
9 (159)	Federal budget	Monthly
10 (183, 187)	Balance on current account	Quarterly
10 (183, 190)	Balance of trade	Monthly
10 (195)	Currency trading	Daily
10 (191)	Foreign exchange	Daily
10 (195)	Key-currency cross rates	Daily
10 (195)	World value of the dollar	Weekly
11 (200)	Leading indicators	Monthly
13 (272)	ADRs	Daily
13 (225)	American Stock Exchange (AMEX)	Daily
13 (249)	Benchmarks for mutual fund investors	Weekly
13 (233)	Breakdown of trading	Daily
13, 15 (250, 326)	Closed-end funds (stocks & bonds)	Daily
13 (276)	Corporate-dividend news	Daily
13 (276)	Digest of corporate-earnings report	Daily
13 (210, 223)	Dow Jones averages	Daily
13 (272)	Dow Jones country indexes	Daily
13 (234)	Dow Jones global sector titans	Daily
13 (249)	Dow Jones hedge benchmark	Daily
13 (225)	Dow Jones indexes	Daily

Chapter (Page)	Series Description	Publication Schedule
13 (272)	Dow Jones specialty indexes	Daily
13 (254)	Exchange-traded portfolios	Daily
13 (249)	Fund leaders and laggards	Weekly
13 (221, 226)	Gainers and losers	Daily
13 (269)	Global stocks	Daily
13 (249)	How fund categories stack up	Daily
13 (246)	How the largest mutual funds did	Daily
13 (261)	Index options	Daily
13 (280)	Insider-trading spotlight	Weekly
13 (272)	International stock market indexes	Daily
13 (269)	International stocks and indexes	Daily
13 (282)	IPO scorecard	Weekly
13 (249)	Largest stock and bond funds	Weekly
13 (233)	Late-trading snapshot	Daily
13 (262)	Leaps—long-term options	Daily
13 (246)	Lipper indexes	Daily
13 (221)	Major stock indexes	Daily
13 (278)	Market by the slice	Daily
13–16 (211)	Markets diary	Daily
13–16 (214)	Markets lineup	Daily
13 (226)	Markets scorecard	Daily
13 (226)	Markets scorecard's diaries	Daily
13 (254)	MITTS—market index target-term securities	Daily
13 (233)	Money flows	Daily
13 (250)	Monthly review of mutual funds	Monthly
13 (226)	Most-active issues	Daily
13 (255)	Most-active listed options	Daily
13 (272)	MSCI indexes	Daily
13 (243)	Mutual funds	Daily
13 (249)	Mutual-fund scorecard	Daily

Chapter (Page)	Series Description	Publication Schedule
13 (225)	NASDAQ	Daily
13 (243)	NASDAQ NM issues under $100 million market cap	Daily
13 (243)	NASDAQ national-market issues	Daily
13 (265)	NASDAQ short-selling highlights	Monthly
13 (243)	NASDAQ small-cap issues	Daily
13 (225)	New York Stock Exchange	Daily
13 (238)	NYSE composite transactions	Daily
13 (233)	NYSE highs/lows	Daily
13 (265)	NYSE and AmEx short-selling highlights	Monthly
13 (234)	Odd-lot trading	Daily
13 (246)	Performance yardsticks	Weekly
13 (243)	Preferred-stock listings	Daily
13 (221, 226)	Price percentage gainers and losers	Daily
13 (225)	Russell 2000	Daily
13 (225)	S&P 500	Daily
13 (233)	Uptick vs. downtick trading by dollar volume	Daily
13 (211)	U.S. stocks	Daily
13 (226)	Volume percentage leaders	Daily
13 (269)	World stock markets	Daily
13 (219, 278)	Yields on Dow components	Weekly
14 (304)	Cash prices (commodities)	Daily
14 (296)	Commodities (article)	Daily
14 (301)	Commodities indexes	Daily
14 (294)	Future prices	Daily
15 (328)	Bond-market data bank	Daily
15, 16 (328, 349)	Bonds and interest	Daily
15 (319)	Corporate bonds	Daily
15, 16 (309, 340)	Credit markets (article)	Daily
15 (329)	Global government-bond index	Weekly

Chapter (Page)	Series Description	Publication Schedule
15 (315)	Government agency & similar issues	Daily
15 (322)	High-yield bonds	Daily
15, 16 (329, 335)	Interest rates & bonds	Daily
15, 16 (315, 355)	Key interest rates	Weekly
15 (323)	Municipal-bond index	Weekly
15 (322)	New-securities issues	Daily
15 (323)	The pipeline/securities-offering calendar	Weekly
15, 16 (312, 345)	Treasury bonds, notes, and bills	Daily
15, 16 (329, 355)	Treasury yield curve	Daily
15, 16 (328, 356)	Yield comparisons	Daily
16 (336)	Bankrate.com money markets and CDs	Weekly
16 (337)	Certificate of deposit yields	Weekly
16 (335)	Consumer rates	Daily
16 (340)	Money-market mutual funds	Weekly
16 (350)	Money rates	Daily

LISTING OF STATISTICAL SERIES ACCORDING TO *THE WALL STREET JOURNAL* PUBLICATION SCHEDULE

Day of Month Usually Published in *The Wall Street Journal*	Series Description	Chapter (Page)
Quarterly		
Middle of last month of quarter	Balance on current account	10 (183, 187)
End of month	GDP	4 (34)
End of last month of quarter	Corporate profits (Commerce Department)	3 (25)
A month after end of quarter	Productivity	4 (51)
One month after close of quarter	Corporate profits (*The Wall Street Journal* survey)	3 (26)
Monthly		
1st	Leading indicators	11 (200)
1st week	Manufacturers' orders	5 (70)

Day of Month Usually Published in *The Wall Street Journal*	Series Description	Chapter (Page)
1st week	Monthly review of mutual funds	13 (250)
1st week	New-home sales	7 (113)
1st week	New-vehicle sales	7 (101)
1st week	Purchasing-managers' index	4 (49)
Monday of 2nd week	Employment	7 (87)
2nd week	Consumer credit	7 (105)
Middle of 2nd week	Retail sales	7 (113)
Midmonth	Capacity utilization	4 (41)
Midmonth	Consumer-price index	7 (83)
Midmonth	Industrial production	4 (41)
Midmonth	Inventories	6 (74)
Midmonth	Producer-price index	4 (58)
3rd week	Balance of trade	10 (183, 190)
17th to 20th	Housing starts	7 (107)
Thursday or Friday of next-to-last week	Durable-goods orders	5 (68)
Last week	Consumer confidence	7 (95)
Last week	Existing-home sales	7 (111)
Last week	Federal budget	9 (159)
Last week	NASDAQ short-selling highlight	13 (265)
Last week	NYSE and AmEx short-selling highlights	13 (265)
Last week	Personal income	7 (89)
Weekly		
Monday	Global government-bond index	15 (329)
Monday	The pipeline/securities-offering calendar	15 (323)
Monday	World value of the dollar	10 (195)
Monday	Yields on Dow components	13 (219, 278)
Tuesday	Key interest rates	15, 16 (315, 355)

Day of Month Usually Published in *The Wall Street Journal*	Series Description	Chapter (Page)
Wednesday	Bankrate.com money markets and CDs	16 (336)
Wednesday	Certificate of deposit yields	6 (337)
Wednesday	Insider trading spotlight	13 (280)
Wednesday	Municipal-bond index	15 (323)
Thursday	Money-market mutual funds	16 (340)
Thursday	IPO scorecard	13 (282)
Friday	Benchmarks for mutual fund investors	13 (249)
Friday	Fund leaders and laggards	13 (249)
Friday	Jobless claims	7 (89)
Friday	Largest stock and bond funds	13 (289)
Friday	Performance yardsticks	13 (246)

Series Description—Daily	Chapter Introduced
ADRs	13 (272)
American Stock Exchange (AMEX)	13 (225)
Bond-market data bank	15 (328)
Bonds and interest	15, 16 (328, 349)
Breakdown of trading	13 (233)
Cash prices (commodities)	14 (304)
Closed-end funds (stocks and bonds)	13, 15 (250, 326)
Commodities (article)	14 (296)
Commodity indexes	14 (301)
Consumer rates	16 (335)
Corporate Bonds	15 (319)
Corporate-dividend news	13 (276)
Credit markets (article)	15, 16 (309, 340)
Currency trading	10 (195)
Digest of corporate-earnings report	13 (276)

D

THE WALL STREET JOURNAL ONLINE WEB SOURCES

Go to the Web site of the *Journal* by typing in the following address: http://online.wsj.com. That will bring up the home page of *The Wall Street Online*. You can subscribe by clicking on the appropriate link at the top of the page. If you store your password, you can avoid providing your password each time you log on.

A facsimile of *The Wall Street Journal Online*'s home page appears on page 8. You may wish to explore the links in the online edition's home page at your leisure. It contains four principal sets of data-gathering procedures: news articles, company information, data on and analysis of the economy, and market information

News-Article Retrieval
The home page has links to current and previous news stories. To retrieve news stories in the *Journal*'s archive, enter the subject where indicated under Article Search and click on the arrow.

Company Information
The home page has links to stock quotes, financial data, and related company information. Type in the company name or stock symbol under Quotes & Research and click on the arrow.

Data on and Analysis of the Economy

Click on Economy on the home page's left-hand menu-bar, and then select one of the following options under Data and Resources at the top right of the linked page (see page 9 for an example from the Thursday, November 4, 2004, edition).

Economic Indicators. Click on *Economic Indicators* for the latest government report. The following array of links will appear. Brief, descriptive information for each of these links is available when you scroll down the source's Web page.

Economic Indicators Archive		
Beige Book Report	Cost-Index (PDF)	Initial Jobless Claims
Business Inventories (PDF)	Employment Situation (PDF)	Leading Indicators
Business Productivity (PDF)	Existing-Home Sales	New-Home Sales (PDF)
Construction Spending (PDF)	Factory Orders (PDF)	Nonmanufacturing Index
Consumer Credit (PDF)	FRsale Trade Sales (PDF)	Personal Income (PDF)
Consumer Price Index (PDF)	Gross Domestic Product (PDF)	Philadelphia Fed Survey (PDF)
Current Account (PDF)	Housing Starts (PDF)	Producer Price Index (PDF)
Durable-Goods Orders (PDF)	Import/Export Price Indexes (PDF)	Purchasing Index
E-Commerce Retail Sales	Industrial Production (PDF)	Retail Sales (PDF)
Employment	International Trade (PDF)	U. Michigan Survey
		Unemployment Report (PDF)

The listing that follows informs you of the chapter that introduces and discusses each of these indicators. An asterisk (*) after the chapter number indicates that the chapter does not directly deal with the indicator, but does cover the general subject.

Economic Indicator	**Chapter (Page)**
Beige Book Report	8* (156)
Business Inventories (PDF)	6 (74)

Economic Indicator	Chapter (Page)
Business Productivity (PDF)	4 (51)
Construction Spending (PDF)	7* (107)
Consumer Credit (PDF)	7 (105)
Consumer Price Index (PDF)	7 (83)
Current Account (PDF)	10 (183, 187)
Durable-Goods Orders (PDF)	5 (68)
E-Commerce Retail Sales	7* (113)
Employment Cost-Index (PDF)	4 (51)
Employment Situation (PDF)	7* (87)
Existing-Home Sales	7 (111)
Factory Orders (PDF)	5 (70)
FRsale Trade Sales (PDF)	6* (74)
Gross Domestic Product (PDF)	4 (34)
Housing Starts (PDF)	7 (107)
Import/Export Price Indexes (PDF)	10* (183, 190)
Industrial Production (PDF)	4 (41)
International Trade (PDF)	10* (183, 190)
Initial Jobless Claims	7 (89)
Leading Indicators	11 (200)
New-Home Sales (PDF)	7 (113)
Nonmanufacturing Index	4* (49)
Personal Income (PDF)	7 (89)
Philadelphia Fed Survey (PDF)	4* (49)
Producer Price Index (PDF)	4 (58)
Purchasing Index	4 (49)
Retail Sales (PDF)	7 (113)
U. Michigan Survey	7 (95)
Unemployment Report (PDF)	7 (87)

* An asterisk (*) indicates that the chapter does not directly deal with the indicator but does cover the general subject.

Chartbook. Click on *Chartbook* for an up-to-date chart. The following listing informs you of the chapter that introduces and discusses each of these charts. An asterisk (*) indicates that the chapter does not directly deal with the information contained in the chart, but does cover the general subject.

Chart	Chapter (Page)
Real GDP	4 (34)
Unemployment Rate	7 (87)
Industrial Production	4 (41)
Purchasing Managers' Index	4 (49)
Retail Sales	7 (113)
Consumer Spending	4* (34)
Consumer Confidence	7 (95)
Consumer Prices	7 (83)
Producer Prices	4 (58)
Housing Starts	7 (107)
Existing-Home Sales	7 (111)
Trade Deficit	10 (183, 190)

* An asterisk (*) indicates that the chapter does not directly deal with the information in the chart but does cover the general subject.

Briefing.com. Click on *Reports from Briefing.com* for this firm's analyses of the economic indicators. The following array of links will appear.

Reports from Briefing.com

• Auto Sales	• Consumer Credit	• Housing Starts
• Average Workweek	• Core CPI	• ISM Index
• Building Permits	• Core PPI	• ISM Services
• Business Inventories	• CPI	• Import Prices ex-oil
• Capacity Utilization	• Durable Orders	• Industrial Production
• Chain Deflator-Final	• Existing Home Sales	• Initial Claims
• Chain Deflator-Prel.	• Export Prices ex-ag.	• Leading Indicators
• Chicago PMI	• Factory Orders	• Mich Sentiment-Prel.
• Construction Spending	• GDP-Final	• Mich Sentiment-Rev.
	• GDP-Prel.	• New Home Sales
• Consumer Confidence	• Hourly Earnings	• Nonfarm Payrolls

Reports from Briefing.com (*continued*)

• PPI	• Productivity-Rev.	• Treasury Budget
• Personal Income	• Retail Sales	• Truck Sales
• Personal Spending	• Retail Sales ex-auto	• Unemployment Rate
• Philadelphia Fed	• Trade Balance	• Wholesale Inventories

The listing that follows informs you of the chapter that introduces and discusses each of these indicators. An asterisk (*) indicates that the chapter does not directly deal with the indicator but does cover the general subject.

Economic Indicator	Chapter (Page)
Auto Sales	7 (101)
Average Workweek	7 (87)
Building Permits	7 (107)
Business Inventories	6 (74)
Capacity Utilization	4 (41)
Chain Deflator-Final	4* (34)
Chain Deflator-Prel.	4* (34)
Chicago PMI	4 (49)
Construction Spending	7* (107)
Consumer Confidence	7 (95)
Consumer Credit	7 (105)
Core CPI	7* (83)
Core PPI	4* (58)
CPI	7 (83)
Durable Orders	5 (68)
Existing Home Sales	7 (111)
Export Prices ex-ag.	10* (183, 190)
Factory Orders	5* (70)
GDP-Final	4 (34)
GDP-Prel.	4 (34)
Hourly Earnings	7* (87)

Economic Indicator	Chapter (Page)
Housing Starts	7 (107)
Import Prices ex-oil	10* (183, 190)
Industrial Production	4 (41)
Initial Claims	7 (87)
ISM Index	4 (49)
ISM Services	4 (49)
Leading Indicators	11 (200)
Mich Sentiment-Prel.	7 (95)
Mich Sentiment-Rev.	7 (95)
New Home Sales	7 (113)
Nonfarm Payrolls	7 (87)
Personal Income	7 (89)
Personal Spending	7* (89)
Philadelphia Fed	4* (49)
PPI	4 (58)
Productivity-Rev.	4 (51)
Retail Sales	7 (113)
Retail Sales ex-auto	7 (113)
Trade Balance	10 (183, 190)
Treasury Budget	9 (159)
Truck Sales	7* (101)
Unemployment Rate	7 (87)
Wholesale Inventories	6 (74)

* An asterisk (*) indicates that the chapter does not directly deal with the indicator, but does cover the general subject.

Federal Reserve Monitor. Click on *Federal Reserve Monitor* to track Federal Reserve policy and actions. The *Monitor* provides minutes of meetings of the Federal Open Market Committee, which sets Federal Reserve interest-rate policy. Recent interest rates are included, as well as a roster of committee members.

Market Information (Stocks, Bonds, Commodities, Currency, etc.)

Click on *Markets and Markets Data Center* on the home page's left-hand menubar. The Markets Data Index, with the following array of links, will appear.

MARKETS DATA INDEX
Data Banks

- Data Bank
- Closing Stock Diary
- Closing Stock Data Bank

U.S. STOCKS
Market Wrap
- Quotes Search
- Most Actives—Summary
- Leaders—Summary
- Losers—Summary
- Volume Percentage Leaders—Summary
- Most Actives—Top 100
- Leaders—Top 100
- Losers—Top 100
- Volume Percentage Leaders—Top 100
- NYSE Highs/Lows
- NMS Highs/Lows
- AMEX Highs/Lows
- OTC Bulletin Board Most Actives
- DJIA Hour by Hour
- Index Charts
- Closing Stock Tables

After Hours
- Most Actives: 4–6:35 p.m.
- Leaders/Losers: 4–6:35 p.m.

Statistics
- Dividends
- Index Components
- Money Flow—Summary
- Money Flow—Top Gainers
- Money Flow—Top Decliners

- New Securities Issues
- New Stock Listings
- Odd Lot Trading
- Short Interest
- Stock Splits
- Yields on Dow Stocks

Historical Index Data
Dow Jones Industrial Average
- One-Day Gains/Losses, All Time
- One-Day Gains/Losses, 2004
- One-Day Gains/Losses, 2003
- One-Day Gains/Losses, 2002
- Intraday Point Swings

S&P 500 Index
- One-Day Gains/Losses, All Time
- One-Day Gains/Losses, 2004
- One-Day Gains/Losses, 2003
- One-Day Gains/Losses, 2002

Nasdaq Composite
- One-Day Gains/Losses, All Time
- One-Day Gains/Losses, 2004
- One-Day Gains/Losses, 2003
- One-Day Gains/Losses, 2002
- Volume Records

NYSE
- Volume Records

Major Indexes
- Highs/Lows, All Time

Options/Futures
- Index Options
- LEAPS

MARKETS DATA INDEX (*continued*)

- Listed Options
- Most Active Options
- Options Summaries
- Unusual Intraday Option Activity
- Unusual Daily Option Activity
- Index Futures, U.S.
- Index Futures, Non-U.S.

INDUSTRY GROUPS/SECTORS

- DJ Industry Group Center
- Map of the Market

Sector Maps

- Basic Materials
- Consumer, Cyclical
- Consumer, Noncyclical
- Energy
- Financial
- Healthcare
- Industrial
- Internet
- Technology
- Telecom
- Utilities

UPGRADES AND DOWNGRADES

- Upgrades and Downgrades

AMERICAS STOCKS

- Argentina
- Brazil
- Brazil Most Actives
- Canada
- Chile
- Mexico

- Mexico Most Actives
- Venezuela

- DJ Global Indexes
- Leading Groups
- Lagging Groups
- Americas Groups

ASIAN/PACIFIC STOCKS

- Australia
- Australia Most Actives
- China - Shanghai
- China - Shenzhen
- Hong Kong
- Hong Kong Most Actives
- India
- Indonesia
- Japan
- Japan Most Actives
- Malaysia
- Malaysia Most Actives
- New Zealand
- Pakistan
- Philippines
- Singapore
- Singapore Most Actives
- South Korea
- Sri Lanka
- Taiwan
- Thailand

- DJ Global Indexes
- Leading Groups
- Lagging Groups
- Asian Groups

MARKETS DATA INDEX (*continued*)

EUROPEAN STOCKS

- Belgium
- Britain
- Britain Most Actives
- Denmark
- France
- France Most Actives
- Germany
- Germany Most Actives
- Italy
- Italy Most Actives
- Netherlands
- Netherlands Most Actives
- Norway
- Portugal
- South Africa
- Spain
- Spain Most Actives
- Sweden
- Switzerland
- Switzerland Most Actives
- Additional Closing Stock Tables

- DJ Global Indexes
- Leading Groups
- Lagging Groups
- European Groups

CORPORATE EARNINGS

- Digest of Earnings
- Earnings Calendar
- Earnings Restatements
- Earnings Surprises
- Going-Concern Statements

Industry Earnings

- 3rd Quarter 2004
- 2nd Quarter 2004
- 1st Quarter 2004
- 4th Quarter 2003

Company Earnings

- 3rd Quarter 2004
- 2nd Quarter 2004
- 1st Quarter 2004
- 4th Quarter 2003

GLOBAL INDEXES

- DJ Global Indexes
- World Leading Groups
- World Lagging Groups
- Americas Groups
- Asian Groups
- European Groups
- U.S. Leading & Lagging Groups
- DJ Global Portfolio Indexes
- DJ Industry Group Center

BOND MARKETS

- Bond Indexes
- Bond Yields
- Bond Diaries
- Federal Reserve Data
- Federal Reserve Monitor
- Guaranteed Investment Contracts
- International Government Bonds
- Returns on International Gov't Bonds
- Key Rates
- Money Rates

MARKETS DATA INDEX (*continued*)

- Mortgage-Backed Securities and CMOs
- Treasury Quotes
- Tax-Exempt Bonds
- Mortgage & Banking Rate Center

COMMODITIES

Agriculture
- Food, Fiber
- Livestock, Meat
- Oats, Corn, Rice
- Oilseeds
- Wheat

Energy
- Electricity
- Petroleum

Index
- U.S.
- Non-U.S.

Interest Rate
- Americas
- Europe
- Euro
- EuroDollar, Yen
- Asian, Pacific

Other
- Currency
- Metals
- Lumber
- Weather
- Commodities Weekly Settlement
- Futures Options
- Agricultural

- Currency
- Index
- Interest Rate
- Livestock
- Metals
- Oil
- Other
- Futures Options Weekly Settlement
- Spot Prices
- Cash Prices
- Electricity Prices
- Oil Statistics
- London Metal Exchange Prices

CURRENCIES
- Exchange Rates
- Hourly Exchange Rates
- Key Cross Rates
- Currency Futures
- Currency Futures Options
- World Value of Dollar

MUTUAL FUNDS
- Annuities
- Closed-End Funds
- Scorecards
- International Funds
- Quotes Search
- Mutual Funds Families Search

IPOs
- Latest IPOs
- IPO Watch
- IPO Pipeline
- Withdrawn Deals
- Securities Offering Calendar

MARKETS DATA INDEX (*continued*)

OTHER STATS

- Auto Sales
- Economic Chartbook
- Economic Indicators Archive
- Federal Interest Rates
- Federal Reserve Monitor
- Going-Concern Statements
- Insider Trading Spotlight
- Reports from Briefing.com

CALENDARS

- U.S. Economic Calendar
- International Economic Calendar
- Securities Offering Calendar
- Earnings Calendar

UPDATE TIMES

- Update Times for Market Data Center

The listing that follows, arranged by chapter, informs you of the chapters and pages in which you can find a discussion of these reports. Chapters 13 (The Stock Market), 14 (Commodities and Precious Metals),15 (Long-Term Interest Rates), and 16 (Money-Market Investments) discuss the reports contained in these links. Repetitive entries, such as the country-by-country list of stock reports, are omitted. In some cases reference is made to the chapters' discussions of the *Journal*'s print-edition publication of these reports when the online and print reports are similar.

Report	Topic/Subject	Page
Most Actives—Top 100	Volume leaders	226
Leaders—Top 100	Price percentage gainers	226
Losers—Top 100	Price percentage losers	226
Volume Percentage Leaders—Top 100	Volume leaders	226
NYSE Highs/Lows	Daily	233
NMS Highs/Lows	Daily	243
AMEX Highs/Lows	Daily	225
OTC Bulletin Board Most Actives	Over the counter	226
DJIA Hour by Hour	For the past week	214
Index Charts	Major indexes	214
Closing Stock Tables	Major domestic and European	238

After Hours

Most Actives: 4–6:35 p.m.	After market closing	233
Leaders/Losers: 4–6:35 p.m.	After market closing	233

Statistics

Dividends	Daily report	276
Index Components	Dow, Nasdaq, and Russell	219
Money Flow—Summary	Uptick vs. downtick	233
Money Flow—Top Gainers	Uptick exceeds downtick	233
Money Flow—Top Decliners	Downtick exceeds uptick	233
New Securities Issues	Daily, stocks and bonds	282
New Stock Listings	On major exchanges	322, 323
Odd Lot Trading	Fewer than 100 shares	234
Short Interest	Borrowed stock outstanding	265
Stock Splits	With prices adjusted	276
Yields on Dow Stocks	Dividend/price	276

Historical Index Data

Dow Jones Industrial Average

Report	Topic/Subject	Page
S&P 500 Index		
Nasdaq Composite		
NYSE		
Major Indexes		
Options/Futures		
Index Options	Evening update	261
LEAPS	Long-term options	262
Listed Options	Evening update	255
Most Active Options	Ranked by trading volume	255
Options Summaries	By exchange	255
Unusual Intraday Option Activity	High volume for the day	255
Unusual Daily Option Activity	High volume recently	255
Index Futures, U.S.	Various domestic contracts	294
Index Futures, Non-U.S.	Various international contracts	294
Industry Groups/Sectors		
DJ Industry Group Center	Sector and industry reports	278
Sector Maps		
Upgrades and Downgrades		
Upgrades and Downgrades	Research reports	210
Americas Stocks		
Asian/Pacific Stocks		
European Stocks		
Corporate Earnings		
Digest of Earnings	Past five days	276
Earnings Calendar	Schedule of reports	276

Report	Topic/Subject	Page
Earnings Restatements	Corrections	276
Earnings Surprises	Actual vs. estimate	276
Going-Concern Statements	Firms in trouble	276
Industry Earnings		
3rd Quarter 2004	Sector/industry	279
Company Earnings		
3rd Quarter 2004	Sector/industry/company	276
Global Indexes		
DJ Global Indexes	Regions and countries	272
World Leading Groups	By sector and firm	234, 269, 272
World Lagging Groups	By sector and firm	234, 269, 272
Americas Groups	By sector and industry	234, 269, 272
Asian Groups	By sector and industry	234, 269, 272
European Groups	By sector and industry	234, 269, 272
U.S. Leading and Lagging Groups	By sector and firm	234, 269, 272
DJ Industry Group Center	Best and worst industries	278
Mutual Funds		
Annuities	Variable annuities	249
Closed-End Funds	Stock and bond funds	250
Scorecards	Ranks funds by categories	249
International Funds	Alphabetically	249
Quotes Search	Companies and funds	249
Mutual Funds Families Search	Grouped by management	249
IPOs		
Latest IPOs	Initial public offerings	282
IPO Watch	Tracks IPOs	282
IPO Pipeline	Planned IPOs	282
Withdrawn Deals	Canceled IPOs	282

Report	Topic/Subject	Page
Guaranteed Investment Contracts	Interest yields	328
International Government Bonds	Japan, UK, Germany, Canada	329
Returns on International Govt. Bonds	Local currency and U.S. dollar	329
Key Rates	Short, medium, and long term	315, 355
Money Rates	Variety of instruments	350
Mortgage-Backed Securities, CMOs	Fannie Mae, Ginnie Mae, etc.	315
Treasury Quotes	Bonds, notes, and bills	312, 345
Tax-Exempt Bonds	State and local issues	323
Mortgage and Banking Rate Center	Consumer finance info	335

E

FURTHER REFERENCES*

These references were selected to assist you with further research into the many topics covered in this book. Given the flood of new Internet-based information in recent years, a special effort was made to highlight timeless classics—and perspective-building information—of particular value in organizing and managing a long-term investment master plan. Many of these books and services enjoy a wide following among private and institutional investors, alike.

In certain cases, a book may be out-of-print, but copies will be available in bookstores, in libraries, or through the catalogs listed herein. All McGraw-Hill titles are available in bookstores, in many catalogs, or directly from McGraw-Hill Publishing at 1-800-2-MCGRAW.

ASSOCIATIONS AND CLUBS

American Association of Individual Investors
(312) 280-0170 / www.AAII.com

Member benefits include the monthly *AAII Journal* with detailed articles on wide ranging investment and financial planning topics. Numerous extra books and support services are also available.

---

*The author gratefully acknowledges the assistance of Robert H. Meier of Chicago, Illinois, in compiling these references.

American Institute for Economic Research
(413) 528-1216 / Fax: (413) 528-0103
www.aier.org

The institute publishes close to 40 special reports and books on investment basics, estate planning, insurance, the behavioral sciences, and economics. The twice-monthly *Research Reports* newsletter is known for its comprehensive business-cycle condition forecasts.

Oxford Club
(800) 992-0205 / Fax: (410) 223-2650
www.oxfordclub.com

The twice-monthly member newsletter includes global portfolio recommendations. In addition, frequent bulletins and chapter meetings keep members current on everything from wealth-protection strategies to foreign real estate. Affiliate clubs are located in London, Paris, and Bonn.

BONDS AND MONEY MARKET

All About Bonds and Bond Mutual Funds
by Esmé Faerber. McGraw-Hill.

Without getting bogged down in needless technicalities, all the basics of bonds and bond funds are covered. This revised edition contains new material on bond mutual funds, tax-free municipal bonds, and international bonds and bond funds.

Bond Market Rules—50 Axioms to Master Bonds for Trading or Income
by Michael B. Sheimo. McGraw-Hill.

The first of its kind, this book is packed with solid, actionable advice and insights to increase bond-portfolio profits — whether for conservative income or aggressive growth.

BOOK CATALOGS

Books of Wall Street
(877) 996-3336 / Fax: (786) 513-2807
www.fraserbooks.com

One of the largest and most comprehensive selections of business and finance catalogs, including new editions of long out-of-print classics. Investment newsletters are also listed, especially those using contrary-opinion decision models.

Laissez Faire Books
(800) 326-0996
http://laissezfaire.org

World's largest selection of books on free-market economics, plus benchmark titles in personal finance, offshore tax and estate planning, socioeconomic trends, and children and money.

CHARTING & TECHNICAL SERVICES

Chartcraft, Inc.
(914) 632-0422 / Fax: (914) 632-0335

The Chartcraft *Point & Figure Monthly Chart Book* includes more than 3,500 common stocks on the New York, American, and OTC exchanges, 42 industry bullish-consensus charts, data for 185 more industry groups, major option and world indexes, and much more. Although not as well-known as bar charting, point & figure charting is considered more reliable by many practitioners.

Technical Analysis of Stocks & Commodities
(800) 832-4642 / Fax: (206) 938-1307
www.traders.com

This monthly magazine is the single best source for "how-to" articles, the latest indicator-reliability studies, and new software and data bases.

Topline Investment Graphics
(800) 347-0157 / Fax: (303) 440-0147
http://topline-charts.com

The company offers an extensive selection of custom chart formats and data combinations for tracking markets and optimizing indicators. The company does not sell data.

CHILDREN AND MONEY

Gifting to People You Love
by Adriane G. Berg. New Market Press. $24.95

The complete family guide to making gifts, bequests, and investments for children.

National Center for Financial Education
(877) 947-3752 / www.ncfe.org

The one-stop source for virtually everything in print to help children learn how to become better savers and investors.

CYCLES

Elliott Wave International
(800) 336-1618 / Fax: (770) 536-2514
www.elliottwave.com

Newsletters and books on the Elliott Wave Theory and cycles in general. For cycle basics, start with *The Wave Principle of Human Social Behavior and the New Science of Socionomics* by Robert Prechter.

FINANCIAL PLANNING

How to Pay Zero Estate Taxes
How to Pay Zero Taxes
by Jeff A. Schnepper. McGraw-Hill.

The two foundation references to discover every practical tax break the IRS allows.

The Financial Planning Association
(800) 322-4237 / (404) 845-3660
www.fpanet.org

The Association provides a set of eight brochures on important planning topics free of charge, including guidelines for choosing a financial adviser. The topics also are covered on their Web site.

Smart Questions to Ask Your Financial Advisers
by Lynn Brenner. Penguin Putnam, Inc.
www.penguinputnam.com

FOREIGN CURRENCIES

Information Line
(800) 831-0007 / Fax: (301) 881-1936
www.assetstrategies.com

This newsletter is published free of charge by Asset Strategies International, a major foreign-currency and precious-metals dealer. Prominent economists and money managers are interviewed, and U.S. dollar and inflation forecasts are regularly issued along with investor protection alerts.

FINANCIAL HISTORY

It Was a Very Good Year—Extraordinary Moments in Stock Market History
by Martin S. Fridson. John Wiley & Sons.

Against the Gods—The Remarkable Story of Risk
by Peter L. Bernstein. John Wiley & Sons.

The fascinating story of how risk has been measured, forecast, and controlled since the Renaissance.

INTERNATIONAL INVESTING

Strategic Investment
Agora Publishing
P.O. Box 925
Frederick, MD 21075
(866) 215-9065
$198 per year

12 monthly issues per year, with many extra global investing special reports and sector studies. Editor Dan Denning travels extensively to meet with company managers and government economic policy officials.

MUTUAL FUNDS

Mutual Fund Rules—50 Essential Axioms to Explain and Examine Mutual Fund Investing
by Michael B. Sheimo. McGraw-Hill.

Covering everything from types of mutual funds and how they differ to tips and techniques for avoiding fraud and hidden charges, it's must reading for anyone owning mutual funds.

ONLINE INVESTING

Computerized Investing Magazine
(800) 428-2244
www.aaii.com
$40 per year; $39 for members

Published bimonthly by the American Association of Individual Investors (AAII). A definitive source with many detailed articles on new software products and comprehensive systems directories by application category.

Mining for Gold on the Internet
by Mary Ellen Bates. McGraw-Hill.

Must reading. Take maximum advantage of hundreds of free financial and software Web sites. Sample Web sites are illustrated, and valuable pointers given on using the Net to manage personal finances.

COMMODITIES FUTURES AND OPTIONS

Options Edge
The RMB Group
Suite 1800A
141 West Jackson Blvd.
Chicago, IL 60604
(800) 345-7026
www.rmbgroup.com

Founded in 1984, the research and brokerage team RMB Group has earned a reputation for superior service and long-term, "big move" option strategies. Their newsletter, *Options Edge,* is published approximately 60 times per year and is only available to clients. Their individual managed accounts are frequently among the top performers in the business.

PRECIOUS METALS

The Moneychanger
(888) 218-9226
http://the-moneychanger.com

A monthly newsletter featuring in-depth interviews with precious-metal economists and portfolio managers, insightful analysis of political forces impacting precious-metals prices, and in-depth technical analysis of gold, silver, platinum, and palladium.

PRIVACY

The Sovereign Individual **newsletter**
5 Catherine Street
Waterford, Ireland
(353) 51-844-068 / info@thesovereignsociety.com
www.youreletters.com
$145 per year

12 monthly issues per year. Edited by Mark Nestmann. One of the most knowledgeable authorities on legal privacy protection. The society also publishes a free e-mail letter, *The Sovereign Society Offshore A-Letter.* It offers extensive analysis of domestic and international privacy and tax issues. The letter has links to dozens of additional information sources.

PSYCHOLOGY

International Institute of Trading Mastery
(919) 852-3994 / Fax: (919) 852-3942
www.iitm.com

One-of-a-kind personal psychological profiling, home-study courses, seminars, and the monthly *Market Mastery* newsletter to successfully overcome the many hidden psychological barriers to profitable trading and investing.

REAL ESTATE

Getting Started in Real Estate, **2nd ed.**
by Michael and Jean Thomsett. John Wiley & Sons.

STOCK MARKET

Alexander Paris Report
(800) 416-7479 / Fax: (312) 634-6350

This newsletter uses a proprietary, free-market credit-cycle model to pinpoint business cycle and stock sector leadership transitions, with specific stock recommendations.

How to Read a Financial Report
by John A. Tracy. John Wiley & Sons.

Now in the fifth edition, this popular guide gives investors the basics needed to intelligently decipher company annual reports and financial statements.

Stock Trader's Almanac
(201) 767-4100 / Fax: (201) 767-7337
www.hirschorganization.com

The annual *Wall Street* classic. Combines a desk calendar, daily diary, and valuable market tips such as the best trading days and calendar periods to buy and sell stocks; also the results of probability studies, and dozens more insights every month of the year.

The Hulbert Financial Digest
(703) 750-9060 / Fax: (703) 750-9220
www.marketwatch.com

The world's most widely followed advisory-services performance tracking service. In addition to ranking over 60 stock, commodity, and mutual fund newsletters, the service features in-depth sector, cyclical, and new-issue performance updates.

Stock Index Futures & Options
by Susan Abbott Gidel. John Wiley & Sons.

The benchmark reference on the most popular stock-index futures and option contracts on 20 U.S. and 18 foreign exchanges. Includes valuable trading guidelines.

What Works on Wall Street, **3rd ed.**
by James P. O'Shaughnessy. McGraw-Hill.

One of the most valuable investment books of all time. Never before have so many factual, unbiased, and surprising findings on what portfolio strategies actually work—and how well—been presented in one place. Importantly, the book also warns of popular market folklore with no basis in fact.

Winning the Loser's Game, **4th ed.**
by Charles D. Ellis. McGraw-Hill.

A revised and updated edition of *Investment Policy*, a financial magnum opus considered essential reading for professionals, this edition is tailored for individual investors. The books details how to manage stock market holdings to maximize lifetime financial success through five stages, from earning and saving through investing and estate planning and gifting.

TECHNOLOGY AND TRENDS

Growth Stock Alert
Jefferson Financial
2400 Jefferson Highway
Jefferson, LA 70121
(800) 877-8847

12 monthly issues per year. Editor James B. Powell is a highly regarded technology and trends forecaster. His trend spotting and technology stock recommendations are noted for their balanced perspectives.

TRADING SYSTEMS

Trade Your Way to Financial Freedom
by Van K. Tharp. McGraw-Hill.

In simple English, the book quickly and simply reveals how to pick the optimum trading system, and details the vital but little known key to trading profits: trading for expectancy rather than accuracy. This book is of exceptional value, no matter what the investment time horizon—from day trading to decades-long master portfolio planning.

I N D E X

ABOUT THE AUTHOR

MICHAEL B. LEHMANN is Emeritus Professor of Economics at the University of San Francisco, where he taught for 38 years, He is a graduate of Grinnell College and received his Ph.D. from Cornell University.

Professor Lehmann lectures extensively on business and investment conditions and has developed a popular seminar, *Be Your Own Economist*®, based on this book, which he offers to investors, the business community, and corporations as an in-house training program. For further information, please visit Professor Lehmann at his web site, www.BeYourOwnEconomist.com.

FREE OFFER—The Oldest and Wisest Investment Newsletter in the Newest and Easiest Format

The Outlook is America's oldest continuously published investment advisory newsletter, and now it's available online! Best of all, because you're reading an S&P book, you're entitled to a free 30-day trial. Outlook Online is perfect for both beginners and expert investors alike. The site contains the latest issue of *The Outlook* as well as a searchable archive of the past year's issues. You'll get everything from Standard & Poor's latest individual investment recommendations and economic forecasts to complete portfolios that can help you build wealth. For more than 80 years, *The Outlook* has been identifying the developments that affect stock performance—and making recommendations on when to buy, sell and hold. With Outlook Online you'll also get:

Features on Sectors, Industries and Technical Analysis—These weekly articles will keep you informed about what sectors are poised to outperform, what industries have been on a roll, a where the market may be headed next.

Supervised Master List of Recommended Issues—Standard & Poor's favorites for long-term capital appreciation and superior long-term total return. These groups of stocks have been helping generations of investors build wealth.

Complete Lists of STARS stocks—The highly regarded *Stock Appreciation Ranking System* offers an easy way to pick stocks that Standard & Poor's believes will do best in the near term—six months to one year. Week after week, STARS ranks 1,200 active stocks so you can track changes at a glance.

Platinum and Neural Fair Value Portfolios—Outlook Online also contains detailed information on two more of Standard & Poor's portfolios, both of which have historically outperformed the market by wide margins.

Global Features—Outlook Online is also helpful to investors looking for news and views from abroad. It contains a number of features on both Europe and Asia, including the best picks from S&P's overseas research departments.

Stock and Fund Reports—You'll even get access to 10 free Standard & Poor's reports every month. Whether you're looking for more information on a company or a mutual fund, these reports will help you make informed decisions.

It's simple to activate your free trial to Outlook Online. Just visit the URL below and follow the directions on the screen. No credit card is required and registration will take only a few minutes. To get the best guidance on Wall Street and specific stock recommendations from the experts in the field, just visit us at:

http://www.spoutlookonline.com/ol_mw1.0.asp?ADID=LEH

The Wall Street Journal

Special Student Rate!

It's Not Just about Business...
But the Business of Life!

Subscribe Now
and Get BOTH the
Print and Online
Editions at Special
Student Rates.

YOU SAVE over 60%!

Universally recognized for accuracy and fairness, THE WALL STREET JOURNAL keeps you on top of the news and gives you an edge in reaching your professional and personal goals. The Journal connects the world's business community. Join them today!

FOR SPECIAL STUDENT RATES
Visit subscribe.wsj.com/textbook
or call toll-free 1-800-975-8602

THE WALL STREET JOURNAL.
— PRINT & ONLINE —

Business. And the Business of Life.